CW00408327

STREET ATLAS

Tyne & Wear

First published in 2001 as
Tyne & Wear Northumberland by

Philip's, a division of
Octopus Publishing Group Ltd
2-4 Heron Quays, London E14 4JP

First edition 2005
First impression 2005

ISBN-10   0-540-08752-1 (spiral)
ISBN-13   978-0-540-08752-5 (spiral)

© Philip's 2005

o|S Ordnance Survey®

This product includes mapping data licensed
from Ordnance Survey® with the permission of
the Controller of Her Majesty's Stationery Office.
© Crown copyright 2005. All rights reserved.
Licence number 100011710.

Printed and bound in Spain
by Cayfosa-Quebecor

Contents

III — **Key to map symbols**

IV — **Key to map pages**

VI — **Route planning**

VIII — **Administrative and Postcode boundaries**

1 — **Street maps** at 3½ inches to 1 mile

98 — **Street maps of Newcastle upon Tyne and Sunderland city centres** at 7 inches to 1 mile

104 — **Index** of towns and villages

106 — **Index** of streets, hospitals, industrial estates, railway stations, schools, shopping centres and universities and places of interest

Digital Data

The exceptionally high-quality mapping found in this atlas is available as digital data in TIFF format, which is easily convertible to other bitmapped (raster) image formats.

The index is also available in digital form as a standard database table. It contains all the details found in the printed index together with the National Grid reference for the map square in which each entry is named.

For further information and to discuss your requirements, please contact Philip's on 020 7644 6932 or james.mann@philips-maps.co.uk

Symbol	Description
	Motorway with junction number
	Primary route – dual/single carriageway
	A road – dual/single carriageway
	B road – dual/single carriageway
	Minor road – dual/single carriageway
	Other minor road – dual/single carriageway
	Road under construction
	Tunnel, covered road
	Rural track, private road or narrow road in urban area
	Gate or obstruction to traffic (restrictions may not apply at all times or to all vehicles)
	Path, bridleway, byway open to all traffic, road used as a public path
	Pedestrianised area
DY7	**Postcode boundaries**
	County and unitary authority boundaries
	Railway, tunnel, railway under construction
	Tramway, tramway under construction
	Miniature railway
Walsall	**Railway station**
	Private railway station
South Shields	**Metro station**
	Tram stop, tram stop under construction
	Bus, coach station

Symbol	Description
	Ambulance station
	Coastguard station
	Fire station
	Police station
	Accident and Emergency entrance to hospital
H	**Hospital**
+	**Place of worship**
i	**Information Centre** (open all year)
	Shopping Centre
P P&R	**Parking, Park and Ride**
PO	**Post Office**
	Camping site, caravan site
	Golf course, picnic site
Prim Sch	**Important buildings, schools, colleges, universities and hospitals**
	Built up area
	Woods
River Medway	**Water name**
	River, weir, stream
	Canal, lock, tunnel
	Water
	Tidal water
Church	**Non-Roman antiquity**
ROMAN FORT	**Roman antiquity**
87	**Adjoining page indicators and overlap bands**
237	The colour of the arrow and the band indicates the scale of the adjoining or overlapping page (see scales below)

Abbr	Full	Abbr	Full	Abbr	Full
Acad	**Academy**	Inst	**Institute**	Recn Gd	**Recreation Ground**
Allot Gdns	**Allotments**	Ct	**Law Court**		
Cemy	**Cemetery**	L Ctr	**Leisure Centre**	Resr	**Reservoir**
C Ctr	**Civic Centre**	LC	**Level Crossing**	Ret Pk	**Retail Park**
CH	**Club House**	Liby	**Library**	Sch	**School**
Coll	**College**	Mkt	**Market**	Sh Ctr	**Shopping Centre**
Crem	**Crematorium**	Meml	**Memorial**	TH	**Town Hall/House**
Ent	**Enterprise**	Mon	**Monument**	Trad Est	**Trading Estate**
Ex H	**Exhibition Hall**	Mus	**Museum**	Univ	**University**
Ind Est	**Industrial Estate**	Obsy	**Observatory**	W Twr	**Water Tower**
IRB Sta	**Inshore Rescue Boat Station**	Pal	**Royal Palace**	Wks	**Works**
		PH	**Public House**	YH	**Youth Hostel**

■ The small numbers around the edges of the maps identify the 1 kilometre National Grid lines
■ The dark grey border on the inside edge of some pages indicates that the mapping does not continue onto the adjacent page

The scale of the maps on the pages numbered in blue is 5.52 cm to 1 km • 3½ inches to 1 mile • 1: 18103

0	¼	½	¾	1 mile
0	250 m	500 m	750 m	1 kilometre

The scale of the maps on pages numbered in red is 11.04 cm to 1 km • 7 inches to 1 mile • 1: 9051

0	220 yards	440 yards	660 yards	½ mile
0	125 m	250 m	375 m	½ kilometre

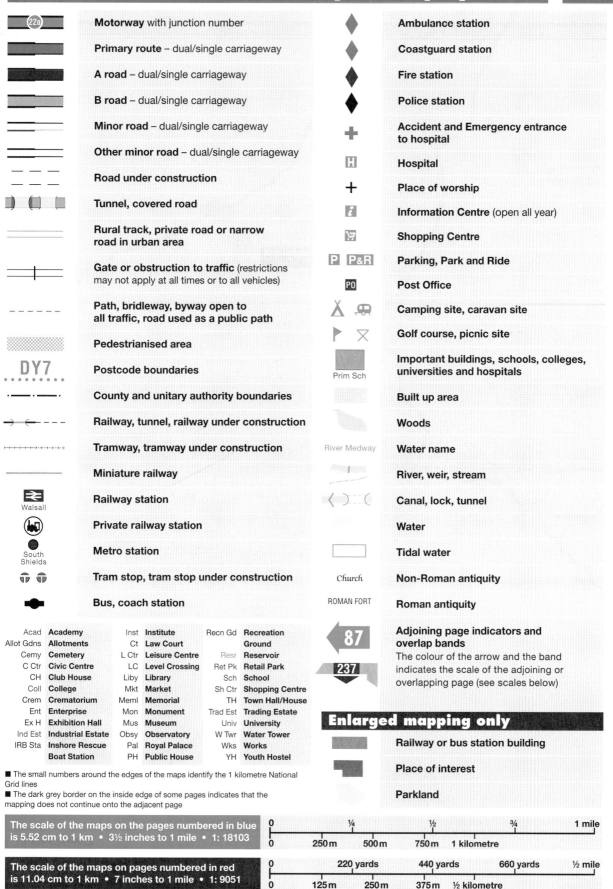

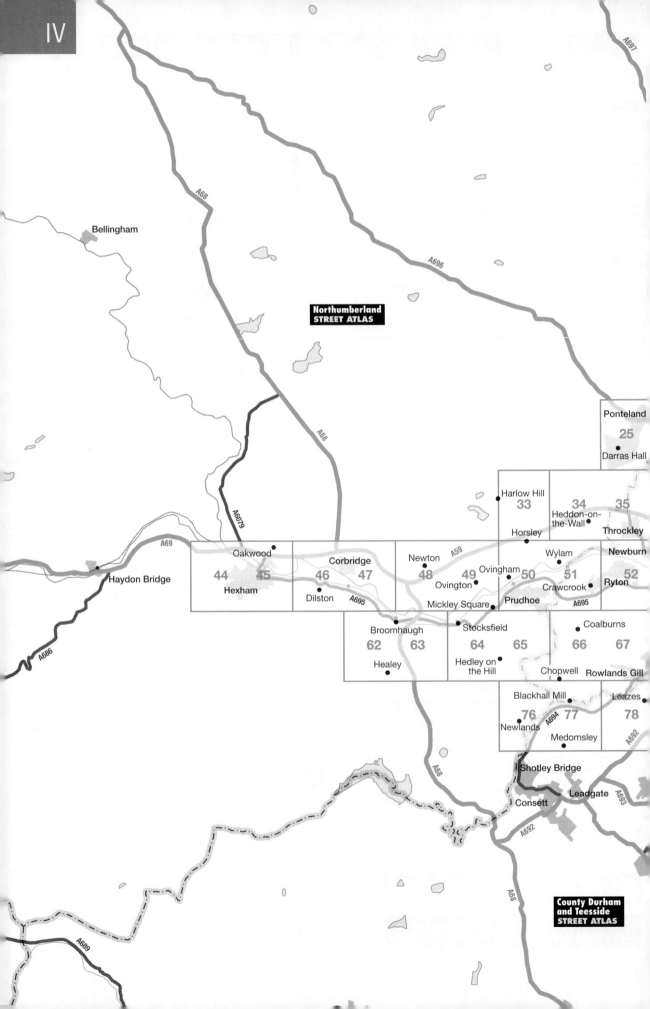

Bellingham

Northumberland
STREET ATLAS

Ponteland
25
Darras Hall

Harlow Hill
33   **34**   **35**
Heddon-on-
the-Wall
Horsley   Throckley

Newton   Wylam   Newburn
48   **49** Ovingham **50** **51** **52**
Ovington   Crawcrook   Ryton
Mickley Square   Prudhoe

Oakwood
44   **45**   **46**   **47**
Hexham   Corbridge
Dilston

Haydon Bridge

Broomhaugh   Stocksfield   Coalburns
62   **63**   **64**   **65**   **66**   **67**
Healey   Hedley on   Chopwell   Rowlands Gill
the Hill

Blackhall Mill   Leazes
76   **77**   **78**
Newlands
Medomsley

Shotley Bridge

Leadgate
Consett

County Durham
and Teesside
STREET ATLAS

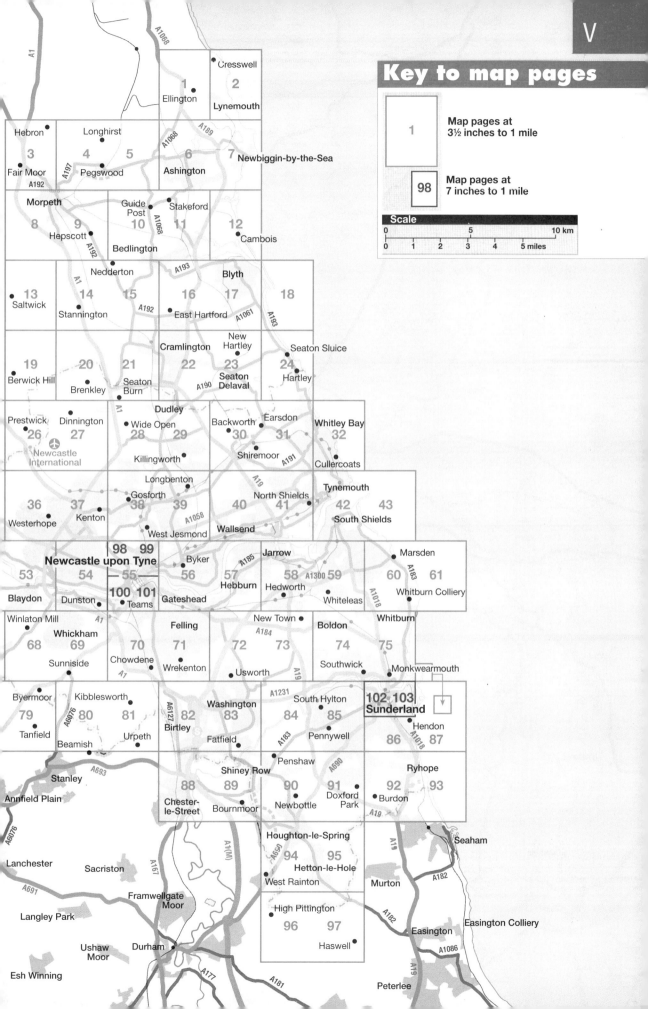

V

Key to map pages

1	Map pages at 3½ inches to 1 mile
98	Map pages at 7 inches to 1 mile

Scale

0 ———————— 5 ———————— 10 km

0 — 1 — 2 — 3 — 4 — 5 miles

A1068

A1

Cresswell

1 Ellington

2 Lynemouth

Hebron

3

Fair Moor

A192

Longhirst

4 Pegswood

A197

5

A1068

A189

6

Ashington

7 Newbiggin-by-the-Sea

Morpeth

8

9 Hepscott

A192

Guide Post

10

A1068

Stakeford

11

Bedlington

12 Cambois

Nedderton

A1

A192

A193

Blyth

13 Saltwick

14 Stannington

15

16 East Hartford

A1061

17

A193

18

Cramlington

19 Berwick Hill

20 Brenkley

21 Seaton Burn

22

A190

New Hartley

23 Seaton Delaval

24 Hartley

Seaton Sluice

Prestwick

26

Newcastle International

Dinnington

27

A1

Dudley

28 Wide Open

29 Killingworth

Backworth

30

Shiremoor

Earsdon

31

A191

Whitley Bay

32

Cullercoats

Longbenton

36 Westerhope

37 Kenton

Gosforth

38

39

A1058

West Jesmond

40

Wallsend

North Shields

41

A19

Tynemouth

42

43 South Shields

98 99

Newcastle upon Tyne

Byker

56

A185

Jarrow

57 Hebburn

58 Hedworth

A1300

59

Whiteleas

Marsden

60

A183

61 Whitburn Colliery

53 Blaydon

54 Dunston

55

100 101 Teams

Gateshead

A1018

Winlaton Mill

A1

Whickham

68

69 Sunniside

Chowdene

70

A1

Felling

71 Wrekenton

72 Usworth

A184

New Town

73

A19

Boldon

74 Southwick

Whitburn

75 Monkwearmouth

Byermoor

79 Tanfield

A6076

Kibblesworth

80 Beamish

81 Urpeth

A6127

Birtley

82

Washington

83 Fatfield

A1231

84

A183

South Hylton

85 Pennywell

102 103

Sunderland

A1018

86

Hendon

87

Stanley

A693

Annfield Plain

Penshaw

Shiney Row

88

Chester-le-Street

89 Bournmoor

90 Newbottle

A690

91 Doxford Park

92 Burdon

Ryhope

93

A19

Seaham

A6076

Lanchester

Sacriston

A167

Framwellgate Moor

A1(M)

Houghton-le-Spring

A690

94 West Rainton

Hetton-le-Hole

95

Murton

A182

A691

Langley Park

Ushaw Moor

Durham

High Pittington

96

97 Haswell

A177

A181

A182

A182

Easington

A1086

Easington Colliery

A19

Esh Winning

Peterlee

Route Planning

Scale

0   5   10 km

0   1   2   3   4   5 miles

STAVANGER 20:45
HAUGESUND 23:00
BERGEN 27:00
KRISTIANSAND 18:00
GOTHENBURG 26:00
AMSTERDAM 15:00

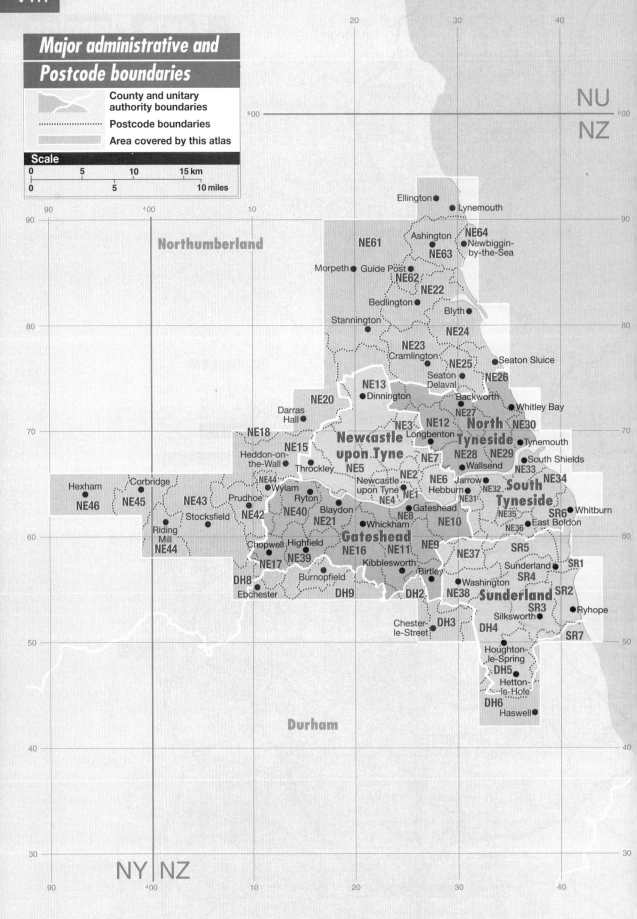

Major administrative and Postcode boundaries

County and unitary authority boundaries

Postcode boundaries

Area covered by this atlas

Scale

| 0 | 5 | 10 | 15 km |

| 0 | 5 | 10 miles |

NU

NZ

Northumberland

Ellington

Lynemouth

NE61

Ashington

NE64

Newbiggin-by-the-Sea

NE63

Morpeth

Guide Post

NE62

NE22

Bedlington

Blyth

Stannington

NE24

NE23

Cramlington

NE25

Seaton Sluice

Seaton Delaval

NE26

NE13

Dinnington

Backworth

NE20

Whitley Bay

Darras Hall

NE27

NE18

NE3

NE12

North

NE30

Longbenton

Tyneside

NE15

Newcastle upon Tyne

Tynemouth

Heddon-on-the-Wall

NE28

NE29

NE5

NE7

Wallsend

South Shields

Throckley

NE2

NE33

Hexham

NE44

NE6

Jarrow

NE34

NE46

Corbridge

Wylam

Newcastle upon Tyne

NE1

Hebburn

South

NE45

NE43

Prudhoe

Ryton

NE4

NE32

Tyneside

NE42

Blaydon

NE8

Gateshead

NE31

Stocksfield

NE40

NE21

Whickham

NE10

NE35

SR6

Whitburn

Riding Mill

Chopwell

Highfield

Gateshead

NE36

East Boldon

NE44

NE16

NE11

NE9

SR5

Kibblesworth

NE37

SR1

NE17

NE39

Birtley

Sunderland

DH8

Burnopfield

Washington

SR4

Ebchester

DH9

DH2

NE38

Sunderland

SR2

Chester-le-Street

DH3

SR3

Ryhope

DH4

Silksworth

SR7

Houghton-le-Spring

DH5

Hetton-le-Hole

DH6

Haswell

Durham

NY NZ

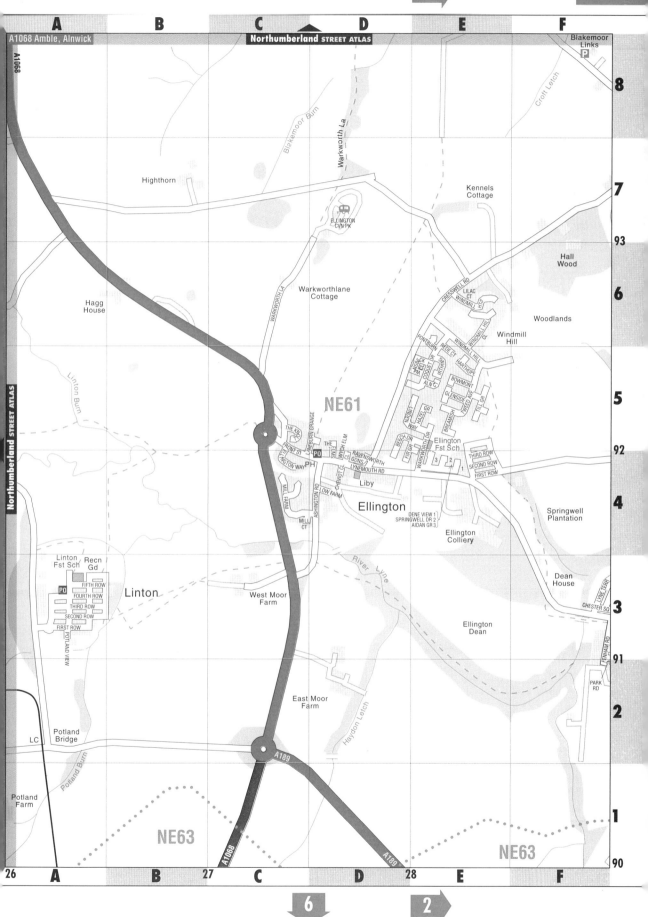

A   B   C   D   E   F

A1068 Amble, Alnwick

A1068

Blakemoor
Links
P

8

Croft Letch

Warkworth La

Highthorn

Kennels
Cottage

7

93

Blakemoor Burn

Hall
Wood

ELLINGTON
CVN PK

CRESSWELL RD

LILAC
CT

WINDMILL

HIGH

Woodlands

6

Warkworthlane
Cottage

WARKWORTH LA

WINDMILL HILL
CL

Windmill
Hill

Hagg
House

Linton Burn

FONTBURN

REDE CT

HARTHOPE

WINDMILL HILL

JACK
RICE
WISDE
PM
COQUET LA
IRTHIN

BOWMONT

ALN CT

GLENSIDE

NE61

REDNIT
HAZEL
GR

TWEED AVE

TILL GR

5

BREAMISH

Northumberland STREET ATLAS

BEECH DR

WAY

WARKWORTH DR

Ellington
Fst Sch

THIRD ROW

92

THE KIL
NEBURN GRANGE

TIR GR
TIR GR

3   2   1

SECOND ROW

FRONT ST

THE
ELMS

WYCH ELM

RAVENSWORTH
GDNS

FIRST ROW

ELLINGTON WAY

PH
PO

ASHINGTON RD

CHEVIOT CL

LOW FARM

LYNEMOUTH RD

Liby

MILL FARM

Ellington

4

MILL
CT

DENE VIEW 1
SPRINGWELL DR 2
AIDAN GR 3

Springwell
Plantation

West Moor
Farm

River Line

Ellington
Colliery

Ellington
Dean

Dean
House

LYNE TERR

CHESTER SQ

3

Linton
Fst Sch

Recn
Gd

FIFTH ROW

PO

FOURTH ROW

Linton

THIRD ROW

SECOND ROW

FIRST ROW

FENHAM RD

91

POTLAND VIEW

PARK
RD

2

LC

Potland
Bridge

East Moor
Farm

Potland Burn

Haydon Letch

Potland
Farm

1

NE63

A1068

A189

NE63

90

26   A   B   27   C   D   28   E   F

A B C D E F

8

St Bartholomews Cl

SOUTH SIDE

+

7

Cresswell

Sea Lodge

P

93

Caravan Site

P

6

Snab Point

NE61

5

92

CRESSWELL HOME FARM COTTS

Cresswell Home Farm

4

Chugdon Wood

Bewick Drift

River Lyne

JUBILEE COTTS

CHESTER SQ

CORONATION COTTS

BOLAND RD

RIVER VIEW

DUNLIN CT

Lynemouth Fst Sch

EDEN TERR

DALTON AVE

Liby

3

INGLEBY TERR

ALBION TERR

+

CHURCH SQ

GUILDFORD SQ

HENLEY SQ

JERSEY SQ

MARKET ST

SEA VIEW

+

PO

91

KINGSLEY RD

OAKLAND TERR

Lynemouth

QUEEN ST

BRIDGE RD

MATLOCK SQ 1

NEVILLE SQ 2

MARKET SQ

Sewage Works

Lyne Hill

2

PARK VIEW

PARK RD

Works

Cemy

1

Power Station

Lyne Sands

NE63

90

Works

29 A B 30 C D 31 E F

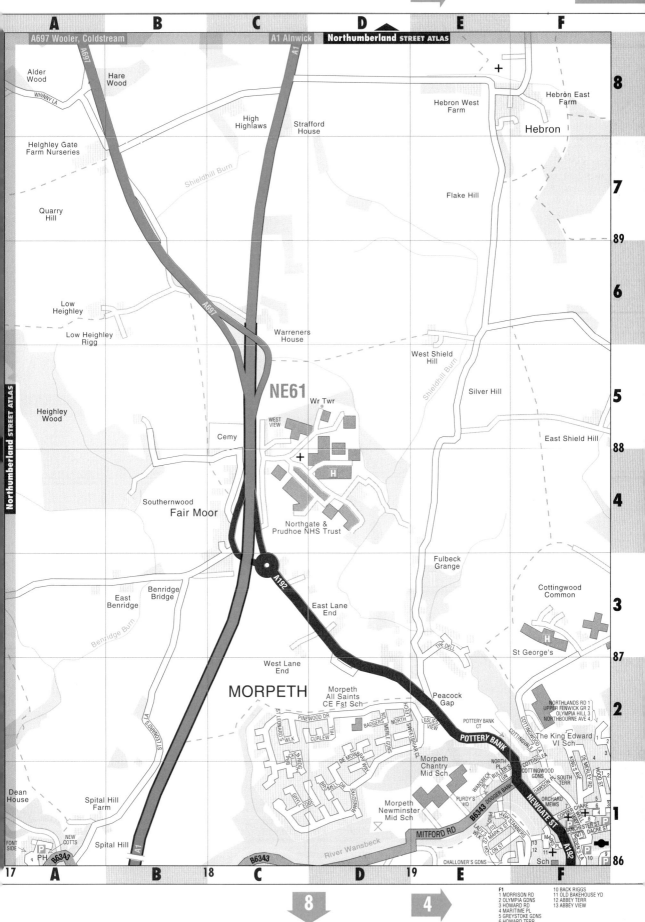

Northumberland STREET ATLAS

A697 Wooler, Coldstream
A1 Alnwick

Alder Wood
Hare Wood
Hebron West Farm
Hebron East Farm
Hebron
Helghley Gate Farm Nurseries
High Highlaws
Strafford House
Flake Hill
Quarry Hill
Low Heighley
Low Heighley Rigg
Warreners House
West Shield Hill
Silver Hill
Heighley Wood
NE61
Wr Twr
WEST VIEW
East Shield Hill
Cemy
Southernwood
Fair Moor
Northgate & Prudhoe NHS Trust
Fulbeck Grange
Cottingwood Common
East Benridge
Benridge Bridge
East Lane End
THE DELL
St George's
NORTHLANDS RD 1
UPPER FENWICK GR 2
OLYMPIA HILL 3
NORTHBOURNE AVE 4
West Lane End
MORPETH
Morpeth All Saints CE Fst Sch
Peacock Gap
POTTERY BANK CT
LESLIES VIEW
POTTERY BANK
The King Edward VI Sch
ST LEONARDS WLK
PINEWOOD DR
CURLEW
BADGERS
MERLE GDNS
NORTH SWEETBRIAR CL
DE MOWBRAY WAY
Morpeth Chantry Mid Sch
COTTINGWOOD GDNS
SOUTH TERR
Dean House
Spital Hill Farm
BLUEBELL
WANSDYKE
EDGE
Morpeth Newminster Mid Sch
PURDY'S HO
DOGGER BANK
ORCHARD MEWS
COPPER CHARE
MANCHESTER ST
DACRE ST
FONT SIDE
NEW COTTS
PH
Spital Hill
MITFORD RD
B6343
River Wansbeck
CHALLONER'S GDNS

F1
1 MORRISON RD
2 OLYMPIA GDNS
3 HOWARD RD
4 MARITIME PL
5 GREYSTOKE GDNS
6 HOWARD TERR
7 ST JAMES TERR
8 WELLWAY CT
9 CORPORATION YD
10 BACK RIGGS
11 OLD BAKEHOUSE YD
12 ABBEY TERR
13 ABBEY VIEW

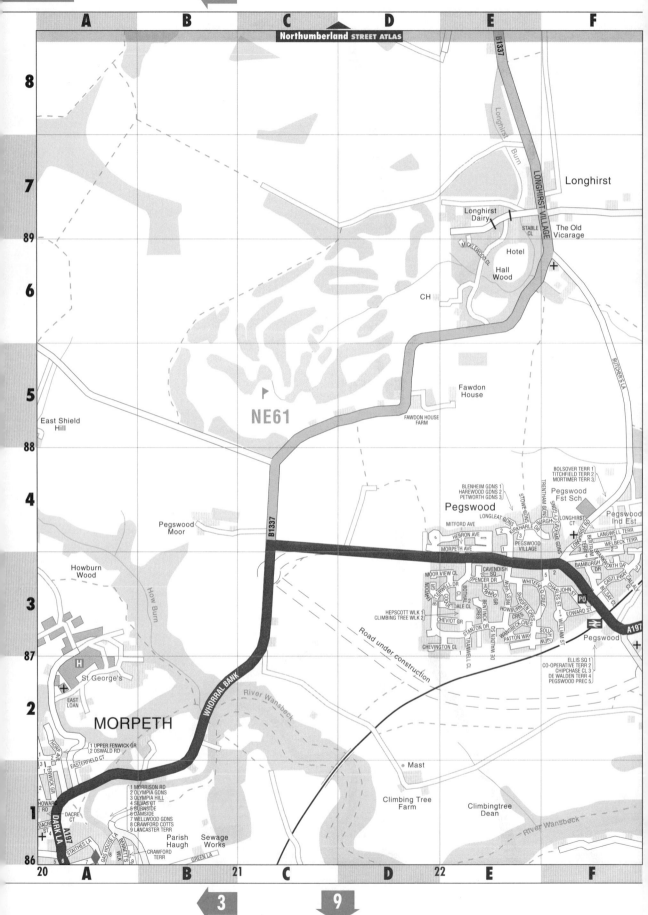

8

7

89

6

5

NE61

88

4

3

87

2

1

86

East Shield
Hill

Howburn
Wood

How Burn

MORPETH

St George's

EAST
LOAN

THORP AVE
FENWICK GR

1 UPPER FENWICK GR
2 OSWALD RD

EASTERFIELD CT

DACRE
CT

HOWARD
RD

DACRE ST

DARK LA

A197

STAITHES LA

GAS HOUSE LA

BENNETT'S
WLK

1 MORRISON RD
2 OLYMPIA GDNS
3 OLYMPIA HILL
4 SILVAS CT
5 BURNSIDE
6 DAMSIDE
7 WELLWOOD GDNS
8 CRAWFORD COTTS
9 LANCASTER TERR

CRAWFORD
TERR

GREEN LA

Parish
Haugh

Sewage
Works

River Wansbeck

WHORRAL BANK

Pegswood
Moor

Longhirst
Burn

Longhirst

LONGHIRST VILLAGE

B1337

Longhirst Dairy

The Old
Vicarage

STABLE
CL

Hotel

MICKLEWOOD CL

Hall
Wood

CH

Fawdon
House

Fawdon
House
Farm

FAWDON HOUSE FARM

B1337

BUTCHER'S LA

Pegswood

BLENHEIM GDNS 1
HAREWOOD GDNS 2
PETWORTH GDNS 3

MITFORD AVE

HEBRON AVE

MORPETH AVE

LONGLEAT GDNS

STOWE GDNS

TRENTHAM GDNS

KIRKHARLE DR

Pegswood
Village

BURGH GDNS

SNOW DROP GDNS

LONGHIRST
CT

Bolsover Terr 1
Titchfield Terr 2
Mortimer Terr 3

Pegswood Fst Sch

Pegswood
Ind Est

LANGWELL TERR

WELBECK TERR

MARKWORTH RD

BERTRAM DR

BAMBURGH
DR

CASTLEWAY

BELSAY CT

MOOR VIEW CL

SPENCER DR

BOTHAL
GR

HOWDON RD

CAVENDISH
SQ

WHITFIELD CRES

HOWARD
DR

BETHNICK
CRES

HOWBURN
CRES

WANSBECK CRES

SHAPFELL CRES

CHARLES ST

JOHN ST

EDWARD ST

WILLIAM ST

SOUTH
VIEW

BUTTERWELL DR

COQUETDALE CL

HEPSCOTT WLK 1
CLIMBING TREE WLK 2

CHEVIOT GR

STANTON DR

TRANWELL CL

PATTON WAY

CHEVINGTON CL

MITFORD GDNS

Road under construction

PO

Pegswood

A197

Ellis Sq 1
Co-operative Terr 2
Chipchase Cl 3
De Walden Terr 4
Pegswood Prec 5

Mast

Climbing Tree
Farm

Climbingtree
Dean

River Wansbeck

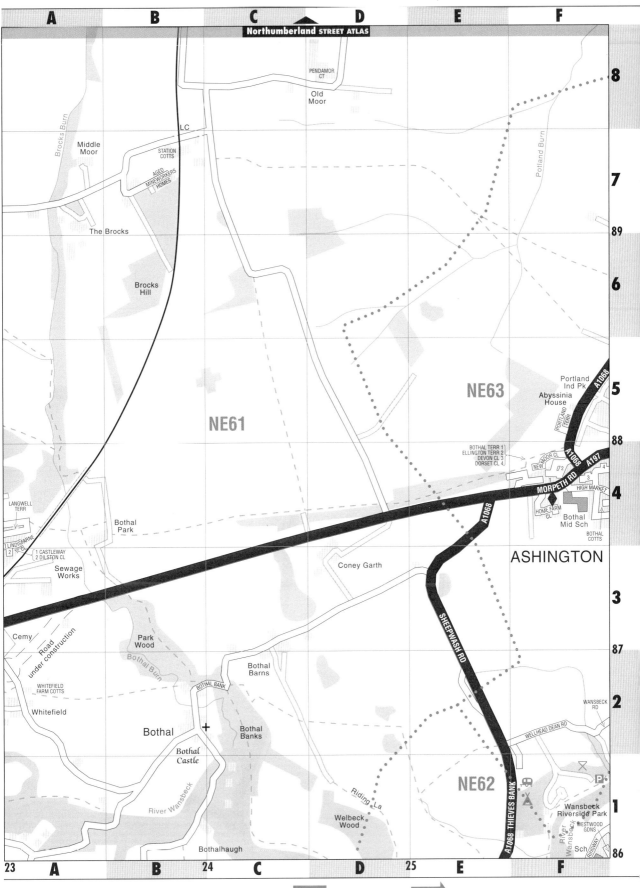

8
7
89
6
5
88
4
3
87
2
1
86

PENDAMOR CT

Old Moor

Brocks Burn

Middle Moor

LC

STATION COTTS

AGED MINEWORKERS HOMES

The Brocks

Brocks Hill

Portland Burn

NE63

Portland Ind Pk

Abyssinia House

A1068

PORTLAND TERR

NE61

BOTHAL TERR 1
ELLINGTON TERR 2
DEVON CL 3
DORSET CL 4

NEW

A1068

A197

A1068

MOOR CL

MORPETH RD

HIGH MARKET

LANGWELL TERR

HOME FARM CL

Bothal Mid Sch

BOTHAL COTTS

1 LINDISFARNE
2

Bothal Park

ASHINGTON

1 CASTLEWAY
2 DILSTON CL

Sewage Works

Coney Garth

A1068

SHEEPWASH RD

Cemy

Road under construction

Park Wood

Bothal Burn

Bothal Barns

WHITEFIELD FARM COTTS

BOTHAL BANK

WANSBECK RD

Whitefield

Bothal Banks

WELLHEAD DEAN RD

Bothal

Bothal Castle

NE62

A1068 THIEVES BANK

Wansbeck Riverside Park

WESTWOOD GDNS

Sch

River Wansbeck

Riding La

Welbeck Wood

River Wansbeck

RIDGWAY

Bothalhaugh

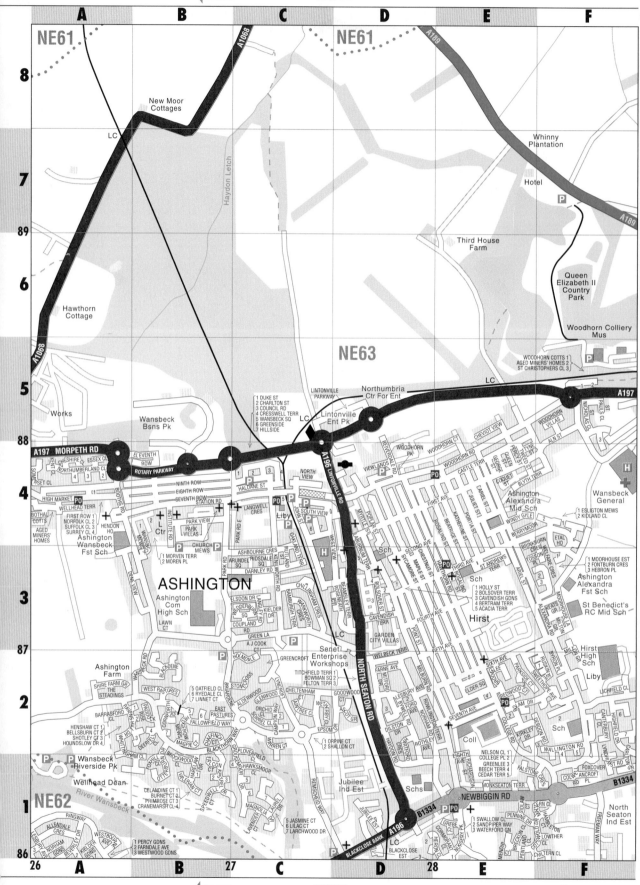

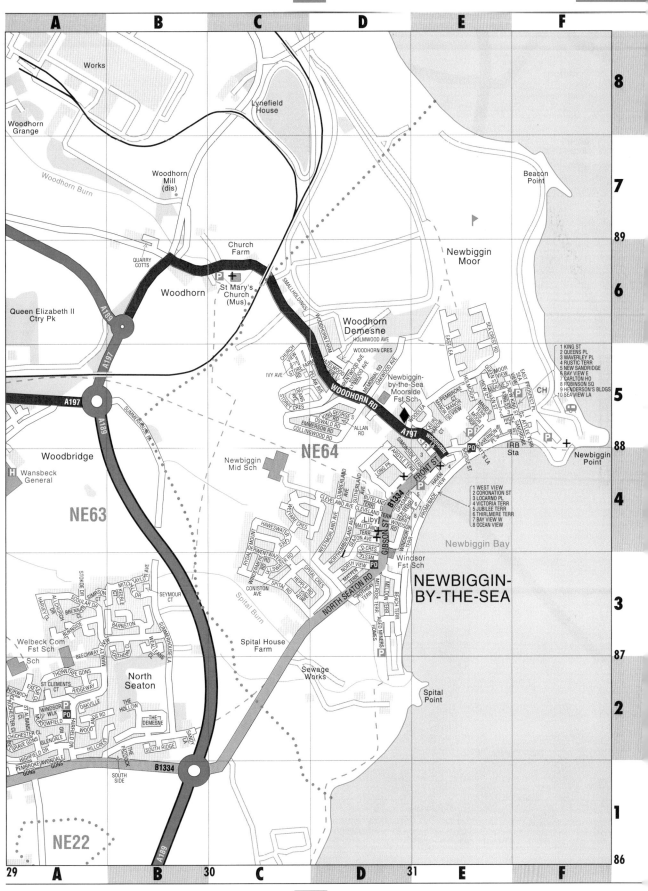

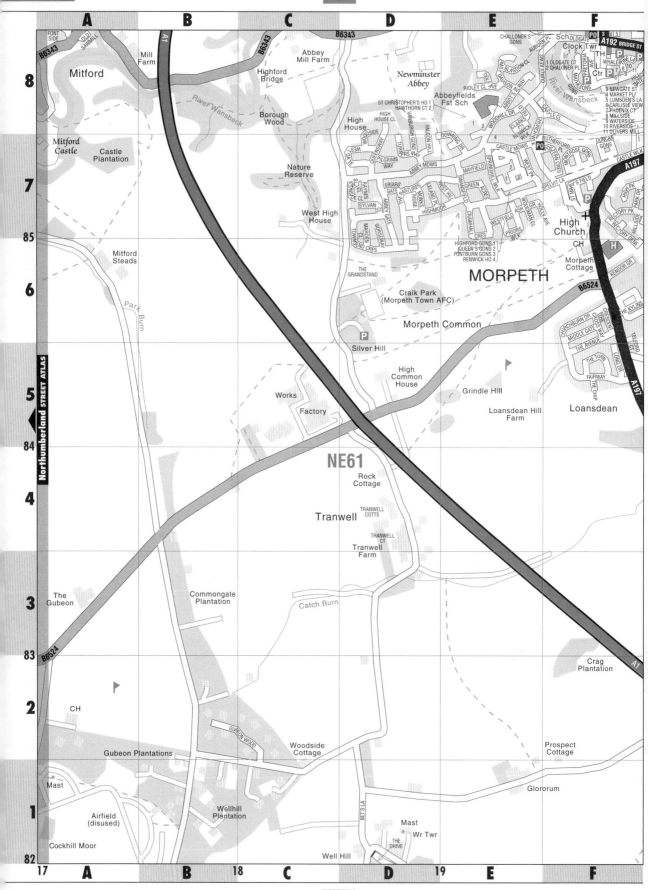

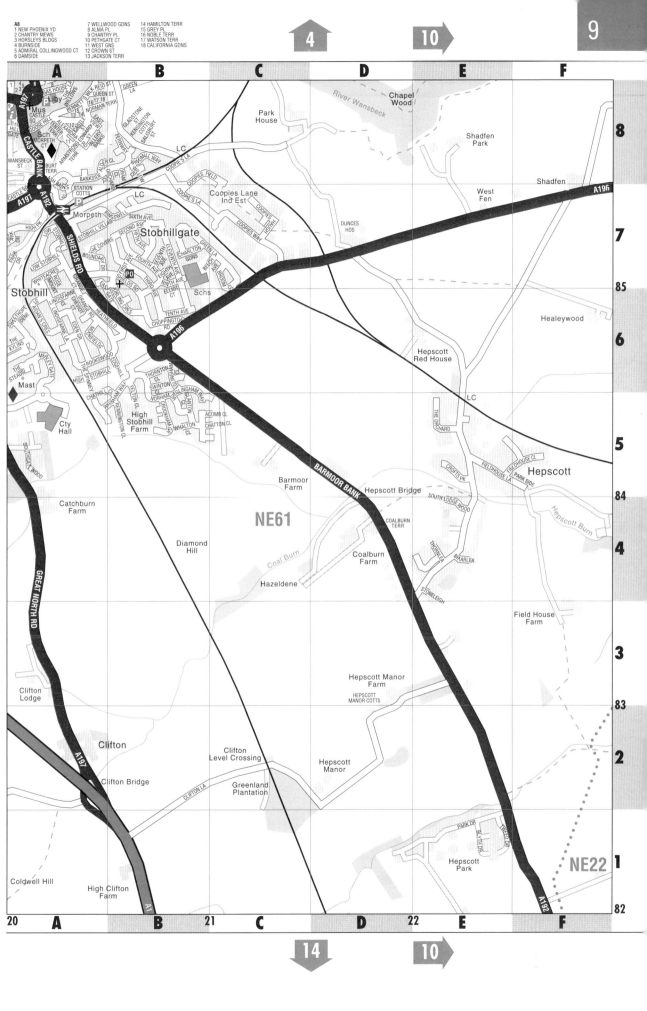

9 5

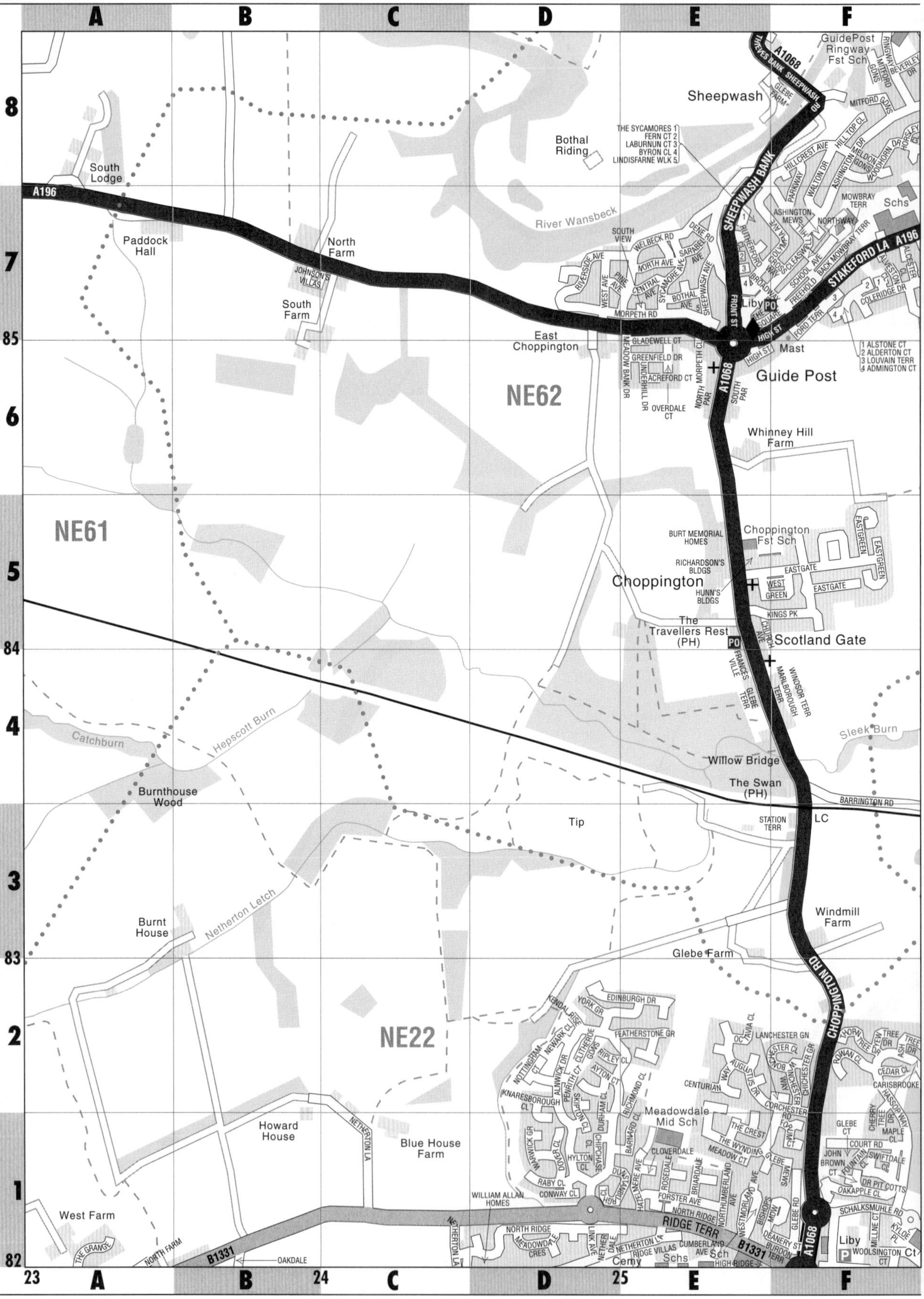
A B C D E F
8 7 85 6 5 84 4 3 83 2 1 82
23 24 25
A196
A1068
B1331
South Lodge
Paddock Hall
North Farm
JOHNSON'S VILLAS
South Farm
Bothal Riding
River Wansbeck
Sheepwash
GuidePost Ringway Fst Sch
SHEEPWASH BANK
THE SYCAMORES 1
FERN CT 2
LABURNUN CT 3
BYRON CL 4
LINDISFARNE WLK 5
HILLCREST AVE
HILL TOP CL
MITFORD GDNS
ASHINGTON MEWS
MOWBRAY TERR
Schs
NORTHWAY
STAKEFORD LA
BACK MOWBRAY TERR
COLERIDGE DR
SOUTH VIEW
WELBECK RD
NORTH AVE
RIVERSIDE AVE
WEST AVE
PINE AVE
CENTRAL AVE
SYCAMORE AVE
BOTHAL AVE
SHEEPWASH AVE
MORPETH RD
FRONT ST
Liby
PO
HIGH ST
Mast
THE SQUARE
FORD TERR
1 ALSTONE CT
2 ALDERTON CT
3 LOUVAIN TERR
4 ADMINGTON CT
East Choppington
GLADEWELL CT
GREENFIELD DR
MEADOW BANK DR
UNDERHILL DR
ACREFORD CT
OVERDALE CT
NORTH MORPETH CL
NORTH PAR
SOUTH PAR
Guide Post
NE62
Whinney Hill Farm
NE61
BURT MEMORIAL HOMES
Choppington Fst Sch
RICHARDSON'S BLDGS
Choppington
HUNN'S BLDGS
EASTGATE
EASTGREEN
WEST GREEN
KINGS PK
The Travellers Rest (PH)
CHURCH AVE
Scotland Gate
FRANCES VILLE
GLEBE TERR
MARLBOROUGH TERR
WINDSOR TERR
Catchburn
Hepscott Burn
Sleek Burn
Willow Bridge
The Swan (PH)
BARRINGTON RD
Burnthouse Wood
Tip
STATION TERR
LC
Burnt House
Netherton Letch
Windmill Farm
Glebe Farm
CHOPPINGTON RD
EDINBURGH DR
KENDAL RISE
YORK GR
FEATHERSTONE GR
LANCHESTER GN
NE22
CENTURIAN WAY
AUGUSTUS DR
CHICHESTER GR
WINCHESTER
CORCHESTER
NOTTINGHAM CT
NEWARK CL
ALNWICK DR
PENRITH CT
CLITHEROE GDNS
RIPLEY CL
AYTON CT
RICHMOND CL
KNARESBOROUGH CL
SKIPTON CL
DURHAM CL
Meadowdale Mid Sch
THE CREST
THE WYNDING
MEADOW CT
GLEBE MEWS
CEDAR CL
CARISBROOKE
GLEBE CT
CHERRY TREE DR
MAPLE CL
COURT RD
JOHN BROWN CT
FOUNTAIN CL
SWIFTDALE CL
DR PIT COTTS
OAKAPPLE CL
SCHALKSMUHLE RD
Howard House
Blue House Farm
NETHERTON LA
WARWICK GR
DOVER CL
HYLTON CL
CHIPCHASE CL
BARNARD CL
CLOVERDALE
ROSEDALE
BRIARDALE
NORTHUMBERLAND AVE
WESTMORLAND AVE
RABY CL
CONWAY CL
WILLIAM ALLAN HOMES
FORSTER AVE
NORTH RIDGE
RIDGE TERR
BISHOPS MDW
DEANERY ST
BURDON TERR
GLEBE RD
MILLNE CT
KYLOE PL
Liby
P
WOOLSINGTON CT
West Farm
THE GRANGE
NORTH FARM
OAKDALE
MEADOWDALE CRES
LINK AVE
NETHERDALE
NETHERTON LA
RIDGE VILLAS
CUMBERLAND AVE
Sch
Cemy
Schs
HIGH RIDGE

9 15

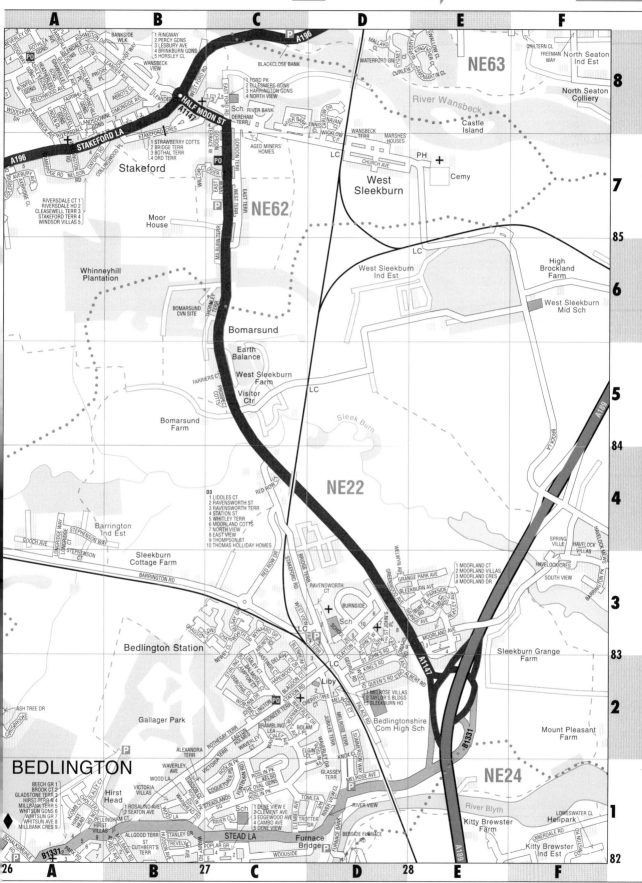

A   B   C   D   E   F

NE22

Ind Est

NE63

SANDY BAY CVN PK

LINKS VIEW

WANSBECK ST

SEA VIEW

River Wansbeck

8

7

Works

Sewage Works

THE PADDOCKS

P

WEST VIEW

SOUTH VIEW

WEMBLEY GDNS

NORTH VIEW

WEMBLEY TERR

85

6

LC

Sleekburn Bsns Ctr

NE24

5

Cambois

Refuse Tip

Cow Gut

84

LC

Cambois Fst Sch

4

NE22

NORTHFIELD RD

SANDFIELD RD

WATERFIELD RD

WILSON AVE

HARBOUR VIEW

1 UNITY TERR
2 RIDLEY TERR
3 AGED MINERS HOMES

1
3 PO
2

East Sleekburn

SELBOURNE TERR

3

Sleek Burn

WEST BRIDGE ST

83

NE22

2

Factory Point

River Blyth

North Beach

Jetties

WORSDELL ST

DALE ST

GRAY ST

1

NE24

BLYTH

Mast

Sewage Works

Kitty Brewster Ind Est

THIRLMERE WAY

COWLEY RD

SPENCER RD

SPENCER

PORTLAND ST 1
THOMPSON ST 2
BALFOUR ST 3
GRIEVE ST 4

MILLFIELD GDNS

CRAWFORD ST

ANN'S ROW

WILLOW AVE

POPLAR AVE

CAMBRE AVE

CHESTNUT

LINKS AVE

North Blyth

5 ARGYLE ST
6 THE CLOSE
7 THOMPSON ST
8 ARGYLE MEWS
9 GOSCHEN ST

GRASMERE WAY

CONISTON RD

1 BUTTERMERE WAY
2 BEECHER ST

TA Ctr

A193

COWPEN RD

B1329

HODGSON'S RD

REGENT ST

B1329

82

29   A   B   30   C   D   31   E   F

A   B   C   D   E   F

Whitehouse
Farm Ctr

Airfield
(disused)

Saltwick
Plantation

Saltwick Moor

Catraw Burn

GREEN LA

BEL'S LA

Point to Point
Course

THE
VILLAS

North
Saltwick

81

Duddo Hill West
Plantation

6

Catraw Burn

Works

Duddo Hill

GREEN LA

5

Saltwick
House

80

Saltwick

NE61

West Duddo

4

Middle
Duddo

West Catraw
Wood

Duddo Burn

3

BELL'S HILL

Shilvington Burn

79

Middle Catraw
Wood

NE20

2

Whinney Hill
Farm

GREEN LA

Bog Hall

1

Church
Wood

Bellasis
Farm

78

Northumberland STREET ATLAS

A B C D E F

8

Netherton Letch

Moor Farm
Estate

LC

STANNINGTON STATION RD

Works

Dovecote Farm

7

Moor
Farm

NE22

Netherton
Wood

81

MOOR LA

Netherton Park
Farm

Mast

Buckie's
Bridge

Lough
House

6

Netherton Park

THE DRIVE

Low Middle
Moor

5

NE61

East
Moor

80

West House
Farm

4

Catraw Valley
North

THE BEECHES

Briery Hill

Stannington
Fst Sch

THE GLEBE

GREEN RD

Catraw

CHURCH RD

BEECH LA

PH

Stannington

Catraw Valley
South

P

PO

THE CLOSE

Town
Farm

THE LIMES

BRIERY LA

3

Catraw Burn

Swan
Farm

Fox
Hill

Plessey Hall
Farm

79

Sewage
Works

Stannington Vale

NE23

Plessey
Wood

Stottford
Dene

2

Stannington
Banks

Greensfield
Plantation

Catraw
Plantation

Victoria
Plantation

River Blyth

STANNINGTON
VALE

Stannington
Bridge

Shotton
North
Farm

1

Ewe Hill
Plantation

Scroggy
Plantation

NE13

Burntland
Plantation

Mill
Banks

SHOTTON LA

78

20 A B 21 C D 22 E F

A1

A192

B1331

A192

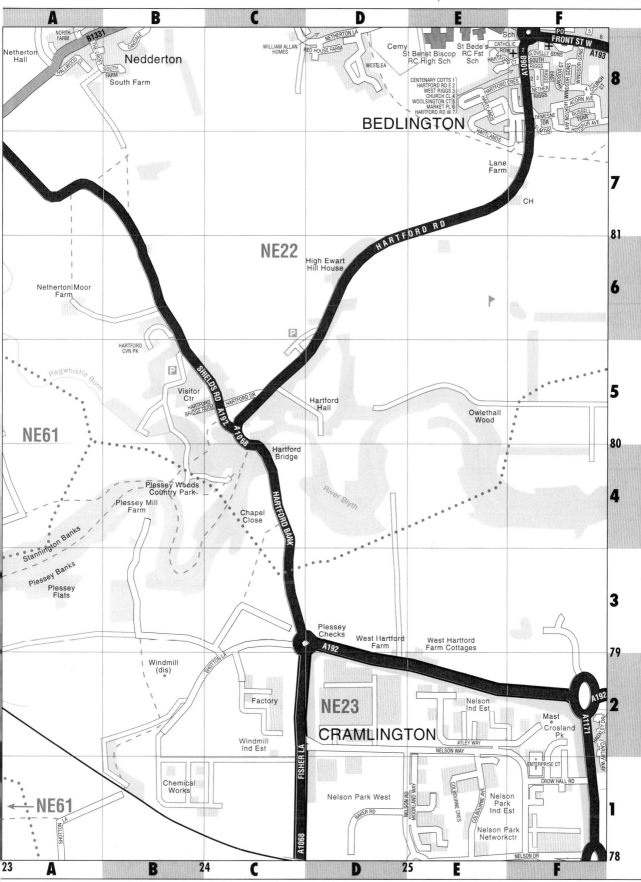

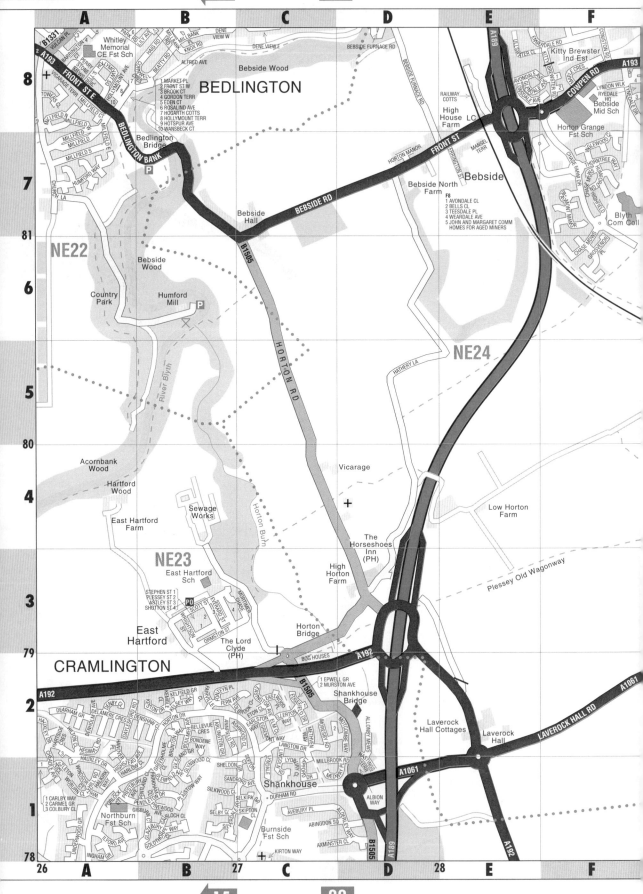

15
11

BEDLINGTON

1 MARKET PL
2 FRONT ST W
3 BROOK CT
4 GORDON TERR
5 EDEN CT
6 ROSALIND AVE
7 HOGARTH COTTS
8 HOLLYMOUNT TERR
9 HOTSPUR AVE
10 WANSBECK CT

Whitley Memorial CE Fst Sch

Bedside Wood

Bedlington Bridge

Bedlington Bank

NE22

Bebside Wood

Country Park

Humford Mill

Bebside Hall

BEBSIDE RD

HORTON RD

River Blyth

Acornbank Wood

Hartford Wood

East Hartford Farm

Sewage Works

Horton Burn

NE23

East Hartford Sch

STEPHEN ST 1
PLESSEY ST 2
ASTLEY ST 3
SHOTTON ST 4

East Hartford

CRAMLINGTON

A192

1 EPWELL GR
2 MURSTON AVE

The Lord Clyde (PH)

Horton Bridge

BOG HOUSES

A192

Shankhouse Bridge

Shankhouse

1 CARLBY WAY
2 CARMEL GR
3 COLBURY CL

Northburn Fst Sch

Burnside Fst Sch

Bebside North Farm

F8
1 AVONDALE CL
2 BELLS CL
3 TEESDALE PL
4 WEARDALE AVE
5 JOHN AND MARGARET COMM
  HOMES FOR AGED MINERS

Bebside

High House Farm

RAILWAY COTTS

HORTON MANOR

FRONT ST

NE24

HATHERY LA

Vicarage

Low Horton Farm

The Horseshoes Inn (PH)

High Horton Farm

Plessey Old Wagonway

Laverock Hall Cottages

Laverock Hall

LAVEROCK HALL RD

A1061

A1061

ALBION WAY

Kitty Brewster Ind Est

Horton Grange Fst Sch

Bebside Mid Sch

RYEDALE HO

Blyth Com Coll

A193

COWPEN RD

B1331

A193

FRONT ST E

A189

B1505

A1061

A192

B1505

15
22

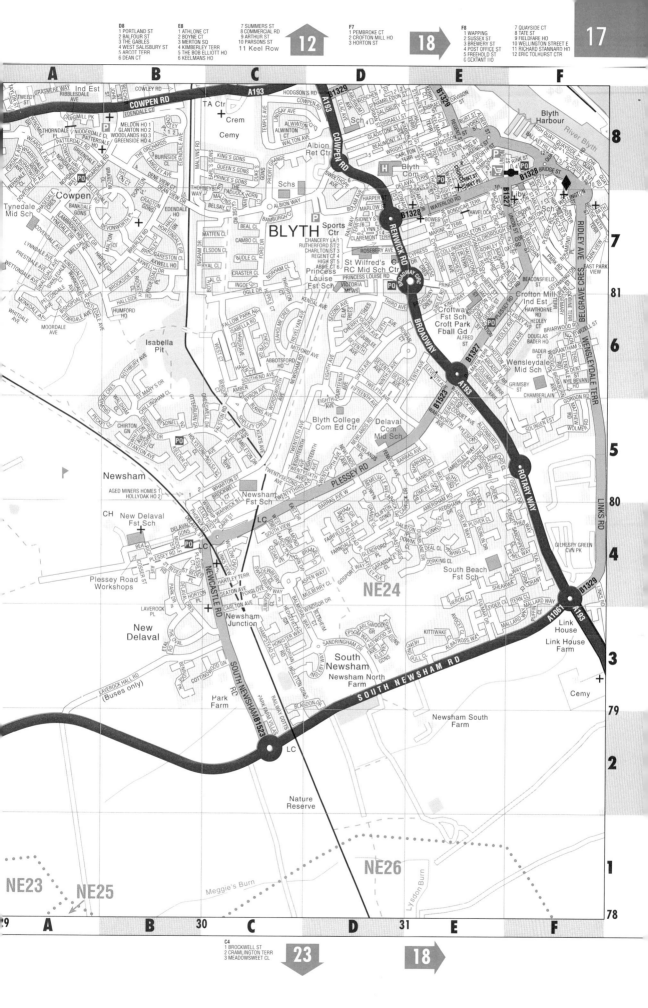

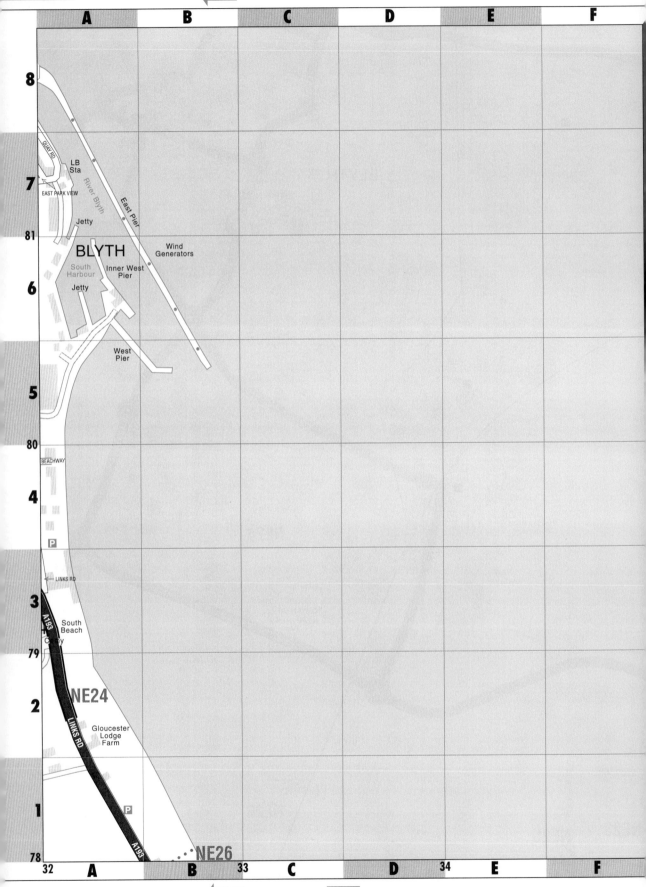

A　B　C　D　E　F

8

QUAY RD

LB
Sta

EAST PARK VIEW

River Blyth

East Pier

Jetty

7

81

BLYTH

Wind
Generators

South
Harbour

Inner West
Pier

Jetty

6

West
Pier

5

80

BEACHWAY

4

P

← LINKS RD

3

A193

South
Beach

Quay

79

NE24

2

LINKS RD

Gloucester
Lodge
Farm

1

P

78

A193

NE26

A B C D E F

NE61

Bellasis
Bridge

8

River Blyth

GREEN LA

River Pont

Pont Ends
Plantation

7

Make me Rich

77

Berwick Hill
Low House

Low Horton
House

Ewe Hill

6

5

NE20

76

NE13

Old Horton
Grange

4

West End
Farm

BERWICK HILL
COTTS.

Gravel La

East
Farm

New Horton
Grange

NEW HORTON
GRANGE COTTS

South East
Farm

Carr House

Berwick Hill

3

Park House Farm
Cottages

75

Park
House

Fox
Covert

PONT PK

DANGER AREA

2

Rifle
Range

Blackpool Drain

1

Carr
Plantation

74

Northumberland STREET ATLAS

A **B** **C** **D** **E** **F**

SHOTTON LA

SHOTTON LA

Shotton

NE61

Shotton South Farm

8

Ewe Hill

Blagdon Lake

NE61

Lake Plantation

Election Plantation

Home Farm

New Kennels

New Cottages

Coal Wood

Lake Wiseman

Old Kennels

7

Cascade Dene

North Wood

77

Twist Plantation

Bog House

Blagdon Hall

Shotton Edge

Snitter Burn

6

Grove Pond

North Wood

Fusilier Plantation

Deer Park Wood

Blagdon Park

LEGGES DR

SOUTH DR

Thornhill Cottage

5

Park House

Shotton Grange

76

Milkhope Plantation

MILKHOPE CTR

NE13

4

Hoys Wood

Shotton Edge South

A1

3

Brenkley

North Farm

Crow Wood

Seven Mile House

75

South Brenkley

East Brenkley Farm

2

Trinidad Plantation

1

Gardener's Houses Farm

74

Carr Grange Farm

PRESTWICK CARR RD

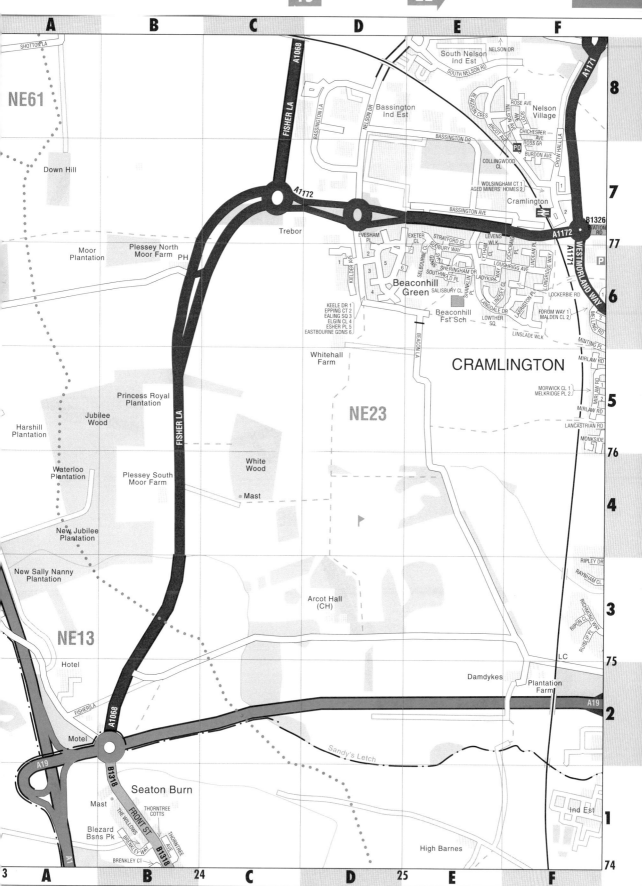

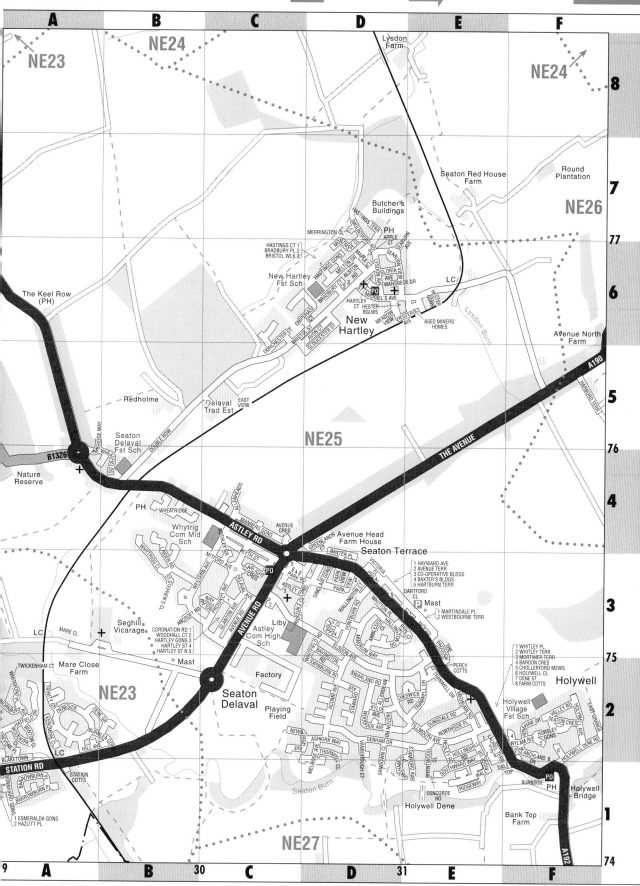

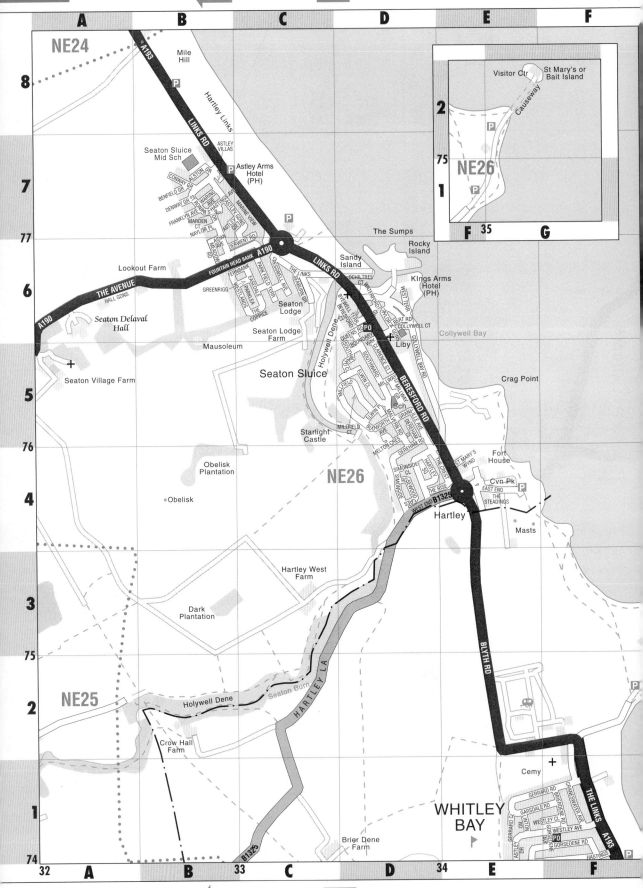

NE24

Mile Hill

Hartley Links

A193

LINKS RD

P

Astley Villas

Seaton Sluice Mid Sch

CONWAY GR
ALSTON GR
BENFIELD GR
ST WARING
DENWAY GR
HASTINGS AV
FRANKLYN AVE
ASTLEY GDNS
MARDEN CT
ST BRIAN'S
NAYLOR PL
AIDAN AVE
DERWENT RD
WESTLANDS

MARINE VIEW

Astley Arms Hotel (PH)

P

Lookout Farm

THE AVENUE
HALL GDNS

A190

A190

FOUNTAIN HEAD BANK

FERNBANK
GREENRIGG
PARK FIELD TERR
EASTDALE
PARKLEA
CRESSWELL AVE
SEABURN GR
THE COPPICE

THE LINKS

Seaton Lodge

Seaton Lodge Farm

LINKS RD

P

The Sumps

Sandy Island

Rocky Island

OCHILTREE CT
WATERFORD
BYWELL GDNS
BERESFORD GDNS
WEST TERR
BEAT RD
COLLYWELL CT

Kings Arms Hotel (PH)

Collywell Bay

Crag Point

QUEENS RD
PO
BOUNDARY
SOUTHWARD
CLARENCE ST
Liby
COLLYWELL BAY RD

Seaton Delaval Hall

Mausoleum

Seaton Village Farm

Seaton Sluice

Starlight Castle

MILLFIELD
ELWIN CT
ELWIN PL
MILLWAY
GRANT
GLEBE AVE
MILLFIELD CT
MILLVIEW
BLUNORTH
MILLFIELD AVE
Sch
BERESFORD RD

MELTON CRES
DERHAM RD

Obelisk Plantation

Obelisk

NE26

SIMONSIDE CL
SIMONSIDE RD
HARTLEY SQ
THE CREST
ROSEWOOD
SIMONSIDE CRES
THE RISE
ST MARY'S WYND

Fort House

Cvn Pk
EAST END
THE STEADINGS

B1325

WEST END

Hartley

Masts

Hartley West Farm

Dark Plantation

BLYTH RD

HARTLEY LA

Seaton Burn

Holywell Dene

NE25

Crow Hall Farm

B1325

Brier Dene Farm

Cemy

WHITLEY BAY

GERRARD RD
GARSDALE RD
BRIERDENE RD
CRANSWATER CT
WESTLEY CL
GORSEDENE RD
WESTLEY AVE
GERRARD CT
ASTLEY DR
WOLSINGTON
GORSEDENE AVE
PO
GORSEDENE RD
HASTINGS

THE LINKS

A193

P

Inset (NE26):

Visitor Ctr

St Mary's or Bait Island

Causeway

P

NE26

P

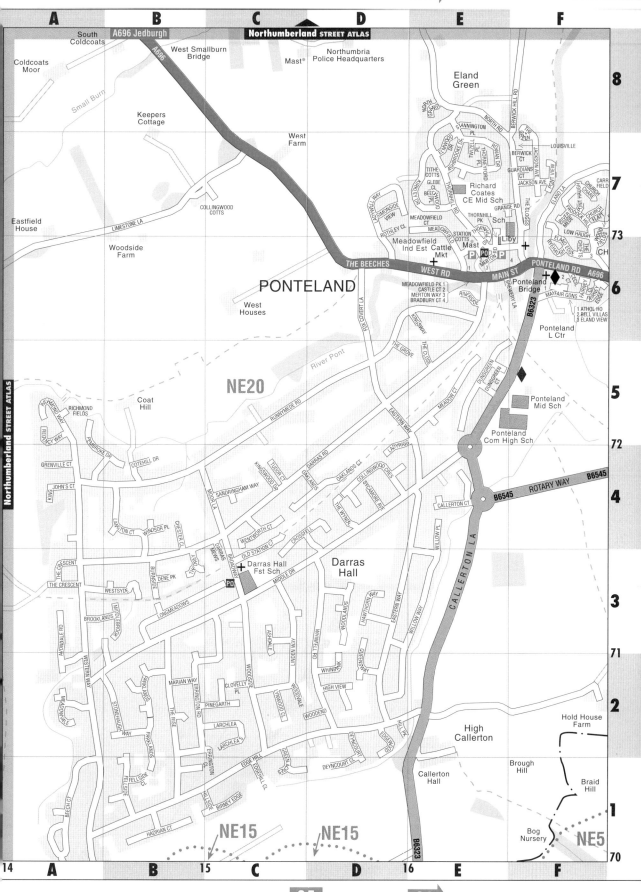

| | 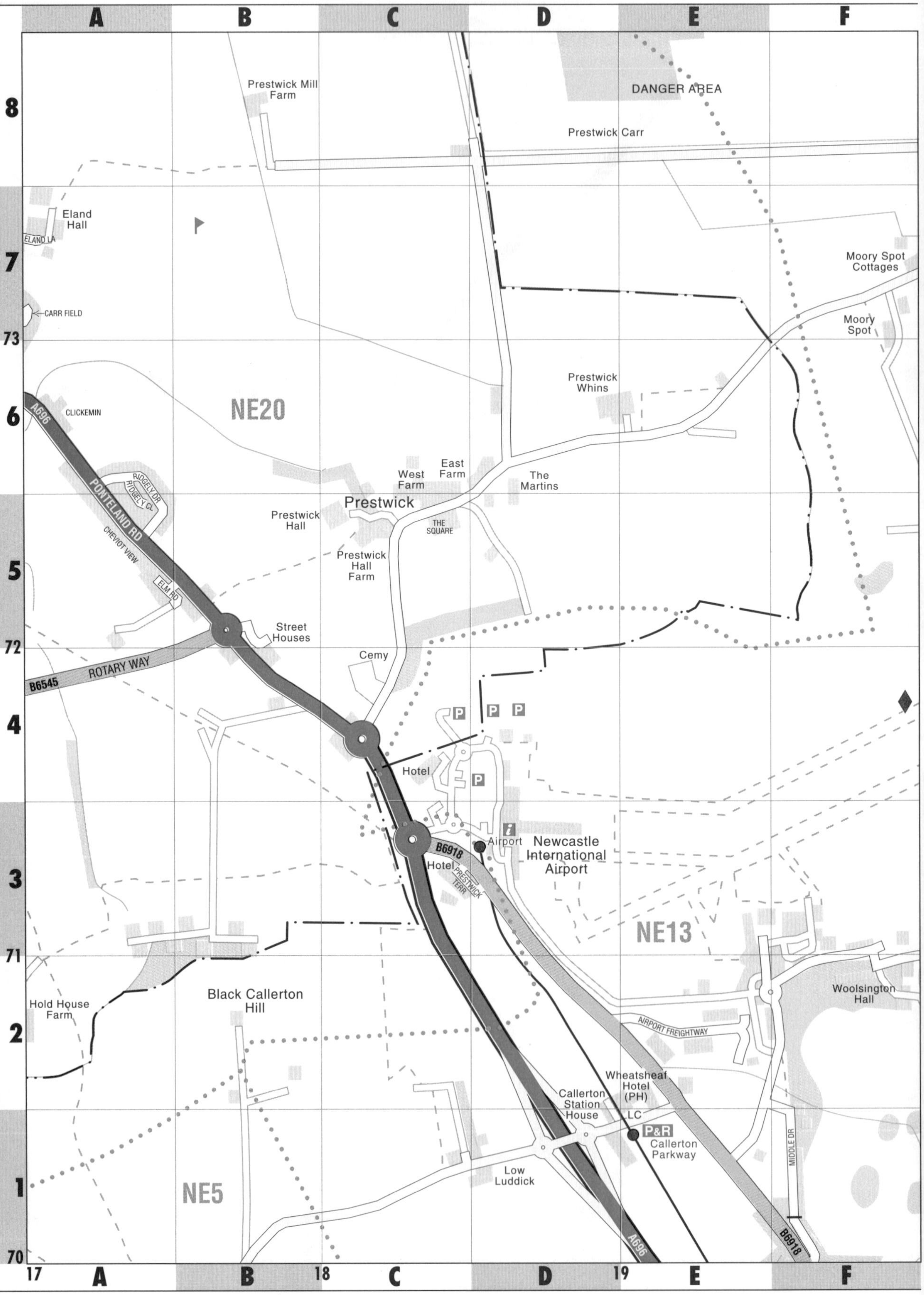 A | B | C | D | E | F |

8

Prestwick Mill Farm

DANGER AREA

Prestwick Carr

Eland Hall

7

ELAND LA

Moory Spot Cottages

Moory Spot

CARR FIELD

73

CLICKEMIN

NE20

Prestwick Whins

6

A696

PONTELAND RD

RIDGELY DR
RIDGELY CL

CHEVIOT VIEW

East Farm

West Farm

The Martins

Prestwick

ELM RD

Prestwick Hall

THE SQUARE

5

Prestwick Hall Farm

Street Houses

72

Cemy

B6545 ROTARY WAY

P P P

4

Hotel

P

Newcastle International Airport

i Airport

3

Hotel
PRESTWICK TERR

B6918

NE13

71

Black Callerton Hill

Woolsington Hall

Hold House Farm

AIRPORT FREIGHTWAY

2

Wheatsheaf Hotel (PH)

Callerton Station House

LC

MIDDLE DR

P&R Callerton Parkway

1

NE5

Low Luddick

A696

B6918

70

| 17 | A | | B | 18 | C | | D | 19 | E | | F |

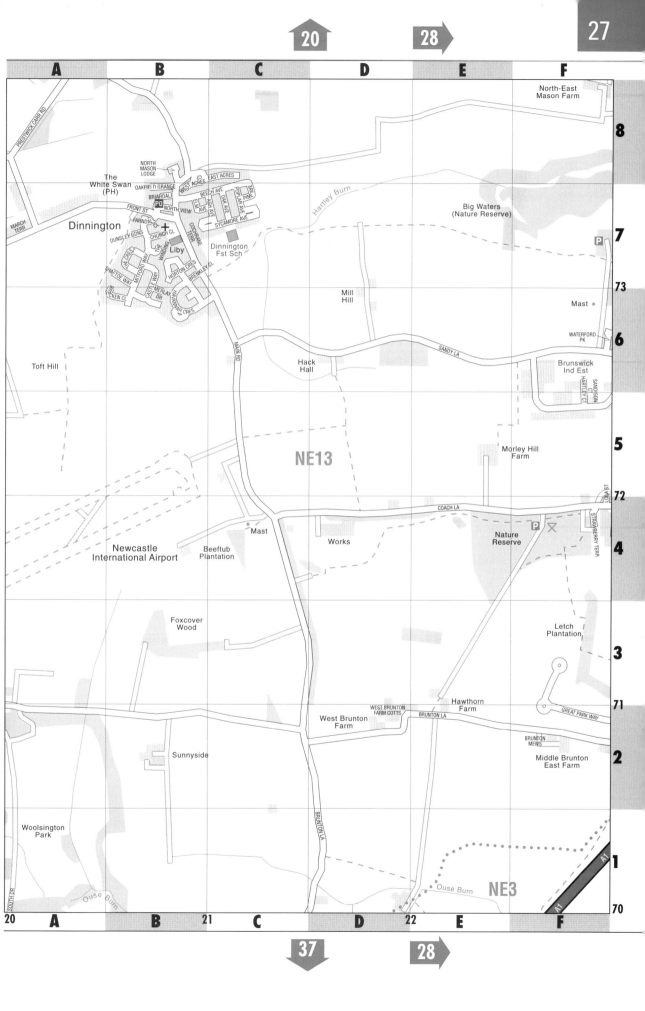

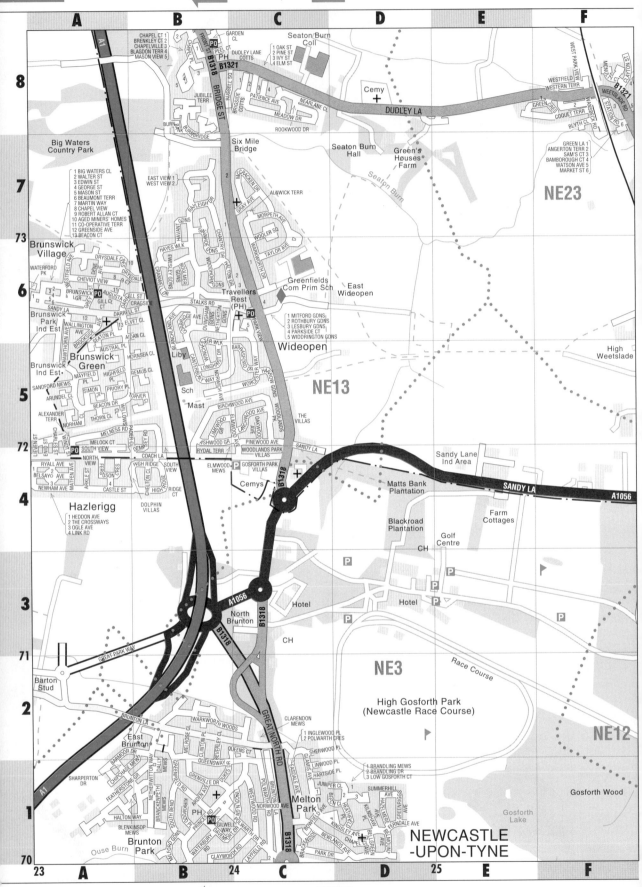

8

7

73

6

5

72

4

3

71

2

1

70

Big Waters
Country Park

1 BIG WATERS CL
2 WALTER ST
3 EDWIN ST
4 GEORGE ST
5 MASON ST
6 BEAUMONT TERR
7 MARTIN WAY
8 CHAPEL VIEW
9 ROBERT ALLAN CT
10 AGED MINERS' HOMES
11 CO-OPERATIVE TERR
12 GREENSIDE AVE
13 BEACON CT

Brunswick
Village

Brunswick
Park
Ind Est

Brunswick
Ind Est

Brunswick
Green

Hazlerigg

1 HEDDON AVE
2 THE CROSSWAYS
3 OGLE AVE
4 LINK RD

Barton
Stud

East
Brunton

Brunton
Park

Seaton Burn
Coll

CHAPEL CT 1
BRENKLEY CT 2
CHAPELVILLE 3
BLAGDON TERR 4
MASON VIEW 5

1 OAK ST
2 PINE ST
3 IVY ST
4 ELM ST

DUDLEY LA

Seaton Burn
Hall

Green's Houses
Farm

Seaton Burn

Six Mile
Bridge

Greenfields
Com Prim Sch

East
Wideopen

Travellers
Rest
(PH)

1 MITFORD GDNS
2 ROTHBURY GDNS
3 LESBURY GDNS
4 PARKSIDE CT
5 WIDDRINGTON GDNS

Wideopen

NE13

THE
VILLAS

Sandy Lane
Ind Area

Matts Bank
Plantation

Blackroad
Plantation

Golf
Centre

Farm
Cottages

SANDY LA

A1056

North
Brunton

A1056

High Gosforth Park
(Newcastle Race Course)

Race Course

NE3

Hotel

Hotel

CH

CH

NE12

Gosforth Wood

Gosforth
Lake

Melton
Park

NEWCASTLE
-UPON-TYNE

NE23

NE13

WEST
PARK VIEW

WESTFIELD
WESTERN TERR

COQUET TERR

BLYTH CL

B1321

GREEN LA 1
ANGERTON TERR 2
SAM'S CT 3
BAMBOROUGH CT 4
WATSON AVE 5
MARKET ST 6

High
Weetslade

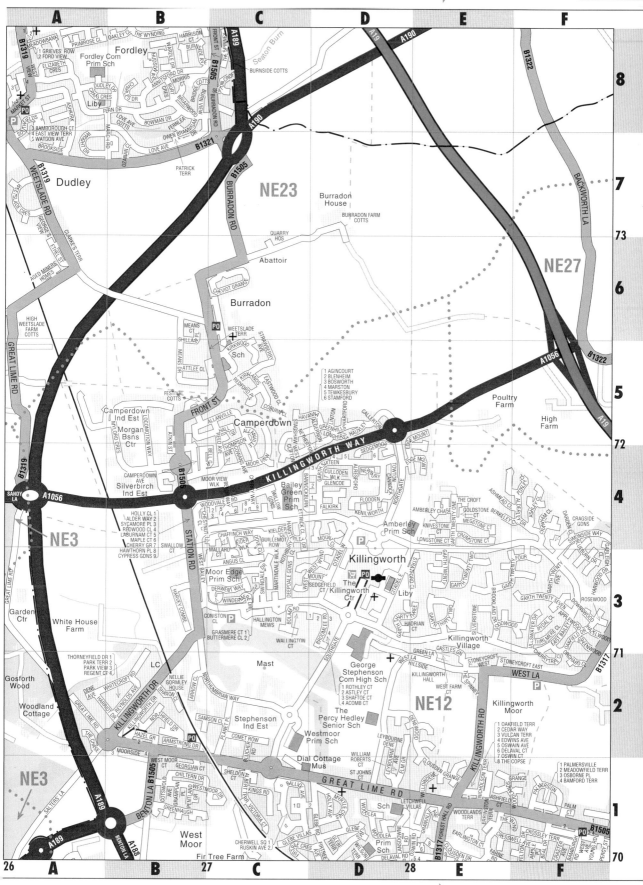

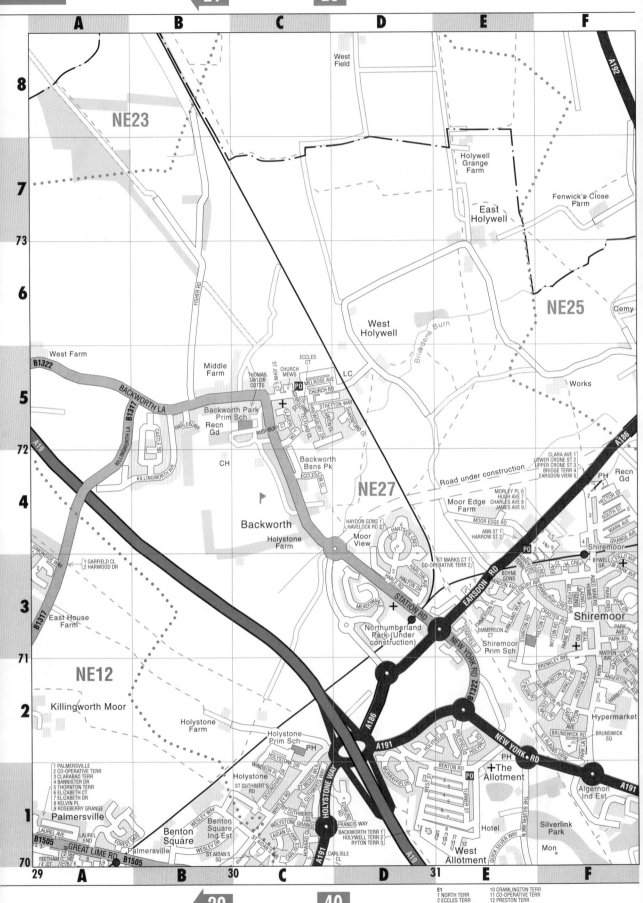

NE23

West Field

NE25

Holywell Grange Farm

Fenwick's Close Farm

East Holywell

Cemy

West Holywell

West Farm

B1322

BACKWORTH LA

Middle Farm

Eccles CT

Church Mews

Thomas Taylor Cotts

LC

Works

B1317

Harlebury

Backworth Park Prim Sch

Recn Gd

Rushbury

Backworth Bsns Pk

CH

Eccles In Cl

NE27

Road under construction

CLARA AVE 1
LOWER CRONE ST 2
UPPER CRONE ST 3
BRIDGE TERR 4
EARSDON VIEW 5

A19

Killingworth Ave

Castle Sq

Moor Edge Farm

MORLEY PL 6
HUGH AVE 7
CHARLES AVE 8
JAMES AVE 9

Recn Gd

PH

HECTOR ST

SOUTH ST

WARK AVE

GRANGE AVE

Shiremoor

HAYDON GDNS 1
HAVELOCK RD 2

Backworth

Holystone Farm

Moor View

HARTSIDE CRES

ANN ST 1
HARROW ST 2

MOOR EDGE RD

BYWELL GR

PARK AVE

AGED MINERS HOMES

Shiremoor

SIMONSIDE WAY

1 GARFIELD CL
2 HARWOOD DR

HARLE RD

HALTON DR

ST MARKS CT 1
CO-OPERATIVE TERR 2

EARSDON RD

BOYNE GDNS

PARK CRES

PARK RD

B1317

East House Farm

MEADOW VALE

Northumberland Park (Under construction)

Shiremoor Prim Sch

MATFEN AVE

NE12

71

NEW YORK RD

BRENKLEY AVE

BRAINTON CL

ANGERTON AVE

HARBOTTLE AVE

NE12

Killingworth Moor

Holystone Farm

B1322

Hypermarket

BRUNSWICK SQ

BRUNSWICK RD

Holystone Prim Sch

PH

A186

A191

NEW YORK RD

ST ALDANS VIEW

PARK LA

Holystone

Windsor Pl

St Cuthbert's Rd

HOLYFIELDS

MURRAYFIELD

BENTON RD

The Allotment

Algernon Ind Est

A191

1 PALMERSVILLE
2 CO-OPERATIVE TERR
3 CLARABAD TERR
4 BANNISTER DR
5 THORNTON TERR
6 ELIZABETH CT
7 ELIZABETH DR
8 KELVIN PL
9 ROSEBERRY GRANGE

HOLYSTONE DR

HOLYSTONE WAY

TURNER ST

Hotel

Silverlink Park

Mon

Palmersville

Benton Square

Benton Square Ind Est

Holystone Grange

FRANCIS WAY

BACKWORTH TERR 1
HOLYWELL TERR 2
RYTON TERR 3

West Allotment

THE SILVERLINK N

QUICK SILVER WAY

LAUREL AVE

B1505

FEETHAM /4 /CT

Benton Square

LAUREL END

FOREST GATE

Palmersville

GREAT LIME RD

B1505

WESLEY WAY

ST AIDAN'S SQ

CARLISLE CL

A19

E1
1 NORTH TERR
2 ECCLES TERR
3 CARLISLE TERR
4 BUDDLE TERR
5 MAUD TERR
6 LAMB TERR
7 GRIFFITH TERR
8 TAYLOR TERR
9 EARSDON TERR
10 CRAMLINGTON TERR
11 CO-OPERATIVE TERR
12 PRESTON TERR

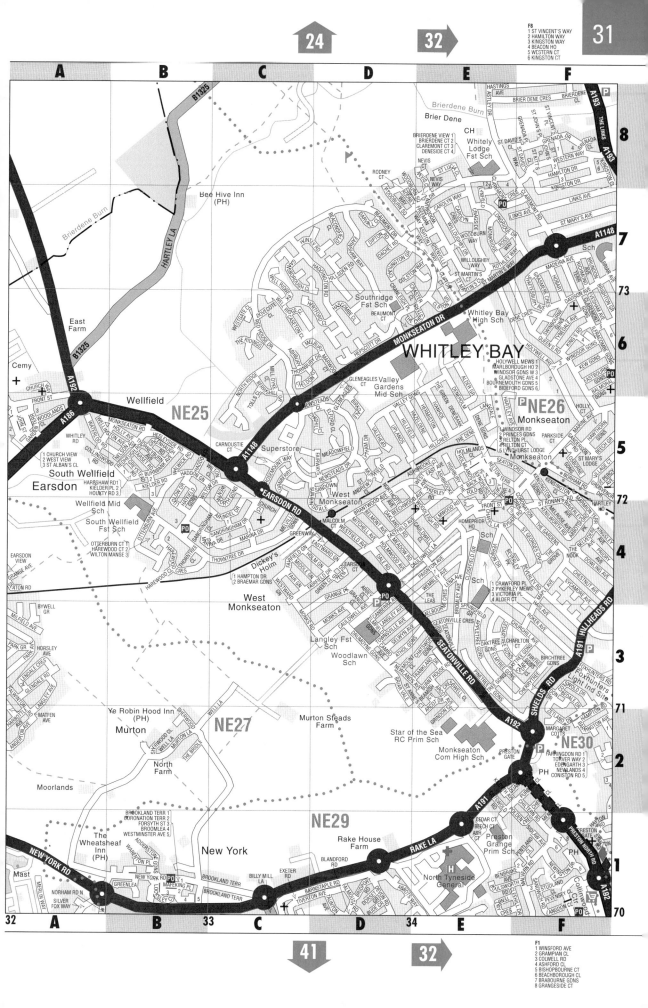

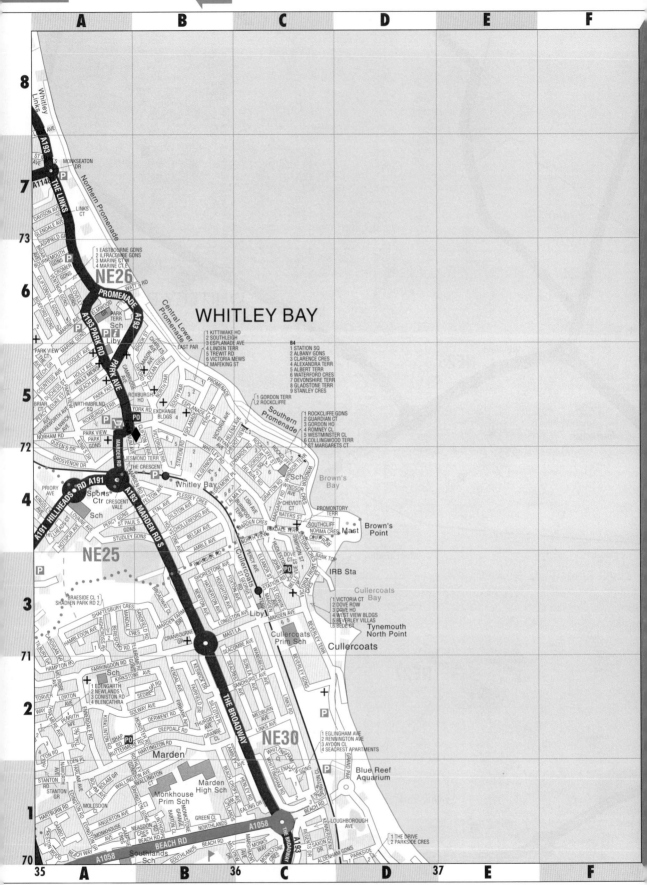

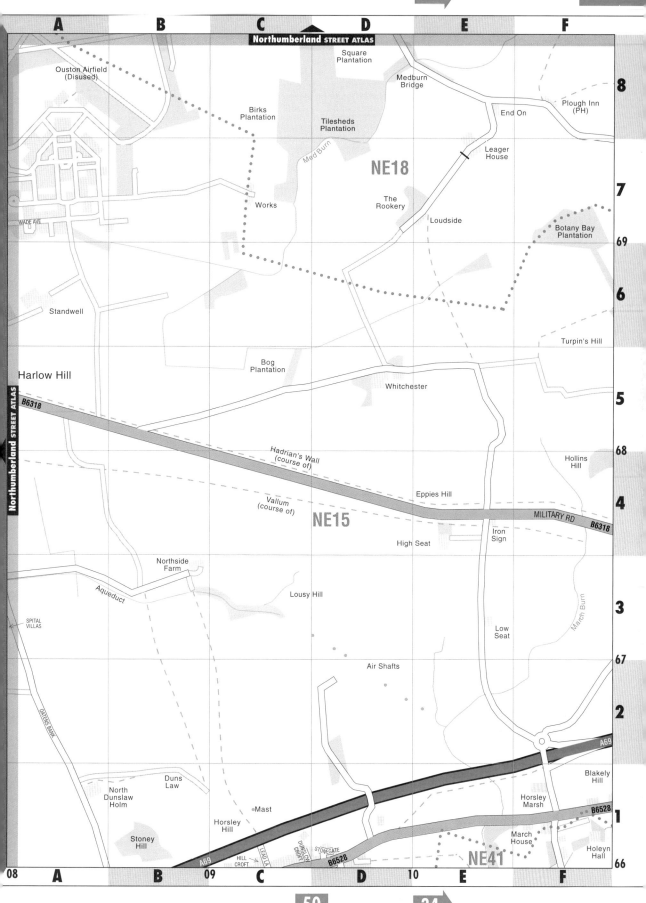

Northumberland STREET ATLAS

Northumberland STREET ATLAS

A **B** **C** **D** **E** **F**

Square Plantation

Ouston Airfield (Disused)

Medburn Bridge

Plough Inn (PH)

8

Birks Plantation

Tilesheds Plantation

End On

Med Burn

NE18

Leager House

7

WADE AVE

Works

The Rookery

Loudside

Botany Bay Plantation

69

Standwell

6

Turpin's Hill

Bog Plantation

Harlow Hill

Whitchester

5

B6318

Hadrian's Wall (course of)

Hollins Hill

68

Vallum (course of)

Eppies Hill

4

NE15

MILITARY RD

B6318

High Seat

Iron Sign

Northside Farm

Aqueduct

Lousy Hill

SPITAL VILLAS

Low Seat

March Burn

3

Air Shafts

67

2

A69

OATENS BANK

Duns Law

Blakely Hill

North Dunslaw Holm

Horsley Marsh

B6528

Mast

Horsley Hill

HILL CROFT

LEAD LA

DUNSLOW CROFT

STONEGATE

B6528

March House

Holeyn Hall

1

Stoney Hill

A69

NE41

66

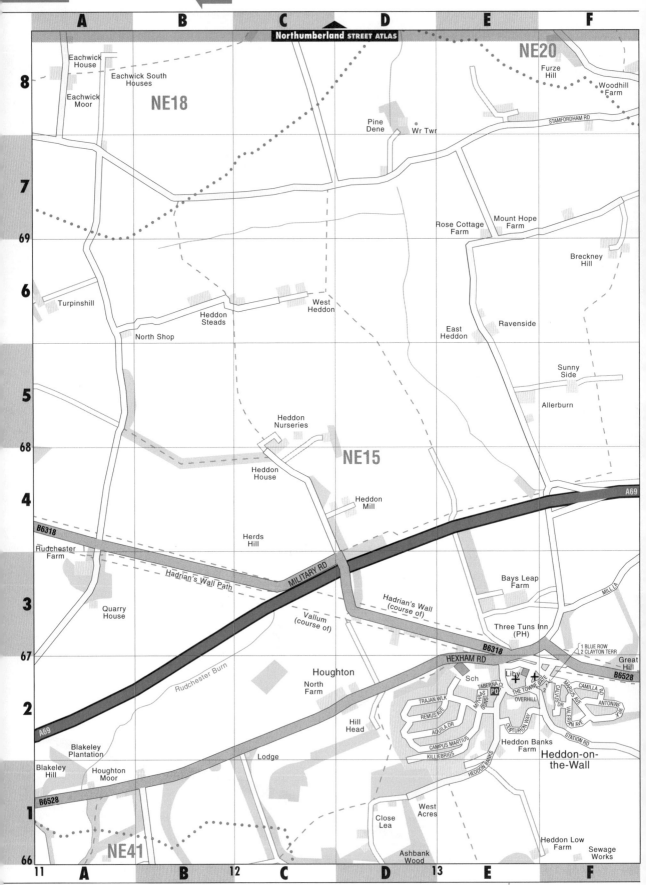

Northumberland STREET ATLAS

A **B** **C** **D** **E** **F**

NE20

NE18

8

Eachwick House
Eachwick South Houses
Eachwick Moor

Furze Hill
Woodhill Farm

Pine Dene
Wr Twr
STAMFORDHAM RD

7

Rose Cottage Farm
Mount Hope Farm
Breckney Hill

69

Turpinshill

6

Heddon Steads
West Heddon
East Heddon
Ravenside

North Shop

Sunny Side
Allerburn

5

Heddon Nurseries

NE15

68

Heddon House

4

Heddon Mill
A69

B6318

Herds Hill

Rudchester Farm
Hadrian's Wall Path
MILITARY RD
Hadrian's Wall (course of)
Bays Leap Farm
MILL LA

3

Quarry House
Vallum (course of)
Three Tuns Inn (PH)
1 BLUE ROW
2 CLAYTON TERR
Great Hill

67

B6318

Rudchester Burn
HEXHAM RD
B6528

Houghton North Farm
Sch
Libv
THE TOWNE GATE
TABERNA CL
PO
OVERHILL
CAMILLA RD
ANTONINE

2

A69
Hill Head
TRAJAN WLK
REMUS AVE
AQUILA DR
CAMPUS MARTIUS
KILLIEBRIGS
MITHRAS GDNS
CENTURIONS WAY
CALVUS DR
VALERIAN WAY
MARIUS AVE
STATION RD
Heddon Banks Farm
Heddon-on-the-Wall

Blakeley Plantation
Lodge
HEDDON BANKS

1

Blakeley Hill
Houghton Moor
B6528

Close Lea
West Acres
Heddon Low Farm
Sewage Works

NE41
Ashbank Wood

66

11 **A** **B** 12 **C** **D** 13 **E** **F**

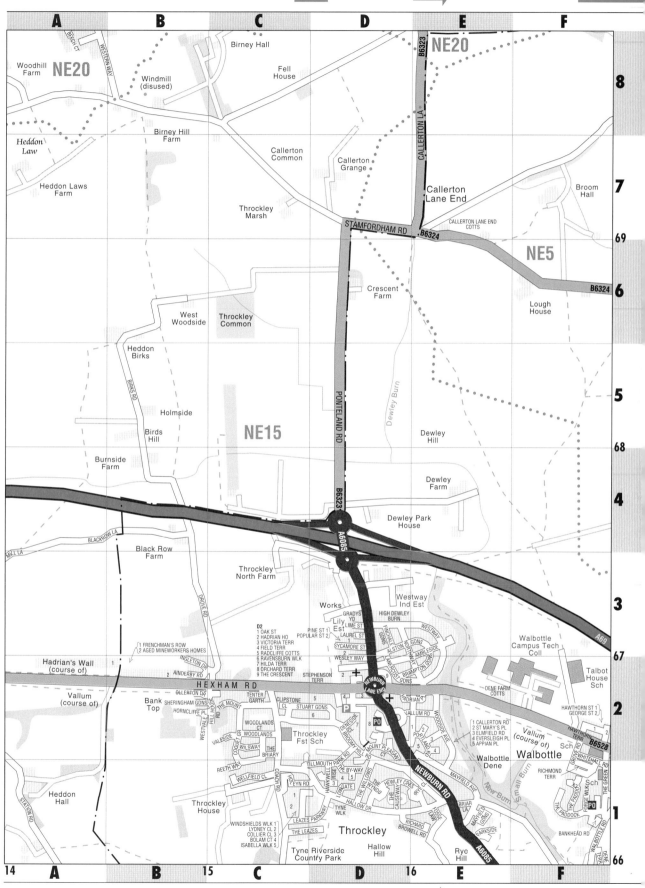

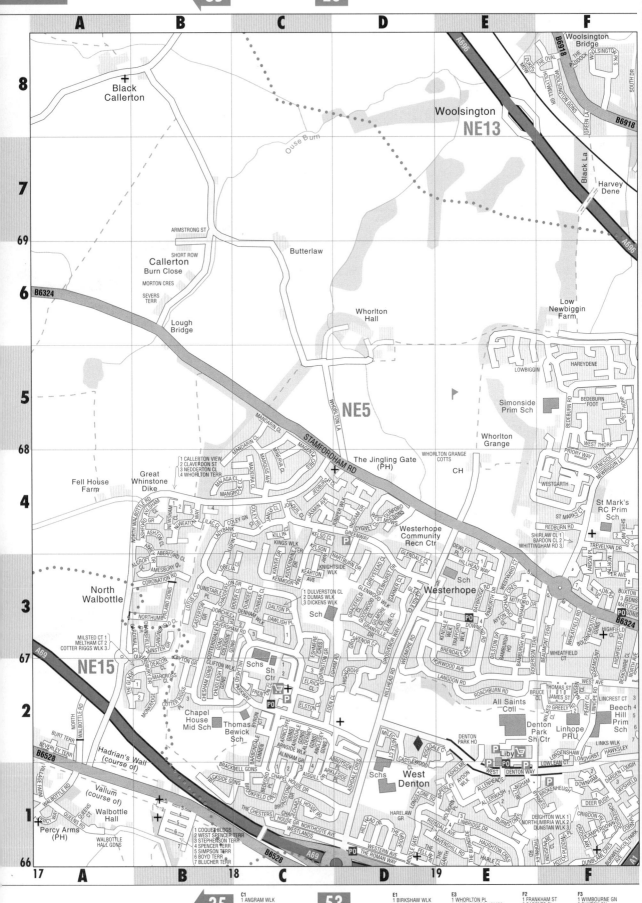

A   B   C   D   E   F

8   Black Callerton

Woolsington
NE13

Woolsington Bridge
Harvey Dene

7

69   Armstrong St
SHORT ROW
Callerton
Burn Close   Butterlaw
MORTON CRES

6   B6324
SEVERS TERR
Lough Bridge
Whorlton Hall   Low Newbiggin Farm

WHORLTON LA
NE5
LOWBIGGIN
HAREYDENE
Simonside Prim Sch
BEDEBURN FOOT
WEST THORP
PRIORY WAY

5   STAMFORDHAM RD
Whorlton Grange
WESTGARTH

68   1 CALLERTON VIEW
2 CLAVERDON ST
3 NEDDERTON CL
4 WHORLTON TERR
The Jingling Gate (PH)
WHORLTON GRANGE COTTS
CH
St Mark's RC Prim Sch
ST MARKS RD

Fell House Farm
Great Whinstone Dike
Westerhope Community Recn Ctr
SHIRLAW CL 1
BARDON CL 2
WHITTINGHAM RD 3
REDBURN RD
TREVELYAN DR

4   1 DULVERSTON CL
2 DUMAS WLK
3 DICKENS WLK
Westerhope
BUXTON GDNS
MATLOCK GDNS

3   North Walbottle
CORONATION RD
Sch
B6324
HIGHFIELD

MILSTED CT 1
MELTHAM CT 2
COTTER RIGGS WLK 3
WHEATFIELD CT
WEST AVE

67   A69
NE15
COTTER RIGGS
Schs
Sh Ctr
PO
All Saints Coll
Beech Hill Prim Sch
LINCREST CT 3

2   BURT TERR
REVERLEY TERR
Chapel House Mid Sch
Thomas Bewick Sch
Denton Park Sh Ctr
Linhope PRU
LINKS WLK
HAWKSLEY

B6528
Hadrian's Wall (course of)
Liby
DENTON WAY
DOWNHAM
DEER BUSH

Vallum (course of)
Walbottle Hall
West Denton
DEIGHTON WLK 1
NORTHUMBRIA WLK 2
DUNSTAN WLK 3

1   Percy Arms (PH)
WALBOTTLE HALL GDNS
THE CHESTERS
NORTHCOTE AVE
WESTLANDS
1 COQUET BLDGS
2 WEST SPENCER TERR
3 STEPHENSON TERR
4 SPENCER TERR
5 SIMPSON TERR
6 BOYD TERR
7 BLUCHER TERR
CRIGDON HILL
DUNBLANE CRES

66   17   A   18   B6528   B   A69   C   18   D   THE ROMAN WAY   19   E   F

C1
1 ANGRAM WLK
2 ASKRIGG WLK
3 AUDLAND WLK
4 AUSTWICK WLK
C2
1 HANOVER WLK
2 HANOVER CL
3 ELGAR AVE

E1
1 BIRKSHAW WLK
2 BICKERTON WLK
3 KNARSDALE PL
4 HIGHWELL LA

E3
1 WHORLTON PL
2 AGED MINERS HOMES
3 MARSHAM RD
4 COUNDEN RD
5 KENSINGTON VILLAS

F2
1 FRANKHAM ST
2 BARENTS CL
3 FAIRSPRING
4 FENTON WLK
5 FORESTBORN CT
6 FOURSTONES
7 FORDMOSS WLK

F3
1 WIMBOURNE GN
2 BUXTON GN
3 CHATSWORTH GDNS
4 PILTON WLK
5 BOYD TERR
6 BELMONT COTTS
7 RAPPERTON CT

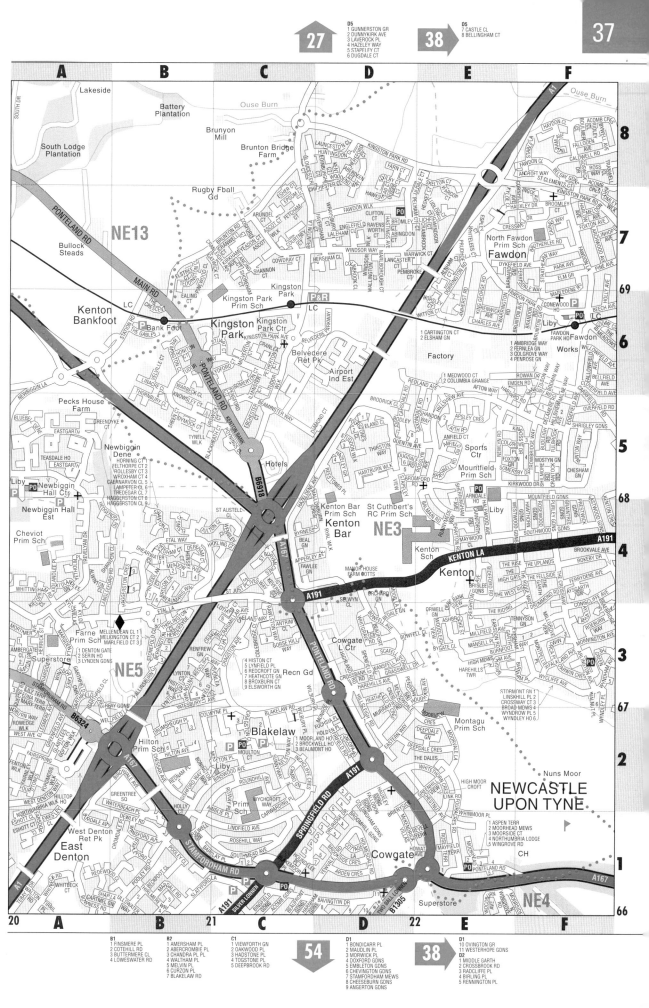

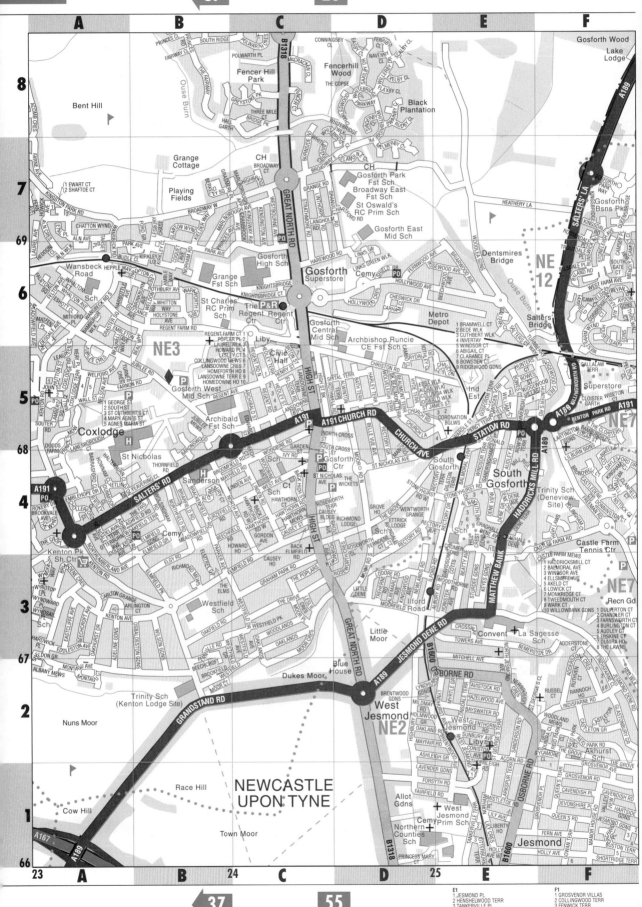

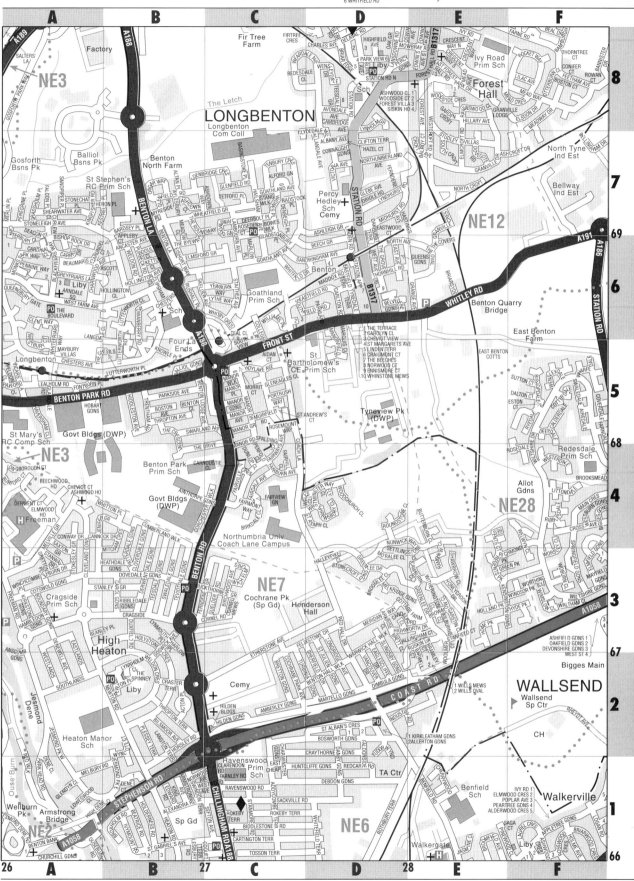

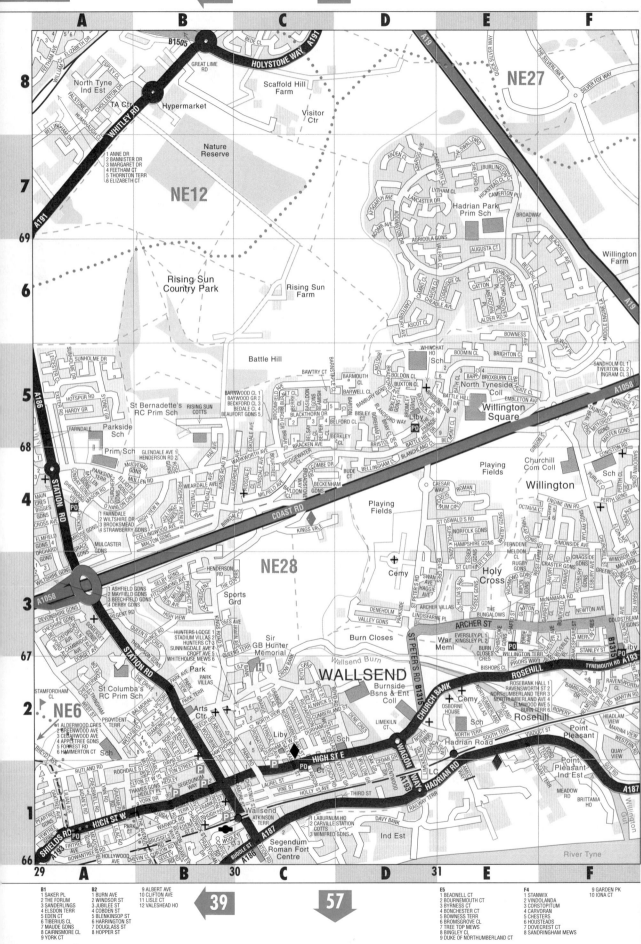

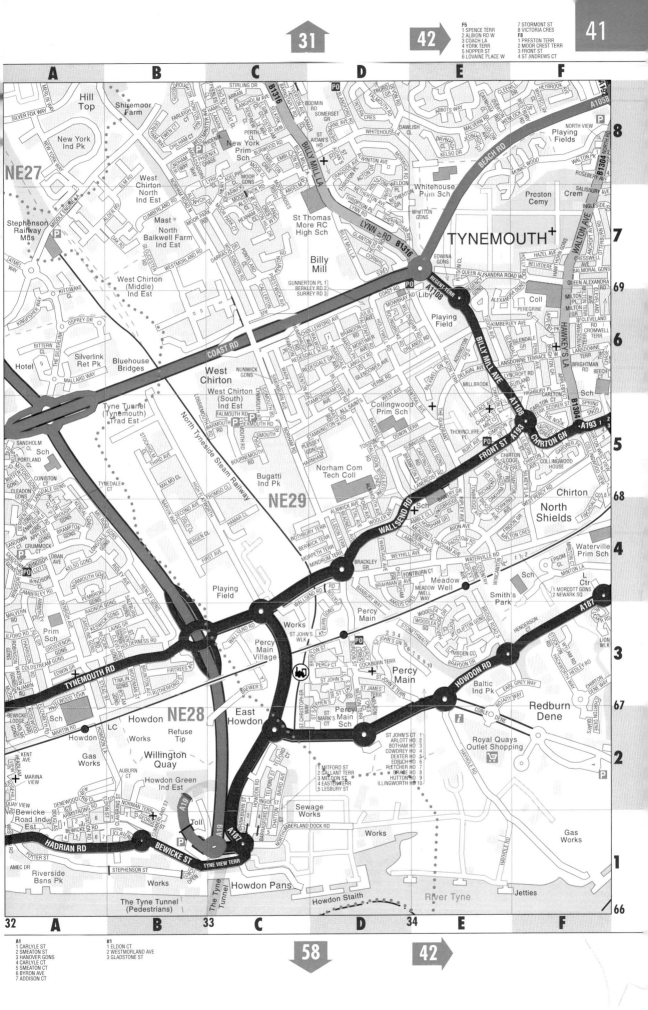

Map

Grid columns A–F (top: 35, 36, 37; rows 8–1, down to 66)

Major labels:
- **TYNEMOUTH** — NE30
- **SOUTH SHIELDS** — NE33
- NE29
- NE34
- Preston
- North Shields
- King Edward's Bay
- Tynemouth Castle / Priory
- Prior's Haven
- North Pier / South Pier
- River Tyne Entrance
- Groyne Lighthouse
- Fish Mkt
- Clifford's Fort
- Low Lights
- South Marine Park / North Marine Park
- Bents Park
- Westoe
- Sports Gd
- Port of Newcastle International Ferry Terminal
- Dock / Marina
- River Tyne — Shields Harbour

Index boxes on map:

C5
1 PENNYFINE CL
2 ORCHARD CT
3 POST OFFICE LA
4 ARGYLE PL
5 BULMAN'S LA
6 POPPLEWELL TERR
7 ARGYLE TERR
8 PRESTON CT
9 CAWTHORNE TERR

B6
1 KENSINGTON GDNS
2 NORTH CHURCH ST
3 BRANDLING TERR
4 NORTHUMBERLAND SQ
5 HARDY CT
6 GEORGE SQ
7 KETTLEWELL TERR
8 BRINKBURN ST
9 FIELD HO
10 NORFOLK CT
11 BACK ALBION RD

D7
1 STEPHENSON ST
2 THE ARCADE
3 COLBECK TERR
4 DAWSON SQ
5 NEWCASTLE TERR
6 TYNEMOUTH PL
7 PRIORY MEWS
8 MARINERS POINT
9 ADMIRAL HO

10 STATION MEWS
11 BACK SHIPLEY RD
12 HORSLEY TERR
13 KNOTT MEMORIAL FLATS
14 NELSON HOUSE
15 VICTORY HOUSE
16 SOVEREIGN HOUSE
17 TRAFALGAR HOUSE
18 KINGSWOOD CT

19 RINGTON CT
20 BACK PRUDHOE TERR
21 ENSIGN HO

(Clifford's Fort area)
1 EDWARD GRAVELING HO
2 THOMAS FERGUSON ST
3 RENAISSANCE POINT
4 CLIFFORD'S FORT

(Fish Quay area)
7 BEDFORD HO
8 BEDFORD CT
9 UNION STAIRS
10 CAWDELL CT
11 BANK CT
12 HOWARD CT
13 STEPHENSON CT
14 JAYCROFT CT
15 LAUREL CT
16 EAST NORFOLK ST

1 YEOMAN ST
2 SIBTHORPE ST
3 RUDYERD CT
4 RUDYERD ST
5 LOWER RUDYERD ST
6 CAMDEN ST

1 PRIORY CT
2 COLLINGWOOD HO
3 GUILLIMOT HO

D4
1 MORTON CT
2 LIVINGSTONE ST
3 CLEVELAND ST
4 URFA TERR
5 WOODLANDS TERR

A4
1 LANGLEY TARN
2 TRINITY CL
3 TRINITY TERR
4 BELLE VUE TERR
5 LANNERWOOD
6 UPPER ELSDON ST
7 ELSDON PL
8 LAWSON ST
9 TRINITY CT
10 HATFIELD HO
11 ACTON HO

A3
1 BLUCHER ST
2 LION WLK
3 CHIRTON DENE WAY
4 WATCH HOUSE CL
5 HENDON CL

C2
1 TEDCO BSNS WORKS
2 READHEAD BLDS
3 MILLBANK IND EST
4 ST HILDA IND EST
5 FOREST RD IND EST
6 MAXWELL ST IND EST
7 WESTERN APP IND EST
8 RAYNHAM CT

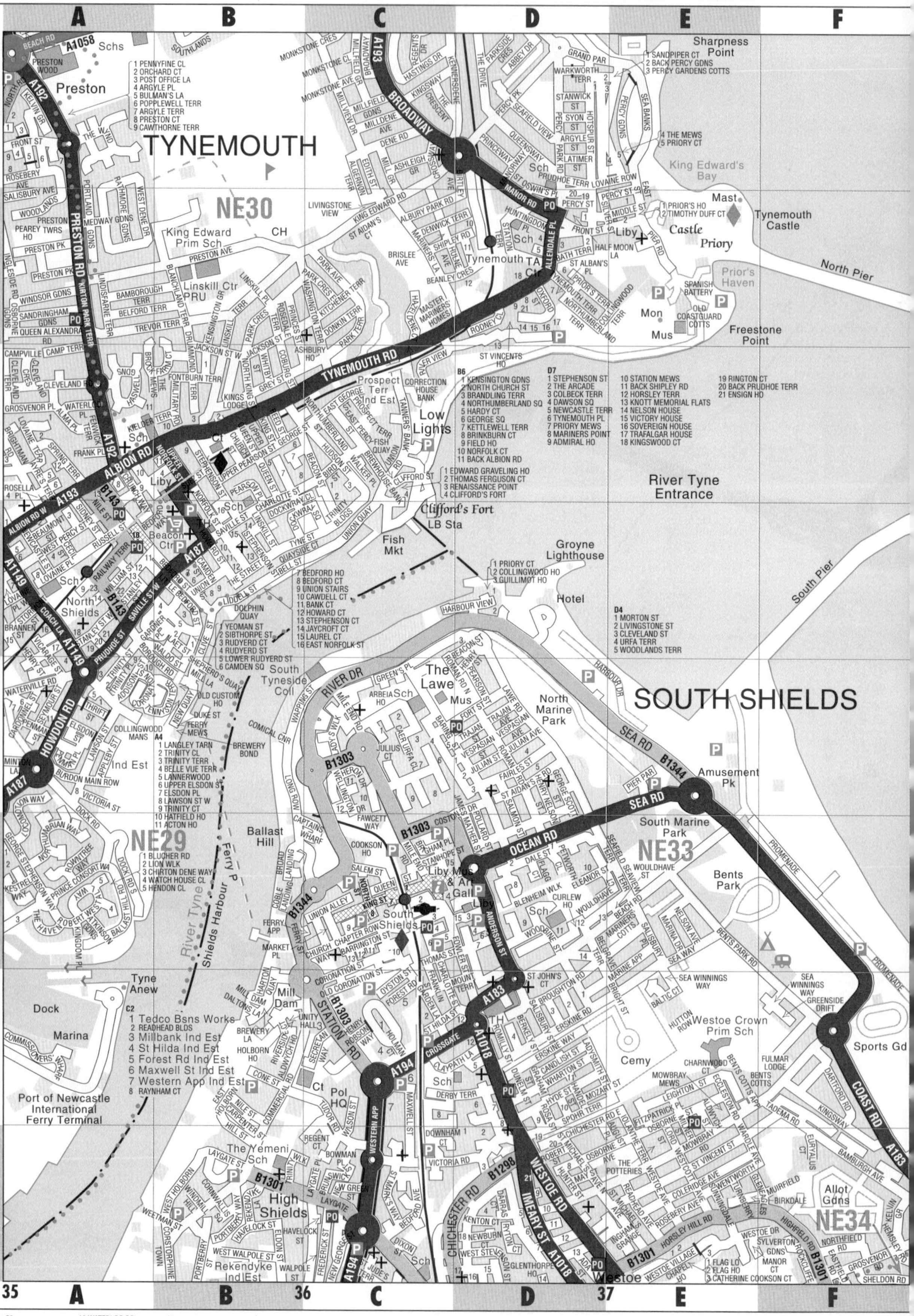

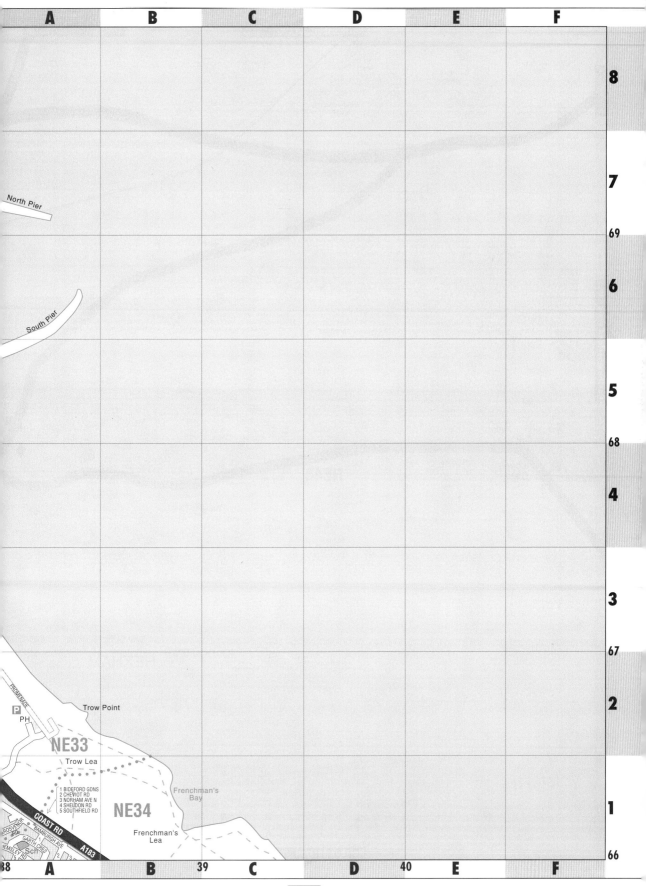

A B C D E F

A6079 Bellingham (B6320)

ALNMOUTH TERR

8

A69 Carlisle

A69

Coastley Burnfoot Farm

Burnfoot Wood

West Boat

Kingshaw Haugh

Westwood House

River Tyne

A69

Old Bridge End

7

B6531

Highwood Farm

LC

65

Cemy

SPITAL LA

CH

6

High Wood

The Shaws Farm

Shaws La

Cobbler's Hall

EILANSGATE HO 1
MILLFIELD GDNS 2
QUATRE BRAS 3
MILLFIELD CT 4
WESTBOURNE GR 5
PORTLAND TERR 6

ST ACCA'S CT

Highside

DUKES RD

THE LINK
THE CROFT
WEST QUARTER

BROADWAY GDNS

EILANSGATE

PARK AVE

5

Northumberland STREET ATLAS

LEAZES LA

LEAZES CRES 7
HIGH BURSWELL 8
BURNLAND TERR 9
LEAZES CT 10
WESTFIELD CT 11

HIGH REINS 1
REINS CT 2

Leazes

Plain Trees Farm

HEATHER HILL

BEECH HILL
BEECH AVE

Alexandra Cres

GLEN TERR

WOODBINE TERR

OSBORNE AV

B6531

RYE TERR

PO

64

Low Gate

Summerrods West Farm

Shaws La

SOUTH VIEWS

Alexandra Terr

TYNEDALE TERR

WHETSTONE GN

FAIRFIELD

Lowgate Fst Sch

Summerrods

NE46

Queen Elizabeth High Sch

ALLENDALE RD

MAIDENS CROFT

B6305

4

B6305

Cockshaw Burn

Summerrods Dean

Woodley Field Farm

St Joseph's RC Mid Sch

CANON SAVAGE DR

HIGHFORD LA

WEST HEXTOL

HEXTOL CT
HEXTO

VALEBROOK

ST PAULS RD

Breckon Hill

High House Farm

IVESON

PATTERSON CL
BISHOPTON WAY

DERBY DR

HENDERSON CL

THE C

ST MATTHEW

JOHN

FALSTONE AV

3

Blossom Hill

DR BAKER DR

CONNISCLIFFE CT

CONNISCLIFFE

BIRCH CL
ELM CL

ASH CL
OAK CL

WEST

THE OAKS

NURSERY GRANGE

WYDON PK

63

Nichols Dean

Low Yarridge

Highford

HOLLY CL

CAUSEY HILL WAY

HEXHAM

Barn End

INTAKE WAY

2

West Plantation

Benson's Fell

Green Hill

1

High Yarridge

Rot Sike

Plover Hill

Hexham Race Course

62

90 A 91 B C 92 D E F

90 A B 91 C D 92 E F

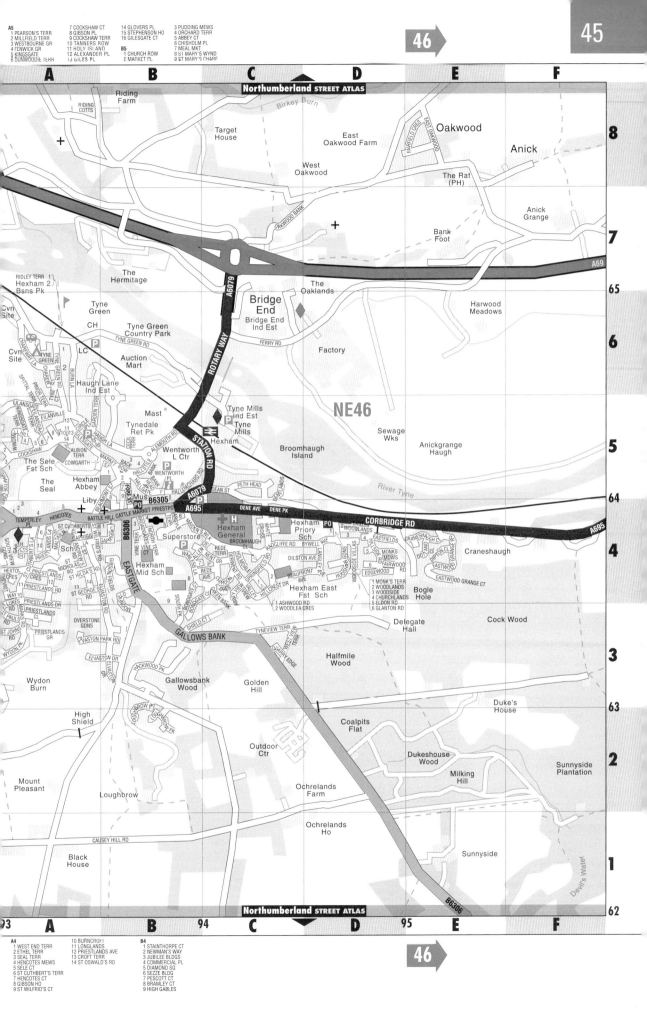

Northumberland STREET ATLAS

NE46

A B C D E F

8

7

65

6

5

64

4

63

3

2

1

62

BEAUFRONT
CASTLE FLATS

Beaufront
Castle

The Park

Knoll
Hill

CORCHESTER LA

Beaufront
Red House

Red House
Plantation

NE46

Prior
Thorns

Redhouse
Haughs

Redhouse Burn

A69

River Tyne

Widehaugh
Nursery

Wide Haugh

Dilston Haughs

Sam's
Island
LC

A695

Dilston Plains

Dilston
Park

Dilston South
Park

Dilston
Park

Park
Wood

Bowlingally
Hill

East
Haugh

Devil's Water

DILSTON
WEST COTTS

Birchside
Wood

West
Haugh

Swallowship Wood

Swallowship
Hill

B6307

Birchy
Wood

Birchy Syke

DILSTON HAUGH
COTTS

Dilston Haugh
Farm

Dilston
Mill

B6321

Dilston
Hall

Dilston

High
Town

West
Fell

Snokoehill
Plantation

Snokoe
Hill

B6307

NE45

Scurl
Hill

Corbridge

The
Scrogs

A695

Cemy

Corbridge
Bridge

STATION RD

TINKLER'S BANK

LADYCUTTERS LA

Roecliff
Lodge

Quarry Cottage
Belt

Temperley Grange
Farm

A68 Jedburgh

Hampstead
House

Cor Burn

A68

A69

B6529

Corbridge
Mid Sch

THE RIGGS

PRIORY GDNS

COW LA

CHANTRY EST

STAGSHAW RD

CORCHESTER
TWRS

LEAZES
TERR

ST HELEN'S LA

PROPHSTONES RD

THE AVENUE

CORCHESTER TERR 1
CORCHESTER AVE 2
TRINITY CT 3

Corbridge
Roman Site

ROMAN WY

TRINITY TERR

PRIOR
TERR

COOKSON CL

ST HELEN'S ST

WEST TERR
PRINCE
ST

MANOR
COTTS

CHAINS
DR

TOWN FARM FIELD

ORCHARD
VIEW

WELL BANK

WATLING ST

HILL ST

B6529

B6321

TYNEDALE
MEWS

MIDDLE ST

FRONT ST

MARKET
PL

MAIN ST

B6307

Northumberland STREET ATLAS

8

Gallow Hill

Gallowhill

Thornbrough High Barns

7

Cor Burn

LEAZES LA

B6321

Thornbrough Kiln House

AYDON RD

CRAGSIDE

JAMESON DR

BEAUFRONT LA

WOODSIDE AVE

BEECH DR

MILKWELL LA

THE RIGGS

65

Aydon Grange

Piperclose House

Quarry Wood

Linn Burn Wood

6

WILLOW DENE

SYNCLEN AVE

MILKWELL

Corbridge CE Fst Sch

SYNCLEN TERR

ST HELEN'S LA

AYDON AVE

AYDON CRES

AYDON GDNS

1 CHANTRY EST
2 ST HELEN'S ST
3 ST WILFREDS CT
4 WINDSOR CT
5 AYDON GR
6 AYDON RD EST
7 AYDON WAY

Crooks Hill

NE45

WOODBINE TERR

BELANDS

WINDSOR TERR

ST WILFRID'S RD

GREENCRO

CROFTS WAY

CROFTS CL

APPLETREE LA

CROFTS AVE

CARL

Thornbrough

PRINCES ST

ORCHARD CRES

✝

Corbridge

Howden Dene Farm

Cricket Plantation

Thornbrough Buildings

5

MAIN ST

B6530

NEWCASTLE RD

SPOUTWELL LA

CARRSFIELD

APPLETREE RISE

STABLE BLOCK

Sidle Hill

Brocks Bushes

Howden Dene

64

Gallow Hill

East Lodge

A69

4

Eales

Thornbrough Haugh

Thornbrough Wood

Styford Toll Bar

Styford Lodge

B6530

Tynedale Park

TINKLER'S BANK

Gravel Pit

River Tyne

3

B6529

Farnley Haughs

NE43

High Barns

ADYCUTTERS LA

Farnley Grange

Gravel Pit

63

Styford Cottages

Whinney Corner

LC

2

Farnley Gate

Grey Court

Abbeybank Wood

Prospect Hill

NE44

Riding Hills

1

Mast

Styford Park

Styford Hall

62

A695

Northumberland STREET ATLAS

NE45

NE43

NE44

Stelling
Hall

The
Rookery

Whittington
Hill

Newton
Hall

Owlet
House

Obsy

Newtonkiln
House

Mast

Round
Hill

Mowden Hall
(Prep Sch)

Newton
High House

Boat
House

Cushatbank
Wood

The
Oaks

Tofts
Hill

Toftshill
Plantation

Newton

Brockhole Burn

Brockhole
Wood

PO
Smithy
OLD FORGE
PH

Shaw
House

North
Acomb

Brocks
Bushes

Newton Burn

Wager
Wood

Planetree
Banks

Planetreebanks
Plantation

A69

B6309

A69

B6530

Stonyverge
Wood

A68

BYWELL
HOME FARM

Styford
Wood

Beam Burn

PEEPY
COTTS

Cottagebank
Wood

Stonyverge Burn

Peepy

Sunny
Bank

Peepy
Dene

Sod
Hall

Bywell
Park

River Tyne

A68

Crookey Burn

B6309

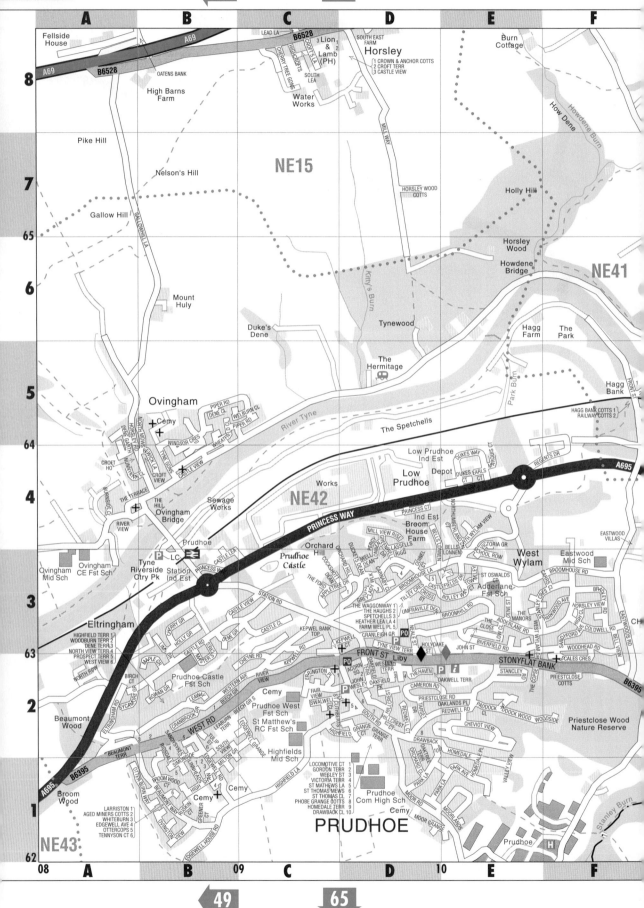

A   B   C   D   E   F

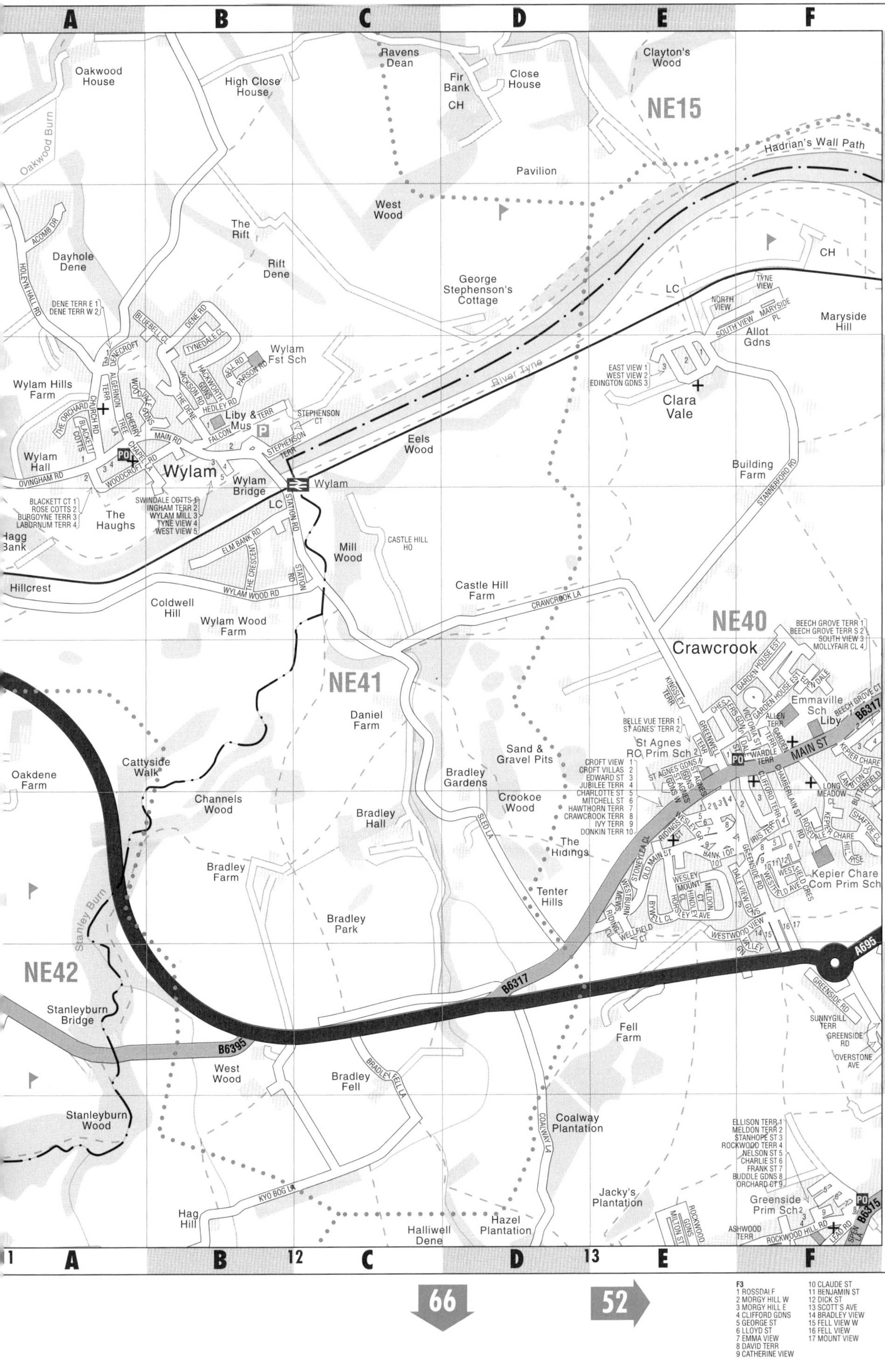

8

Oakwood House

Ravens Dean

Fir Bank CH

Close House

Clayton's Wood

NE15

Hadrian's Wall Path

High Close House

Pavilion

CH

7

The Rift

West Wood

George Stephenson's Cottage

LC

TYNE VIEW

NORTH VIEW

MARYSIDE PL

65

Dayhole Dene

Rift Dene

DENE TERR E 1
DENE TERR W 2

EAST VIEW 1
WEST VIEW 2
EDINGTON GDNS 3

SOUTH VIEW

Allot Gdns

Maryside Hill

Wylam Hills Farm

BLUEBELL CL
DENE RD

Wylam Fst Sch

6

WOODCROFT

HACKWORTH GDNS

HEDLEY RD

FALCON TERR

PARSON RD

Liby & TERR Mus

STEPHENSON CT

Clara Vale

Wylam Hall

MAIN RD

CHERRY TREE

THE TERR

JACKSON RD

STEPHENSON TERR

Eels Wood

Building Farm

OVINGHAM RD

PO

WOODCROFT

WYLAM

Wylam Bridge

LC

Wylam

River Tyne

STANNERFORD RD

5

BLACKETT CT 1
ROSE COTTS 2
BURGOYNE TERR 3
LABURNUM TERR 4

SWINDALE COTTS 1
INGHAM TERR 2
WYLAM MILL 3
TYNE VIEW 4
WEST VIEW 5

ELM BANK RD

STATION RD

Mill Wood

CASTLE HILL HO

Hagg Bank

THE CRESCENT

Hillcrest

Coldwell Hill

WYLAM WOOD RD

Castle Hill Farm

CRAWCROOK LA

NE40

BEECH GROVE TERR 1
BEECH GROVE TERR S 2
SOUTH VIEW 3
MOLLYFAIR CL 4

64

Wylam Wood Farm

NE41

Crawcrook

GARDEN HOUSES

BEECH GROVE CT

B6317

4

Daniel Farm

KINSLEY

CHEERS GDNS

GARDEN HOUSE

EMZ DALE

Emmaville Sch Liby

Oakdene Farm

Cattyside Walk

Sand & Gravel Pits

BELLE VUE TERR 1
ST AGNES' TERR 2

ST AGNES RD Prim Sch

GREENDEL

ALLEN TERR

WARDLE TERR

PO

MAIN ST

KEPIER CHARE

Channels Wood

Bradley Gardens

Crookoe Wood

CROFT VIEW 1
CROFT VILLAS 2
EDWARD ST 3
JUBILEE TERR 4
CHARLOTTE ST 5
MITCHELL ST 6
HAWTHORN TERR 7
CRAWCROOK TERR 8
IVY TERR 9
DONKIN TERR 10

ST AGNES GDNS

CLIFFORD RD

CHAMBERLAIN ST

STOCKDALE RD

LONG MEADOW CL

BITTERFIELD

STARTFIELD

KEPIER CHARE

Kepier Chare Com Prim Sch

3

Bradley Hall

Bradley Farm

SLED LA

The Hidings

STONEYLEA RD

OLD MAIN ST

BANK TOP

WESLEY MOUNT

MELDON

RIDINGS

DALE VIEW

GREENSIDE RD

OLD RD

WEST

Bradley Park

Tenter Hills

WELLFIELD CT

BYWELL CL

CHINGLEY

RIDING

MEWS

WESTWOOD

WESTWOOD GDNS

A695

63

NE42

Stanley Burn

B6317

Stanleyburn Bridge

GREENSIDE RD

SUNNYGILL TERR

2

B6395

West Wood

Bradley Fell

BRADLEY FELL LA

Fell Farm

GREENSIDE RD

OVERSTONE AVE

Stanleyburn Wood

KYO BOG LA

COALWAY LA

Coalway Plantation

ELLISON TERR 1
MELDON TERR 2
STANHOPE ST 3
ROCKWOOD TERR 4
NELSON ST 5
CHARLIE ST 6
FRANK ST 7
BUDDLE GDNS 8
ORCHARD CT 9

PO

B6315

1

Hag Hill

Halliwell Dene

Hazel Plantation

Jacky's Plantation

ROCKWOOD GDNS

MILTON ST

Greenside Prim Sch

ASHWOOD TERR

ROCKWOOD HILL RD

62

1   A   B   12   C   D   13   E   F

F3
1 ROSSDAI F
2 MORGY HILL W
3 MORGY HILL E
4 CLIFFORD GDNS
5 GEORGE ST
6 LLOYD ST
7 EMMA VIEW
8 DAVID TERR
9 CATHERINE VIEW
10 CLAUDE ST
11 BENJAMIN ST
12 DICK ST
13 SCOTT'S AVE
14 BRADLEY VIEW
15 FELL VIEW W
16 FELL VIEW
17 MOUNT VIEW

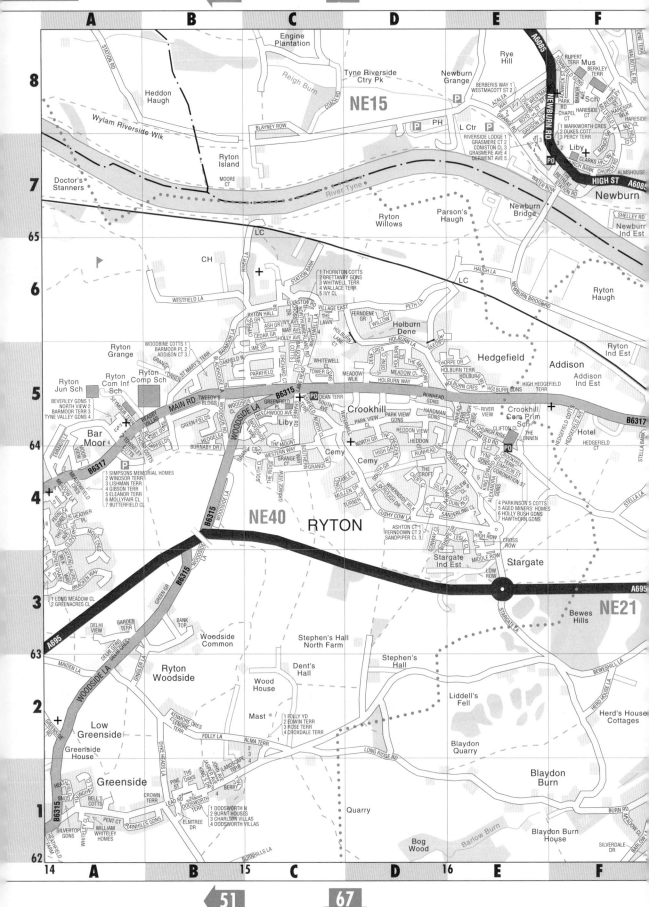

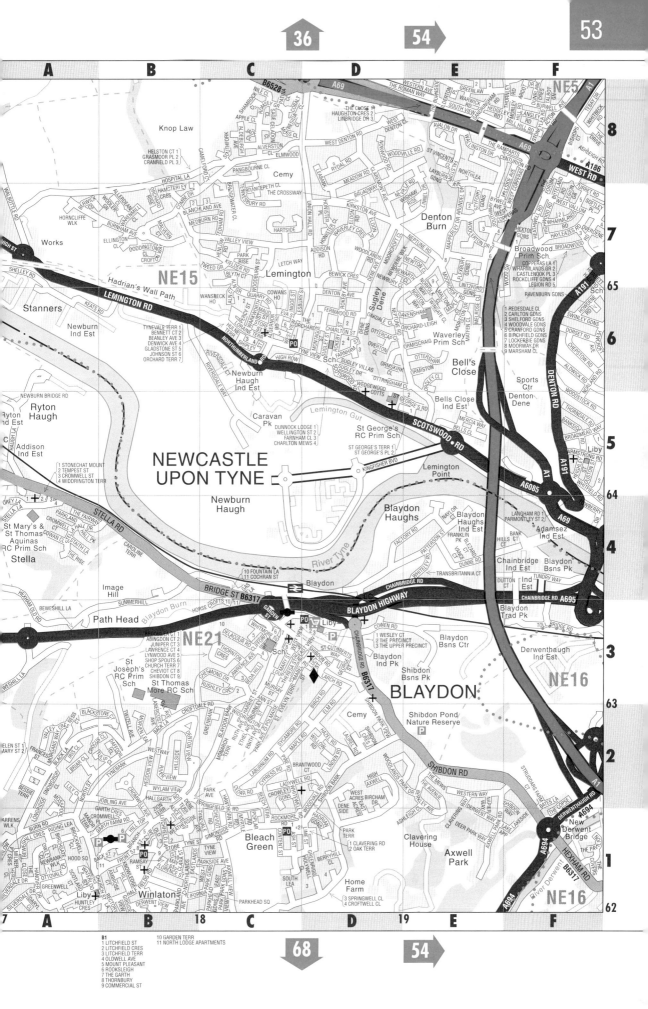

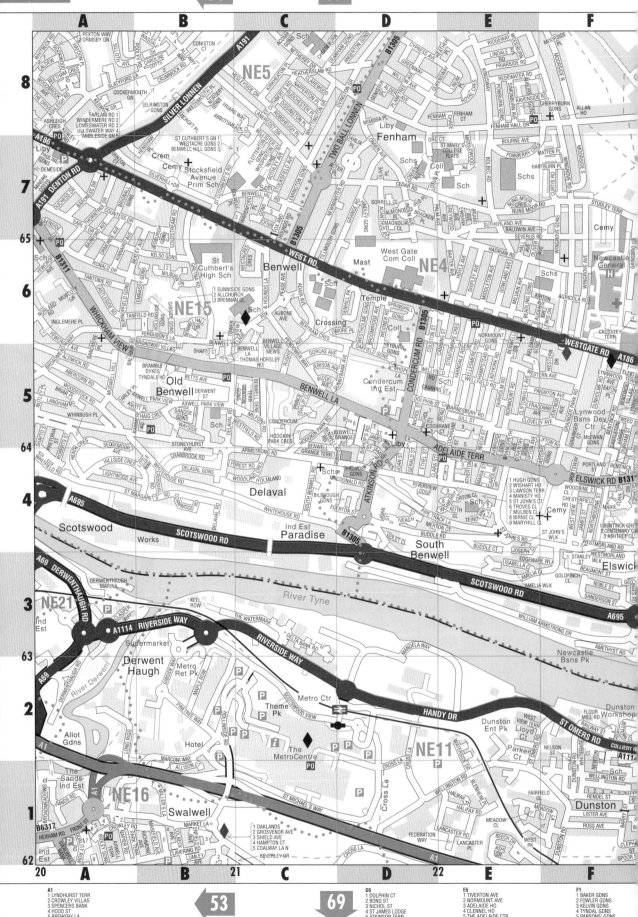

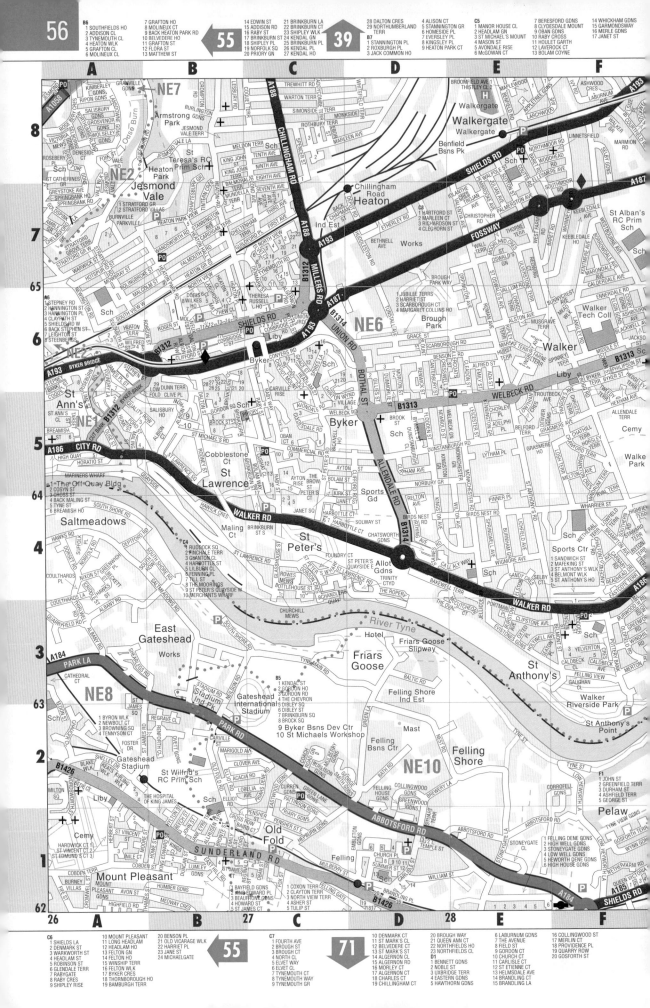

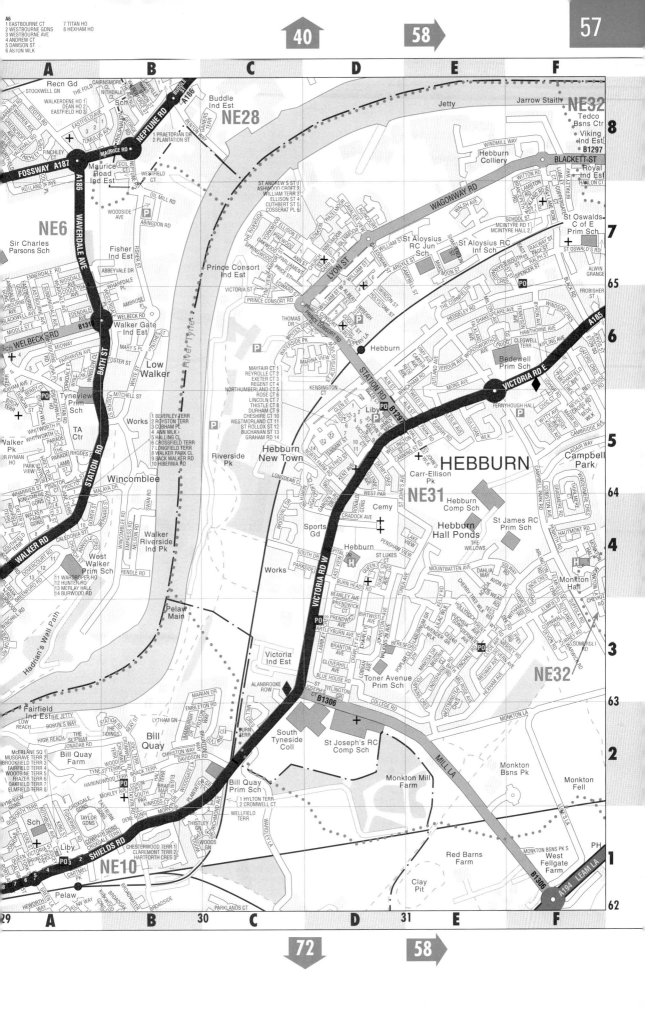

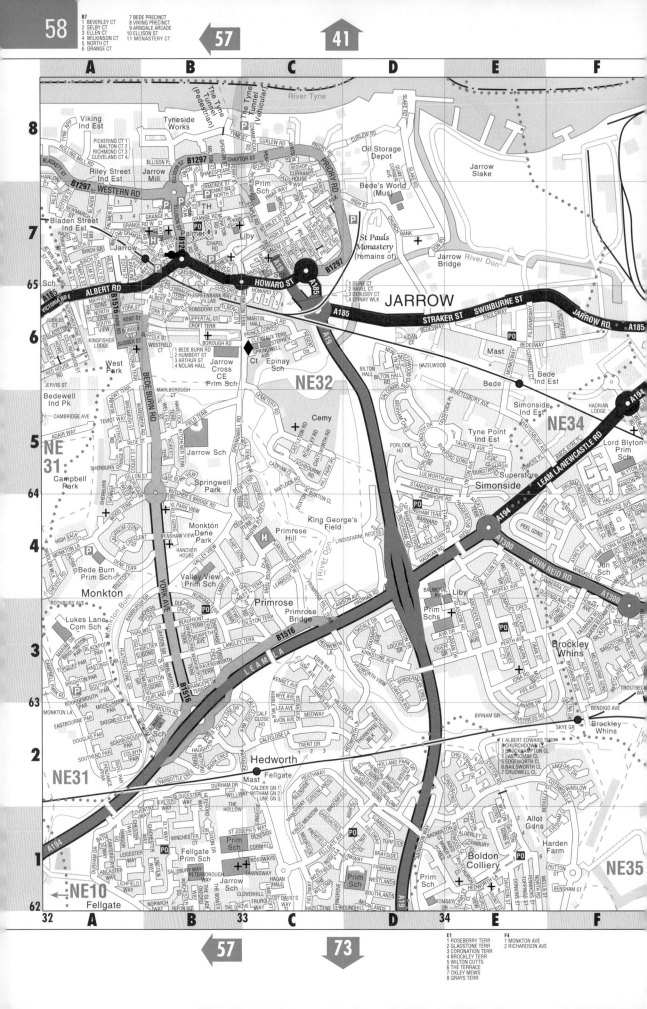

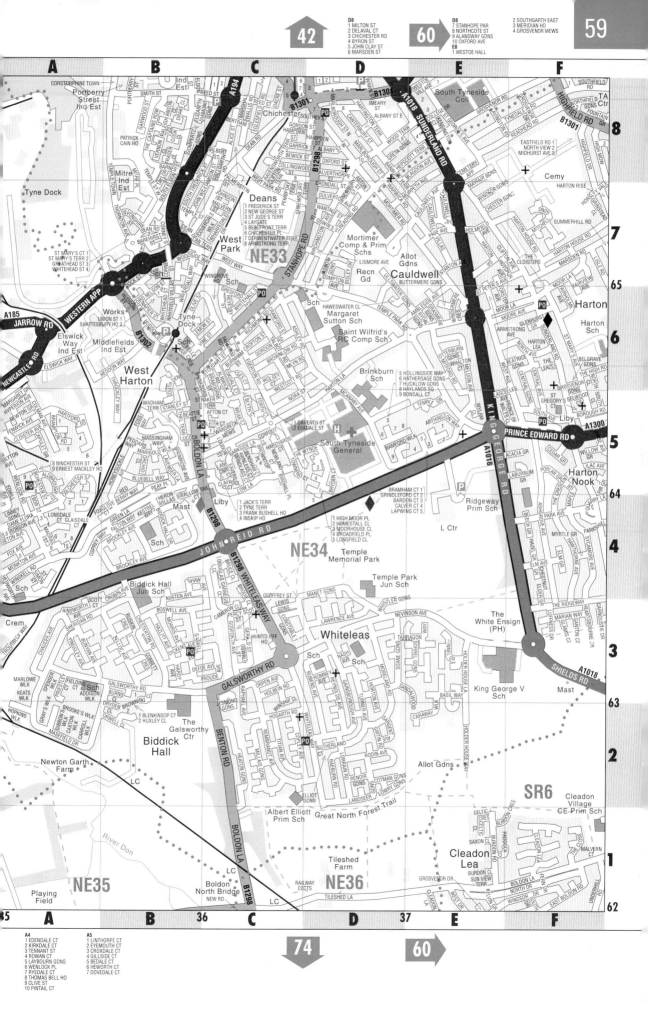

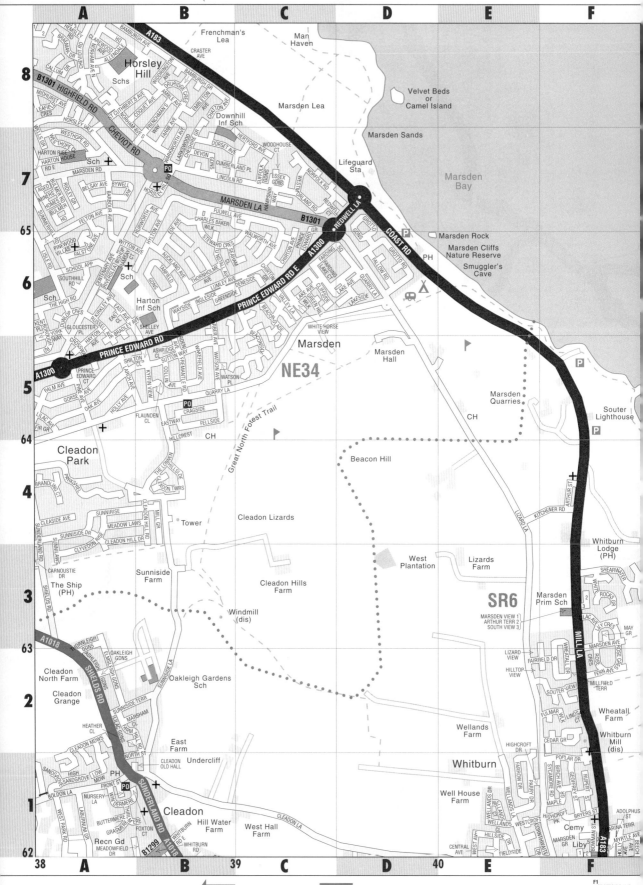

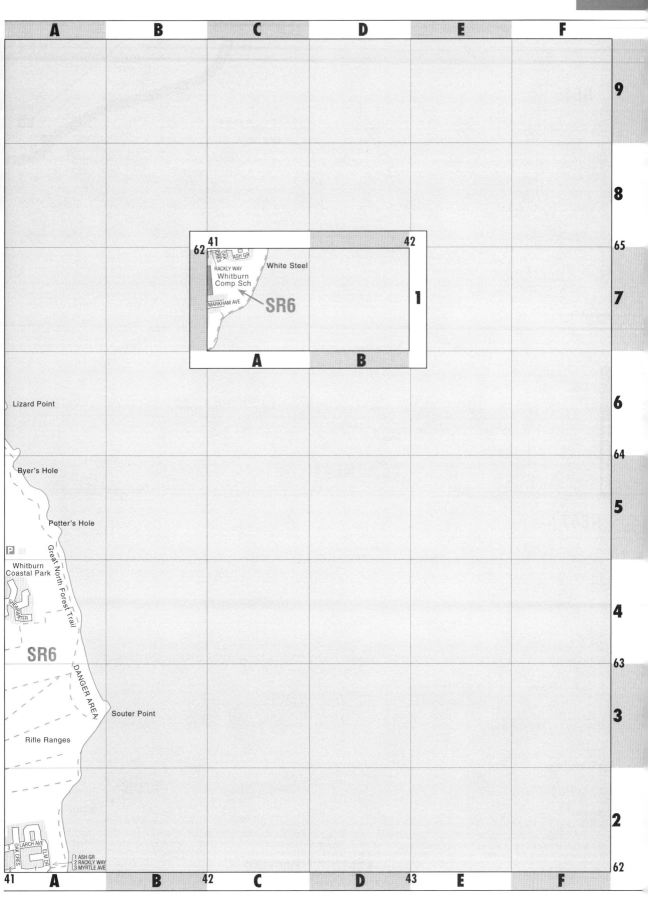

A   B   C   D   E   F

9

8

65

41   42

62

RACKLY WAY
Whitburn
Comp Sch

White Steel

1

MARKHAM AVE

SR6

7

A   B

6

Lizard Point

64

Byer's Hole

5

Potter's Hole

P

Whitburn
Coastal Park

Great North Forest Trail

SHEARWATER

SR6

4

DANGER AREA

63

Souter Point

3

Rifle Ranges

2

OAK CRES

3 LARCH AVE

ELM DR

1 ASH GR
2 RACKLY WAY
3 MYRTLE AVE

62

41   A   B   42   C   D   43   E   F

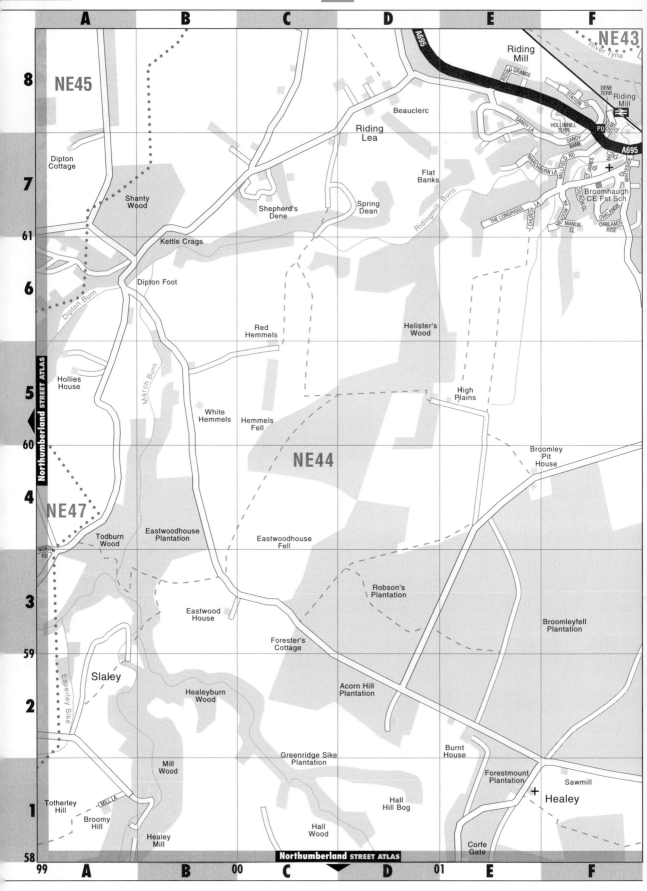

NE43

River Tyne

Riding
Mill

NE45

8

Dipton
Cottage

Beauclerc

Riding
Lea

RIDING GRANGE

STATION CL

DENE
TERR

Riding
Mill

PO

7

Shanty
Wood

Shepherd's
Dene

Spring
Dean

Flat
Banks

SANDY LA

HOLLINHILL
TERR

SANDY
BANK

MARCHBURN LA

MILLFIELD RD

ST JAMES
CL

A695

MILL CL

WHITESIDE

Broomhaugh
CE Fst Sch

61

Kettle Crags

Ridingmill Burn

THE LONGRIGGS

CHURCH LA

CHURCH PK

MEADOW PK

MANOR
CL

OAKLANDS

OAKLANDS
RISE

6

Dipton Foot

Red
Hemmels

Helister's
Wood

Dipton Burn

March Burn

Hollies
House

High
Plains

5

White
Hemmels

Hemmels
Fell

60

Broomley
Pit
House

NE44

4

NE47

Todburn
Wood

Eastwoodhouse
Plantation

Eastwoodhouse
Fell

NORTH
RD

Robson's
Plantation

Broomleyfell
Plantation

3

Eastwood
House

Forester's
Cottage

59

Slaley

Healeyburn
Wood

Acorn Hill
Plantation

Esperley Sike

2

Mill
Wood

Greenridge Sike
Plantation

Burnt
House

Forestmount
Plantation

Sawmill

1

Totherley
Hill

MILL LA

Hall
Hill Bog

Healey

Broomy
Hill

Hall
Wood

Healey
Mill

Corfe
Gate

58

99   A   B   00   C   D   01   E   F

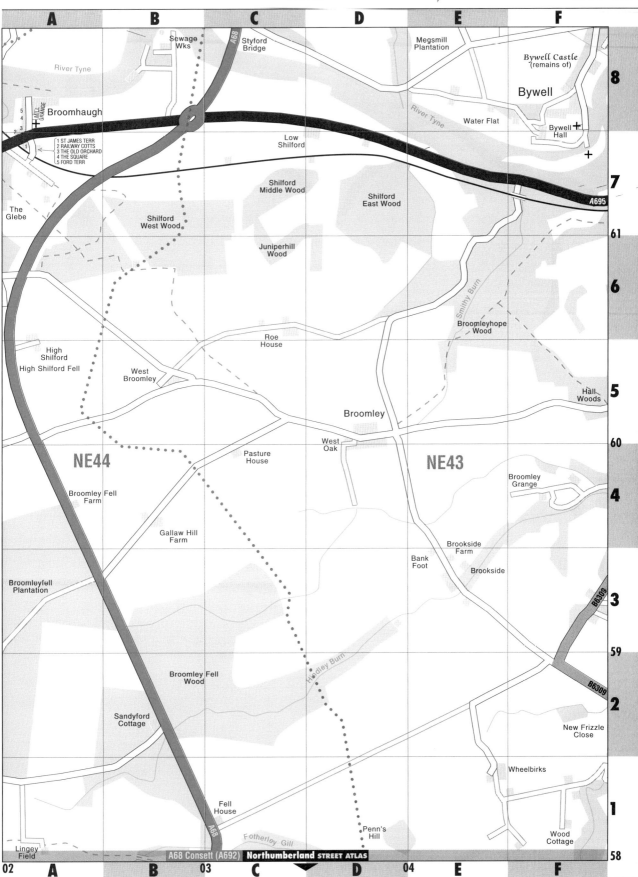

A B C D E F

River Tyne

Sewage
Wks

Styford
Bridge

Megsmill
Plantation

Bywell Castle
(remains of)

Bywell

8

Broomhaugh

Low
Shilford

River Tyne

Water Flat

Bywell
Hall

1 ST JAMES TERR
2 RAILWAY COTTS
3 THE OLD ORCHARD
4 THE SQUARE
5 FORD TERR

A695

7

The
Glebe

Shilford
Middle Wood

Shilford
East Wood

61

Shilford
West Wood

Juniperhill
Wood

Smithy Burn

6

Broomleyhope
Wood

Roe
House

High
Shilford

High Shilford Fell

West
Broomley

Broomley

Hall
Woods

5

West
Oak

60

NE44

Pasture
House

NE43

Broomley
Grange

4

Broomley Fell
Farm

Gallaw Hill
Farm

Bank
Foot

Brookside
Farm

Brookside

Broomleyfell
Plantation

B6309

3

Broomley Fell
Wood

Hadley Burn

59

B6309

Sandyford
Cottage

2

New Frizzle
Close

Wheelbirks

Fell
House

A68

Penn's
Hill

Wood
Cottage

1

Lingey
Field

Fotherley Gill

58

02 A B 03 C D 04 E F

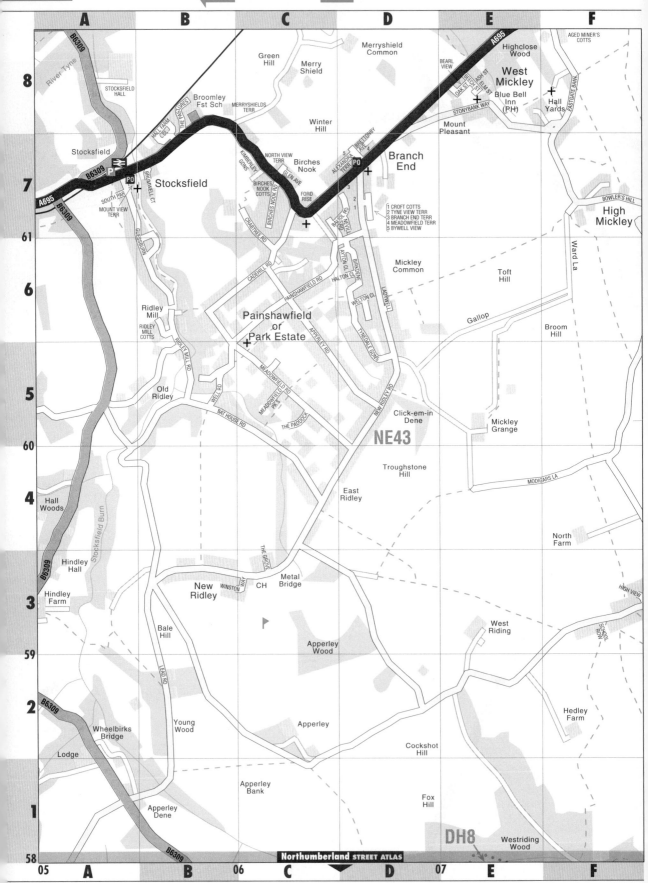

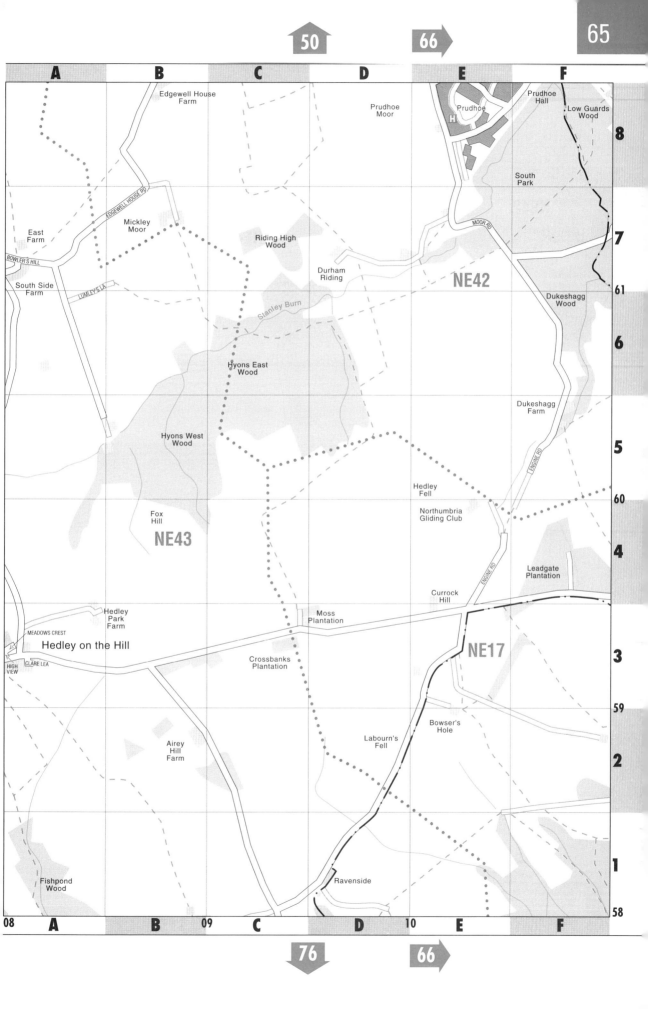

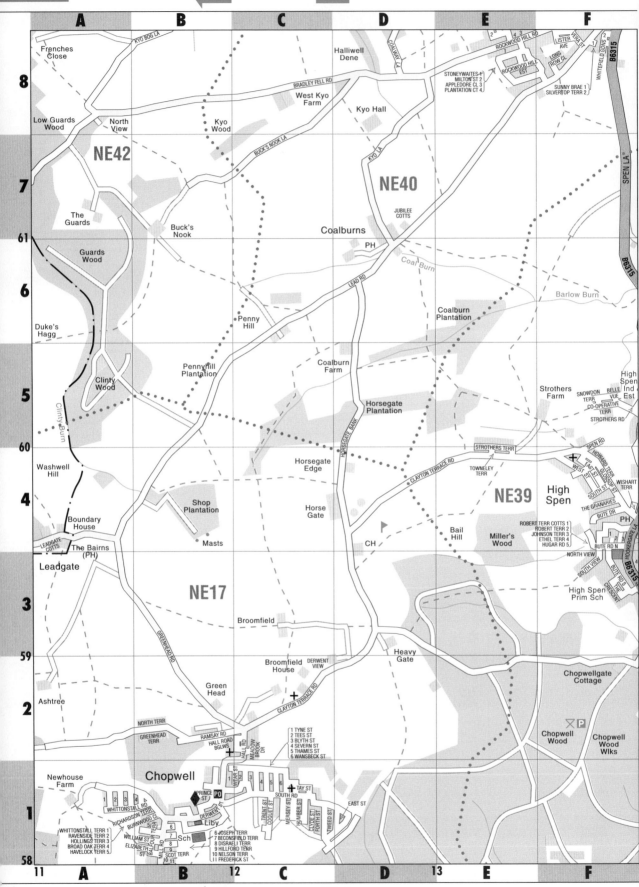

A B C D E F

8

Frenches
Close

Low Guards
Wood

North
View

NE42

7

The
Guards

Buck's
Nook

61

Guards
Wood

6

Duke's
Hagg

Penny
Hill

Clinty
Wood

Pennyhill
Plantation

5

Washwell
Hill

60

4

Boundary
House

LEADGATE
COTTS

The Bairns
(PH)

Leadgate

NE17

Shop
Plantation

Masts

KYO BOG LA

West Kyo
Farm

BRADLEY FELL RD

Halliwell
Dene

Kyo
Wood

BUCK'S NOOK LA

Kyo Hall

COLWAY LA

NE40

KYO LA

JUBILEE
COTTS

Coalburns

PH

LEAD RD

Coal Burn

Coalburn
Plantation

Coalburn
Farm

HORSEGATE BANK

Horsegate
Plantation

Horsegate
Edge

Horse
Gate

CH

Bail
Hill

CLAYTON TERRACE RD

Barlow Burn

STROTHERS TERR

Strothers
Farm

Towneley
Terr

NE39

Miller's
Wood

ROCKWOOD HILL RD

ROCKWOOD HILL
EST

STONEYWAITES 1
MILTON ST 2
APPLEDORE CL 3
PLANTATION CT 4

WHITEFIELD GDNS

LISTER
AVE

LONG
ROW CL

VERA ST

B6315

SUNNY BRAE 1
SILVERTOP TERR 2

SPEN LA

B6315

High Spen
Ind Est

SNOWDON
TERR

BELLE
VUE

CO-OPERATIVE
TERR

STROTHERS RD

SPEN RD

High
Spen

HOWARD ST

EAST ST

GLOSTER ST

WEST ST

SOUTH ST

WISHART
TERR

THE GRANARIES

BUTE DR

PH

ROBERT TERR COTTS 1
ROBERT TERR 2
JOHNSON TERR 3
ETHEL TERR 4
HUGAR RD 5

NORTH VIEW

SOUTH VIEW

BUTE RD N

BUTE RD S

HOOKERGATE LA

CRESCENT

High Spen
Prim Sch

3

Broomfield

GREENHEAD RD

59

Ashtree

Green
Head

Broomfield
House

DERWENT
VIEW

CLAYTON TERRACE RD

Heavy
Gate

Chopwellgate
Cottage

2

NORTH TERR

Greenhead
Terr

RAMSAY RD

HALL ROAD
BGLWS

HALL RD

MEADOW
BROOK DR

1 TYNE ST
2 TEES ST
3 BLYTH ST
4 SEVERN ST
5 THAMES ST
6 WANSBECK ST

Chopwell
Wood

Chopwell
Wood
Wlks

Newhouse
Farm

Chopwell

WEAR ST

PRINCE
ST

PO

Liby

DERWENT ST

TRENT ST

COQUET ST

MERSEY ST

HUMBER ST

TAY ST

SOUTH RD

CLYDE ST

FORTH ST

EAST ST

TWEED ST

1

WHITTONSTALL RD

RICHARDSON TERR

BURNWOOD CL

WILLIAM ST

BILFOUR ST

MILL RD

ELIZABETH ST

SCOT TERR

Sch

WHITTONSTALL TERR 1
RAVENSIDE TERR 2
HOLLINGS TERR 3
BROAD OAK TERR 4
HAVELOCK TERR 5

6 JOSEPH TERR
7 BECONSFIELD TERR
8 DISRAELI TERR
9 HILLFORD TERR
10 NELSON TERR
11 FREDERICK ST

58

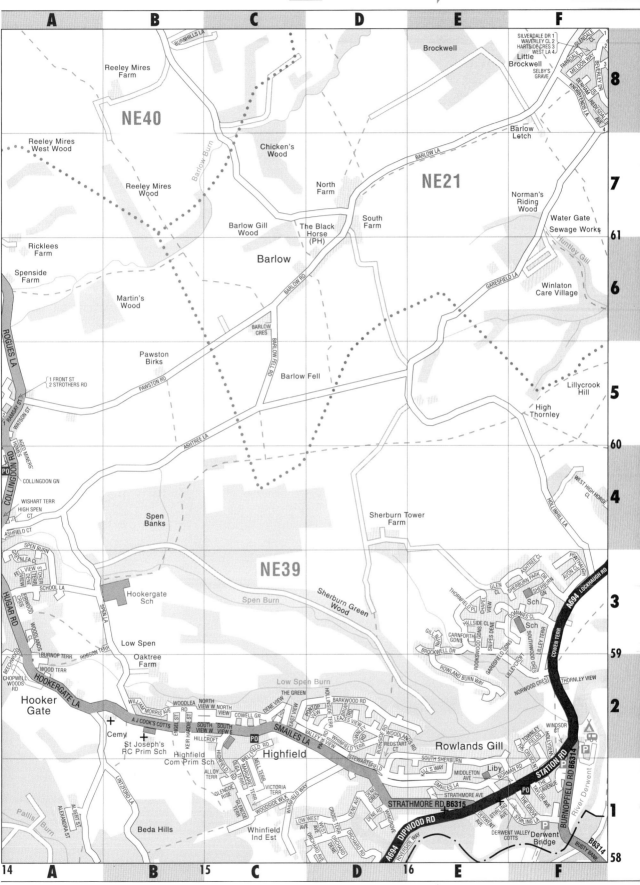

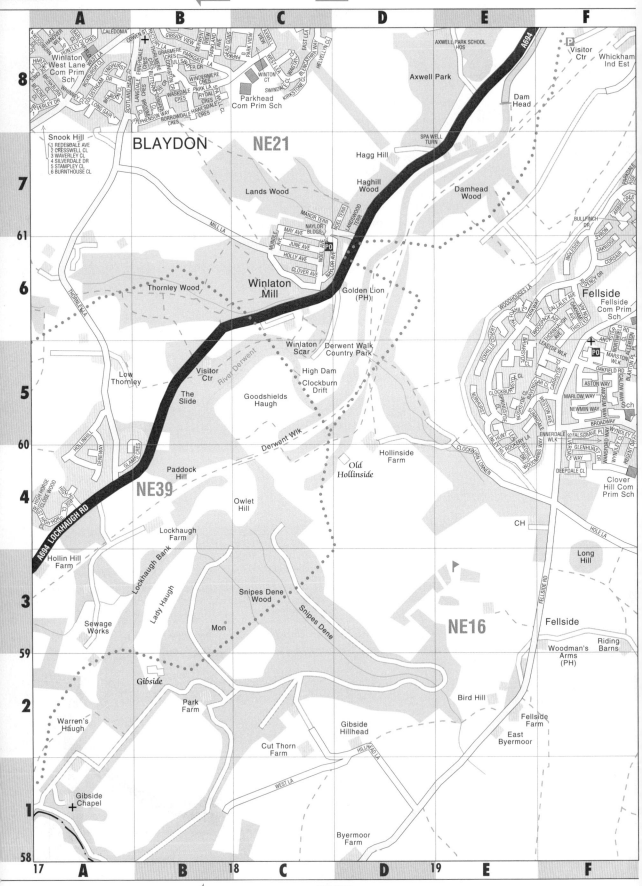

A B C D E F

8

Winlaton West Lane Com Prim Sch

CALEDONIA

BLAYDON

NE21

Axwell Park School Hos

Visitor Ctr

Whickham Ind Est

Axwell Park

Dam Head

Snook Hill
1 REDESDALE AVE
2 CRESSWELL CL
3 WAVERLEY CL
4 SILVERDALE DR
5 STAMPLEY CL
6 BURNTHOUSE CL

Parkhead Com Prim Sch

SPA WELL TURN

7

Lands Wood

Hagg Hill

Haghill Wood

Damhead Wood

61

MILL LA

MANOR TERR
NOEL TERR
LANDSWOOD TERR

MUNDLE AVE
MAY AVE
JUNE AVE
HOLLY AVE
CLOVER AVE
NOEL AVE
NAYLOR BLDGS
PO

Bullfinch Dr

6

Thornley Wood

Winlaton Mill

Golden Lion (PH)

Fellside

Fellside Com Prim Sch

PO

THORNLEY LA

Winlaton Scar

Derwent Walk Country Park

River Derwent

5

Low Thornley

Visitor Ctr

The Slide

High Dam
Clockburn Drift

Goodshields Haugh

Sch

MARLOW WAY
NEWMIN WAY
BROADWAY

60

HOLLINHILL

DENEWAY

GLAMIS CRES

Derwent Wlk

Old Hollinside

Hollinside Farm

CLOCKBURN LONNEN

DEEPDALE CL

Clover Hill Com Prim Sch

4

HIGH HORSE CLOSE WOOD
WEST HIGH HORSE

A694 LOCKHAUGH RD

Paddock Hill

NE39

Owlet Hill

CH

HOLE LA

FELLSIDE RD

Long Hill

3

Hollin Hill Farm

Lockhaugh Farm

Lockhaugh Bank

Lady Haugh

Snipes Dene Wood

Snipes Dene

NE16

Fellside

59

Sewage Works

Gibside

Park Farm

Mon

Woodman's Arms (PH)

Riding Barns

2

Warren's Haugh

Gibside Hillhead

Bird Hill

Fellside Farm

East Byermoor

Cut Thorn Farm

HILL FOOT LA

1

Gibside Chapel

WEST LA

Byermoor Farm

58

17 A B 18 C D 19 E F

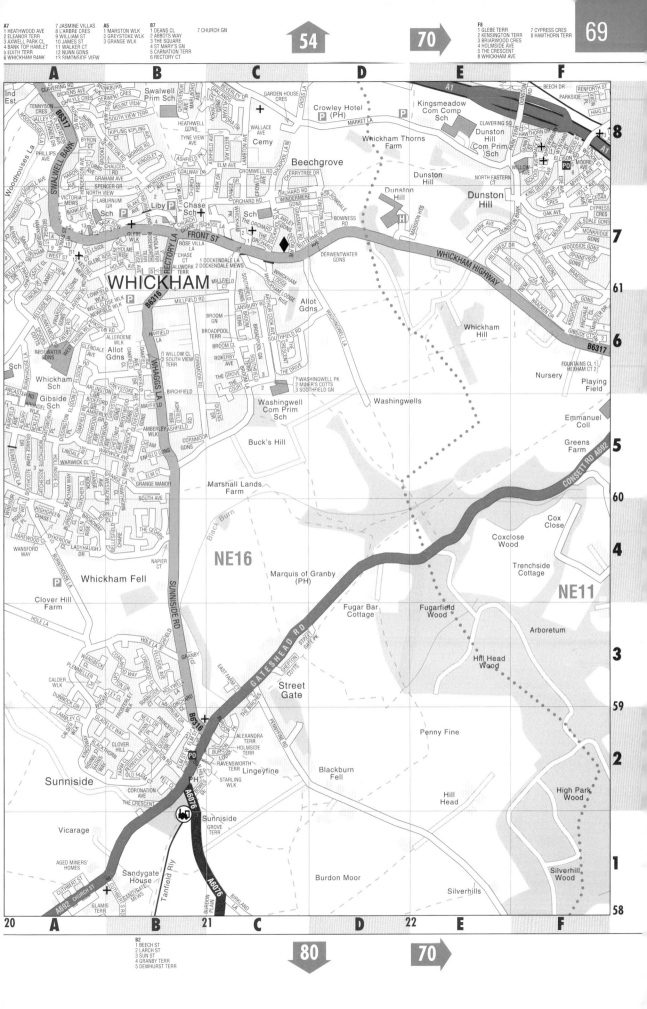

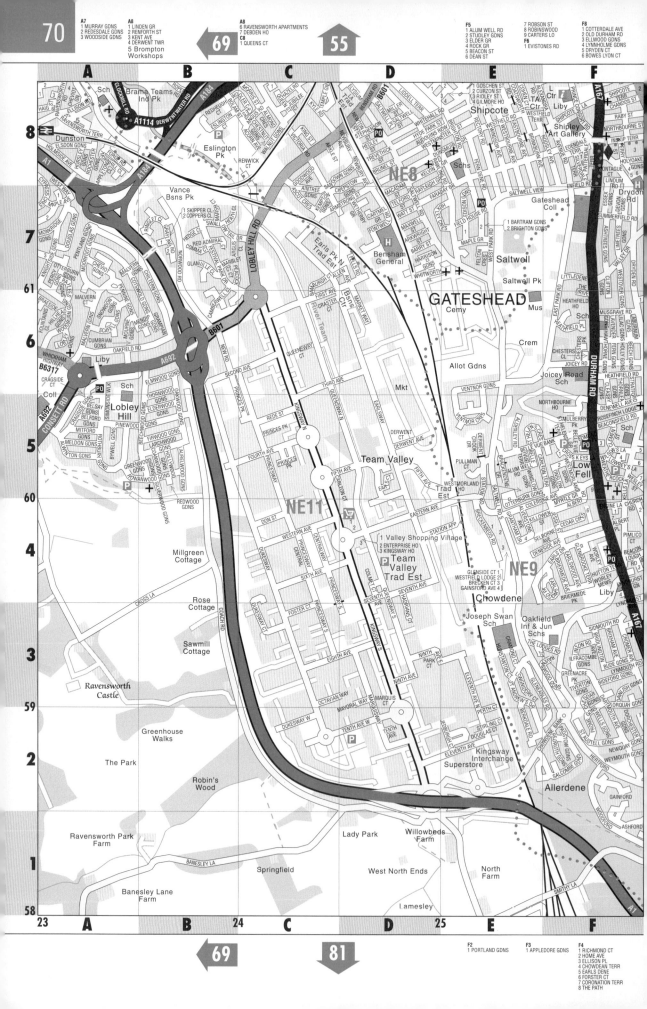

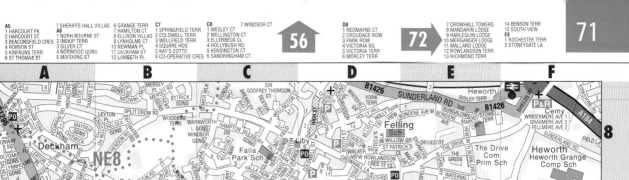
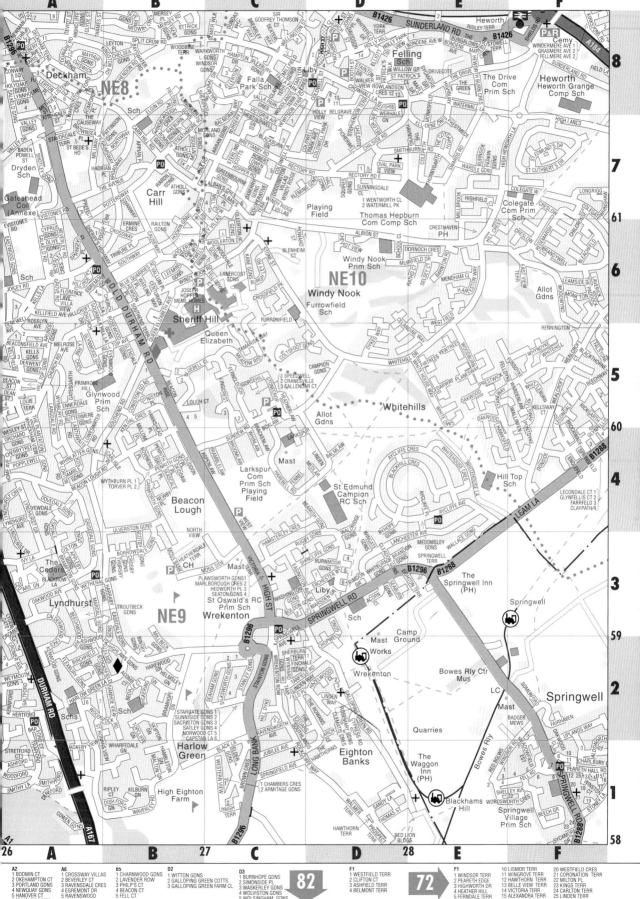

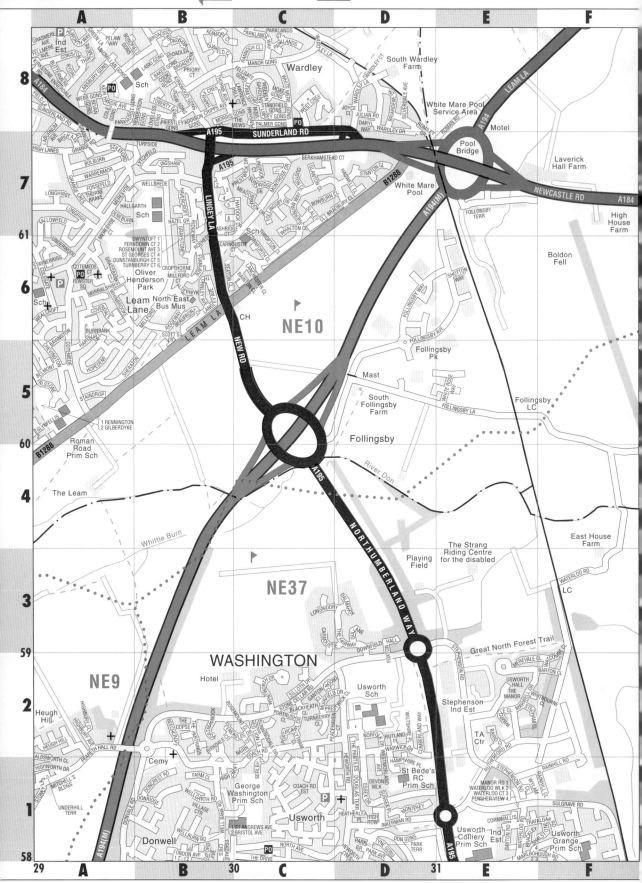

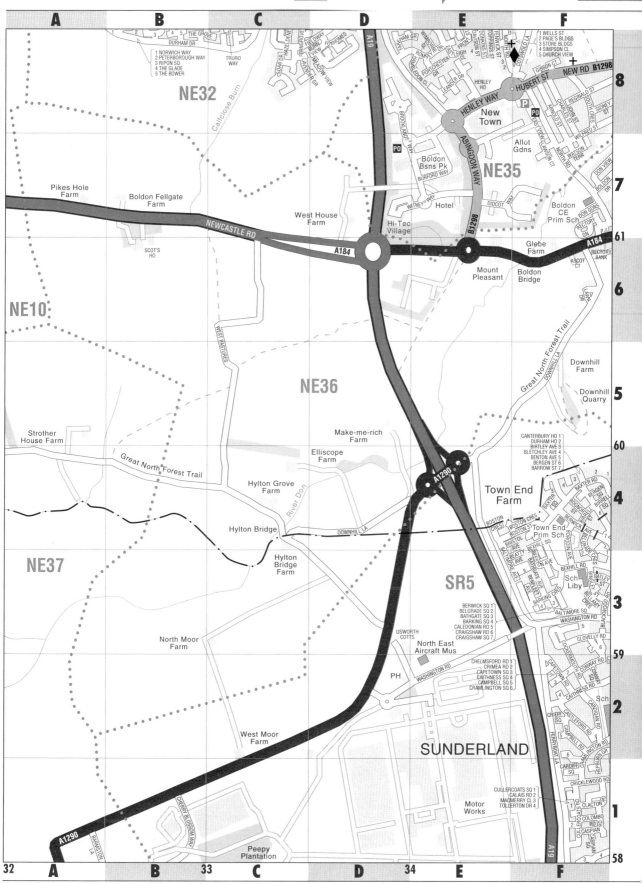

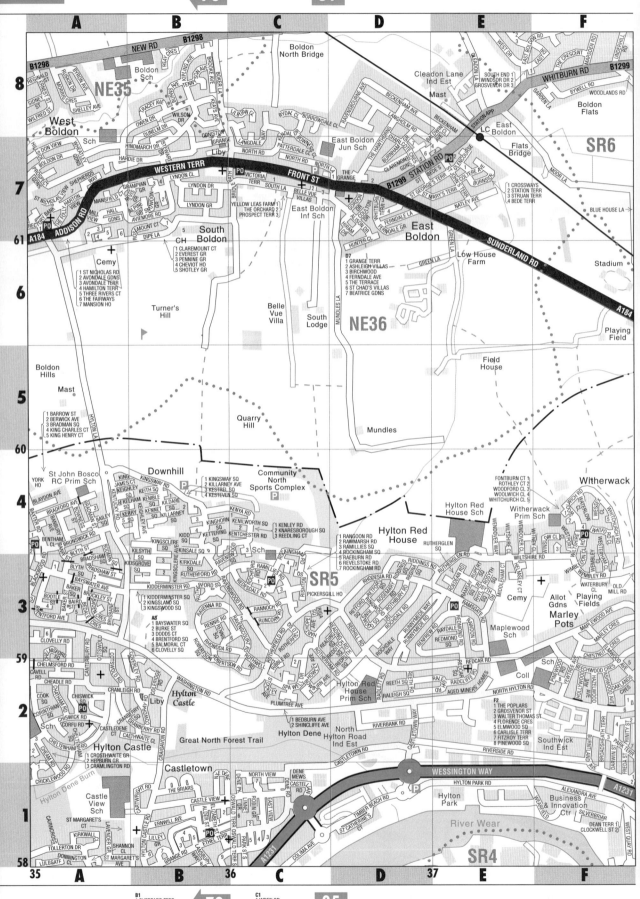

B1
1 SHEPPARD TERR
2 STANLEY ST
3 WEST VIEW
4 ASHWOOD GR
5 JOYCE TERR
6 THE GROVE
7 THOMPSON CRES
8 PARKHOUSE AVE
9 JENNIFER AVE

C1
1 WREN GR
2 THRUSH GR
3 EAST VIEW S
4 CASTLE ST S
5 BARRON ST S
6 CHAFFINCH RD
7 THE VILLAS

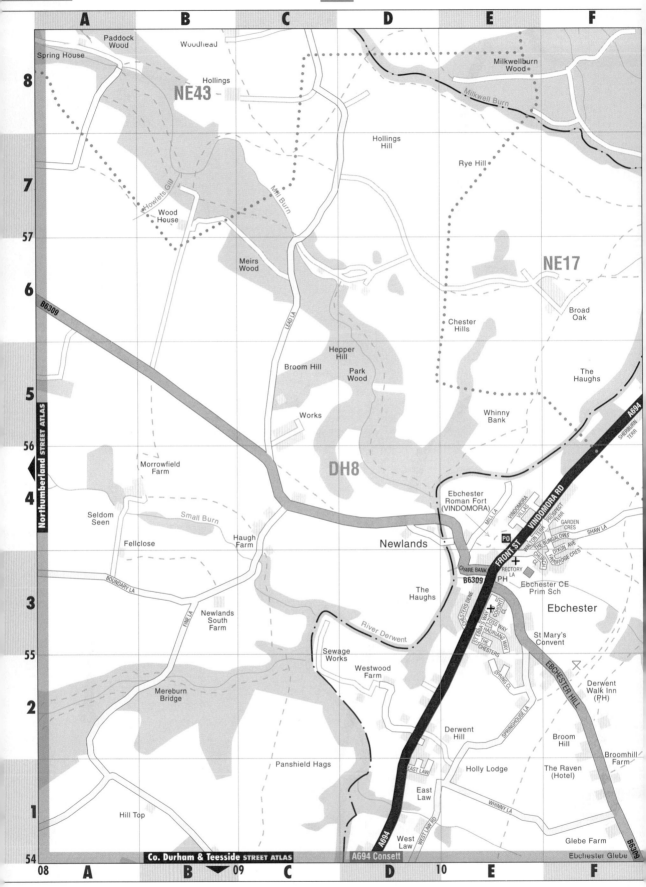

A B C D E F

8

Spring House
Paddock Wood
Woodhead
Hollings
NE43
Milkwellburn Wood
Milkwell Burn

7

Hollings Hill
Rye Hill

57

Howlets Gill
Wood House
Meirs Wood
NE17

6

B6309
Chester Hills
Broad Oak

Hepper Hill
Lead La
Broom Hill
Park Wood
The Haughs

5

Works
Whinny Bank

56

Morrowfield Farm
DH8
Ebchester Roman Fort (VINDOMORA)
VINDOMORA VILLAS
VINDOMORA RD
PROSPECT TERR
GARDEN CRES
SHAW LA

Northumberland STREET ATLAS

4

Seldom Seen
Small Burn
Haugh Farm
Newlands
PO
FRONT ST
WALTON TERR
THE BUNGALOWS
CHURCH TERR
DIXON AVE
BRIDGE CRES

Fellclose

Boundary La
The Haughs
CHARE BANK
RECTORY LA
PH
B6309
Ebchester CE Prim Sch
Ebchester

3

Fine La
Newlands South Farm
River Derwent
CHESTERS DENE
EBBA'S WAY
FOSS WAY
COHORT CL
HADRIAN'S WAY
THE CHESTERS
St Mary's Convent
EBCHESTER HILL
Derwent Walk Inn (PH)

55

Sewage Works
Westwood Farm
SPRING CL

2

Mereburn Bridge
Derwent Hill
SPRINGHOUSE LA
Broom Hill
Broomhill Farm

Panshield Hags
EAST LAW
Holly Lodge
The Raven (Hotel)

1

Hill Top
East Law
WEST LAW RD
WHINNY LA
Glebe Farm
B6309

54

A694
West Law

A694 Consett
Ebchester Glebe

08 A B 09 C D 10 E F

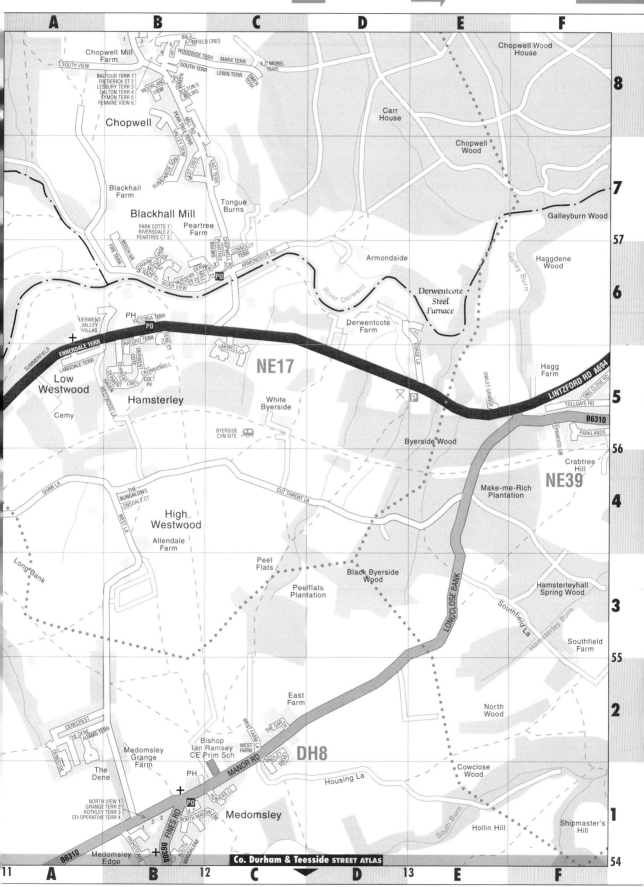

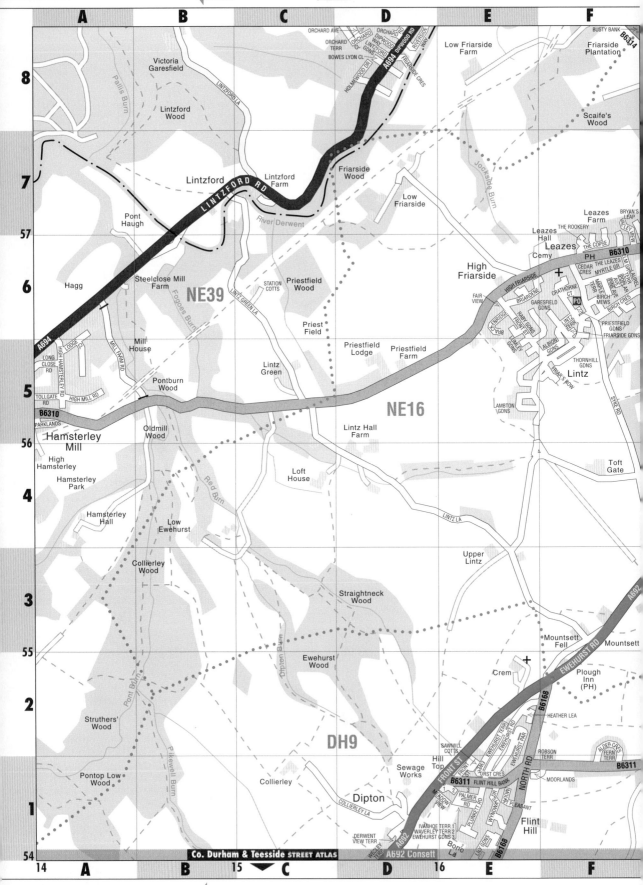

A B C D E F

8

7

57

6

57

5

56

4

3

55

2

1

54

Busty Bank
B6314

ORCHARD AVE
ORCHARD TERR
BOWES LYON CL
ORCHARD GDNS
LINTZFORD
DIPWOOD WAY
DIPWOOD RD
RIVERSIDE
A694
HOLMWOOD DRIVE
FRIARSIDE CRES

Low Friarside Farm

Friarside Plantation

Scaife's Wood

Victoria Garesfield

Lintzford Wood

Pallis Burn

LINTZFORD LA

Lintzford

Lintzford Farm

LINTZFORD RD

Friarside Wood

Jockside Burn

Low Friarside

Pont Haugh

River Derwent

Leazes Farm
Bryan's Leap
VALLEY VIEW
THE ROOKERY
Leazes Hall
Leazes
THE COPSE
B6310
Cemy
PH
Hagg

Steelclose Mill Farm

Fogoes Burn

NE39

STATION COTTS
Priestfield Wood

High Friarside

High Friarside
FAIR VIEW
CEDAR CRES
CRATHORNE CT
THE LEAZES
ELM GARTH
LAUREL GR
MYRTLE GR
PO
BIRCH MEWS
BIRCH CRES

LINTZ GREEN LA

Priest Field

GARESFIELD GDNS
BRIARDENE
RUBY GDNS
FRON GDNS
LINTZ TERR
TEMPLEY GDNS
BRACK
ALBION GDNS
FRIAR'S ROW
THORNHILL GDNS
FRIARSIDE GDNS
PRIESTFIELD GDNS

Mill House

Priestfield Lodge

Priestfield Farm

Lintz

Lintz Green

Pontburn Wood

NE16

LAMBTON GDNS

SYKE RD

LONG CLOSE RD
HIGH HAMSTERLEY RD
MILL FARM RD
LODGE

A694

TOLLGATE RD
HIGH MILL RD
PARKLANDS
B6310

Hamsterley Mill

Oldmill Wood

Lintz Hall Farm

Toft Gate

High Hamsterley

Red Burn

Loft House

Hamsterley Park

LINTZ LA

Hamsterley Hall

Low Ewehurst

Collierley Wood

Straightneck Wood

Upper Lintz

A692

Pont Burn

Ewehurst Wood

Mountsett Fell

Mountsett

Chopwell Burn

EWEHURST RD

Crem

Plough Inn (PH)

Struthers' Wood

DH9

Sewage Works

SAWMILL COTTS
Hill Top
B6168
HEATHER LEA
EWEHURST TERR
EWEHURST PAR
EWEHURST GDNS
ROBSON TERR
MOORLANDS
ALDER CRES
FERN TERR
B6311

Pikewell Burn

Pontop Low Wood

Collierley

COLLIERLEY LA

Dipton

FRONT ST
B6311
Flint Hill Bank
MEADOW VIEW
FURST CRES
PALMER RD
PLUNKETT RD
WYNYARD ST
MT PLEASANT
NORTH RD
Flint Hill

IVANHOE TERR
WAVERLEY TERR
EWEHURST GDNS
DERWENT VIEW TERR
WESLEY TERR
Bono La
LION GDNS
B6168

A692

A692 Consett

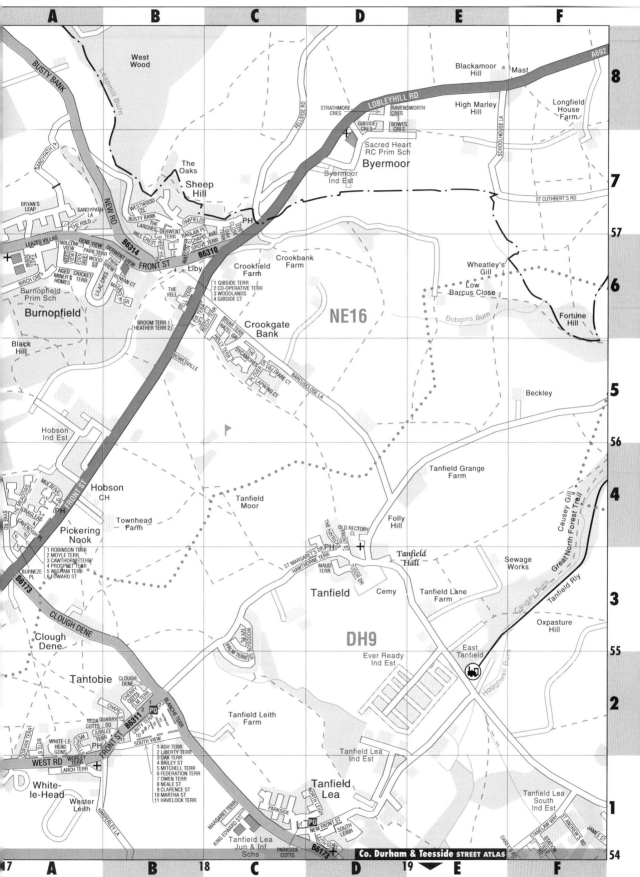

Co. Durham & Teesside STREET ATLAS

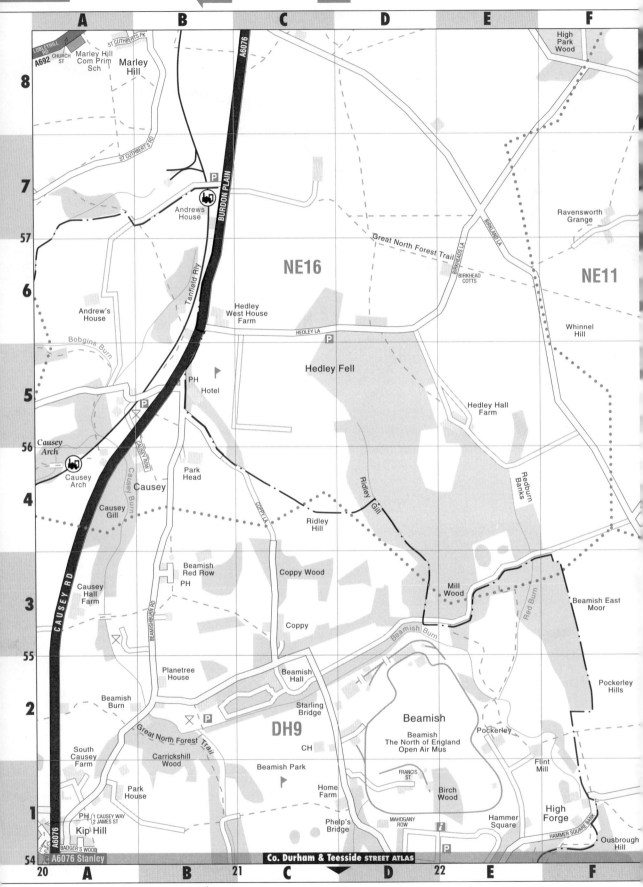

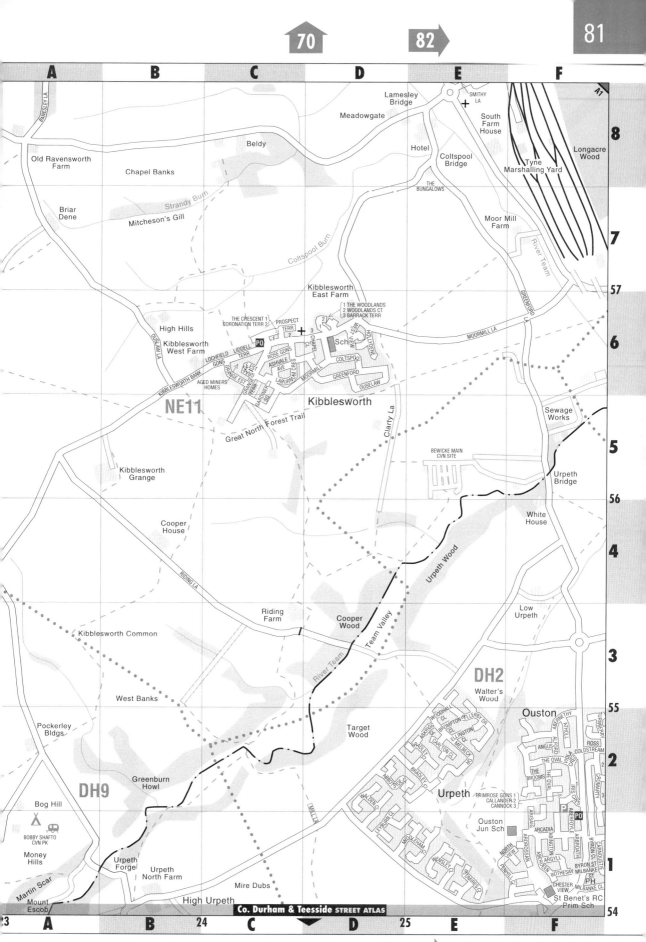

A B C D E F

8
7
57
6
5
56
4
3
55
2
1
54

A1

BANESLEY LA

Old Ravensworth
Farm

Briar
Dene

Chapel Banks

Mitcheson's Gill

Strandy Burn

Beldy

Meadowgate

Lamesley
Bridge

SMITHY
LA

South Farm
House

Hotel

Coltspool
Bridge

Coltspool
Bridge

Tyne
Marshalling Yard

Longacre
Wood

The Bungalows

Coltspool Burn

Moor Mill
Farm

River Team

GREENFORD LA

High Hills

DISLAW LA

Kibblesworth
West Farm

Kibblesworth
East Farm

THE CRESCENT 1
CORONATION TERR 2

PROSPECT
TERR

1 THE WOODLANDS
2 WOODLANDS CT
3 BARRACK TERR

SSM VIEW

HOLYDENE

MOORMILL LA

57

THE CRESCENT

LOCHFIELD
GDNS

LIDDELL
TERR

ROSE GDNS

ASHVALE
AVE

CHAPEL
CL

Sch

PO

KIBBLESWORTH BANK

GRANGE EST

GRANGE
TERR

GARDINER SQ

LABURNUM CRES

MOORMILL

COLTSPO

GREENFORD

OUSELAW

6

AGED MINERS'
HOMES

NE11

Kibblesworth

Great North Forest Trail

Clarty La

Sewage
Works

Urpeth
Bridge

5

Kibblesworth
Grange

BEWICKE MAIN
CVN SITE

White
House

56

Cooper
House

Urpeth Wood

4

RIDING LA

Low
Urpeth

DH2

Riding
Farm

Cooper
Wood

Team Valley

River Team

Kibblesworth Common

Walter's
Wood

55

West Banks

Target
Wood

Ouston

WOODHALL CL

PELLERBY DR

ABRIGG CL

BROMPTON CL

ELLINGTON CL

CARLTON CL

MELBECK CL

BRADLEY CL

ABBEY CL

ANGUSTON
ALFORD
ABERNETHY
AITHOLL
TURNBERRY
ROSS
COLDSTREAM
CROMARTY

THE OVAL

IRIS CRES

THE
BROOMS

Urpeth

PRIMROSE GDNS 1
CALLANDER 2
CANNOCK 3

ARISAIG
ARCADIA
ABINGTON

Pockerley
Bldgs

Bog Hill

BOBBY SHAFTO
CVN PK

Money
Hills

Martin Scar

Mount
Escob

DH9

Greenburn
Howl

Urpeth
Forge

Urpeth
North Farm

Mire Dubs

MILL LA

WALDEN CL

LEYBURN CL

MOORSHAM

WENSLEY CL

PENRITH CL

POMFRET CL

Ouston
Jun Sch

ARDROSSAN
ARGYLL

NORTH VIEW

PENRITH CL

ABERFOYLE
ARBROATH

ARGYLL
AYCLIFFE
ROTHESAY CL

CHESTER
VIEW

ARDINGTON

P

PO

CARNOUSTIE

BYRON ST
MILBANKE ST

CROMARTY

PH

St Benet's RC
Prim Sch

54

High Urpeth

F3
1 WHEATEAR CL
2 FIELDFARE CL
3 STONECHAT CL
4 CORMORANT CL
5 PLOVER CL
6 WHITETHROAT CL
7 GLENHOLME CL
8 TEAL CL
9 WREN CL

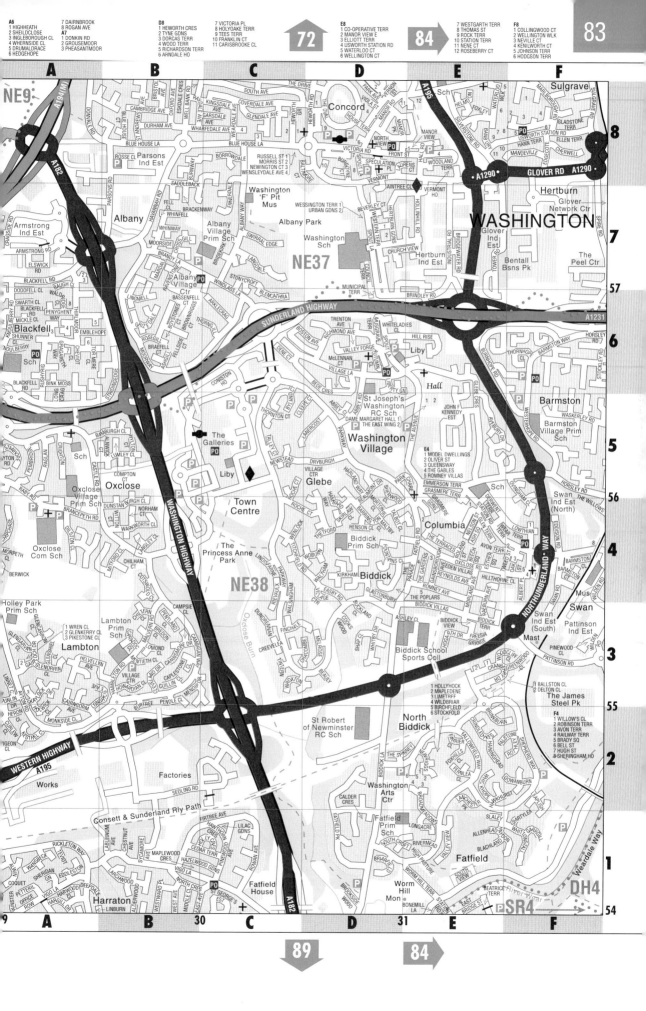

83
73

A   B   C   D   E   F

8   A1290
LC

Peepy
Plantation

Works

MACMERRY CL 1
TOLLERTON DR 2
MAYDOWN CL 3

SR5

Sunrise
Ent Pk

SEVERN
HOS

Hilltorn
Farm

Glover
Network
Ctr

Hylton
Plantation

RINGWAY

Inn

Works

NE37

WESSINGTON WAY

A1231

A19

7

Wood
House

FERRYBOAT
LA

57

A1231

SUNDERLAND HIGHWAY

BARMSTON LA

6   WASHINGTON

Pattison
Ind Est

NE38

Low
Barmston
Farm

Offerton Haugh

High Wood

Manor
House
Farm

Nab
End

OFFERTON CL 1
MAYFIELD RD 2

White
Heugh

ALSTON RD

Middle
Barmston
Farm

FARADAY CL

Weardale Way

Washington
Waterfowl and
Wetlands Ctr

River Wear

Weardale Way

Stony Heugh

5

56

Sewage
Works

4

Pennywell
Ind Est

Offerton
Grange
Farm

WILDEN RD

Wood House
Farm

CH

SR4

Offerton

THE GRANARIES

Offerton

3   Glebe House
Farm

PH

Ayton's
Wood

Offerton
Hall Farm

A183

STAITHES RD

ALICE WELL VILLAS

Cox
Green

55

JUBILEE TERR

The James
Steel Park

Low
Lambton

Dawson's
Plantation

CHESTER RD

ARNHAM GR 1
KINGSWOOD GR 2
CHALFONT GR 3

2

Penshaw
Wood

Victoria Viaduct

DH4

Penshaw
Hill

Flinton Hill
Farm

Great North Forest Trail

Low
Lambton
Farm

COXGREEN RD

Penshaw
Monument

Carr Hill

1

The
Bottoms

HILL LA

BACK LA

East Barnwell
Farm

A183

54

32   A   B   33   C   A183   D   34   E   F

83
90

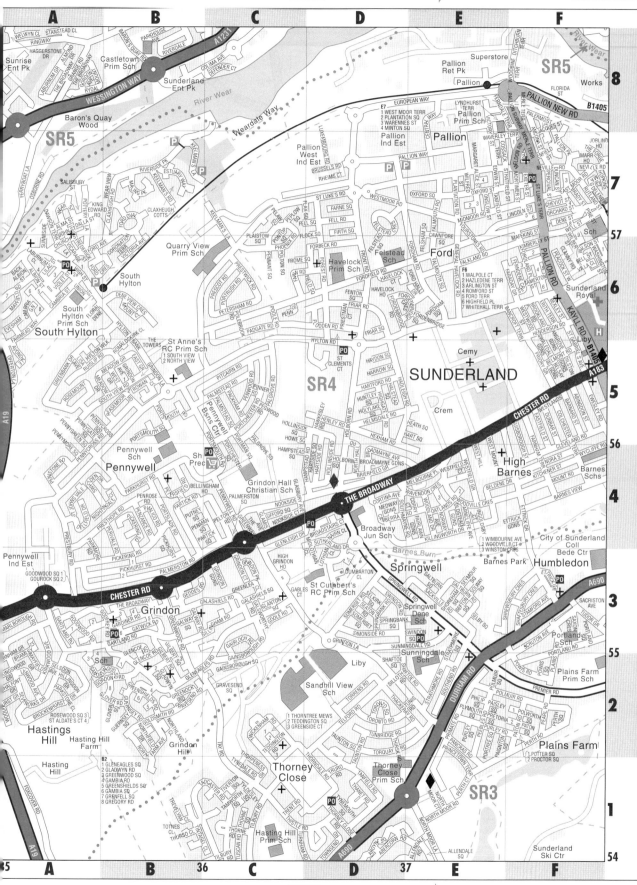

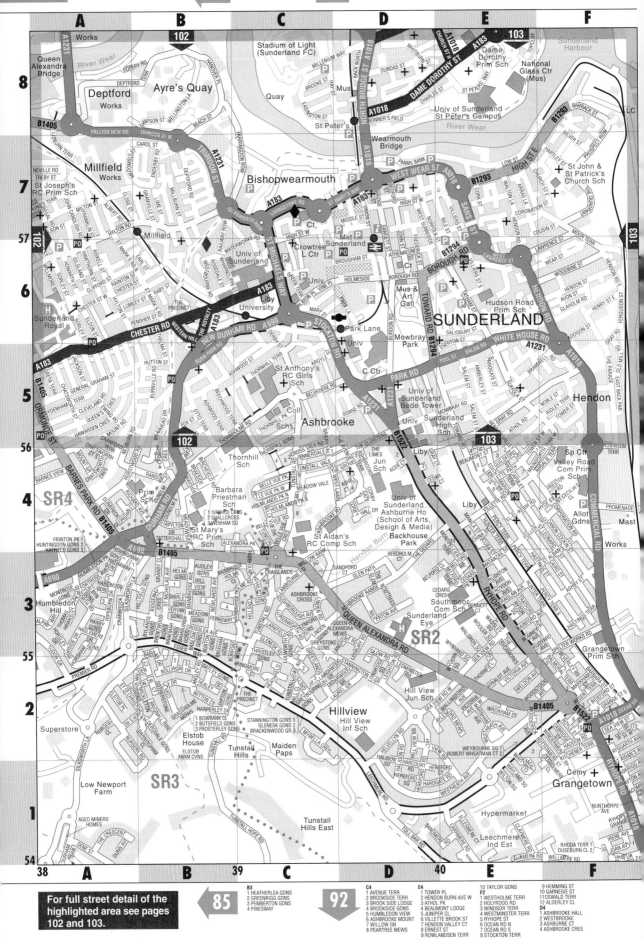

For full street detail of the highlighted area see pages 102 and 103.

B3
1 HEATHERLEA GDNS
2 GREENRIGG GDNS
3 PEMBERTON GDNS
4 PINESWAY

C4
1 AVENUE TERR
2 BROOKSIDE TERR
3 BROOK SIDE LODGE
4 BROOKSIDE GDNS
5 HUMBLEDON VIEW
6 ASHBROOKE MOUNT
7 WILLOW GN
8 PEARTREE MEWS

E4
1 TOWER PL
2 HENDON BURN AVE W
3 ATHOL PK
4 BEAUMONT LODGE
5 JUNIPER CL
6 VILLETTE BROOK ST
7 HENDON VALLEY CT
8 ERNEST ST
9 ROWLANDSEN TERR

10 TAYLOR GDNS
F2
1 WESTHOLME TERR
2 HOLYROOD RD
3 WINDSOR TERR
4 WESTMINSTER TERR
5 RYHOPE ST
6 OCEAN RD N
7 OCEAN RD S
8 STOCKTON TERR

9 HEMMING ST
10 GARNEGIE ST
11 OSWALD TERR
12 ALDERLEY CL
D4
1 ASHBROOKE HALL
2 WESTBROOKE
3 ASHBURNE CT
4 ASHBROOKE CRES

Maud's Hole

Hudson Dock

SR1

North East Pier

South West Breakwater

Dock

Sewage Works

Roker Pier

North Pier

SR1

New South Pier

P

PROMENADE

LC

OCEAN RD
MARGARET ST

IVOR ST

1 ST AIDAN'S AVE
2 ASKRIGG AVE

AYTON AVE
ACKLAM AVE
APPLEGARTH AVE
ASKERN AVE
NETHERBY RD

MILLTHORP CL

SR2

HOWL

ANGH

RYHOPE RD

A1018

Salterfen Rocks

Road under construction

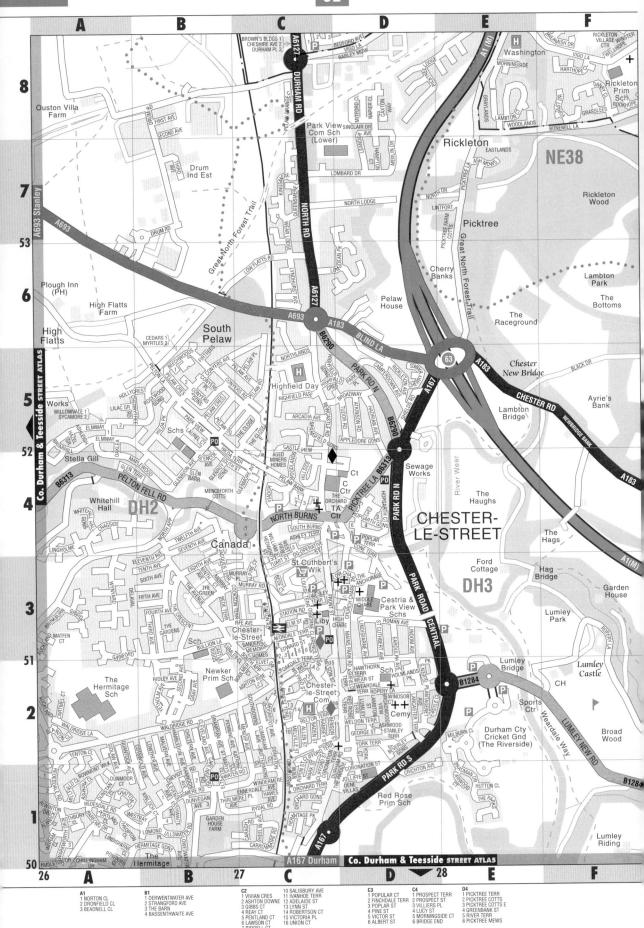

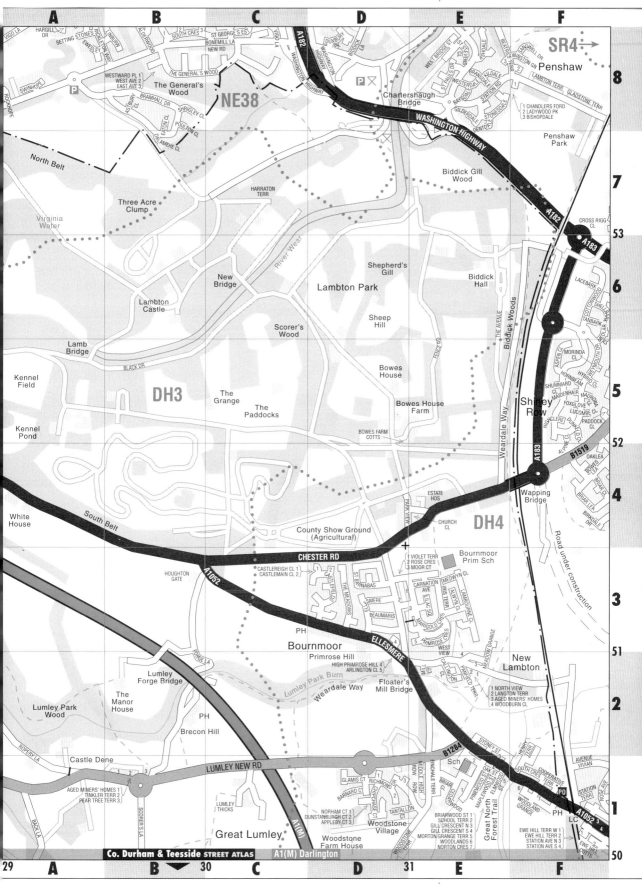

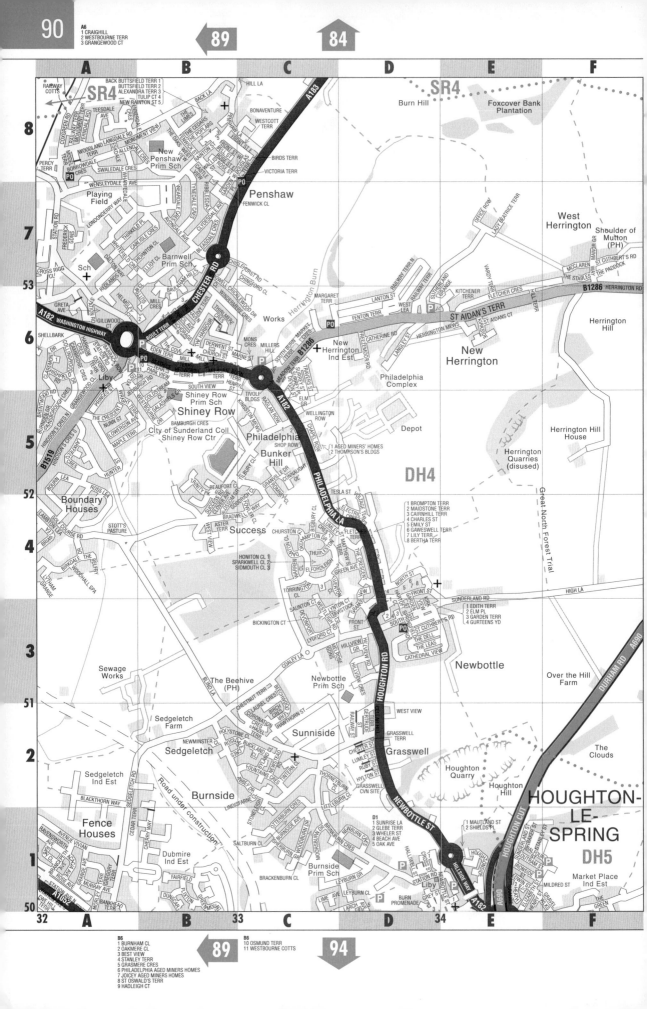

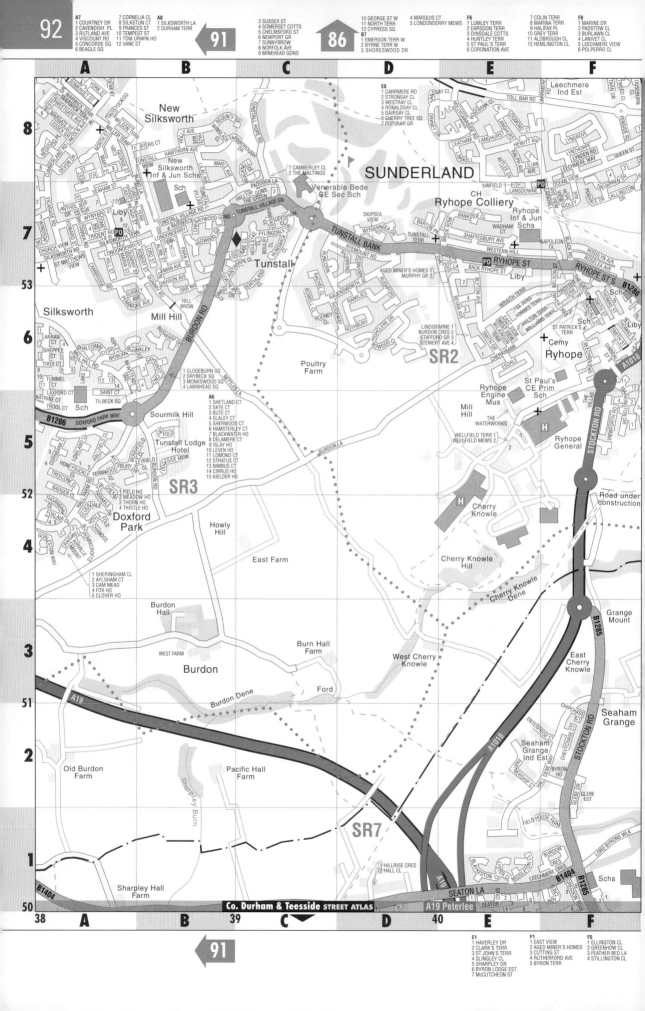

A1018

Ryhope Nook

SALTERFEN RD
SALTERFEN LA

1 TOLLBAR RD
2 MARINE DR
3 TOLLBAR HO
4 LEECHMERE WAY
5 QUEEN ST
6 LADOCK CL
7 POLPERRO CL

Maiden's Flat

Road under construction

BYONY TOFT
ATHELSTAN RIGG
CLIFF VIEW

RYHOPE RD

SEAHAM RD

Halliwell Banks

THE VILLAGE
PO
B1287
CLIFF TERR
STATION RD
SCOTLAND
GEORGE
SEA VIEW

1 FLORALIA AVE
2 GREY TERR
3 GORDON TERR
4 KILBURN CL
5 SOUTH FARM
6 ERNEST TERR
7 RICHARDSON TERR
8 FAWCETT TERR
9 THOMPSON TERR
10 CRANSTON PL
11 ROBSON PL
12 ARTHUR ST
13 MOIR TERR
14 CHARLES ST
15 JOHN ST

Pincushion

HEDLEY
FEATHER BED
ETHEL
ARTHUR AVE
ATHOL GDNS
REGENT RD

MARVILLE W
MARVILLE E

FEATHER BED LA

SR2

Road under construction

Ryhope Dene House
(Convent)

Ryhope Dene

SR7

Hall Farm

Seaham Hall

BYRON'S CT

LC

LORD BYRONS WLK

Seaham Dene

NEW DR

1 BURNWAY
2 NEWLANDS RD W
3 NEWARK CRES
4 NAVENBY CL

WOODLANES

P

BURNHALL DR

NORFOLK CL

NORTON AVE

NORMANBY

SEAHAM RD

Seaham Sch

Northlea

SEAHAM

1 SUTHERLAND ST
2 EMBANKMENT RD

STONEYCROFT WAY 1
ROCKINGHAM CL 2

P

PROMENADE

B1287

NORTH RD

RUNSWICK DR

THE CASTLEREAGH HOMES

53
52
51
50

8
7
6
5
4
3
2
1

41 A B 42 C D 43 E F

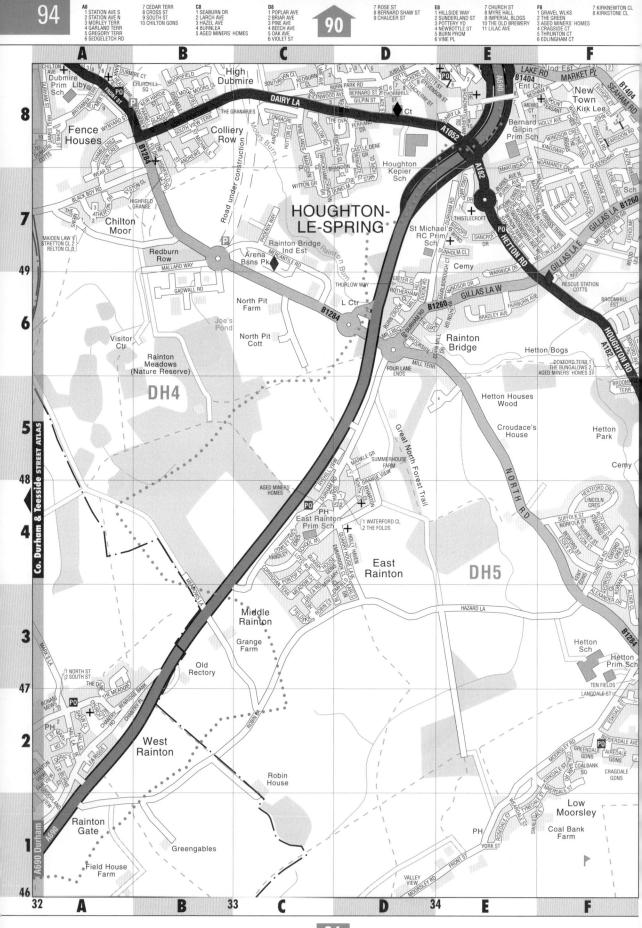

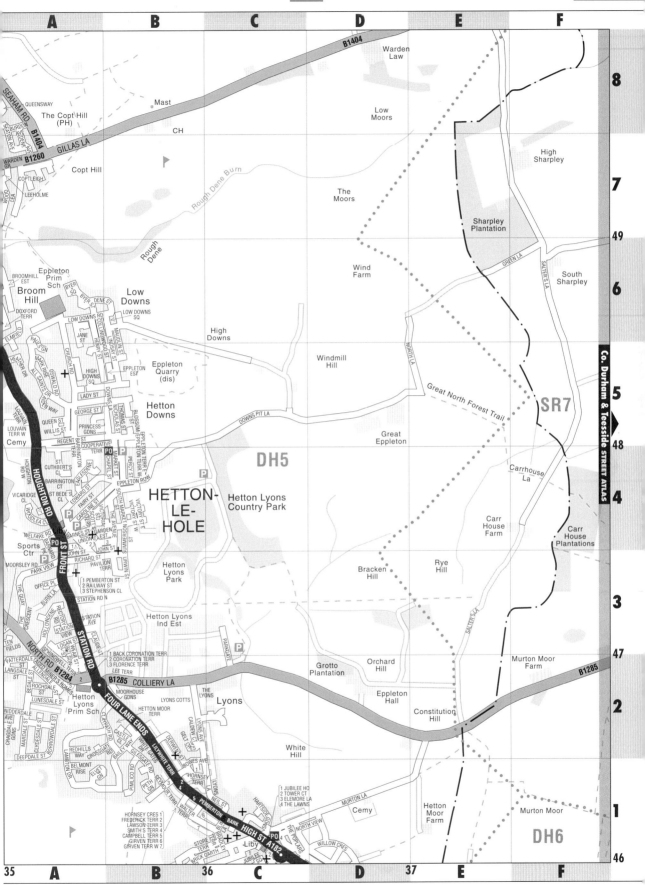

94

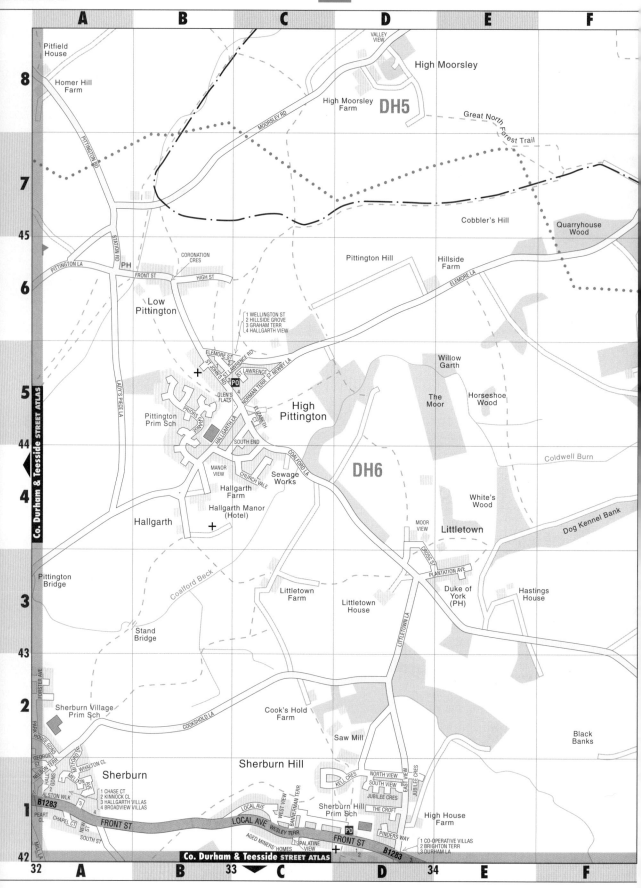

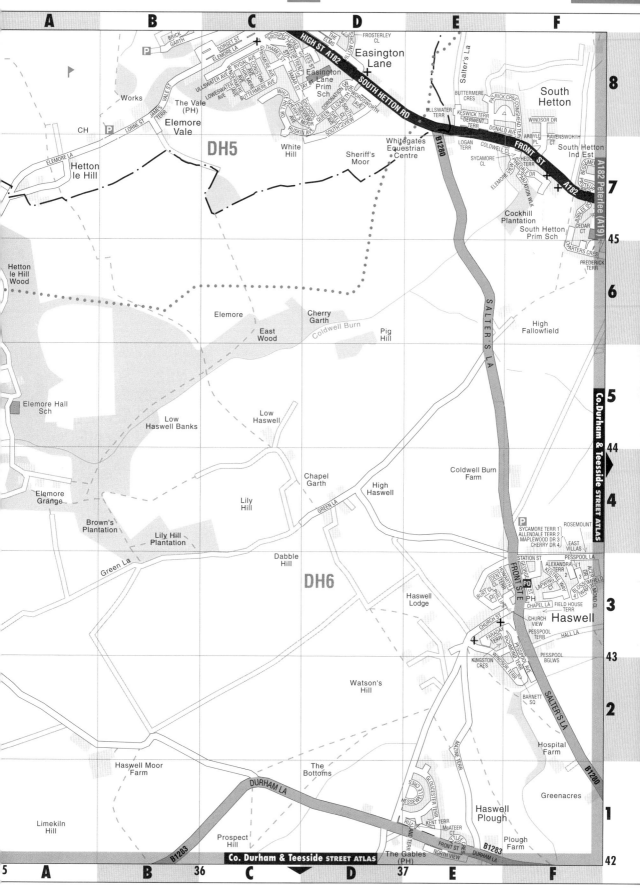

A B C D E F

8
7
45
6
5
44
4
3
43
2
1
42

DH5

Hetton le Hill

Hetton le Hill Wood

Works
The Vale (PH)
CH
Elemore Vale
ELEMORE LA
JAMES VALE TERR
LORNE ST
P

BRICK GARTH
DORSET ST
ELEMORE LA
ULLSWATER AVE
LOWESWATER AVE
GRASMERE AVE
WINDERMERE AVE
BUTTERMERE AVE
RYDAL AVE
CONISTON AVE
THAMES ST
TAMAR ST
TAY ST
WHIT HILL RD
SHERIFF AVE
SEVERN ST
RUSKIN AV
QUEEN ST
CORONATION ST
QUEEN ELIZABETH CT
WORDSWORTH AVE
SOUTH VIEW
SOUTHDENE
PROSPECT CRES
WESTERN TERR
DALE ST
HIGH ST A182
SOUTH HETTON RD
THE ELMS
WILLOW CRES
FROSTERLEY CL

Easington Lane
Easington Lane Prim Sch

White Hill

Sheriff's Moor

Whitegates Equestrian Centre

Salter's La

South Hetton

BUTTERMERE CRES
P RICK CRES
CONISHEAD DR
KESWICK TERR
DERWENT TERR
DONALD AVE
ULLSWATER TERR
LOGAN TERR
COLDWELL CL
SYCAMORE CL
ELEMORE VIEW
HEDLEY TERR
AIREDALE DR
PLANTATION WALK
ARGYLE PL
FRONT ST
WINDSOR DR
RAVENSWORTH CT
South Hetton Ind Est
A182
JUBILEE ST
KESSINGTON
PESSCROFT
CEDAR CT
CARTERS CRES
FREDERICK TERR

A182 Peterlee (A19)

Cockhill Plantation
South Hetton Prim Sch

B1280

SALTER'S LA

Elemore
East Wood
Cherry Garth
Coldwell Burn
Pig Hill

High Fallowfield

Elemore Hall Sch

Low Haswell Banks
Low Haswell

Coldwell Burn Farm

ROSEMOUNT
SYCAMORE TERR 1
ALLENDALE TERR 2
MAPLEWOOD DR 3
CHERRY DR 4
EAST VILLAS
P

Elemore Grange
Brown's Plantation
Lily Hill
Chapel Garth
High Haswell
GREEN LA

Lily Hill Plantation

Green La
Dabble Hill

DH6

Haswell Lodge

STATION ST
GEORGE ST
DENT ST
BURT CT
PILE ST
PEEL ST
FRONT ST E
PO
PH
CHAPEL LA
ALEXANDRA TERR
KESWICK WAY
LAPWING CT
ACRE LA
RAYMOND CL
BLOSSOMFIELD WAY
PESSPOOL LA
FIELD HOUSE TERR
CHURCH VIEW
Haswell
PESSPOOL TERR
HALL LA
PESSPOOL BGLWS
CHURCH ST
FARADAY TERR
RICHMOND TERR
WINDSOR TERR
KINGSTON CRES
SALTER'S LA
BARNETT SQ

Watson's Hill

Haswell Moor Farm
The Bottoms

DURHAM LA

Prospect Hill

B1283

Limekiln Hill

Hospital Farm
Greenacres

MITRE TERR
GLOUCESTER TERR
LITTLE CRES
MESSEW
KENT TERR
MCATEER CT
CLYDE CRES
RUSHYFORD CT
FRONT ST
NORTH VIEW
The Gables (PH)

Haswell Plough
Plough Farm
B1283
DURHAM LA
B1280

5 A B 36 C D 37 E F

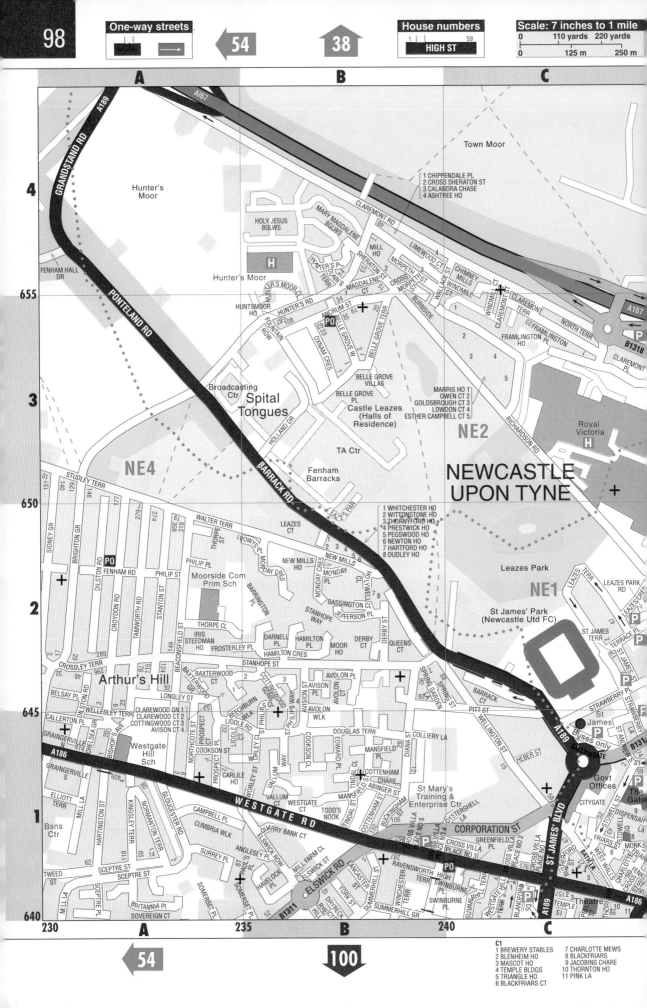

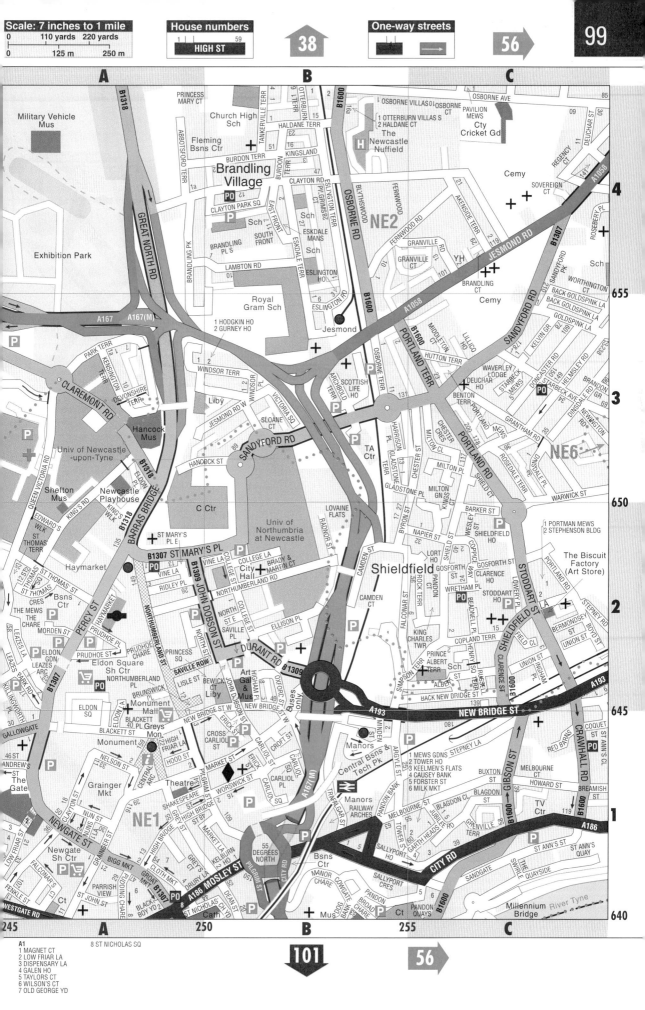

Scale: 7 inches to 1 mile

0 — 110 yards — 220 yards
0 — 125 m — 250 m

House numbers
1 — 59
HIGH ST

38

One-way streets

56

A1
1 MAGNET CT
2 LOW FRIAR LA
3 DISPENSARY LA
4 GALEN HO
5 TAYLORS CT
6 WILSON'S CT
7 OLD GEORGE YD

8 ST NICHOLAS SQ

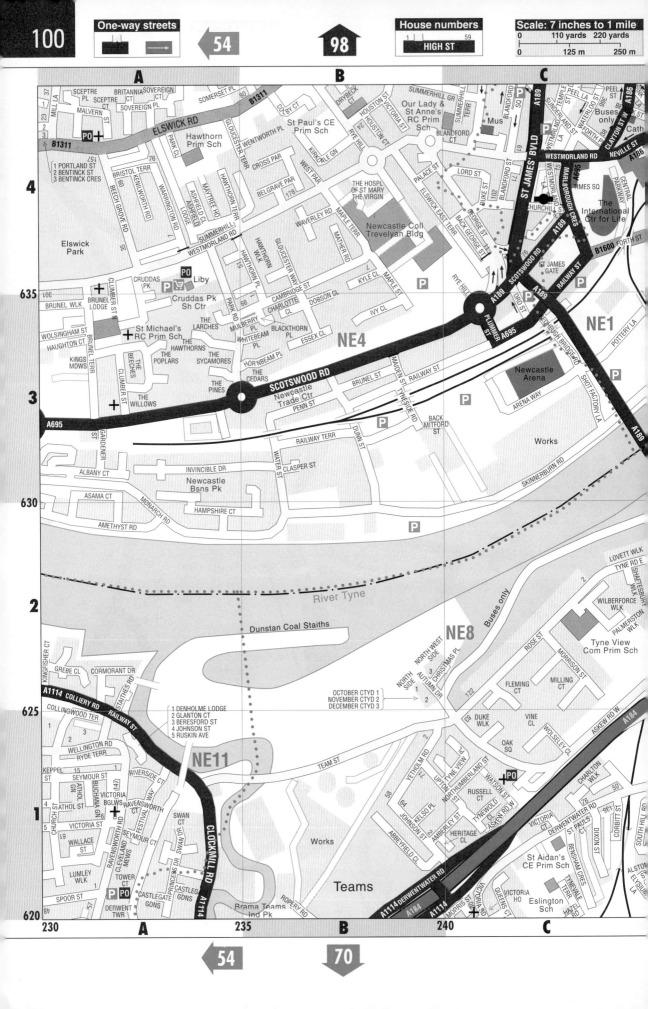

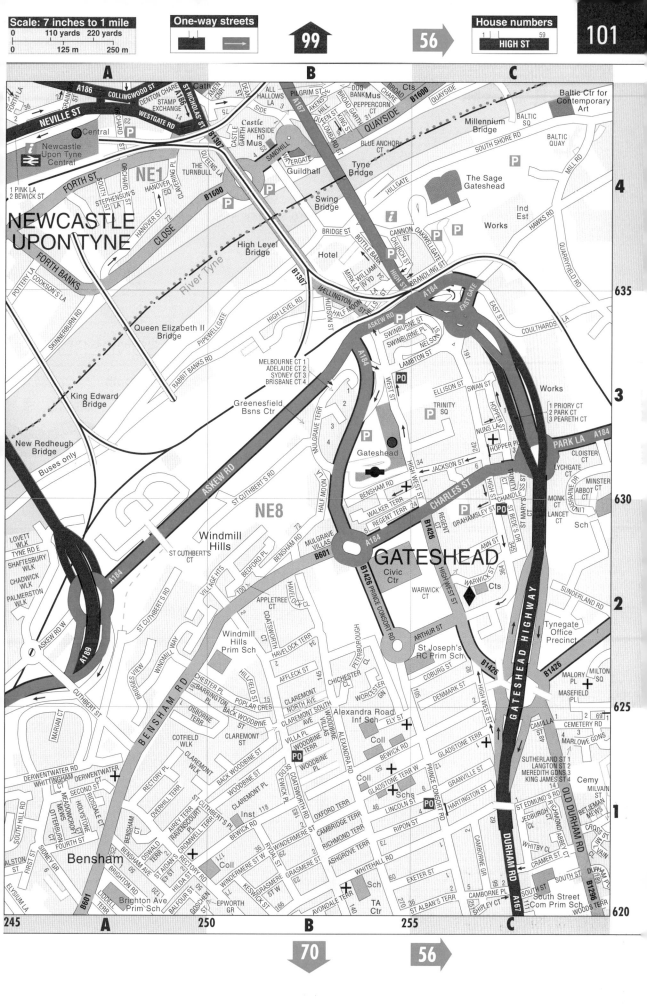

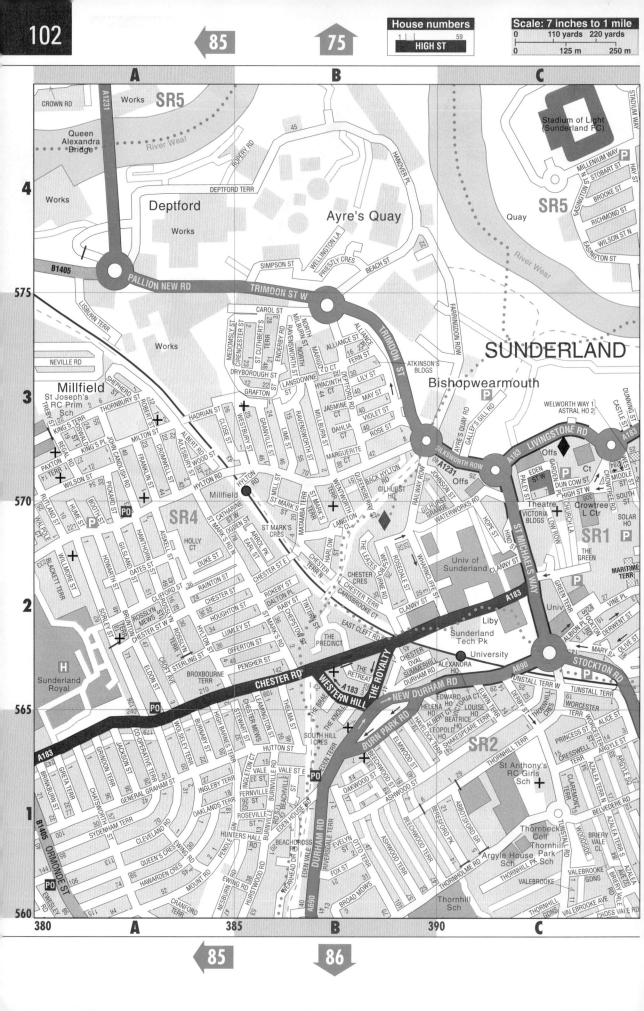

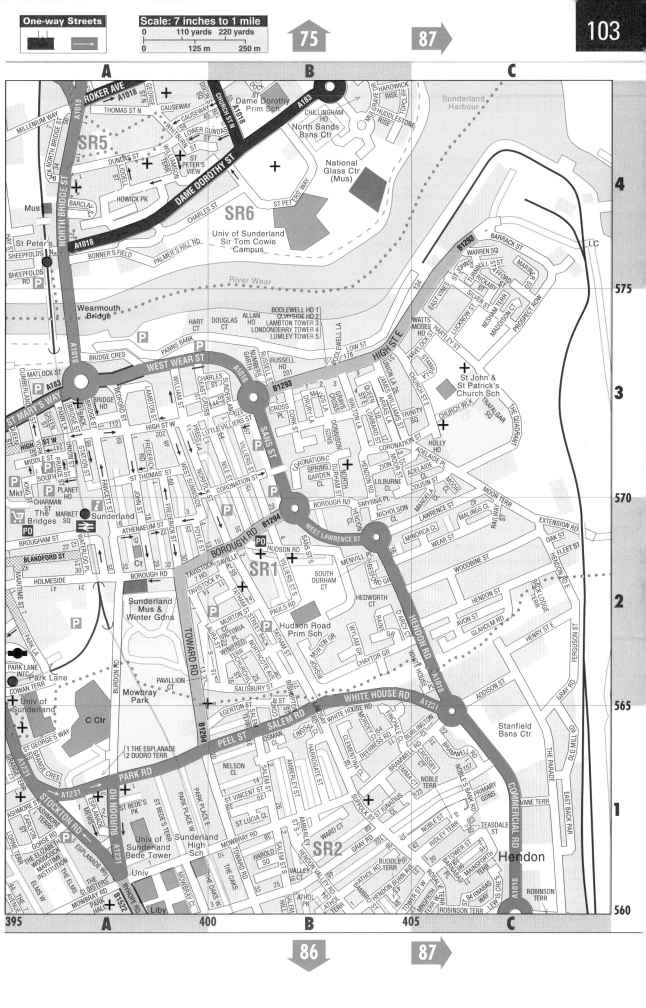

Index

Church Rd **6** Beckenham BR2..........**53** C6

Place name	**Location number**	**Locality, town or village**	**Postcode district**	**Page and grid square**
May be abbreviated on the map	Present when a number indicates the place's position in a crowded area of mapping	Shown when more than one place has the same name	District for the indexed place	Page number and grid reference for the standard mapping

Public and commercial buildings are highlighted in **magenta**   **Places of interest** are highlighted in blue with a star ★

Abbreviations used in the index

Acad	**Academy**	Comm	**Common**	Gd	**Ground**	L	**Leisure**	Prom	**Prom**
App	**Approach**	Cott	**Cottage**	Gdn	**Garden**	La	**Lane**	Rd	**Road**
Arc	**Arcade**	Cres	**Crescent**	Gn	**Green**	Liby	**Library**	Recn	**Recreation**
Ave	**Avenue**	Cswy	**Causeway**	Gr	**Grove**	Mdw	**Meadow**	Ret	**Retail**
Bglw	**Bungalow**	Ct	**Court**	H	**Hall**	Meml	**Memorial**	Sh	**Shopping**
Bldg	**Building**	Ctr	**Centre**	Ho	**House**	Mkt	**Market**	Sq	**Square**
Bsns, Bus	**Business**	Ctry	**Country**	Hospl	**Hospital**	Mus	**Museum**	St	**Street**
Bvd	**Boulevard**	Cty	**County**	HQ	**Headquarters**	Orch	**Orchard**	Sta	**Station**
Cath	**Cathedral**	Dr	**Drive**	Hts	**Heights**	Pal	**Palace**	Terr	**Terrace**
Cir	**Circus**	Dro	**Drove**	Ind	**Industrial**	Par	**Parade**	TH	**Town Hall**
Cl	**Close**	Ed	**Education**	Inst	**Institute**	Pas	**Passage**	Univ	**University**
Cnr	**Corner**	Emb	**Embankment**	Int	**International**	Pk	**Park**	Wk, Wlk	**Walk**
Coll	**College**	Est	**Estate**	Intc	**Interchange**	Pl	**Place**	Wr	**Water**
Com	**Community**	Ex	**Exhibition**	Junc	**Junction**	Prec	**Precinct**	Yd	**Yard**

Index of localities, towns and villages

A

Addison 52 F5
Albany 83 B7
Allerdene 70 F2
Anick 45 F8
Annitsford 22 B1
Arthur's Hill 98 A2
Ashbrooke 86 C5
Ashington 6 B3
Axwell Park 53 E1
Ayre's Quay 102 B4
Ayton 82 F2

B

Backworth 30 C4
Barley Mow 82 C2
Barlow 67 C6
Bar Moor 52 A5
Barmston 83 F5
Beaconhill Green 21 E6
Beacon Lough 71 B4
Beamish 80 D2
Bebside 16 E7
Bedlington 11 A1
Bedlington Station 11 B3
Beechgrove 69 C8
Bell's Close 53 E6
Bensham 101 A1
Benton Square 30 B1
Benwell 54 C6
Berwick Hill 19 A3
Biddick 83 D4
Biddick Hall 59 B2
Bill Quay 57 B2
Billy Mill 41 D7
Birtley 82 C3
Bishopwearmouth 102 C3
Black Callerton 36 A8

Blackfell 83 A6
Blackhall Mill 77 B7
Blakelaw 37 C2
Blaydon 53 E3
Blaydon Burn 52 E1
Blaydon Haughs 53 E4
Bleach Green 53 C1
Blyth 17 C7
Boldon 74 A8
Boldon Colliery 58 E1
Bomarsund 11 C6
Bothal 5 B2
Boundary Houses 90 A4
Bournmoor 89 D3
Branch End 64 D7
Brandling Village 99 B4
Brenkley 20 D3
Bridge End 45 C6
Brockley Whins 58 F3
Broomhaugh 63 A8
Broom Hill 95 A6
Bromley 63 D5
Brunswick Green 28 A5
Brunswick Village 28 A6
Brunton Park 28 B1
Bunker Hill 90 C5
Burdon 92 B3
Burnopfield 79 A6
Burnside 90 B2
Burradon 29 C6
Byermoor 79 D7
Byker 56 C5
Bywell 63 F8

C

Callerton 36 B6
Callerton Lane End ...35 E7
Cambois 12 C5
Campbell Park 57 F5
Camperdown 29 C5

Canada 88 B4
Carley Hill 75 A4
Carr Hill 71 B7
Castletown 74 B1
Cauldwell 59 E7
Causey 80 C4
Chester-le-Street 88 E4
Chilton Moor 94 A7
Chirton 41 F5
Choppington 10 E5
Chopwell 66 B1
Chowdene 70 E4
Clara Vale 51 E6
Cleadon 60 B1
Cleadon Lea 59 E1
Cleadon Park 60 A4
Clifton 9 A2
Coalburns 66 D7
Colliery Row 94 B8
Collingwood 22 B4
Columbia 83 E4
Concord 83 D8
Corbridge 47 B5
Cowgate 37 D1
Cowpen 17 A7
Coxlodge 38 A5
Cramlington 21 F5
Cramlington Village ..22 B7
Crawcrook 51 E4
Cresswell 2 A7
Crookgate Bank 79 C6
Crookhill 52 D5
Cullercoats 32 D3

D

Darras Hall 25 D3
Deans 59 C7
Deckham 71 A8
Delaval 54 C4
Denton Burn 53 E7

Deptford 102 A4
Derwent Haugh 54 B2
Dilston 46 D3
Dinnington 27 A7
Dipton 78 D1
Donwell 72 B1
Downhill 74 B4
Doxford Park 91 E6
Dudley 29 A7
Dunston 54 F1
Dunston Hill 69 E7

E

Earsdon 31 A5
Easington Lane 97 D8
East Boldon 74 D7
East Cramlington 22 E5
East Denton 37 A1
Eastfield 22 D8
East Gateshead 56 B3
East Hartford 16 B3
East Herrington 91 C6
East Holywell 30 E7
East Howdon 41 C2
East Rainton 94 D4
East Sleekburn 12 A3
Ebchester 76 F3
Eighton Banks 71 D1
Eland Green 25 E8
Elemore Vale 97 B8
Ellington 1 D4
Elswick 54 F3
Eltringham 50 A3

F

Fair Moor 3 C4
Farringdon 91 D8

Fatfield 83 E1
Fawdon 37 E7
Felling 71 D8
Felling Shore 56 E2
Fellside 68 F6
Fence Houses 94 A8
Fenham 54 D7
Flint Hill 78 E1
Follingsby 72 D5
Ford 85 E6
Fordley 29 B8
Forest Hall 39 E8
Friars Goose 56 D3
Fulwell 75 C4

G

Gateshead 55 E2
Glebe 83 D5
Gosforth 38 C6
Grangetown 86 F1
Grasswell 90 D2
Great Lumley 89 C1
Greenside 52 A1
Grindon 85 B3
Guide Post 10 F6

H

Hall Close 22 B6
Hallgarth 96 B4
Hamsterley 77 B5
Hamsterley Mill 78 A5
Harlow Green 71 B1
Harlow Hill 33 A5
Harraton 83 B1
Hartley 24 E4
Harton 59 F6
Harton Nook 59 F5

Hastings Hill 85 A2
Haswell 97 F3
Haswell Plough 97 E1
Hazlerigg 28 A4
Healey 62 F1
Heaton 56 D7
Hebburn 57 E5
Hebburn Hall Ponds 57 E4
Hebburn New Town 57 C5
Hebron 3 F8
Heddon-on-the-Wall ...34 F2
Hedgefield 52 E5
Hedley on the Hill 65 A3
Hedworth 58 C2
Hendon 103 C1
Hepscott 9 F5
Hertburn 83 F7
Hetton Downs 95 B5
Hetton le Hill 97 A7
Hetton-le-Hole 95 B4
Heworth 71 F8
Hexham 44 E2
High Barnes 85 E4
High Callerton 25 E2
High Church 8 F7
High Dubmire 94 B8
Highfield 67 C2
High Flatts 88 A6
High Forge 80 F1
High Friarside 78 E6
High Heaton 39 A3
High Mickley 64 F7
High Moorsley 96 D8
High Pittington 96 C5
High Shields 42 B1
High Southwick 75 B3
High Spen 66 F4
High Urpeth 81 B1
High Westwood 77 B4
Hill Top 41 A8
Hillview 86 C2
Hirst 6 E3
Hobson 79 A4
Holy Cross 40 E3
Holywell 23 F2
Hooker Gate 67 A2
Horsley 50 D8
Horsley Hill 60 B8
Houghton 34 D2
Houghton-le-Spring ...94 D7
Howdon 41 B2
Howdon Pans 41 C1
Humbledon 85 F4
Hylton Castle 74 A2
Hylton Red House 74 D4

Klondyke 22 C5

J

Jarrow 58 D6
Jesmond 38 E1
Jesmond Vale 56 A7

K

Kenton 37 E4
Kenton Bankfoot 37 A6
Kenton Bar 37 D4
Kibblesworth 81 D5
Killingworth 29 D3
Kingston Park 37 C6
Kip Hill 80 A1

L

Lambton 83 A3
Leadgate 66 A3
Leam Lane 72 A6
Leazes 78 F6
Lemington 53 C7
Linton 1 B3
Lintz 78 F5
Lintzford 78 B7
Littletown 96 E4
Loansdean 8 F5
Lobley Hill 70 A5
Longbenton 39 C8
Longhirst 4 F7
Low Downs 95 B6
Low Fell 70 F5
Low Gate 44 A4
Low Greenside 52 A2
Low Lights 42 C6
Low Moorsley 94 F1
Low Pittington 96 B6
Low Prudhoe 50 D4
Low Southwick 75 A1
Low Walker 57 B6
Low Westwood 77 A5
Lyndhurst 71 A3
Lynemouth 2 B2
Lyons 95 C2

M

Marden 32 B2
Marley Hill 80 A8
Marley Pots 74 F3
Marsden 60 C5
Mayfield 22 C6
Medomsley 77 C1
Melton Park 28 C1
Mickley Square 49 E1
Middle Herrington ...91 B8
Middle Rainton 94 C3
Millfield 102 A3
Mill Hill 92 B6
Mitford 8 A8
Monkseaton 31 F5
Monkton 58 A4
Monkwearmouth 75 D1
Moor Farm Estate ...14 D8
Moorside 91 D5
Morpeth 8 E6
Mount Pleasant 56 A1
Murton 31 B2

N

Nedderton 15 B8
Newbiggin-by-the-Sea ...7 E3
Newbottle 90 E3
Newburn 52 F7
Newburn Haugh 53 C4
Newcastle upon Tyne ...55 C6
New Delaval 17 B3
New Hartley 23 D6
New Herrington 90 E6
New Lambton 89 F2
Newlands 76 D4

New Ridley 64 B3
Newsham 17 B5
New Silksworth 92 B8
Newton 48 C6
Newton Hall 48 D7
New Town
  Houghton-le-Spring ...94 F8
New Town West Boldon ...73 E8
North Biddick 83 E2
North Blyth 12 E1
Northlea 93 B1
North Seaton 7 B2
North Shields 41 F4
North Side 82 D6
North Walbottle 36 A3

O

Oakwood 45 E8
Offerton 84 F3
Old Benwell 54 B5
Old Fort 56 C1
Ouston 81 F2
Ovingham 50 B5
Ovington 49 C4
Oxclose 83 B5

P

Painshawfield 64 C6
Pallion 85 E7
Palmersville 30 A1
Paradise 54 C4
Park Estate 64 C6
Parkside 22 B7
Path Head 53 B3
Pegswood 4 E4
Pelaw 56 F1
Pennywell 85 B4
Penshaw 90 C7
Percy Main 41 D3
Philadelphia 90 C5
Pickering Nook 79 A4
Picktree 88 E7
Plains Farm 85 F2
Ponteland 25 D6
Portobello 82 E4
Preston 42 A8
Prestwick 26 C5
Primrose 58 C3
Prudhoe 50 D1

R

Rainton Bridge 94 E6
Rainton Gate 94 A1
Redburn Dene 41 F2
Rickleton 88 E7
Riding Lea 62 D8
Riding Mill 62 E8
Roker 75 F2
Rosehill 40 E2
Rowlands Gill 67 E2
Ryhope 92 F6
Ryhope Colliery ...92 E7
Ryton 52 C4
Ryton Haugh 53 A5
Ryton Woodside ...52 B2

S

St Ann's 56 A5
St Anthony's 56 E3
St Lawrence 56 B5
St Peter's 56 C4
Saltmeadows 56 A4
Saltwick 13 A4
Scotland Gate 10 F5
Scotswood 54 A4
Seaburn 75 F4
Seaham 93 C1
Seaham Grange ...92 F2
Seaton Burn 21 B1
Seaton Delaval ...23 C2
Seaton Sluice 24 C5
Seaton Terrace ...23 D4
Sedgeletch 90 B2
Seghill 22 F1
Shankhouse 16 C1
Sheep Hill 79 B7
Sheepwash 10 E8
Sherburn 96 A1
Sherburn Hill 96 C1
Sheriff Hill 71 B6
Shieldfield 99 B2
Shiney Row 90 B5
Shipcote 70 E8
Shiremoor 30 F3
Shotton 20 E8
Silksworth 91 F7
Simonside 58 E5
Slaley 62 A2
South Bents 75 E3
South Benwell ...54 D4
South Boldon ...74 B7
Southfield 22 B3
South Gosforth ..38 E4
South Hetton ...97 F8
South Hylton ...85 A6
South Newsham ..17 D3
South Pelaw 88 B6
South Shields ...42 E4
South Wellfield ..31 A5
Southwick 75 A2
Spital Tongues ..98 B3
Springwell Sunderland ...85 D3
Springwell Washington ...71 F2
Stakeford 11 B7
Stanners 53 A6
Stannington 14 D3
Stargate 52 E3
Stella 53 A4
Stobhill 9 A6
Stobhillgate 9 B7
Stocksfield 64 B7
Stonelaw 22 A5
Street Gate 69 C3
Success 90 C4
Sulgrave 83 F8
Sunderland 86 E6
Sunniside
  Houghton-le-Spring ...90 C2
Sunniside Whickham ...69 A2
Swalwell 54 B1
Swan 83 F3

T

Tanfield 79 D3
Tanfield Lea 79 D1
Tantobie 79 A2

Teams 100 B1
Team Valley 70 D5
The Lawe 42 C4
Thorney Close ...85 C1
Throckley 35 D1
Town Centre 83 C4
Town End Farm ..73 E4
Tranwell 8 C4
Tunstall 92 C7
Tynemouth 42 B8

U

Urpeth 81 E2
Usworth 72 C1

W

Walbottle 35 F2
Walker 56 F6
Walkergate 56 E8
Walkerville 39 F1
Wallsend 40 D2
Wardley 72 C8
Washington 83 F7
Washington Village ...83 D5
Wellfield 31 B5
West Allotment ..30 E1
West Boldon ...74 A8
West Chirton ...41 C6
West Denton ...36 D1
Westerhope 36 E3
West Harton ...59 B6
West Herrington ..90 F7
West Holywell ..30 D6
West Jesmond ..38 D2
West Mickley ...64 E8
West Monkseaton ...31 C4
West Moor 29 B1
West Rainton ...94 B2
West Sleekburn ..11 D7
West Wylam 50 E3
Whickham 69 B7
Whitburn 60 E1
Whitehills 71 D5
Whitelea 22 A5
Whiteleas 59 D3
White-le-Head ...79 A1
Whitley Bay 32 C6
Wideopen 28 C5
Willington 40 F4
Willington Quay ..41 B2
Willington Square ...40 E5
Wincomblee 57 B5
Windmill Hills ...101 B2
Windy Nook 71 D6
Winlaton 53 B1
Winlaton Mill ...68 C6
Witherwack 74 F4
Woodbridge 7 A4
Woodhorn 7 B6
Woodhorn Demesne ...7 D6
Woodstone Village ...89 D1
Woolsington 36 E8
Wrekenton 71 C3
Wylam 51 B6

5

55 Degrees N NE1 . . . . . .99 B1

A

A J Cook Ct NE63 . . . . .6 C3
A J Cook's Cotts NE39 . . . .67 B2
Abbay St SR5 . . . . .75 A1
Abbey Cl Washington NE38 83 D5
  Whitley Bay NE25 . . . . . . .31 D4
Abbey Ct Gateshead NE8 .101 C1
  5 Hexham NE46 . . . . . . .45 B5
Abbey Dr Burnside DH4 . . .90 C2
  Jarrow NE32 . . . . .58 C7
  Newcastle-u-T NE5 . . . . . .36 B4
  Tynemouth NE30 . . . . . . .42 D8
Abbey Gate NE61 . . . . .8 D7
Abbey Mdws NE61 . . . . .8 D7
Abbey Rd NE38 . . . . .83 D5
Abbey Terr
  12 Morpeth NE61 . . . . .3 F1
  Shiremoor NE27 . . . . .30 E3
  13 Morpeth NE61 . . . . .3 F1
Abbey View Hexham NE46 .45 C4
Abbeyfield Cl NE8 . . . . . . .100 B1
Abbeyfields Fst Sch NE61 .8 E8
Abbeyvale Dr NE6 . . . . . . .57 B7
Abbie Ct NE24 . . . . .17 D7
Abbot Ct NE8 . . . . .101 C3
Abbot's Way NE61 . . . . . . .8 E8
Abbots Cl NE62 . . . . .11 B8
Abbots Way
  Tynemouth NE29 . . . . . . .41 E8
  2 Whickham NE16 . . . . . .69 B7
Abbotsfield Cl SR3 . . . . . .91 F5
Abbotsford Gr SR2 . . . . . .102 C1
Abbotsford Ho NE24 . . . . .17 C6
Abbotsford Pk NE25 . . . . .31 F4
Abbotsford Rd NE10 . . . . .56 D1
Abbotsford Terr NE2 . . . . .99 A4
Abbotside Cl DH2 . . . . . . .81 D2
Abbotside Pl NE5 . . . . .36 D2
Abbotsmeade Cl NE5 . . . .54 C8
Abbs St SR5 . . . . .75 D1
Abercorn Pl NE28 . . . . . . .40 E6
Abercorn Rd
  Newcastle-u-T NE15 . . . . .54 A5
  Sunderland SR3 . . . . .91 D8
Abercrombie Pl **2** NE5 . .37 B2
Aberdare Rd SR3 . . . . .91 E7
Aberdeen DH2 . . . . .81 F1
Aberdeen Ct NE3 . . . . .37 D8
Aberdeen Dr NE32 . . . . . . .58 E3
Aberdeen Twr SR3 . . . . . . .91 E8
Aberford Cl NE5 . . . . .36 B3
Aberfoyle DH2 . . . . .81 F1
Abernethy DH2 . . . . .81 F2
Abigail Ct NE3 . . . . .38 E5
Abingdon Ct
  Blaydon NE21 . . . . .53 C3
  Newcastle-u-T NE3 . . . . . .37 D7
Abingdon Rd NE6 . . . . . . .57 B7
Abingdon Sq NE23 . . . . . .16 C1
Abingdon St SR4 . . . . .85 F5
Abingdon Way NE35 . . . . .73 E7
Abinger St NE4 . . . . .98 B1
Abington DH2 . . . . .81 F1
Aboyne Sq SR3 . . . . .85 D1
Acacia Ave DH4 . . . . .90 A4
Acacia Gr Hebburn NE31 .57 E4
  South Shields NE34 . . . . .59 F5
Acacia Rd NE10 . . . . .56 B2
Acacia Terr NE63 . . . . .6 D3
Acanthus Ave NE4 . . . . . . .54 D7
Acer Ct SR2 . . . . .86 D4
Acer Dr DH6 . . . . .97 F3
Acklam Ave SR2 . . . . .87 A1
Acomb Ave
  Seaton Delaval NE25 . . . .23 D2
  Wallsend NE28 . . . . .40 D7
Acomb Cl NE61 . . . . .9 C5
Acomb Cres NE3 . . . . .38 A8
Acomb Ct Bedlington NE22 11 A1
  Gateshead NE9 . . . . .71 B2
  Killingworth NE12 . . . . . . .29 D3
  Sunderland SR2 . . . . .86 F1
Acomb Dr NE41 . . . . .51 A7
Acomb Gdns NE5 . . . . . . .37 C1
Acorn Ave Bedlington NE22 15 F8
  Gateshead NE8 . . . . .70 C8
Acorn Ct NE9 . . . . .71 D3
Acorn Rd NE2 . . . . .38 E2
Acorn Sq NE42 . . . . .50 D2
Acreford Ct NE2 . . . . .10 E6
Acton Dr NE29 . . . . .41 D8
Acton Ho **11** NE29 . . . . . .42 A4
Acton Pl NE7 . . . . .39 B2
Acton Rd NE5 . . . . .53 F8
Ada St Newcastle-u-T NE6 .56 E6
  South Shields NE33 . . . . .42 D1
Adair Ave NE15 . . . . .54 C6
Adair Way NE31 . . . . .58 A5
Adams Terr DH8 . . . . .77 A2
Adamsez Ind Est NE15 . . .53 F4
Adderlane Fst Sch NE42 .50 E3
Adderlane Rd NE42 . . . . . .50 E3
Addington Cres NE29 . . . .41 E6

Addington Dr Blyth NE24 . .17 E5
  Wallsend NE28 . . . . .40 D7
Addison Cl **2** NE6 . . . . . .56 B6
Addison Ct Ryton NE40 . . .52 B5
  7 Wallsend NE28 . . . . . .41 A1
Addison Gdns NE10 . . . . . .72 B8
Addison Ind Est
  Ryton NE21 . . . . .52 F5
  Ryton NE21 . . . . .53 A5
Addison Rd
  North Shields NE29 . . . . .42 A4
  Sunderland SR2 . . . . . . .103 C2
Addison Wlk NE34 . . . . . . .59 A3
Addycombe Terr NE6 . . . . .39 C1
Adelaide Cl SR1 . . . . .103 C3
Adelaide Ct NE8 . . . . .101 B3
Adelaide Ctr The **5** NE4 .54 E5
Adelaide Ho **3** NE4 . . . . .54 E5
Adelaide Pl SR1 . . . . .103 C3
Adelaide St **12** DH3 . . . . .88 C2
Adelaide Terr NE4 . . . . . . .54 E4
Adeline Gdns NE3 . . . . . . .38 A3
Adelphi Cl NE29 . . . . .41 C8
Adelphi Pl NE6 . . . . .56 E5
Aden Twr SR3 . . . . .91 E8
Admington Ct NE62 . . . . . .10 F7
Admiral Collingwood Ct **5**
  NE1 . . . . .9 A8
Admiral Ho **9** NE30 . . . . .42 D7
Admiral Way SR3 . . . . .91 C5
Adolphus St SR6 . . . . .60 F1
Affleck St NE8 . . . . .101 B2
Afton Ct NE34 . . . . .59 C5
Afton Way NE3 . . . . .37 E6
Agar Rd SR3 . . . . .91 E8
Aged Miner's Cotts NE43 64 F8
Aged Miner's Homes
  Boldon Colliery NE35 . . . .58 D1
  Burnopfield NE16 . . . . . . .79 A6
  Hetton le H DH5 . . . . .95 A2
  3 Houghton-le-S,New Town
  DH5 . . . . .94 F8
  Ryhope SR2 . . . . .92 E7
  2 Seaham SR7 . . . . .92 F1
Aged Miners Cotts NE42 .50 B1
Aged Miners Homes
  Blyth NE24 . . . . .17 B5
  Cambois NE24 . . . . .12 D4
  Chester le S DH2 . . . . . . .88 C4
  Newbiggin-by-t-S NE64 . . .7 D3
  2 Newcastle-u-T NE5 . . . .36 E3
Aged Miners' Homes
  Annitsford NE23 . . . . .22 B1
  Ashington NE63 . . . . .6 A4
  Ashington,Woodbridge NE63 .6 F5
Aged Miners' Homes
  DH4 . . . . .89 E2
Aged Miners' Homes
  Brunswick Village NE13 . . .28 A6
  Cramlington NE23 . . . . . . .21 F7
  Dudley NE23 . . . . .29 A6
  East Rainton DH5 . . . . . . .94 C4
Aged Miners' Homes
  DH3 . . . . .89 B1
Aged Miners' Homes
  DH5 . . . . .94 F6
Aged Miners' Homes
  NE39 . . . . .67 A4
Aged Miners' Homes **5**
  DH4 . . . . .94 C8
Aged Miners' Homes
  NE11 . . . . .81 C6
Aged Miners' Homes
  New Hartley NE25 . . . . . .23 E6
  New Silksworth SR3 . . . . .86 A1
Aged Miners' Homes
  NE39 . . . . .67 F1
Aged Miners' Homes
  NE40 . . . . .52 E4
Aged Miners' Homes
  Sherburn Hill DH6 . . . . . .96 C1
  Shiney Row DH4 . . . . . . .90 C5
  South Shields NE34 . . . . .60 A7
Aged Miners' Homes
  Stakeford NE62 . . . . .11 C8
  Sunderland SR5 . . . . .74 E2
Aged Miners' Homes
  NE16 . . . . .69 A1
Aged Miners' Homes
  NE27 . . . . .30 F3
Aged Mineworkers Homes
  Longhirst NE61 . . . . .5 B7
  Throckley NE15 . . . . .35 B8
Agincourt Hebburn NE31 . .57 D7
  Killingworth NE12 . . . . . . .29 D4
Agnes Maria St NE3 . . . . .38 A5
Agricola Ct **1** NE33 . . . . .42 C4
Agricola Gdns NE28 . . . . .40 D7
Agricola Rd NE4 . . . . .54 F6
Aidan Ave NE26 . . . . .24 D4
Aidan Cl
  Brunswick Village NE13 . . .28 A6
  Wallsend NE27 . . . . .30 C1
Aidan Ct Jarrow NE32 . . . .58 D6
  Longbenton NE7 . . . . .39 C5
Aidan Gr NE61 . . . . .1 E4
Aidan Wlk NE3 . . . . .38 E5
Aiden Way DH5 . . . . .95 A5
Ailesbury St SR4 . . . . . . .102 A3
Ainderby Rd NE15 . . . . . . .35 B2
Ainsdale Gdns NE5 . . . . . .36 C2
Ainslie Pl NE5 . . . . .37 C2
Ainsworth St NE34 . . . . . .59 A3

Ainthorpe Cl SR3 . . . . .92 B7
Ainthorpe Gdns NE7 . . . . .39 C4
Aintree Cl Ashington NE63 . .6 C2
  Washington NE37 . . . . . . .83 D7
Aintree Gdns NE8 . . . . . . .70 C7
Aintree Rd SR3 . . . . .91 D8
Airedale NE28 . . . . .39 F5
Airedale Gdns DH5 . . . . . .94 F2
Airey Terr
  Gateshead NE8 . . . . .101 A1
  Newcastle-u-T NE6 . . . . . .57 A5
Aireys Cl DH4 . . . . .94 C8
Airport Freightway NE13 .26 E2
Airport Ind Est NE3 . . . . . .37 D6
Airport Sta NE13 . . . . .26 D3
Airville Mount SR3 . . . . . .92 A4
Aisgill Cl NE23 . . . . .22 B6
Aisgill Dr NE5 . . . . .36 C1
Aiskell St SR4 . . . . .102 A2
Akeld Cl NE23 . . . . .22 B5
Akeld Ct NE3 . . . . .38 E4
Akeld Mews **7** SR6 . . . . .75 E1
Akenside Hill NE1 . . . . . .101 B4
Akenside Ho NE1 . . . . . . .101 B4
Akenside Terr NE2 . . . . . . .99 C4
Akhurst Sch NE2 . . . . .38 F2
Alamein Ave DH5 . . . . .94 F8
Alanbrooke Row NE31 . . . .57 C3
Alansway Gdns **9** NE33 .59 D8
Albany Ave NE12 . . . . .39 D7
Albany Ct NE4 . . . . .100 A3
Albany Gdns **2** NE26 . . . .32 B4
Albany Ho SR5 . . . . .75 C1
Albany Mews 38 A2
Albany Rd NE8 . . . . .56 A3
Albany St E NE33 . . . . .59 D8
Albany St W NE33 . . . . . . .59 D8
Albany Village Ctr NE37 .83 B7
Albany Village Prim Sch
  NE37 . . . . .83 C7
Albany Way NE37 . . . . .83 C7
Albatross Way NE24 . . . . .17 E3
Albemarle Ave NE2 . . . . . .38 D3
Albemarle St **4** NE33 . . .42 C3
Albert Ave **9** NE28 . . . . .40 B2
Albert Ct NE2 . . . . .102 B1
Albert Dr NE9 . . . . .70 F4
Albert Edward Terr NE35 .58 E2
Albert Elliott Prim Sch
  NE34 . . . . .59 C2
Albert Pl Gateshead NE9 . .70 F4
  Washington NE38 . . . . . . .83 F4
Albert Rd Bedlington NE22 .11 E2
  Jarrow NE32 . . . . .58 A6
  Jarrow NE32 . . . . .58 B6
  Seaton Sluice NE26 . . . . .24 D6
  Sunderland SR4 . . . . . . .102 A3
Albert St Blyth NE24 . . . . .17 E8
  6 Chester le S DH3 . . . .88 C3
  Hebburn NE31 . . . . .57 D6
  Newcastle-u-T NE2 . . . . . .99 C2
  Rowlands Gill NE39 . . . . .67 A1
Albert Terr
  Longbenton NE12 . . . . . . .29 C1
  5 Whitley Bay NE26 . . . .32 B4
Albion Ct
  Newcastle-u-T NE6 . . . . . .56 B5
  10 South Shields NE33 . . .42 C4
Albion Gdns NE16 . . . . . . .78 F5
Albion Ho **3** NE29 . . . . . .42 A5
Albion Pl SR1 . . . . .102 C2
Albion Rd W NE29,NE30 . .42 A6
Albion Rd W NE29 . . . . . . .42 A5
Albion Ret Ctr NE24 . . . . .17 D8
Albion Row
  Newcastle-u-T NE6 . . . . . .56 B6
  Newcastle-u-T,St Lawrence
  NE6 . . . . .56 B5
Albion St Gateshead NE10 .71 D6
  Sunderland SR4 . . . . .85 A6
Albion Terr
  6 Gateshead NE9 . . . . . .71 F1
  Hexham NE46 . . . . .45 A5
  Lynemouth NE61 . . . . .2 A3
  8 North Shields NE29 . . .42 A6
Albion Way Blyth NE24 . . .17 C7
  Cramlington NE23 . . . . . . .16 D1
Albury Park Rd NE30 . . . . .42 C7
Albury Pl NE16 . . . . .69 A5
Albury Rd NE2 . . . . .38 E3
Albyn Gdns SR3 . . . . .86 A3
Alcester Cl NE62 . . . . .10 F7
Alconbury Cl NE24 . . . . . .17 E5
Alcroft Ct NE5 . . . . .36 B3
Aldborough St NE24 . . . . .17 E8
Aldbrough Cl **11** SR2 . . . .92 F6
Aldbrough St NE34 . . . . . .59 A5
Aldeburgh Ave NE15 . . . . .53 C8
Aldenham Gdns NE30 . . . .32 C1
Aldenham Rd SR3 . . . . . . .91 E8
Aldenham Terr SR3 . . . . . .91 E8
Alder Ave NE4 . . . . .54 D8
Alder Cl Hetton le H DH5 . .94 F3
  Morpeth NE61 . . . . .9 A8
Alder Cres DH9 . . . . .78 F2
Alder Ct NE25 . . . . .31 E4
Alder Gr NE25 . . . . .31 E6
Alder Rd Shiremoor NE29 .41 B7
  Wallsend NE28 . . . . .40 E6
Alder St SR5 . . . . .74 B1
Alder Way NE12 . . . . .29 C4
Alderley Cl
  Boldon Colliery NE35 . . . .58 D1
  12 Sunderland SR2 . . . . .86 F2
Alderley Dr NE12 . . . . .29 F4
Alderley Rd NE9 . . . . .70 E5
Alderley Way NE23 . . . . . .16 D1
Alderney Gdns NE5 . . . . . .36 C2

Aldershot Rd SR3 . . . . . . .91 D7
Aldershot Sq SR3 . . . . . . .91 D7
Alderton Dr NE38 . . . . .6 C2
Alderwood Ashington NE63 .6 C2
  Washington NE38 . . . . . . .89 B8
Alderwood Cres NE6 . . . . .39 F1
Alderwyk NE10 . . . . .72 B6
Aldsworth Cl NE9 . . . . . . .72 A1
Aldwych Dr NE29 . . . . .41 B7
Aldwych Ho NE33 . . . . . . .42 B2
Aldwych Rd SR3 . . . . .91 D7
Aldwych Sq SR3 . . . . .91 D6
Aldwych St NE33 . . . . .42 C2
Alemouth Rd NE46 . . . . . .45 B5
Alexander Dr DH5 . . . . . . .94 F3
Alexander Pl **12** NE46 . . .45 A5
Alexander Terr
  Hazlerigg NE13 . . . . .28 A5
  Sunderland SR6 . . . . .75 D3
Alexandra Ave SR5 . . . . . .74 F1
Alexandra Cres NE46 . . . .44 F5
Alexandra Dr NE16 . . . . . .69 C8
Alexandra Gdns
  North Shields NE29 . . . . .41 E6
  Ryton NE40 . . . . .52 E4
Alexandra Ho SR2 . . . . . .102 C2
Alexandra Pk SR2 . . . . . . .86 C4
Alexandra Rd
  Ashington NE63 . . . . .6 F3
  Gateshead NE8 . . . . .101 B1
  Morpeth NE61 . . . . .9 A8
  Newcastle-u-T NE6 . . . . . .39 B1
Alexandra Road Inf Sch
  NE8 . . . . .101 B1
Alexandra St
  Rowlands Gill NE39 . . . . .67 A1
  Wallsend NE28 . . . . .40 C2
Alexandra Terr
  Bedlington NE22 . . . . .11 B1
  Haswell DH6 . . . . .97 F3
  Hexham NE46 . . . . .44 F5
  Penshaw DH4 . . . . .90 B8
  15 Springwell NE9 . . . . .71 F1
  Stocksfield NE43 . . . . . . .64 D7
  Sunnyside NE16 . . . . . . .69 C2
  4 Whitley Bay NE26 . . . .32 B4
Alexandra Way NE23 . . . . .22 B5
Alford DH2 . . . . .81 F2
Alford Gn NE12 . . . . .39 C7
Alfred Ave NE22 . . . . .11 B1
Alfred St Blyth NE24 . . . . .17 E6
  Hebburn NE31 . . . . .57 D5
  Newcastle-u-T NE6 . . . . . .56 E6
Algernon NE12 . . . . .29 D5
Algernon **14** NE6 . . . . . . .56 C7
Algernon Ct **17** NE6 . . . .56 C7
Algernon Ind Est NE27 . . .30 F1
Algernon Pl NE26 . . . . . . .32 B4
Algernon Rd
  15 Newcastle-u-T,Heaton
  NE6 . . . . .56 C7
  Newcastle-u-T,Lemington
  NE15 . . . . .53 C6
Algernon Terr
  Tynemouth NE30 . . . . . . .42 C8
  Wylam NE41 . . . . .51 A6
Algiers Rd SR3 . . . . .91 C7
Alice St Blaydon NE21 . . . .53 B1
  South Shields NE33 . . . . .59 C8
  Sunderland SR2 . . . . . . .102 C1
Alice Well Villas SR4 . . . .84 B3
Alison Ct SR3 . . . . .91 C8
Alison Ct **4** NE6 . . . . . . .56 B7
Alison Dr NE36 . . . . .74 D7
All Hallows La NE1 . . . . . .101 B4
All Saints Bsns Ctr NE1 .99 B1
All Saints CE Prim Sch
  NE34 . . . . .59 B4
All Saints Coll NE5 . . . . . .36 E2
All Saints Dr
  North Shields NE29 . . . . .41 D6
  Sunderland SR6 . . . . .75 D1
All Saints Dr DH5 . . . . . . .95 A5
All Saints Ho **6** SR6 . . . .75 D1
Allan Ho
  Newcastle-u-T NE4 . . . . . .54 F8
  Sunderland SR1 . . . . . . .103 B3
Allan Rd NE64 . . . . .7 D5
Allandale Ave NE12 . . . . . .39 D7
Allanville NE12 . . . . .29 C5
Allchurch NE15 . . . . .54 B6
Allchurch Dr NE63 . . . . . . .7 A3
Allen Ave NE11 . . . . .70 D7
Allen Dr NE46 . . . . .45 B4
Allen St DH3 . . . . .88 C2
Allen Terr NE40 . . . . .51 F4
Allendale Ave NE28 . . . . . .40 B4
Allendale Cres
  Penshaw DH4 . . . . .90 B8
  Shiremoor NE27 . . . . .31 A3
  Stakeford NE62 . . . . .6 A1
Allendale Dr NE34 . . . . . . .60 A8
Allendale Pl NE30 . . . . . . .42 D7
Allendale Rd Blyth NE24 . .17 F6
  Hexham NE46 . . . . .44 F4
  Newcastle-u-T NE6 . . . . . .56 D5
  Sunderland SR3 . . . . .91 D8
Allendale Sq SR3 . . . . . . .91 E8
Allendale St DH5 . . . . .95 A2
Allendale Terr
  Haswell DH6 . . . . .97 F3
  Newcastle-u-T NE6 . . . . . .56 F5
Allenheads NE38 . . . . .83 E1
Allenheads
  Newcastle-u-T NE5 . . . . . .36 E1
  Seaton Delaval NE25 . . . .23 C4
Allensgreen NE23 . . . . . . .22 B6

Allerdean Cl
  Newcastle-u-T NE15 . . . . .53 B7
  Seaton Delaval NE25 . . . .23 D2
Allerdene Wlk NE16 . . . . . .69 B6
Allerhope NE23 . . . . .22 B5
Allerton Gdns NE6 . . . . . . .39 C2
Allerton Pl NE16 . . . . .68 F5
Allerwash NE5 . . . . .36 E1
Allery Banks NE61 . . . . . . .9 A8
Allgood Terr NE22 . . . . . . .11 B1
Allhusen Terr NE8 . . . . . . .56 B1
Alliance Pl SR4 . . . . .102 B3
Alliance St SR4 . . . . .102 B3
Allingham Ct NE7 . . . . . . .39 C3
Allison Ct NE16 . . . . .54 B1
Alloa Rd SR3 . . . . .91 D8
Allonby Mews NE23 . . . . .16 D2
Allonby Way NE5 . . . . .54 B8
Alloy Terr NE39 . . . . .67 C1
Allwork Terr NE16 . . . . . . .69 B7
Alma Pl **8** Morpeth NE61 . .9 A8
  North Shields NE29 . . . . .42 A6
  Whitley Bay NE26 . . . . . . .32 C4
Alma St SR4 . . . . .85 A7
Alma Terr NE40 . . . . .52 C2
Almond Cl DH6 . . . . .97 F3
Almond Cres NE8 . . . . . . .70 C8
Almond Dr SR5 . . . . .85 A8
Almond Gr NE24 . . . . .17 C4
Almond Pl NE4 . . . . .54 D7
Almshouses NE15 . . . . . . .52 F7
Aln Ave NE3 . . . . .38 A7
Aln Cres NE3 . . . . .38 A7
Aln Ct Ellington NE61 . . . . .1 E5
  Newcastle-u-T NE15 . . . . .53 C6
Aln Gr NE15 . . . . .53 C7
Aln St Ashington NE63 . . . .6 F5
  Hebburn NE31 . . . . .57 D6
Aln Wlk NE3 . . . . .38 A6
Alnham Ct NE3 . . . . .37 E7
Alnham Gr NE5 . . . . .36 C2
Alnmouth Ave NE29 . . . . .41 D4
Alnmouth Dr NE3 . . . . . . .38 E4
Alnmouth Terr NE46 . . . . .44 F8
Alnwick Ave
  North Shields NE29 . . . . .41 D4
  Whitley Bay NE26 . . . . . . .32 A4
Alnwick Cl
  Chester le S DH2 . . . . . . .88 A1
  Whickham NE16 . . . . .69 A7
Alnwick Ct NE38 . . . . .83 B8
Alnwick Dr NE22 . . . . .10 D2
Alnwick Gr NE32 . . . . .58 B2
Alnwick Rd
  South Shields NE34 . . . . .59 C6
  Sunderland SR3 . . . . .91 E8
Alnwick Sq SR3 . . . . .91 E8
Alnwick St Newburn NE15 .52 F8
  Wallsend NE28 . . . . .40 C2
Alnwick Terr NE13 . . . . . . .28 C7
Alpine Ct DH4 . . . . .89 F5
Alpine Ct DH2 . . . . .88 C3
Alpine Gr NE36 . . . . .74 B7
Alpine Way SR3 . . . . .86 A3
Alresford NE12 . . . . .29 D4
Alston Ave
  East Cramlington NE23 . . .22 D5
  Newcastle-u-T NE6 . . . . . .56 F5
Alston Cl Tynemouth NE29 .41 C7
  Wallsend NE28 . . . . .41 A4
Alston Cres SR6 . . . . .75 C4
Alston Gdns NE15 . . . . . . .35 D3
Alston Gr NE26 . . . . .24 B7
Alston Rd
  New Hartley NE25 . . . . . .23 D6
  Washington NE38 . . . . . . .84 B6
Alston St **3** NE8 . . . . . .101 A1
Alstone Ct NE62 . . . . .10 F7
Altan Pl NE12 . . . . .39 B7
Altree Grange SR5 . . . . . .75 C3
Altrincham Twr SR3 . . . . .91 E8
Alum Well Rd
  Gateshead NE9 . . . . .70 E5
  1 Gateshead,Low Fell NE9 .70 F5
Alverston Cl NE15 . . . . . . .53 C8
Alverstone Ave NE6 . . . . . .70 E4
Alverstone Rd SR3 . . . . . .91 D7
Alverthorpe St NE33 . . . . .59 D8
Alveston Cl NE62 . . . . .10 F7
Alwin NE38 . . . . .83 A1
Alwin Grange
  Hebburn NE31 . . . . .57 F7
  Jarrow NE32 . . . . .58 A7
Alwinton Ave NE29 . . . . . .41 D8
Alwinton Cl Blyth NE24 . . .17 C8
  Newcastle-u-T NE5 . . . . . .37 A4
Alwinton Ct NE24 . . . . . . .17 C8
Alwinton Dr DH2 . . . . .88 A1
Alwinton Gdns NE11 . . . . .70 A5
Alwinton Rd NE27 . . . . . . .31 A3
Alwinton Sq **5** NE63 . . . . .6 F2
Alwinton Terr NE3 . . . . . . .38 D5
Alwyn Cl DH4 . . . . .89 E3
Amalfi Twr SR3 . . . . .91 E8
Amara Sq SR3 . . . . .91 E8
Ambassadors Way NE29 .41 B8
Amber Ct SR4 . . . . .17 C6
Ambergate Cl NE5 . . . . . . .37 A3
Amberley Chase NE12 . . .29 E4
Amberley Cl NE28 . . . . . . .41 A3
Amberley Gdns NE7 . . . . .39 C2
Amberley Prim Sch NE12 29 E4
Amberley St
  Gateshead NE8 . . . . .100 C1
  Sunderland SR2 . . . . . . .103 B1
Amberley St S SR2 . . . . .103 B1
Amberley Way NE24 . . . . .17 E5

Amberley Wlk NE16 69 B5
Amberly Gr NE16 69 A5
Amble Ave
South Shields NE34 60 B8
Whitley Bay NE25 32 D4
Amble Cl Blyth NE24 17 C5
North Shields NE29 41 E4
Amble Gr NE2 56 A7
Amble Pl NE12 29 F1
Amble Twr SR3 91 E8
Amble Way NE3 38 B6
Ambleside NE15 35 E3
Ambleside Ave NE34 59 E6
Ambleside Cl NE25 23 D3
Ambleside Gdns NE9 71 A4
Ambleside Gn NE5 54 B8
Ambleside Terr SR6 75 C4
Ambridge Way
Newcastle-u-T NE3 37 F5
Seaton Delaval NE25 23 A4
Ambrose Ct NE21 53 B1
Ambrose Pl NE6 57 B6
Ambrose Rd SR3 91 D8
Amec Dr NE28 41 A1
Amec Way NE28 40 E1
Amelia Cl NE4 54 E3
Amelia Gdns SR3 91 C7
Amelia Wlk NE4 54 E3
Amen Cnr NE1 101 B4
Amersham Pl 1 NE5 37 B2
Amersham Rd NE24 17 E4
Amesbury Cl NE5 36 B3
Amethyst Rd NE4 100 A2
Amethyst St 1 SR4 85 F7
Amherst Rd NE3 37 E6
Amos Ayre Pl NE34 58 F5
Amsterdam Rd SR3 91 E8
Amy St SR5 75 B2
Ancaster Ave NE12 39 B6
Ancaster Rd NE16 68 F6
Anchorage The
Chester le S DH3 88 D3
Penshaw DH4 90 B6
Ancona St SR4 85 F7
Ancroft Ave NE29 41 F7
Ancroft Pl Ashington NE63 6 F1
Newcastle-u-T NE5 54 B8
Ancroft Rd NE25 23 B3
Ancroft Way NE3 37 F8
Ancrum St NE2 98 B3
Ancrum Way NE16 68 F5
Anderson St NE33 42 D3
Andover Pl NE28 40 E6
Andrew Ct 4 NE6 57 A6
Andrew Rd SR3 91 D7
Andrews House Sta*
NE16 80 B7
Anfield Ct NE3 37 E5
Anfield Rd NE3 37 E5
Angel of the North* NE9 82 A8
Angerton Ave
Shiremoor NE27 30 F2
Tynemouth NE30 32 A1
Angerton Gdns NE5 54 D8
Angerton Terr NE23 28 F8
Angle Terr NE28 40 F2
Anglesey Gdns NE5 36 C2
Anglesey Pl NE4 98 B1
Anglesey Rd SR3 91 D7
Anglesey Sq SR3 91 D7
Angram Dr SR2 87 A1
Angram Wlk 1 NE5 36 C1
Angrove Gdns SR4 85 F5
Angus DH2 81 F2
Angus Cl NE12 29 C3
Angus Cres NE29 41 D3
Angus Rd NE8 70 C8
Angus Sq SR3 91 D7
Ann St Blaydon NE21 53 C3
Gateshead NE8 101 C2
Hebburn NE31 57 C7
Shiremoor NE27 30 E4
Ann Wlk NE6 57 A4
Ann's Row NE24 12 E1
Anne Dr NE12 40 A8
Annfield Rd NE23 16 B2
Annie St SR6 75 E4
Annitsford Dr NE23 29 B8
Annitsford Rd NE23 22 E1
Annville Cres NE6 57 A4
Anscomb Gdns NE7 39 A2
Anson Cl NE33 59 B8
Anson Pl NE5 36 F3
Anstead Cl NE23 22 B6
Anthony Rd SR3 91 D8
Anton Pl NE23 22 B5
Antonine Wlk NE15 34 F2
Antrim Cl NE5 37 C3
Antwerp Rd SR3 91 C7
Apex Bsns Village NE23 22 B1
Apperley NE5 36 E1
Apperley Ave NE3 37 C4
Apperley Rd NE43 64 C6
Appian Pl Gateshead NE9 71 B7
Throckley NE15 35 E2
Apple Cl NE15 53 C8
Apple Ct NE25 23 D6
Appleby Ct
Bournmoor DH4 89 D1
Longbenton NE12 39 B6
North Shields NE29 41 F5
Appleby Gdns
Gateshead NE9 71 A3
Wallsend NE28 41 A4
Appleby Pk NE29 41 F6
Appleby Rd SR3 91 D7
Appleby Sq SR3 91 D7
Appleby St NE29 42 A4
Appledore Cl NE40 66 E8
Appledore Gdns
Chester le S DH3 88 D5
1 Gateshead NE9 70 F3
Appledore Rd NE24 17 C5
Appleforth Ave SR2 87 A1
Appleton Cl NE11 70 A8
Appletree Ct NE8 101 B2
Appletree Dr NE42 50 D3
Appletree Gardens Fst Sch
NE25 31 E4
Appletree Gdns
Newcastle-u-T NE6 39 F1
Whitley Bay NE25 31 E3
Appletree La NE45 47 A5
Appletree Rise NE45 47 A5
Applewood NE12 29 F3
Appley Terr SR6 75 E2
Apsley Cres NE3 37 E5
Aqua Terr NE64 7 D4
Aquila Dr NE15 34 E2
Arbeia Ho NE33 42 C4
Arbeia Roman Fort Mus*
NE33 42 C4
Arbroath DH2 81 F1
Arbroath Rd SR3 91 D8
Arcade The 2 NE30 42 D7
Arcadia DH2 81 F1
Arcadia Ave DH3 88 C5
Arcadia Terr NE24 17 E6
Archbishop Runcie CE Fst
Sch NE3 38 D5
Archbold Terr NE2 99 B3
Archer Rd SR3 91 D8
Archer Sq SR3 91 D8
Archer St NE28 40 E3
Archer Villas NE28 40 D3
Archibald Fst Sch NE3 38 C5
Archibald St NE3 38 C5
Arcot Ave
Cramlington NE23 21 E8
Whitley Bay NE25 31 E3
Arcot Dr
Newcastle-u-T NE5 53 F8
Whitley Bay NE25 31 E3
Arcot Terr 5 NE24 17 D8
Arden Ave NE3 28 B1
Arden Cl NE28 40 D7
Arden Cres NE5 37 D1
Arden Sq SR3 91 E8
Ardrossan DH2 81 F1
Ardrossan Rd SR3 91 D7
Arena Bsns Pk DH4 94 C7
Arena Way NE4 100 C3
Argus Cl NE11 70 B7
Argyle Ct DH9 80 A1
Argyle House Sch SR2 102 C1
Argyle Mews NE24 12 E1
Argyle Pl South Hetton DH6 97 F7
Tynemouth NE29 42 A8
Argyle Sq SR2 102 C1
Argyle St Blyth NE24 12 E1
Hebburn NE31 57 D7
Newcastle-u-T NE1 99 B1
Sunderland SR2 102 C1
Tynemouth NE30 42 D8
Argyle Terr Hexham NE46 45 B4
Newbiggin-by-t-S NE64 7 D4
Tynemouth NE29 42 A8
Argyll DH2 81 F1
Ariel St NE63 6 E3
Arisaig DH2 81 F1
Arkle Rd SR3 91 D7
Arkle St Gateshead NE8 70 C8
Hazlerigg NE13 28 A4
Arklecrag NE37 83 C6
Arkleside Pl NE5 36 D1
Arkwright St NE8 70 D7
Arlington Ave NE3 37 F3
Arlington Cl DH4 89 E3
Arlington Ct NE3 38 A3
Arlington Gr
Cramlington NE23 16 B2
Whickham NE16 69 A6
Arlington Rd NE31 57 F4
Arlington St 3 SR4 85 F6
Arlott Ho NE29 41 D3
Armitage Gdns NE9 71 C1
Armondside Rd NE17 77 C6
Armstrong Ave
Newcastle-u-T NE6 39 B1
South Shields NE34 59 E6
Armstrong Cl NE46 44 F3
Armstrong Dr NE12 29 B2
Armstrong Ind Est NE37 83 A7
Armstrong Rd
Newcastle-u-T NE15,NE4 54 C4
Wallsend NE28 41 A1
Washington NE37 83 A7
Armstrong St
Gateshead NE8 70 D7
Woolsington NE5 36 B7
Armstrong Terr
Morpeth NE61 9 A8
South Shields NE33 59 C8
Arncliffe Ave SR4 85 E4
Arncliffe Gdns NE5 36 C2
Arndale Arc 9 NE32 58 B7
Arndale Ho 14 Birtley DH3 82 C4
Newcastle-u-T NE3 37 E5
6 Washington NE37 83 D8
Arndale Sq NE12 39 A6
Arnold Rd SR3 91 D8
Arnold St NE35 73 F8
Arnside Wlk NE5 36 C2
Arran Ct SR3 92 A6
Arran Dr NE32 58 E3
Arran Gdns NE10 71 C7
Arran Pl NE29 41 C8
Arras La SR1 103 B3
Arrol Pk SR4 102 B2
Arrow Cl NE12 29 B2
Arthington Way NE34 59 E5
Arthur Ave SR2 93 A6
Arthur Cook Ave NE16 69 C6
Arthur St 9 Blyth NE24 17 E8
Gateshead NE8 101 C2
Jarrow NE32 58 B6
Ryhope SR2 93 A6
Whitburn SR6 60 F4
Arthur Terr SR6 60 F3
Arundel Cl
Bedlington NE22 11 C3
Brunswick Village NE13 28 A5
Arundel Ct
Longbenton NE12 39 A6
Newcastle-u-T NE3 37 C7
Arundel Dr
Newcastle-u-T NE15 53 E7
Whitley Bay NE25 31 C4
Arundel Gdns
Gateshead NE9 71 A5
Sunderland SR3 91 C7
Arundel Rd SR3 91 D8
Arundel Sq NE63 6 C3
Arundel Wlk NE16 69 A5
Asama Ct NE4 100 A3
Ascham House Sch NE3 38 C4
Ascot Cl NE28 40 D6
Ascot Cres NE8 70 C7
Ascot Ct
Newcastle-u-T NE3 37 C7
Sunderland SR3 91 D7
West Boldon NE36 73 F6
Ascot Gdns NE34 59 D7
Ascot Gr NE63 6 D2
Ascot Wlk NE3 37 C7
Ascott Ct NE12 39 B6
Ash Ave NE13 27 C7
Ash Banks NE61 9 A7
Ash Cl NE46 44 E3
Ash Ct NE29 31 E1
Ash Gr Dunston NE11 54 E1
Morpeth NE61 8 E7
Ryton NE40 52 C6
Wallsend NE28 40 D1
Whitburn SR6 61 A2
Ash Mdws NE38 88 E7
Ash Sq NE38 83 E4
Ash St Blaydon NE21 53 C1
Mickley Square NE43 64 E8
Ash Terr DH9 79 B2
Ash Tree Dr NE22 10 F2
Ashberry Gr SR6 75 D1
Ashbourne Ave NE6 56 F6
Ashbourne Cl NE27 30 C5
Ashbourne Cres NE63 6 C3
Ashbourne Rd NE32 58 C5
Ashbrooke NE25 31 E5
Ashbrooke Cl NE25 31 E5
Ashbrooke Cres 4 SR2 86 D4
Ashbrooke Cross SR2 86 C3
Ashbrooke Dr NE20 25 E7
Ashbrooke Gdns NE28 40 E3
Ashbrooke Hall 1 SR2 86 D4
Ashbrooke Mount 6
SR2 86 C4
Ashbrooke Range SR2 86 D3
Ashbrooke Rd SR2 86 C4
Ashbrooke St NE3 37 E3
Ashbrooke Terr SR2 86 D4
Ashburn Rd NE28 40 E6
Ashburne Ct 3 SR2 86 D4
Ashburton Rd NE3 38 A4
Ashbury NE25 31 C6
Ashbury Ho NE30 42 C6
Ashby St SR2 86 F3
Ashcroft Dr NE12 39 E7
Ashdale Penshaw DH4 89 E8
Ponteland NE20 25 C3
Ashdale Cres NE5 36 D1
Ashdale Ct SR6 75 E2
Ashdown Cl NE12 39 B7
Ashdown Rd SR3 91 D7
Ashdown Way NE12 39 B7
Asher St NE10 56 C1
Ashfield NE32 58 D2
Ashfield Ave NE16 69 C8
Ashfield Cl NE4 100 A4
Ashfield Ct
High Spen NE39 67 A4
Killingworth NE12 29 E1
Ashfield Gdns NE28 40 A3
Ashfield Gr
6 North Shields NE29 42 A6
Whitley Bay NE26 32 A7
Ashfield Lodge NE4 100 A4
Ashfield Pk NE16 69 B8
Ashfield Rd
Newcastle-u-T NE3 38 A4
Whickham NE16 69 B5
Ashfield Rise NE16 69 B5
Ashfield Terr
Chester le S DH3 88 D2
4 Gateshead NE10 56 F1
Ryton NE40 52 C5
3 Springwell NE9 71 E1
Ashford NE9 71 A1
Ashford Cl Blyth NE24 17 E5
4 Tynemouth NE29 31 F1
Ashford Gr NE5 36 B4
Ashford Rd SR3 91 D7
Ashgill NE37 83 B6
Ashgrove Ave NE34 59 F4
Ashgrove Terr Birtley DH3 82 B5
Gateshead NE8 101 B1
Ashill Ct SR2 86 D4
Ashington Alexandra Fst Sch
NE63 6 F3
Ashington Alexandra Mid Sch
NE63 6 E4
Ashington Central Fst Sch
NE63 6 D3
Ashington Com High Sch
NE63 6 B3
Ashington Dr NE62 11 A8
Ashington Hirst Park Mid Sch
NE63 6 E3
Ashington Hospl NE63 6 C3
Ashington Mews NE62 10 F7
Ashington Rd NE61 1 D4
Ashington Wansbeck Fst Sch
NE63 6 A4
Ashkirk Dudley NE23 29 A8
Sunderland SR3 91 E8
Ashkirk Cl DH2 88 A1
Ashkirk Way NE25 23 D2
Ashleigh DH2 88 A5
Ashleigh Cl NE21 53 E1
Ashleigh Cres NE5 54 A8
Ashleigh Gdns SR6 60 A2
Ashleigh Gr
Longbenton NE12 39 D7
Newcastle-u-T NE2 38 D2
Sunderland SR6 75 E4
Tynemouth NE30 42 C8
Ashleigh Rd NE5 54 A8
Ashleigh Sch NE30 42 B5
Ashleigh Special Sch
NE30 42 A6
Ashleigh Terr 7 SR6 75 E4
Ashleigh Villas 2 NE36 74 D7
Ashley Cl Killingworth NE12 29 F4
Washington NE38 83 D3
Ashley Gdns NE62 11 A8
Ashley Prim Sch NE34 59 C6
Ashley Rd NE34 59 C6
Ashley Terr DH3 88 C4
Ashmead Cl NE12 29 E4
Ashmore Ho SR6 75 F4
Ashmore St SR2 103 A1
Ashmore Terr SR2 103 A1
Asholme NE5 36 E1
Ashridge Cl NE34 60 B5
Ashridge Ct NE10 72 C7
Ashton Cl NE5 36 B4
Ashton Ct NE40 52 D4
Ashton Downe 2 DH2 88 C2
Ashton Rise DH2 88 C2
Ashton Way
Sunderland SR3 91 C6
Whitley Bay NE26 31 E7
Ashtree Cl
Newcastle-u-T NE4 54 F4
Rowlands Gill NE39 67 F3
Ashtree Gdns NE25 31 E3
Ashtree Ho NE2 98 B4
Ashtree La NE21,NE39 67 B5
Ashtrees Gdns NE9 70 F7
Ashvale Ave NE11 81 C6
Ashwell Rd SR3 91 D7
Ashwood DH3 88 D2
Ashwood Ave SR5 74 F2
Ashwood Cl
Cramlington NE23 16 C2
Longbenton NE12 39 E8
Ashwood Cres NE6 39 F1
Ashwood Croft NE31 57 D7
Ashwood Gdns NE9 71 A2
Ashwood Gr
4 Sunderland SR5 74 B1
Wideopen NE13 28 B5
Ashwood Ho NE7 39 A4
Ashwood Rd NE46 45 C4
Ashwood St SR2 102 B1
Ashwood Terr
Greenside NE40 51 F1
Sunderland SR2 102 B1
Askern Ave SR2 87 A1
Askew Rd NE8 101 B3
Askew Rd W NE8 100 C1
Askrigg Ave
Sunderland SR2 86 F1
Wallsend NE28 40 D7
Askrigg Cl DH2 81 E2
Askrigg Wlk 2 NE5 36 C1
Aspen Cl DH4 89 F5
Aspen Ct SR3 91 E6
Aspen Terr NE5 37 E1
Aspen Way NE24 17 D4
Aspenlaw NE9 71 C4
Aspley Cl SR3 92 A6
Association Rd 4 SR6 75 E2
Astbury Cl NE38 89 B8
Aster Pl NE4 54 C7
Aster Terr DH4 90 B4
Astley Com High Sch
NE25 23 C3
Astley Ct NE12 29 D3
Astley Dr NE26 31 E8
Astley Gdns
Seaton Delaval NE25 23 C3
Seaton Sluice NE26 24 B7
Astley Gr NE26 24 B7
Astley Rd NE25 23 C4
Astley St NE23 16 B3
Astley Villas NE26 24 B7
Aston Sq SR3 91 D7
Aston St NE33 59 D7
Aston Way NE16 68 F5
Aston Wlk 6 NE6 57 A6
Astral Ho SR1 102 C3
Athelhampton NE38 84 A5
Athelstan Rigg SR2 93 A7
Athenaeum St SR1 103 A2
Atherton Dr
Fence Houses DH4 94 A7
Newcastle-u-T NE4 54 E4
Athlone Ct 1 NE24 17 E8
Athlone Pl DH3 82 D1
Athol Gdns Ryhope SR2 93 A6
Whitley Bay NE25 31 D3
Athol Gn NE11 100 A1
Athol Gr SR3 92 A7
Athol Ho NE20 25 F6
Athol Pk 3 SR2 86 E4
Athol Rd SR2 103 B1
Athol St NE11 100 A1
Athol Terr SR2 103 B1
Atholl DH2 81 F2
Atholl Gdns NE9 71 B7
Atkin St NE12 29 B5
Atkinson Gdns NE29 42 A3
Atkinson House Sch
NE23 22 F2
Atkinson Rd
Chester le S DH3 88 D5
Newcastle-u-T NE4 54 D4
Sunderland SR6 75 E4
Atkinson Road Prim Sch
NE4 54 D4
Atkinson St NE28 40 B1
Atkinson Terr
5 Newcastle-u-T NE4 54 D5
Wallsend NE28 40 B1
Atkinson's Bldgs SR4 102 B3
Atlantis Rd SR3 91 C8
Atley Way NE23 15 E2
Atmel Way NE28 41 A7
Attlee Cl NE23 29 B5
Attlee Cres DH6 97 E1
Attlee Gr SR2 92 E8
Attlee Terr NE64 7 F5
Attwood Gr SR5 75 B2
Aubone Ave NE15 54 C6
Auburn Cl NE28 41 A2
Auburn Ct NE28 41 B2
Auburn Gdns NE4 54 E8
Auburn Pl NE61 8 E8
Auckland DH2 88 A3
Auckland Ave NE34 60 B6
Auckland Rd NE31 57 F7
Auckland Terr NE32 58 E4
Auden Gr NE4 54 E6
Audland Wlk 3 NE5 36 C1
Audley Ct NE2 38 F2
Audley Gdns SR3 86 B3
Audley Rd NE3 38 E4
Audouins Row NE8 70 E8
August Pl NE33 42 D1
Augusta Cl NE13 28 A6
Augusta Ct NE28 40 E6
Augusta Sq SR3 91 D7
Augustus Dr NE22 10 E2
Austen Ave NE34 59 B4
Austin Sq SR5 75 B2
Austral Pl NE13 28 A5
Australia Gr NE34 58 F3
Australia Twr SR3 91 E8
Austwick Wlk 4 NE5 36 C1
Autumn Cl NE38 83 D6
Autumn Dr NE8 100 B2
Avalon Dr NE15 53 E8
Avalon Rd SR3 91 D8
Avebury Ave NE62 11 A7
Avebury Dr NE38 83 E5
Avebury Pl NE23 16 C1
Avenue Cres NE25 23 C4
Avenue Rd Gateshead NE8 70 F8
Seaton Delaval NE25 23 C3
Avenue Terr
Seaton Delaval NE25 23 D3
1 Sunderland SR2 86 C4
Avenue The Birtley DH3 82 C4
Blaydon NE21 53 E2
Bournmoor DH3 89 E6
Chester le S DH2 88 B3
Corbridge NE45 46 F6
Gateshead,Carr Hill NE9 71 B7
7 Gateshead,Felling NE10 56 D1
Hetton le H DH5 95 B4
Morpeth NE61 8 F6
Rowlands Gill NE39 67 F1
Seaton Delaval NE25,NE26 23 E5
Seaton Sluice NE26 24 A6
Sunderland SR2 103 A1
Wallsend NE28 40 B1
Washington NE38 83 E5
Whitley Bay NE26 32 A5
Avenue Vivian
Fence Houses DH4 90 A1
Great Lumley DH4 89 F1
Aviemore Rd NE36 74 B7
Avis Ave NE64 7 C3
Avison Ct NE4 98 B2
Avison Pl NE4 98 B2
Avison St NE4 98 B2
Avocet Cl NE24 17 E3
Avocet Ho 23 NE29 42 A5
Avolon Ct NE4 98 B2
Avolon Pl NE4 98 B2
Avolon Wlk NE4 98 B2
Avon Ave Hedworth NE32 58 C2
North Shields NE29 41 E4
Avon Cl Rowlands Gill NE39 67 F3
Wallsend NE28 40 D6
Avon Cres DH4 94 A8
Avon Ct NE25 23 D6
Avon Rd NE31 57 F4

Avon St Gateshead NE8 ...56 A1
Sunderland SR2 ....103 C2
Avon Terr
Washington NE38 ....83 E4
3 Washington NE38 .....83 F4
Avondale SR4 ....85 A5
Avondale Ave Blyth NE24 .16 E8
Longbenton NE12 ....39 D8
Penshaw DH4 ....90 B7
Avondale Cl 1 NE24 .....16 F8
Avondale Ct NE3 ....38 D4
Avondale Gdns
Ashington NE63 ....7 A2
West Boldon NE36 ....74 A7
Avondale Rd
Newcastle-u-T NE6 ......56 C5
Ponteland NE20 ....25 A2
Avondale Rise 5 NE6 ...56 C5
Avondale Terr
Chester le S DH3 ....88 C3
Gateshead NE8 ....101 B1
West Boldon NE36 ....74 A7
Avonlea Way NE5 ....37 C3
Avonmouth Rd SR3 .....91 D7
Avonmouth Sq SR3 .....91 D7
Awnless Ct NE34 ....59 C5
Axbridge Cl NE62 ....11 A7
Axbridge Gdns NE4 .....54 E5
Axford Terr NE17 ....77 B6
Axminster Cl NE23 ......16 D1
Axwell Dr NE24 ....17 B7
Axwell Ho NE24 ....17 B7
Axwell Park Cl 3 NE16 ..69 A7
Axwell Park Rd NE21 ....53 E1
Axwell Park School Hos
NE21 ....68 C8
Axwell Park View NE15 ..54 B5
Axwell Terr NE16 ....54 A1
Axwell View Blaydon NE21 53 C1
Whickham NE16 ....69 A7
Aycliffe Ave NE9 ....71 E4
Aycliffe Cres NE9 ....71 D4
Aycliffe Pl NE9 ....71 E4
Aydon Ave NE45 ....47 A6
Aydon Cl NE30 ....32 C1
Aydon Cres NE45 ....47 B6
Aydon Dr NE45 ....47 A6
Aydon Gdns
Corbridge NE45 ....47 A6
Longbenton NE12 ....38 F6
Aydon Gr Corbridge NE45 .47 A6
Jarrow NE32 ....58 B3
Aydon Ho SR3 ....91 E7
Aydon Rd NE45 ....47 C7
Aydon Rd Est NE45 ......47 A6
Aydon Way NE45 ....47 B6
Aydon Wlk NE5 ....36 E1
Aylesbury Dr SR3 ....92 A5
Aylesbury Pl NE12 ....39 B7
Aylesford Mews SR2 ....86 E2
Aylesford Sq NE24 ......17 E5
Aylsham Cl NE5 ....36 B4
Aylsham Ct SR3 ....92 A4
Aylyth Pl NE3 ....37 F3
Ayr Dr NE32 ....58 E3
Ayre's Quay Rd SR1 ....102 C3
Ayre's Terr NE29 ....42 A6
Ayrey Ave NE34 ....58 F4
Aysgarth Ave
Sunderland SR2 ....86 F2
Wallsend NE28 ....40 D7
Aysgarth Gn NE3 ....37 F4
Ayton Ave SR2 ....87 A1
Ayton Cl
Newcastle-u-T NE5 ....36 E3
Stocksfield NE43 ....64 D6
Ayton Ct NE22 ....10 D2
Ayton Prim Sch NE38 ....82 F3
Ayton Rd NE38 ....82 F4
Ayton Rise NE6 ....56 C5
Ayton St NE6 ....56 D5
Azalea Ave SR2 ....102 C1
Azalea Terr N SR2 .....102 C1
Azalea Terr S SR2 .....102 C1
Azalea Way NE15 ....52 E8

B

Back Albion Rd 11 NE30 .42 B6
Back Albion St SR4 .....85 A6
Back Beaumont Terr
NE3 ....38 D5
Back Bridge St SR1 ....103 A3
Back Buttsfield Terr DH4 90 B8
Back Chapman St NE6 ..56 C7
Back Coronation Terr
DH5 ....95 A2
Back Croft Rd NE24 .....17 E7
Back Elmfield Rd NE3 ...38 C4
Back George St NE4 ...100 C4
Back Goldspink La NE2 ..99 C3
Back Hawthorn Rd W
NE3 ....38 C4
Back Heaton Park Rd 9
NE6 ....56 B6
Back High St NE3 ....38 C4
Back Hylton Rd SR4 ....102 D3
Back La Blaydon NE21 ...53 B2
Great Lumley DH3 ....89 A1
Penshaw DH4 ....90 B8
Whitley Bay NE25 ....31 E5
Back Lodge Terr SR1 ...103 C2
Back Maling St NE6 .....56 A5
Back Mitford St NE4 ...100 B3
Back Mowbray Terr NE62 10 F7
Back New Bridge St NE1,
NE2 ....99 C2
Back North Bridge St
SR5 ....103 A4
Back Percy Gdns NE30 ..42 D8
Back Prudhoe Terr 20
NE30 ....42 D7
Back Riggs 10 NE61 ......3 F1
Back Row Hexham NE46 ..45 B5
Whickham NE16 ....69 B7
Back Ryhope St SR2 ....92 E7
Back Shipley Rd 11 NE30 42 D7
Back St NE21 ....53 B1
Back Stephen St 6 NE6 .56 A6
Back Walker Rd NE6 ....57 A4
Back Woodbine St NE8 .101 B1
Backworth Bsns Pk NE27 30 C4
Backworth La NE23,NE27 .29 F7
Backworth Park Prim Sch
NE27 ....30 C5
Backworth Terr NE27 ....30 D1
Baden Cres SR5 ....74 A3
Baden Powell St NE9 ....71 A7
Baden St DH3 ....88 C2
Bader Ct NE24 ....17 F6
Badger Cl SR3 ....92 A5
Badger Mews NE9 ....71 F2
Badger's Wood DH9 .....80 A1
Badgers Gn NE61 ....3 D2
Badminton Cl NE35 .....58 E1
Baffin Ct SR3 ....91 F6
Baildon Cl NE28 ....40 C4
Bailey Green Prim Sch
NE12 ....29 C4
Bailey Sq SR5 ....74 A4
Bailey St DH9 ....79 B2
Bailey Way DH5 ....95 B2
Bainbridge Ave
South Shields NE34 ......58 F4
Sunderland SR3 ....86 B3
Bainbridge Holme Cl
SR3 ....86 B3
Bainbridge Holme Rd
SR3 ....86 C3
Bainford Ave NE15 ......54 A7
Baird Ave NE28 ....41 C2
Baird Cl NE37 ....72 E2
Baird Ct NE8 ....56 B1
Baird St SR5 ....74 A3
Baker Gdns
1 Dunston NE11 ....54 F1
Gateshead NE10 ....72 B8
Baker Rd NE23 ....15 D1
Baker Sq SR5 ....74 A3
Baker St
Houghton-le-S DH5 ....90 E1
Sunderland SR5 ....74 A3
Bakewell Terr NE6 ......56 D4
Baldersdale Gdns SR2 ..86 B2
Baldwin Ave Cleadon NE36 74 E8
Newcastle-u-T NE4 ....54 F7
Balfour Rd NE15 ....54 A6
Balfour St 2 Blyth NE24 ..17 D8
Gateshead NE8 ....101 A1
Houghton-le-S DH5 ....90 E1
Balfour Terr NE17 ....66 B1
Balgonie Cotts NE40 ....52 C5
Baliol Rd NE43 ....64 D7
Balkwell Ave NE29 ......41 D5
Balkwell Gn NE29 ....41 E6
Ballast Hill NE24 ....17 F8
Ballast Hill Rd NE29 ....42 A3
Balliol Ave NE12 ....29 C1
Balliol Bsns Pk NE12 ....39 A7
Balliol Gdns NE7 ....39 B5
Balliol Prim Sch NE12 ...39 B6
Ballston Cl NE38 ....83 E3
Balmain Rd NE5 ....37 E4
Balmlaw NE9 ....71 D4
Balmoral Ave
Brockley Whins NE32 .....58 E3
Newcastle-u-T NE3 ....38 E4
Balmoral Cl NE22 ....11 C2
Balmoral Cres DH5 ......94 F7
Balmoral Ct 5 SR5 ....74 A3
Balmoral Dr NE10 ....71 C8
Balmoral Gdns
Tynemouth NE29 ....41 F7
Whitley Bay NE26 ....31 F6
Balmoral St NE28 ....40 B2
Balmoral Terr
Newcastle-u-T,Heaton NE6 .56 B8
Newcastle-u-T,South Gosforth
NE3 ....38 E4
Sunderland,East Herrington
SR3 ....91 C7
Sunderland,Grangetown
SR2 ....86 F2
Balmoral Way Blyth NE24 .17 C3
Gateshead NE10 ....71 C8
Balroy Ct NE12 ....39 E7
Baltic Ct NE33 ....42 E2
Baltic Ctr for Contemporary Art★ NE8 ....101 C4
Baltic Ind Pk NE28 ......41 E3
Baltic Quay NE8 ....101 C4
Baltic Rd NE10 ....56 D3
Baltic Sq NE8 ....101 C4
Baltimore Ave SR5 ......73 E3
Baltimore Ct NE37 ......83 C8
Baltimore Sq SR5 ....73 F3
Bamborough Ct NE23 ...29 A8
Bamborough Terr NE30 ..42 A7
Bambro' St SR2 ....103 B1
Bamburgh Ave NE33,
NE34 ....43 A1
Bamburgh Cl Blyth NE24 .17 C7
Bamburgh Cl *continued*
Washington NE38 ....83 B5
Bamburgh Cres
Shiney Row DH4 ....90 B5
Shiremoor NE27 ....30 F3
Bamburgh Ct
Gateshead NE8 ....70 C7
Newcastle-u-T NE7 ....38 F5
Bamburgh Dr
Gateshead NE10 ....57 B2
Pegswood NE61 ....4 F3
Wallsend NE28 ....40 F2
Bamburgh Gdns SR3 ....86 B3
Bamburgh Gr
Jarrow NE32 ....58 A3
South Shields NE34 ......60 B8
Bamburgh Ho NE5 ....36 E3
Bamburgh Rd
Longbenton NE12 ....29 F1
Newcastle-u-T NE5 ....36 E3
Bamburgh Sch NE34 .....60 A8
Bamburgh Terr
Ashington NE63 ....6 C3
19 Newcastle-u-T NE6 .....56 C6
Bamburgh Wlk NE3 .....38 A6
Bamford Terr NE12 ......29 F1
Bamford Wlk NE34 ......59 D5
Bampton Ave SR6 ....75 C5
Banbury NE37 ....83 E8
Banbury Ave SR5 ....74 A4
Banbury Gdns NE28 .....40 D5
Banbury Rd NE3 ....37 F6
Banbury Terr NE33,NE34 ..59 D8
Banbury Way Blyth NE24 ..17 E5
North Shields NE29 ....41 D4
Bancroft Terr SR4 ....85 F6
Banesley La NE11 ....70 B1
Banff St SR5 ....74 A4
Bangor Sq NE32 ....58 A1
Bank Ave NE16 ....69 A7
Bank Ct Blaydon NE21 ....53 F4
North Shields NE30 ......42 B5
Bank Foot Sta NE13 .....37 B6
Bank Head NE46 ....45 B5
Bank Top Crawcrook NE40 .51 E3
Greenside NE40 ....52 B3
Tynemouth NE30 ....32 C3
Bank Top Hamlet 4
NE16 ....69 A7
Bankdale Gdns NE24 ....17 A7
Bankhead Rd NE15 ......35 F1
Bankhead Terr DH4 .....94 A8
Bankside NE61 ....9 A8
Bankside Cl SR2 ....92 E7
Bankside La NE34 ......59 C5
Bankside Rd NE15 ......53 F5
Bankside Wlk NE62 .....11 B8
Bankwell La NE8 ....101 B4
Bannerman Terr DH6 ....96 C1
Bannister Dr NE12 ......40 A8
Bannockburn NE12 ......29 C4
Barbara Priestman Sch
SR2 ....86 B4
Barbara St SR2 ....86 F2
Barbary Dr SR6 ....75 F2
Barbondale Lonnen NE5 .36 C2
Barbour Ave NE34 ....60 A7
Barclay Pl NE5 ....37 B1
Barclay St SR6 ....103 A4
Barcusclose La DH9,NE16 79 D5
Bardolph Rd NE29 ....41 D6
Bardon Cl NE5 ....36 F4
Bardon Cres NE25 ....23 F2
Bardon Ct NE34 ....59 E5
Bardsey Pl NE12 ....39 B7
Barehirst St NE33 ....59 B7
Barents Cl 2 NE5 ....36 F2
Baret Rd
Newcastle-u-T,Walker NE6 .56 F7
Newcastle-u-T,Walkergate
NE6 ....56 E8
Barford Ct NE9 ....71 A2
Barford Dr DH2 ....88 A1
Baring St NE33 ....42 D4
Barker St NE2 ....99 C2
Barking Cres SR5 ....73 F3
Barking Sq SR5 ....73 F3
Barkwood Rd NE39 ......67 D2
Barley Mow DH3 ....88 D8
Barley Mow Prim Schs
DH3 ....82 D1
Barlow Cres NE21 ....67 C6
Barlow Fell Rd NE21 ....67 C5
Barlow La NE21 ....67 E7
Barlow Rd NE21 ....67 C6
Barlowfield Cl NE21 .....68 A8
Barmoor Bank NE61 ......9 D5
Barmoor Dr NE3 ....28 A2
Barmoor La NE40 ....52 B5
Barmoor Pl NE40 ....52 B5
Barmoor Terr NE40 ......52 A5
Barmouth Cl NE28 ....40 D5
Barmouth Rd NE29 ......41 C5
Barmston Cl NE38 ....83 F4
Barmston Ct NE38 ....83 F4
Barmston La NE38 ....84 C6
Barmston Rd NE38 ....84 A4
Barmston Village Prim Sch
NE38 ....83 F5
Barmston Way NE38 .....83 F6
Barn The 3 DH2 ....88 B1
Barnabas Pl SR2 ....103 C1
Barnard Cl NE22 ....10 E1
Barnard Cres NE31 ......57 E7
Barnard Ct DH4 ....89 D1
Barnard Gn NE3 ....37 E7
Barnard Gr NE32 ....58 D4
Barnard Pk DH5 ....95 A4
Barnard St Blyth NE24 ....17 E7
Sunderland SR4 ....85 F5
Barnes Jun & Inf Schs
SR4 ....85 F4
Barnes Park Rd SR4 .....86 A4
Barnes St DH5 ....95 A4
Barnes View SR4 ....85 F4
Barnes' Rd NE33 ....59 B8
Barnesbury Rd NE4 .....54 E5
Barnett Ct SR5 ....75 B2
Barnett Sq DH6 ....97 F2
Barningham NE38 ....84 A5
Barningham Cl SR3 .....86 B2
Barns Cl NE32 ....58 A4
Barnstaple Cl NE28 .....40 C5
Barnstaple Rd NE29 .....31 D1
Barnston NE63 ....7 B3
Barnton Rd NE10 ....71 E6
Barnwell Prim Sch DH4 .90 B7
Barnwood Cl NE28 ......40 C5
Baron's Quay Rd SR5 ...85 B8
Baroness Dr NE15 ....54 A7
Baronswood NE3 ....38 B5
Barr Cl NE28 ....40 E5
Barrack Ct NE4 ....98 C2
Barrack Rd NE2,NE4 .....98 B3
Barrack Row DH4 ....90 A6
Barrack St SR1 ....103 C4
Barrack Terr NE11 ......81 D6
Barras Ave
Annitsford NE23 ....22 B1
Blyth NE24 ....17 E5
Barras Ave W NE24 .....17 D5
Barras Bridge NE1 ......99 A2
Barras Dr SR3 ....86 B3
Barras Gdns NE23 ....22 B1
Barras Mews NE23 ......22 F1
Barrasford Cl
Ashington NE63 ....6 A2
Newcastle-u-T NE3 ....38 A4
Barrasford Dr NE13 .....28 C5
Barrasford Rd NE23 .....22 C6
Barrasford St NE28 ......41 C1
Barrass Ave NE23 ....22 F1
Barrie Sq SR5 ....75 B2
Barrington Ave NE30 ....31 F2
Barrington Ct
Bedlington NE22 ....16 A8
Hetton le H DH5 ....95 A4
Barrington Dr NE38 .....83 D4
Barrington Ind Est NE22 .11 A4
Barrington Pk NE22 .....11 F3
Barrington Pl
Gateshead NE8 ....101 A2
Newcastle-u-T NE4 ....98 B2
Barrington Rd NE22 .....11 B3
Barrington St NE33 .....42 C3
Barrington Terr DH5 ....95 A5
Barron St S 5 SR5 ......74 C1
Barrow St SR5 ....73 F4
Barrowburn Pl NE23 ....23 A1
Barry St Dunston NE11 ...54 F1
Gateshead NE8 ....70 D7
Barton Cl Tynemouth NE30 32 B1
Wallsend NE28 ....40 D5
Washington NE37 ....72 F2
Barton Ct SR6 ....75 C5
Barton Pk SR2 ....92 D7
Bartram Gdns NE8 ......70 E7
Bartram St SR5 ....75 C3
Barwell Cl NE28 ....40 D5
Barwell Ct NE7 ....39 E3
Basil Way NE34 ....59 E3
Basildon Gdns NE28 .....40 C5
Basingstoke Pl NE12 ....39 C7
Baslow Gdns SR3 ....86 B3
Bassenfell Ct NE37 ......83 B6
Bassenthwaite Ave 4
DH2 ....88 B1
Bassington Ave NE23 ....21 E7
Bassington Cl NE4 ......98 B2
Bassington Dr NE23 .....21 E8
Bassington Ind Est NE23 .21 D8
Bassington La NE23 .....21 D8
Bat House Rd NE43 .....64 B5
Bates La NE21 ....53 F2
Bath Cl NE28 ....40 E5
Bath La Blyth NE24 ....17 F7
Newcastle-u-T NE1,NE4 ...98 C1
Bath Rd Gateshead NE10 ..56 D2
Hebburn NE31 ....57 E3
Bath Sq NE32 ....58 A1
Bath St NE6 ....57 B6
Bath Terr Blyth NE24 .....17 F7
Newcastle-u-T NE3 ....38 D5
Tynemouth NE30 ....42 D7
Bathgate Ave SR5 ....73 F3
Bathgate Cl NE28 ....40 E5
Bathgate Sq SR5 ....73 F3
Batley St SR5 ....73 F3
Battle Hill NE46 ....45 B4
Battle Hill Dr NE28 ......40 D5
Battle Hill Prim Sch
NE28 ....40 D5
Baugh Cl NE37 ....83 A7
Baulkham Hills DH4 .....90 B7
Bavington NE10 ....72 A5
Bavington Dr NE5 ....37 D1
Bavington Gdns NE30 ...32 B1
Bavington Rd NE25 ......23 D2
Bawtry Ct NE28 ....40 C5
Bawtry Gr NE29 ....41 E5
Baxter Ave NE4 ....54 E6
Baxter Pl NE25 ....23 D3
Baxter Rd SR5 ....73 F4
Baxter Sq SR5 ....73 F4
Baxter's Bldgs NE25 .....23 D3
Baxterwood Ct NE4 ......98 A2
Baxterwood Gr NE4 .....98 A2
Bay View E NE64 ....7 E5
Bay View W NE64 ....7 E4
Baybridge Rd NE5 ......36 E3
Bayfield Gdns NE8 ......56 B1
Baysdale DH4 ....89 E8
Bayswater Ave SR5 .....74 A3
Bayswater Rd
Gateshead NE8 ....71 B8
Newcastle-u-T NE2 ....38 E2
Bayswater Sq 1 SR5 .....74 A3
Baytree Gdns NE25 .....31 F3
Baywood Gr NE28 ....40 C5
Beach Ave
Whitley Bay NE26 ....32 A5
4 Houghton-le-S DH4 ....90 D1
Beach Croft Ave NE30 ...32 B1
Beach Rd
South Shields NE33 ....42 E3
Tynemouth NE29 ....42 A8
Beach St SR4 ....102 B4
Beach Terr NE64 ....7 D3
Beach Way NE30 ....32 A1
Beachborough Cl 6
NE29 ....31 F1
Beachcross Rd SR4 ....102 B1
Beaches The NE4 ......100 A3
Beachville St SR4 .....102 B1
Beachway NE24 ....18 A4
Beacon Ct
Brunswick Village NE13 ...28 A6
4 Gateshead NE9 ....71 B5
Beacon Ctr NE29 ....42 B5
Beacon Dr
Brunswick Village NE13 ...28 A5
Sunderland SR6 ....75 F1
Beacon Glade NE34 .....60 C6
Beacon Ho 4 NE26 ......31 F8
Beacon La NE23 ....21 E6
Beacon Lough Rd NE9 ..71 A4
Beacon Rise NE9 ....71 B5
Beacon St Gateshead NE9 .71 A5
North Shields NE30 ......42 C6
South Shields NE33 ......42 D5
Beaconsfield Ave NE9 ...71 A5
Beaconsfield Cl NE25 ...31 D7
Beaconsfield Cres 3
NE9 ....71 A5
Beaconsfield Rd NE9 ....70 F5
Beaconsfield St
Blyth NE24 ....17 F7
Newcastle-u-T NE4 ....98 A2
Beaconsfield Terr
Birtley DH3 ....82 B4
Chopwell NE17 ....66 B1
Beaconside NE34 ....60 C5
Beadling Gdns NE4 .....54 E6
Beadnell Ave NE29 ......41 D4
Beadnell Cl Blaydon NE21 .68 A8
3 Chester le S DH2 ......88 A1
Beadnell Ct 1 NE28 .....40 E5
Beadnell Gdns NE27 .....30 F3
Beadnell Pl NE2 ....99 C2
Beadnell Rd NE24 ....17 B5
Beadnell Way NE3 ......38 A6
Beagle Sq 6 SR3 ....92 A7
Beal Cl NE24 ....17 C7
Beal Dr NE12 ....29 F1
Beal Gdns NE28 ....40 F5
Beal Gn NE5 ....37 C4
Beal Rd NE27 ....30 F3
Beal Terr NE6 ....56 F4
Beal Way NE3 ....38 B6
Beaminster Way NE3 ...37 C5
Beamish Cl NE28 ....40 C5
Beamish Ct NE25 ....31 E3
Beamish Gdns NE9 ......71 D4
Beamish The North of England Open Air Mus★
DH9 ....80 D2
Beamish View DH3 ......82 E5
Beamishburn Rd DH9,
NE16 ....80 B3
Beamsley Terr NE63 ......6 D3
Beanley Ave
Hebburn NE31 ....57 D4
Newcastle-u-T NE15 ......53 C6
Beanley Cres NE30 ......42 D7
Beanley Pl NE7 ....39 A3
Bearl Farm Cotts NE43 ..49 B5
Bearl View NE43 ....64 E8
Beatrice Ave NE24 ......17 B4
Beatrice Gdns
7 East Boldon NE36 .....74 D7
South Shields NE34 ......59 F6
Beatrice Ho SR2 ....102 C1
Beatrice Rd NE6 ....39 B1
Beatrice St Ashington NE63 .6 E4
Sunderland SR6 ....75 E2
Beatrice Terr
Penshaw DH4 ....89 E8
Shiney Row DH4 ....90 B6
Beattie St NE34 ....59 B5
Beatty Ave
Newcastle-u-T NE2 ....38 E3
Sunderland SR5 ....73 F3
Beatty Rd NE22 ....16 B8
Beaufort Cl
Newcastle-u-T NE5 ....37 D3
Shiney Row DH4 ....90 B5
Beaufort Gdns NE28 .....40 C5
Beaufront Ave NE46 .....45 D4
Beaufront Castle Flats
NE46 ....46 A8
Beaufront Cl NE10 ......72 B6
Beaufront Gdns
Gateshead NE8 ....56 B1
Newcastle-u-T NE5 ....37 C1

Bea – Bir 109

Beaufront Terr
Jarrow NE32 ....58 B3
South Shields NE33 ....59 C8
Beauly NE38 ....83 D3
Beaumaris DH4 ....89 D3
Beaumaris Ct NE12 ....39 A6
Beaumaris Gdns SR3 ....91 C7
Beaumaris Way NE5 ....37 B4
Beaumont Ct NE25 ....31 D6
Beaumont Dr
Washington NE38 ....83 D5
Whitley Bay NE25 ....31 D7
Beaumont Ho NE5 ....37 C2
Beaumont Lodge 4 SR2 .86 E4
Beaumont Manor NE24 ..16 F7
Beaumont St Blyth NE24 .17 D8
Hexham NE46 ....45 B5
Newcastle-u-T NE4 ....54 F3
North Shields NE29 ....42 A5
Sunderland,Hendon SR2 ..86 E4
Sunderland,Southwick SR5 .75 A2
Beaumont Terr
Brunswick Village NE13 ..28 A6
Jarrow NE32 ....58 A5
Newcastle-u-T NE5 ....36 F3
Newcastle-u-T,Gosforth
NE3 ....38 D5
Prudhoe NE42 ....50 A2
Beaumont Way NE42 ....50 B1
Bebdon Ct NE24 ....17 C6
Bebside Furnace Rd
NE24 ....16 D8
Bebside Mid Sch NE24 ..16 F8
Bebside Rd NE24 ....16 C7
Beckenham Ave NE36 ..74 D8
Beckenham Cl NE36 ....74 E8
Beckenham Gdns NE28 ..40 C4
Beckett St NE8 ....56 A4
Beckfoot Cl NE5 ....37 B1
Beckford NE38 ....84 A4
Beckford Cl NE28 ....40 C5
Beckside Gdns NE5 ....36 B1
Beckwith Rd SR3 ....91 C8
Beda Cotts DH9 ....79 A2
Beda Hill NE21 ....53 C3
Bedale Cl NE28 ....40 C5
Bedale Cres SR5 ....74 A3
Bedale Ct Gateshead NE9 .71 B2
5 South Shields NE34 ....59 A5
Bedale Dr NE25 ....31 F3
Bedale Gn NE5 ....37 D3
Bedale St DH5 ....95 A2
Bedburn NE38 ....82 F1
Bedburn Ave SR5 ....74 C2
Bede Burn Prim Sch
NE32 ....58 A4
Bede Burn Rd NE32 ....58 B5
Bede Burn View NE32 ..58 B5
Bede Cl NE12 ....40 C8
Bede Com Prim Sch
NE10 ....56 B2
Bede Cres Wallsend NE28 .40 E3
Washington NE38 ....83 D6
Bede Ct Chester le S DH3 .88 C3
Gateshead NE8 ....56 A2
Tynemouth NE30 ....32 C3
Bede Ho 9 SR3 ....91 D7
Bede Ind Est NE32 ....58 E6
Bede Prec 7 NE32 ....58 B7
Bede St SR6 ....75 E2
Bede Sta NE32 ....58 E6
Bede Terr
Chester le S DH2 ....88 B3
East Boldon NE36 ....74 E7
Jarrow NE32 ....58 C5
Bede Wlk Hebburn NE31 ..57 F5
Newcastle-u-T NE3 ....38 E5
Bede's World (Mus)★
NE32 ....58 D7
Bedeburn Foot NE5 ....36 F5
Bedeburn Rd NE5 ....36 F5
Bedesway NE32 ....58 E6
Bedewell Ind Pk NE31 ..58 A5
Bedewell Prim Sch NE31 .57 F6
Bedford Ave Birtley DH3 ..82 D1
Chester le S DH3 ....88 D8
South Shields NE33 ....42 C1
Wallsend NE28 ....40 A3
Bedford Ct NE30 ....42 B5
Bedford Ho NE30 ....42 B5
Bedford Pl
Gateshead NE8 ....101 B2
New Silksworth SR3 ....92 A8
Newcastle-u-T NE5 ....36 C1
Bedford St
Hetton le H DH5 ....94 F4
North Shields NE29,NE30 ..42 B5
Sunderland SR1 ....103 A3
Bedford Terr 13 NE29 ....42 A6
Bedford Way NE29 ....42 B5
Bedlington Bank NE22,
NE24 ....16 A7
Bedlington West End Fst Sch
NE22 ....10 E1
Bedlingtonshire Com High
Sch NE22 ....11 D2
Beech Ave
Cramlington NE23 ....22 D5
Dinnington NE13 ....27 B7
Hexham NE46 ....44 E5
4 Houghton-le-S DH4 ....94 D8
Morpeth NE61 ....9 C7
Newcastle-u-T NE3 ....37 F6
Whickham NE16 ....69 C8
Whitburn SR6 ....60 F1
Beech Cl NE3 ....28 C1
Beech Ct
Newcastle-u-T NE3 ....38 C4
Beech Ct *continued*
North Shields NE29 ....41 F6
Ponteland NE20 ....25 A1
Tynemouth NE29 ....31 E1
Beech Dr Corbridge NE45 .47 B6
Dunston NE11 ....54 E1
Ellington NE61 ....1 D5
Beech Gdns NE9 ....70 F6
Beech Gr Bedlington NE22 .11 A1
Blackhall Mill NE17 ....77 B6
Longbenton NE12 ....39 D6
Prudhoe NE42 ....50 B2
South Shields NE34 ....59 F4
Springwell NE9 ....71 F1
Wallsend NE28 ....40 B2
Whitley Bay NE26 ....31 F5
Beech Gr S NE42 ....50 B2
Beech Grove Ct NE40 ....51 F4
Beech Grove Rd NE4 ...100 A4
Beech Grove Terr NE40 ..51 F4
Beech Grove Terr S NE40 51 F4
Beech Hill NE46 ....44 E5
Beech Hill Prim Sch NE5 36 F2
Beech Sq NE38 ....83 E4
Beech St Gateshead NE8 ..56 B1
Jarrow NE32 ....58 A7
Mickley Square NE43 ....64 E8
Newcastle-u-T NE4 ....54 E5
1 Sunniside NE16 ....69 B2
Beech Terr Ashington NE63 .6 E2
Blaydon NE21 ....53 C2
Burnopfield NE16 ....79 C6
Beech Way NE12 ....29 C4
Beechbrooke SR2 ....92 F6
Beechburn Wlk NE4 ....98 A1
Beechcroft
Newcastle-u-T NE3 ....38 B2
Washington NE37 ....72 B2
Beechcroft Ave NE3 ....38 A3
Beecher St NE24 ....17 B8
Beeches The
Longbenton NE12 ....39 D6
Ponteland NE20 ....25 D6
Stannington NE61 ....14 C4
Beechfield Gdns NE28 ..40 A3
Beechfield Rd NE3 ....38 B4
Beechlea NE61 ....14 C3
Beecholm Ct SR2 ....86 D3
Beechway Ashington NE63 ..7 A3
Gateshead NE10 ....71 F5
Beechwood NE39 ....67 A2
Beechwood Ave
Gateshead NE9 ....71 A3
Newcastle-u-T NE3 ....38 E6
Ryton NE40 ....52 C5
Stakeford NE62 ....11 A8
Whitley Bay NE25 ....31 D4
Beechwood Cl NE32 ....58 D6
Beechwood Cres SR5 ....74 F2
Beechwood Gdns NE11 ..70 B5
Beechwood Ho NE7 ....39 A4
Beechwood Pl NE20 ....25 E7
Beechwood St SR2 ....102 B1
Beechwood Terr
Burnside DH4 ....90 C2
Sunderland SR2 ....102 B1
Beechwoods DH2 ....88 B5
Beeston Ave SR5 ....73 F3
Beetham Cres NE5 ....54 A8
Beethoven St 10 NE33 ..42 D2
Begonia Cl NE31 ....57 E3
Beldene Dr SR4 ....85 E4
Belford Ave NE27 ....30 F3
Belford Cl Sunderland SR2 86 D3
Wallsend NE28 ....40 D5
Belford Gdns NE11 ....70 A5
Belford Rd SR2 ....86 E3
Belford Terr
Newcastle-u-T NE6 ....56 E5
Sunderland SR2 ....86 E3
Tynemouth NE30 ....42 A7
Belfry The DH4 ....90 A4
Belgrade Cres SR5 ....73 F4
Belgrade Sq SR5 ....73 F3
Belgrave Cres NE24 ....17 F6
Belgrave Ct NE10 ....71 D8
Belgrave Gdns
Ashington NE63 ....7 A2
South Shields NE34 ....59 F6
Belgrave Par NE4 ....100 B4
Belgrave Terr
Gateshead NE10 ....71 D7
South Shields NE33 ....42 D3
Bell Gr NE12 ....29 B4
Bell House Rd SR5 ....75 A5
Bell Rd NE41 ....51 B6
Bell St Hebburn NE31 ....57 D6
North Shields NE30 ....42 B5
Penshaw DH4 ....90 B8
Sunderland SR4 ....85 F6
6 Washington NE38 ....83 F4
Bell View NE42 ....50 F3
Bell Villas NE20 ....25 F6
Bell's Cotts NE40 ....52 A1
Bell's Hill NE61 ....13 D3
Bell's Pl NE22 ....16 A8
Bellamy Cres SR5 ....73 F3
Bellburn Ct NE23 ....22 D8
Belle Grove Pl NE2 ....98 B3
Belle Grove Terr NE2 ....98 B3
Belle Grove Villas NE2 ..98 B3
Belle Grove W NE2 ....98 B3
Belle View Terr 13 NE9 ..71 F1
Belle Vue NE39 ....66 F5
Belle Vue Ave NE3 ....38 D5
Belle Vue Bank NE9 ....70 E5
Belle Vue Cres
South Shields NE33 ....59 B6
Belle Vue Cres *continued*
Sunderland SR2 ....86 C4
Belle Vue Dr SR2 ....86 C4
Belle Vue Gr NE9 ....70 F5
Belle Vue Pk SR2 ....86 C4
Belle Vue Pk W SR2 ....86 C4
Belle Vue Rd SR2 ....86 C4
Belle Vue St NE30 ....32 C3
Belle Vue Terr
Crawcrook NE40 ....51 F4
Gateshead NE9 ....70 E5
4 North Shields NE29 ..42 A4
Belle Vue Villas NE36 ..74 C7
Bellerby Dr DH2 ....81 E2
Bellevue Cres NE23 ....16 B2
Bellfield Ave NE3 ....37 F6
Bellgreen Ave NE3 ....28 D1
Bellingham Cl NE28 ....40 D4
Bellingham Ct
Bedlington NE22 ....11 A1
8 Newcastle-u-T NE3 ....37 D5
Bellingham Dr NE12 ....40 A8
Bellingham Ho SR4 ....85 B4
Bellister Gr NE5 ....54 C7
Bellister Rd NE29 ....41 D6
Belloc Ave NE34 ....59 B3
Bells Cl 2 Blyth NE24 ..16 F8
Newcastle-u-T NE15 ....53 E5
Bells Close Ind Est NE15 .53 E5
Bells Lonnen NE42 ....50 D4
Bellsburn Ct NE63 ....6 B2
Bellshill Cl NE28 ....40 E6
Bellway Ind Est NE12 ..39 F7
Belmont NE10 ....72 A5
Belmont Ave NE25 ....31 D4
Belmont Cl NE28 ....40 E5
Belmont Cotts 6 NE5 ..36 F3
Belmont Rd SR4 ....85 F5
Belmont Rise DH5 ....95 A1
Belmont St NE6 ....56 F3
Belmont Terr 4 NE9 ....71 E1
Belmont Wlk NE6 ....56 F3
Belmount Ave NE3 ....28 D1
Belper Cl NE28 ....40 C5
Belsay NE38 ....82 F4
Belsay Ave Hazlerigg NE13 28 A4
South Shields NE34 ....60 A7
Whitley Bay NE25 ....32 B4
Belsay Cl Pegswood NE61 ..4 F3
Wallsend NE28 ....40 C5
Belsay Ct NE24 ....17 C7
Belsay Gdns
Dunston NE11 ....70 A5
Newcastle-u-T NE3 ....37 F8
Sunderland SR4 ....85 F5
Belsay Gr NE22 ....11 C3
Belsay Ho 7 SR3 ....91 D7
Belsay Pl NE4 ....98 A2
Belsfield Gdns NE32 ....58 B4
Belsize Pl NE6 ....56 F8
Beltingham NE5 ....36 E1
Belvedere NE29 ....41 F7
Belvedere Ave NE25 ....31 F4
Belvedere Ct 12 NE6 ....56 C7
Belvedere Gdns NE12 ....39 D6
Belvedere Ho 10 NE6 ....56 B6
Belvedere Parkway NE3 .37 D6
Belvedere Rd SR2 ....102 C1
Belvedere Ret Pk NE3 ..37 C6
Bemersyde Dr NE2 ....38 E3
Benbrake Ave NE29 ....31 E1
Bendigo Ave NE34 ....58 F3
Benedict Biscop CE Prim Sch
SR3 ....91 D5
Benedict Rd SR6 ....75 F2
Benfield Bsns Pk NE6 ..56 E8
Benfield Gr NE26 ....24 B7
Benfield Rd NE6 ....39 E1
Benfield Sch NE6 ....39 E1
Benfleet Ave SR5 ....73 F3
Benjamin Rd NE28 ....41 A3
Benjamin St 11 NE40 ....51 F3
Bennett Ct
Newcastle-u-T NE15 ....53 C6
Sunderland SR2 ....86 E3
Bennett Gdns 1 NE10 ..56 D1
Bennett's Wlk NE61 ....9 A8
Benridge Bank DH4 ....94 A2
Benridge Pk NE24 ....17 B3
Bensham Ave NE8 ....101 A1
Bensham Cres NE8 ....100 C1
Bensham Ct
Gateshead NE8 ....101 A1
South Shields NE34 ....59 C5
Bensham General Hospl
NE8 ....70 D7
Bensham Rd
Gateshead NE8 ....101 B3
Gateshead,Bensham NE8 .101 A1
Gateshead,Windmill Hills
NE8 ....101 B2
Bensham St NE35 ....58 F1
Bensham Trad Est NE8 ..70 D8
Benson Cl NE46 ....44 E4
Benson Pl 20 NE6 ....56 C6
Benson Rd NE6 ....56 D6
Benson St DH3 ....88 C2
Benson Terr 14 NE10 ....71 D8
Bentall Bsns Pk NE37 ....83 F7
Bentham Cl SR5 ....74 A4
Bentinck Cres
Newcastle-u-T NE4 ....54 F4
Pegswood NE61 ....4 E3
Bentinck Rd NE4 ....54 F5
Bentinck St NE4 ....54 F4
Bentinck Villas NE4 ....54 F5
Benton Ave SR5 ....73 F4
Benton Bank NE2 ....39 A1
Benton Cl NE7 ....39 B5
Benton Hall Wlk NE7 ....39 D2
Benton La NE12 ....39 B7
Benton Lodge Ave NE7 ..39 B5
Benton Park Prim Sch
NE7 ....39 B4
Benton Park Rd NE7 ....39 A5
Benton Rd
Biddick Hall NE34 ....59 C2
Newcastle-u-T NE7 ....39 B3
Shiremoor NE27 ....30 E1
Benton Square Ind Est
NE12 ....30 B1
Benton Sta NE12 ....39 D6
Benton Terr NE2 ....99 C3
Benton Way
Wallsend NE28 ....40 B1
Wallsend NE28 ....57 B8
Bents Cotts NE33 ....42 E2
Bents Cotts App NE33 ..42 E2
Bents Park Rd NE33 ....42 E3
Bents The SR6 ....75 F7
Benwell Dene Terr NE15 .54 C5
Benwell Gr NE4 ....54 E5
Benwell Grange 9 NE15 .54 D5
Benwell Grange Ave
NE15 ....54 D5
Benwell Grange Cl 8
NE15 ....54 D5
Benwell Grange Rd NE15 54 C5
Benwell Grange Terr
NE15 ....54 C5
Benwell Hall Dr NE15 ..54 B6
Benwell Hill Gdns NE5 ..54 C7
Benwell Hill Rd NE5 ....54 C7
Benwell La
Newcastle-u-T NE15 ....54 C5
Newcastle-u-T,Old Benwell
NE15 ....54 B5
Benwell Roman Temple★
NE15 ....54 D6
Benwell Vallum Crossing★
NE15 ....54 D6
Benwell Village NE15 ....54 B6
Benwell Village Mews
NE15 ....54 C6
Berberis Way NE15 ....52 E8
Beresford Ave NE31 ....57 E3
Beresford Ct NE26 ....24 D6
Beresford Gdns 7 NE6 ..56 C5
Beresford Pk SR2 ....102 C1
Beresford Rd
Seaton Sluice NE26 ....24 D5
Tynemouth NE30 ....32 A3
Beresford St NE11 ....100 A1
Bergen Cl NE29 ....41 B4
Bergen Sq SR5 ....73 F4
Bergen St SR5 ....73 F4
Berkdale Rd NE9 ....70 E2
Berkeley Cl
Boldon Colliery NE35 ....58 E2
Killingworth NE12 ....29 E4
Sunderland SR3 ....91 C7
Berkeley Sq NE3 ....38 B7
Berkely St NE33 ....42 D2
Berkhamstead Ct NE10 ..72 C7
Berkley Ave NE21 ....53 E2
Berkley Cl NE28 ....40 C5
Berkley Rd NE29 ....41 D6
Berkley St NE15 ....52 F8
Berkley Terr NE15 ....52 F8
Berkley Way NE31 ....57 F8
Berkshire Cl NE5 ....36 F2
Bermondsey St NE2 ....99 C2
Bernard Gilpin Prim Sch
DH5 ....94 E8
Bernard Shaw St 8 DH4 94 D8
Bernard St
Houghton-le-S DH4 ....94 D8
Newcastle-u-T NE6 ....57 B4
Berrington Dr NE5 ....37 B3
Berrishill Gr NE25 ....31 C6
Berry Cl
Newcastle-u-T NE6 ....57 A6
Wallsend NE28 ....40 C5
Berry Hill NE40 ....52 B1
Berryfield Cl SR3 ....92 A5
Berryhill Cl NE21 ....53 D1
Berrymoor NE63 ....6 E4
Bertha Terr DH4 ....90 D4
Bertram Cres NE15 ....54 C6
Bertram St 3 Birtley DH3 .82 C4
South Shields NE33 ....59 C8
Bertram Terr
Ashington NE63 ....6 D3
Pegswood NE61 ....4 F4
Berwick NE38 ....82 F4
Berwick Ave SR5 ....73 F4
Berwick Cl NE15 ....53 A7
Berwick Ct NE20 ....25 F7
Berwick Dr NE28 ....40 D5
Berwick Hill Cotts NE20 .19 A4
Berwick Hill Rd NE20 ....25 F8
Berwick Sq SR5 ....73 F3
Berwick Terr NE29 ....41 D4
Besford Gr SR1 ....103 B2
Bessemer Rd DH6 ....97 F7
Bessie Surtees House Mus★
NE1 ....101 B4
Bessie Terr NE21 ....53 A2
Best View 3 DH4 ....90 B6
Bet's La NE61 ....13 D8
Bethnell Ave NE6 ....56 D7
Betjeman Mews NE8 ...101 C1
Betts Ave NE15 ....54 B5
Bevan Ave SR2 ....92 E6
Bevan Dr NE12 ....38 F6
Bevan Gdns NE10 ....72 A8
Beverley Cl NE3 ....28 B2
Beverley Cres NE9 ....71 A6
Beverley Ct
2 Gateshead NE9 ....71 A6
1 Jarrow NE32 ....58 B7
Washington NE37 ....83 D7
Beverley Dr Blaydon NE21 .67 F8
Stakeford NE62 ....6 A1
Whickham NE16,NE21 ....69 C8
Beverley Gdns
Chester le S DH3 ....88 D2
Ryton NE40 ....52 A5
Tynemouth NE30 ....32 C2
Beverley Pk NE25 ....31 E4
Beverley Pl NE28 ....40 F3
Beverley Rd
Gateshead NE9 ....71 A6
Sunderland SR2 ....86 F2
Whitley Bay NE25 ....31 F4
Beverley Terr
Newcastle-u-T NE6 ....57 A5
Tynemouth NE30 ....32 C3
Walbottle NE15 ....36 A2
Beverley Villas NE30 ....32 C3
Beweshill Cres NE21 ....53 A1
Beweshill La NE21 ....53 A3
Bewick Cres NE15 ....53 D7
Bewick Ct NE1 ....99 B2
Bewick Garth NE43 ....49 E1
Bewick La NE42 ....50 B4
Bewick Pk NE28 ....40 F5
Bewick Rd NE8 ....101 B1
Bewick St
Newcastle-u-T NE1 ....101 A4
South Shields NE33 ....59 C8
Bewicke Lodge NE28 ....41 A2
Bewicke Main Cvn Site
DH2 ....81 E5
Bewicke Rd NE28 ....41 A1
Bewicke Road Ind Est
NE28 ....41 A1
Bewicke St NE28 ....41 B1
Bewicke View DH3 ....82 D5
Bexhill Prim Sch SR5 ....73 F3
Bexhill Rd SR5 ....73 F3
Bexhill Sq Blyth NE24 ....17 E5
Sunderland SR5 ....73 F4
Bexley Ave NE15 ....54 B6
Bexley Gdns NE28 ....40 D5
Bexley Pl NE16 ....69 A5
Bexley St SR4 ....85 F6
Bickerton Wlk 2 NE5 ....36 E1
Bickington Ct DH4 ....90 C3
Bicknell Ho NE6 ....56 C5
Biddick Hall Dr NE34 ....59 B4
Biddick Hall Inf Sch
NE34 ....59 A3
Biddick Hall Jun Sch
NE34 ....59 B4
Biddick La NE38 ....83 D2
Biddick Prim Sch NE38 ..83 D4
Biddick School Sports Coll
NE38 ....83 E3
Biddick Terr NE38 ....83 E3
Biddick View NE38 ....83 E3
Biddick Villas NE38 ....83 E3
Biddlestone Cres NE29 ..41 D5
Biddlestone Rd NE6 ....39 C1
Bideford Gdns
Gateshead NE9 ....70 F3
Jarrow NE32 ....58 E5
South Shields NE34 ....43 A1
Whitley Bay NE26 ....32 A6
Bideford Gr NE16 ....69 A5
Bideford Rd NE3 ....37 E4
Bideford St SR2 ....86 F2
Big Waters Cl NE13 ....28 A6
Big Waters Ctry Pk★
NE13 ....28 A7
Bigbury Cl DH4 ....90 C4
Bigg Mkt NE1 ....99 A1
Bigges Gdns NE28 ....39 F4
Bilbrough Gdns NE4 ....54 D4
Bill Quay Prim Sch NE10 57 C2
Billy Mill Ave NE29 ....41 E6
Billy Mill La NE29 ....41 D8
Bilsdale SR6 ....75 F7
Bilsdale Pl NE12 ....38 F6
Bilsmoor Ave NE7 ....39 B2
Bilton Hall NE32 ....58 D6
Bilton Hall Rd NE32 ....58 D6
Binchester St NE34 ....59 A5
Bingfield Gdns NE5 ....37 C1
Bingley Cl 8 NE28 ....40 E5
Bingley St SR5 ....73 F3
Bink Moss NE37 ....83 A6
Binsby Gdns NE9 ....71 B2
Binswood Ave NE5 ....37 C2
Birch Ave Gateshead NE10 72 A7
Whitburn SR6 ....60 F1
Birch Cl NE46 ....44 E3
Birch Cres
Burnopfield NE16 ....79 A6
Burnside DH4 ....90 C2
Birch Ct Prudhoe NE42 ....50 A2
Silksworth SR3 ....91 E6
Birch Gr Jarrow NE32 ....58 A7
Wallsend NE28 ....40 C5
Birch Mews NE16 ....78 F6
Birch Rd NE21 ....53 D3
Birch St NE32 ....58 A7
Birch Terr Birtley DH3 ....82 B5
Newcastle-u-T NE6 ....57 A5
Bircham Dr NE21 ....53 D1
Birches Nook Cotts NE43 64 C7

Birches Nook Rd NE43 64 C7
Birches The NE16 69 C3
Birchfield NE16 69 B5
Birchfield Gdns
Gateshead NE9 71 A2
Newcastle-u-T NE15 53 E7
Birchfield Rd SR2 86 B4
Birchfield NE38 83 E2
Birchgate Cl NE21 53 A1
Birchington Ave NE33 59 D7
Birchtree Gdns NE25 31 F3
Birchvale Ave NE5 37 B2
Birchwood 3 NE36 74 D7
Birchwood Ave
Newcastle-u-T NE7 39 C3
Whickham NE16 69 A5
Wideopen NE13 28 C5
Birchwood Cl NE23 22 F1
Bird St NE30 42 C6
Birdhill Pl NE34 59 C5
Birds Nest Rd
Newcastle-u-T NE6 56 D4
Newcastle-u-T NE6 56 E4
Birds Terr DH4 90 C8
Birkdale
South Shields NE33 42 E1
Whitley Bay NE25 31 D5
Birkdale Ave SR6 75 E7
Birkdale Cl
Newcastle-u-T NE7 39 C4
Wallsend NE28 40 C4
Washington NE37 72 B2
Birkdale Dr DH4 90 A4
Birkdene NE43 64 D6
Birkhead Cotts NE16 80 E6
Birkheads La NE11,NE16 80 E6
Birkland La DH9,NE11, NE16 80 E7
Birks Rd NE15 35 B5
Birkshaw Wlk 1 NE5 36 E1
Birling Pl 4 NE5 37 D2
Birnam Gr NE32 58 E2
Birney Edge NE20 25 C1
Birnham Pl NE3 37 F3
Birnie Cl NE4 54 E4
Birrell Sq SR5 73 F4
Birrell St SR5 73 F4
Birtley Ave Sunderland SR5 73 F4
Tynemouth NE30 42 D8
Birtley Cl NE3 38 A4
Birtley East Com Prim Sch DH3 82 C6
Birtley Golf Course DH3 82 D2
Birtley La DH3 82 D3
Birtley Villas 1 DH3 82 C5
Birtwistle Ave NE31 57 D3
Biscop Terr NE32 58 C4
Biscuit Factory (Art Store) The NE2 99 C2
Bishop Cres NE32 58 C8
Bishop Harland CE Prim Sch SR5 74 C3
Bishop Ian Ramsey CE Prim Sch DH8 77 C1
Bishop Morton Gr SR1 103 B2
Bishop Ramsay Ct NE34 60 A6
Bishop Rock Dr NE12 39 A6
Bishop's Ave NE4 98 A1
Bishop's Rd NE15 54 D5
Bishopbourne Ct 5 NE29 31 F1
Bishopdale Penshaw DH4 89 E8
Wallsend NE28 39 F5
Bishopdale Ave NE24 17 A6
Bishops Cl NE28 40 E2
Bishops Ct NE5 53 F8
Bishops Dr NE40 52 D4
Bishops Mdw NE22 10 F1
Bishops Way SR3 91 E5
Bishops Wynd DH5 94 E7
Bishopton St Blyth NE24 17 E6
Sunderland SR2 103 B1
Bishopton Way NE46 44 E3
Bisley Ct NE28 40 D5
Bisley Dr NE34 59 D7
Bittern Cl Dunston NE11 54 F2
Shiremoor NE28 41 A6
Biverfield Rd NE42 50 E3
Black Boy Rd DH4 94 A7
Black Boy Yd NE1 99 A1
Black Dr DH3 89 B5
Black La Blaydon NE21 53 A2
Gateshead NE9 71 C1
Black Rd Hebburn NE31 57 F6
Sunderland SR2 92 F7
Blackberries The 18 NE9 71 F1
Blackburn Gn NE10 71 C7
Blackcap Cl NE38 82 F3
Blackclose Bank NE63 6 D1
Blackclose Est NE63 6 D1
Blackdene NE63 6 B2
Blackett Cotts NE41 51 A6
Blackett Ct NE41 51 A6
Blackett Pl NE1 99 A1
Blackett St
Hebburn NE31,NE32 57 F8
Newcastle-u-T NE1 99 A1
Blackett Terr SR4 102 A2
Blackfell Prim Sch NE37 83 A6
Blackfell Rd NE37 82 F6
Blackfriars 3 NE1 98 C1
Blackfriars Ct 6 NE1 98 C1
Blackfriars Way NE12 39 A6
Blackhams Hill Sta★ NE9 71 E1
Blackheath Cl NE37 72 C2
Blackheath Ct NE3 37 B5
Blackhill Ave NE28 40 F6
Blackhill Cres NE9 71 D4
Blackhouse La NE40 52 B5
Blackpool Par NE31 58 A3
Blackrow La
Gateshead NE9 71 A3
Heddon-on-t-W NE15 35 A4
Blackstone Ct NE21 53 A2
Blackthorn Cl NE16 69 A2
Blackthorn Dr Blyth NE24 17 C4
Wallsend NE28 40 C5
Blackthorn Pl NE4 100 B3
Blackthorn Way
Ashington NE63 6 B2
Fence Houses DH4 90 A2
Blackthorne NE10 71 F5
Blackwater Ho 7 SR3 92 A6
Blackwell Ave NE6 57 A6
Blackwood Rd SR5 74 A3
Bladen St NE32 58 A7
Bladen Street Ind Est NE32 58 A7
Blagdon Ave NE34 59 E8
Blagdon Cl Morpeth NE61 8 E8
Newcastle-u-T NE1 99 C1
Blagdon Cres NE23 21 E8
Blagdon Ct NE22 11 C2
Blagdon Dr NE24 17 C3
Blagdon St NE1 99 C1
Blagdon Terr
Cramlington NE23 22 B6
Seaton Burn NE13 28 B8
Blake Ave NE16 69 B7
Blake Wlk NE8 56 A2
Blakelaw Rd
7 Newcastle-u-T NE5 37 B2
Newcastle-u-T NE5 37 C2
Blakemoor Pl NE5 37 C1
Blaketown NE23 23 A1
Blanche Terr DH9 79 B2
Blanchland NE38 83 E1
Blanchland Ave
Newcastle-u-T NE15 53 C7
Wideopen NE13 28 B6
Blanchland Cl NE28 40 D5
Blanchland Dr
Holywell NE25 23 F2
Sunderland SR5 75 C3
Blanchland Terr NE30 42 B7
Blandford Ct NE4 100 C4
Blandford Rd NE29 41 D8
Blandford Sq NE1 100 C4
Blandford St
Newcastle-u-T NE1 100 C4
Sunderland SR1 103 A2
Blandford Way NE28 40 D5
Blaxton Pl NE16 68 F5
Blaydon Ave SR5 74 A4
Blaydon Bank NE21 53 C2
Blaydon Bsns Ctr NE21 53 E3
Blaydon Bsns Pk NE21 53 F4
Blaydon Haughs Ind Est NE21 53 E4
Blaydon Highway NE21 53 D3
Blaydon Ind Pk NE21 53 D3
Blaydon Trad Pk NE21 53 F3
Blaydon West Prim Sch NE21 53 C3
Blaykeston Cl SR7 92 E1
Blayney Row NE15 52 C8
Bleachfeld NE10 71 F6
Bleasdale Cres DH4 90 B7
Blencathra
Tynemouth NE30 32 A2
Washington NE37 83 C6
Blencathra Way NE21 68 C8
Blenheim NE12 29 D4
Blenheim Ct Blyth NE24 17 D3
Gateshead NE10 71 C6
Blenheim Dr NE22 11 C2
Blenheim Gdns NE61 4 E4
Blenheim Ho 2 NE1 98 C1
Blenheim Pl NE11 54 E1
Blenheim Wlk NE33 42 D3
Blenkinsop Ct NE34 59 B3
Blenkinsop Gr NE32 58 B3
Blenkinsop Mews NE3 28 A1
Blenkinsop St 5 NE28 40 B2
Bletchley Ave SR5 73 F4
Blezard Bsns Pk NE13 21 B1
Blezard Ct NE21 53 E4
Blind La Burnside DH4 90 B3
Chester le S DH3 88 D6
New Silksworth SR3 92 B7
Blindy La DH5 95 C1
Bloomfield Ct SR6 75 F2
Bloomfield Dr DH5 94 D3
Bloomsbury Ct NE3 38 B4
Blossom Gr DH4 90 B4
Blossom St DH5 95 B5
Blossomfield Way DH6 97 F3
Blount St NE6 56 D6
Blucher Rd
Killingworth NE12 29 C2
North Shields NE29 41 F3
Blucher Terr NE15 36 B1
Blue Anchor Ct NE8 101 B4
Blue House Ct NE37 83 B8
Blue House La
Cleadon SR5,SR6 75 A6
Washington NE37 83 C8
Blue House Rd NE31 57 D3
Blue Quarries Rd NE9 71 B6
Blue Reef Aquarium★ NE30 32 D1
Blue Row NE15 34 F2
Blue Top Cotts NE23 22 D6
Bluebell Cl Gateshead NE9 71 B5
Wylam NE41 51 B7
Bluebell Dene NE5 37 A5
Bluebell Way NE34 59 B5
Blueburn Dr NE12 29 F3
Blumer St DH4 94 A8
Blyth Cl NE23 28 F8
Blyth College Com Ed Ctr NE24 17 D5
Blyth Com Coll NE24 16 F7
Blyth Community Hospl NE24 17 D8
Blyth Ct
Newcastle-u-T NE15 53 C7
South Shields NE34 59 C5
Blyth Dr NE61 9 E1
Blyth Rd NE26 24 E2
Blyth Sq SR5 74 A3
Blyth St Chopwell NE17 66 C1
Seaton Delaval NE25 23 C3
Sunderland SR5 74 A4
Blyth Terr Ashington NE63 6 E4
Birtley DH3 82 B4
Blythswood NE2 99 B4
Blyton Ave Ryhope SR2 92 E6
South Shields NE34 58 F5
Bob Elliott Ho The 5 NE24 17 E8
Bobby Shafto Cvn Pk DH9 81 A1
Bodlewell Ho SR1 103 B3
Bodlewell La SR1 103 B3
Bodley Cl NE3 37 D5
Bodmin Cl NE28 40 E5
Bodmin Ct 1 NE9 71 A2
Bodmin Rd NE29 41 C8
Bodmin Sq SR5 74 A4
Bodmin Way NE3 37 F6
Bog Houses NE23 16 C2
Bognor St SR5 73 F4
Bohemia Terr NE24 17 E6
Boker La NE35 74 B8
Bolam NE38 82 F4
Bolam Ave Blyth NE24 17 D7
Tynemouth NE30 32 A1
Bolam Coyne 13 NE6 56 C5
Bolam Ct NE15 35 D1
Bolam Dr NE63 6 E2
Bolam Gdns NE28 41 B3
Bolam Gr NE30 32 A1
Bolam Pl NE22 11 C2
Bolam Rd NE12 29 C3
Bolam St Gateshead NE8 70 B8
Newcastle-u-T NE6 56 C5
Bolam Way
Newcastle-u-T NE6 56 C5
Seaton Delaval NE25 23 C3
Boland Rd NE61 2 A3
Bolbec Rd NE4 54 E7
Bolburn NE10 72 A7
Boldon Bsns Pk NE35 73 E7
Boldon CE Prim Sch NE36 73 F7
Boldon Cl NE28 40 D5
Boldon Dr NE36 74 A7
Boldon Gdns NE9 71 C3
Boldon La Cleadon SR6 59 F1
East Boldon NE34,NE36 59 C1
South Shields NE34 59 B5
Boldon Sch NE35 74 B8
Bolingbroke Rd NE29 41 D6
Bolingbroke St
Newcastle-u-T NE6 56 A7
4 South Shields NE33 42 D2
Bollihope Dr SR3 86 B2
Bolsover St NE63 6 D3
Bolsover Terr
Ashington NE63 6 D3
Pegswood NE61 4 F4
Bolton's Bglws NE17 77 B8
Bomarsund Cvn Site NE22 11 B6
Bonaventure DH4 90 C8
Bonchester Cl NE22 10 F2
Bonchester Ct 4 NE28 40 E5
Bonchester Pl NE23 22 D8
Bond Cl SR5 75 C1
Bond Ct NE4 54 E5
Bond St 2 NE4 54 D5
Bondene Ave NE10 71 E8
Bondene Ave W NE10 71 E8
Bondene Way NE23 16 B2
Bondfield Cl NE28 40 F3
Bondfield Gdns NE10 72 A8
Bondgate Cl NE46 45 B4
Bondgate Ct NE46 45 B4
Bondicar Terr NE24 17 E7
Bondicarr Pl 1 NE5 37 D1
Bonemill La
Chester le S NE38 88 F8
Washington NE38 89 C8
Bonington Way NE5 37 B2
Bonner's Field SR6 103 A4
Bonnivard Gdns NE23 23 A1
Bonsall Ct NE34 59 D5
Booth St Gateshead NE10 71 D8
Sunderland SR4 102 A2
Booths Rd NE63 6 A4
Bootle St SR5 74 A3
Bordeaux Cl SR3 91 E6
Border History Mus★ NE46 45 B5
Border Rd NE28 40 B1
Boreham Cl NE28 40 D5
Borodin Ave SR5 73 F4
Borough Rd Jarrow NE32 58 B6
North Shields NE29 42 A5
South Shields NE34 60 A5
Borough Rd *continued*
Sunderland SR1 103 B2
Borrowdale Birtley DH3 82 D1
Washington NE37 83 C8
Whickham NE16 69 D7
Borrowdale Ave
Blyth NE24 17 A8
Newcastle-u-T NE6 56 F7
Sunderland SR6 75 D5
Borrowdale Cl NE36 74 C8
Borrowdale Cres
Blaydon NE21 68 B8
Penshaw DH4 90 A8
Borrowdale Gdns NE9 71 B3
Borrowdale St DH5 95 A2
Boscombe Dr NE28 40 C4
Boston Ave
Newcastle-u-T NE7 39 B5
Washington NE38 83 D6
Boston Cl NE28 40 D5
Boston Cres SR5 73 E4
Boston Ct NE12 39 F8
Boston St SR5 73 F4
Bosun's Way NE10 57 A2
Boswell Ave NE34 59 B3
Bosworth NE12 29 D4
Bosworth Gdns NE6 39 D2
Bothal Ave NE62 10 E7
Bothal Bank NE61 5 C2
Bothal Cl Blyth NE24 17 C7
Pegswood NE61 4 E3
Bothal Cotts NE63 5 F4
Bothal Mid Sch NE63 5 F4
Bothal St NE6 56 D6
Bothal Terr Ashington NE63 5 F4
Stakeford NE62 11 B8
Botham Ho NE29 41 D3
Bottle Bank NE8 101 B4
Bottlehouse St NE6 56 C4
Boulby Cl SR3 92 C7
Boulevard The NE12 39 A6
Boulmer Ave NE23 16 B2
Boulmer Cl NE3 37 F8
Boulmer Ct DH2 88 C2
Boulmer Gdns NE13 28 B6
Boulsworth Rd NE29 31 E1
Boult Terr DH4 90 B6
Boundary Dr NE61 9 A7
Boundary Gdns NE7 39 A3
Boundary La DH8 76 A3
Boundary St SR5 75 C2
Boundary Way NE26 24 D6
Bourn Lea DH4 90 A5
Bourne Ave NE4 54 E7
Bournemouth Ct 2 NE28 40 E5
Bournemouth Gdns
Newcastle-u-T NE5 36 F3
Whitley Bay NE26 32 A6
Bournemouth Par NE31 58 A3
Bournemouth Rd NE29 41 C5
Bournmoor Prim Sch DH4 89 E3
Bourtree Cl NE28 40 C4
Bowbank Cl SR3 86 B2
Bowburn Ave SR5 74 C2
Bowburn Cl NE10 72 C7
Bower St SR6 75 D4
Bower The NE32 73 B8
Bowes Ave DH5 95 B1
Bowes Cl NE16 69 B2
Bowes Cres NE16 79 D8
Bowes Ct Blyth NE24 17 E7
Newcastle-u-T NE3 38 E5
Bowes Farm Cotts DH3 89 D5
Bowes Ho 8 SR3 91 D7
Bowes Lea DH4 89 F4
Bowes Lyon Cl NE39 78 D8
Bowes Lyon Ct 6 NE9 70 F8
Bowes Rly★ NE9 82 E8
Bowes Rly Ctr Mus★ NE9 71 E2
Bowes St Blyth NE24 17 E8
Newcastle-u-T NE3 38 E5
Bowes Wlk NE12 39 C7
Bowesville NE16 79 B5
Bowfell Ave NE5 37 D3
Bowfell Cl NE5 37 D3
Bowfell Gdns NE62 11 A8
Bowfield Ave NE3 28 C1
Bowler's Hill NE43 64 F7
Bowlynn Cl SR3 91 E6
Bowman Dr NE23 29 B8
Bowman Pl NE33 42 C1
Bowman Sq NE63 6 D2
Bowman St SR6 60 F1
Bowmont NE61 1 E5
Bowmont Dr NE23 22 D8
Bowmont Wlk DH2 88 A1
Bowness Ave NE28 40 E6
Bowness Cl NE36 74 C7
Bowness Pl NE9 71 B4
Bowness Rd
Newcastle-u-T NE5 37 A1
Whickham NE16 69 D7
Bowness St SR5 74 A4
Bowness Terr 5 NE28 40 E5
Bowood Cl SR2 92 D6
Bowsden Ct NE3 38 E5
Bowsden Terr NE3 38 E5
Bowtrees SR2 86 D3
Boxlaw NE9 71 C5
Boyd Cres NE28 40 C2
Boyd Rd NE28 40 D2
Boyd St Newburn NE15 52 E8
Newcastle-u-T NE2 99 C2
Boyd Terr
Newcastle-u-T,Walbottle NE15 36 B1
Boyd Terr *continued*
5 Newcastle-u-T,Westerhope NE5 36 F3
Boyne Ct 2 NE24 17 E8
Boyne Gdns NE27 30 E3
Boystones Ct NE37 83 B6
Brabourne Gdns 7 NE29 31 F1
Brabourne St NE34 59 C6
Brack Terr NE10 57 B2
Bracken Ave NE28 40 C5
Bracken Cl NE13 27 B6
Bracken Dr NE11 69 F6
Bracken Pl NE4 54 D7
Bracken Ridge NE61 3 C1
Bracken Way NE40 52 A3
Brackenburn Cl DH4 90 C1
Brackendene Dr NE9 70 E5
Brackenfield Rd NE3 38 B4
Brackenlaw NE9 71 C3
Brackenridge NE16 78 E6
Brackenside NE3 28 C1
Brackenway NE37 83 B7
Brackenwood Gr SR2 86 C2
Brackley NE37 72 E1
Brackley Gr NE29 41 D4
Bracknell Cl SR3 92 C8
Bracknell Gdns NE5 36 C1
Bradbury Cl NE10 72 D7
Bradbury Ct
New Hartley NE25 23 D6
Ponteland NE20 25 F6
Bradbury Pl NE25 23 D6
Bradford Ave
Sunderland SR5 74 A4
Wallsend NE28 40 D5
Bradley Ave
Houghton-le-S DH5 94 E6
South Shields NE34 60 A6
Bradley Cl DH2 81 E2
Bradley Fell La NE41 51 C2
Bradley Fell Rd NE40, NE42 66 C8
Bradley Rd NE42 50 F3
Bradley Terr DH5 95 C1
Bradley View 14 NE40 51 F3
Bradman Dr DH3 88 E1
Bradman Sq SR5 74 A4
Bradman St SR5 74 A4
Bradshaw Sq SR5 74 A3
Bradshaw St SR5 74 A3
Bradwell Rd NE3 37 E5
Bradwell Way DH4 90 C4
Brady & Martin Ct NE1 99 B2
Brady Sq 5 NE38 83 F4
Brady St SR4 85 F7
Brae The SR2 102 B2
Braebridge Pl NE3 37 F3
Braefell Ct NE37 83 B6
Braemar Ct NE10 57 B2
Braemar Dr NE34 60 A8
Braemar Gdns
Sunderland,East Herrington SR3 91 C6
Sunderland,Hillview SR3 86 B3
Whitley Bay NE25 31 C4
Braeside Dunston NE11 69 F7
Sunderland SR2 86 B4
Braeside Cl NE30 32 A3
Brahman Ave NE29 41 D4
Braintree Gdns NE3 37 F4
Brama Teams Ind Pk NE8 70 B8
Bramble Cl NE24 17 D4
Bramble Dykes NE15 54 B6
Bramblelaw NE9 71 C4
Brambles The DH3 82 D6
Brambling Lea NE22 11 C2
Bramhall Dr NE38 89 B8
Bramham Ct NE34 59 E5
Bramhope Gn NE9 71 B2
Bramley Cl SR4 85 A3
Bramley Ct
8 Hexham NE46 45 B4
Newcastle-u-T NE7 39 E3
Brampton Ave NE6 56 F4
Brampton Ct NE23 22 C8
Brampton Gdns
Gateshead NE9 71 A3
Throckley NE15 35 E2
Wallsend NE28 41 A4
Brampton Pl NE29 41 E5
Brampton Rd NE34 59 A5
Bramwell Ct NE3 38 E5
Bramwell Rd SR2 103 B1
Brancepeth Ave
Fence Houses DH4 90 A1
Newcastle-u-T NE4 54 E5
Brancepeth Cl NE15 53 C7
Brancepeth Rd
Hebburn NE31 57 F7
Washington NE38 83 A4
Brancepeth Terr NE32 58 B3
Branch End Terr NE43 64 D7
Branch St NE21 53 B1
Branckenpeth Mews NE3 28 B1
Brand Ave NE4 54 E7
Brandling Ct
14 Gateshead NE10 56 D1
Newcastle-u-T NE2 99 C4
South Shields NE34 60 A4
Brandling Dr NE3 28 D1
Brandling La 15 NE10 56 D1
Brandling Mews NE3 28 D1
Brandling Pk NE2 99 A4
Brandling Pl NE10 56 D1
Brandling Pl S NE2 99 B4
Brandling Prim Sch NE10 56 D1

Brandling St
Gateshead NE8 101 C4
Sunderland SR6 75 E2
Brandling St S SR6 75 E1
Brandling Terr 3 NE30 42 B6
Brandon Ave NE27 30 E3
Brandon Cl Blaydon NE21 68 A8
Blyth NE24 17 B8
Houghton-le-S DH4 94 D7
Brandon Gdns NE9 71 D3
Brandon Gr NE2 99 C3
Brandon Rd
Newcastle-u-T NE3 37 F6
North Shields NE29 41 D6
Brandy La NE37 83 B7
Brandywell NE10 71 F6
Brannen St NE29 42 A5
Bransdale DH4 89 E8
Bransdale Ave SR6 75 F7
Branston St SR5 75 B2
Branton Ave NE31 57 D3
Brantwood Ave NE25 31 D4
Brantwood Ct NE21 53 D2
Branxton Cres NE6 56 F5
Bray Cl NE28 40 D5
Braydon Dr NE29 41 E3
Brayside NE32 58 D1
Breamish NE61 1 E5
Breamish Dr NE38 88 F8
Breamish Ho NE1 56 A5
Breamish St Jarrow NE32 58 A5
Newcastle-u-T NE1 56 A5
Brearley Way NE10 71 C8
Brecken Ct NE9 70 E4
Breckenbeds Rd NE9 70 E4
Breckon Cl NE63 6 E1
Brecon Cl NE5 37 B4
Bredon Cl NE38 83 B3
Brendale Ave NE5 36 E3
Brenkley Ave NE27 30 F2
Brenkley Cl NE13 27 B7
Brenkley Ct NE13 28 B8
Brenkley Way NE13 21 B1
Brenlynn Cl SR3 91 E6
Brennan Cl Ashington NE63 7 A3
Newcastle-u-T NE15 54 B6
Brentford Ave SR5 74 A3
Brentford Sq 4 SR5 74 A3
Brentwood Ave
Newbiggin-by-t-S NE64 7 D5
Newcastle-u-T NE2 38 E2
Brentwood Cl NE25 23 E2
Brentwood Gdns
Newcastle-u-T NE2 38 D2
Sunderland SR3 86 B3
Whickham NE16 69 B5
Brentwood Gr NE28 40 D1
Brentwood Pl 6 NE33 42 D2
Brentwood Rd DH4 90 A5
Brett Cl NE7 39 D3
Brettanby Gdns NE40 52 C6
Brettanby Rd NE10 71 C7
Bretton Gdns NE7 39 C2
Brettonby Ave NE43 64 D7
Brewer Terr SR2 93 A6
Brewer's La NE28,NE29 41 C3
Brewery Bank 6 NE16 54 A1
Brewery Bond NE29 42 B4
Brewery La
Gateshead NE10 56 D2
Ponteland NE20 25 E6
South Shields NE33 42 B2
5 Whickham NE16 54 A1
Brewery St 3 NE24 17 F8
Brewery Stables 1 NE1 98 C1
Brewhouse Bank NE30 42 C6
Briar Ave
2 Houghton-le-S DH4 94 D8
Whitley Bay NE26 32 A6
Briar Cl Blaydon NE21 53 A2
Great Lumley DH4 89 E1
Shiney Row DH4 89 F4
Wallsend NE28 40 C5
Briar Ct NE26 32 A5
Briar Edge NE12 39 D8
Briar La NE15 35 E1
Briar Lea DH4 89 F4
Briar Pl NE15 54 A5
Briar Rd NE39 67 D2
Briar Terr NE16 79 C6
Briar Vale NE25 31 D3
Briardale Bedlington NE22 10 E1
Dinnington NE13 27 B7
Briardale Rd NE24 17 A8
Briardene Ashington NE63 6 B2
Burnopfield NE16 78 E6
Briardene Cl SR3 91 C6
Briardene Cres NE3 38 A3
Briardene Dr NE10 72 D8
Briarfield NE38 83 D1
Briarfield Rd NE3 38 B4
Briarhill DH2 88 A5
Briarlea NE61 9 E4
Briars The SR5 74 B1
Briarside NE5 37 A3
Briarsyde NE12 39 E6
Briarsyde Cl NE16 68 E5
Briarwood NE23 29 B8
Briarwood Ave NE3 38 E6
Briarwood Cres
3 Dunston NE11 69 F8
Newcastle-u-T NE6 39 F1
Briarwood Rd NE24 17 F6
Briarwood St DH4 89 E1
Briary The NE15 35 C2
Brick Garth DH5 95 C1
Brick Row SR2 92 E7
Bridekirk NE37 83 C7
Bridge Cotts NE23 29 B8
Bridge Cres SR1 103 A3
Bridge End 6 DH3 88 C4
Bridge End Ind Est NE46 45 C6
Bridge Ho SR1 103 A3
Bridge Pk NE3 38 C8
Bridge Rd NE61 2 A2
Bridge Road S NE29 41 E3
Bridge St Blaydon NE21 53 C4
Blyth NE24 17 F7
Blyth NE24 17 F8
Gateshead NE8 101 B4
Morpeth NE61 8 F8
Newbiggin-by-t-S NE64 7 E4
Seaton Burn NE13 28 B8
Sunderland SR1 103 A3
Bridge Terr
Bedlington NE22 11 C3
Shiremoor NE27 30 F4
Stakeford NE62 11 B8
Bridges The
19 South Shields NE33 42 D1
Sunderland SR1 103 A2
Bridges View NE8 101 A2
Bridgewater Cl
Newcastle-u-T NE15 53 C7
Wallsend NE28 40 C4
Bridgewater Rd NE37 83 E7
Bridle Path
East Boldon NE36 74 C7
Sunderland SR3 91 C8
Bridle The NE27 31 B2
Bridlington Ave NE9 70 F3
Bridlington Cl NE28 40 D5
Bridlington Par NE31 58 A3
Bridport Rd NE29 31 D1
Brier Dene Cres NE26 31 F8
Brierdene Cl NE26 31 F8
Brierdene Ct NE26 31 E8
Brierdene Rd NE26 24 F1
Brierdene View NE26 31 E8
Brierfield Gr SR4 85 D4
Brierley Cl NE24 17 B7
Brierley Rd NE24 17 B7
Briermede Ave NE9 70 F4
Briermede Pk NE9 70 F4
Briery Hill La NE61 14 C3
Briery Vale Cl SR2 102 C1
Briery Vale Rd SR2 86 C4
Brieryside NE5 37 D2
Brigham Ave NE3 37 E3
Brigham Pl NE33 42 C3
Bright St
South Shields NE33 42 E2
Sunderland SR6 75 E1
Brightlea DH3 82 E5
Brightman Rd NE29 42 A6
Brighton Ave Prim Sch
NE8 101 A1
Brighton Cl NE28 40 E5
Brighton Gdns NE8 70 E7
Brighton Gr
Newcastle-u-T NE4 98 A2
North Shields NE29 41 F6
Whitley Bay NE26 31 F6
Brighton Par NE31 58 A3
Brighton Rd NE8 70 E8
Brighton Terr DH6 96 D1
Brignall Gdns NE15 54 A7
Brignall Rise SR3 86 B2
Brigside Cotts NE13 28 C8
Brindley Rd NE37 83 E6
Brinkburn
Chester le S DH2 88 A3
Washington NE38 83 E2
Brinkburn Ave Blyth NE24 17 F6
Cramlington NE23 22 C6
Gateshead NE8 70 E8
Newcastle-u-T NE3 38 B6
Whickham NE16 69 B8
Brinkburn Cl
Blaydon NE21 68 A8
Newcastle-u-T NE6 56 B6
Brinkburn Cres
Ashington NE63 6 E4
Burnside DH4 90 C1
Brinkburn Ct
22 Newcastle-u-T NE6 56 B6
8 North Shields NE30 42 B6
Brinkburn Gdns NE62 11 A8
Brinkburn La 21 NE6 56 B6
Brinkburn Pl 25 NE6 56 B6
Brinkburn Sch NE34 59 D6
Brinkburn Sq 7 NE6 56 B5
Brinkburn St
17 Newcastle-u-T NE6 56 B6
Newcastle-u-T,St Lawrence
NE6 56 B5
North Shields NE28 41 C1
South Shields NE34 59 B6
Sunderland SR4 102 A1
Brinkburn St S NE6 56 C4
Brisbane Ave NE34 58 F3
Brisbane Ct NE8 101 B3
Brisbane St SR5 74 A3
Brislee Ave NE30 42 C7
Brislee Gdns NE3 37 E4
Bristlecone SR3 91 E5
Bristol Ave Sunderland SR5 73 F4
Washington NE37 83 B8
Bristol Dr NE28 40 D5
Bristol St NE25 23 D6
Bristol Terr NE4 100 A4
Bristol Wlk NE25 23 D6
Britannia Ct NE4 100 A4
Britannia Pl NE4 98 A1
Britannia Rd SR3 92 A7
Britannia Terr DH4 94 A8
Brittania Ho NE28 40 F1
Brixham Ave NE9 70 F3
Brixham Cres NE32 58 D5
Brixham Gdns SR3 86 B3
Broad Chare NE1 101 B4
Broad Garth NE1 101 B4
Broad Landing NE33 42 B3
Broad Mdws
Newcastle-u-T NE3 37 F3
Sunderland SR2 102 B1
Broad Oak Terr NE17 66 B1
Broadbank NE10 72 B8
Broadfield Pl NE34 59 D5
Broadgates NE46 45 B4
Broadlands SR6 75 A7
Broadlea NE10 72 B8
Broadmayne Ave SR4 85 D4
Broadmayne Gdns SR4 85 D4
Broadmead Way NE15 54 A5
Broadmeadows
Sunderland SR3 91 B6
Washington NE38 83 E2
Broadmeadows Cl NE16 54 A1
Broadoak NE10 57 B1
Broadpark NE10 72 B8
Broadpool Gn NE16 69 C6
Broadpool Terr NE16 69 C6
Broadsheath Terr SR5 74 F2
Broadside NE10 72 B8
Broadstairs Ct SR4 85 D4
Broadstone Gr NE5 36 C1
Broadstone Way NE28 40 C4
Broadview Villas DH6 96 A1
Broadwater NE10 57 B1
Broadway Blyth NE24 17 E6
Chester le S DH3 88 D5
Gateshead NE9 71 B7
Guide Post NE62 10 F7
Newcastle-u-T NE15 53 D7
Ponteland NE20 25 C3
Whickham NE16 69 A4
Broadway Circ NE24 17 E7
Broadway Cl NE30 32 B3
Broadway Cres NE24 17 E6
Broadway Ct
Newcastle-u-T NE3 38 C7
Wallsend NE28 40 E6
Broadway E NE3 38 C7
Broadway East Fst Sch
NE3 38 D7
Broadway Gdns NE46 44 F5
Broadway Jun Sch SR4 85 D4
Broadway The
Houghton-le-S DH4 94 E8
Sunderland,Castletown SR5 85 A8
Sunderland,Grindon SR4 85 B3
Sunderland,Springwell SR4 85 D4
Tynemouth NE30 32 B2
Broadway Villas NE15 54 B6
Broadway W NE3 38 B7
Broadwell Ct NE3 38 F4
Broadwood Prim Sch
NE15 53 F7
Broadwood Rd NE15 53 F7
Broadwood View DH3 88 D2
Brock Farm Ct NE30 42 B6
Brock La NE22,NE62 11 F5
Brock Sq 8 NE6 56 B5
Brock St NE6 56 B5
Brockenhurst Dr SR4 85 A2
Brockhampton Cl NE35 58 E2
Brockley Ave NE34 59 B4
Brockley St SR5 74 A3
Brockley Terr 4 NE35 58 E1
Brockley Whins Sta NE32 58 F2
Brockwade NE10 71 F4
Brockwell Cl NE21 53 A1
Brockwell Ct NE24 17 C5
Brockwell Ctr The NE23 22 B8
Brockwell Dr NE39 67 E3
Brockwell Ho NE5 37 C2
Brockwell Mid Sch NE23 22 B8
Brockwell Rd NE38 82 F5
Brockwell St 1 NE24 17 C4
Brockwood Cl NE63 6 B1
Brodie Cl NE34 59 C4
Brodrick Cl NE3 37 D5
Brodrick St 13 NE33 42 D3
Brokenheugh NE5 36 F1
Bromarsh Ct SR6 75 F1
Bromford Rd NE3 37 D5
Bromley Ave NE25 31 E4
Bromley Ct NE3 37 D7
Bromley Gdns Blyth NE24 17 E5
Wallsend NE28 40 D5
Brompton Cl DH2 81 E2
Brompton Terr DH4 90 D4
Brompton Workshops 5
NE11 70 A8
Bromsgrove Cl 6 NE28 40 E5
Bronte St NE8 56 B1
Brook Ct Bedlington NE22 11 A1
Bedlington NE22 16 A8
Brook Side Lodge 3
SR2 86 C4
Brook St
Newcastle-u-T NE6 56 D5
Whitley Bay NE26 32 B6
Brookbank Cl SR3 91 F5
Brooke Ave
West Boldon NE35 74 B8
Whickham NE16 69 A8
Brooke St SR5 102 C4
Brooke's Wlk NE34 59 A2
Brookfield NE3 38 B2
Brookfield Cres NE5 36 C1
Brookfield Terr NE10 57 A1
Brookland Dr NE12 29 E3
Brookland Rd SR4 85 F6
Brookland Terr NE29 31 B1
Brooklands NE20 25 A3
Brooklands Way NE35 73 D8
Brookside Dudley NE23 29 A7
Houghton-le-S DH5 94 D6
Brookside Ave Blyth NE24 17 B7
Brunswick Village NE13 28 A6
Brookside Cres NE5 37 D1
Brookside Gdns 4 SR2 86 C4
Brookside Terr 2 SR2 86 C4
Brookside Wood NE38 83 D1
Brooksmead NE28 40 A4
Brookvale Ave NE3 38 A4
Broom Cl Blaydon NE21 68 B8
Morpeth NE61 9 C7
Whickham NE16 69 C6
Broom Ct NE9 82 F8
Broom Gn NE16 69 C6
Broom La NE16 69 C6
Broom Terr
Burnopfield NE16 79 C6
Whickham NE16 69 C6
Broom Wood Ct NE42 50 B1
Broome Cl NE3 37 F6
Broomfield NE32 58 C2
Broomfield Ave
Newcastle-u-T NE6 39 E1
Wallsend NE28 40 C5
Broomfield Cres NE17 77 B8
Broomfield Rd NE3 38 B4
Broomhaugh CE Fst Sch
NE44 62 F7
Broomhaugh Cl NE46 45 C4
Broomhill Est DH5 94 F6
Broomhill Gdns NE5 37 D1
Broomhill Rd NE42 50 E3
Broomhill Terr DH5 94 F5
Broomhouse La NE42 50 D3
Broomhouse Rd NE42 50 F3
Broomlaw NE9 71 C4
Broomlea NE29 31 B1
Broomlea Ct NE21 53 C3
Broomlee NE63 6 E2
Broomlee Cl NE7 39 D3
Broomlee Rd NE12 29 D3
Broomley Ct NE3 37 F7
Broomley Fst Sch NE43 64 B8
Broomley Wlk NE3 37 F7
Broomridge Ave NE15 54 D6
Brooms The DH2 81 F2
Broomshields Ave SR5 75 B3
Broomshields Cl SR5 75 B3
Broomy Hill Rd NE15 35 D2
Broomylinn Pl NE23 22 C8
Brotherlee Rd NE3 37 F7
Brough Ct 3 NE6 56 C7
Brough Gdns NE28 41 A4
Brough Park Way NE6 56 D7
Brough St 2 NE6 56 C7
Brough Way 20 NE6 56 C7
Brougham St SR1 103 A2
Broughton Rd NE33 42 D2
Brow The NE6 56 C5
Brown Cres NE9 71 C1
Brown's Bldgs DH3 82 C1
Browne Rd SR6 75 E3
Browning Cl NE34 59 B3
Browning Sq NE8 56 A2
Brownlow Cl NE7 39 E3
Brownlow Rd NE34 59 C6
Brownrigg Dr NE23 22 C5
Brownriggs Ct NE37 83 B6
Brownsea Pl NE9 71 A7
Browntop Pl NE34 59 C5
Broxbourne Terr SR4 102 A2
Broxburn Cl NE28 40 E5
Broxburn Ct NE5 37 C3
Broxholm Rd NE6 39 B1
Bruce Cl
Newcastle-u-T NE5 36 F2
Whiteleas NE34 59 C4
Bruce Gdns NE5 54 C7
Brumell Dr NE61 3 D1
Brumwell Ct NE43 64 B7
Brundon Ave NE26 31 F7
Brunel Dr SR6 75 F2
Brunel Lodge NE4 100 A3
Brunel St Gateshead NE8 70 D8
Newcastle-u-T NE4 100 B3
Brunel Terr NE4 100 A3
Brunel Wlk NE4 100 A3
Brunswick Gr NE13 28 A6
Brunswick Ind Est NE13 27 F6
Brunswick Park Ind Est
NE13 28 A6
Brunswick Pl NE1 99 A2
Brunswick Rd
Shiremoor NE27 30 F2
Sunderland SR5 74 A4
Brunswick Sq NE27 30 F2
Brunswick St NE33 42 C1
Brunton Ave
Newcastle-u-T NE3 37 F6
Wallsend NE28 41 B3
Brunton Cl NE27 30 F2
Brunton Gr NE3 37 F6
Brunton La Hazlerigg NE13 27 E2
Newcastle-u-T,Brunton Park
NE3,NE13 28 B2
Newcastle-u-T,Kingston Park
NE3 37 C7
Brunton Mews NE13 27 F2
Brunton Rd NE3 37 C7
Brunton St NE29 41 D3
Brunton Terr SR4 102 A2
Brunton Way
Cramlington NE23 16 B2
Brunton Way continued
Gateshead NE10 57 B2
Brussels Rd
Sunderland SR4 85 D7
Wallsend NE28 40 B1
Bryan's Leap NE16 79 A7
Bryden Ct NE34 59 D5
Bryers St SR6 60 F1
Buchanan Gn NE11 100 A1
Buchanan St NE31 57 D5
Buck's Nook La NE40 66 C7
Buckingham SR3 91 E8
Buckingham Cl 1 SR6 75 F8
Buckingham St NE4 98 B1
Buckland Cl Burnside DH4 90 C2
Washington NE38 83 D3
Buckthorne Gr NE7 39 C3
Buddle Ct NE4 54 E4
Buddle Ind Est NE28 57 C8
Buddle Rd NE4 54 D4
Buddle St NE28 40 C1
Buddle Terr
4 Shiremoor NE27 30 E1
Sunderland SR2 103 B1
Bude Ct NE28 40 C4
Bude Gdns NE9 70 F3
Bude Gr NE29 31 D1
Budle Cl Blyth NE24 17 C7
Newcastle-u-T NE3 38 A6
Budleigh Rd NE3 37 F5
Budworth Ave NE26 24 D5
Bugatti Ind Pk NE29 41 C5
Buller's Gn NE61 3 E1
Bullfinch Dr NE16 69 A7
Bullion La DH2 88 B3
Bullion La Prim Sch DH2 88 B3
Bulman's La NE29 42 A8
Bulmer Ho NE34 60 A7
Bulmer Rd NE34 60 A7
Bungalows The
Birtley DH3 82 B6
Ebchester DH8 76 F4
Gateshead NE10 71 E8
Hetton le H DH5 94 F6
Kibblesworth NE11 81 E8
Medomsley NE17 77 B4
Wallsend NE28 40 F3
Bunyan Ave NE34 59 A3
Burdale Ave NE5 37 A1
Burdon Ave
Cramlington NE23 21 F7
Houghton-le-S DH5 95 A8
Burdon Cl SR6 59 E1
Burdon Cres Cleadon SR6 59 E1
Ryhope SR2 92 E6
Seaham SR7 92 F1
Burdon La
Ryhope SR2,SR3 92 C5
Silksworth SR3 91 F3
Burdon Lodge NE16 69 C2
Burdon Main Row NE29 42 A4
Burdon Pk NE16 69 C2
Burdon Plain NE16 80 B7
Burdon Rd Cleadon SR6 59 E1
Silksworth,Doxford Park
SR3 92 B5
Silksworth,Mill Hill SR3 92 B6
Sunderland SR1,SR2 103 A1
Burdon St NE29 41 D3
Burdon Terr
Bedlington NE22 10 F1
Newcastle-u-T NE2 99 B4
Burford Ct NE7 39 A4
Burford Gdns SR3 86 B3
Burford Way NE35 73 E7
Burghley Gdns NE61 4 F4
Burghley Rd NE10 71 C6
Burgoyne Ct NE37 83 D8
Burgoyne Terr NE41 51 A6
Burke St 2 SR5 74 A3
Burlawn Cl 3 SR2 92 F8
Burleigh St 9 NE33 42 D2
Burlington Cl SR2 103 C1
Burlington Ct
Newcastle-u-T NE2 38 F2
Wallsend NE28 40 E7
Burlington Gdns NE6 56 B8
Burlison Gdns NE10 56 C2
Burn Ave
2 Longbenton NE12 39 D8
1 Wallsend NE28 40 B2
Burn Closes Cres NE28 40 E3
Burn Crook DH5 94 D6
Burn Heads Rd NE31 57 D4
Burn La Hetton le H DH5 95 A3
Hexham NE46 45 A6
Burn Park Rd
Houghton-le-S DH4 94 D8
Sunderland SR2 102 B1
Burn Prom 5 DH4 94 E8
Burn Rd NE21 53 A1
Burn Terr Hebburn NE31 57 C2
Shiney Row DH4 90 B6
Wallsend NE28 40 F2
Burn View Dudley NE23 29 B8
Hedworth NE32 73 D8
Burnaby Dr NE40 52 B4
Burnaby St SR4 102 A1
Burnbank Gateshead NE10 72 A6
Seaton Burn NE13 28 B8
5 Sunderland SR5 75 B2
Burnbank Ave NE25 31 B5
Burnbridge NE13 28 B8
Burncroft 10 NE46 45 A4
Burnden Gr DH4 90 A5

Burnet Cl NE28 ....40 C5
Burnet Ct NE63 ....6 B1
Burney Villas NE8 ....56 A1
Burneze Pl NE16 ....79 A4
Burnfoot Terr NE26 ......32 C4
Burnfoot Way NE3 ....37 E3
Burnhall Dr SR7 ....93 A1
Burnham Ave NE15 ......53 B7
Burnham Cl Blyth NE24 ..17 E5
1 Penshaw DH4 ....90 B6
Burnham Gr
  East Boldon NE36 ......74 D7
  Newcastle-u-T NE6 .....56 E4
Burnham St NE34 ....59 C6
Burnhills Gdns NE40 .....52 A1
Burnhills La NE40 ....67 B8
Burnhope Dr SR5 ....75 B3
Burnhope Gdns **1** NE9 ..71 D3
Burnhope Rd NE38 ....83 E6
Burnland Terr NE46 ......44 F5
Burnlea **4** DH4 ....94 C8
Burnlea Gdns NE23 ......23 B2
Burnley St NE21 ....53 C2
Burnmoor Gdns NE9 ......71 D3
Burnopfield Gdns NE15 ...54 A6
Burnopfield Prim Sch
  NE16 ....79 A6
Burnopfield Rd NE39 .....67 F1
Burns Ave Blyth NE24 ....17 C5
  West Boldon NE35 ......74 B8
Burns Ave N DH5 ....94 E7
Burns Ave S DH5 ....94 E7
Burns Cl Biddick Hall NE34 59 B3
  West Rainton DH4 ......94 A2
  Whickham NE16 ....69 B5
Burns Cres NE16 ....69 A8
Burns St NE32 ....58 B2
Burnside Ashington NE63 ..7 A3
  Bedlington NE22 ....11 D3
  East Boldon NE36 ......74 E7
  Gateshead NE10 ....71 E7
  Holywell NE25 ....23 F1
  Jarrow NE32 ....58 C4
  Morpeth NE61 ....4 A1
  Newcastle-u-T NE2 .....98 B3
  Ovington NE42 ....49 D4
  Ponteland NE20 ....25 B3
Burnside Ave
  Burnside DH4 ....90 C1
  Dudley NE23 ....29 B8
Burnside Bsns & Ent Coll
  NE28 ....40 D2
Burnside Cl Blyth NE24 ...17 B8
  Ovingham NE42 ....50 A4
  Seghill NE23 ....22 E1
  Whickham NE16 ....69 A4
Burnside Cotts
  Annitsford NE23 ....29 C8
  Mickley Square NE43 ...49 E1
Burnside Fst Sch NE23 ...16 C1
Burnside Prim Sch DH4 ...90 D1
Burnside Rd
  Newcastle-u-T NE3 .....38 C7
  Rowlands Gill NE39 .....67 D2
  Tynemouth NE30 ....32 B3
Burnside The NE5 ....36 E1
Burnside View NE23 .....22 E1
Burnstones NE5 ....36 E1
Burnt House Rd NE25 ....31 E3
Burnt Houses NE40 .....52 B1
Burnthouse Cl NE21 .....68 A8
Burnthouse La
  Whickham NE16 ....69 A5
  Whickham NE16 ....69 A6
  Whickham,Whickham Fell
  NE16 ....69 A4
Burntland Ave SR5 ......74 F2
Burnville NE6 ....56 A7
Burnville Rd SR4 ....102 B1
Burnville Rd S SR4 ......102 B1
Burnway Seaham SR7 ....93 A1
  Washington NE37 ....83 B8
Burnwood Cl NE17 ......66 B1
Burradon Farm Cotts
  NE23 ....29 D7
Burradon Prim Sch NE23 29 C5
Burradon Rd NE23 ......29 C7
Burrow St **5** NE33 .....42 C3
Burscough Cres SR6 ....75 D2
Burstow Ave NE6 ....56 E3
Burswell Ave NE46 ......44 F5
Burswell Villas NE46 ....44 F5
Burt Ave NE29 ....41 E5
Burt Cl DH6 ....97 E3
Burt Cres NE23 ....29 B8
Burt Meml Homes NE62 ..10 E5
Burt Rd NE22 ....11 E3
Burt St NE24 ....17 E8
Burt Terr Morpeth NE61 ...9 A4
  Walbottle NE15 ....36 A2
Burtree NE38 ....83 B3
Burwell Ave NE5 ....53 F8
Burwood Cl NE6 ....57 A4
Burwood Rd
  Newcastle-u-T NE6 .....56 F3
  Tynemouth NE29 ......41 C8
Business & Innovation Ctr
  SR5 ....74 F1
Buston Terr NE2 ....38 F1
Busty Bank
  Burnopfield NE16 ....79 B7
  Burnopfield NE16,NE39 ..79 A8
Butcher's Bridge Rd
  NE32 ....58 B4

Butcher's La NE61 ....4 F5
Bute Ct **3** SR3 ....92 A6
Bute Dr NE39 ....66 F4
Bute Rd N NE39 ....66 F4
Bute Rd S NE39 ....66 F3
Bute St NE39 ....79 A2
Buteland Rd NE15 ....53 F7
Buteland Terr NE64 ......7 D4
Butsfield Gdns SR3 .....86 B2
Butterburn Cl NE7 ......39 E4
Butterfield Cl NE40 .....51 F4
Buttermere Cleadon SR6 ..60 A1
  Gateshead NE10 ....72 A8
Buttermere Ave
  Easington Lane DH5 ....97 C8
  Whickham NE16 ....69 D7
Buttermere Cl
  Chester le S DH2 ......88 C2
  Killingworth NE12 ......29 C3
  3 Newcastle-u-T NE5 ..37 B1
Buttermere Cres
  Blaydon NE21 ....68 B8
  South Hetton DH6 ......97 E8
Buttermere Gdns
  Gateshead NE9 ....71 A5
  South Shields NE34 ....59 E6
Buttermere Rd NE30 ....32 A2
Buttermere St SR2 ......86 E2
Buttermere Way NE24 ...12 B1
Buttsfield Terr DH4 ......90 B8
Buxton Cl Jarrow NE32 ...58 C5
  Wallsend NE28 ....40 D5
Buxton Gdns
  Newcastle-u-T NE5 .....36 F3
  Sunderland SR3 ....86 B3
Buxton Gn **2** NE5 .....36 F3
Buxton Rd NE32 ....58 C5
Buxton St NE1 ....99 C1
By-Way The NE15 ....35 D1
Byer Sq DH5 ....95 A6
Byer St DH5 ....95 A6
Byermoor Ind Est NE16 ..79 D7
Byers St SR3 ....92 B8
Byerside Cvn Site NE17 ..77 C5
Byeways The NE12 ......39 B6
Bygate Cl NE3 ....37 E3
Bygate Rd NE25 ....31 E4
Byker Bank NE6 ....56 A5
Byker Bridge NE1,NE6 ...56 A6
Byker Bsns Development Ctr
  9 NE6 ....56 B5
Byker Cres **17** NE6 ....56 C6
Byker Prim Sch NE6 .....56 B5
Byker St NE6 ....56 F6
Byker Sta NE6 ....56 C6
Byker Terr NE6 ....56 F6
Byland Cl DH4 ....90 C2
Byland Ct NE38 ....83 C5
Byland Rd NE12 ....38 F6
Bylands Gdns SR3 ......86 B3
Byony Toft SR2 ....93 A7
Byrne Terr W **2** SR3 ...92 B7
Byrness Cl NE5 ....36 E1
Byrness Ct NE34 ....37 C4
Byrness St **3** NE28 ....40 E5
Byrness Row NE23 ......22 C8
Byron Ave Blyth NE24 ...17 C6
  Hebburn NE31 ....57 F6
  6 Wallsend NE28 .....41 A1
  West Boldon NE35 .....74 A8
Byron Cl Guide Post NE62 .10 E7
  Ouston DH2 ....82 A1
Byron Ct
  Newcastle-u-T NE5 .....36 C2
  Whickham NE16 ....69 A8
Byron Ho SR7 ....92 F2
Byron Lodge Est **6** SR7 92 E1
Byron Pl NE63 ....6 F2
Byron Rd SR5 ....75 A2
Byron St
  Newcastle-u-T NE2 .....99 B2
  Ouston DH2 ....81 F1
  4 South Shields NE33 ..59 D8
  Sunderland SR5 ....75 C1
Byron Terr
  Houghton-le-S DH5 .....94 E7
  5 Seaham SR7 ....92 F1
Byron Wlk NE8 ....56 A2
Byron's Ct SR7 ....93 C2
Bywell Ave Hexham NE46 .45 D4
  Newcastle-u-T,Denton Burn
  NE15 ....53 E7
  Newcastle-u-T,Fawdon NE3 37 F8
  South Shields NE34 ....60 A7
  Sunderland SR5 ....75 C3
Bywell Cl NE40 ....51 E3
Bywell Gdns
  Dunston NE11 ....70 A5
  Gateshead NE9 ....71 B6
Bywell Gr NE27 ....31 A3
Bywell Home Farm NE43 48 F3
Bywell Rd Ashington NE63 ..6 D2
  Cleadon SR6 ....74 F8
Bywell St NE6 ....56 D5
Bywell Terr NE32 ....58 B3
Bywell View NE43 ......64 D7

C

Cadehill Rd NE43 ....64 C6
Cadlestone Ct NE23 ....22 D8
Caedmon Com Prim Sch
  NE8 ....101 B1
Caer Urfa Cl NE33 ......42 C4
Caernarvon Cl NE5 .....37 B4

Caernarvon Dr SR3 ......91 C6
Caesar Way NE28 ......40 E4
Caesar's Wlk **3** NE33 ..42 C4
Cairncross SR5 ....74 A1
Cairnglass Gn NE23 .....22 D8
Cairngorm Ave NE38 ....83 A2
Cairnhill Terr DH4 ....90 D4
Cairns Rd SR5 ....75 C4
Cairns Sq SR5 ....75 C4
Cairns Way NE3 ....37 F7
Cairnside SR3 ....91 C7
Cairnside S SR3 ....91 B7
Cairnsmore Cl
  Cramlington NE23 .....22 B4
  Newcastle-u-T NE6 .....57 B8
Cairnsmore Dr NE38 ....83 B3
Cairo St SR2 ....86 F3
Caithness Rd SR5 ......73 F2
Caithness Sq SR5 ......73 F2
Calais Rd SR5 ....73 F1
Calandra Chase NE2 ....98 B4
Caldbeck Ave NE6 ......56 F3
Caldbeck Cl NE6 ....56 F3
Calder Cres NE38 ....83 D1
Calder Ct **13** SR3 .....91 F6
Calder Gn NE32 ....58 C2
Calder Wlk
  Sunniside NE16 ....69 A2
  Sunniside NE16 ....69 A3
Calderbourne Ave **6**
  SR6 ....75 C4
Calderdale NE28 ....39 F5
Calderdale Ave NE6 .....56 F7
Calderwood Cres NE9 ...71 A3
Caldew Cres NE5 ....54 A8
Caldew Ct DH5 ....95 B2
Caldwell Rd NE3 ....37 F8
Caledonia NE21 ....68 A8
Caledonia St NE6 ....57 A4
Caledonian Rd SR5 .....73 F3
Caledonian St NE31 ....57 D7
Calf Close Dr NE32 .....58 B2
Calf Close Ho NE32 .....58 C2
Calf Close Wlk NE32 ....58 C2
Calfclose La NE32 ......58 C2
California NE21 ....53 B1
California Gdns **18** NE61 .9 A8
Callalley Ave NE16 ......68 F6
Callaly Ave NE23 ....22 C6
Callaly Cl NE61 ....4 F3
Callaly Way NE6 ....56 D4
Callander DH2 ....82 A2
Callendar Ct NE9 ....71 C5
Callerdale Rd NE24 .....17 A7
Callerton NE12 ....29 D5
Callerton Ave NE29 .....41 C6
Callerton Cl
  3 Ashington NE63 .....6 F2
  Cramlington NE23 .....22 C6
Callerton Ct NE20 ......25 E4
Callerton La NE5,NE15,
  NE20 ....25 E3
Callerton Lane End Cotts
  NE5 ....35 E7
Callerton Parkway Sta
  NE13 ....26 E1
Callerton Pl NE4 ....98 A1
Callerton Rd NE15 .....35 E2
Callerton View NE5 .....36 B4
Callington Cl DH4 ......89 E2
Callington Dr SR2 ......92 F7
Callum Dr NE34 ....60 A8
Calow Way NE16 ....68 F5
Calthwaite Cl SR5 ......74 B2
Calver Ct NE34 ....59 E5
Calvus Dr NE15 ....34 F2
Cam Mead SR3 ....92 A4
Camberley Cl SR3 ......92 C8
Camberley Rd NE28 ....41 A4
Camberwell Cl NE11 ....70 B6
Camberwell Way SR3 ...91 D5
Cambo Ave
  Bedlington NE22 ....11 C1
  Whitley Bay NE25 ......31 D3
Cambo Cl Blyth NE24 ....17 C7
  Newcastle-u-T NE3 .....38 D5
  Wallsend NE28 ....40 D6
Cambo Dr NE23 ....22 C6
Cambo Gn NE5 ....37 C2
Cambo Pl NE30 ....32 A1
Cambois Fst Sch NE24 ..12 C4
Camborne Gr NE8 .....101 C1
Camborne Pl NE8 .....101 C1
Cambourne Ave **4** SR6 .75 E4
Cambria Gn SR4 ....85 A6
Cambria St SR4 ....85 A6
Cambrian Way NE38 ....83 B3
Cambridge Ave
  Hebburn NE31 ....57 F5
  Longbenton NE12 ......39 D8
  Wallsend NE28 ....40 A3
  Washington NE37 ......83 B8
  Whitley Bay NE26 .....32 A5
Cambridge Cres SR4 ...90 A6
Cambridge Pl DH3 .....82 C1
Cambridge Rd
  New Silksworth SR3 ....92 A7
  Stakeford NE62 ....11 A7
Cambridge St NE4 ....100 B4
Cambridge Terr NE8 ...101 B1
Camden Ct NE1 ....99 B2
Camden Sq NE30 ......42 B5
Camden St
  Newcastle-u-T NE1,NE2 .99 B2
  North Shields NE30 ....42 B5
  Sunderland SR5 ....75 A1
Camelford Ct NE15 .....53 C8
Cameron Cl NE34 ......59 C3

Cameron Rd NE42 .....50 D2
Camerton Pl NE28 .....40 E7
Camilla Rd NE15 ....34 F2
Camilla St NE8 ....101 C1
Camp Terr NE29 ....42 A6
Campbell Park Rd NE31 .57 F5
Campbell Pl NE4 ....98 A1
Campbell Rd SR5 ......73 F2
Campbell Sq SR5 ......73 F2
Campbell St NE31 .....57 E7
Campbell Terr DH5 .....95 B1
Camperdown NE5 ......36 F1
Camperdown Ave
  Chester le S DH3 ......88 D5
  Killingworth NE12 .....29 B4
Camperdown Ind Est
  NE12 ....29 B5
Campion Gdns NE10 ....71 D5
Campion Way NE63 .....6 C2
Campsie Cl NE38 ......83 B3
Campsie Cres NE30 ....32 A1
Campus Martius NE15 ..34 E2
Campville NE29 ....42 A6
Camsey Cl NE12 ....38 F7
Camsey Pl NE12 ....38 F7
Canberra Ave NE25 ....31 D3
Canberra Dr NE34 .....58 F4
Canberra Rd SR4 ......85 D4
Candelford Cl NE7 .....39 D3
Candlish St NE33 ......42 D2
Canning St Hebburn NE31 57 E5
  Newcastle-u-T NE4 .....54 E5
Canning Street Prim Sch
  NE4 ....54 D5
Cannock Killingworth NE12 29 D4
  Ouston DH2 ....82 A2
Cannock Dr NE7 ....39 A4
Cannon St NE8 ....101 A4
Canon Cockin St SR2 ...86 F4
Canon Gr NE32 ....58 C7
Canon Savage Dr NE46 .44 A4
Canonbie Sq NE23 .....22 D8
Canonsfield Cl
  Newcastle-u-T NE15 ....36 B3
  Silksworth SR3 ....91 F5
Canterbury Ave NE28 ..40 D6
Canterbury Cl
  Ashington NE63 ....6 F2
  Longbenton NE12 .....39 A7
Canterbury Ho SR5 ....73 F4
Canterbury Rd SR5 ....74 A3
Canterbury St
  Newcastle-u-T NE6 .....56 D6
  South Shields NE33 ....59 D8
Canterbury Way
  Hedworth NE32 ....58 A1
  Wideopen NE13 ....28 B5
Capercaillie Lodge NE23 .22 B1
Capetown Rd SR5 ......73 F2
Capetown Sq SR5 .....73 F2
Caplestone Cl NE38 ....83 B3
Capstan La NE9 ....71 F2
Captains Row The NE33 .59 B8
Captains Wharf NE33 ...42 C3
Capulet Gr NE34 ....59 A5
Capulet Terr SR2 ....86 E4
Caradoc Cl NE38 ......83 B3
Caragh Rd DH2 ....88 C1
Caraway Wlk NE34 ....59 E2
Carden Ave NE34 .....60 B5
Cardiff Sq SR5 ....73 F1
Cardigan Gr NE30 .....32 A3
Cardigan Rd SR5 ......73 F2
Cardigan Terr NE6 .....56 B7
Cardinal Cl
  Longbenton NE12 .....39 A6
  Newcastle-u-T NE15 ....36 B3
Cardinals Cl **5** SR5 ...91 F5
Cardonnel St NE29 ....42 A4
Cardwell St SR6 ....75 E1
Careen Cres SR3 ......91 B7
Carew Ct NE23 ....22 B5
Carham Ave NE23 .....22 C6
Carham Cl Corbridge NE45 47 B5
  Newcastle-u-T NE3 .....38 D6
Caris St NE8,NE9 ......71 A8
Carisbrooke NE12 .....41 A2
Carisbrooke Cl **11** NE37 .83 D8
Carisbrooke Ct SR1 ...102 B2
Carlcroft **8** SR6 ......75 E1
Carlcroft Pl NE23 ......22 C5
Carley Hill Rd SR5 .....75 B3
Carley Lodge SR5 .....75 B3
Carley Rd SR5 ....75 B2
Carlile Ho NE4 ....98 A1
Carlingford Rd DH2 ....88 B1
Carliol Pl NE1 ....99 B1
Carliol Sq NE1 ....99 B1
Carliol St NE1 ....99 B1
Carlisle Cl NE27 ....30 C1
Carlisle Cres DH4 .....90 B7
Carlisle Cres **11** NE10 ..56 D1
Carlisle Ho **4** SR3 ....91 D7
Carlisle Pl NE9 ....71 B4
Carlisle St NE10 ....56 D1
Carlisle Terr
  3 Shiremoor NE27 ....30 E1
  6 Sunderland SR5 ....74 F2
Carlisle View NE61 .....8 F8
Carlisle Way NE27 ....30 C1
Carlow Dr NE62 ....11 D8
Carlton Ave NE24 .....17 C3
Carlton Cl DH2 ....88 A1
Carlton Cres SR3 ......91 C7
Carlton Gdns NE15 ....53 E7

Carlton Gr NE63 ....6 F1
Carlton Grange NE3 ...38 A3
Carlton Ho NE64 ....7 E5
Carlton Rd NE12 ......39 D6
Carlton St NE24 ....17 F7
Carlton Terr Blyth NE24 ..17 D8
  Gateshead NE9 ....70 F5
  North Shields NE29 ....41 F5
  24 Springwell NE9 ....71 F1
Carlyle Cres NE16 .....69 A8
Carlyle Ct **4** NE28 ....41 A1
Carlyle St **1** NE28 ....41 A1
Carlyon St SR2 ....103 A1
Carmel Gr NE23 ....16 A1
Carnaby Cl NE42 ......50 D3
Carnaby Rd NE6 ......56 F4
Carnation Ave DH4 ....89 E3
Carnation Terr **5** NE16 .69 B7
Carnegie Cl NE34 .....59 C4
Carnegie St **10** SR2 ...86 F2
Carnforth Cl NE28 .....40 E7
Carnforth Gdns
  Gateshead NE9 ....71 B4
  Rowlands Gill NE39 ....67 E3
Carnforth Gn NE3 .....37 E7
Carnoustie Ouston DH2 .82 A1
  Washington NE37 .....72 C3
Carnoustie Cl NE7 .....39 C4
Carnoustie Ct
  Gateshead NE10 ......72 B6
  Whitley Bay NE25 .....31 C5
Carnoustie Dr NE34 ...59 F3
Carol Gdns NE7 ......39 B3
Carol St SR4 ....102 B3
Caroline Cotts NE5 ....54 B8
Caroline Gdns NE28 ...41 A3
Caroline St
  Hetton le H DH5 ......95 A4
  Jarrow NE32 ....58 A7
  Newcastle-u-T NE4 .....54 E4
Caroline Terr NE21 ....53 B4
Carolyn Cl NE12 ......39 C6
Carolyn Cres NE26 ....31 E7
Carolyn Way NE26 ....31 E7
Carpenter St NE33 ....42 B2
Carr Field NE20 ....25 F7
Carr Hill Com Prim Sch
  NE9 ....71 B7
Carr Hill Rd N10,NE9 ...71 B7
Carr St Blyth NE24 .....17 C4
  Hebburn NE31 ....57 D7
Carrfield Rd NE3 ......37 F5
Carrick Dr NE24 ......17 C4
Carrigill Dr NE12 .....39 A6
Carrington Cl NE23 ...22 F1
Carrmere Rd SR2 ......86 E1
Carrock Ct SR3 ....91 F6
Carroll Wlk NE34 .....59 A2
Carrowmore Rd DH2 ..88 C1
Carrs Cl NE42 ....50 F3
Carrsfield NE45 ....47 A5
Carrsyde Cl NE16 .....68 F5
Carsdale Rd NE3 ......37 D5
Carter Ave NE31 ......57 E6
Carters Lo **9** NE9 ....70 F5
Cartington Ave NE27 ..30 F2
Cartington Cl NE3 .....37 E7
Cartington Rd NE29 ...41 E5
Cartington Terr NE6 ...39 C1
Cartmel Ct DH2 ....88 A2
Cartmel Gn NE5 ......37 A1
Cartmel Gr NE8 ....70 D7
Cartmel Pk NE10 .....57 A1
Cartwright Rd SR5 ....74 B1
Carville Gdns NE28 ....57 B8
Carville Prim Sch NE28 ..57 B8
Carville Rd NE28 ......40 B1
Carville Rise NE6 .....56 C6
Carville St NE10 ......56 B6
Carville Station Cotts
  NE28 ....40 C4
Carvoran **4** NE28 ....40 F4
Carwarding Pl NE5 ....37 C2
Caseton Cl NE25 .....31 C6
Caspian Cl NE32 ......58 C5
Caspian Rd SR5 ......73 F1
Caspian Sq SR5 ......73 F1
Castellian Rd SR5 .....74 C1
Casterton Gr NE5 .....36 B3
Castle Bank NE61 ......9 A8
Castle Cl Chester le S DH3 88 D2
  Hetton le H DH5 ......95 B2
  Morpeth NE61 ....8 F8
  7 Newcastle-u-T NE3 ..37 D5
  Prudhoe NE42 ....50 D4
  Whickham NE16 ......69 A4
Castle Ct NE20 ....25 E6
Castle Dene Gr DH4 ...94 D8
Castle Farm Mews NE2 .38 F3
Castle Garth NE1 .....101 B4
Castle Gn **10** SR3 ....91 D7
Castle Hill Ho NE41 ...51 C5
Castle Lea NE42 ......50 B3
Castle Leazes (Halls of
  Residence) NE2 ......98 B3
Castle Mdws NE61 .....8 E7
Castle Mews SR3 .....91 D7
Castle Rd Prudhoe NE42 .50 B3
  Washington NE38 .....83 A5
Castle Riggs DH2 ......88 B3
Castle Sq Backworth NE27 .30 D5
  Morpeth NE61 ....9 A8
Castle St Hazlerigg NE13 ..28 A4
  Morpeth NE61 ....9 A8
  Sunderland SR1 ......102 C3
Castle St S **4** SR5 ....74 C1
Castle Terr NE63 ....6 E4

Castle View
Chester le S DH3 . . . . .88 C5
Horsley NE15 . . . . .50 C8
Ovingham NE42 . . . . .50 B4
Penshaw DH4 . . . . .90 B8
Prudhoe NE42 . . . . .50 C3
Sunderland SR5 . . . . .74 B1
Castle View Sch SR5 . . . .74 A1
Castle Way NE13 . . . . . . .27 B7
Castle Wlk NE61 . . . . .9 A7
Castledale Ave NE24 . . . .17 A6
Castledene Ct
Newcastle-u-T NE3 . . . . . . .38 F4
Sunderland SR5 . . . . .74 A2
Castlefields DH4 . . . . . . .89 D3
Castlefields Dr NE42 . . . .50 E3
Castleford Rd SR5 . . . . . .73 F2
Castlegate Gdns NE8 . . .100 A1
Castlemain Cl DH4 . . . . . .89 D3
Castlenook Pl NE15 . . . . .53 F7
Castlereagh Homes The
SR7 . . . . .93 D1
Castlereagh St SR3 . . . . .92 A7
Castlereigh Cl DH4 . . . . . .89 D3
Castles Farm Rd NE2,NE7 . .38 F5
Castles Gn NE12 . . . . .29 E3
Castleside Rd NE15 . . . . .54 A6
Castleton Cl
Cramlington NE23 . . . . .16 A1
Newcastle-u-T NE2 . . . . . . .38 F2
Castleton Gr NE2 . . . . . . .38 F2
Castleton Lodge NE4 . . . .54 F5
Castleton Rd NE32 . . . . . .58 C5
Castletown Prim Sch
SR5 . . . . .85 B8
Castletown Rd SR5 . . . . . .74 C1
Castletown Way SR5 . . . . .74 D2
Castleway NE61 . . . . .4 F3
Castlewood Cl NE5 . . . . . .36 D2
Catcheside Cl NE16 . . . . .69 A5
Cateran Way NE23 . . . . . .22 C4
Catharine St W SR4 . . . . .102 A2
Cathedral Ct NE8 . . . . . . .56 A3
Cathedral View DH4 . . . . .90 D3
Catherine Cookson Ct
NE33 . . . . .42 E1
Catherine Rd DH4 . . . . . . .90 D6
Catherine St ☒ NE33 . . . .42 D3
Catherine View ☒ NE40 . .51 F3
Catholic Row NE22 . . . . . .15 E8
Catkin Wlk NE40 . . . . .52 A3
Cato Sq SR5 . . . . .75 A2
Cato St SR5 . . . . .75 A2
Catrail Pl NE23 . . . . .22 C8
Cattle Market NE46 . . . . . .45 B4
Catton Gr NE16 . . . . .69 B3
Catton Pl NE28 . . . . .40 E6
Cauldwell Ave
South Shields NE34 . . . . . . .59 E7
Whitley Bay NE25 . . . . .31 D3
Cauldwell Cl NE31 . . . . . .31 E4
Cauldwell La NE25 . . . . . .31 E4
Cauldwell Pl NE34 . . . . . .59 E7
Cauldwell Villas NE34 . . . .59 E7
Causeway Gateshead NE9 .71 B6
Sunderland SR6 . . . . .103 A4
Causeway The
Gateshead NE9 . . . . .71 A8
Throckley NE15 . . . . .35 D1
Causey Arch ★ DH9 . . . . . .80 A4
Causey Arch Sta ★ NE16 . .80 A4
Causey Bank NE1 . . . . . . .99 B1
Causey Bldgs NE3 . . . . . .38 C4
Causey Brae NE46 . . . . . .44 F3
Causey Hill Rd
Hexham NE46 . . . . .44 F3
Hexham NE46 . . . . .45 B1
Causey Hill Way NE46 . . . .44 F3
Causey Ho NE3 . . . . .38 C3
Causey Pk NE46 . . . . .44 F4
Causey Rd DH9,NE16 . . . . .80 A3
Causey Row NE16 . . . . . . .80 B4
Causey St NE3 . . . . .38 C4
Causey Way Hexham NE46 .44 F3
Kip Hill DI9 . . . . .80 A1
Cavalier View NE31 . . . . . .57 D7
Cavalier Way SR3 . . . . . . .91 F7
Cavell Rd SR5 . . . . .74 A2
Cavendish Gdns NE63 . . . . .6 D3
Cavendish Pl
Burnopfield NE16 . . . . .79 A4
New Silksworth SR3 . . . . . . .91 F7
Newcastle-u-T NE2 . . . . . . .38 F1
Cavendish Rd NE2 . . . . . . .38 F1
Cavendish Sq NE61 . . . . . .4 E3
Cavendish Terr NE63 . . . . . .6 D3
Caversham Rd NE5 . . . . . .36 B3
Cawburn Cl NE7 . . . . .39 E3
Cawdel Ct NE30 . . . . .42 B5
Cawfields Ct NE12 . . . . . .38 F6
Cawnpore Sq SR4 . . . . . . .85 E7
Cawthorne Terr NE16 . . . .79 A4
Caxton Way DH3 . . . . .88 D8
Caxton Wlk NE34 . . . . . . .59 A2
Caynham Ct NE29 . . . . . . .41 E8
Cayton Gr NE5 . . . . .36 B2
Cecil Ct Ponteland NE20 . .25 F6
Wallsend NE28 . . . . .57 B8
Cecil St NE29 . . . . .42 A5
Cecil Terr NE46 . . . . .45 B5
Cedar Cl Bedlington NE22 .10 C2
Whitley Bay NE25 . . . . .31 F3
Cedar Cres
Burnopfield NE16 . . . . .78 F6
Dunston NE11 . . . . .69 F7
Gateshead NE9 . . . . .70 F4
Cedar Ct South Hetton DH6 .97 F7
Sunderland SR2 . . . . .86 D4

Cedar Ct continued
Tynemouth NE29 . . . . .31 E1
Cedar Dr NE32 . . . . .73 C8
Cedar Gr Blyth NE24 . . . . .17 C4
Hebburn NE31 . . . . .57 E3
Ryton NE40 . . . . .52 C6
South Shields NE34 . . . . . .59 F5
Wallsend NE28 . . . . .40 D2
Whitburn SR6 . . . . .60 F2
Cedar Rd Blaydon NE21 . . .53 C2
Newcastle-u-T NE4 . . . . . . .54 D7
Cedar Terr Ashington NE63 .6 C4
Fence Houses DH4 . . . . . . .90 A1
Washington NE38 . . . . .83 C1
Cedar Way NE12 . . . . .29 E1
Cedars DH2 . . . . .88 B5
Cedars Cres SR2 . . . . . . .86 E3
Cedars Gn NE9 . . . . .71 A3
Cedars Pk SR2 . . . . .86 E3
Cedars Sch The NE9 . . . .71 A3
Cedars The
Gateshead NE9 . . . . .71 C2
Newcastle-u-T NE4 . . . . . .100 B3
Penshaw DH4 . . . . .90 B8
Sunderland SR2 . . . . .86 D4
Whickham NE16 . . . . .69 B4
Cedartree Gdns NE25 . . . .31 E3
Cedarway NE10 . . . . .71 E5
Cedarwood DH4 . . . . .89 E1
Cedarwood Ave NE6 . . . . .40 A1
Cedarwood Gr SR2 . . . . . .86 D2
Cedric Cres SR2 . . . . .86 B4
Celadon Cl NE15 . . . . .53 C8
Celandine Cl NE3 . . . . . . .38 D7
Celandine Ct NE63 . . . . . . .6 B1
Celandine Way NE10 . . . . .71 E5
Cellar Hill Terr DH4 . . . . .90 D2
Celtic Cl SR6 . . . . .59 E1
Celtic Cres SR6 . . . . .59 E1
Cemetery App NE34 . . . . . .59 E8
Cemetery Rd
Gateshead NE8 . . . . .101 C1
Jarrow NE32 . . . . .58 C5
Centenary Ave NE34 . . . . .60 A6
Centenary Cotts NE22 . . . .15 F8
Centenary Ct NE4 . . . . . . .54 F4
Central Arc NE1 . . . . .99 A1
Central Ave
Guide Post NE62 . . . . .10 E7
North Shields NE29 . . . . . . .41 E5
South Shields NE34 . . . . . .59 F6
Whitburn SR6 . . . . .60 F2
Central Bsns & Tech Pk
NE1 . . . . .99 B1
Central Gdns NE34 . . . . . .59 F6
Central Newcastle High Sch
NE2 . . . . .99 A4
**Central Newcastle High Sch
(Jun Dept)** NE3 . . . . . . .38 C4
Central Parkway NE1 . . . .100 C4
Central Sta (Metro)
NE1 . . . . .101 A4
Central Way SR4 . . . . .85 E8
Centralway NE11 . . . . .70 C4
Centurian Way NE22 . . . . .10 E2
Centurion Rd NE15 . . . . . .53 F8
Centurion Way
Gateshead NE9 . . . . .71 B6
Heddon-on-t-W NE15 . . . . . .34 E2
Ceolfrid Terr NE32 . . . . . .58 C4
Cestria Prim Sch DH3 . . . .88 D3
Chacombe NE38 . . . . .83 D3
Chadderton Dr NE5 . . . . . .36 B3
Chadwick St NE28 . . . . . . .40 B1
Chadwick Wlk NE8 . . . . . .101 A4
Chaffinch Ct NE63 . . . . . . .6 B2
Chaffinch Rd ☒ SR5 . . . . .74 C1
Chaffinch Way NE12 . . . . .29 C4
Chainbridge Ind Est
NE21 . . . . .53 F4
Chainbridge Rd
Blaydon NE21 . . . . .53 D3
Blaydon,Derwenthaugh
NE21 . . . . .53 F4
Chainbridge Road Ind Est
NE21 . . . . .53 F4
Chains Dr NE45 . . . . .46 F6
Chalfont Gr SR4 . . . . .85 A2
Chalfont Rd NE6 . . . . .56 C6
Chalford Rd ☒ SR5 . . . . . .75 B2
Challoner's Gdns NE61 . . . .3 E1
Chaloner Pl NE61 . . . . .8 F7
Chamberlain St
Blyth NE24 . . . . .17 F6
Crawcrook NE40 . . . . .51 F4
Chambers Cres NE9 . . . . .71 C1
Chancery La NE24 . . . . . . .17 D7
Chandler Ct NE2 . . . . .38 F2
Chandlers Ford DH4 . . . . .89 F8
Chandlers Quay NE6 . . . . .56 C4
Chandless St NE8 . . . . . .101 C3
Chandos SR3 . . . . .92 A4
Chandos St NE8 . . . . .70 F8
Chandra Pl ☒ NE5 . . . . . .37 B2
Chantry Cl SR3 . . . . .91 E5
Chantry Dr NE13 . . . . .28 B6
Chantry Est NE45 . . . . . . .46 F6
Chantry Ho DH4 . . . . .94 A2
Chantry Mews ☒ NE61 . . . .9 A8
Chantry Pl
☒ Morpeth NE61 . . . . .9 A8
West Rainton DH4 . . . . .94 A2
Chapel Ave NE16 . . . . .79 B6
Chapel Cl
Kibblesworth NE11 . . . . .81 D6
Newcastle-u-T NE3 . . . . . . .28 D1
Chapel Ct Newburn NE15 . .52 E8
Seaton Burn NE13 . . . . .28 B8

Chapel Ct continued
Sherburn DH6 . . . . .96 A1
Chapel Ho NE33 . . . . .42 E1
Chapel House Dr NE5 . . . .36 C1
Chapel House Gr NE5 . . . .36 C1
Chapel House Mid Sch
NE5 . . . . .36 B2
Chapel House Rd NE5 . . . .36 C1
Chapel La Haswell DH6 . . .97 F3
Whitley Bay NE25 . . . . .31 E4
Wylam NE41 . . . . .51 A6
Chapel Park Mid Sch
NE5 . . . . .36 C3
Chapel Pl NE32 . . . . .28 B8
Chapel Row Birtley DH3 . . .82 E3
Mickley Square NE43 . . . . . .49 E1
Penshaw DH4 . . . . .90 C5
Chapel St Hetton le H DH5 .95 B4
North Shields NE29 . . . . . . .41 E5
Tantobie DH9 . . . . .79 B2
Chapel View
Brunswick Village NE13 . . . .28 A6
Rowlands Gill NE39 . . . . . . .67 E3
Chapelville NE13 . . . . .28 B8
Chapman St SR6 . . . . .75 C4
Chapter Row NE33 . . . . . .42 C3
Chare Bank DH8 . . . . .76 E3
Chare The NE1 . . . . .99 A2
Chareway NE46 . . . . .45 A6
Chareway La NE46 . . . . . . .45 A6
Charlbury Cl NE9 . . . . .71 F1
Charlcote Cres NE36 . . . . .74 D7
Charles Ave
Longbenton NE12 . . . . .39 D8
Newcastle-u-T NE3 . . . . . . .37 C6
Shiremoor NE27 . . . . .30 F4
Whitley Bay NE26 . . . . .32 B5
Charles Baker Wlk NE34 . .60 B7
Charles Ct ☒ NE6 . . . . . . .56 C7
Charles Dr NE23 . . . . .29 B8
**Charles Perkins Meml
Cottage Homes** DH3 . . . .82 C3
Charles St
Boldon Colliery NE35 . . . . . .73 F8
Gateshead NE8 . . . . .101 C2
Hazlerigg NE13 . . . . .28 A5
Newbottle DH4 . . . . .90 D4
Pegswood NE61 . . . . .4 F3
Ryhope SR2 . . . . .93 A6
Sunderland SR1 . . . . .103 B3
Sunderland,Monkwearmouth
SR6 . . . . .103 A4
Charleswood NE3 . . . . . . .38 D8
Charlie St NE40 . . . . .51 F1
Charlotte Cl NE4 . . . . . . .100 B3
Charlotte Mews ☒ NE1 . . .98 C1
Charlotte Sq NE1 . . . . . . .98 C1
Charlotte St
Crawcrook NE40 . . . . .51 E3
North Shields NE30 . . . . . . .42 B6
South Shields NE33 . . . . . .42 C2
Wallsend NE28 . . . . .40 A3
Charlotte Terr ☒ NE33 . . . .42 D2
Charlton Cl NE46 . . . . .44 F2
Charlton Ct NE25 . . . . .31 E3
Charlton Gdns NE61 . . . . . .9 B7
Charlton Gr SR6 . . . . .75 A8
Charlton Mews NE15 . . . . .53 D6
Charlton Rd SR5 . . . . .75 C2
Charlton St Ashington NE63 .6 C4
Blyth NE24 . . . . .17 D7
Newcastle-u-T NE15 . . . . . .53 D6
Charlton Villas NE40 . . . . .52 B1
Charlton Wlk NE8 . . . . . .100 C1
Charman St SR1 . . . . .103 A3
Charminster Gdns NE6 . . .39 C1
Charnwood Ave NE12 . . . .39 A6
Charnwood Ct NE33 . . . . .42 E2
Charnwood Gdns ☒ NE9 . .71 B8
Charter Dr SR3 . . . . .91 C7
Charters Cres DH6 . . . . . .97 F6
Chase Ct Sherburn DH6 . . .96 A1
Whickham NE16 . . . . .69 B7
Chase Farm Dr NE24 . . . . .16 F7
Chase Mdws NE24 . . . . . .16 F6
Chase Mews NE24 . . . . . .16 F7
Chase Sch NE16 . . . . .69 B7
Chase The Hexham NE46 . .44 F3
Longbenton NE12 . . . . .29 A4
North Shields NE29 . . . . . . .41 F6
Washington NE38 . . . . .82 F1
Chasedale Cres NE24 . . . .17 A7
Chatham Cl NE25 . . . . .23 D1
Chatham Rd SR5 . . . . .74 A2
Chathill Cl NE25 . . . . .23 D1
Chathill Terr NE6 . . . . .56 F5
Chatsworth Cres SR4 . . . .86 A4
Chatsworth Ct ☒ NE33 . . .42 D3
Chatsworth Dr NE22 . . . . .11 C3
Chatsworth Gdns
☒ Newcastle-u-T NE5 . . . . .36 F3
Newcastle-u-T,Walker NE6 . .56 D4
Whitley Bay NE25 . . . . .31 E3
Chatsworth Pl NE16 . . . . .69 A5
Chatsworth Rd NE32 . . . . .58 C5
Chatsworth St SR4 . . . . .102 A1
Chatsworth St S SR4 . . . .86 A1
Chatterton St SR5 . . . . . . .75 C4
Chatton Ave
Cramlington NE23 . . . . .22 C6
South Shields NE34 . . . . . .60 B8
Chatton Cl
Chester le S DH2 . . . . .88 A1
Morpeth NE61 . . . . .9 C5
Chatton St NE28 . . . . .41 C1
Chatton Wynd NE3 . . . . . .38 A7

Chaucer Ave NE34 . . . . . .59 A3
Chaucer Cl NE8 . . . . .56 A3
Chaucer Rd NE16 . . . . .69 B8
Chaucer St ☒ DH4 . . . . . .94 D8
Chaytor Gr SR1 . . . . .103 B2
Chaytor St NE32 . . . . .58 B8
Cheadle Ave
Cramlington NE23 . . . . .16 A1
Wallsend NE28 . . . . .40 E6
Cheadle Rd SR5 . . . . .74 A2
Cheam Cl NE16 . . . . .69 B5
Cheam Rd SR5 . . . . .74 A2
Cheddar Gdns NE9 . . . . . .70 F3
Cheldon Cl NE25 . . . . .31 C6
Chelford Cl NE28 . . . . .40 E7
Chelmsford Gr NE2 . . . . . .56 A7
Chelmsford Rd SR5 . . . . . .74 A2
Chelmsford Sq SR5 . . . . . .74 A3
Chelmsford St ☒ SR3 . . . .92 A8
Chelsea Gdns NE8 . . . . . .71 B8
Chelsea Gr NE4 . . . . .98 A1
Cheltenham Ct NE63 . . . . . .6 C2
Cheltenham Dr NE35 . . . . .58 E2
Cheltenham Rd SR5 . . . . . .74 A2
Cheltenham Sq SR5 . . . . . .74 A2
Cheltenham Terr NE6 . . . .56 B7
Chelton Cl NE13 . . . . .28 B4
Chepstow Gdns NE8 . . . . .70 D7
Chepstow Rd NE15 . . . . . .53 F6
Chepstow St SR4 . . . . . . .102 B2
Cherribank SR2 . . . . .92 E6
Cherry Banks DH3 . . . . . . .88 D5
Cherry Blossom Way
NE37 . . . . .73 B1
Cherry Cotts DH9 . . . . . . .79 B2
Cherry Dr DH6 . . . . .97 F3
Cherry Gr
Killingworth NE12 . . . . .29 C4
Prudhoe NE42 . . . . .50 B3
Cherry Knowle Hospl
SR2 . . . . .92 E4
Cherry Tree Dr NE22 . . . . .10 F1
Cherry Tree Gdns NE25 . . .50 C8
Cherry Tree La NE41 . . . . .51 A6
Cherry Tree Sq SR2 . . . . . .92 E8
Cherry Tree Wlk NE31 . . . .57 E4
Cherry Trees NE24 . . . . . .17 D6
Cherry Way
Fence Houses DH4 . . . . . . .90 B1
Killingworth NE12 . . . . .29 C4
Cherrytree Cl NE12 . . . . . .29 F2
Cherrytree Ct NE22 . . . . . .11 D2
Cherrytree Dr NE16 . . . . . .69 C8
Cherrytree Gdns
Gateshead NE9 . . . . .71 A4
Whitley Bay NE25 . . . . .31 F3
Cherrytree Rd DH2 . . . . . . .88 A5
Cherrywood NE6 . . . . .39 E1
Cherrywood Gdns SR3 . . .92 B7
Cherwell NE37 . . . . .83 F8
Cherwell Sq NE12 . . . . . . .29 C1
Chesham Gdns NE5 . . . . . .36 B2
Chesham Gr NE3 . . . . .37 F5
Cheshire Ave DH3 . . . . . . .82 C1
Cheshire Cl NE63 . . . . .6 A4
Cheshire Ct NE31 . . . . .57 D5
Cheshire Gdns NE28 . . . . .40 A3
Cheshire Gr NE34 . . . . . . .60 B7
Chesils The NE12 . . . . .39 A5
Chesmond Dr NE21 . . . . . .53 C3
Chessar Ave NE5 . . . . .37 B2
Chester Ave NE28 . . . . . . .40 F3
Chester Cl NE20 . . . . .25 B4
Chester Cres
Newcastle-u-T NE2 . . . . . . .99 C3
Sunderland SR3 . . . . .102 B2
Chester Gdns NE34 . . . . . .59 E7
Chester Gr Blyth NE24 . . . .17 C6
Seghill NE23 . . . . .22 E1
Chester Mews SR4 . . . . . .102 B2
Chester Oval SR2 . . . . . . .102 B2
Chester Pl NE8 . . . . .101 B2
Chester Rd
Bournmoor DH3,DH4 . . . . . .89 D8
Chester le S DH3 . . . . .88 F5
Penshaw DH4 . . . . .90 B7
Shiney Row DH4 . . . . .90 B7
Sunderland SR1,SR4 . . . . .102 B2
Sunderland,Grindon SR4 . . .85 B3
Sunderland,High Barnes
SR1,SR2,SR4 . . . . .85 F5
Chester Sq NE61 . . . . .2 A3
Chester St Newbottle DH4 .90 D4
Newcastle-u-T NE2 . . . . . . .99 C3
Sunderland NE2 . . . . .102 A3
Chester St E SR4 . . . . . . .102 A2
Chester St W SR4 . . . . . . .102 A2
Chester Terr SR1 . . . . . . .102 B2
Chester Terr N SR4 . . . . .102 B2
Chester View DH2 . . . . . . .81 D7
Chester Way NE32 . . . . . . .58 A2
**Chester-le-Street CE Jun
Sch** DH2 . . . . .88 B5
Chester-le-Street Com Hospl
DH3 . . . . .88 C2
Chester-le-Street Sta
DH3 . . . . .88 C3
Chesterfield Rd NE4 . . . . .54 F4
Chesterhill NE23 . . . . .22 B5
Chesters ☒ NE28 . . . . .40 F4
Chesters Ave NE12 . . . . . .39 A5
Chesters Cl NE9 . . . . .70 F6
Chesters Ct NE12 . . . . . . .39 B6
Chesters Dene DH8 . . . . . .76 E3

Cas – Chi 113

Chesters Gdns NE40 . . . . .51 E4
Chesters Pk NE9 . . . . .70 F6
Chesters The
Ebchester DH8 . . . . .76 E3
Newcastle-u-T NE5 . . . . . . .36 C1
Whitley Bay NE25 . . . . .31 E6
Chesterton Rd NE34 . . . . .59 B3
Chesterwood Dr NE28 . . . .40 A2
Chesterwood Terr NE10 . . .57 B1
Chestnut Ave Blyth NE24 . .12 D1
Newcastle-u-T NE5 . . . . . . .37 E2
Washington NE38 . . . . .83 B1
Whickham NE16 . . . . .69 B5
Whitley Bay NE25 . . . . .31 F4
Chestnut Cl
Hedworth NE32 . . . . .58 D1
Killingworth NE12 . . . . .29 B4
Chestnut Cres SR5 . . . . . .74 F3
Chestnut Gdns NE8 . . . . . .70 C8
Chestnut Gr NE34 . . . . . . .59 F4
Chestnut St Ashington NE63 .6 D3
Wallsend NE28 . . . . .40 C5
Chestnut Terr DH4 . . . . . . .90 C3
Cheswick Dr NE3 . . . . .38 D6
Cheswick Rd NE25 . . . . . . .23 E2
Chevin Cl NE6 . . . . .40 B1
Chevington NE10 . . . . .72 A5
Chevington Cl NE61 . . . . . . .4 E3
Chevington Gdns ☒ NE5 . .37 D1
Chevington Gr SR5 . . . . . .31 D2
Cheviot Cl Ellington NE61 . . .1 D4
Tynemouth NE29 . . . . .31 F2
Washington NE37 . . . . .83 A6
Cheviot Ct Blaydon NE21 . .53 C3
Morpeth NE61 . . . . .9 A6
Newcastle-u-T NE7 . . . . . . .39 A4
Whitley Bay NE26 . . . . .32 C4
Cheviot Gdns NE11 . . . . . .70 A7
Cheviot Gn NE11 . . . . .70 A8
Cheviot Gr NE61 . . . . .4 E3
Cheviot Grange NE23 . . . .29 C8
Cheviot Ho NE36 . . . . .74 B7
Cheviot Jun Sch NE34 . . . .60 A8
Cheviot La SR2 . . . . .92 E7
Cheviot Mount NE6 . . . . . .56 C6
Cheviot Prim Sch NE5 . . . .37 A4
Cheviot Rd Blaydon NE21 . .53 C3
Chester le S DH2 . . . . .88 B1
Hebburn NE32 . . . . .58 A4
South Shields NE34 . . . . . .60 A7
South Shields NE34 . . . . . .60 A8
Cheviot St SR43 . . . . .85 F7
Cheviot View
Ashington NE63 . . . . .6 E5
Brunswick Village NE13 . . . .28 A6
Gateshead NE10 . . . . .71 D6
Longbenton NE12 . . . . .39 C6
Ponteland NE20 . . . . .26 A5
Prudhoe NE42 . . . . .50 E2
Seghill NE23 . . . . .22 F1
Whitley Bay NE26 . . . . .32 B5
Cheviot Way
Hexham NE46 . . . . .45 A4
Stakeford NE62 . . . . .11 B8
Chevron The ☒ NE6 . . . . . .56 B5
Chevychase Ct SR7 . . . . . .92 F2
Cheyne Rd NE42 . . . . .50 C2
Cheyne The SR3 . . . . .92 A5
Chichester Ave NE23 . . . . .21 F8
Chichester Cl
Ashington NE63 . . . . .7 A2
Gateshead NE8 . . . . .101 B2
Newcastle-u-T NE3 . . . . . . .37 D8
Chichester Gr NE22 . . . . . .10 F2
Chichester Pl NE33 . . . . . .59 C8
Chichester Rd
South Shields NE33 . . . . . .42 D1
Sunderland SR6 . . . . .75 E4
Chichester Rd E NE33 . . . .42 D1
Chichester Sta NE33 . . . . .59 C8
Chichester Way NE32 . . . .58 B1
Chick's La ☒ NE25 . . . . . .31 F8
Chicken Rd NE28 . . . . .40 A4
Chigwell Cl DH4 . . . . .90 B7
Chilcote NE10 . . . . .71 D7
Chilcrosse NE10 . . . . .71 F6
Chilham Ct
Tynemouth NE29 . . . . .41 B8
Washington NE38 . . . . .83 B4
Chillingham Cl NE24 . . . . .17 B5
Chillingham Cres NE63 . . . .6 C3
Chillingham Ct ☒ NE6 . . . .56 C7
Chillingham Dr
Chester le S DH2 . . . . .88 A1
North Shields NE29 . . . . . . .41 D4
Chillingham Ho NE6 . . . . .103 B4
Chillingham Ind Est NE6 . .56 C7
Chillingham Rd NE6 . . . . . .56 C6
Chillingham Road Prim Sch
NE6 . . . . .56 C8
Chillingham Road Sta
NE6 . . . . .56 D7
Chillingham Terr NE32 . . . .58 D4
Chilside Rd NE10 . . . . .71 D7
Chiltern Ave DH3 . . . . .88 B2
Chiltern Cl Ashington NE63 . .6 F1
Washington NE38 . . . . .83 B3
Chiltern Dr NE12 . . . . .29 B1
Chiltern Gdns NE11 . . . . . .70 B7
Chiltern Rd NE29 . . . . .31 F2
Chilton Ave DH4 . . . . .94 A8
Chilton Gdns ☒ DH4 . . . . .94 A8
Chilton St ☒ SR5 . . . . .75 C1
Chimney Mills NE2 . . . . . . .98 C4
China St SR2 . . . . .86 E4

Chingford Cl DH4 ....90 C7
Chip The NE61 ....8 F5
Chipchase NE38 ....82 F4
Chipchase Ave NE23 .....22 B6
Chipchase Cl
Bedlington NE22 ....10 D1
Pegswood NE61 ....4 F3
Chipchase Cres NE5 .....36 E3
Chipchase Ct
Bournmoor DH4 ....89 D1
New Hartley NE25 ....23 D6
Seaham SR7 ....92 F2
Chipchase Mews NE3 ...28 A1
Chipchase Terr NE32 ....58 B3
Chippendale Pl NE2 ......98 B4
Chirdon Cres NE46 ......45 C4
Chirnside NE23 ....22 B4
Chirton Ave
North Shields NE29 ....41 F5
South Shields NE34 ....60 C6
Chirton Dene Quays
NE28 ....41 F2
Chirton Dene Way NE29 .42 A3
Chirton Gn Blyth NE24 ....17 B5
North Shields NE29 ....41 F5
Chirton Gr NE34 ....60 C6
Chirton Hill Dr NE29 ....41 C7
Chirton La NE29 ....41 E5
Chirton Lodge NE28 .....41 E5
Chirton West View NE29 .41 F5
Chirton Wynd NE6 ....56 C5
Chisholm Pl 6 NE46 .....45 B5
Chislehurst Rd DH4 .....90 B7
Chiswick Gdns NE8 .....71 A8
Chiswick Rd SR5 ....74 A2
Chiswick Sq SR5 ....74 A2
Chollerford Ave
North Shields NE29 ....41 D6
Whitley Bay NE25 ....32 B4
Chollerford Cl NE3 ......38 A4
Chollerford Mews NE25 ..23 F2
Chollerton Dr
Bedlington NE22 ....11 A1
Longbenton NE12 ....40 A8
Choppington Fst Sch
NE62 ....10 E5
Choppington Rd
Bedlington NE22,NE62 .....10 F2
Morpeth NE61 ....9 B6
Chopwell Gdns NE9 .....71 D2
Chopwell Prim Sch NE17 66 B1
Chopwell Rd NE17 ....77 C6
Chopwell Wood Wlks*
NE39 ....66 F2
Chopwell Woods Rd
NE39 ....67 A3
Chorley Pl NE6 ....56 E5
Chowdean Terr 4 NE9 ...70 F4
Chowdene Bank NE11,
NE9 ....70 F2
Christ Church CE Prim Sch
Newcastle-u-T NE2 ....99 C2
North Shields NE30 ....42 A6
Christal Terr SR6 ....75 D3
Christie Terr NE6 ....56 F5
Christmas Pl NE8 ......100 B2
Christon Cl NE3 ....38 E5
Christon Rd NE3 ....38 D5
Christon Way NE10 ......57 B2
Christopher Rd NE6 .....56 E7
Chudleigh Gdns NE5 ....36 B2
Church Ave
Choppington NE62 ....10 E5
Newcastle-u-T NE3 ....38 D5
West Sleekburn NE62 .....11 D7
Church Bank Jarrow NE32 58 D7
Newburn NE15 ....52 F7
Sunderland SR5 ....75 A1
Wallsend NE28 ....40 D2
Church Chare
Chester le S DH3 ....88 D3
Ponteland NE20 ....25 F7
Whickham NE16 ....69 B7
Church Cl Bedlington NE22 15 F8
Bournmoor DH4 ....89 E4
Dinnington NE13 ....27 B7
Ebchester DH8 ....76 E3
Riding Mill NE44 ....62 F7
Whitley Bay NE25 ....31 C4
Church Ct Bedlington NE22 15 F8
10 Gateshead NE10 ....56 D1
Church Dr NE9 ....71 A6
Church Flatt NE20 ....25 F7
Church Gn 7 NE16 ......69 B7
Church High Sch NE2 ...99 B4
Church La
Bedlington NE22 ....16 A7
Gateshead NE9 ....71 B6
Newcastle-u-T NE3 ....38 D5
Riding Mill NE44 ....62 E7
Sunderland SR1 ....102 C2
Whitburn SR6 ....75 F8
Church Mews
Ashington NE63 ....6 B4
Backworth NE27 ....30 C5
Church Pl NE10 ....56 D1
Church Rd
Backworth NE27 ....30 C5
Gateshead NE9 ....71 A5
Hetton le H DH5 ....95 A5
Newburn NE15 ....52 F7
Newcastle-u-T NE3 ....38 D5
Stannington NE61 ....14 C3
Wylam NE41 ....51 A6
Church Rise Ryton NE40 ..52 E5
Church Rise *continued*
Whickham NE16 ....69 B7
Church Row 1 NE46 .....45 B5
Church Sq NE61 ....2 B3
Church St Birtley DH3 ....82 C4
Blaydon NE21 ....53 B1
Blyth NE24 ....17 E8
Cramlington NE23 ....22 B6
Dunston NE11 ....100 A1
Gateshead NE8 ....101 B4
Gateshead,Felling NE10 ...71 D8
Haswell DH6 ....97 E3
Hebburn NE31 ....57 D7
7 Houghton-le-S DH4,DH5 .94 E8
Newcastle-u-T NE6 ....57 A4
North Shields NE30 ....42 B6
Penshaw DH4 ....90 B6
9 Sunderland SR5 ....75 B2
Sunderland,South Hylton
SR4 ....85 A6
Sunniside NE16 ....69 A1
West Rainton DH4 ....94 A2
Church St E SR1 ....103 C3
Church St N SR6 ....103 B4
Church Terr NE21 ....53 C3
Church Vale DH6 ....96 C4
Church View
Boldon Colliery NE35 ......58 E1
Earsdon NE25 ....31 A5
Haswell DH6 ....97 F3
New Silksworth SR3 ......92 A7
Newbiggin-by-t-S NE64 .....7 C5
Wallsend NE28 ....40 D2
Washington NE37 ....83 D7
Church Way Earsdon NE25 31 A6
North Shields NE29,NE30 ..42 A6
South Shields NE33 ....42 C3
Church Wlk Morpeth NE61 .8 E8
Newcastle-u-T NE6 ....57 A5
Sunderland SR1 ....103 C3
Churchburn Dr NE61 .....8 F6
Churchdown Cl NE35 ....58 E2
Churcher Gdns NE28 ....40 A4
Churchill Ave
Sunderland SR5 ....75 A2
Whitley Bay NE25 ....31 F3
Churchill Com Coll NE28 .40 F4
Churchill Gdns NE2 .....39 A1
Churchill Mews NE6 .....56 C4
Churchill Sq DH4 ....94 B8
Churchill St
Newcastle-u-T NE1 ......100 C4
Sunderland SR1 ....103 B2
Wallsend NE28 ....40 F4
Churchlands NE46 ......45 D4
Churchwalk Ho NE6 .....57 A5
Churston Cl DH4 ....90 C4
Cicero Terr 4 SR5 ......75 A2
Cinderford Cl NE35 .....58 E2
Circle Pl NE46 ....45 A5
Circle The NE32 ....58 C4
Cirencester St SR4 .....102 B3
Cirrus Ho 14 SR3 ....92 A6
Citadel E NE12 ....29 D3
Citadel W NE12 ....29 D3
City Hall NE1 ....99 B2
City of Sunderland Coll
(Hylton Ctr) SR5 ....74 E2
City of Sunderland Coll Bede
Ctr SR3 ....85 F3
City of Sunderland Coll
Shiney Row Ctr DH4 ...90 B5
City Rd NE1 ....99 C1
City Way SR3 ....91 C6
Citygate NE4 ....98 C1
Civic Ct NE31 ....57 F5
Clacton Rd SR5 ....73 F1
Clanfield Ct NE3 ....38 F4
Clanny Ho SR4 ....85 F6
Clanny St Sunderland SR1 102 B2
Sunderland SR1 ....102 C2
Clapham Ave NE6 ....56 D5
Clara Ave NE27 ....30 F4
Clara St Blaydon NE21 ...53 B1
Newcastle-u-T NE4 ....54 D4
Clarabad Terr NE12 .....30 A1
Clarance Pl NE3 ....38 E5
Clare Lea NE43 ....65 A3
Claremont Ave
Newcastle-u-T NE15 ......53 D7
Sunderland SR6 ....75 E3
Claremont Cres NE26 ....31 E7
Claremont Ct NE26 ......31 E8
Claremont Dr DH4 ......90 A6
Claremont Gdns
East Boldon NE36 ....74 D7
Whitley Bay NE26 ....31 F6
Claremont North Ave
NE8 ....101 B2
Claremont Pl
Gateshead NE8 ....101 B1
Newcastle-u-T NE2 ....98 C3
Claremont Rd
Newcastle-u-T NE2 ....98 B4
Sunderland SR6 ....75 E3
Whitley Bay NE26 ....31 F7
Claremont South Ave
NE8 ....101 B1
Claremont St
Gateshead NE8 ....101 B1
Newcastle-u-T NE2 ....98 C3
Claremont Terr
Blyth NE24 ....17 D7
Gateshead NE10 ....57 B1
Newcastle-u-T NE2 ....98 C3
9 Springwell NE9 ....71 F1
Sunderland SR2 ....102 C1
Claremont Wlk NE8 ....101 A1
Claremount Ct NE36 .....74 B7
Clarence Cres 3 NE26 ...32 B4
Clarence Ho NE2 ....99 C2
Clarence St
Newcastle-u-T NE1,NE2 ...99 C2
Seaton Sluice NE26 ....24 D5
2 Sunderland SR5 ....75 A2
Tantobie DH9 ....79 B2
Clarence Terr DH3 ......88 C3
Clarendon Mews NE3 ...28 C2
Clarendon Rd NE6 ......39 C1
Clarendon Sq SR5 ......75 B3
Clarewood Ave NE34 ....60 A8
Clarewood Ct NE4 ......98 B2
Clarewood Gn NE4 ......98 A2
Clarewood Pl NE5 ......54 C8
Clark's Terr 2 SR7 ......92 E1
Clarke Terr NE10 ....71 C8
Clarke's Terr NE23 ......29 A6
Clarks Field NE61 ....8 E8
Clarks Hill Wlk NE15 ....52 F7
Clasper Ct 11 NE33 ......42 C4
Clasper St NE4 ....100 B3
Clasper Way NE16 ......54 A3
Claude St
10 Crawcrook NE40 ....51 F3
Hetton le H DH5 ....95 A3
Claudius Ct 4 NE33 .....42 C4
Claverdon St NE5 ....36 B4
Clavering Pl NE1 ....101 A4
Clavering Rd
Blaydon NE21 ....53 C1
Whickham NE16 ....54 B1
Clavering Sq NE11 ......69 F8
Clavering St NE28 ....41 B1
Clavering Way NE21 .....53 E2
Claverley Dr NE27 ......30 C5
Claxheugh Cotts SR4 ....85 B7
Claxheugh Rd SR4 ......85 B7
Claymere Rd SR2 ....86 E1
Claypath NE10 ....71 F4
Claypath La NE33 ....42 D2
Claypath Rd DH5 ....95 B2
Claypath St 4 NE6 ......56 A6
Claypool Ct NE34 ....59 C5
Clayside Ho 4 NE33 .....42 D1
Clayton Park Sq NE2 ....99 B4
Clayton Rd NE2 ....99 B4
Clayton St
Bedlington NE22 ....11 D3
Dudley NE23 ....28 F8
Jarrow NE32 ....58 B7
Newcastle-u-T NE1 ....99 A1
Clayton St W NE1 ......100 C4
Clayton Terr
Gateshead NE8 ....56 C1
Heddon-on-t-W NE15 .....34 F2
Clayton Terrace Rd
Chopwell NE17 ....66 C2
High Spen NE13,NE39 .....66 D4
Clayworth Rd NE3 ......28 B1
Cleadon Gdns
Gateshead NE9 ....71 D3
Wallsend NE28 ....41 A5
Cleadon Hill Dr NE34 ...60 A4
Cleadon Hill Rd NE34 ...60 B4
Cleadon La Cleadon SR6 ..60 C1
East Boldon NE36,SR6 .....74 E8
Cleadon Lane Ind Est
NE36 ....74 E8
Cleadon Lea SR6 ....59 F1
Cleadon Mdws SR6 .....60 A2
Cleadon Old Hall SR6 ...60 A1
Cleadon St NE6 ....56 E6
Cleadon Twrs NE34 .....60 B4
Cleadon Village CE Prim Sch
SR6 ....59 F1
Cleasby Gdns NE9 ......70 F6
Cleasewell Terr NE62 ....11 A7
Cleaside Ave NE34 ......60 A4
Cleaswell Hill NE62 .....10 F7
Cleaswell Hill Special Sch
NE62 ....10 F7
Cleehill Dr NE29 ....31 F1
Cleeve Ct NE38 ....83 C5
Cleghorn St 4 NE6 .....56 C8
Clegwell Terr NE31 .....57 F6
Clematis Cres NE9 ......71 D2
Clement Ave NE22 ......11 C1
Clement St NE9 ....70 F5
Clementina Cl SR2 .....103 B1
Clennel Ave NE31 ......57 D5
Clennel Ho 4 NE4 ....54 E5
Clent Way NE12 ....39 A6
Clephan St NE11 ....54 F1
Clervaux Terr NE32 .....58 C6
Cleveland Ave
Chester le S DH2 ....88 B2
Newbiggin-by-t-S NE64 .....7 D4
North Shields NE29 ....41 F6
Cleveland Cres NE29 ....42 A6
Cleveland Ct Jarrow NE32 58 A7
9 South Shields NE33 ....42 C4
Cleveland Dr NE38 .....83 B3
Cleveland Gdns
Newcastle-u-T NE7 ....39 A3
Wallsend NE28 ....41 B3
Cleveland Mews NE11 ..100 A1
Cleveland Rd
North Shields NE29 ....42 A6
Sunderland SR4 ....85 F5
Cleveland St 3 NE33 ....42 D4
Cleveland Terr
Newbiggin-by-t-S NE64 .....7 D4
North Shields NE29 ....42 A6
Cleveland View SR6 .....75 E6
Clickemin NE20 ....26 A4
Cliff Rd SR2 ....93 A6
Cliff Row NE26 ....32 C4
Cliff Terr SR2 ....93 A6
Cliff View SR2 ....93 A6
Cliffe Ct SR6 ....75 F4
Cliffe Pk SR6 ....75 F4
Clifford Gdns 4 NE40 ...51 F3
Clifford Rd NE6 ....56 D5
Clifford St Blaydon NE21 ..53 C3
Chester le S DH3 ....88 C1
Newcastle-u-T NE6 ....56 B6
North Shields NE30 ....42 C6
Sunderland SR4 ....102 A2
Clifford Terr
Chester le S DH3 ....88 C2
Crawcrook NE40 ....51 F3
Clifford's Fort NE30 .....42 C6
Cliffside NE34 ....60 C6
Clifton Ave
South Shields NE34 ....59 E7
10 Wallsend NE28 ....40 B2
Clifton Cl Ryton NE40 ....52 E4
Stakeford NE62 ....11 A8
Clifton Ct
2 Gateshead NE9 ....71 E1
Newcastle-u-T NE3 ....37 D7
Whitley Bay NE26 ....31 E7
Clifton Gdns Blyth NE24 ..17 D4
Gateshead NE9 ....70 F7
North Shields NE29 ....41 E3
Clifton Gr NE25 ....31 E6
Clifton La NE61 ....9 B2
Clifton Rd
Cramlington NE23 ....22 C5
Newcastle-u-T NE4 ....54 F5
Sunderland SR6 ....75 E4
Clifton Terr
Longbenton NE12 ....39 D7
South Shields NE33 ....59 C8
Whitley Bay NE26 ....32 B5
Clifton Wlk NE5 ....36 B2
Cliftonbourne Ave 2
SR6 ....75 E4
Cliftonville Ave NE4 .....54 E5
Cliftonville Gdns NE26 ..32 A6
Climbing Tree Wlk NE61 ...4 E3
Clintburn Ct NE23 ....22 C8
Clinton Pl
Newcastle-u-T NE3 ....28 B2
Sunderland SR3 ....91 C6
Clipsham Cl NE12 ....39 B6
Clipstone Ave NE6 ......56 E3
Clipstone Cl NE15 ....35 C2
Clitheroe Gdns NE22 ....10 D2
Clive Pl NE6 ....56 B5
Clive St North Shields NE29 42 B5
9 South Shields NE34 ....59 A4
Clockburn Lonnen NE16 .68 E4
Clockburnsyde Cl NE16 ..68 E5
Clockmill Rd NE11,NE8 .100 A1
Clockstand Cl 8 SR6 ....75 E2
Clockwell St SR5 ....74 F1
Cloggs The NE20 ....25 F7
Cloister Ave NE34 ....59 A5
Cloister Ct NE8 ....101 C3
Cloister Garth NE7 ......38 F5
Cloister Wlk NE32 ....58 C7
Cloisters The
Newcastle-u-T NE7 ....38 F5
South Shields NE34 ....59 F7
Sunderland SR2 ....103 A1
Close NE1 ....101 A4
Close E The DH2 ....88 C5
Close St
4 Sunderland SR5 ....75 B1
Sunderland,Millfield SR4 ..102 A3
Close The Blaydon NE21 ..53 A1
Blyth NE24 ....12 E1
Burnopfield NE16 ....79 C7
Chester le S DH2 ....88 C5
Cleadon SR6 ....59 F1
Houghton-le-S DH5 ....94 F8
Newcastle-u-T NE5 ....53 E8
Ponteland NE20 ....25 E5
Prudhoe NE42 ....50 E3
Seghill NE23 ....22 F1
Stannington NE61 ....14 C3
Closeburn Sq SR3 ....92 B6
Closefield Gr NE25 ......31 E4
Cloth Mkt NE1 ....99 A1
Clough Dene
Tantobie DH9 ....79 B2
Tantobie,Pickering Nook
NE16 ....79 A3
Clough La NE1 ....99 A1
Clousden Dr NE12 ....29 E1
Clousden Grange NE12 ..29 E1
Clovelly Ave NE4 ....54 E5
Clovelly Gdns
Bedlington NE22 ....15 F8
Whitley Bay NE26 ....32 A6
Clovelly Pl Jarrow NE32 ...58 E5
Ponteland NE20 ....25 C2
Clovelly Sq 6 SR5 ......74 A3
Clover Ave
Gateshead NE10 ....56 B2
Shiney Row DH4 ....90 B4
Winlaton Mill NE21 ....68 C6
Clover Hill NE16 ....69 B2
Clover Hill Com Prim Sch
NE16 ....68 F4
Clover Ho SR3 ....92 A4
Cloverdale NE22 ....10 E1
Cloverdale Gdns
Newcastle-u-T NE7 ....39 B3
Whickham NE16 ....69 B5
Cloverfield Ave NE3 .....37 F6
Cloverhill NE32 ....58 C1
Cloverhill Ave NE31 .....57 D3
Cloverhill Cl NE23 ....22 A1
Cloverhill Dr NE40 ......52 A4
Clumber St NE4 ....100 A3
Clumber St N NE4 .....100 A3
Clyde Ave NE31 ....57 E3
Clyde Ct 10 SR3 ....91 F6
Clyde St Chopwell NE17 ...66 C1
Gateshead NE8 ....71 A8
Clydedale Ave NE12 .....39 D8
Clydesdale Ave DH4 .....90 B7
Clydesdale Mount 8
NE6 ....56 C5
Clydesdale Rd NE6 ......56 C5
Clydesdale St DH5 ......95 A2
Clyvedon Rise NE34 ....60 A3
Co-operative Bldgs
NE25 ....23 D3
Co-operative Cres 6
NE10 ....71 C7
Co-operative St DH3 ....88 C4
Co-Operative Terr
Backworth NE27 ....30 E3
Brunswick Village NE13 ...28 A6
Burnopfield NE16 ....79 B6
Gateshead NE10 ....71 C7
High Spen NE39 ....66 F5
Longbenton NE12 ....30 A1
Medomsley DH8 ....77 B1
Pegswood NE61 ....4 F3
11 Shiremoor NE27 ....30 E1
Sunderland SR4 ....102 A1
1 Washington NE37 ......83 E8
Co-operative Villas DH6 .96 D1
Coach La
Brunswick Village NE13 ....27 E4
Hazlerigg NE13 ....28 B4
Newcastle-u-T NE7 ....39 C4
North Shields NE29 ....42 A5
Coach Open NE28 ....41 B1
Coach Rd
Kibblesworth NE11 ....70 B3
Throckley NE15 ....35 C1
Wallsend NE28 ....40 C1
Washington NE37 ....72 C2
Coach Rd Est NE37 ......72 C1
Coach Road Gn NE10 ....56 C2
Coal La NE42 ....49 D4
Coalbank Rd DH5 ....94 F2
Coalbank Sq DH5 ....94 F2
Coalburn Terr NE61 ......9 D4
Coaley La DH4 ....90 C3
Coalford La DH6 ....96 C4
Coalway Dr NE16 ....69 B8
Coalway La
Greenside NE40,NE41 .....51 D1
Whickham NE16 ....69 B7
Coalway La N NE16 .....54 B1
Coanwood Dr NE23 .....22 C5
Coanwood Gdns NE11 ...70 B5
Coanwood Rd NE15 .....54 B4
Coanwood Way NE16 ....69 B3
Coast Rd
Newcastle-u-T NE6,NE7,
NE28 ....39 E2
North Shields NE28,NE29 ..41 C6
South Shields NE34,SR6 ...60 D6
Wallsend NE28,NE29 ......40 C4
Coatsworth Ct NE8 .....101 B2
Coatsworth Rd NE8 ....101 B1
Cobalt Cl NE15 ....53 C8
Cobbett Cres NE34 ......59 B3
Cobbler's La NE43 ......49 B8
Cobblestone Ct NE6 .....56 B5
Cobden Rd NE23 ....22 C4
Cobden St Gateshead NE8 .56 A1
4 Wallsend NE28 ....40 B2
Cobden Terr NE8 ....56 A1
Cobham Pl NE6 ....57 A4
Cobham Sq SR5 ....75 B2
Coble Dene NE29 ....41 E2
Coble Landing NE33 .....42 B3
Coburg St Blyth NE24 ....17 F7
Gateshead NE8 ....101 C2
North Shields NE30 ....42 B6
Coburn Cl NE23 ....29 C5
Cochran St NE21 ....53 C4
Cochrane Ct NE4 ....54 E5
Cochrane Park Ave NE7 .39 C2
Cochrane St NE4 ....54 E5
Cochrane Terr NE13 .....27 B7
Cockburn Terr NE29 .....41 D3
Cockermouth Gn NE5 ....54 A8
Cockermouth Rd SR5 ....73 F2
Cockshaw NE46 ....45 A5
Cockshaw Ct 7 NE46 ....45 A5
Cockshaw Terr 9 NE46 ...45 A5
Cockshott Dean NE42 ...50 C3
Cohen Ct NE8 ....70 E8
Cohort Cl DH8 ....76 E3
Colbeck Ave NE16 ....54 B1
Colbeck Terr 3 NE30 ....42 D7
Colbourne Ave NE23 .....15 E1
Colbourne Cres NE23 ....15 E1
Colbury Cl NE23 ....16 A2
Colby Ct NE4 ....100 B4
Colchester St NE34 ......59 A5
Colchester Terr SR4 .....85 F5
Coldbeck Ct NE23 ....22 C5
Coldingham Gdns NE5 ...37 D2
Coldside Gdns NE5 ......36 B3
Coldstream DH2 ....82 A2
Coldstream Ave SR5 ....75 B2
Coldstream Cl DH4 .....90 B5
Coldstream Dr NE21 .....68 A8
Coldstream Gdns NE28 ..41 A3
Coldstream Rd NE15 .....54 B7
Coldstream Way NE29 ...41 C8
Coldwell Cl DH6 ....97 F7

Col – Cra 115

Coldwell La NE10 .71 C7
Coldwell Park Ave NE10 .71 D7
Coldwell Park Dr NE10 .71 D7
Coldwell Rd NE42 .50 F3
Coldwell St NE10 .71 D8
Coldwell Terr 2 NE10 .71 C7
Cole Gdns NE10 .72 A8
Colebridge Cl NE5 .37 C3
Colebrooke DH3 .82 D2
Colegate NE10 .71 F7
Colegate Com Prim Sch NE10 .71 F7
Colegate W NE10 .71 F7
Colepeth NE10 .71 E7
Coleridge Ave
Gateshead NE9 .70 E4
South Shields NE33 .42 E1
Coleridge Rd SR5 .74 B2
Coleridge Sq NE31 .57 E6
Coley Gn NE5 .36 B4
Coley Hill Cl NE5 .36 C4
Coley Terr SR6 .75 E3
Colgrove Pl NE3 .37 E5
Colgrove Way NE3 .37 F5
Colima Ave SR5 .85 C8
Colin Pl NE6 .57 A8
Colin Terr 7 SR2 .92 F6
College Burn Rd SR3 .91 E5
College Dr NE33 .59 E8
College La
Longbenton NE12 .39 C6
Newcastle-u-T NE1 .99 B2
College Pl NE63 .6 E2
College Rd Ashington NE63 .6 E2
Hebburn NE31 .57 D2
College St NE1 .99 B2
College View 4 SR5 .75 C1
Collier Cl NE15 .35 D1
Collierley La DH9 .78 D1
Colliery La
Hetton le H DH5 .95 B2
Newcastle-u-T NE4 .98 B1
Colliery Rd NE11 .54 F2
Collin Ave NE34 .60 B5
Collingdon Gn NE39 .67 A4
Collingdon Rd NE39 .67 A4
Collingwood Ave NE28 .40 B4
Collingwood Cl NE23 .21 F8
Collingwood Cotts NE20 .25 B7
Collingwood Cres NE20 .25 D4
Collingwood Ct 1 NE37 .83 F8
Collingwood Ctr NE29 .31 F1
Collingwood Dr
Hexham NE46 .44 F2
Shiney Row DH4 .90 A6
Collingwood Gdns NE10 .56 D2
Collingwood Ho
North Shields NE29 .41 F5
South Shields NE33 .42 D5
Collingwood Mans NE29 .42 B4
Collingwood Mews NE3 .38 C5
Collingwood Pl NE62 .11 A7
Collingwood Prim Sch NE29 .41 D5
Collingwood Rd
Earsdon NE25 .31 A5
Newbiggin-by-t-S NE64 .7 D5
Collingwood St
16 Gateshead NE10 .56 D1
Hebburn NE31 .58 A6
Hetton le H DH5 .95 A6
Newcastle-u-T NE1 .101 A4
South Shields NE33 .59 C8
3 Sunderland SR5 .75 B2
Collingwood Terr
Blyth NE24 .17 E7
Dunston NE11 .100 A1
1 Newcastle-u-T NE2 .38 F1
Tynemouth NE30 .42 D7
Whitley Bay NE26 .32 C4
Collingwood View NE29 .41 F5
Collywell Bay Rd NE26 .24 D5
Collywell Ct NE26 .24 D6
Colman Ave NE34 .59 A5
Colmet Ct NE11 .70 D4
Colnbrook Cl NE3 .37 D7
Colombo Rd SR5 .73 F1
Colston St NE4 .54 D6
Colston Way NE25 .31 D7
Colt Pk NE17 .77 B5
Coltere Ave NE36 .74 E7
Colton Gdns NE9 .71 A3
Coltpark NE5 .36 F1
Coltpark Pl NE23 .22 B5
Coltsfoot Gdns NE10 .71 C5
Coltspool NE11 .81 D6
Columba St SR5 .75 B2
Columba Wlk NE3 .38 E5
Columbia Grange NE3 .37 E5
Columbia Terr NE24 .17 E6
Colwell Pl NE5 .54 B7
Colwell Rd Ashington NE63 .6 F1
Shiremoor NE27 .30 F2
3 Tynemouth NE29 .31 F1
Colwyn Par NE31 .58 A2
Colwyne Pl NE5 .37 B2
Combe Dr NE15 .53 B7
Comet Row NE12 .29 C2
Comet Sq SR3 .92 A7
Comical Cnr NE33 .42 B4
Comma Ct NE11 .70 B7
Commercial Pl 4 NE46 .45 B4
Commercial Rd
8 Blyth NE24 .17 E8
Jarrow NE32 .58 C8
Newcastle-u-T,Byker NE6 .56 C5
Newcastle-u-T,South Gosforth NE3 .38 E5

Commercial Rd *continued*
South Shields NE33 .42 B1
Sunderland SR2 .86 F4
Commercial St 9 NE21 .53 B1
Commissioners' Wharf NE29 .42 A2
Compton Ave NE34 .59 D7
Compton Ct NE38 .83 B5
Compton Rd NE29 .41 F5
Concorde Ho NE25 .23 E1
Concorde Sq 5 SR3 .92 A7
Concorde Way NE32 .58 B6
Condercum Ct NE15 .54 C5
Condercum Ind Est NE4 .54 D5
Condercum Rd NE4 .54 D5
Cone St NE33 .42 B2
Cone Terr DH3 .88 D4
Conewood Ho NE3 .37 F6
Conhope La NE15,NE4 .54 D5
Conifer Cl NE21 .68 B8
Conifer Ct NE12 .39 F8
Coniscliffe Ave NE3 .37 F4
Coniscliffe Pl 1 SR6 .75 E1
Conishead Terr DH6 .97 F8
Coniston Birtley DH3 .82 D2
Gateshead NE10 .72 A8
Coniston Ave
Easington Lane DH5 .97 C8
Hebburn NE31 .57 F4
Newbiggin-by-t-S NE64 .7 C3
Newcastle-u-T NE2 .38 E2
Sunderland SR5 .75 C4
Whickham NE16 .69 D7
Coniston Cl
Chester le S DH2 .88 C2
Killingworth NE12 .29 C3
Newburn NE15 .52 E7
Coniston Cres NE21 .68 B8
Coniston Ct
Newcastle-u-T NE5 .54 B8
Wallsend NE28 .41 A4
Coniston Dr NE32 .58 D3
Coniston Gdns NE9 .71 B5
Coniston Grange NE36 .74 B7
Coniston Ho NE38 .83 C6
Coniston Pl NE9 .71 B5
Coniston Rd Blyth NE24 .12 A1
Tynemouth NE30 .32 A2
Wallsend NE28 .41 A4
Connaught Cl DH4 .90 C5
Connaught Gdns NE12 .39 D7
Connaught Terr NE32 .58 B6
Conningsby Cl NE3 .38 D8
Conniscliffe Ct NE46 .44 F3
Conniscliffe Rd NE46 .44 F3
Connolly Terr NE17 .77 C6
Consett Rd NE11 .70 A5
Constable Cl NE40 .52 C4
Constable Gdns NE34 .59 C3
Constables Garth 7 DH3 82 C4
Content St NE21 .53 C1
Convent Rd NE4 .54 D7
Conway Cl
Bedlington NE22 .10 D1
Ryton NE40 .52 D4
Conway Dr NE7 .39 A4
Conway Gdns
Sunderland SR3 .91 C7
Wallsend NE28 .40 B4
Conway Gr NE26 .24 B7
Conway Rd SR5 .73 F2
Conway Sq Gateshead NE9 71 A8
Sunderland SR5 .73 F2
Conyers Ave DH2 .88 B5
Conyers Gdns DH2 .88 B5
Conyers Pl DH2 .88 B5
Conyers Rd
Chester le S DH2 .88 C5
Newcastle-u-T NE6 .56 C6
Cook Cl NE33 .59 B8
Cook Gdns NE10 .72 B8
Cook Sq SR5 .74 A2
Cooks Wood NE38 .83 D3
Cookshold La DH6 .96 B2
Cookson Cl
Corbridge NE45 .46 F6
Newcastle-u-T NE4 .98 B1
Cookson Ho NE33 .42 C3
Cookson St NE4 .98 A1
Cookson Terr DH2 .88 B3
Cookson's La NE1 .101 A4
Coomassie Rd NE24 .17 E7
Coomside NE23 .22 C4
Coop Bldgs 13 DH3 .82 C4
Cooper St SR6 .75 E1
Cooperative Terr
Great Lumley DH4 .89 F1
Hetton le H DH5 .95 A5
Coopie's La NE61 .9 B7
Coopies Field NE61 .9 B8
Coopies Haugh NE61 .9 C7
Coopies Lane Ind Est NE61 .9 C7
Coopies Way NE61 .9 C7
Copland Terr NE2 .99 C2
Copley Ave NE34 .59 C2
Copley Dr SR3 .86 B2
Copper Chare NE61 .3 F1
Copperas La NE15 .53 F7
Coppergate Ct NE31 .57 F7
Coppers Cl NE11 .70 B7
Coppice The NE26 .24 C6
Coppice Way NE2 .99 C2
Coppy La DH9,NE16 .80 C4
Copse The Blaydon NE21 .53 F2
Burnopfield NE16 .78 F6
Longbenton NE12 .29 E1
Newcastle-u-T NE3 .38 D8

Copse The *continued*
Prudhoe NE42 .50 E2
Washington NE37 .72 B2
Coptleigh DH5 .95 A7
Coquet NE38 .82 F1
Coquet Ave Blyth NE24 .17 E5
Newcastle-u-T NE3 .38 B6
South Shields NE34 .60 B8
Whitley Bay NE26 .32 A5
Coquet Bldgs NE15 .36 B1
Coquet Dr NE61 .1 E5
Coquet Gr NE15 .35 C2
Coquet Ho 16 SR3 .91 F6
Coquet Park Fst Sch NE26 .31 F7
Coquet St Ashington NE63 .6 E4
Chopwell NE17 .66 C1
Hebburn NE31 .57 D6
Jarrow NE32 .58 A5
Newcastle-u-T NE1 .56 A6
Coquet Terr Dudley NE23 .28 F8
Newcastle-u-T NE6 .56 B8
Coquetdale Ave NE6 .57 A6
Coquetdale Cl NE61 .4 E3
Coquetdale Pl NE22 .11 C1
Coquetdale Villas 5 SR6 .75 E2
Corbiere Cl SR3 .91 E6
Corbitt St NE8 .100 C1
Corbridge Ave NE13 .28 B6
Corbridge CE Fst Sch NE45 .47 A6
Corbridge Cl NE28 .40 E6
Corbridge Ct NE12 .38 F6
Corbridge Mid Sch NE45 .46 F7
Corbridge Rd
Hexham NE46 .45 D4
Newcastle-u-T NE6 .56 C6
Corbridge Roman Site★ NE45 .46 E6
Corbridge St NE6 .56 B6
Corbridge Sta NE45 .46 F4
Corby Gate SR2 .86 D4
Corby Gdns NE6 .56 F6
Corby Hall Dr SR2 .86 D4
Corchester Ave NE45 .46 F6
Corchester La NE46,NE45 .46 C7
Corchester Rd NE22 .10 F2
Corchester Terr NE45 .46 F6
Corchester Twrs NE45 .46 E7
Corchester Wlk NE7 .39 C4
Corfu Rd SR5 .74 A2
Corinthian Sq SR5 .74 A2
Cork St SR1 .103 B3
Cormorant Cl
Ashington NE63 .6 E1
Blyth NE24 .17 F4
4 Washington NE38 .82 F3
Cormorant Dr NE11 .100 A2
Corn Mill Dr DH5 .94 D6
Cornbank Cl SR3 .92 A5
Corndean NE38 .84 A4
Cornel Mews NE7 .39 C3
Cornel Rd NE7 .39 C3
Cornelia Cl 7 SR3 .92 A7
Corney St NE33 .59 B7
Cornfields The NE31 .57 E6
Cornforth Cl
Ashington NE63 .6 B2
Gateshead NE10 .72 C6
Cornhill Hedworth NE32 .58 C1
Newcastle-u-T NE5 .36 F1
Cornhill Ave NE3 .37 F7
Cornhill Cres NE29 .41 D7
Cornhill Rd
Cramlington NE23 .22 C6
6 Sunderland SR5 .75 B2
Cornmoor Gdns NE16 .69 B5
Cornmoor Rd NE16 .69 B6
Cornthwaite Dr SR6 .75 E8
Cornwall Rd NE31 .57 F3
Cornwallis NE37 .72 E1
Cornwallis Sq NE33 .42 B1
Cornwallis St 13 NE33 .42 C3
Cornwell Cres NE22 .16 B8
Cornwell Ct NE3 .38 F4
Coronation Ave
6 Ryhope SR2 .92 F6
Sunniside NE16 .69 B2
Coronation Bglws NE3 .38 D5
Coronation Cl SR1 .103 B3
Coronation Cotts NE61 .2 A3
Coronation Cres
Burnside DH4 .90 C2
High Pittington DH6 .96 B6
Whitley Bay NE25 .31 F4
Coronation Gn DH5 .97 D8
Coronation Rd
Newcastle-u-T NE5 .36 B3
Seaton Delaval NE25 .23 C3
Sunniside NE16 .69 B2
Coronation St
Annitsford NE23 .22 B1
Blyth NE24 .17 E6
Chester le S DH3 .88 D1
Newbiggin-by-t-S NE64 .7 E5
North Shields NE29 .42 A4
Ryton NE40 .52 E4
South Shields NE33 .42 C2
Sunderland SR1 .103 B3
Wallsend NE28 .40 C2
Coronation Terr
3 Boldon Colliery NE35 .58 E1
Chester le S DH3 .88 C2
7 Gateshead NE9 .70 F4
Hetton le H DH5 .95 A2
Kibblesworth NE11 .81 C6
21 Springwell NE9 .71 F1
Sunderland SR4 .85 B6

Coronation Terr *continued*
Tynemouth NE29 .31 B1
Corporation Rd SR2 .86 F4
Corporation St NE4 .98 C1
Corporation Yd 9 NE61 .3 F1
Corpus Christi RC Prim Sch NE8 .70 E8
Correction House Bank NE30 .42 C6
Corrighan Terr DH5 .94 C4
Corrofell Gdns NE10 .56 F1
Corry Ct SR4 .85 E4
Corsair NE16 .68 F6
Corsenside NE5 .36 F1
Corstopitum 3 NE28 .40 F4
Corstorphine Town NE33 .42 B1
Cortina Ave SR4 .85 D4
Corvan Terr DH9 .79 A2
Cosford Ct NE3 .37 C7
Cossack Terr SR4 .85 E7
Cosser St NE24 .17 B4
Cosserat Pl NE31 .57 D7
Coston Dr NE33 .42 C3
Cosyn St NE6 .56 A5
Cotehill Dr NE20 .25 B4
Cotehill Rd 2 NE5 .37 B1
Cotemede NE10 .72 A5
Cotemede Ct NE10 .72 A6
Cotfield Wlk NE8 .101 A1
Cotgarth The NE10 .71 E7
Cotherstone Ct SR3 .86 B2
Cotman Gdns NE34 .59 D2
Cotswold Ave
Chester le S DH2 .88 B1
Longbenton NE12 .29 B1
Cotswold Cl NE38 .83 B4
Cotswold Dr
Ashington NE63 .6 F1
Whitley Bay NE25 .31 F3
Cotswold Gdns
Dunston NE11 .70 A7
Newcastle-u-T NE7 .39 A3
Cotswold La NE35 .58 F2
Cotswold Rd
Sunderland SR5 .74 A2
Tynemouth NE29 .31 E2
Cotswold Sq SR5 .74 A3
Cottage Farm NE7 .39 D3
Cottage La NE5 .37 D1
Cottenham Chare NE4 .98 B1
Cottenham St NE4 .98 B1
Cotter Riggs Pl NE5 .36 B2
Cotter Riggs Wlk NE5 .36 B2
Cotterdale NE28 .39 F5
Cotterdale Ave 1 NE8 .70 F8
Cottersdale Gdns NE5 .36 B3
Cottinglea NE61 .3 F2
Cottingvale NE61 .3 F2
Cottingwood Ct NE4 .98 B2
Cottingwood Gdns
Morpeth NE61 .3 F1
Newcastle-u-T NE4 .98 B2
Cottingwood Gn NE24 .17 C3
Cottingwood La NE61 .3 F2
Cottonwood
Shiney Row DH4 .89 F6
Silksworth SR3 .91 E5
Coulson Cl NE46 .44 F2
Coulson Park Fst Sch NE63 .6 F2
Coulthards La NE8 .101 C3
Coulthards Pl NE8 .56 A4
Coulton Dr NE36 .74 D7
Council Ave DH4 .90 B6
Council Rd NE63 .6 C4
Council Terr NE37 .83 D7
Counden Rd 4 NE5 .36 E3
Countess Ave NE26 .32 A5
Countess Dr NE15 .54 A7
Coupland Gr NE32 .58 B3
Coupland Rd NE63 .6 C3
Court Rd NE22 .10 F1
Court The NE16 .69 C6
Courtfield Rd NE6 .56 F8
Courtney Ct NE3 .37 C7
Courtney Dr SR3 .91 F8
Cousin St SR1 .103 C3
Coutts Rd NE6 .56 E8
Cove The DH4 .90 B6
Coventry Gdns
Newcastle-u-T NE4 .54 E4
North Shields NE29 .41 E4
Coventry Way NE32 .58 B1
Coverdale Gateshead NE10 72 A6
Wallsend NE28 .39 F5
Coverdale Ave Blyth NE24 17 A7
Washington NE37 .83 C8
Coverdale Wlk NE33 .59 C7
Coverley Rd SR5 .74 B2
Covers The
Longbenton NE12 .39 E6
Morpeth NE61 .9 A7
Wallsend NE28 .40 B3
Whickham NE16 .53 F1
Cow La NE45 .46 F7
Cowan Cl NE21 .53 A4
Cowan Terr SR2 .103 A2
Cowans Ave NE12 .29 C4
Cowans Ho NE15 .53 C6
Cowdray Ct NE3 .37 C7
Cowdray Rd SR5 .74 B2
Cowdrey Ho NE29 .41 D3
Cowell Gr NE39 .67 C2
Cowen Gdns NE9 .71 A1
Cowen Rd NE21 .53 D3
Cowen St Blaydon NE21 .68 B8
Newcastle-u-T NE6 .56 F6
Cowen Terr NE39 .67 F3

Cowgarth NE46 .45 A5
Cowgate NE1 .99 B1
Cowley Cres DH5 .94 C4
Cowley Pl NE24 .17 B8
Cowley Rd NE24 .12 B1
Cowpath Gdns NE10 .57 A1
Cowpen Hall Rd NE24 .17 A8
Cowpen Rd NE24 .17 C8
Coxfoot Cl NE34 .59 C5
Coxgreen Rd DH4,SR4 .84 B2
Coxlodge Rd NE3 .38 A5
Coxlodge Terr NE3 .38 A5
Coxon St Gateshead NE10 .57 B2
Sunderland SR2 .103 B1
Coxon Terr NE8 .56 C1
Crabtree Rd NE43 .64 C7
Cradock Ave NE31 .57 D4
Craggyknowe NE37 .82 F6
Craghall Dene NE2 .38 E4
Craghall Dene Ave NE2 .38 E4
Cragleas NE16 .79 A4
Cragside
Brunswick Village NE13 .28 B6
Chester le S DH2 .88 A4
Corbridge NE45 .47 B7
Cramlington NE23 .22 C4
Newcastle-u-T NE7 .39 B3
South Shields NE34 .60 B5
Whitley Bay NE26 .31 E7
Cragside Ave NE29 .41 D8
Cragside CE Fst Sch NE23 .22 B4
Cragside Ct Dunston NE11 70 A6
4 Houghton-le-S DH5 .94 F8
Cragside Gdns
Bedlington NE22 .11 C3
Dunston NE11 .70 A5
Killingworth NE12 .29 F4
Wallsend NE28 .40 F3
Cragside Ho 5 SR3 .91 D7
Cragside Prim Sch NE7 .39 A3
Cragside Rd NE37 .83 A7
Cragston Ave NE5 .37 C3
Cragston Cl NE5 .37 C2
Cragton Gdns NE24 .17 B7
Craig Cres NE23 .29 A8
Craig St 2 DH3 .82 C4
Craigavon Rd SR5 .74 B2
Craigend NE23 .22 B5
Craighill 1 DH4 .90 A6
Craiglands The SR3 .86 C3
Craigmill Pk NE24 .17 A8
Craigmillar Ave NE5 .37 C3
Craigmillar Cl NE5 .37 C3
Craigmont Ct NE12 .39 D6
Craigshaw Rd SR5 .73 F3
Craigshaw Sq SR5 .73 F3
Craigwell Dr SR3 .92 A4
Craik Park (Morpeth Town AFC) NE61 .8 D6
Crake Way NE38 .82 F2
Cramer St NE8 .101 C1
Cramlington Beaconhill Fst Sch NE23 .21 E6
Cramlington Com High Sch NE23 .22 A4
Cramlington Eastlea Fst Sch NE23 .22 C8
Cramlington Hareside Fst Sch NE23 .22 A5
Cramlington Hillcrest Sch NE23 .22 B6
Cramlington Kramel Fst Sch NE23 .22 C5
Cramlington Parkside Mid Sch NE23 .22 B7
Cramlington Rd SR5 .73 F2
Cramlington Shanklea Fst Sch NE23 .22 B7
Cramlington Sq SR5 .73 F2
Cramlington Sta NE23 .21 F7
Cramlington Terr
2 Blyth NE24 .17 C4
10 Shiremoor NE27 .30 E1
Cramond Ct NE9 .70 E3
Cramond Way NE23 .22 B4
Cranberry Dr NE38 .83 E3
Cranberry Rd SR5 .74 B2
Cranberry Sq SR5 .74 A2
Cranborne SR3 .91 C6
Cranbourne Gr NE30 .32 B3
Cranbrook SR3 .86 A3
Cranbrook Ave NE3 .38 C7
Cranbrook Ct NE3 .37 E7
Cranbrook Dr NE42 .50 B2
Cranbrook Rd NE15 .54 B4
Cranemarsh Cl NE63 .6 C1
Craneshaugh Cl NE46 .45 E4
Cranesville NE9 .71 C5
Craneswater Ave NE26 .24 F1
Cranfield Pl NE15 .53 C7
Cranford Gdns NE15 .53 E7
Cranford St NE34 .59 C6
Cranford Terr SR4 .102 A1
Cranham Cl NE12 .29 F4
Cranlea NE3 .37 C6
Cranleigh Ave NE3 .37 C7
Cranleigh Gr NE42 .50 D3
Cranleigh Pl NE25 .31 D6
Cranleigh Rd SR5 .74 A2
Cranshaw Pl NE23 .22 C5
Cranston Pl SR2 .93 A6
Crantock Rd NE3 .37 F5
Cranwell Ct NE3 .37 C7
Cranwell Dr NE13 .28 B6

Craster Ave
Longbenton NE12 . . . . .29 F1
Shiremoor NE27 . . . . .30 F3
South Shields NE34 . . . . . .60 B8
Craster Cl Blyth NE24 . . .17 C7
Whitley Bay NE25 . . . . .31 D7
Craster Ct NE11 . . . . .70 C6
Craster Gdns NE28 . . . . .40 F3
Craster Rd NE29 . . . . . . .41 D5
Craster Sq NE3 . . . . .38 A6
Craster Terr NE7 . . . . . . .39 B2
Crathie DH3 . . . . .82 C7
Crathorne Ct NE16 . . . . .78 F6
Craven Ct SR6 . . . . .75 F1
Crawcrook La NE40,NE41 .51 D5
Crawcrook Terr NE40 . . . .51 E3
Crawford Cotts NE61 . . . . .4 A1
Crawford Ct SR3 . . . . .91 F6
Crawford Pl NE25 . . . . . . .31 E4
Crawford St NE24 . . . . . . .12 D1
Crawford Terr
Morpeth NE61 . . . . .4 A1
Newcastle-u-T NE6 . . . . . . .56 F5
Crawhall Cres NE61 . . . . . .8 E7
Crawhall Rd NE1 . . . . . . .99 C1
Crawley Ave NE31 . . . . . . .57 D3
Crawley Gdns NE16 . . . . .69 C2
Crawley Rd NE28 . . . . . . .40 B1
Crawley Sq NE31 . . . . . . .57 D3
Craythorne Gdns NE6 . . . .39 D2
Creevelea NE38 . . . . .83 C3
Creighton Ave NE3 . . . . . .37 E4
Creland Way NE15 . . . . . .37 C3
Crescent Ave NE46 . . . . . .44 F5
Crescent The
Chester le S DH2 . . . . .88 B3
Cleadon SR6 . . . . .74 F8
5 Dunston NE11 . . . . . . .69 F8
High Spen NE39 . . . . .95 A3
Hetton le H DH5 . . . . .95 A3
Jarrow NE32 . . . . .58 A4
Kibblesworth NE11 . . . . . . .81 C6
Morpeth NE61 . . . . .8 F6
New Silksworth SR3 . . . . . .86 A1
Newbottle DH4 . . . . .90 D4
Newcastle-u-T NE7 . . . . . . .39 B5
Newcastle-u-T,Kenton Bankfoot
NE13 . . . . .37 B6
Ponteland NE20 . . . . .25 A3
Rowlands Gill NE39 . . . . . . .67 F2
Ryton NE40 . . . . .52 D5
Seghill NE23 . . . . .22 F1
Shiney Row DH4 . . . . .90 A5
South Shields NE34 . . . . . .59 F5
Sunniside NE16 . . . . .69 B2
9 Throckley NE15 . . . . . . .35 D2
Tynemouth NE30 . . . . .42 C8
Wallsend NE28 . . . . .40 B3
Whickham NE16 . . . . .69 C6
Whitley Bay NE26 . . . . .32 B4
Wylam NE41 . . . . .51 B5
Crescent Vale NE26 . . . . .32 A4
Crescent Way NE12 . . . . .39 E8
Crescent Way N NE12 . . .39 E8
Crescent Way S NE12 . . .39 E8
Creslow NE10 . . . . .71 F4
Cressbourne Ave 5 SR6 .75 E4
Cresswell Ave
Longbenton NE12 . . . . .29 F1
Seaton Sluice NE26 . . . . . .24 C6
Tynemouth NE29 . . . . .41 F7
Cresswell Cl Blaydon NE21 68 A8
Whitley Bay NE25 . . . . .31 E3
Cresswell Dr Blyth NE24 . .17 C5
Newcastle-u-T NE3 . . . . . . .37 E7
Cresswell Home Farm Cotts
NE61 . . . . .2 B4
Cresswell Rd Ellington NE61 1 E6
Wallsend NE28 . . . . .40 A1
Cresswell St NE6 . . . . . . .56 D6
Cresswell Terr
Ashington NE63 . . . . .6 C4
Sunderland SR2 . . . . .102 C1
Crest The Bedlington NE22 .10 E1
Dinnington NE13 . . . . .27 B7
Seaton Sluice NE26 . . . . . .24 E4
Cresthaven NE10 . . . . . . .71 E6
Crichton Ave DH3 . . . . . . .88 D1
Cricket Terr NE16 . . . . . . .79 A6
Cricklewood Dr DH4 . . . .90 B6
Cricklewood Rd SR5 . . . .74 A1
Criddle St NE8 . . . . .56 A4
Crieff Gr NE32 . . . . .58 D3
Crieff Sq SR5 . . . . .73 F2
Crigdon Hill NE5 . . . . . . .36 F1
Crighton NE38 . . . . .83 A5
Crimdon Gr DH4 . . . . .94 C7
Crimea Rd SR5 . . . . .73 F2
Crindledykes NE38 . . . . . .83 E2
Cripps Ave NE10 . . . . .72 B8
Crocus Cl NE21 . . . . .53 A2
Croft Ave Longbenton NE12 39 E7
Sunderland SR4 . . . . .102 A2
Wallsend NE28 . . . . .40 C2
Croft Cl NE40 . . . . .52 D4
Croft Cotts NE43 . . . . . . .64 D7
Croft Ho NE42 . . . . .50 A4
Croft Rd NE24 . . . . .17 E7
Croft St NE1 . . . . .99 B1
Croft Terr
13 Hexham NE46 . . . . . . .45 A4
Horsley NE15 . . . . .50 C6
Jarrow NE32 . . . . .58 B6
Croft The Hexham NE46 . .44 F5
Killingworth NE12 . . . . .29 E4

Croft The continued
Nedderton NE22 . . . . .15 A8
Newcastle-u-T NE3 . . . . . . .38 A4
Ryton NE40 . . . . .52 D4
Sherburn Hill DH6 . . . . . . .96 D1
Croft View
Crawcrook NE40 . . . . .51 E3
Ovingham NE42 . . . . .50 B4
Croft Villas 2 NE40 . . . . .51 E3
Croft's La NE15 . . . . .50 C8
Croftdale Rd NE21 . . . . . .53 B2
Crofter Ct NE23 . . . . .22 A1
Crofthead Dr NE23 . . . . . .22 B4
Crofton Mill Ho 2 NE24 . .17 F7
Crofton Mill Ind Est NE24 17 F7
Crofton St
South Shields NE34 . . . . . .59 C6
Crofton Way NE15 . . . . . .53 B7
Crofts Ave NE45 . . . . .47 B5
Crofts Cl NE45 . . . . .47 B5
Crofts Pk NE61 . . . . .9 E5
Crofts The NE20 . . . . .25 F6
Crofts Way NE45 . . . . . . .47 A6
Croftside DH3 . . . . .82 C5
Croftside Ave 2 SR6 . . . .75 F8
Croftsway NE4 . . . . .54 F4
Croftway Fst Sch NE24 . . .17 E6
Croftwell Cl NE21 . . . . . . .53 D1
Cromarty DH2 . . . . .81 F2
Cromarty St SR6 . . . . .75 D2
Cromdale Pl NE5 . . . . .37 B1
Cromer Ave NE9 . . . . .70 F3
Cromer Ct NE9 . . . . .71 A3
Cromer Gdns
Newcastle-u-T NE2 . . . . . . .38 E3
Whitley Bay NE26 . . . . .32 A6
Crompton Rd NE6 . . . . . . .56 B8
Cromwell Ave NE21 . . . . .53 B2
Cromwell Ct
Newcastle-u-T NE10 . . . . . .57 C2
Ryton NE21 . . . . .53 A4
Cromwell Pl NE21 . . . . . . .53 A1
Cromwell Rd
Gateshead NE10 . . . . .57 B2
Whickham NE16 . . . . .69 C8
Cromwell St
Gateshead NE8 . . . . .56 A1
Ryton NE21 . . . . .53 A4
Sunderland SR4 . . . . .102 A3
Cromwell Terr
Gateshead NE8 . . . . .101 A1
Newcastle-u-T NE10 . . . . . .57 B2
North Shields NE29 . . . . . .41 F6
Crondall St NE33 . . . . . . .59 D7
Cronin Ave NE34 . . . . . . .59 B4
Cronniewell NE17 . . . . . . .77 B5
Crookham Gr NE61 . . . . . . .9 B5
Crookham Way NE23 . . . .22 C4
Crookhill Com Prim Sch
NE40 . . . . .52 E5
Crookhill Terr NE40 . . . . .52 E4
Croome Gdns NE61 . . . . . .4 F4
Cropthorne NE10 . . . . . . .72 B6
Crosby Gdns NE9 . . . . . . .71 B3
Crosland Pk NE23 . . . . . . .15 F2
Cross Ave NE28 . . . . .39 F4
Cross Carliol St NE1 . . . .99 B1
Cross Dr NE40 . . . . .52 C6
Cross Keys La NE9 . . . . . .70 F5
Cross La Dunston NE11 . . .54 D2
Kibblesworth NE11 . . . . . . .70 B4
Cross Morpeth St NE2 . . .98 B4
Cross Par NE4 . . . . .100 B4
Cross Pl SR1 . . . . .103 B3
Cross Rigg Cl
Penshaw DH4 . . . . .90 A7
Shiney Row DH4 . . . . .89 F7
Cross Row Gateshead NE8 56 B1
Ryton NE40 . . . . .52 C6
Cross Sheraton St NE2 . .98 B4
Cross St
8 Fence Houses DH4 . . . .94 A8
Gateshead NE8 . . . . .101 C1
High Pittington DH6 . . . . . .96 D3
Houghton-le-S DH4 . . . . . .90 D1
Newcastle-u-T NE1 . . . . . . .98 C1
Newcastle-u-T,St Ann's NE6 56 A5
Prudhoe NE42 . . . . .50 D3
Cross Terr NE39 . . . . .67 C1
Cross Vale Rd SR2 . . . . . .86 C4
Cross Villa Place No 1
NE4 . . . . .98 C1
Cross Villa Place No 2
NE4 . . . . .98 C1
Cross Villa Place No 3
NE4 . . . . .98 C1
Cross Villa Place No 4
NE4 . . . . .98 B1
Cross Villa Place No 5
NE4 . . . . .98 B1
Cross Way The NE61 . . . . .8 F6
Crossbank NE5 . . . . .37 D3
Crossbrook Rd 2 NE5 . . .37 D2
Crossby Ct SR2 . . . . .103 C1
Crossfell NE20 . . . . .25 C4
Crossfell Gdns NE62 . . . .11 A8
Crossfield Pk NE10 . . . . . .71 C6
Crossfield Terr NE6 . . . . .57 A4
Crossgate NE33 . . . . .42 C2
Crossgate Rd DH5 . . . . . .95 A2
Crossgill NE37 . . . . .83 B7
Crosshill Rd NE15 . . . . . . .54 B4
Crosslaw NE5 . . . . .36 F1
Crosslea Ave SR3 . . . . . . .86 B3

Crossley Terr
Longbenton NE12 . . . . .29 F1
Newcastle-u-T NE4 . . . . . . .98 A2
Crossway Gateshead NE9 .71 B6
Guide Post NE62 . . . . .10 F7
Newcastle-u-T NE2 . . . . . . .38 E3
South Shields NE34 . . . . . .60 A5
Tynemouth NE30 . . . . .42 C8
Crossway Ct NE5 . . . . . . .37 F3
Crossway The
Newcastle-u-T,Kenton NE3 . .37 F4
Newcastle-u-T,Lemington
NE15 . . . . .53 D7
Crossway Villas 1 NE9 . .71 A6
Crossways
East Boldon NE36 . . . . . . .74 E7
Hedworth NE32 . . . . .58 C1
New Silksworth SR3 . . . . . .91 F5
Crossways The NE13 . . . .28 A4
Crosthwaite Gr SR5 . . . . .74 A1
Croudace Row 2 NE10 . .71 D8
Crow Bank NE28 . . . . .40 C2
Crow Hall La NE23 . . . . . .21 F7
Crow Hall Rd NE23 . . . . . .15 F1
Crow La SR3 . . . . .91 B7
Crowhall La NE10 . . . . . . .71 D8
Crowhall Twrs 7 NE10 . . .71 D8
Crowley Ave NE16 . . . . . . .69 C8
Crowley Gdns NE21 . . . . .53 C2
Crowley Rd NE16 . . . . . . .54 A1
Crowley Villas 2 NE16 . . .54 A1
Crown & Anchor Cotts
NE15 . . . . .50 C8
Crown Rd SR5 . . . . .75 A1
Crown St Blyth NE24 . . . . .17 F7
12 Morpeth NE61 . . . . .9 A4
Crown Terr NE40 . . . . .52 B2
Crowther Ind Est
Birtley NE37 . . . . .82 F4
Washington NE38 . . . . .82 F5
Crowther Rd NE38 . . . . . .82 F5
Crowtree L Ctr SR1 . . . . .102 C2
Crowtree Rd SR1 . . . . . . .102 C3
Croxdale Ct 3 NE34 . . . . .59 A5
Croxdale Gdns NE10 . . . .57 A2
Croxdale Terr
Gateshead NE10 . . . . .57 A1
Greenside NE40 . . . . .52 C1
Croydon Rd NE4 . . . . .98 A2
Crozier St SR5 . . . . .75 C1
Cruddas Pk NE4 . . . . . . .100 A4
Cruddas Pk Sh Ctr NE4 .100 A4
Crudwell Cl NE35 . . . . . . .58 E2
Crummock Ave SR6 . . . . .75 C4
Crummock Ct NE28 . . . . . .41 A4
Crummock Rd NE5 . . . . . .54 B8
Crumstone Ct NE12 . . . . .29 E4
Crusade Wlk NE32 . . . . . .58 A5
Cty Cricket Gd NE2 . . . . . .99 C4
Cuba St SR2 . . . . .86 E4
Cuillin Cl NE38 . . . . .83 B3
Culford Pl NE28 . . . . .40 E6
Cullercoats Prim Sch
NE30 . . . . .32 C3
Cullercoats Rd NE15 . . . .73 F1
Cullercoats Sq SR5 . . . . .73 F1
Cullercoats St NE6 . . . . . .56 E6
Cullercoats Sta NE30 . . . .32 C3
Culloden Wlk NE12 . . . . . .29 D4
Culzean Ho 6 SR3 . . . . . .91 D7
Cumberland Ave
Bedlington NE22 . . . . .10 C1
Newbiggin-by-t-S NE64 . . . . .7 D4
Cumberland Pl
Birtley DH3 . . . . .82 D1
South Shields NE34 . . . . . .60 B7
Cumberland Rd
New Silksworth SR3 . . . . . .92 A8
Shiremoor NE29 . . . . .41 B7
Cumberland St
Sunderland SR1 . . . . .103 A3
Wallsend NE28 . . . . .40 C2
Wallsend,Willington Quay
NE28 . . . . .41 B1
Cumberland Way NE37 . . .72 D2
Cumberland Wlk NE7 . . . .39 B4
Cumbria Wlk NE4 . . . . . . .98 A1
Cumbrian Ave
Chester le S DH2 . . . . .88 C2
Sunderland SR6 . . . . .75 C5
Cumbrian Gdns NE11 . . . .70 A6
Cummings St NE24 . . . . . .17 E8
Curlew Cl Ashington NE63 .11 E8
Longbenton NE12 . . . . .39 A7
Ryton NE40 . . . . .52 E4
Washington NE38 . . . . .83 A2
Curlew Hill NE61 . . . . .3 D2
Curlew Ho NE33 . . . . .42 D3
Curlew Rd Jarrow NE32 . . .58 C8
Jarrow NE32 . . . . .58 D8
Curlew Way NE24 . . . . . . .17 E4
Curly Kews NE61 . . . . .8 E8
Curran Ho NE32 . . . . .58 C8
Curren Gdns NE10 . . . . . .56 C2
Curtis Rd NE4 . . . . .54 F7
Curzon Pl 6 NE5 . . . . . . .37 B2
Curzon Rd W NE28 . . . . . .40 B1
Curzon St NE28 . . . . .70 E8
Cushat Cl NE6 . . . . .56 C5
Cushy Cow La NE40 . . . . .52 D4
Cut Bank NE1 . . . . .56 A5
Cut Throat La NE17,NE39 .77 C4
Cuthbert Ct NE32 . . . . . . .58 E6
Cuthbert St
Gateshead NE8 . . . . .101 A2
Hebburn NE31 . . . . .57 D7
Sunniside NE16 . . . . .69 A1
Cuthbert Wlk NE3 . . . . . . .38 E5

Cuthbertson Ct SR6 . . . . .75 E5
Cutting St 3 SR7 . . . . . . .92 F1
Cygnet Cl Ashington NE63 .11 D8
Newcastle-u-T NE5 . . . . . . .36 D4
Cyncopa Way NE5 . . . . . .37 D2
Cypress Ave NE4 . . . . .54 D8
Cypress Cres Blyth NE24 . .17 E7
Dunston NE11 . . . . .70 A7
Cypress Dr NE24 . . . . .17 E7
Cypress Gdns Blyth NE24 .17 E7
Killingworth NE12 . . . . .29 C4
Cypress Rd Blaydon NE21 .53 C2
Gateshead NE9 . . . . .71 D2
Cypress Sq 12 SR3 . . . . . .92 A8
Cyprus Gdns NE9 . . . . . . .71 A6

D

D'arcy Ct SR1 . . . . .103 B2
Dachet Rd NE25 . . . . .31 D7
Dacre Cl NE45 . . . . .4 A1
Dacre Rd SR6 . . . . .75 D4
Dacre St Morpeth NE61 . . . .3 F1
South Shields NE33 . . . . . .59 C8
Daffodil Cl NE21 . . . . .53 B2
Dahlia Cl SR4 . . . . .102 B3
Dahlia Pl NE4 . . . . .54 D7
Dahlia Way NE31 . . . . . . .57 E4
Dainton Cl DH4 . . . . .90 C4
Dairnbrook 7 NE37 . . . . .83 A6
Dairy La DH4 . . . . .94 C8
Daisy Cotts 10 DH3 . . . . .82 C4
Dalamere Cl NE38 . . . . . . .89 B7
Dale NE25 . . . . .31 D4
Dale St Cambois NE24 . . . .12 E1
Crawcrook NE40 . . . . .51 F4
South Shields NE33 . . . . . .42 D3
Dale Terr SR6 . . . . .75 E2
Dale Top NE25 . . . . .23 F1
Dale View Gdns NE40 . . . .51 F3
Dalegarth Gr SR6 . . . . . . .75 C5
Dales The NE5 . . . . .37 E2
Dalla St SR4 . . . . .85 A7
Dally Mews NE3 . . . . .28 B1
Dalmahoy NE37 . . . . .72 D3
Dalmatia Terr NE24 . . . . . .17 E6
Dalston Pl NE24 . . . . .17 E4
Dalton Ave NE61 . . . . .2 A3
Dalton Cl NE23 . . . . .22 B6
Dalton Cres 28 NE6 . . . . .56 B6
Dalton Ct NE28 . . . . .39 F5
Dalton Pl
Newcastle-u-T NE5 . . . . . . .36 C3
Sunderland SR4 . . . . .102 B2
Dalton St
Newcastle-u-T NE6 . . . . . . .56 B5
Newcastle-u-T NE6 . . . . . . .56 B6
Dalton Terr NE17 . . . . .77 B8
Dalton Way DH4 . . . . .90 A7
Daltons La NE33 . . . . .42 B2
Dame Allan's Boys Sch
NE4 . . . . .54 E7
Dame Allan's Girls Sch
NE4 . . . . .54 E7
Dame Dorothy Cres 5
SR6 . . . . .75 E1
Dame Dorothy Prim Sch
SR6 . . . . .103 B4
Dame Dorothy St SR6 . . .103 A4
Dame Flora Robson Ave
NE34 . . . . .58 F4
Dame Margaret Hall
NE38 . . . . .83 E5
Damside 6 NE61 . . . . .9 A8
Danby Cl Silksworth SR3 . .92 B6
Washington NE38 . . . . .88 F8
Danby Gdns NE6 . . . . . . .39 D1
Danville Rd SR6 . . . . .75 E4
Darden Cl NE12 . . . . .29 F4
Darden Lough NE5 . . . . . .36 F1
Darenth St NE34 . . . . .59 C6
Darien Ave SR6 . . . . .75 D4
Dark La NE61 . . . . .4 A1
Darley Ct 15 SR3 . . . . . . .91 F6
Darley Pl NE15 . . . . .54 A5
Darnell Pl NE4 . . . . .98 B2
Darnley Rd NE63 . . . . .6 C3
Darras Ct NE33 . . . . .42 D1
Darras Dr NE29 . . . . .41 F7
Darras Hall Fst Sch NE20 25 C3
Darras Mews NE20 . . . . . .25 C4
Darras Rd NE20 . . . . .25 D4
Darrell St NE13 . . . . .28 A6
Dartford Cl NE25 . . . . .23 E3
Dartford Rd
South Shields NE33 . . . . . .42 D1
Sunderland SR6 . . . . .75 D4
Dartmouth Ave NE9 . . . . .70 F2
Darvall Cl NE25 . . . . .31 C4
Darwin Cres NE3 . . . . .37 F3
Darwin St SR5 . . . . .74 F2
Daryl Cl NE21 . . . . .53 A1
Daryl Way NE10 . . . . .72 D8
Davenport Dr NE3 . . . . . . .28 B1
Davenport Sch DH5 . . . . .94 F6
David Adams Ho 7 NE15 54 D5
David Gdns SR6 . . . . .75 F3
David St NE28 . . . . .40 B2
David Terr 8 NE40 . . . . . .51 F3
Davidson Cotts NE2 . . . . .38 C3
Davidson Rd NE10 . . . . . . .57 B2
Davidson St NE10 . . . . . . .71 D8
Davison Ave
New Silksworth SR3 . . . . . .92 B7
Whitley Bay NE26 . . . . .31 F6
Davison St Blyth NE24 . . . .17 E8

Davison St continued
Boldon Colliery NE35 . . . . .58 E1
Newburn NE15 . . . . .52 E8
Davison Terr 3 SR5 . . . . .75 A2
Davy Bank NE28 . . . . .40 D1
Dawlish Cl NE29 . . . . .41 D8
Dawlish Gdns NE9 . . . . . .70 F3
Dawlish Pl NE5 . . . . .36 C3
Dawson Pl NE61 . . . . .3 F1
Dawson Sq 4 NE30 . . . . .42 D7
Dawson St 5 NE6 . . . . . . .57 A6
Dawson Terr SR4 . . . . . . .85 A7
Daylesford Dr NE3 . . . . . . .38 A4
Daylesford Rd NE23 . . . . .16 A2
Dayshield NE5 . . . . .36 F1
De Merley Rd NE61 . . . . . . .3 E2
De Mowbray Way NE61 . . .3 D2
De Walden Sq NE61 . . . . . .4 E3
De Walden Terr NE61 . . . . .4 F3
Deacon Cl NE15 . . . . .36 B2
Deacon Ct NE12 . . . . .39 A7
Deaconsfield Cl SR3 . . . . .91 F5
Deadridge La NE45 . . . . . .47 B7
Deal Cl NE24 . . . . .17 E4
Dean Ct 6 NE24 . . . . .17 D8
Dean Ho NE6 . . . . .57 A8
Dean Rd
South Shields NE33 . . . . . .59 B7
South Shields,Dean NE33 . .59 C8
Dean St Gateshead NE9 . . .71 A5
Hexham NE46 . . . . .45 C5
Newcastle-u-T NE1 . . . . . . .99 B1
Dean Terr Ryton NE40 . . . .52 C5
South Shields NE33 . . . . . .59 B7
Sunderland SR5 . . . . .75 A1
Dean View Dr NE24 . . . . . .17 B8
Deanery St NE22 . . . . .10 F1
Deanham Gdns NE5 . . . . .54 D8
Deans Ave NE64 . . . . .7 C5
Deans Cl 1 NE16 . . . . .69 B7
Deansfield Cl SR3 . . . . . . .91 F5
Deansfield Gr NE15 . . . . . .36 B3
Dearham Gr NE23 . . . . . . .16 A2
Debden Ho 7 NE11 . . . . . .70 A8
Debdon Gdns NE6 . . . . . . .39 D1
Debdon Pl NE23 . . . . .22 B6
Debdon Rd NE63 . . . . .6 F2
Debussy Ct NE32 . . . . . . .58 C6
December Ctyd NE8 . . . .100 B2
Deckham St 11 NE8 . . . . .71 A8
Deckham Terr NE8,NE9 . . .71 A8
Dee Rd NE31 . . . . .57 F3
Dee St NE32 . . . . .58 C7
Deel Ho 2 SR3 . . . . .91 D7
Deepbrook Rd 5 NE5 . . . .37 C1
Deepdale Wallsend NE28 . .39 F5
Washington NE38 . . . . .83 A1
Deepdale Cl NE16 . . . . . . .68 F4
Deepdale Cres NE5 . . . . . .37 E2
Deepdale Gdns NE12 . . . .29 C3
Deepdale Gn NE5 . . . . . . .37 E2
Deepdale Rd NE30 . . . . . .32 B2
Deepdale St DH5 . . . . .95 A2
Deepdene Gr SR6 . . . . . . .75 E5
Deepdene Rd SR6 . . . . . . .75 D5
Deer Bush NE5 . . . . .36 F1
Deer Park Way NE21 . . . . .53 E1
Deerbolt Pl NE12 . . . . .39 C7
Deerfell Cl NE63 . . . . .6 B2
Deerness Rd SR2 . . . . . .103 B1
Dees Ave NE28 . . . . .40 B3
Defender Ct SR5 . . . . .85 C8
Deighton Wlk NE5 . . . . . . .36 F1
Delacour Rd NE21 . . . . . . .53 C3
Delamere Cres NE23 . . . .16 A2
Delamere Ct 8 SR3 . . . . .92 A6
Delamere Rd NE3 . . . . . . .37 F5
Delaval DH2 . . . . .88 A3
Delaval Ave
North Shields NE29 . . . . . .41 E6
Seaton Delaval NE25 . . . . .23 C3
Delaval Com Mid Sch
NE24 . . . . .17 D5
Delaval Com Prim Sch
NE15 . . . . .54 B8
Delaval Cres NE24 . . . . . .17 B4
Delaval Ct
Bedlington NE22 . . . . .11 C2
Longbenton NE12 . . . . .29 E1
15 South Shields NE33 . . .42 D1
Delaval Gdns Blyth NE24 . .17 B4
Newcastle-u-T NE15 . . . . . .54 B4
Delaval Rd
Newcastle-u-T,Delaval NE15 54 B4
Newcastle-u-T,Old Benwell
NE15 . . . . .54 B5
Whitley Bay NE26 . . . . .32 C4
Longbenton NE12 . . . . .29 D1
Delaval St NE24 . . . . .17 B4
Delaval Terr Blyth NE24 . . .17 B4
Newcastle-u-T NE3 . . . . . . .38 A3
Delaval Trad Est NE25 . . .23 C5
Delhi Cres NE40 . . . . .52 A3
Delhi Gdns NE40 . . . . .52 A3
Delhi View NE40 . . . . .52 A3
Dell The Morpeth NE61 . . . .3 E3
Newbottle DH4 . . . . .90 D3
Dellfield Dr SR4 . . . . .85 A4
Delton Cl NE38 . . . . .83 E3
Delton Cl NE38 . . . . .83 E3
Demesne Dr NE22 . . . . . . .15 F8
Demesne The NE63 . . . . . .7 B2
Dempsey Rd NE13 . . . . . . .28 C4
Denbeigh Pl NE12 . . . . . . .39 C7
Denbigh Ave
Sunderland SR6 . . . . .75 D4
Wallsend NE28 . . . . .41 A3

Denbigh Com Prim Sch
NE28 41 A3
Denby Cl NE23 16 A2
Dene Ave
Brunswick Village NE13 28 A6
Hexham NE46 45 C4
Houghton-le-S DH5 95 A7
Killingworth NE12 29 A2
Newcastle-u-T,Denton Burn
NE15 53 D7
Newcastle-u-T,South Gosforth
NE3 38 E4
Rowlands Gill NE39 67 D1
Dene Bank View NE3 37 E3
Dene Cl Newcastle-u-T NE7 39 A1
Ovingham NE42 50 B5
Riding Mill NE44 62 F8
Ryton NE40 52 D5
Dene Cres
Newcastle-u-T NE3 38 E4
Rowlands Gill NE39 67 D1
Ryton NE40 52 D5
Wallsend NE28 40 D2
Whitley Bay NE26 31 F6
Dene Ct Birtley DH3 82 C7
Hamsterley NE17 77 B6
Newcastle-u-T NE7 39 B1
Washington NE38 83 C6
Dene Farm Cotts NE15 35 E2
Dene Garth NE42 50 A5
Dene Gdns
Gateshead NE10 57 B1
Houghton-le-S DH5 94 F7
Newcastle-u-T NE15 53 D6
Whitley Bay NE25 31 E5
Dene Gr
Newcastle-u-T NE3 38 E4
Prudhoe NE42 50 B3
Seghill NE23 23 B2
Dene La Cleadon SR6 75 C7
Sunderland SR6 75 D4
Dene Mews SR5 74 C1
Dene Pk Hexham NE46 45 C4
Ponteland NE20 25 B3
Sunderland SR5 74 C1
Dene Rd Blaydon NE21 53 D3
Guide Post NE62 10 E7
Rowlands Gill NE39 67 D1
Sunderland SR5 74 C1
Tynemouth NE30 42 C8
Wylam NE41 51 B7
Dene Side NE21 53 D2
Dene St Hetton le H DH5 95 B6
Holywell NE25 23 F2
New Silksworth SR3 86 A1
Prudhoe NE42 50 E3
Sunderland SR4 85 F7
Dene Terr Blaydon NE21 53 B2
Jarrow NE32 58 A4
Newburn NE15 52 F8
Newcastle-u-T NE3 38 E4
Ovington NE42 49 D4
Riding Mill NE44 62 F8
Dene Terr E NE41 51 A7
Dene Terr W NE41 51 A7
Dene The Medomsley DH8 77 A2
West Rainton DH4 94 A2
Whitley Bay NE25 31 E5
Wylam NE41 51 B6
Dene View Ashington NE63 6 B3
Bedlington NE22 11 C1
Burnopfield NE16 79 A6
Ellington NE61 1 E4
High Spen NE39 67 A3
Newcastle-u-T NE3 38 E4
Rowlands Gill NE39 67 C2
Dene View Cres SR4 85 B6
Dene View Ct NE24 17 B7
Dene View Dr NE24 17 B8
Dene View E NE22 11 C1
Dene View W NE22 16 B8
Dene Villas DH3 88 D1
Denebank NE25 31 E5
Deneburn NE10 72 A7
Denecrest DH8 77 A2
Denecroft NE41 51 A6
Deneford NE9 71 A1
Deneholm Wallsend NE28 40 D3
Whitley Bay NE25 31 E5
Denelands NE46 45 C5
Deneside Dunston NE11 69 F7
Hedworth NE32 58 C1
Newcastle-u-T NE5 36 F4
Newcastle-u-T,Denton Burn
NE15 54 A7
Seghill NE23 23 A2
South Shields NE34 60 C6
Deneside Ave NE9 70 F4
Deneside Cl NE15 35 D2
Deneside Ct
Newcastle-u-T NE2 56 A8
Whitley Bay NE26 31 E8
Denesyde DH8 77 A2
Deneway NE39 68 A4
Denewell Ave
Gateshead NE9 70 F5
Newcastle-u-T NE7 39 A3
Denewood NE12 29 E2
Denewood Ct NE28 41 A2
Denham Ave SR6 75 D4
Denham Dr NE25 23 D2
Denham Gr NE21 67 F8
Denham Wlk NE5 36 C3
Denhill Pk NE15 54 D6
Denholm Ave NE23 16 A2
Denholme Lodge NE11 100 A1
Denmark Ct 10 NE6 56 C7
Denmark Ctr 14 NE33 42 C3
Denmark St
Gateshead NE8 101 C2
2 Newcastle-u-T NE6 56 C6
Dennison Cres DH3 82 C6
Denshaw Cl NE23 16 B2
Dent Cl DH6 97 E3
Dent St Blyth NE24 17 F6
Sunderland SR6 75 D4
Dentdale DH4 89 E8
Denton Ave
Newcastle-u-T NE15 53 D6
North Shields NE29 41 C6
Denton Chare NE1 101 A4
Denton Ct NE5 54 A7
Denton Gate NE5 37 A3
Denton Gdns NE15 54 C5
Denton Gr NE5 37 A3
Denton Park Ho NE5 36 E2
Denton Park Sh Ctr NE5 36 E2
Denton Rd NE15 53 F6
Denton View NE21 53 B2
Denver Gdns NE6 56 E5
Denway Gr NE26 24 B7
Denwick Ave NE15 53 C6
Denwick Terr NE30 42 C7
Depot Rd NE6 56 D7
Deptford Rd
Gateshead NE8 56 A4
Sunderland SR4 102 B3
Deptford Terr SR4 102 A4
Derby Cres NE31 57 D5
Derby Ct NE4 98 B2
Derby Gdns NE28 40 A3
Derby St Jarrow NE32 58 C7
Newcastle-u-T NE4 98 B2
South Shields NE33 42 C2
Sunderland SR2 102 C2
Derby Terr NE33 42 D2
Dereham Cl NE26 24 D5
Dereham Ct NE5 37 B4
Dereham Rd NE26 24 D5
Dereham Terr NE62 11 C8
Dereham Way NE29 41 B8
Derry Ave SR6 75 E4
Derwent Ave
Gateshead NE11 70 D5
Hebburn NE31 57 E3
Newburn NE15 52 E7
Rowlands Gill NE39 67 E1
Derwent Cote NE17 77 B5
Derwent Cres
Hamsterley NE17 77 B5
Whickham NE16 69 B8
Derwent Crook Dr NE9 70 E5
Derwent Ct
Gateshead NE11 70 D5
Newcastle-u-T NE7 39 A4
Derwent Gdns
Gateshead NE9 71 A5
Wallsend NE28 41 A4
Derwent Haven NE17 77 B5
Derwent Rd Hexham NE46 45 C4
Seaton Sluice NE26 24 C6
Tynemouth NE30 32 B2
Derwent St
Blackhall Mill NE17 77 C6
Chopwell NE17 66 B1
Hetton le H DH5 95 B2
Newcastle-u-T NE15 54 B5
Penshaw DH4 90 B6
Sunderland SR1 102 C2
Derwent Terr
Burnopfield NE16 79 B7
South Hetton DH6 97 E8
Washington NE38 83 E4
Derwent Twr NE11 100 A1
Derwent Valley Cotts
NE39 67 F1
Derwent Valley Villas
NE17 77 A6
Derwent View
Blaydon NE21 53 B1
Burnopfield NE16 79 B6
Chopwell NE17 66 C2
Derwent View Terr DH9 78 D1
Derwent Walk Cty Pk★
NE16,NE21,NE39 68 C5
Derwent Way
Blaydon NE21 53 E1
Killingworth NE12 29 C3
Derwentcote Steel Furnace★
NE17 77 E6
Derwentdale Gdns NE7 39 B3
Derwenthaugh Ind Est
NE16 53 F3
Derwenthaugh Marina
NE21 54 A3
Derwenthaugh Rd NE21 54 A3
Derwentwater Ave 1
DH2 88 B1
Derwentwater Ct NE8 101 A1
Derwentwater Gdns
NE16 69 D7
Derwentwater Rd
Gateshead NE8 100 C1
Newbiggin-by-t-S NE64 7 C3
Gateshead NE9 70 B8
Derwentwater Terr NE33 59 C8
Deuchar Ho NE2 99 C3
Deuchar St NE2 99 C4
Devon Ave NE16 69 C7
Devon Cl NE63 5 F4
Devon Cres DH3 82 B6
Devon Dr SR3 92 A8
Devon Gdns
Gateshead NE9 70 F7
South Shields NE34 60 B7
Devon Rd Hebburn NE31 57 F3
Devon Rd *continued*
Tynemouth NE29 31 D1
Devon St Hetton le H DH5 94 F4
Penshaw DH4 90 C6
Devon Wlk NE37 72 D1
Devonport DH4 90 C3
Devonshire Dr NE27 30 C1
Devonshire Gdns NE28 40 A3
Devonshire Pl NE2 38 F1
Devonshire St
South Shields NE33 59 B7
Sunderland SR5 75 C1
Devonshire Terr
Newcastle-u-T NE2 99 A3
7 Whitley Bay NE26 32 B4
Devonshire Twr 1 SR5 75 D1
Devonworth Pl NE24 17 A7
Dewberry Cl NE24 17 C4
Dewhurst Terr 5 NE16 69 B2
Dewley NE23 22 B5
Dewley Ct NE23 22 B5
Dewley Pl NE5 36 E4
Dewley Rd NE5 37 B1
Dewsgreen NE23 22 B6
Dexter Ho NE29 41 D3
Dexter Way NE10 71 C8
Deyncourt NE20 25 D2
Deyncourt Cl NE20 25 D1
Dial Cottage Mus★ NE12 29 C1
Diamond Ct NE3 37 D5
Diamond Hall Jun & Inf Sch
SR4 85 F7
Diamond Sq 5 NE46 45 B4
Diamond St NE28 40 B2
Diana St NE4 98 B1
Dibley Sq 5 NE6 56 B5
Dibley St 6 NE6 56 B5
Dick St 12 NE40 51 F3
Dickens Ave
Biddick Hall NE34 59 B3
Whickham NE16 69 A8
Dickens St
Houghton-le-S DH4 94 D8
Sunderland SR5 75 A1
Dickens Wlk NE5 36 C3
Dickson Dr NE46 44 E3
Didcot Ave NE29 41 E4
Didcot Way NE36 73 E7
Dillon St NE32 58 A5
Dilston Ave Hexham NE46 45 D4
Whitley Bay NE25 32 B4
Dilston Cl Pegswood NE61 5 A3
Shiremoor NE27 30 F2
Washington NE38 83 A4
Dilston Dr Ashington NE63 6 D2
Newcastle-u-T NE5 36 E3
Dilston Gdns SR4 85 F5
Dilston Haugh Cotts
NE45 46 D4
Dilston Rd NE4 98 A2
Dilston Terr Jarrow NE32 58 C3
Newcastle-u-T NE3 38 E4
Dilston West Cotts NE45 46 C2
Dimbula Gdns NE7 39 D2
Dinmont Pl NE23 22 B5
Dinnington Fst Sch NE13 27 C7
Dinsdale Ave NE28 40 C4
Dinsdale Cotts 3 SR2 92 F6
Dinsdale Pl NE2 99 C3
Dinsdale Rd
Newcastle-u-T NE2 99 C3
2 Sunderland SR6 75 E2
Dinsdale St SR2 92 F6
Dinsdale St S SR2 92 F6
Dipe La NE36 74 B7
Dipton Ave NE4 54 E4
Dipton Cl NE46 45 E4
Dipton Gdns SR3 86 B2
Dipton Gr NE23 22 B6
Dipton Rd NE25 31 D7
Dipwood Rd NE39 67 E1
Dipwood Way NE39 78 D8
Discovery Ct SR3 91 F7
Dishforth Gn NE9 71 B1
Dispensary La 3 NE1 99 A1
Disraeli St Blyth NE24 17 D8
Blyth NE24 17 E8
Fence Houses DH4 94 B8
Disraeli Terr NE17 66 B1
Dissington Pl
Newcastle-u-T NE5 54 C8
Whickham NE16 69 A5
Ditchburn Terr SR4 85 F8
Dixon Ave DH8 76 F4
Dixon Pl NE11 69 F8
Dixon Rd DH5 94 D6
Dixon St Gateshead NE8 100 C1
South Shields NE33 42 C1
Dixon's Sq SR6 103 A4
Dobson Cl NE4 100 B3
Dobson Cres NE6 56 C4
Dock Rd NE29 42 A4
Dock Rd S NE29 42 A3
Dock St South Shields NE33 59 B7
Sunderland SR6 75 E1
Dockendale La NE16 69 C7
Dockendale Mews NE16 69 C7
Dockwray Cl NE30 42 C6
Dockwray Sq NE30 42 B5
Doddfell Cl NE37 83 A6
Doddington Cl NE15 53 B7
Doddington Dr NE23 22 B6
Doddington Villas NE10 71 C7
Dodds Ct 3 SR5 74 A3
Dodds Farm NE3 38 A5
Dodds Terr DH3 82 C6
Dodsworth N NE40 52 B1
Dodsworth Terr NE40 52 B1
Dodsworth Villas NE40 52 B1
Dog Bank NE1 101 B4
Dogger Bank NE61 3 E1
Dolphin Ct 1 NE4 54 D5
Dolphin Quay NE29 42 B5
Dolphin St NE4 54 D5
Dolphin Villas NE13 28 B4
Dominies Cl NE39 67 F3
Don Dixon Dr NE32 58 B1
Don Gdns
Washington NE37 72 D1
West Boldon NE36 73 F7
Don Rd NE32 58 D7
Don St NE11 70 C4
Don View NE36 74 A7
Donald Ave DH6 97 F8
Donald St NE3 38 E5
Doncaster Rd NE2 99 C3
Doncrest Rd NE37 72 B1
Donkin Rd NE37 82 F7
Donkin Terr
Crawcrook NE40 51 E3
North Shields NE30 42 C7
Donkins St NE35 58 E1
Donnington Ho 1 SR3 91 D7
Donnington Cl SR5 74 A1
Donnington Ct NE3 38 F4
Donnison Gdns SR1 103 B3
Donridge NE37 72 B1
Donside NE10 71 F4
Donvale Rd NE37 72 A1
Dorcas Ave NE15 54 C5
Dorcas Terr 3 NE37 83 D8
Dorchester Cl NE5 36 B3
Dorchester Ct NE25 23 C6
Dorchester Gdns NE9 70 F2
Doris Wilkes Ho NE6 56 B6
Dorking Ave NE29 41 E4
Dorking Cl NE24 17 E4
Dorking Rd SR6 75 E4
Dornoch Cres NE10 71 E6
Dorrington Rd NE3 37 E7
Dorset Ave Birtley DH3 82 D1
Hebburn NE31 57 F5
South Shields NE34 60 B7
Sunderland SR6 75 E4
Wallsend NE28 40 A3
Dorset Cl NE63 5 F4
Dorset Gr NE29 31 D1
Dorset Rd Gateshead NE8 56 A4
Newcastle-u-T NE15 53 F6
Dorset St DH5 97 C8
Dotland Cl NE46 45 E4
Double Row NE25 23 B5
Douglas Ave NE3 38 A4
Douglas Bader Ho NE24 17 F6
Douglas Cl NE34 59 C4
Douglas Ct
Gateshead NE11 70 E2
Sunderland SR1 103 B3
Douglas Gdns NE11 70 A7
Douglas Par NE31 58 A2
Douglas Rd SR6 75 E4
Douglas St NE28 41 A1
Douglas Terr
Newcastle-u-T NE4 98 B1
Penshaw DH4 90 C8
Washington NE37 72 D1
Douglass St 7 NE28 40 B2
Doulting Cl NE12 39 B6
Dove Ave NE32 58 C3
Dove Cl NE12 29 C4
Dove Ct 10 Birtley DH3 82 C5
Tynemouth NE30 32 C3
Dove Ho NE30 32 C3
Dove Row NE30 32 C3
Dovecote Cl NE25 31 C6
Dovecote Rd NE12 39 E7
Dovecrest Ct 7 NE28 40 F4
Dovedale Ave NE24 17 A8
Dovedale Ct 7 NE34 59 A5
Dovedale Gdns
Gateshead NE9 71 A4
Newcastle-u-T NE7 39 B3
Dovedale Rd SR6 75 C5
Dover Cl Bedlington NE22 10 D1
Newcastle-u-T NE5 36 C3
Dovercourt Rd NE6 57 A4
Dowling Ave NE25 31 F4
Downe Cl NE24 17 E4
Downend Rd NE5 36 E3
Downfield NE37 72 D3
Downham NE5 36 F1
Downham Ct NE33 42 C1
Downhill Inf Sch NE34 60 B7
Downhill La
Sunderland SR5,NE36 73 F5
West Boldon NE36 73 D4
Downing Dr NE61 8 E7
Downs La DH5 95 B5
Downs Pit La DH5 95 C5
Downswood NE12 29 F3
Doxford Ave DH5 94 F6
Doxford Gdns 4 NE5 37 D1
Doxford Park Way SR3 91 E6
Doxford Pl NE23 22 B5
Doxford Terr DH5 94 F6
Dr Pit Cotts NE22 10 F1
Dr Ryman Ho NE6 57 A5
Drake Cl NE33 59 B8
Drawback NE42 50 D2
Drawback Cl NE42 50 D2
Drayton Rd
Newcastle-u-T NE3 37 E4
Sunderland SR6 75 D4
Drey The NE20 25 B3
Drive Com Prim Sch The
NE10 71 E8
Drive The Birtley DH3 82 D1
Gateshead,Felling NE10 71 E8
Gateshead,Saltwell NE9 70 F6
Newcastle-u-T NE7 39 B4
Newcastle-u-T,East Denton
NE5 54 A8
Newcastle-u-T,Gosforth
NE3 38 C3
Stannington NE61 14 D6
Tranwell NE61 8 D1
Tynemouth NE30 42 D8
Wallsend NE28 40 B2
Washington NE37 72 C1
Whickham NE16 69 C6
Drivecote NE10 71 E8
Dronfield Cl 2 DH2 88 A1
Drove Rd NE15 35 B3
Drum Ind Est DH2 88 B7
Drum Rd DH2,DH3 88 B8
Drumaldrace 5 NE37 83 A6
Drummond Cres NE34 58 F5
Drummond Rd NE3 37 F4
Drummond Terr NE30 42 B6
Drumoyne Cl SR3 91 B6
Drumoyne Gdns NE25 31 D3
Drumsheugh Pl NE5 37 B2
Druridge Ave SR6 75 E5
Druridge Cres Blyth NE24 17 B5
South Shields NE34 60 B8
Druridge Dr Blyth NE24 17 B5
Newcastle-u-T NE5 37 D1
Drury La
Newcastle-u-T NE1 99 A1
Sunderland SR1 103 B3
Tynemouth NE29 41 C7
Drybeck Ct
Cramlington NE23 22 D8
Newcastle-u-T NE4 98 B1
Drybeck Sq SR3 92 B6
Drybeck Wlk NE23 22 D8
Dryborough St SR4 102 B3
Dryburgh NE38 83 D5
Dryburgh Cl NE29 41 E8
Dryden Cl NE34 59 B2
Dryden Ct 5 NE9 70 F8
Dryden Rd NE9 70 F7
Dryden Road Hospl NE9 70 F8
Dryden Sch NE9 71 A7
Dryden St SR5 75 A2
Drysdale Cres NE13 28 A6
Drysdale Ct NE13 28 B6
Dubmire Cotts DH4 94 A8
Dubmire Ct DH4 94 A8
Dubmire Ind Est DH4 90 B1
Dubmire Prim Sch DH4 94 A8
Duchess Cres NE32 58 B3
Duchess Cres E NE32 58 B3
Duchess Dr NE15 54 A7
Duchess St NE26 32 A5
Duckets Dean NE42 50 D3
Duckpool La NE16 69 C7
Duckpool La N NE16 69 C8
Duddon Pl NE9 71 B4
Dudley Ave SR6 75 D4
Dudley Bsns Ctr NE23 22 A2
Dudley Dr NE23 29 A8
Dudley Gdns SR3 91 C7
Dudley Ho NE4 98 B2
Dudley La Annitsford NE23 22 A2
Cramlington,Collingwood
NE23 22 A4
Cramlington,Hall Close
NE23 22 A6
Seaton Burn NE13,NE23 28 D8
Dudley Lane Cotts NE13 28 C8
Dugdale Ct 6 NE3 37 D5
Dugdale Rd NE3 37 D5
Duke of Northumberland Ct
9 NE28 40 E5
Duke St Ashington NE63 6 C4
Gateshead NE10 57 A1
Newcastle-u-T NE1 100 C4
North Shields NE29 42 B4
Sunderland SR4 102 A2
Whitley Bay NE26 32 A5
Duke St N SR6 75 D2
Duke Wlk NE8 100 C1
Duke's Ave NE31 57 D4
Duke's Gdns NE24 17 C8
Dukes Cott NE15 52 F7
Dukes Ct NE42 50 E4
Dukes Dr NE3 28 B1
Dukes Mdw NE13 36 E8
Dukes Rd NE46 44 E5
Dukes Way NE42 50 E4
Dukesfield NE23 22 B6
Dukesway NE11 70 C4
Dukesway Ct NE11 70 C3
Dukesway W NE11 70 C2
Dulverston Cl NE5 36 C3
Dulverton Ave NE33 59 D7
Dulverton Ct NE2 38 F2
Dumas Wlk NE5 36 C3
Dumbarton Cl SR4 85 D3
Dumfries Cres NE32 58 E3
Dun Cow St SR1 102 C3
Dunbar Cl NE5 36 C3
Dunbar St SR4 85 F5
Dunblane Cres NE5 36 F1
Dunblane Dr NE24 17 E4
Dunblane Rd SR6 75 E4
Dunbreck Gr SR4 86 A4
Duncan Gdns NE61 8 F7
Duncan St Gateshead NE8 56 B1
Newcastle-u-T NE6 57 A5

Duncan St continued
Sunderland SR4 . . . . .85 F7
Dunces Hos NE61 . . . . .9 D7
Dundas St SR6 . . . . .103 A4
Dundas Way NE10 . . . . . . .71 C8
Dundee Cl NE5 . . . . .36 C3
Dundee Ct NE32 . . . . .58 E3
Dundrennan NE38 . . . . . . .83 C3
Dunelm SR2 . . . . .86 B4
Dunelm Cl 6 DH3 . . . . . .82 C4
Dunelm Dr
Houghton-le-S DH4 . . . . .94 D7
West Boldon NE36 . . . . . .74 B8
Dunelm Rd DH5 . . . . .94 F4
Dunelm S SR4 . . . . .86 B4
Dunelm St NE33 . . . . .42 D2
Dunford Gdns NE5 . . . . . .36 C4
Dunholm Cl DH5 . . . . .94 E7
Dunholme Rd NE4 . . . . . . .54 F5
Dunira Cl NE2 . . . . .38 F2
Dunira Ho NE2 . . . . .38 F2
Dunkeld Cl Blyth NE24 . . .17 E4
Gateshead NE10 . . . . .72 B8
Shiney Row DH4 . . . . . . .89 F5
Dunkirk Ave DH5 . . . . . . .94 F7
Dunlin Cl NE40 . . . . .52 E4
Dunlin Ct NE61 . . . . .2 A3
Dunlin Dr Blyth NE24 . . . .17 E4
Washington NE38 . . . . . . .82 F3
Dunlop Cl NE7 . . . . .39 C4
Dunlop Cres NE34 . . . . . .60 A6
Dunmoor Cl NE3 . . . . . . .38 A4
Dunmoor Ct DH2 . . . . . . .88 A1
Dunmore Ave SR6 . . . . . .75 E4
Dunmorlie St NE6 . . . . . .56 D6
Dunn Ave SR3 . . . . .86 A1
Dunn St NE4 . . . . .100 B3
Dunn Street Prim Sch
NE32 . . . . .58 C7
Dunn Terr NE6 . . . . .56 B6
Dunn's Terr NE2 . . . . . . .98 B4
Dunne Rd NE21 . . . . .53 E4
Dunning St SR1 . . . . . . .102 C3
Dunnlynn Cl SR3 . . . . . . .91 E6
Dunnock Dr
Sunniside NE16 . . . . .69 A3
Washington NE38 . . . . . . .82 F2
Dunnock Lodge NE15 . . .53 D6
Dunnykirk Ave 2 NE3 . .37 C5
Dunscar DH4 . . . . .90 B1
Dunsdale Dr NE23 . . . . . .22 D8
Dunsdale Rd NE25 . . . . . .23 E2
Dunsgreen NE20 . . . . . . .25 E5
Dunsgreen Ct NE20 . . . . .25 E5
Dunsley Gdns NE13 . . . . .27 B7
Dunslow Croft NE15 . . . .33 C1
Dunsmuir Gr NE8 . . . . . . .70 D8
Dunstable Pl NE5 . . . . . . .36 B3
Dunstan Cl DH2 . . . . .88 A1
Dunstan Wlk NE5 . . . . . . .36 F1
Dunstanburgh Cl
Bedlington NE22 . . . . . . .10 D1
Newcastle-u-T NE6 . . . . .56 D5
Washington NE38 . . . . . . .83 B4
Dunstanburgh Ct
Bournmoor DH4 . . . . . . .89 D2
Gateshead NE10 . . . . .72 B7
Jarrow NE32 . . . . .58 E5
Dunstanburgh Rd NE6 . .56 D5
Dunster Ho 3 SR3 . . . . .91 D7
Dunston Bank NE11 . . . . .69 F7
Dunston Ent Pk NE11 . . . .54 F2
Dunston Hill Com Prim Sch
NE11 . . . . .69 F8
Dunston Hill Hospl NE11 69 D7
Dunston Pl NE24 . . . . . . .17 B8
Dunston Rd NE11 . . . . . . .54 F1
Dunston Riverside Prim Sch
NE11 . . . . .54 F1
Dunston Sta NE11 . . . . . . .70 A8
Dunston Workshops
NE11 . . . . .54 F2
Dunvegan DH3 . . . . .82 E2
Dunvegan Ave DH2 . . . . .88 B1
Dunwoodie Terr 6 NE46 .45 A5
Duoro Terr SR2 . . . . .103 A1
Durant Rd NE1 . . . . .99 B2
Durban St NE24 . . . . .17 D8
Durham Ave NE37 . . . . . . .83 B8
Durham Cl NE22 . . . . .10 D2
Durham Ct NE31 . . . . .57 D5
**Durham Cty Cricket Gd (The
Riverside)** DH3 . . . . .88 C2
Durham Dr NE32 . . . . .58 B2
Durham Gr NE32 . . . . .58 B2
Durham Ho SR5 . . . . .73 F4
Durham La Haswell DH6 . .97 C1
Sherburn Hill DH6 . . . . . .96 D1
Durham Pl Birtley DH3 . . .82 D1
Gateshead NE8 . . . . .101 C1
Durham Rd Birtley DH3 . .82 C3
Chester le S DH3 . . . . . . .88 C1
Chester le S,Barley Mow
DH3 . . . . .88 C2
Cramlington NE23 . . . . . .16 C1
East Rainton DH5 . . . . . .94 C4
Gateshead NE8,NE9 . . . . .70 F6
Houghton-le-S DH5 . . . . .90 F3
Houghton-le-S DH5 . . . . .94 E7
Sunderland SR3 . . . . .85 E2
Durham St
Fence Houses DH4 . . . . . .94 A8
3 Gateshead NE10 . . . . . .56 F1
Newcastle-u-T NE4 . . . . .54 F5
Wallsend NE28 . . . . .40 C2

Durham Street W NE28 . .40 C2
Durham Terr SR3 . . . . . . .86 A1
Durken Bsns Pk NE23 . . . .12 E5
Dutton Ct NE21 . . . . .53 E4
Duxbury Pk NE38 . . . . . . .89 D8
Duxfield Rd NE7 . . . . .39 B3
Dwyer Cres SR2 . . . . .92 F6
Dyer Sq SR5 . . . . .75 B2
Dyke Heads La NE40 . . . .52 B1
Dykefield Ave NE13 . . . . .37 E7
Dykelands Rd SR6 . . . . . .75 E5
Dykelands Way NE34 . . . .58 F3
Dykenook Cl NE16 . . . . . .69 A4
Dykes Way NE10 . . . . .71 D5
Dymock Ct NE3 . . . . .37 B5

E

E D Morel Terr NE17 . . . . .77 C8
Eaglescliffe Dr NE7 . . . . .39 D2
Eaglesdene DH5 . . . . .95 A4
Ealing Ct NE3 . . . . .37 B6
Ealing Dr NE30 . . . . .32 C1
Ealing Sq NE23 . . . . .21 D6
Eardulph Ave DH3 . . . . . .88 D3
Earl St SR4 . . . . .102 B2
Earl Grey Way NE29 . . . . .41 F3
Earl's Dr NE15 . . . . .54 A7
Earl's Gdns NE24 . . . . . . .17 C8
Earlington Ct NE12 . . . . . .29 E1
Earls Ct Gateshead DH98 .70 D5
Prudhoe NE42 . . . . .50 E4
Sunderland SR5 . . . . .75 A4
Earls Dene 5 NE9 . . . . . .70 F4
Earls Dr NE9 . . . . .70 F4
Earls Gn DH5 . . . . .94 D3
Earls Pk N Trad Est NE11 70 C7
Earlston St SR5 . . . . .75 A4
Earlston Way NE23 . . . . . .16 C2
Earlsway DH98,NE11,NE82 .70 D5
Earlswood Ave NE9 . . . . . .70 F4
Earlswood Gr NE24 . . . . . .17 D3
Earlswood Pk NE9 . . . . . .70 F4
Earnshaw Way NE25 . . . . .31 D7
Earsdon Cl NE5 . . . . .37 A1
Earsdon Ct NE25 . . . . . . .31 D4
Earsdon Rd
Houghton-le-S DH5 . . . . .94 F8
Newcastle-u-T NE3 . . . . .37 E3
Shiremoor NE27 . . . . .30 E4
Whitley Bay NE25 . . . . . . .31 C4
Earsdon Terr
2 Ryhope SR2 . . . . .92 F6
9 Shiremoor NE27 . . . . . .30 E1
Earsdon View NE27 . . . . . .30 F4
Easby Cl NE3 . . . . .38 D8
Easby Rd NE38 . . . . .83 D4
Easdale Ave NE3 . . . . .28 C1
Easedale NE24 . . . . .24 C6
Easedale Gdns NE9 . . . . .71 B3
Easington Ave
Cramlington NE23 . . . . . .16 C2
Gateshead NE9 . . . . .71 C3
Easington Lane Prim Sch
DH5 . . . . .97 D8
Easington St SR5 . . . . . .102 C4
Easington St N SR5 . . . .102 C4
East Acres Blaydon NE21 .53 D1
Dinnington NE13 . . . . . . .27 C8
East Ave Longbenton NE12 .39 D6
South Shields NE34 . . . . .60 A6
Washington NE38 . . . . . . .83 B1
Whitley Bay NE25 . . . . . . .31 E5
East Back Par SR2 . . . . .103 C1
East Bailey NE12 . . . . . . .29 F3
East Benton Cotts NE12 . .39 E5
East Boldon Inf Sch
NE36 . . . . .74 D7
East Boldon Jun Sch
NE36 . . . . .74 D7
East Boldon Rd SR6 . . . . .59 F1
East Boldon Sta NE36 . . . .74 E8
East Bridge St DH4 . . . . . .83 E1
East Cl NE34 . . . . .60 A6
East Cleft Rd SR2 . . . . . .102 B2
East Cres NE22 . . . . .11 D2
East Cross St SR1 . . . . . .103 A3
East Dr Blyth NE24 . . . . . .17 C4
Cleadon SR6 . . . . .74 F8
East End NE26 . . . . .24 E4
East Farm Ct NE16 . . . . . .69 C3
East Farm Terr NE23 . . . .22 B6
East Fields SR6 . . . . .75 F8
East Ford Rd NE62 . . . . . .11 C8
East Forest Hall Rd NE12 39 E8
East Front NE2 . . . . .99 B4
East Gate Gateshead NE8 101 C1
Morpeth NE61 . . . . .9 A6
East George Potts St 13
NE33 . . . . .42 D1
East George St NE30 . . . . .42 C6
East Gr SR4 . . . . .85 B5
East Grange
Holywell NE25 . . . . .23 F2
Sunderland SR5 . . . . .75 C3
East Hartford Sch NE23 . .16 B3
East Herrington Prim Sch
SR3 . . . . .91 C7
East Hill Rd NE8 . . . . .56 B1
East Holborn NE33 . . . . . .42 B2
East Law DH8 . . . . .76 D1
East Lea Blaydon NE21 . . .68 C8
Newbiggin-by-t-S NE64 . . .7 C5
East Loan NE61 . . . . .4 A2
East Moffett St 11 NE33 . .42 D1
East Moor Rd SR4 . . . . . . .85 F7

East Oakwood NE46 . . . . .45 E8
East Par NE26 . . . . .32 B5
East Park Gdns NE21 . . . .53 C1
East Park Rd NE9 . . . . . . .70 F6
East Park View NE24 . . . .18 A7
East Pastures NE63 . . . . . .6 B2
East Percy St NE30 . . . . . .42 C6
East Rainton Prim Sch
DH5 . . . . .94 C4
East Riggs NE22 . . . . .15 F8
East Sea View NE64 . . . . . .7 F5
East St Chopwell NE17 . . .66 D1
Gateshead NE8 . . . . .101 C3
Hebburn NE31 . . . . .57 F7
High Spen NE39 . . . . .66 F4
Mickley Square NE43 . . . .49 F1
9 South Shields NE33 . . . .42 C3
Tynemouth NE30 . . . . . . .42 E7
Whitburn SR6 . . . . .75 F8
East Stainton St 10 NE33 42 D1
East Stevenson St 12
NE33 . . . . .42 D1
East Tanfield Sta ★ DH9 .79 E2
East Terr Chopwell NE17 . .77 C7
Stakeford NE62 . . . . .11 C7
East Thorp NE5 . . . . .36 F5
East View
8 Bedlington NE22 . . . . . .11 D3
Blaydon NE21 . . . . .53 D3
Boldon Colliery NE35 . . . .73 F8
Burnopfield NE16 . . . . . . .79 A6
Crawcrook NE40 . . . . .51 E6
Hebburn NE31 . . . . .57 D4
Morpeth NE61 . . . . .9 A8
New Hartley NE25 . . . . . .23 C5
Rowlands Gill NE39 . . . . .67 C2
Ryhope SR2 . . . . .92 E6
1 Seaham SR7 . . . . .92 F1
Seghill NE23 . . . . .22 F1
Sherburn Hill DH6 . . . . . .96 D1
Stakeford NE62 . . . . .11 C7
Sunderland,Castletown SR5 74 C1
Sunderland,Monkwearmouth
SR6 . . . . .75 C3
Wideopen NE13 . . . . .28 B7
East View Ave NE23 . . . . . .22 B6
East View S 3 SR5 . . . . . .74 C1
East View Terr
Dudley NE23 . . . . .29 A8
Gateshead NE10 . . . . .71 F6
Whickham NE16 . . . . .69 B8
East Villas DH6 . . . . .97 F4
East Vines SR1 . . . . .103 C3
East Wing The NE38 . . . . .83 E5
East Woodlands NE46 . . . .45 D4
Eastbourne Ave
Gateshead NE8 . . . . .70 E8
Newcastle-u-T NE6 . . . . .57 A6
Eastbourne Ct 1 NE6 . . . .57 A6
Eastbourne Gdns
Cramlington NE23 . . . . . .21 D6
Newcastle-u-T NE6 . . . . .57 A6
Whitley Bay NE25 . . . . . . .31 D4
Eastbourne Gr 12 NE33 . .42 D3
Eastbourne Par NE31 . . . .58 A2
Eastbourne Sq SR5 . . . . . .75 A4
Eastburn Gdns NE10 . . . .57 B2
Eastcheap NE6 . . . . .39 C1
Eastcliffe Ave NE3 . . . . . .38 A3
Eastcombe Cl NE35 . . . . . .58 E2
Eastcote Terr NE6 . . . . . . .56 F4
Easten Terr NE28 . . . . . . .41 C1
Easterfield Ct NE61 . . . . . .4 A1
Eastern Ave NE11,NE9 . . .70 D4
Eastern Gdns 4 NE10 . . . .56 D1
Eastern Way
Newcastle-u-T NE5 . . . . .37 D2
Ponteland NE20 . . . . .25 D3
Eastfield Ave
Newcastle-u-T NE28,NE6 . .57 A8
Whitley Bay NE25 . . . . . . .31 D4
Eastfield Ho NE6 . . . . .57 A8
Eastfield Rd
Longbenton NE12 . . . . . . .39 D6
South Shields NE34 . . . . .59 F8
Eastfield St SR4 . . . . .85 F5
Eastfield Terr NE12 . . . . . .39 D6
Eastfields NE46 . . . . .45 D4
Eastgarth NE5 . . . . .37 B3
Eastgate Choppington NE62 10 F5
Hexham NE46 . . . . .45 B4
Eastgate Bank NE43 . . . . .64 D8
Eastgate Gdns NE4 . . . . . .54 E4
Eastgreen NE62 . . . . .10 F5
Eastlands Blaydon NE21 . .53 B1
Chester le S NE38 . . . . . .88 E7
Newcastle-u-T NE7 . . . . .39 A3
Eastleigh Cl NE35 . . . . . . .73 E8
Eastmoor Rd SR4 . . . . . . .85 F6
Eastward Gn NE25 . . . . . . .31 D4
Eastway NE34 . . . . .60 B5
Eastwood Ave NE24 . . . . .17 D3
Eastwood Cl NE23 . . . . . . .29 C5
Eastwood Ct NE12 . . . . . . .39 D7
Eastwood Gdns
Gateshead,Low Fell NE9 . .71 A6
Gateshead,Old Fold NE10 . .56 F2
Newcastle-u-T NE3 . . . . .37 F4
Eastwood Grange Ct
NE46 . . . . .45 E4
Eastwood Grange Rd
NE46 . . . . .45 E4
Eastwood Mid Sch NE42 .50 F3
Eastwood Pl NE23 . . . . . . .16 C2
Eastwood Villas NE42 . . . .50 F4
Eastwoods Rd NE42 . . . . .50 F3
Eaton Cl NE38 . . . . .89 B8
Eaton Pl NE4 . . . . .54 F7

Eavers Ct NE34 . . . . .59 C5
Ebba Wlk NE3 . . . . .38 D5
Ebchester Ave NE9 . . . . . .71 D3
Ebchester CE Prim Sch
DH8 . . . . .76 E3
Ebchester Ct NE3 . . . . . . .37 C5
Ebchester Hill DH8 . . . . . .76 F2
Ebchester St NE34 . . . . . .59 A5
Ebdon La SR6 . . . . .75 D4
Ebor St Newcastle-u-T NE6 56 C8
South Shields NE34 . . . . .59 A4
Eccles Ct NE27 . . . . .30 C5
Eccles Terr 2 NE27 . . . . .30 E1
Eccleston Cl NE27 . . . . . . .30 C4
Eccleston Rd NE33 . . . . . .42 E2
Ecgfrid Terr NE32 . . . . . . .58 C4
Eddison Rd NE38 . . . . . . .83 F4
Eddleston NE38 . . . . .83 A1
Eddleston Ave NE3 . . . . . .38 A3
Eddrington Gr NE5 . . . . . .36 C2
Ede Ave Dunston NE11 . . .69 F8
South Shields NE34 . . . . .60 B7
Eden Ave NE16 . . . . .79 A6
Eden Cl NE5 . . . . .36 C2
Eden Ct Bedlington NE22 . .16 A8
5 Wallsend NE28 . . . . . . .40 B1
Eden Dale NE40 . . . . .51 F4
Eden Gr NE61 . . . . .9 A8
Eden House Rd SR2,SR4 .102 B1
Eden Pl NE30 . . . . .32 A1
Eden St NF28 . . . . .40 B1
Eden St W SR1 . . . . .102 C3
Eden Terr Lynemouth NE61 . .2 A3
Penshaw DH4 . . . . .90 B6
Sunderland SR2 . . . . . . .102 B1
Eden Vale SR2 . . . . .102 B1
Eden Villas NE38 . . . . .83 E4
Eden Wlk NE32 . . . . .58 C3
Edenbridge Cres NE12 . . .39 B7
Edendale Ave Blyth NE24 .17 B8
Newcastle-u-T NE6 . . . . .57 A6
Edendale Ct Blyth NE24 . .17 B8
1 South Shields NE34 . . . .59 A4
Edendale Ho NE24 . . . . . .17 B7
Edendale Terr NE8 . . . . . .70 F8
Edengarth NE30 . . . . .32 A2
Edgar St NE3 . . . . .38 F5
Edge Hill NE20 . . . . .25 C1
Edge Mount NE12 . . . . . . .29 E4
Edgecote NE37 . . . . .83 F8
Edgefield NE27 . . . . .30 E3
Edgefield Ave NE3 . . . . . .37 F5
Edgefield Dr NE23 . . . . . .16 C2
Edgehill NE61 . . . . .9 B6
Edgehill Cl NE20 . . . . .25 C1
Edgeware Ct SR5 . . . . . . .75 A3
Edgeware Wlk NE4 . . . . . .54 E3
Edgewell Ave NE42 . . . . . .50 B1
Edgewell Grange NE42 . . .50 C2
Edgewell House Rd NE42,
NE43 . . . . .65 B8
Edgewell Rd NE42 . . . . . .50 B1
Edgewood Hexham NE46 . .45 D4
Ponteland NE20 . . . . .25 D2
Edgeworth Cl NE35 . . . . . .58 E2
Edgeworth Cres SR6 . . . . .75 D2
Edgmond Ct SR2 . . . . .92 E8
Edgware Rd NE8 . . . . .71 A8
Edhill Ave NE34 . . . . .59 A4
Edhill Gdns NE34 . . . . . . .58 F4
Edinburgh Ct NE3 . . . . . . .37 D8
Edinburgh Dr NE22 . . . . . .10 E2
Edinburgh Rd NE32 . . . . . .58 E4
Edinburgh Sq 3 SR5 . . . .75 A3
Edington Gdns NE40 . . . . .51 E6
Edington Gr NE30 . . . . . . .32 A1
Edington Rd NE30 . . . . . . .32 A1
Edison Gdns NE8 . . . . .70 E7
Edith Ave NE21 . . . . .53 C2
Edith Moffat Ho 7 NE29 .42 A6
Edith St Jarrow NE32 . . . . .58 A7
Sunderland,Hendon SR2 . .86 E4
Sunderland,Monkwearmouth
SR5 . . . . .75 C2
Tynemouth NE30 . . . . . . .42 C6
Edith Terr Newbottle DH4 .90 D3
5 Whickham NE16 . . . . . .69 A7
Edlingham Cl NE3 . . . . . . .38 F4
Edlingham Ct 6 DH5 . . . .94 F8
Edmonton Sq 1 SR5 . . . .75 A3
Edmund Pl NE9 . . . . .70 F5
Edmund Rd NE27 . . . . . . .30 D1
Edna Terr NE5 . . . . .37 A3
Edrich Ho NE29 . . . . .41 D3
Edward Burdis St SR5 . . .75 B2
Edward Graveling Ho
NE30 . . . . .42 C6
Edward Ho SR2 . . . . .102 C2
Edward Pl NE4 . . . . .98 B1
Edward Rd
Bedlington NE22 . . . . . . .11 D3
Birtley DH3 . . . . .82 B5
Wallsend NE28 . . . . .40 F3
Edward St Blyth NE24 . . . .17 D7
Burnopfield NE16 . . . . . . .79 A4
Chester le S DH3 . . . . . . .88 C3
Crawcrook NE40 . . . . .51 E3
Hebburn NE31 . . . . .57 C6
Hetton le H DH5 . . . . .95 A4
Morpeth NE61 . . . . .9 A8
New Silksworth SR3 . . . . .92 A7
Newcastle-u-T NE3 . . . . .38 C5
Pegswood NE61 . . . . .4 F3
Edward's Wlk NE1 . . . . . . .99 A2
Edwards Rd NE26 . . . . . . .32 C4
Edwin Gr NE28 . . . . .41 A3

Edwin St
Brunswick Village NE13 . . .28 A6
Houghton-le-S DH5 . . . . .90 E1
14 Newcastle-u-T NE6 . . . .56 B6
Sunderland SR4 . . . . .85 E7
Edwin Terr NE40 . . . . .52 C2
Edwin's Ave S NE12 . . . . .39 E8
Edwina Gdns NE29 . . . . . .41 E7
Edwins Ave NE12 . . . . . . .39 E8
Egerton Rd NE34 . . . . . . .59 C6
Egerton St
Newcastle-u-T NE4 . . . . .54 D4
Sunderland SR2 . . . . . . .103 B1
Eggleston Dr SR3 . . . . . . .86 A2
Egham Rd NE5 . . . . .36 C2
Eglesfield Rd NE33 . . . . . .59 C8
Eglingham Ave NE30 . . . .32 C1
Eglingham Cl NE61 . . . . . .9 B6
Eglingham Way NE61 . . . .9 B6
Eglinton St SR5 . . . . .75 C1
Eglinton St N SR5 . . . . . . .75 C1
Eglinton Twr 2 SR5 . . . . .75 D1
Egremont Dr 4 NE9 . . . . .71 A6
Egremont Gdns NE9 . . . . .71 A6
Egremont Pl NE26 . . . . . . .32 B4
Egremont Way NE23 . . . . .16 C2
Egton Terr DH3 . . . . .82 C5
Eider Cl NE24 . . . . .17 E3
Eider Wlk NE12 . . . . .29 C4
Eighteenth Ave NE24 . . . .17 E5
Eighth Ave Ashington NE63 . .6 E2
Blyth NE24 . . . . .17 D6
Chester le S DH2 . . . . . . .88 B3
Gateshead NE11 . . . . .70 D3
Morpeth NE61 . . . . .9 B7
Newcastle-u-T NE6 . . . . .56 C8
Eighth Row NE63 . . . . .6 B4
Eighton Terr NE9 . . . . .71 E3
Eilansgate NE46 . . . . .45 A5
Eilansgate Ho NE46 . . . . .44 F5
Eilansgate Terr NE46 . . . .45 A5
Eilanville NE46 . . . . .45 A5
Eishort Way NE12 . . . . . . .39 B6
Eland Cl NE3 . . . . .37 D5
Eland Edge NE20 . . . . .25 F6
Eland La NE20 . . . . .25 F7
Eland Rd NE20 . . . . .25 F6
Elberfeld Ct NE32 . . . . . . .58 B6
Elder Gdns NE9 . . . . .71 C4
Elder Gr 3 Gateshead NE9 70 F5
South Shields NE34 . . . . .59 F3
Elder Sq NE63 . . . . .6 E2
Elderwood Gdns NE11 . . .70 B5
Eldon Ct 1 NE28 . . . . . . .41 B1
Eldon Gr NE1 . . . . .99 A2
Eldon La NE1 . . . . .99 A1
Eldon Pl
Newcastle-u-T NE1 . . . . .99 A3
Newcastle-u-T,Lemington
NE15 . . . . .53 D7
Eldon Rd Hexham NE46 . . .45 D7
Newcastle-u-T NE15 . . . . .53 D7
Eldon Sq NE1 . . . . .99 A2
Eldon Square Sh Ctr NE1 99 A2
Eldon St Gateshead NE8 . .56 A2
South Shields NE33 . . . . .42 B3
Sunderland SR4 . . . . . . .102 A2
Wallsend NE28 . . . . .41 B2
Eleanor St
South Shields NE33 . . . . .42 D3
Tynemouth NE30 . . . . . . .32 C3
Eleanor Terr
Crawcrook NE40 . . . . .52 A4
2 Whickham NE16 . . . . . .69 A7
Electric Cres DH4 . . . . . . .90 D4
Elemore Hall Sch DH6 . . .97 A5
Elemore La
Easington Lane DH5 . . . . .97 A7
High Pittington DH6 . . . . .96 B6
Elemore St DH6 . . . . .96 B5
Elemore View DH6 . . . . . .97 F7
Elenbel Ave NE22 . . . . . . .11 C1
Eleventh Ave Blyth NE24 .17 E6
Chester le S DH2 . . . . . . .88 B3
Gateshead NE11 . . . . .70 E2
Morpeth NE61 . . . . .9 B7
Eleventh Ave N NE11 . . . .70 E3
Eleventh Row NE63 . . . . . .6 B4
Elford Cl NE25 . . . . .31 D5
Elfordleigh DH4 . . . . .90 C4
Elgar Ave 3 NE5 . . . . . . .36 C2
Elgin Ave NE28 . . . . .40 F4
Elgin Cl Bedlington NE22 . .11 D2
Cramlington NE23 . . . . . .21 D6
Tynemouth NE29 . . . . . . .41 C8
Elgin Ct NE10 . . . . .57 B2
Elgin Gdns NE6 . . . . .56 F6
Elgin Pl DH3 . . . . .82 D2
Elgin Rd NE9 . . . . .71 B8
Elgin St NE32 . . . . .58 E4
Elgy Rd NE3 . . . . .38 B3
Elisabeth Ave DH3 . . . . . .82 B6
Elizabeth Cres NE23 . . . . .29 A8
Elizabeth Ct
High Pittington DH6 . . . . .96 C5
Longbenton NE12 . . . . . . .30 A1
Elizabeth Diamond Gdns
NE33 . . . . .59 B8
Elizabeth Dr NE12 . . . . . . .40 A8
Elizabeth Rd NE28 . . . . . . .41 A2
Elizabeth St
Chopwell NE17 . . . . .66 B1
East Cramlington NE23 . . .22 F5
Houghton-le-S DH5 . . . . .90 E1
Newcastle-u-T NE6 . . . . .56 A6
7 South Shields NE33 . . . .42 D2
Sunderland,Castletown SR5 74 B1

Elizabeth St *continued*
Sunderland,Monkwearmouth SR5 75 C3
Elizabeth Woodcock Maritime Inst The SR2 103 A1
Ell-Dene Cres NE10 71 E7
Ellen Ct 3 NE32 58 B7
Ellen Terr NE37 83 F8
Ellerbeck Cl 3 NE10 71 C8
Ellersmere Gdns NE30 32 B2
Ellerton Way
Cramlington NE23 16 C2
Gateshead NE10 71 C8
Ellesmere DH4 89 D3
Ellesmere Ave
Newcastle-u-T,South Gosforth NE3 38 E4
Newcastle-u-T,Walkergate NE6 56 E8
Newcastle-u-T,Westerhope NE5 37 A2
Ellesmere Ct SR2 86 E1
Ellesmere Gdns NE62 11 C8
Ellesmere Rd NE4 54 E5
Ellesmere Terr SR6 75 E3
Ellington Cl
Newcastle-u-T NE15 53 B7
1 Ryhope SR2 92 F5
Urpeth DH2 81 E2
Ellington Cvn Pk NE61 1 D7
Ellington Fst Sch NE61 1 E5
Ellington Terr NE63 5 F4
Ellington Way NE61 1 C4
Elliot Cl DH4 90 B7
Elliot Ct NE61 9 B7
Elliot Gdns NE34 59 D2
Elliot Rd NE10 56 B1
Elliott Dr NE10 71 D8
Elliott Gdns NE28 40 A4
Elliott St NE24 17 C4
Elliott Terr
Newcastle-u-T NE4 98 A1
3 Washington NE37 83 E8
Ellis Rd SR5 75 A3
Ellis Sq Pegswood NE61 4 F3
Sunderland SR5 75 B3
Ellison Pl
3 Gateshead NE9 70 F4
Jarrow NE32 58 B8
Newcastle-u-T NE1 99 B2
Ellison Rd NE11,NE8 69 F8
Ellison St Gateshead NE8 101 C3
Hebburn NE31 57 C7
Hebburn NE31 57 D6
10 Jarrow NE32 58 B7
Ellison Terr NE40 51 F1
Ellison Villas 8 NE8 71 A8
Ellwood Gdns 3 NE9 70 F8
Elm Ave Dinnington NE13 27 B7
Dunston NE11 69 F7
South Shields NE34 59 F4
Whickham NE16 69 C8
Elm Bank Rd NE41 51 B5
Elm Cl Cramlington NE23 16 C2
Hexham NE46 44 E3
Elm Ct NE16 69 B5
Elm Dr Bedlington NE22 15 F8
Whitburn SR6 61 A2
Elm Gr Burnopfield NE16 78 F6
Killingworth NE12 29 D1
Newcastle-u-T NE3 37 F7
Shiney Row DH4 90 C5
South Shields NE34 59 F4
Elm Pl DH4 90 D3
Elm Rd Blaydon NE21 53 D2
Ponteland NE20 26 A5
Tynemouth NE29 41 B8
Elm St Chester le S DH3 88 C3
Jarrow NE32 58 A7
Mickley Square NE43 64 E8
Seaton Burn NE13 28 C8
Sunniside NE16 69 B2
Elm St W NE16 69 B2
Elm Terr Birtley DH3 82 B5
Tantobie DH9 79 B2
Elm Trees NE24 17 D6
Elmcroft Rd NE12 39 E7
Elmfield DH5 95 A6
Elmfield Cl SR3 91 C6
Elmfield Gdns
Newcastle-u-T NE3 38 B4
Wallsend NE28 39 F4
Whitley Bay NE25 31 D3
Elmfield Gr NE3 38 B4
Elmfield Pk NE3 38 B3
Elmfield Rd Hebburn NE31 57 F3
Newcastle-u-T NE3 38 C3
Throckley NE15 35 E2
Elmfield Terr
Gateshead NE10 57 A1
Hebburn NE31 57 F4
Elms The
Easington Lane DH5 97 D8
Ellington NE61 1 D4
Newcastle-u-T NE3 38 B3
Sunderland SR2 103 A1
Elms W SR2 103 A1
Elmsford Gr NE12 39 B6
Elmsleigh Gdns SR6 60 A2
Elmtree Dr NE40 52 B1
Elmtree Gdns NE25 31 E3
Elmtree Gr NE3 38 B3
Elmway DH2 88 A5
Elmwood NE15 53 C8
Elmwood Ave
Sunderland SR5 74 F3
Wallsend NE28 40 F2
Wideopen NE13 28 C5
Elmwood Cres NE6 39 F1
Elmwood Dr NE20 25 E7
Elmwood Gdns NE11 70 B6
Elmwood Gr NE26 32 A6
Elmwood Ho NE7 39 A4
Elmwood Mews NE13 28 B4
Elmwood Rd NE25 31 E4
Elmwood Sq 5 SR5 74 F2
Elmwood St
Great Lumley DH4 89 E1
Sunderland SR2 102 B1
Elrick Cl NE5 36 C2
Elrington Gdns NE5 54 B8
Elsdon Ave NE25 23 D3
Elsdon Cl NE24 17 C7
Elsdon Ct NE16 69 A5
Elsdon Dr Ashington NE63 6 C3
Longbenton NE12 39 F8
Elsdon Gdns NE11 70 A8
Elsdon Pl 7 NE29 42 A4
Elsdon Rd
Newcastle-u-T NE3 38 C5
Whickham NE16 69 A6
Elsdon St NE29 42 A4
Elsdon Terr
North Shields NE29 41 D4
4 Wallsend NE28 40 B1
Elsdonburn Rd SR3 91 E5
Elsham Gn NE3 37 E6
Elsing Cl NE5 37 B4
Elstob Farm Cvns SR3 86 B2
Elstob Pl
Newcastle-u-T NE6 56 E4
Sunderland SR3 86 A2
Elston Cl NE5 36 C2
Elstree Ct NE3 37 B7
Elstree Gdns NE24 17 D3
Elstree Sq SR5 75 A3
Elswick East Terr NE4 100 B4
Elswick Rd
Newcastle-u-T NE4 100 A4
Washington NE37 83 A7
Elswick Row NE4 98 B1
Elswick St NE4 98 B1
Elswick Way NE34 59 A6
Elswick Way Ind Est NE34 59 A6
Elsworth Gn NE5 37 C3
Elterwater Rd DH2 88 B1
Elton St E NE28 40 B1
Elton St W NE28 40 B1
Eltringham Cl NE28 40 A2
Eltringham Cotts NE43 49 F1
Eltringham Rd NE42 50 A2
Elvaston Dr NE46 45 B3
Elvaston Gr NE46 45 B3
Elvaston Park Rd NE46 45 A3
Elvaston Rd Hexham NE46 45 B4
Ryton NE40 52 C6
Elvet Cl
Brunswick Village NE13 28 B6
6 Newcastle-u-T NE6 56 C7
Elvet Ct NE6 56 C7
Elvet Gn Chester le S DH2 88 C2
Hetton le H DH5 95 A1
Elvet Way 5 NE6 56 C7
Elvington St SR6 75 E3
Elwin Cl NE26 24 D5
Elwin Pl NE26 24 D5
Elwin Terr SR2 102 C2
Ely Cl NE12 39 D4
Ely St NE8 101 B1
Ely Way NE32 58 B1
Elysium La NE8 101 A1
Embankment Rd SR7 93 B1
Embassy Gdns NE15 54 B6
Emblehope NE37 83 A6
Emblehope Dr NE3 38 A4
Emblehope Ho SR3 91 E8
Embleton Ave
Newcastle-u-T NE3 38 A6
South Shields NE34 60 B8
Wallsend NE28 40 E5
Embleton Cres NE29 41 C8
Embleton Dr Blyth NE24 17 C5
Chester le S DH2 88 A1
Embleton Gdns
Gateshead NE10 56 D1
5 Newcastle-u-T NE5 37 D1
Embleton Rd
Gateshead NE10 57 B2
Tynemouth NE29 41 C8
Emden Rd NE3 37 F6
Emily Davison Ave NE61 8 E8
Emily St Gateshead NE8 56 B1
Newbottle DH4 90 D4
Newcastle-u-T NE6 56 E6
Emlyn Rd NE34 59 C6
Emma Ct SR2 103 B1
Emma View 7 NE40 51 F3
Emmanuel Coll NE11 70 A5
Emmaville NE40 52 A4
Emmaville Prim Sch NE40 51 F4
Emmbrook Cl DH5 94 D4
Emmerson Ct NE27 30 E3
Emmerson Pl NE27 30 E3
Emmerson Rd NE64 7 D5
Emmerson Terr NE38 83 E5
Emmerson Terr W 1 SR3 92 B7
Emperor Way SR3 91 C5
Empress Rd NE6 57 B4
Empress St 3 SR5 75 C1
Emsworth Rd SR5 75 A3
Enderby Dr NE46 44 E3
Enderby Rd SR4 102 B3
Enfield Ave NE16 54 B1
Enfield Gdns NE16 69 B5
Enfield Rd NE9 70 F8
Enfield St SR4 85 F7
Engel St NE39 67 B2
Engine Inn Rd NE28 40 F4
Engine La NE9 70 F4
Engine Rd
Hedley on t H NE17 65 E4
Prudhoe NE42 65 F5
Englefeld NE10 71 F4
Englefield Cl NE3 37 D7
Englemann Way SR3 91 E5
English Martyrs RC Prim Sch SR5 74 F2
English Martyrs' RC Prim Sch NE5 54 C8
Enid Ave SR6 75 D3
Enid St NE13 28 A4
Ennerdale Birtley DH3 82 D2
Gateshead NE10 72 A8
Sunderland SR2 86 C4
Washington NE37 83 C7
Ennerdale Cres
Blaydon NE21 68 B8
Penshaw DH4 90 A8
Ennerdale Gdns
Gateshead NE9 71 A5
Wallsend NE28 41 A4
Ennerdale Pl DH2 88 C1
Ennerdale Rd Blyth NE24 16 F8
Newcastle-u-T NE6 56 F6
Tynemouth NE30 32 A2
Ennerdale St DH5 94 F2
Ennerdale Terr NE17 77 A5
Ennerdale Wlk NE16 68 F5
Ennis Cl NE62 11 D8
Ennismore Ct NE12 39 D6
Ensign Ho 21 NE30 42 D7
Enslin St NE6 56 F3
Enterprise Ct
Cramlington NE23 15 F1
Seaham SR7 92 F2
Enterprise Ho NE11 70 D4
Epinay Sch NE32 58 C6
Epinay Wlk NE32 58 C6
Epping Ct NE23 21 D6
Epping Sq 4 SR5 75 A3
Eppleton Est DH5 95 B5
Eppleton Prim Sch DH5 95 A6
Eppleton Row DH5 95 B4
Eppleton Terr E DH5 95 B4
Eppleton Terr W DH5 95 B4
Epsom Cl NE29 41 F4
Epsom Ct NE3 37 C7
Epsom Dr NE63 6 C2
Epsom Sq 5 SR5 75 A3
Epsom Way NE24 17 D3
Epwell Gr NE23 16 C2
Epworth Gr NE8 101 B1
Equitable St NE28 40 B1
Eric Tolhurst Ctr 12 NE24 17 F8
Erick St NE1 99 B1
Erin Sq SR5 75 B3
Erith Terr SR4 85 F6
Ermine Cres NE9 71 B6
Ernest Mackley Ho NE34 59 A5
Ernest St
8 Sunderland SR2 86 E4
West Boldon NE35 74 A8
Ernest Terr
Chester le S DH3 88 C2
Ryhope SR2 93 A6
Ernwill Ave SR5 74 B1
Errington Cl NE20 25 C2
Errington Pl NE42 50 C2
Errington Rd NE20 25 B2
Errington St NE24 16 E7
Errington Terr NE12 29 E1
Errol Pl DH3 82 D2
Erskine Ct NE2 38 F2
Erskine Rd NE33 42 D2
Erskine Way NE33 42 D2
Esdale SR2 92 E6
Esher Ct NE3 37 C7
Esher Gdns NE24 17 D3
Esher Pl NE23 21 D6
Eshmere Cres NE5 36 C3
Eshott Cl
Newcastle-u-T,East Denton NE5 37 A1
Newcastle-u-T,Fawdon NE3 38 A6
Eshott Ct NE5 37 A1
Esk Ct 12 SR3 91 F6
Esk St N10,NE9 71 B7
Esk Terr 9 DH3 82 C5
Eskdale Birtley DH3 82 E1
Penshaw DH4 90 A8
Eskdale Ave Blyth NE24 17 A8
Wallsend NE28 40 C5
Eskdale Cres NE37 72 B1
Eskdale Ct NE34 59 C6
Eskdale Dr NE32 58 D3
Eskdale Gdns NE9 71 A3
Eskdale Mans NE2 99 B4
Eskdale Rd SR6 75 F6
Eskdale St Hetton le H DH5 94 F2
South Shields NE34 59 C5
Eskdale Terr
Newcastle-u-T NE2 99 B4
Whitley Bay NE26 32 C4
Eslington Ct NE8 70 B8
Eslington Ho NE2 99 B4
Eslington Mews NE63 6 F4
Eslington Rd NE2 99 B3
Eslington Sch NE8 100 C1
Eslington Terr NE2 99 B4
Esmeralda Gdns NE23 22 F1
Esplanade NE26 32 B5
Esplanade Ave NE26 32 B5
Esplanade Mews SR2 103 A1
Esplanade Pl NE26 32 B5
Esplanade The SR2 103 A1
Esplanade W SR2 103 A1
Espley Cl NE12 40 A8
Espley Ct NE3 37 E7
Essen Way SR3 86 B3
Essex Cl Ashington NE63 6 A4
Newcastle-u-T NE4 100 B3
Essex Dr NE37 72 D1
Essex Gdns Gateshead NE9 70 F7
South Shields NE34 60 C7
Wallsend NE28 40 E3
Essex Gr SR3 92 A8
Essex St DH5 94 F4
Estate Houses DH4 89 E4
Esther Campbell Ct NE2 98 C3
Esther Sq NE38 83 E4
Esthwaite Ave DH2 88 B1
Eston Ct Blyth NE24 17 B8
Wallsend NE28 39 F5
Eston Gr SR5 75 C3
Estuary Way SR4 85 B7
Etal Ave
North Shields NE29 41 D4
Whitley Bay NE25 32 B4
Etal Cl NE27 30 F3
Etal Cres Jarrow NE32 58 E4
Shiremoor NE27 30 F3
Etal Ct 2 NE29 42 A6
Etal Ho NE63 6 F4
Etal La NE5 37 B3
Etal Pl NE3 38 A7
Etal Rd NE24 17 B3
Etal Way NE5 37 B4
Ethel Ave Blaydon NE21 53 C2
Ryhope SR2 93 A6
Ethel St Dudley NE23 29 A6
Newcastle-u-T NE4 54 D4
Ethel Terr
2 Hexham NE46 45 A4
High Spen NE39 66 F3
South Shields NE34 59 B5
Sunderland SR5 74 B1
Etherley Rd NE6 56 D7
Etherstone Ave NE7 39 C3
Eton Cl NE23 16 C2
Eton Sq NE31 57 F6
Ettrick Cl NE12 29 C4
Ettrick Gdns
Gateshead NE8 71 B8
Sunderland SR4 85 F4
Ettrick Gr SR3 85 F4
Ettrick Lodge NE3 38 D4
Ettrick Rd NE32 58 A5
European Way SR4 85 E8
Euryalus Ct NE33 42 F1
Eustace Ave NE29 41 E5
Euston Ct SR5 75 A4
Eva St NE15 53 C6
Evanlade NE10 72 B6
Evelyn St SR2 102 B1
Evelyn Terr NE21 53 C3
Evenwood Gdns NE9 71 B5
Ever Ready Ind Est DH9 79 D2
Everard St NE23 16 B3
Everest Gr NE36 74 B7
Everest Sq SR5 75 A4
Eversleigh Pl NE15 35 E2
Eversley Cres SR5 75 B3
Eversley Pl
7 Newcastle-u-T NE6 56 B7
Wallsend NE28 40 F3
Everton La SR5 75 A3
Evesham SR4 85 A6
Evesham Ave NE26 31 F6
Evesham Cl NE35 58 F1
Evesham Garth NE3 37 E3
Evesham Pl NE23 21 D7
Evistones Gdns NE6 56 E3
Evistones Rd NE9 71 A7
Ewart Cres NE34 58 E4
Ewart Ct NE3 38 A7
Ewbank Ave NE4 54 E7
Ewe Hill Cotts DH4 89 F1
Ewe Hill Terr DH4 89 F1
Ewe Hill Terr W DH4 89 F1
Ewehurst Cres DH9 78 E1
Ewehurst Gdns DH9 78 E1
Ewehurst Par DH9 78 E2
Ewehurst Rd DH9 78 E2
Ewehurst Terr DH9 78 E2
Ewen Ct NE29 41 B8
Ewesley NE38 89 A8
Ewesley Cl NE5 37 A1
Ewesley Gdns NE13 28 B6
Ewesley Rd SR4 85 F5
Ewing Rd SR4 102 A1
Exchange Bldgs NE26 32 B5
Exelby Cl NE3 38 D8
Exeter Cl Ashington NE63 7 A2
Cramlington NE23 21 E6
Exeter Ct NE31 57 D5
Exeter Rd Tynemouth NE29 31 C1
Wallsend NE28 40 A5
Exeter St Gateshead NE8 101 C1
Newcastle-u-T NE6 57 A4
Sunderland SR4 85 F7
Exeter Way NE32 58 B2
Exmouth Rd NE29 41 C5
Exmouth Sq SR5 75 A3
Exmouth St 2 SR5 75 A3
Extension Rd SR1 103 C2
Eyemouth Ct 2 NE34 59 A5
Eyemouth La SR5 75 A4
Eyemouth Rd NE29 41 C5

F

Faber Rd SR5 75 A3
Factory Rd NE21 53 D4
Fair Gn NE25 31 C4
Fair View Burnopfield NE16 78 E6
Prudhoe NE42 50 C2
West Rainton DH4 94 A2
Fairburn Ave
Houghton-le-S DH5 94 E6
Newcastle-u-T NE7 39 C4
Fairdale Ave NE7 39 C4
Fairfield
Fence Houses DH4 90 B1
Hexham NE46 44 F4
Longbenton NE12 38 F6
Fairfield Ave Blyth NE24 17 D4
3 Longbenton NE12 39 D8
Whickham NE16 69 A5
Fairfield Cl NE11 54 E1
Fairfield Cres NE46 45 E8
Fairfield Dr Ashington NE63 7 A2
Tynemouth NE30 32 B2
Whitburn SR6 60 F2
Whitley Bay NE25 31 D4
Fairfield Gn NE25 31 C4
Fairfield Ind Est NE10 57 A2
Fairfield Rd NE2 38 D1
Fairfield Terr NE10 57 A1
Fairfields NE40 52 B5
Fairgreen Cl SR3 91 F5
Fairhaven NE9 71 F2
Fairhaven Ave NE6 57 A6
Fairhill Cl NE7 39 C4
Fairholm Rd NE4 54 E5
Fairholme Ave NE34 59 F6
Fairholme Rd SR3 86 C3
Fairisle DH2 82 A1
Fairlands E SR6 75 D2
Fairlands W SR6 75 D2
Fairlawn Gdns SR4 85 E4
Fairles St NE33 42 D4
Fairmead Way SR4 85 A6
Fairmile Dr SR3 92 A4
Fairmont Way NE7 39 C4
Fairney Cl NE20 25 F6
Fairney Edge NE20 25 F6
Fairnley Wlk NE5 37 A2
Fairspring NE5 37 A2
Fairview Ave NE34 59 F7
Fairview Gn NE7 39 C4
Fairville Cl NE23 16 B2
Fairville Cres NE7 39 C4
Fairway Morpeth NE61 8 F5
Stakeford NE62 11 A8
Fairway Cl NE3 38 B8
Fairway The
Newcastle-u-T NE3 38 B8
Ryton NE21 53 A4
Washington NE37 72 D3
Fairways
New Silksworth SR3 92 B7
Whitley Bay NE25 31 D5
Fairways Ave NE7 39 C4
Fairways The NE36 74 A7
Fairwood Rd NE46 45 D4
Fairy St DH5 95 A4
Falcon Ct NE63 6 B1
Falcon Hill NE61 8 D7
Falcon Pl NE12 39 A7
Falcon Terr NE41 51 B6
Falcon Way NE34 59 B4
Falconar St NE2 99 B2
Falconar's Ct NE1 99 A1
Faldonside NE6 39 D2
Falkirk NE12 29 D4
Falkland Ave
Hebburn NE31 57 E6
Newcastle-u-T NE3 37 F3
Falkland Rd SR4 85 E6
Falla Park Com Prim Sch NE10 71 C8
Falla Park Cres NE10 71 C8
Falla Park Rd NE10 71 C8
Falloden Ave NE3 37 F8
Fallodon Gdns NE5 37 D2
Fallodon Rd NE29 41 D5
Fallow Park Ave NE24 17 C6
Fallow Rd NE34 60 D6
Fallowfeld NE10 72 A7
Fallowfield Ave NE3 37 F6
Fallowfield Way
Ashington NE63 6 B2
Washington NE38 83 E2
Falmouth Dr NE32 58 D5
Falmouth Rd
Newcastle-u-T NE6 56 B7
North Shields NE29 41 C5
Sunderland SR4 85 E7
Tynemouth NE29 41 D8
Falmouth Sq SR4 85 E6
Falmouth Wlk NE23 22 A8
Falsgrave Pl NE16 68 F5
Falstaff Rd NE29 41 D6
Falston Rd NE24 17 C5
Falstone Gateshead NE10 72 A5
Washington NE38 83 F2
Falstone Ave
Newcastle-u-T NE15 53 E8
South Shields NE34 60 A6
Falstone Cl NE12 40 A8
Falstone Cres NE63 6 E1
Falstone Sq NE3 38 A6

Falstone Way NE46 . . . . .44 F3
Faraday Cl NE38 . . . . .84 B5
Faraday Gr Gateshead NE8 70 E7
 Sunderland SR4 . . . . .85 F6
Faraday Terr DH6 . . . . .97 E3
Farbridge Cres DH8 . . . . . .76 F3
Farding Lake Ct NE34 . . . . .60 C6
Farding Sq NE34 . . . . .60 C6
Fareham Gr NE35 . . . . .73 D8
Fareham Way NE23 . . . . . . .22 B7
Farlam Ave NE30 . . . . .32 A1
Farlam Rd NE5 . . . . .54 B8
Farleigh Ct NE29 . . . . .41 B8
Farm Cl Sunniside NE16 . . . .69 B2
 Washington NE37 . . . . .72 B1
Farm Cotts NE25 . . . . .23 F2
Farm Hill Rd SR6 . . . . .60 A2
Farm St SR5 . . . . .75 B1
Farm View Ho NE23 . . . . . . .22 E5
Farm Well Pl NE42 . . . . .50 D3
Farn Ct NE3 . . . . .37 D8
Farnborough Cl NE23 . . . . . .22 B8
Farnborough Dr SR3 . . . . . .92 B8
Farndale NE28 . . . . .39 F5
Farndale Ave
 Stakeford NE62 . . . . .11 A8
 Sunderland SR6 . . . . .75 F6
Farndale Cl Blaydon NE21 .67 F8
 Dinnington NE13 . . . . .27 B7
Farndale Ct NE24 . . . . .17 D4
Farndale Rd NE4 . . . . .54 E5
Farne Ave Ashington NE63 . .6 D2
 Newcastle-u-T NE3 . . . . . . .38 A7
 South Shields NE34 . . . . . . .60 B8
Farne Prim Sch NE5 . . . . . .37 A3
Farne Rd NE27 . . . . .30 F3
Farne Sq SR4 . . . . .85 D7
Farne Terr NE6 . . . . .56 E6
Farnham Cl NE15 . . . . .53 D6
Farnham Gr NE24 . . . . .17 D4
Farnham Rd NE34 . . . . .59 C6
Farnham St NE15 . . . . .53 D6
Farnham Terr SR4 . . . . .85 F4
Farnley Rd NE6 . . . . .39 C1
Farnon Rd NE3 . . . . .38 A5
Farnsworth Ct NE2 . . . . .38 F2
Farquhar St 4 NE2 . . . . . . .38 F1
Farrfeld NE10 . . . . .71 F4
Farrier Cl NE38 . . . . .83 E2
Farriers Ct NE22 . . . . .11 C5
Farringdon Com Sports Coll
 SR3 . . . . .91 D7
Farringdon Prim Sch
 SR3 . . . . .91 D8
Farringdon Rd NE30 . . . . . .32 A2
Farringdon Row SR3 . . . .102 C3
Farrington Ave SR3 . . . . . . .91 C8
Farrow Dr SR6 . . . . .60 E1
Farthings The NE37 . . . . . . .72 B2
Fatfield Pk NE38 . . . . .83 D1
Fatfield Prim Sch NE38 . .83 D1
Fatfield Rd NE38 . . . . .83 E4
Fatherly Terr DH4 . . . . .94 B8
Faversham Ct NE3 . . . . .37 D7
Faversham Pl NE23 . . . . . . .22 B8
Fawcett St SR1 . . . . .103 A2
Fawcett Terr SR2 . . . . .93 A6
Fawcett Way NE33 . . . . .42 C3
Fawdon Cl NE3 . . . . .37 F8
Fawdon Gr NE61 . . . . .4 D3
Fawdon House Farm NE61 4 D5
Fawdon La NE3 . . . . .37 F7
Fawdon Park Ho NE3 . . . . .37 F6
Fawdon Park Rd NE3 . . . . .37 F6
Fawdon Pl NE29 . . . . .41 C6
Fawdon Sta NE3 . . . . .37 F6
Fawdon Wlk NE3 . . . . .37 D7
Fawlee Gn NE5 . . . . .37 C4
Fawley Cl NE35 . . . . .58 E1
Fawn Rd SR4 . . . . .85 C6
Feather Bed La NE9 . . . . . .93 A6
Featherstone NE38 . . . . .82 F5
Featherstone Gr
 Bedlington NE22 . . . . .10 E2
 Jarrow NE32 . . . . .58 A3
 Newcastle-u-T NE3 . . . . . . .28 A1
Featherstone St SR6 . . . . . .75 F2
Federation Terr DH9 . . . . . .79 B2
Federation Way NE11 . . . . . .54 E1
Fee Terr SR2 . . . . .92 E6
Feetham Ave NE12 . . . . .40 A8
Feetham Ct NE12 . . . . .30 A1
Felixstowe Dr NE7 . . . . .39 D3
Fell Bank DH3 . . . . .82 D4
Fell Cl Birtley DH3 . . . . .82 E3
 Sunniside NE16 . . . . .69 B2
 Washington NE37 . . . . .83 B7
Fell Ct 5 NE9 . . . . .71 B5
Fell Dyke Com Prim Sch
 NE9 . . . . .71 D3
Fell Pl 7 NE9 . . . . .71 F1
Fell Rd Springwell NE9 . . . . .71 F1
 Sunderland SR4 . . . . .85 D7
Fell Sq SR4 . . . . .85 D7
Fell Terr NE16 . . . . .79 B6
Fell The NE16 . . . . .79 B6
Fell View
 16 Crawcrook NE40 . . . . . .51 F3
 High Spen NE39 . . . . .67 A3
Fell View W 15 NE40 . . . . .51 F3
Fell Way The NE5 . . . . .36 D1
Fellcross DH3 . . . . .82 C5
Felldyke NE10 . . . . .71 F5
Fellgate Ave NE32 . . . . .58 C1
Fellgate Gdns NE10 . . . . . . .72 C8

Fellgate Prim Sch NE32 . .58 B1
Fellgate Sta NE32 . . . . .58 C2
Felling Bsns Ctr NE10 . . . . .56 B1
Felling Dene Gdns NE10 . .56 E1
Felling Gate NE10 . . . . .56 C1
Felling House Gdns
 NE10 . . . . .56 D2
Felling Shore Ind Est
 NE10 . . . . .56 D3
Felling Sta NE10 . . . . .56 D1
Felling View NE6 . . . . .56 F3
Fellmere Ave NE10 . . . . .72 A8
Fells Rd NE11 . . . . .70 D7
Fells The 6 NE9 . . . . .71 A6
Fellsdyke Ct NE9 . . . . .71 C6
Fellside Birtley DH3 . . . . . . .82 D3
 Ponteland NE20 . . . . .25 B1
 South Shields NE34 . . . . . . .60 B5
Fellside Ave NE16 . . . . .69 B3
Fellside Cl NE20 . . . . .25 B1
Fellside Com Prim Sch
 NE16 . . . . .69 A6
Fellside Ct
 Washington NE37 . . . . .83 B6
 Whickham NE16 . . . . .69 A7
Fellside Rd
 Byermoor NE16 . . . . .79 C8
 Whickham NE16 . . . . .68 F3
Fellside The NE3 . . . . .37 F4
Felsham Sq SR4 . . . . .85 E7
Felstead Cres SR4 . . . . . . .85 D7
Felstead Pl NE24 . . . . .17 D4
Felstead Sch SR4 . . . . .85 D6
Felstead Sq SR4 . . . . .85 D6
Felthorpe Ct NE5 . . . . .37 B4
Felton Ave
 Newcastle-u-T NE3 . . . . . . .38 A6
 South Shields NE34 . . . . . . .60 A7
 Whitley Bay NE25 . . . . .32 B4
Felton Cl Morpeth NE61 . . . .9 B7
 Shiremoor NE27 . . . . .30 F3
Felton Cres NE8 . . . . .70 E7
Felton Dr NE12 . . . . .29 F1
Felton Gn 18 NE6 . . . . .56 C6
Felton Ho 14 NE6 . . . . .56 C6
Felton Terr NE63 . . . . .6 D2
Felton Wlk 16 NE6 . . . . . . .56 C6
Fence Rd DH3 . . . . .89 E5
Fencer Ct NE3 . . . . .38 C8
Fenham Chase NE4 . . . . . . .54 E8
Fenham Ct NE4 . . . . .54 E8
Fenham Hall Dr NE4 . . . . . .54 E8
Fenham Rd Lynemouth NE61 1 F3
 Newcastle-u-T NE4 . . . . . . .98 A2
Fenkle St NE1 . . . . .99 A1
Fennel NE9 . . . . .71 C4
Fennel Gr NE3 . . . . .59 E3
Fenning Pl 6 NE6 . . . . .56 C4
Fenside Rd SR2 . . . . .92 F8
Fenton Cl DH2 . . . . .88 A2
Fenton Sq SR4 . . . . .85 D6
Fenton Terr DH4 . . . . .90 D6
Fenton Wlk NE5 . . . . .37 A2
Fenwick Ave Blyth NE24 . . .17 D5
 South Shields NE34 . . . . . . .59 A5
Fenwick Cl
 3 Newcastle-u-T NE2 . . . . .38 F1
 Penshaw NE38 . . . . .90 B8
Fenwick Gr
 4 Hexham NE46 . . . . .45 A5
 Morpeth NE61 . . . . .4 A1
Fenwick St Penshaw DH4 .90 B8
 Boldon Colliery NE35 . . . . . .73 E8
Fenwick Terr
 2 Newcastle-u-T NE2 . . . . .38 F1
 North Shields NE29 . . . . . . .42 A6
Fenwicks St NE35 . . . . .58 E1
Ferguson Cres NE13 . . . . . .28 A4
Ferguson St SR2 . . . . .103 C2
Ferguson's La NE15 . . . . . . .54 B6
Fern Ave Cramlington NE23 16 B2
 Newcastle-u-T,Fawdon NE3 .38 A7
 Newcastle-u-T,Jesmond
 NE2 . . . . .38 F1
 North Shields NE29 . . . . . . .41 F6
 Sunderland SR5 . . . . .75 A2
 Whitburn SR6 . . . . .60 F2
Fern Ct NE62 . . . . .10 E7
Fern Dene Rd NE8 . . . . .70 E8
Fern Dr Cleadon SR6 . . . . . .59 F1
 Dudley NE23 . . . . .29 B8
Fern Gdns NE9 . . . . .70 F6
Fern St SR4 . . . . .102 B3
Fern Terr DH9 . . . . .78 F1
Fernbank NE26 . . . . .24 C6
Fernclough NE9 . . . . .71 C5
Ferndale Ave
 4 East Boldon NE36 . . . . . .74 D7
 Newcastle-u-T NE3 . . . . . . .28 D1
 Wallsend NE28 . . . . .40 C2
Ferndale Ct NE24 . . . . .17 A8
Ferndale Gr NE36 . . . . .74 D7
Ferndale La NE36 . . . . .74 D7
Ferndale Rd DH4 . . . . .90 A8
Ferndale Terr
 5 Springwell NE9 . . . . .71 F1
 Sunderland SR4 . . . . .85 E8
Ferndene
 Longbenton NE12 . . . . .39 D7
 Wallsend NE28 . . . . .40 E4
Ferndene Cres SR4 . . . . . . .85 F6
Ferndene Ct NE3 . . . . .38 C4
Ferndene Gr
 Newcastle-u-T NE7 . . . . . . .39 C3
 Ryton NE40 . . . . .52 D6
Ferndown Ct
 Gateshead NE10 . . . . .72 B7
 Ryton NE40 . . . . .52 D4

Ferngrove NE32 . . . . .73 C8
Fernhill Ave NE16 . . . . .69 A7
Fernlea NF23 . . . . .29 B8
Fernlea Cl NE38 . . . . .83 E2
Fernlea Gdns NE40 . . . . . . .52 A4
Fernlea Gn NE3 . . . . .37 F5
Fernley Villas NE23 . . . . . . .22 D6
Fernsway SR3 . . . . .86 B3
Fernville Ave NE16 . . . . .69 B2
Fernville Rd NE3 . . . . .38 B3
Fernville St SR4 . . . . .102 B1
Fernway NE61 . . . . .9 B8
Fernwood NE2 . . . . .99 B4
Fernwood Ave NE3 . . . . .38 D6
Fernwood Cl SR3 . . . . .92 A5
Fernwood Gr NE39 . . . . .77 F5
Fernwood Rd
 Newcastle-u-T,Jesmond
 NE2 . . . . .99 B4
 Newcastle-u-T,Lemington
 NE15 . . . . .53 D6
Fernyhough Hall NE31 . . . . .57 F5
Ferrand Dr DH4 . . . . .94 D8
Ferriby Cl NE3 . . . . .38 D8
Ferrisdale Way NE3 . . . . . . .37 F7
Ferry App NE33 . . . . .42 C3
Ferry Landing NE42 . . . . . . .49 F3
Ferry Mews
 North Shields NE29 . . . . . . .42 B4
 South Shields NE33 . . . . . . .42 B3
Ferry Rd NE46 . . . . .45 C6
Ferry St Jarrow NE32 . . . . . .58 B8
 South Shields NE33 . . . . . . .42 B3
Ferryboat La
 Sunderland,Castletown SR5 85 A7
 Sunderland,Hylton Castle
 SR5 . . . . .73 F2
Ferrydene Ave NE3 . . . . .37 F4
Festival Cotts NE12 . . . . . . .29 B5
Festival Park Dr NE11 . . . . .70 B7
Festival Way NE11,NE8 . .100 A1
Fetcham Ct NE3 . . . . .37 C7
Fewster Sq NE10 . . . . .72 A6
Field Ho
 9 North Shields NE30 . . . .42 B6
 Silksworth SR3 . . . . .92 A5
Field House Farm SR7 . .92 F1
Field House Rd NE8 . . . . . . .70 E7
Field House Terr DH6 . . . . .97 F3
Field La NE10 . . . . .72 A8
Field Sq SR4 . . . . .85 D6
Field St
 8 Gateshead NE10 . . . . . .56 D1
 Newcastle-u-T NE3 . . . . . . .38 E5
Field Terr Jarrow NE32 . . . . .58 B5
 4 Throckley NE15 . . . . . . .35 D2
Fieldfare Cl 2 NE38 . . . . . .82 F3
Fieldfare Ct NE16 . . . . .79 C5
Fieldfare Ho 9 NE24 . . . . . .17 F8
Fieldhouse Cl NE61 . . . . .9 F5
Fieldhouse La NE61 . . . . .9 E5
Fielding Ct NE34 . . . . .59 A3
Fielding Pl NE9 . . . . .71 B8
Fieldside East Rainton DH5 94 C3
 Whitburn SR6 . . . . .60 E1
Fieldway NE32 . . . . .73 D8
Fife Ave
 Brockley Whins NE32 . . . . .58 E3
 Chester le S DH2 . . . . .88 C3
Fife St NE8 . . . . .56 A1
Fife Terr NE17 . . . . .77 B6
Fifteenth Ave NE24 . . . . . . .17 D6
Fifth Ave Ashington NE63 . . .6 E3
 Blyth NE24 . . . . .17 D6
 Chester le S DH2 . . . . .88 B3
 Gateshead NE98,NE11 . . . .70 D5
 Morpeth NE61 . . . . .9 B7
 Newcastle-u-T NE6 . . . . . . .56 C7
Fifth Row NE61 . . . . .1 A3
Filey Ct NE23 . . . . .22 B8
Filton Cl NE23 . . . . .22 B8
Finchale NE38 . . . . .83 C3
Finchale Cl Dunston NE11 .69 F6
 Houghton-le-S DH4 . . . . . . .94 D8
 Sunderland SR2 . . . . .103 B1
Finchale Gdns
 Gateshead NE9 . . . . .71 C2
 Throckley NE15 . . . . .35 D3
Finchale Rd NE31 . . . . .57 E3
Finchale Terr
 Great Lumley DH4 . . . . .89 E1
 Jarrow NE32 . . . . .58 D4
 2 Newcastle-u-T NE6 . . . . .56 C4
Finchdale Cl NE29 . . . . .41 F4
Finchdale Terr 2 DH3 . . . .88 C3
Finchley Cres NE6 . . . . .57 A8
Finchley Ct NE6 . . . . .57 A8
Findon Gr NE29 . . . . .41 E4
Fine La DH8 . . . . .76 B3
Fines Rd DH8 . . . . .77 B1
Finsbury Ave NE6 . . . . .56 E6
Finsbury St 2 SR5 . . . . . . .75 C1
Finsmere Pl 1 NE5 . . . . . . .37 B1
Finstock Ct NE3 . . . . .38 F4
Fir Gr Ellington NE61 . . . . . . .1 D4
 South Shields NE34 . . . . . . .59 F5
Fir St NE32 . . . . .58 A7
Fir Terr NE16 . . . . .79 B6
Firbank Ave NE30 . . . . .32 B2
Firbanks NF32 . . . . .58 D1
Fire Station Cotts SR6 . . .75 D4
Firfield Rd NE5 . . . . .37 D2
Firs The NE3 . . . . .38 B4
First Ave Ashington NE63 . . .6 E4
 Blyth NE24 . . . . .17 D6
 Chester le S DH2 . . . . .88 B8
 Gateshead NE11 . . . . .70 C6

First Ave continued
 Morpeth NE61 . . . . .9 B7
 Newcastle-u-T NE6 . . . . . . .56 C7
 North Shields NE29 . . . . . . .41 C4
First Row Ashington NE63 . .6 A4
 Ellington NE61 . . . . .1 E4
 Linton NE61 . . . . .1 A3
First St NE8 . . . . .101 A1
Firth Sq SR4 . . . . .85 D7
Firtree Ave
 Longbenton NE12 . . . . .29 D1
 Wallsend NE6 . . . . .40 A1
 Washington NE38 . . . . .83 C1
Firtree Cres NE12 . . . . .29 C1
Firtree Gdns NE25 . . . . .31 F3
Firtree Rd NE16 . . . . .69 A6
Firtrees Chester le S DH2 .88 B5
 Gateshead NE10 . . . . .71 E5
Firtrees Ave NE28 . . . . .41 B3
Firwood Cres NE39 . . . . . . .67 A3
Firwood Gdns NE11 . . . . . . .70 B5
Fish Quay NE30 . . . . .42 C6
Fisher Ind Est NE6 . . . . .57 B7
Fisher La NE13,NE23 . . . . .21 B5
Fisher Rd NE27 . . . . .30 B6
Fisher St NE6 . . . . .57 A5
Fisherwell Rd NE10 . . . . . . .57 A1
Fitzpatrick Pl SR3 . . . . .92 E2
Fitzroy Terr 7 SR5 . . . . . . .74 F2
Fitzsimmons Ave NE28 . . . .40 B3
Flag Ho NE33 . . . . .42 E1
Flag Lo NE33 . . . . .42 E1
Flagg Ct NE33 . . . . .42 D3
Flaunden Cl NE34 . . . . .60 B5
Flax Sq SR4 . . . . .85 C7
Flaxby Cl NE3 . . . . .38 D8
Fleet St SR1 . . . . .103 C2
Fleming Bsns Ctr NE2 . . . .99 B4
Fleming Ct NE8 . . . . .100 C2
Fleming Gdns NE10 . . . . . . .71 D7
Fletcher Cres DH4 . . . . .90 E6
Fletcher Ho NE29 . . . . .41 E3
Fletcher Terr DH4 . . . . .90 D4
Flexbury Gdns
 Gateshead,Lyndhurst NE9 . .71 A2
 Gateshead,Mount Pleasant
 NE10 . . . . .71 C8
 Newcastle-u-T NE15 . . . . . .53 E7
Flint Hill Bank DH9 . . . . . . .78 E1
Flixton NE38 . . . . .90 B1
Flock Sq SR4 . . . . .85 D7
Flodden NE38 . . . . .29 D4
Flodden Rd SR4 . . . . .85 D6
Flodden St NE6 . . . . .56 D5
Flora St 12 NE6 . . . . .56 B6
Floral Dene SR4 . . . . .85 A6
Floralia Ave SR2 . . . . .93 A6
Florence Ave NE9 . . . . .71 A6
Florence Cres 4 SR5 . . . . .74 F2
Florence St NE21 . . . . .53 B1
Florence Terr DH5 . . . . .95 A2
Florida St SR4 . . . . .85 F8
Flotterton Gdns NE5 . . . . . .54 C7
Flour Mill Rd NE11 . . . . .54 F2
Fold The Burnopfield NE16 .79 A7
 Newcastle-u-T NE6 . . . . . . .57 A8
 Silksworth SR3 . . . . .92 B5
 Whitley Bay NE25 . . . . .31 E5
Folds The
 East Rainton DH5 . . . . .94 D4
 Fence Houses DH4 . . . . . . .94 B8
Folldon Ave NE6 . . . . .75 D3
Follingsby Ave NE10 . . . . . .72 D6
Follingsby Dr NE10 . . . . . . .72 C7
Follingsby La NE10 . . . . . . .72 E5
Follingsby Pk NE10 . . . . . . .72 D5
Follingsby Way NE10 . . . . . .72 D6
Follonsby Terr NE10 . . . . . .72 E7
Folly La NE40 . . . . .52 B2
Folly The NE36 . . . . .74 A7
Folly Yd NE40 . . . . .52 C2
Font Side NE61 . . . . .3 A1
Fontburn NE61 . . . . .1 E6
Fontburn Cres NE63 . . . . . . .6 F3
Fontburn Ct
 North Shields NE29 . . . . . . .41 D4
 Sunderland SR5 . . . . .74 F4
Fontburn Gdns NE61 . . . . . .8 E7
Fontburn Pl NE7 . . . . .39 A5
Fontburn Rd
 Bedlington NE22 . . . . .11 C1
 Seaton Delaval NE25 . . . . . .23 D3
Fontburn Terr NE30 . . . . . . .42 B6
Fonteyn Pl NE23 . . . . .16 B2
Fontwell Dr NE8 . . . . .70 D7
Forbeck Rd SR4 . . . . .85 D6
Forber Ave NE34 . . . . .60 B6
Forbes St SR2 . . . . .92 E6
Ford Ave Ashington NE63 . . .6 D2
 North Shields NE29 . . . . . . .41 D4
 Sunderland SR4 . . . . .85 A6
Ford Cres Jarrow NE32 . . . .58 B3
 Shiremoor NE27 . . . . .30 C3
 Sunderland SR4 . . . . .85 A6
Ford Dr NE24 . . . . .17 C7
Ford Gr NE3 . . . . .38 B7
Ford Hall Dr SR4 . . . . .85 E6
Ford Oval SR4 . . . . .85 B7
Ford Pk NE62 . . . . .11 C8
Ford Rise NE43 . . . . .64 C7
Ford St Gateshead NE8 . . . .56 B1
 Newcastle-u-T NE6 . . . . . . .56 B4
Ford Terr Guide Post NE62 .10 F7
 Riding Mill NE44 . . . . .63 A8
 5 Sunderland SR4 . . . . . . .85 F6
 Wallsend NE28 . . . . .40 F2
Ford The NE42 . . . . .50 C2
Ford View NE23 . . . . .22 A1

Fordenbridge Cres SR4 . .85 E6
Fordenbridge Rd SR4 . . . .85 E6
Fordenbridge Sq SR4 . . . .85 E6
Fordfield Rd SR4 . . . . .85 E6
Fordham Rd SR4 . . . . .85 E6
Fordham Sq SR4 . . . . .85 E6
Fordland Pl SR4 . . . . .85 F6
Fordley Com Prim Sch
 NE23 . . . . .29 A8
Fordmoss Wlk NE5 . . . . . . .37 A2
Fore St Hexham NE46 . . . . .45 B5
 Newcastle-u-T NE2 . . . . . . .56 A8
Forest Ave NE12 . . . . .39 E8
Forest Dr NE38 . . . . .88 F8
Forest Gate NE12 . . . . .30 A1
Forest Hall Prim Sch
 NE12 . . . . .29 D1
Forest Hall Rd NE12 . . . . . .29 E1
Forest Rd
 Newcastle-u-T NE15 . . . . . .54 C4
 South Shields NE33 . . . . . . .42 C2
 Sunderland SR4 . . . . .85 D6
Forest Rd Ind Est 5
 NE33 . . . . .42 C2
Forest Villa NE12 . . . . .39 E8
Forest Way NE23 . . . . .22 F1
Forestborn Ct 5 NE5 . . . . .36 F2
Forfar St SR6 . . . . .75 D2
Forge Cl NE17 . . . . .77 B6
Forge La Bournmoor DH3 . .89 B2
 Hamsterley Mill NE17 . . . . .77 E5
Forge Rd NE11,NE8 . . . . . . .70 A8
Forge The NE4 . . . . .85 F7
Forge Wlk NE15 . . . . .35 F1
Forres Pl NE23 . . . . .22 B8
Forrest Rd NE28 . . . . .40 A1
Forster Ave
 Bedlington NE22 . . . . .10 E1
 Sherburn DH6 . . . . .96 A3
 South Shields NE34 . . . . . . .59 E6
Forster Ct 6 NE9 . . . . .70 F4
Forster St Blyth NE24 . . . . . .17 F7
 Newcastle-u-T NE1 . . . . . . .99 C1
 Sunderland SR6 . . . . .75 E1
Forsyth Rd NE2 . . . . .38 E1
Forsyth St NE29 . . . . .31 B1
Fort Sq 2 NE33 . . . . .42 C4
Fort St NE33 . . . . .42 D4
Forth Banks NE1 . . . . .101 A4
Forth Ct 7 Silksworth SR3 91 F1
 South Shields NE34 . . . . . . .59 C5
Forth La NE1 . . . . .101 A4
Forth Pl NE1 . . . . .100 C1
Forth St Chopwell NE17 . . . .66 C1
 Newcastle-u-T NE1 . . . . . .101 A4
Fortrose Ave SR3 . . . . .86 A3
Forum Ct NE22 . . . . .10 F1
Forum The
 Newcastle-u-T NE15 . . . . . .53 F7
 2 Wallsend NE28 . . . . .40 B1
Forum Way NE23 . . . . .22 E6
Foss Way Ebchester DH8 . .76 E3
 South Shields NE34 . . . . . . .59 B5
Fossdyke NE10 . . . . .71 F5
Fosse Law NE15 . . . . .35 E1
Fosse Terr NE9 . . . . .71 B6
Fossefeld NE10 . . . . .72 A7
Fossway NE6 . . . . .56 E7
Foster Ct NE11 . . . . .70 C3
Foster Dr NE8 . . . . .56 B2
Foster St
 Newcastle-u-T,Low Walker
 NE6 . . . . .57 B6
 Newcastle-u-T,Wincomblee
 NE6 . . . . .57 B5
Foundary Ct NE6 . . . . .56 C4
Foundry Ct NE6 . . . . .56 C4
Foundry La NE6 . . . . .56 A6
Fountain Cl NE22 . . . . .10 F1
Fountain Gr NE34 . . . . .59 F8
Fountain Head Bank
 NE26 . . . . .24 C6
Fountain La NE21 . . . . .53 C3
Fountain Row NE2 . . . . .98 B3
Fountains Cl
 Dunston NE11 . . . . .69 F6
 Washington NE38 . . . . .83 D4
Fountains Cres
 Burnside DH4 . . . . .90 C2
 Hebburn NE31 . . . . .57 D7
Four Lane Ends
 Hetton le H DH5 . . . . .95 B2
 Houghton-le-S DH5 . . . . . . .94 E7
Four Lane Ends Sta NE7 .39 C5
Fouracres Rd NE5 . . . . .37 E2
Fourstones NE5 . . . . .37 A2
Fourstones Cl NE3 . . . . .37 D5
Fourstones Rd SR4 . . . . . . .85 E6
Fourteenth Ave NE24 . . . . .17 D6
Fourth Ave Ashington NE63 . .6 D3
 Blyth NE24 . . . . .17 D6
 Chester le S DH2 . . . . .88 B3
 Gateshead NE11 . . . . .70 C5
 Morpeth NE61 . . . . .9 B7
 1 Newcastle-u-T NE6 . . . . .56 C7
Fourth Row NE61 . . . . .1 A3
Fourth St NE8 . . . . .101 A1
Fowberry Cres NE4 . . . . . . .54 E7
Fowberry Rd NE15 . . . . .53 F4
Fowler Cl DH4 . . . . .90 C4
Fowler Gdns 2 NE11 . . . . .54 F1
Fowler St NE33 . . . . .42 C4
Fox & Hounds La NE15 . . . .54 C6
Fox & Hounds Rd NE5 . . . .54 C6
Fox Ave NE34 . . . . .59 A4
Fox Covert La NE20 . . . . . .25 D6
Fox Ho SR3 . . . . .92 A4
Fox Lea Wlk NE23 . . . . .22 C1

Fox St Gateshead NE10 . . .56 C1
Sunderland SR2 . . . . .102 B1
Foxcover NE63 . . . . .6 F1
Foxcover La SR3 . . . . .91 B7
Foxcover Rd
  Sunderland,Middle Herrington
  SR3 . . . . .91 A4
  Sunderland,Offerton SR4 . .84 F2
Foxglove DH4 . . . . .89 F5
Foxglove CI NE24 . . . . .17 C4
Foxglove Ct NE34 . . . . .59 B4
Foxhill CI NE63 . . . . .6 B1
Foxhills CI NE38 . . . . .83 E2
Foxhills Covert NE16 . . . . . .68 E5
Foxhills The NE16 . . . . .68 E6
Foxhomes NE32 . . . . .73 D8
Foxhunters Light Ind Site
  NE25 . . . . .31 F3
Foxhunters Rd NE25 . . . . . .31 F3
Foxlair CI SR3 . . . . .92 A4
Foxley NE37 . . . . .83 E8
Foxley CI NE12 . . . . .29 E5
Foxton Ave
  Newcastle-u-T NE3 . . . . . . .37 F7
  Tynemouth NE30 . . . . .32 B3
Foxton CI NE29 . . . . .41 E3
Foxton Ct SR6 . . . . .60 A1
Foxton Gn NE3 . . . . .37 E5
Foxton Hall NE37 . . . . .72 D3
Foxton Way NE10 . . . . .57 B2
Foyle St SR1 . . . . .103 A2
Framlington Ho NE2 . . . . . . .98 C3
Framlington PI NE2 . . . . .98 C3
Frances St Blaydon NE21 . . .53 A2
  9 New Silksworth SR3 . . .92 A7
Frances Ville NE62 . . . . .10 E4
Francis St Beamish DH9 . . . .80 D1
  Sunderland SR6 . . . . .75 D2
Francis Way NE27 . . . . .30 D1
Frank Bushell Ho NE34 . . . .59 C5
Frank PI NE29 . . . . .42 A6
Frank St Greenside NE40 . . .51 F1
  Sunderland SR5 . . . . .75 B2
  Wallsend NE28 . . . . .40 B1
Frankham St **1** NE5 . . . . . .36 F2
Frankland Dr NE25 . . . . .31 E3
Franklin Ct **10** NE37 . . . . . .83 D8
Franklin Pk NE21 . . . . .53 E4
Franklin St
  South Shields NE33 . . . . . .42 C2
  Sunderland SR4 . . . . .102 A3
Franklyn Ave NE26 . . . . .24 B7
Fraser CI NE33 . . . . .59 B8
Frazer Terr NE10 . . . . .57 A1
Freda St SR5 . . . . .74 F1
Frederick Gdns DH4 . . . . . . .90 A7
Frederick Rd SR1 . . . . .103 A3
Frederick St
  Chopwell NE17 . . . . .77 B8
  South Shields NE33 . . . . . .42 C1
  Sunderland SR1 . . . . .103 A2
  Sunderland,South Hylton
  SR4 . . . . .85 A6
Frederick Terr
  Hetton le H DH5 . . . . .95 B1
  South Hetton DH6 . . . . . . .97 F6
  3 Whitburn SR6 . . . . .60 F1
Freehold Ct NE62 . . . . .10 F7
Freehold St **5** NE24 . . . . . .17 F8
Freeman Hospl NE7 . . . . . . .39 A4
Freeman Rd NE3,NE7 . . . . . .38 F7
Freeman Way
  Ashington NE63 . . . . .6 F1
  Whitley Bay NE26 . . . . .31 E7
Freesia Grange NE38 . . . . . .83 E3
Freezemoor Rd DH4 . . . . . . .90 D6
Fremantle Rd NE34 . . . . .60 B5
French St NE24 . . . . .17 C4
Frenchman's Row NE15 . . . .35 B2
Frenchman's Way NE34 . . . .60 B8
Frensham NE38 . . . . .84 A4
Frenton CI NE5 . . . . .36 C2
Friar Rd SR4 . . . . .85 D6
Friar Sq SR4 . . . . .85 D6
Friar Way NE32 . . . . .58 C7
Friar's Row NE16 . . . . .78 F5
Friarage Ave SR6 . . . . .75 D3
Friars NE1 . . . . .98 C1
Friars Dene Rd NE10 . . . . . .56 C2
Friars Gate NE61 . . . . .8 D7
Friars St NE1 . . . . .98 C1
Friars Way NE5 . . . . .54 C8
Friarsfield CI SR3 . . . . .91 E5
Friarside Cres NE39 . . . . . . .78 D8
Friarside Gdns
  Burnopfield NE16 . . . . .78 F6
  Whickham NE16 . . . . .69 A6
Friarside Rd NE4 . . . . .54 E8
Friary Gdns NE10 . . . . .56 C1
Frinton Pk SR3 . . . . .86 A3
Frobisher Ct SR3 . . . . .91 F6
Frobisher St NE31 . . . . .58 A6
Frome Gdns NE9 . . . . .70 F2
Frome PI NE23 . . . . .22 B8
Frome Sq SR4 . . . . .85 C6
Front Rd SR4 . . . . .85 D6
Front St Annitsford NE23 . . .22 B1
  Blaydon NE21 . . . . .53 B1
  Blyth NE24 . . . . .16 E7
  Boldon Colliery NE35 . . . . .58 E1
  Burnopfield NE16 . . . . .79 B6
  Burnopfield,Hobson NE16 . .79 A4
  Burnopfield,Lintz NE16 . . . .78 E6
  Cleadon SR6 . . . . .60 A1
  Corbridge NE45 . . . . .46 F5
  Cramlington NE23 . . . . . . .22 B6
  Dinnington NE13 . . . . .27 B7

Front St continued
Dipton DH9 . . . . .78 E1
Earsdon NE25 . . . . .31 A5
East Boldon NE36 . . . . .74 C7
Ebchester DH8 . . . . .76 E3
Ellington NE61 . . . . .1 C5
Fence Houses DH4 . . . . .94 A8
Guide Post NE62 . . . . .10 E7
Haswell DH6 . . . . .97 E1
Hetton le H DH5 . . . . .95 A3
Hetton le Hole,Low Moorsley
  DH5 . . . . .94 E1
High Pittington DH6 . . . . .96 B6
High Spen NE39 . . . . .67 A5
Killingworth NE12,NE23 . . . .29 B5
Longbenton NE7,NE12 . . . . .39 C5
Newbiggin-by-t-S NE64 . . . . .7 E4
Newbottle DH4 . . . . .90 D3
Newbottle DH4 . . . . .90 A4
North Shields NE29 . . . . .41 E5
Prudhoe NE42 . . . . .50 D2
Prudhoe,Hagg Bank NE41 . .50 F5
Seghill NE23 . . . . .22 F2
Sherburn DH6 . . . . .96 A1
Sherburn Hill DH6 . . . . .96 D1
South Hetton DH6 . . . . .97 F7
Tanfield DH9 . . . . .79 B3
Tantobie DH9 . . . . .79 B2
Tynemouth NE30 . . . . .42 D7
Tynemouth,Cullercoats
  NE30 . . . . .32 C3
Tynemouth,Preston NE29 . . .42 A8
Washington NE37 . . . . .83 D8
Whickham NE16 . . . . .69 B7
Whickham,Swalwell NE16 . . .54 A1
Whitburn SR6 . . . . .75 F8
Whitley Bay NE25,NE26 . . . .31 C6
Front St E Bedlington NE22 . .16 A8
  Haswell DH6 . . . . .97 F3
  Prudhoe NE42 . . . . .90 B8
Front St W
  Bedlington NE22 . . . . .15 F8
  Penshaw DH4 . . . . .90 B8
Front Street Com Prim Sch
  NE16 . . . . .69 A7
Frosterley CI DH5 . . . . .97 D8
Frosterley Gdns SR3 . . . . . .86 B2
Frosterley PI NE4 . . . . .98 A2
Frosterley Wlk NE16 . . . . . . .69 B3
Froude Ave NE34 . . . . .59 C3
Fuchsia Gdns NE31 . . . . . . .57 E3
Fuchsia PI NE5 . . . . .37 D2
Fulbrook CI NE23 . . . . .16 B2
Fulbrook Rd NE3 . . . . .37 F5
Fuller Rd SR2 . . . . .86 E4
Fullerton PI NE9 . . . . .71 A8
Fulmar Dr Blyth NE24 . . . . . .17 E3
  Washington NE38 . . . . .82 F3
Fulmar Lodge NE33 . . . . . . .42 F2
Fulmar Wlk SR6 . . . . .60 F2
Fulwell Ave NE34 . . . . .60 B7
Fulwell Gn NE5 . . . . .37 B1
Fulwell Inf Sch SR6 . . . . . . .75 D4
Fulwell Jun Sch SR6 . . . . . .75 E4
Fulwell Mill★ SR5 . . . . .75 C3
Fulwell Rd SR6 . . . . .75 D2
Furnace Bank NE22 . . . . . . .11 D1
Furness Ct **1** SR3 . . . . .91 F6
Furrowfield NE10 . . . . .71 C6
Furrowfield Jun Sch
  DH3 . . . . .82 D3
Furrowfield Sch NE10 . . . . . .71 C6
Furzefield Rd SR3 . . . . .38 B4
Fyling Ho **3** SR3 . . . . .91 F5
Fylingdale Dr SR3 . . . . .92 C7

G

Gables Ct SR4 . . . . .85 C3
Gables The **3** Blyth NE24 . .17 D8
  Newcastle-u-T NE13 . . . . . .37 B7
  4 Washington NE38 . . . . .83 E4
Gadwall Rd DH4 . . . . .94 B6
Gainers Terr NE28 . . . . .57 C8
Gainford Chester le S DH2 . .88 A3
  Gateshead NE9 . . . . .70 F2
Gainsborough Ave
  Washington NE38 . . . . .83 E4
  Whiteleas NE34 . . . . .59 D2
Gainsborough CI NE25 . . . . .31 C1
Gainsborough Cres
  Gateshead NE9 . . . . .71 B7
  Shiney Row DH4 . . . . .90 A1
Gainsborough PI NE23 . . . . .22 B3
Gainsborough Rd SR4 . . . . .85 C2
Gainsborough Sq SR4 . . . . .85 C2
Gainsbro Gr NE4 . . . . .54 F6
Gainsford Ave NE9 . . . . .70 E4
Gairloch CI NE23 . . . . .16 B1
Gairloch Dr NE38 . . . . .83 A3
Gairloch Rd SR4 . . . . .85 C3
Gairsay CI SR2 . . . . .92 E8
Galashiels Gr DH4 . . . . .90 B5
Galashiels Rd SR4 . . . . .85 C3
Galashiels Sq SR4 . . . . .85 C3
Galen Ho **4** NE1 . . . . .99 A1
Gallalaw Terr NE3 . . . . .38 F5
Gallant Terr NE28 . . . . .41 C1
Galleries The NE38 . . . . .83 C5
Galley's Gill Rd SR1 . . . . . .102 C2
Galloping Green Cotts **2**
  NE9 . . . . .71 D2
Galloping Green Farm CI **3**
  NE9 . . . . .71 D2
Galloping Green Rd NE9 . . . .71 D2
Gallowgate NE1 . . . . .98 C1
Gallowhill La NE15,NE42 . . .50 B7

Gallows Bank NE46 . . . . .45 B3
Galsworthy Ctr The NE34 . . .59 B2
Galsworthy Rd
  Biddick Hall NE34 . . . . .59 B3
  Sunderland SR4 . . . . .85 C3
  Whiteleas NE34 . . . . .59 C3
Galway Rd SR4 . . . . .85 B3
Galway Sq SR4 . . . . .85 B3
Gambia Rd **4** SR4 . . . . .85 B2
Gambia Sq NE4 . . . . .85 B2
Ganton Ave NE23 . . . . .22 B4
Ganton CI NE37 . . . . .72 C2
Ganton Ct NE34 . . . . .59 F3
Gaprigg Ct NE46 . . . . .45 B4
Gaprigg La NE46 . . . . .45 A4
Garasdale CI NE24 . . . . .17 D4
Garcia Terr **3** SR6 . . . . .75 E1
Garden City Villas NE63 . . . . .6 D3
Garden CI NE13 . . . . .28 B8
Garden Cres DH8 . . . . .76 F4
Garden Croft NF12 . . . . .39 F8
Garden Dr NE31 . . . . .57 D4
Garden Est DH5 . . . . .95 B4
Garden House Cres NE16 .69 C8
Garden House Est NE40 . . . .51 E4
Garden House Farm DH2 .88 E1
Garden La Cleadon SR6 . . . .74 F8
  South Shields NE33 . . . . . .42 C2
Garden Pk **9** NE28 . . . . . . .40 F4
Garden PI Penshaw DH4 . . . .90 B7
  Sunderland SR1 . . . . .102 C3
Garden St Blaydon NE21 . . . .53 C3
  Newbottle DH4 . . . . .90 D3
  Newcastle-u-T NE3 . . . . . . .38 C4
Garden Terr
  10 Blaydon NE21 . . . . . . .53 B1
  Crawcrook NE40 . . . . .51 F4
  Crawcrook,Ryton Woodside
  NE40 . . . . .52 A3
  Earsdon NE25 . . . . .31 A5
  Hexham NE46 . . . . .45 A5
  Newbottle DH4 . . . . .90 D3
Gardener St NE4 . . . . .100 A3
Gardens The
  Chester le S DH2 . . . . .88 B3
  Washington NE38 . . . . .83 E4
  Whitley Bay NE25 . . . . .31 F4
Gardiner Rd SR4 . . . . .85 B3
Gardiner Sq
  Kibblesworth NE11 . . . . . . .81 C6
  4 Sunderland SR4 . . . . . .85 B3
Gardner Pk NE29 . . . . .41 F5
Gardner PI NE29 . . . . .42 B5
Garesfield Gdns
  Burnopfield NE16 . . . . .78 F6
  Rowlands Gill NE39 . . . . . . .67 E8
Garesfield La NE21,NE39 . . .67 E6
Gareston CI NE24 . . . . .17 B7
Garfield St **6** SR4 . . . . .85 F7
Garland Terr **4** DH4 . . . . . .94 A8
Garleigh CI NE12 . . . . .29 F3
Garmondsway **15** NE6 . . . .56 C5
Garner CI NE11 . . . . .36 D3
Garnet St **3** SR4 . . . . .85 F7
Garrett CI NE28 . . . . .40 F3
Garrick CI NE29 . . . . .41 C7
Garrick St NE33 . . . . .59 C8
Garrigill NE38 . . . . .83 F1
Garsdale DH3 . . . . .82 E1
Garsdale Ave NE37 . . . . .83 C8
Garsdale Rd NE26 . . . . .24 E1
Garside Ave DH3 . . . . .82 C6
Garstin CI NE7 . . . . .39 E3
Garth Cotts NE46 . . . . .45 A5
Garth Cres Blaydon NE21 . . .53 B1
  South Shields NE34 . . . . . .43 A1
Garth Farm Rd NE21 . . . . . . .53 B1
Garth Heads NE1 . . . . .99 C1
Garth Sixteen NE12 . . . . . . .29 D4
Garth The
  7 Blaydon NE21 . . . . .53 B1
  Medomsley DH8 . . . . .77 C2
  Newcastle-u-T NE5 . . . . . . .36 E1
  Newcastle-u-T,Kenton NE3 .37 F4
Garth Thirty Three NE12 . . .29 D3
Garth Thirty Two NE12 . . . . .29 E3
Garth Twenty NE12 . . . . .29 E3
Garth Twenty Five NE12 . . . .29 E3
Garth Twenty Four NE12 . . .29 E3
Garth Twenty One NE12 . . . .29 E4
Garth Twenty Seven
  NE12 . . . . .29 E3
Garth Twenty Two NE12 . . . .29 E3
Garthfield CI NE5 . . . . .37 A3
Garthfield Cnr NE5 . . . . .37 A3
Garthfield Cres NE5 . . . . . . .37 A3
Gartland Rd SR4 . . . . .85 B3
Garvey Villas N10,NE9 . . . . .71 C6
Garwood St NE33 . . . . .59 B8
Gas House La NE61 . . . . .4 A1
Gas La NE21 . . . . .53 C4
Gaskell Ave NE34 . . . . .59 B3
Gatacre St NE24 . . . . .17 E8
Gate The NE1 . . . . .98 C1
Gateley Ave NE24 . . . . .17 D4
Gatesgarth NE9 . . . . .71 A5
Gatesgarth Gr SR6 . . . . .75 D5
Gateshead Coll NE9 . . . . . . .70 F7
Gateshead Coll (Annexe)
  NE9 . . . . .71 A7
Gateshead Highway
  NE8 . . . . .101 C2
Gateshead International Stad
  (Athletics Gd) NE10 . . . . .56 C2
Gateshead Jewish Boarding
  Sch NE8 . . . . .101 B1

Gateshead Jewish Prim Sch
  NE8 . . . . .101 B1
Gateshead Jewish Teachers
  Training Coll NE8 . . . . . . .101 B1
Gateshead Rd NE16 . . . . . . .69 C3
Gateshead Sta NE8 . . . . . . .101 B1
Gateshead Stadium Sta
  NE8 . . . . .56 A2
Gateshead Talmudical Coll
  NE8 . . . . .101 B1
Gatwick Ct NE3 . . . . .37 C7
Gatwick Rd SR4 . . . . .85 B3
Gaughan CI NE6 . . . . .56 F3
Gaweswell Terr DH4 . . . . . . .90 D4
Gayhurst Cres SR3 . . . . .92 B6
Gayton Rd NE37 . . . . .72 E1
Geddes Rd SR4 . . . . .85 B3
Gellesfield Chare NE16 . . . .69 B4
Gelt Cres DH5 . . . . .95 A5
General Graham St SR4 . . .102 A1
General Havelock Rd
  SR4 . . . . .85 E6
General's Wood The
  NE38 . . . . .89 B8
Geneva Rd **5** SR4 . . . . .85 B3
Genister PI NE4 . . . . .54 D8
Geoffrey St Whitburn SR6 . .60 F1
  Whiteleas NE34 . . . . .59 C3
George Rd
  Bedlington NE22 . . . . .11 C3
  Wallsend NE28 . . . . .57 B8
George Scott St NE33 . . . . .42 D4
George Smith Gdns
  NE10 . . . . .56 C2
George Sq **6** NE30 . . . . . . .42 B6
George St Ashington NE63 . . .6 F4
  Blaydon NE21 . . . . .53 D3
  Blyth NE24 . . . . .17 E6
  Brunswick Village NE13 . . .28 A6
  Chester le S DH3 . . . . .88 D2
  5 Crawcrook NE40 . . . . . .51 F3
  5 Gateshead NE10 . . . . . .56 F1
  Haswell DH6 . . . . .97 F3
  Hetton le H DH5 . . . . .95 A5
  Newcastle-u-T NE1,NE4 . .100 C4
  Newcastle-u-T,Coxlodge
  NE3 . . . . .38 A5
  North Shields NE30 . . . . . .42 B6
  Ryhope SR2 . . . . .93 A6
  Sherburn DH6 . . . . .96 A1
  Walbottle NE15 . . . . .35 F2
  Wallsend NE28 . . . . .41 B1
  Whickham NE16 . . . . .69 A7
George St E SR3 . . . . .92 A8
George St N SR6 . . . . .103 A4
George St W **10** SR3 . . . . . .92 A8
George Stephenson Com
  High Sch NE12 . . . . .29 D3
George Stephenson Way
  NE29 . . . . .42 A3
George Stephenson's
  Cottage★ NE41 . . . . .51 D7
George Washington Prim Sch
  NE37 . . . . .72 C1
George's View NE23 . . . . . . .29 A7
Georges Rd
  Newcastle-u-T NE4 . . . . . . .54 D4
  Newcastle-u-T,Elswick NE4 .54 F3
Georgian Ct
  Longbenton NE12 . . . . .29 B1
  Sunderland SR4 . . . . .86 A4
Gerald St
  Newcastle-u-T NE4 . . . . . . .54 D4
  Whiteleas NE34 . . . . .59 C3
Gerrard CI
  Cramlington NE23 . . . . . . .22 B4
  Whitley Bay NE26 . . . . .24 E1
Gerrard Rd
  6 Sunderland SR4 . . . . . .85 B3
  Whitley Bay NE26 . . . . .24 F1
Gertrude St DH4 . . . . .90 D2
Ghyll Edge NE61 . . . . .3 C1
Gibbon's Wlk NE34 . . . . .59 A2
Gibbs Ct **3** DH2 . . . . .88 C2
Gibside Chester le S DH2 . . .88 A3
  ★ Rowlands Gill NE16 . . . . .68 B2
Gibside Chapel★ NE16 . . . . .68 A1
Gibside Cres NE16 . . . . .79 D8
Gibside Ct
  Burnopfield NE16 . . . . .79 B6
  Dunston NE11 . . . . .69 F6
Gibside Gdns NE15 . . . . .54 B6
Gibside Sch NE16 . . . . .69 A5
Gibside Terr NE16 . . . . .79 B6
Gibside View NE21 . . . . .68 B8
Gibside Way NE11 . . . . .54 B2
Gibson Ct NE35 . . . . .73 F8
Gibson Fields NE46 . . . . . . .45 B4
Gibson Ho **8** NE46 . . . . . . .45 A5
Gibson St
  Newbiggin-by-t-S NE64 . . . . .7 D4
  Newcastle-u-T NE1 . . . . . . .99 C1
  Wallsend NE28 . . . . .40 F5
Gibson Terr NE40 . . . . .52 A4
Gifford Sq SR4 . . . . .85 C4
Gilberdyke NE10 . . . . .72 A5
Gilbert Rd SR4 . . . . .85 B2
Gilbert Sq SR4 . . . . .85 B3
Gilbert St NE33 . . . . .59 C8
Gilderdale DH4 . . . . .89 E8
Gilderdale Way NE23 . . . . . .22 A3
Giles PI **13** NE46 . . . . .45 A5
Gilesgate Fields NE46 . . . . .45 A5
Gilesgate Ct **16** NE46 . . . . .45 A5
Gilesgate Rd DH5 . . . . .95 B1

Gilhespy Green Cvn Pk
  NE24 . . . . .17 F4
Gilhurst Grange SR1 . . . . . .102 D2
Gill Burn NE39 . . . . .67 E3
Gill Crescent N DH4 . . . . . . .89 E1
Gill Crescent S DH4 . . . . . . .89 E1
Gill Ct NE13 . . . . .28 A6
Gill Side Gr SR6 . . . . .75 E2
Gill St NE4 . . . . .54 E5
Gillas La DH5 . . . . .95 A7
Gillas La E DH5 . . . . .94 F7
Gillas La W DH5 . . . . .94 E6
Gillas Lane Prim Sch
  DH5 . . . . .94 F7
Gillhurst Ho SR1 . . . . .102 A3
Gillies St NE6 . . . . .56 D6
Gilliland Cres DH3 . . . . .82 C6
Gillingham Rd SR4 . . . . .85 C3
Gillside Ct **4** NE34 . . . . .59 A3
Gillwood Ct DH4 . . . . .90 A6
Gilmore CI NE5 . . . . .36 D3
Gilmore Ho NE8 . . . . .70 E6
Gilpin St DH4 . . . . .94 D8
Gilsland Ave NE28 . . . . .40 F3
Gilsland Gr NE23 . . . . .16 B1
Gilsland St SR4 . . . . .102 A2
Gilwell Way NE3 . . . . .28 B1
Gingler La NE40 . . . . .52 A2
Girtin Rd NE34 . . . . .59 D2
Girven Terr DH5 . . . . .95 B1
Girven Terr W DH5 . . . . .95 B1
Gisburn Ct NE23 . . . . .16 B1
Gishford Way NE5 . . . . .37 B2
Givens St SR6 . . . . .75 E2
Glade The Hedworth NE32 . .73 B8
  Walbottle NE15 . . . . .36 A4
Gladeley Way NE16 . . . . .69 B2
Gladewell Ct NE62 . . . . .10 E7
Gladstonbury PI NE12 . . . . .39 C7
Gladstone Ave NE26 . . . . . . .31 F6
Gladstone PI NE2 . . . . .99 B3
Gladstone St Blyth NE24 . . . .17 D8
  Fence Houses DH4 . . . . . . .94 B8
  Hebburn NE31,NE32 . . . . . .58 A6
  Morpeth NE61 . . . . .9 B8
  Newcastle-u-T NE15 . . . . . .53 C6
  Sunderland SR5 . . . . .75 D1
  3 Wallsend NE28 . . . . . . .41 B1
Gladstone Terr
  Bedlington NE22 . . . . .11 A1
  Birtley DH3 . . . . .82 B4
  2 Boldon Colliery NE35 . .58 E1
  Gateshead NE8 . . . . .101 C1
  Newcastle-u-T NE2 . . . . . . .99 B3
  Penshaw DH4 . . . . .89 F8
  Washington NE37 . . . . .83 F8
  8 Whitley Bay NE26 . . . . .32 B4
Gladstone Terr W NE8 . . . .101 B1
Gladwyn Rd **2** SR4 . . . . . . .85 B2
Gladwyn Sq SR4 . . . . .85 B2
Glaholm Rd SR2 . . . . .103 C2
Glaisdale Ct NE34 . . . . .59 A4
Glaisdale Dr SR6 . . . . .75 E6
Glaisdale Rd NE7 . . . . .39 A5
Glamis Ave
  Newcastle-u-T NE3 . . . . . . .28 C1
  Sunderland SR4 . . . . .85 C4
Glamis Cres NE39 . . . . .68 C4
Glamis Ct Bournmoor DH4 . .89 D1
  South Shields NE34 . . . . . .59 F3
Glamis Terr NE16 . . . . .69 A1
Glamis Villas DH3 . . . . .82 C6
Glanmore Rd **3** SR4 . . . . . .85 B3
Glantlees NE5 . . . . .37 A2
Glanton Ave NE25 . . . . .23 C3
Glanton CI
  Chester le S DH2 . . . . .88 A2
  Gateshead NE10 . . . . .72 C7
  Morpeth NE61 . . . . .9 B5
  3 Newcastle-u-T NE6 . . . .56 C4
  Wallsend NE28 . . . . .40 F3
Glanton CI NE11 . . . . .100 A1
Glanton Ho NE24 . . . . .17 B8
Glanton Rd Hexham NE46 . . .45 D7
  Tynemouth NE29 . . . . .41 D7
Glanton Sq SR4 . . . . .85 C3
Glanton Wynd NE3 . . . . .38 B7
Glanville CI NE11 . . . . .70 B7
Glanville Rd SR3 . . . . .91 D5
Glasbury Ave SR4 . . . . .85 C4
Glasgow Rd NE32 . . . . .58 E3
Glassey Terr NE22 . . . . .11 D1
Glasshouse St NE6 . . . . .56 C4
Glastonbury NE38 . . . . .83 D4
Glastonbury Gr NE2 . . . . . . .38 F2
Glazebury Way NE23 . . . . . .16 B1
Glebe Ave
  Longbenton NE12 . . . . .39 D7
  Whickham NE16 . . . . .69 B7
Glebe CI
  Newcastle-u-T NE5 . . . . . . .36 D3
  Ponteland NE20 . . . . .25 E7
Glebe Cres
  Longbenton NE12 . . . . .29 D1
  Washington NE38 . . . . .83 E6
Glebe Ct NE22 . . . . .10 F1
Glebe Dr SR7 . . . . .92 F2
Glebe Est SR7 . . . . .92 F2
Glebe Farm NE62 . . . . .10 F8
Glebe Mews NE22 . . . . .10 F1
Glebe Rd Bedlington NE22 . .10 F1
  Longbenton NE12 . . . . .29 D1
Glebe Rise NE16 . . . . .69 B7
Glebe St NE4 . . . . .54 E6

Glebe Terr
Choppington NE62 10 E4
1 Dunston NE11 69 F8
2 Houghton-le-S DH4 90 D1
Longbenton NE12 29 D1
Glebe The
21 South Shields NE33 42 D1
Stannington NE61 14 C4
Glebe Village Prim Sch NE38 83 D5
Glebe Villas NE12 29 C1
Glebe Wlk NE16 69 B7
Glebelands NE45 47 A6
Glen Ave NE43 64 C7
Glen Barr DH2 88 B4
Glen Cl NE39 67 E3
Glen Ct NE31 57 D5
Glen Luce Dr SR2 86 F2
Glen Path SR2 86 D3
Glen St NE31 57 D5
Glen Terr Chester le S DH2 88 A4
Hexham NE46 44 F5
Washington NE38 83 E4
Glen The SR2 86 D3
Glen Thorpe Ave SR6 75 E2
Glen's Flats DH6 96 B5
Glenallen Gdns NE30 32 C1
Glenavon Ave DH2 88 B4
Glenbrooke Terr NE9 70 F4
Glenburn Cl NE38 82 F3
Glencarron Cl NE38 83 A3
Glencoe NE12 29 D4
Glencoe Ave
Chester le S DH2 88 B4
Cramlington NE23 22 B3
Glencoe Rd SR4 85 B2
Glencoe Rise NE39 67 C2
Glencoe Sq SR4 85 B3
Glencoe Terr NE39 67 C1
Glencourse NE36 74 E7
Glendale Ave Blyth NE24 16 E8
Newcastle-u-T NE3 38 A4
North Shields NE29 41 F6
Stakeford NE62 11 A8
Wallsend NE28 40 B4
Washington NE37 83 C8
Whickham NE16 69 A6
Whitley Bay NE26 32 A7
Glendale Cl Blaydon NE21 67 F8
Newcastle-u-T NE5 36 D3
Sunderland SR3 91 C6
Glendale Gdns
Gateshead NE9 71 B5
Stakeford NE62 11 A8
Glendale Gr NE29 41 F6
Glendale Rd
Ashington NE63 7 A2
Shiremoor NE27 31 A3
Glendale Terr 6 NE6 56 C6
Glendford Pl NE24 17 D4
Glendower Ave NE29 41 D6
Glendyn Cl NE7 39 A1
Gleneagle Cl NE5 36 D3
Gleneagles
South Shields NE33 42 F1
Whitley Bay NE25 31 D6
Gleneagles Cl NE7 39 C5
Gleneagles Ct NE25 31 D6
Gleneagles Dr NE37 72 C2
Gleneagles Rd
Gateshead NE9 70 E3
Sunderland SR4 85 B2
Gleneagles Sq 1 SR4 85 B2
Glenesk Gdns SR2 86 C2
Glenesk Rd SR2 86 C3
Glenfield Ave NE23 16 B1
Glenfield Rd
Longbenton NE12 39 B7
Longbenton NE12 39 C7
Glengarvan Cl NE38 83 A3
Glenholme Cl 7 NE38 82 F3
Glenhurst Dr
Newcastle-u-T NE5 36 D3
Whickham NE16 68 F4
Glenhurst Gr NE34 59 F6
Glenkerry Cl NE38 83 A3
Glenleigh Dr SR4 85 C4
Glenluce Ct NE23 22 B4
Glenluce Dr NE23 22 B3
Glenmoor NE31 57 D7
Glenmore Ave DH2 88 C4
Glenmuir Ave NE23 22 A3
Glenorrin Cl NE38 83 A3
Glenridge Ave 2 NE6 39 B1
Glenroy Gdns DH2 88 B4
Glenshiel Cl NE38 83 A3
Glenside Ellington NE61 1 E5
Hedworth NE32 58 C2
Glenside Ct NE9 70 E4
Glenthorn Rd NE2 38 E2
Glenthorne Rd 1 SR6 75 E2
Glenthorpe Ho NE33 42 D1
Glenuce DH3 82 E3
Glenwood NE63 6 C2
Glenwood Wlk NE5 36 D3
Gloria Ave NE25 23 D6
Glossop St NE39 66 F4
Gloucester Ave SR6 75 E4
Gloucester Ct NE3 37 C8
Gloucester Pl NE34 60 A5
Gloucester Rd
Newcastle-u-T NE4 98 A1
Shiremoor NE29 41 B7
Gloucester St NE25 23 D6
Gloucester Terr
Haswell DH6 97 E1
Newcastle-u-T NE4 100 A4
Gloucester Way
Hedworth NE32 58 B2
Newcastle-u-T NE4 100 B4
Glover Ind Est NE37 83 E7
Glover Network Ctr NE37 83 F7
Glover Rd Sunderland SR4 85 B2
Washington NE37 83 F8
Glover Sq SR4 85 B2
Glovers Pl 14 NE46 45 A5
Glynfellis NE10 71 F4
Glynfellis Ct NE10 71 F5
Glynwood Cl NE23 16 B1
Glynwood Com Prim Sch NE9 71 A5
Glynwood Gdns NE9 71 A5
Goalmouth Cl 6 SR6 75 E2
Goathland Ave NE12 39 C6
Goathland Cl SR3 92 C7
Goathland Dr SR3 92 B6
Goathland Prim Sch NE12 39 C6
Godfrey Rd SR4 85 B3
Gofton Wlk NE5 37 A2
Goldcrest Rd NE38 82 F3
Goldfinch Cl NE4 54 F4
Goldlynn Dr SR3 91 E6
Goldsbrough Ct NE2 98 C3
Goldsmith Rd SR4 85 B2
Goldspink La NE2 56 A7
Goldstone Ct NE12 29 E4
Goldthorpe Cl NE23 16 B1
Golf Course Rd DH4 90 A4
Gompertz Gdns NE33 59 B8
Gooch Ave NE22 11 A4
Goodrich Cl DH4 90 C5
Goodwood NE12 29 E3
Goodwood Ave NE8 70 C8
Goodwood Cl NE5 36 D3
Goodwood Ct NE63 6 D2
Goodwood Rd SR4 85 A3
Goodwood Sq SR4 85 A3
Goole Rd SR4 85 C3
Goose Hill NE61 9 A8
Gordon Ave
Newcastle-u-T NE3 38 C4
Sunderland SR5 85 A8
Gordon Ct 9 NE10 56 D1
Gordon Dr NE36 74 D7
Gordon Ho
2 Newcastle-u-T NE6 56 B5
Whitley Bay NE26 32 C4
Gordon Rd Blyth NE24 17 F6
3 Newcastle-u-T NE6 56 B6
South Shields NE34 59 C6
Sunderland SR4 85 B2
Gordon Sq
Newcastle-u-T NE6 56 B5
Whitley Bay NE26 32 C4
Gordon St NE33 59 D8
Gordon Terr
Bedlington NE22 16 A8
Prudhoe NE42 50 D2
Ryhope SR2 93 A6
Stakeford NE62 11 C7
Sunderland SR5 75 A2
Whitley Bay NE26 32 C5
Gordon Terrace W NE62 11 C7
Gorleston Way SR3 92 A4
Gorse Ave NE34 60 A5
Gorse Hill Way NE5 37 C3
Gorse Rd SR2 103 A1
Gorsedene Ave NE26 24 F1
Gorsedene Rd NE26 24 F1
Gorsehill NE9 71 C5
Gorseway NE61 8 D7
Goschen St Blyth NE24 17 D8
Gateshead NE8 70 D8
Sunderland SR5 75 A2
Gosforth Ave NE34 59 C3
Gosforth Bsns Pk NE12 38 F7
Gosforth Central Mid Sch NE3 38 D6
Gosforth Ctr NE3 38 C4
Gosforth East Mid Sch NE3 38 D7
Gosforth High Sch NE3 38 C6
Gosforth Park Fst Sch NE3 38 D7
Gosforth Park Villas NE13 28 C4
Gosforth Park Way NE3 39 A8
Gosforth St
20 Gateshead NE10 56 D1
Newcastle-u-T NE2 99 C2
Gosforth Terr
Gateshead NE10 56 F1
Newcastle-u-T NE3 38 E5
Gosforth West Mid Sch NE3 38 B5
Gosport Way NE24 17 D4
Gossington NE38 84 A5
Goswick Ave NE7 39 B3
Goswick Dr NE3 37 F8
Goundry Ave SR2 93 A6
Gourock Sq SR4 85 A3
Govt Bldgs (DSS) NE98 39 A5
Gowan Terr NE2 38 F1
Gowanburn
Cramlington NE23 22 A3
Washington NE38 83 F2
Gower Rd SR5 75 A2
Gower St NE6 57 A4
Gower Wlk NE10 71 C8
Gowland Ave NE4 54 E6
Grace Gdns NE28 40 A4
Grace Ho NE29 41 E3
Grace St Dunston NE11 69 F8
Newcastle-u-T,Byker NE6 56 C6
Newcastle-u-T,Walker NE6 56 D6
Gracefield Cl NE5 36 D3
Gradys Yd NE15 35 D3
Grafton Cl 5 NE6 56 B6
Grafton Ho 7 NE6 56 B6
Grafton Rd NE26 32 C4
Grafton St
11 Newcastle-u-T NE6 56 B6
Sunderland SR4 102 B3
Gragareth Way NE37 83 A6
Graham Ave NE16 69 B8
Graham Park Rd NE3 38 C3
Graham Rd NE31 57 D5
Graham St NE33 42 D2
Graham Terr DH6 96 B5
Grahamsley St NE8 101 C2
Grainger Ct NE4 54 F5
Grainger Mkt NE1 99 A1
Grainger Park Rd NE4 54 F5
Grainger St NE1 99 A1
Graingerville N NE4 98 A1
Graingerville S NE4 98 A1
Grampian Ave DH2 88 B2
Grampian Cl 2 NE29 31 F1
Grampian Gdns NE11 70 B6
Grampian Gr NE36 74 B7
Grampian Pl NE12 29 B1
Granaries The
Fence Houses DH4 94 B8
High Spen NE39 66 F4
Sunderland SR4 84 F3
Granby Cl Sunderland SR3 86 B3
Sunniside NE16 69 B3
Granby Terr 4 NE16 69 B2
Grand Par NE30 32 D1
Grandstand Rd NE2 38 B2
Grandstand The NE61 8 D6
Grange Ave
Bedlington NE22 11 E3
Fence Houses DH4 90 A1
Longbenton NE12 39 E6
Shiremoor NE27 30 F4
Grange Cl Blyth NE24 17 D4
Tynemouth NE30 32 B2
Wallsend NE28 40 C2
Whitley Bay NE25 31 D4
Grange Cres
Gateshead NE10 72 A7
Ryton NE40 52 C4
Sunderland SR2 103 A1
Grange Ct Gateshead NE10 72 A7
6 Jarrow NE32 58 B7
Morpeth NE61 9 A7
Prudhoe NE42 50 D2
Ryton NE40 52 C4
Grange Dr NE40 52 C4
Grange Est NE11 81 C6
Grange Farm Dr NE16 69 A5
Grange Fst Sch NE3 38 B6
Grange La NE16 69 B5
Grange Lonnen NE40 52 B5
Grange Manor NE16 69 B5
Grange Nook NE16 69 A5
Grange Park Ave
Bedlington NE22 11 E3
Sunderland SR5 75 C3
Grange Park Prim Sch SR5 75 C2
Grange Pk NE25 31 D4
Grange Pl NE32 58 B7
Grange Rd
Gateshead NE10 72 A7
Jarrow NE32 58 B7
Morpeth NE61 9 A6
Newburn NE15 52 E8
Newcastle-u-T,Fenham NE4 54 D7
Newcastle-u-T,Gosforth NE3 38 C7
Ponteland NE20 25 F7
Ryton NE40 52 C5
Sunderland SR5 85 A8
Grange Rd W NE32 58 B7
Grange St S SR2 86 F2
Grange Terr
1 East Boldon NE36 74 D7
6 Gateshead NE9 71 A8
Kibblesworth NE11 81 C6
Medomsley DH8 77 B1
Prudhoe NE42 50 D2
Sunderland SR2 103 A1
2 Sunderland,High Southwick SR5 75 B2
Grange The
Bedlington NE22 10 A1
East Boldon NE36 74 D7
Grange View
East Rainton DH5 94 D5
Newbottle DH4 90 D3
Ryton NE40 52 C4
Sunderland SR5 75 C3
Grange Villas NE28 40 C2
Grange Wlk 1 NE16 69 A5
Grangemere Cl SR2 86 F1
Grangeside Ct 8 NE29 31 F1
Grangetown Prim Sch SR2 86 F3
Grangewood Cl DH4 90 A5
Grangewood Ct 3 DH4 90 A6
Grant St NE32 58 A7
Grantham Dr NE9 70 E4
Grantham Pl NE23 22 A4
Grantham Rd
Newcastle-u-T NE2 99 C3
Sunderland SR6 75 E2
Grantham St NE24 17 F6
Granville Ave
Longbenton NE12 29 E1
Seaton Sluice NE26 24 D5
Granville Cres NE12 39 E7
Granville Ct NE2 99 C4
Granville Dr
Longbenton NE12 39 E7
Newcastle-u-T NE5 36 D3
Shiney Row DH4 90 C5
Granville Gdns
Newcastle-u-T NE2 56 A8
Stakeford NE62 11 A8
Granville Lodge NE12 39 E8
Granville Rd
Newcastle-u-T,Gosforth NE3 38 D7
Newcastle-u-T,Jesmond NE2 99 C4
Granville St
Gateshead NE8 101 C1
Sunderland SR4 102 B3
Grasmere Birtley DH3 82 E2
Cleadon SR6 60 A1
Grasmere Ave
Easington Lane DH5 97 C8
Gateshead NE10 71 F8
Hedworth NE32 58 D3
Newburn NE15 52 E7
Newcastle-u-T NE6 56 F5
Grasmere Cres
Blaydon NE21 68 B8
5 Penshaw DH4 90 B6
Sunderland SR5 75 C3
Whitley Bay NE26 31 F7
Grasmere Ct
Killingworth NE12 29 C3
Newburn NE15 52 E7
Grasmere Gdns
South Shields NE34 59 E6
Washington NE38 83 E4
Grasmere Ho NE6 56 E5
Grasmere Pl NE3 38 C7
Grasmere Rd
Chester le S DH2 88 B1
Hebburn NE31 57 F4
Wallsend NE28 40 A1
Whickham NE16 69 C7
Grasmere St NE8 101 B1
Grasmere St W NE8 101 B1
Grasmere Terr
Newbiggin-by-t-S NE64 7 D4
Washington NE38 83 E5
Grasmere Way NE24 17 A8
Grasmoor Pl NE15 53 B7
Grassbanks NE10 72 A6
Grassholm Pl NE12 39 A7
Grassholme Mdws SR3 86 B2
Grassington Dr NE23 22 A4
Grasslees NE38 88 F8
Grasswell Cvn Site DH4 90 D2
Grasswell Dr NE5 37 D3
Grasswell Terr DH4 90 D2
Gravel Wlks DH5 90 F1
Gravesend Rd SR4 85 B2
Gravesend Sq SR4 85 C2
Gray Ave Chester le S DH2 88 B2
Wideopen NE13 28 C7
Gray Ct SR2 86 D4
Gray Rd Sunderland SR2 103 B1
Sunderland SR2 103 C2
Gray St NE24 12 E1
Gray's Wlk NE34 59 A2
Graylands NE38 88 E8
Grayling Ct SR3 91 C5
Grayling Rd NE11 70 B7
Grays Cross SR1 103 B3
Grays Terr 8 NE35 58 E1
Graystones NE10 72 B6
Great Lime Rd
Dudley NE12,NE13,NE23 29 A5
Longbenton NE12 29 D1
Great North Rd
Newcastle-u-T,Gosforth NE3 38 C7
Newcastle-u-T,West Jesmond NE2 38 D2
Stannington NE61 9 A4
Great Park Way
Hazlerigg NE13 27 F2
Newcastle-u-T NE13 28 A3
Greathead St NE33 59 B7
Grebe Cl Ashington NE63 6 E1
Blyth NE24 17 E5
Dunston NE11 100 A2
Grebe Ct NE2 38 F1
Greely Rd NE5 36 F2
Green Acres Morpeth NE61 8 E7
Ponteland NE20 25 C1
Green Ave DH4 90 D4
Green Bank NE46 45 C4
Green Cl Stannington NE61 14 C4
Tynemouth NE30 32 B1
Whitley Bay NE25 31 D4
Green Cres NE23 28 F8
Green Gr NE40 52 B3
Green Hill Wlk NE34 60 C6
Green La Ashington NE63 6 C3
Dudley NE23 28 F8
East Boldon NE36 74 E6
Gateshead,Felling NE10 56 D2
Gateshead,Pelaw NE10 57 A1
Haswell DH6 97 B3
Killingworth NE12 29 E2
Morpeth NE61 4 B1
Seaham SR7 95 F6
South Shields NE34 59 B4
Stannington NE61 13 D2
Green La *continued*
Stannington,Duddo Hill NE61 13 D5
Woolsington NE13 36 F8
Morpeth,Stobhillgate NE61 9 B7
Green Lane Gdns NE10 56 C2
Green Pk NE28 39 E3
Green Sq NE25 31 D4
Green St SR1 103 A3
Green Terr SR1 102 C2
Green The
Chester le S DH2 88 B3
Chopwell NE17 77 B8
Gateshead NE10 71 E8
Houghton-le-S DH5 90 F1
New Silksworth SR3 92 C7
Newcastle-u-T NE3 37 F3
Ovington NE42 49 C4
Ponteland NE20 25 F7
Rowlands Gill NE39 67 C2
Sunderland,Bishopwearmouth SR1 102 C2
Sunderland,Southwick SR5 75 A1
Walbottle NE15 35 F1
Whitley Bay NE25 31 E6
Green's Pl NE33 42 C4
Green-Fields NE40 52 B5
Greenacre Pk NE9 70 E3
Greenacres Cl NE40 52 A3
Greenbank Blaydon NE21 53 C2
Jarrow NE32 58 B7
Greenbank Dr SR4 85 A5
Greenbank St 4 DH3 88 D4
Greenbank Villas NE32 58 B7
Greenbourne Gdns NE10 71 C7
Greencroft NE63 6 C2
Greencroft Ave
Corbridge NE45 47 A6
Newcastle-u-T NE6 57 A8
Greendale Cl NE24 17 A8
Greendale Gdns DH5 94 F2
Greendyke Ct NE5 37 A5
Greener Ct NE42 50 B1
Greenesfield Bsns Ctr NE8 101 B3
Greenfield Ave NE5 37 A2
Greenfield Dr NE62 10 E6
Greenfield Pl
Newcastle-u-T NE4 98 C1
Ryton NE40 52 D5
Greenfield Rd NE3 28 B1
Greenfield Terr 2 NE10 56 F1
Greenfields DH2 82 A2
Greenfields Com Prim Sch NE13 28 C6
Greenfields Sch NE31 58 A6
Greenfinch Cl NE38 82 F3
Greenford NE11 81 D6
Greenford La DH2,NE11 81 F6
Greenford Rd NE6 57 A4
Greenhaugh NE12 29 B1
Greenhaugh Rd NE25 31 B5
Greenhead NE38 82 F4
Greenhead Rd NE17 66 B3
Greenhead Terr NE17 66 B2
Greenhill View NE5 37 E2
Greenhills NE12 29 D5
Greenholme Cl NE23 16 B1
Greenhow Cl 2 SR2 92 F5
Greenlands NE32 58 C2
Greenlands Ct NE25 23 D4
Greenlaw NE5 53 E8
Greenlaw Rd NE23 22 A3
Greenlea NE29 31 B1
Greenlea Cl
High Spen NE39 67 A3
Sunderland SR4 85 C3
Greenlee NE63 6 E2
Greenlee Dr NE7 39 D3
Greenmount DH4 90 B1
Greenock Rd SR4 85 B2
Greenrigg Blaydon NE21 53 D1
Seaton Sluice NE26 24 C6
Greenrigg Gdns 2 SR3 86 B3
Greenriggs Ave NE3 28 D1
Greenrising NE42 49 D4
Greenshields Rd SR4 85 B2
Greenshields Sq 5 SR4 85 B2
Greenside Ashington NE63 6 C4
South Shields NE34 60 B6
Greenside Ave
Brunswick Village NE13 28 A6
Wallsend NE28 40 F3
Greenside Cres NE15 54 A7
Greenside Ct SR3 85 C2
Greenside Drift NE33 42 F2
Greenside Ho NE24 17 B8
Greenside Prim Sch NE40 51 F1
Greenside Rd
Crawcrook NE40 51 F3
Greenside NE40 51 F2
Greentree Sq NE5 37 B2
Greenway
Newcastle-u-T NE5 36 D4
Newcastle-u-T,Fenham NE4 54 D8
Whitley Bay NE25 31 D4
Greenway The SR4 85 C4
Greenwell Cl NE21 53 A1
Greenwell Dr NE42 50 D3
Greenwell Terr NE40 51 E4
Greenwich Pl NE8 56 A4
Greenwood NE12 29 F3
Greenwood Ave
Bedlington NE22 11 D3
Houghton-le-S DH4 94 C8
Wallsend NE6 40 A1
Greenwood Cl NE38 83 F3

Greenwood Gdns
Dunston NE11 . . . . .70 B5
Gateshead NE10 . . . . .56 D2
Greenwood Rd SR4 . . . . .85 B3
Greenwood Sq 2 SR4 . . . .85 B2
Greetlands Rd SR2 . . . . . .86 C2
Gregory Rd 8 SR4 . . . . . .85 B2
Gregory Terr SR7 . . . . . . .92 F1
Gregson Terr SR7 . . . . . . .92 F1
Grenada Cl NE26 . . . . .31 F8
Grenada Dr NE26 . . . . . . .31 F8
Grenada Pl NE26 . . . . . . .31 F8
Grenfell Sq 7 SR4 . . . . . .85 B2
Grenville Ct
Cramlington NE23 . . . . . . .22 A5
Ponteland NE20 . . . . .25 A4
Grenville Dr NE3 . . . . .28 B1
Grenville Terr NE1 . . . . . .99 C1
Grenville Way NE26 . . . . .31 E7
Gresford St NE33 . . . . . . .59 C6
Gresham NF73 . . . . .22 B4
Greta Ave DH4 . . . . .90 A6
Greta Gdns NE33 . . . . . . .59 D8
Greta Terr SR4 . . . . .102 A1
Gretna Dr NE32 . . . . .58 F2
Gretna Rd NE15 . . . . .54 B6
Gretton Pl NE7 . . . . .39 A3
Grey Ave NE23 . . . . .22 A3
Grey Lady Wlk NE42 . . . . .50 D3
Grey Pl 15 NE61 . . . . .9 A8
Grey St
Brunswick Village NE13 . . .28 A6
Houghton-le-S DH4 . . . . . .90 D1
Newcastle-u-T NE1 . . . . . .99 A1
North Shields NE30 . . . . . .42 B6
Wallsend NE28 . . . . .40 C2
Grey Terr 10 SR2 . . . . . . .92 F6
Grey's Ct NE1 . . . . .99 A1
Greybourne Gdns SR2 . . .86 C2
Greyfriars La NE12 . . . . . .39 A6
Greystead Cl NE5 . . . . . . .36 D3
Greystead Rd NE25 . . . . .31 B5
Greystoke Ave
Newcastle-u-T NE2 . . . . . .56 A7
Sunderland SR2 . . . . .86 C2
Whickham NE16 . . . . .69 B5
Greystoke Gdns
Gateshead NE9 . . . . .71 B2
5 Morpeth NE61 . . . . .3 F1
Newcastle-u-T NE2 . . . . . .56 A8
Sunderland SR2 . . . . .86 C3
Whickham NE16 . . . . .69 B5
Greystoke Pk NE3 . . . . . . .38 C8
Greystoke Pl NE23 . . . . . .38 C8
Greystoke Wlk 2 NE16 . .69 A5
Greystone Pl SR5 . . . . . . .75 A2
Greywood Ave NE4 . . . . . .54 E7
Grieve St NE24 . . . . .12 D1
Grieves' Row NE23 . . . . . .22 A1
Griffith Terr 7 NE27 . . . . .30 E1
Grimsby St NE24 . . . . . . .17 E6
Grindleford Ct NE34 . . . . .59 E5
Grindon Ave SR4 . . . . . . .85 B5
Grindon Cl
Cramlington NE23 . . . . . . .22 A3
Whitley Bay NE25 . . . . . . .31 E2
Grindon Ct SR4 . . . . .85 C3
Grindon Gdns SR4 . . . . . .85 C3
Grindon Hall Christian Sch
SR4 . . . . .85 C4
Grindon Inf Sch SR4 . . . . .85 B2
Grindon La
Sunderland,South Hylton
SR4 . . . . .85 B5
Sunderland,Springwell SR3,
SR4 . . . . .85 D3
Grindon Pk SR4 . . . . .85 C3
Grindon Terr SR4 . . . . . .102 A1
Grinstead Cl NE34 . . . . . .59 F7
Grisedale Gdns NE9 . . . . .71 A3
Grizedale NE37 . . . . .83 B6
Grizedale Ct SR4 . . . . . . .75 C5
Groat Mkt NE1 . . . . .99 A1
Grosvenor Ave
Newcastle-u-T NE2 . . . . . .38 F1
Whickham NE16 . . . . .69 B8
Grosvenor Cl NE23 . . . . . .22 A3
Grosvenor Cres NE31 . . . .57 F4
Grosvenor Ct NE5 . . . . . . .36 D3
Grosvenor Dr Cleadon SR6 74 E8
South Shields NE34 . . . . . .59 F8
Whitley Bay NE26 . . . . . . .32 A4
Grosvenor Gdns
Newcastle-u-T NE2 . . . . . .56 A8
South Shields NE34 . . . . . .59 F6
Wallsend NE28 . . . . .41 A3
Grosvenor Mews
1 North Shields NE29 . . . .42 A6
4 South Shields NE33 . . . .59 E8
Grosvenor Pl Blyth NE24 . .16 F6
Newcastle-u-T NE2 . . . . . .38 F1
North Shields NE29 . . . . . .42 A6
Grosvenor Rd
Newcastle-u-T NE2 . . . . . .38 F1
South Shields NE33 . . . . . .59 E8
Grosvenor St SR5 . . . . . . .75 A2
Grosvenor Villas NE2 . . . .38 F1
Grosvenor Way NE5 . . . . .36 D3
Grotto Gdns NE34 . . . . . . .60 D6
Grotto Rd NE34 . . . . .60 D6
Grousemoor 2 NE37 . . . .83 A7
Grousemoor Dr NE63 . . . . .6 C1
Grove Ave NE3 . . . . .38 D4
Grove Cotts 9 DH3 . . . . .82 C4
Grove Ho NE3 . . . . .38 D4
Grove Rd Gateshead NE9 . .71 A6
Walbottle NE15 . . . . .35 F2

Grove Terr
Burnopfield NE16 . . . . . . .79 B6
Sunniside NE16 . . . . .69 B1
Grove The Hedworth NE32 .73 B8
Houghton-le-S DH5 . . . . . .94 D6
Longbenton NE12 . . . . . . .39 D6
Newcastle-u-T NE5 . . . . . .36 D1
Newcastle-u-T,Gosforth
NE3 . . . . .38 D4
Newcastle-u-T,Jesmond
NE2 . . . . .38 F2
Ponteland NE20 . . . . .25 D5
Rowlands Gill NE39 . . . . . .67 F1
Ryhope SR2 . . . . .92 F6
Stocksfield NE43 . . . . .64 C3
6 Sunderland SR5 . . . . . . .74 B1
Sunderland,Ashbrooke SR2 .86 D4
Whickham NE16 . . . . .69 C6
Whitley Bay NE25 . . . . . . .31 F4
Guardian Ct NE26 . . . . . . .32 C4
Guardians Ct NE20 . . . . . .25 F7
Gubeon Wood NE61 . . . . . .8 C2
Guelder Rd NE7 . . . . .39 C3
Guernsey Rd SR4 . . . . . . .85 B2
Guernsey Sq SR4 . . . . . . .85 B2
Guessburn NE43 . . . . .64 B6
Guide Post Mid Sch
NE62 . . . . .10 F7
Guide Post Ringway Fst Sch
NE62 . . . . .10 F8
Guildford Pl NE6 . . . . .56 B7
Guildford Sq NE61 . . . . . . .2 A3
Guildford St SR2 . . . . .86 E4
Guillemot Cl NE24 . . . . . . .17 E5
Guillemot Row NE12 . . . . .29 C4
Guillimot Ho NE33 . . . . . . .42 D5
Guisborough Dr NE29 . . . .41 B8
Guisborough St SR4 . . . . .85 F5
Gullane NE37 . . . . .72 D3
Gullane Cl NE10 . . . . .57 C2
Gunn St NE11 . . . . .69 F8
Gunnerston Gr 1 NE3 . . .37 D5
Gunnerton Cl NE23 . . . . . .22 B4
Gunnerton Pl NE29 . . . . . .41 D6
Gurney Ho NE2 . . . . .99 B3
Gurteen Yd DH4 . . . . .90 D3
Gut Rd NE28 . . . . .40 F1
Guyzance Ave NE3 . . . . . .38 B6

H

Hackwood Pk NE46 . . . . . .45 B3
Hackworth Gdns NE41 . . . .51 B6
Hackworth Way NE29 . . . .41 F3
Haddington Rd NE25 . . . . .31 D7
Haddon Cl NE25 . . . . .31 B5
Haddon Gn NE25 . . . . .31 B5
Haddon Rd SR2 . . . . .86 F2
Hadleigh Ct 9 DH4 . . . . . .90 B6
Hadleigh Rd SR4 . . . . .85 D5
Hadrian Ave DH3 . . . . .88 D5
Hadrian Ct
Killingworth NE12 . . . . . . .29 E3
Ponteland NE20 . . . . .25 B1
Hadrian Gdns NE21 . . . . . .53 D1
Hadrian Ho 2 NE15 . . . . .35 D2
Hadrian Lodge NE34 . . . . .58 F5
Hadrian Park Prim Sch
NE28 . . . . .40 E7
Hadrian Pl Gateshead NE9 .71 B7
Throckley NE15 . . . . .35 E2
Hadrian Prim Sch NE33 . .42 C4
Hadrian Rd Blyth NE24 . . . .17 C3
Jarrow NE32 . . . . .58 D4
Newcastle-u-T NE4 . . . . . .54 E6
Wallsend NE28 . . . . .40 D1
Hadrian Road Sta NE28 . . .40 E2
Hadrian Sch NE15 . . . . . . .54 C6
Hadrian St NE4 . . . . .102 A3
Hadrians Ct NE11 . . . . . . .70 D3
Hadrians Way DH8 . . . . . .76 E3
Hadstone Pl 3 NE5 . . . . . .37 C1
Hagan Hall NE32 . . . . .58 C1
Hagg Bank Cotts NE41 . . .50 F5
Haggerston Cl NE5 . . . . . .37 B4
Haggerston Cres NE5 . . . .37 B4
Haggerston St NE5 . . . . . .37 B4
Haggerston Terr NE32 . . . .58 E4
Haggerstone Dr SR5 . . . . .85 B8
Haggie Ave NE28 . . . . .40 D3
Hahnemann Ct SR5 . . . . . .75 B2
Haig Ave NE25 . . . . .31 F3
Haig Cres NE15 . . . . .54 B5
Haig Rd NE22 . . . . .16 B8
Haig St NE11 . . . . .69 F8
Haigh Terr NE10 . . . . .71 C1
Hailsham Ave NE12 . . . . . .39 C7
Haininghead NE38 . . . . . . .83 E2
Hainingwood Terr NE10 . . .57 B2
Haldane Ct NE2 . . . . .99 B4
Haldane St NE63 . . . . .6 C4
Haldane Terr NE2 . . . . . . .99 B4
Halewood Ave NE3 . . . . . .37 E4
Half Fields Rd NE21 . . . . .53 B1
Half Moon La
Gateshead NE8 . . . . .101 B2
Tynemouth NE30 . . . . .42 D7
Half Moon St NE62 . . . . . . .11 B8
Halidon Rd SR2 . . . . .86 D1
Halidon Sq SR2 . . . . .86 D1
Halifax Pl Dunston NE11 . .54 E1
9 Ryhope SR2 . . . . .92 F6
Halifax Rd NE11 . . . . .54 E1
Halkirk Way NE23 . . . . . . .16 A1

Hall Ave NE4 . . . . .54 E6
Hall Cl Seaham SR7 . . . . . .92 D1
West Rainton DH4 . . . . . . .94 A2
Hall Dene Way SR7 . . . . . .92 F2
Hall Dr NF12 . . . . .29 C5
Hall Farm Cl NE43 . . . . . . .64 B8
Hall Farm Rd SR3 . . . . . . .92 A5
Hall Garth NE3 . . . . .38 C8
Hall Gdns Gateshead NE10 71 D7
Seaton Sluice NE26 . . . . . .24 A6
Sherburn DH6 . . . . .96 A1
West Boldon NE36 . . . . . . .74 A7
Hall Gn NE24 . . . . .17 B7
Hall La Haswell DH6 . . . . . .97 F3
Houghton-le-S DH5 . . . . . .94 F7
West Rainton DH4 . . . . . . .94 A3
Hall Pk NE21 . . . . .53 A4
Hall Rd Chopwell NE17 . . . .66 C2
Hebburn NE31 . . . . .57 E5
Washington NE37 . . . . . . .83 E8
Hall Road Bglws NE17 . . . .66 B2
Hall Terr Blyth NE24 . . . . . .17 E8
Gateshead NE10 . . . . .57 B2
Hall View SR6 . . . . .75 F8
Halleypike Cl NE7 . . . . . . .39 D3
Hallfield Cl SR3 . . . . .92 A5
Hallgarth NE10 . . . . .72 A7
Hallgarth Ct SR6 . . . . .75 F1
Hallgarth Ho NE33 . . . . . .59 C8
Hallgarth La DH6 . . . . .96 B5
Hallgarth Rd NE21 . . . . . . .53 B2
Hallgarth View DH6 . . . . . .96 C5
Hallgarth Villas DH6 . . . . .96 A1
Hallgate NE46 . . . . .45 B5
Halling Cl NE6 . . . . .57 A4
Hallington Dr NE25 . . . . . .23 D3
Hallington Mews NE12 . . .29 C3
Halliwell St DH4 . . . . .90 D1
Hallorchard Rd NE46 . . . . .45 B5
Hallow Dr NE15 . . . . .35 D1
Hallside Rd NE24 . . . . .17 B6
Hallstile Bank NE46 . . . . . .45 B5
Hallwood Cl NE22 . . . . . . .15 A8
Halstead Pl 2 NE33 . . . . .42 D1
Halstead Sq SR4 . . . . .85 D5
Halterburn Cl NE3 . . . . . . .38 A4
Halton Cl NE43 . . . . .64 D6
Halton Dr Backworth NE27 30 D3
Wideopen NE13 . . . . .28 B6
Halton Way NE3 . . . . .28 A1
Hamar Cl NE29 . . . . .41 C4
Hambard Way NE38 . . . . .83 D4
Hambledon Ave
Chester le S DH2 . . . . .88 B2
Tynemouth NE30 . . . . .32 A3
Hambledon Cl NE35 . . . . . .73 E8
Hambledon Gdns NE7 . . . .39 A3
Hambleton Cl NE24 . . . . . .17 D8
Hambleton NE63 . . . . .6 F1
Hambleton Gn NE9 . . . . . . .71 B1
Hambleton Rd NE38 . . . . . .83 B3
Hamilton Cres
Newcastle-u-T NE4 . . . . . .98 B2
Tynemouth NE29 . . . . .41 C8
Hamilton Ct
7 Gateshead NE8 . . . . . . .71 A8
Sunderland SR6 . . . . .75 F2
Hamilton Dr NE26 . . . . . . .31 F8
Hamilton Pl NE4 . . . . .98 B2
Hamilton Terr
14 Morpeth NE61 . . . . .9 A8
West Boldon NE36 . . . . . . .74 A7
Hamilton Way 2 NE26 . . . .31 F8
Hammer Square Bank
DH9 . . . . .80 F1
Hammerton Ct NE28 . . . . .40 A1
Hampden Rd SR6 . . . . .75 E2
Hampden St NE33 . . . . . . .59 C8
Hampshire Ct NE4 . . . . . .100 A2
Hampshire Gdns NE28 . . . .40 E4
Hampshire Pl NE37 . . . . . .72 D1
Hampshire Way NE34 . . . .60 F7
Hampstead Cl NE24 . . . . . .17 C3
Hampstead Gdns NE32 . . .58 D2
Hampstead Rd
Newcastle-u-T NE4 . . . . . .54 E5
Sunderland SR4 . . . . .85 D4
Hampstead Sq SR4 . . . . . .85 C4
Hampton Cl NE23 . . . . . . .22 D7
Hampton Ct
Chester le S DH3 . . . . .88 D7
Whickham NE16 . . . . .54 B1
Hampton Dr
Gateshead NE10 . . . . .71 C8
Whitley Bay NE25 . . . . . . .31 C4
Hampton Rd NE30 . . . . . . .32 A2
Hamsterley Cres
Gateshead NE9 . . . . .71 C3
Newcastle-u-T NE15 . . . . .53 B7
Hamsterley Ct 6 SR3 . . . .92 A6
Hamsterley Dr NE12 . . . . .29 C4
Hanby Gdns SR3 . . . . .86 A3
Hancock Mus NE1,NE2 . . .99 A3
Hancock St NE1,NE2 . . . . .99 A3
Handel St NE33 . . . . .42 D2
Handley Cres DH5 . . . . . . .94 C4
Handley Cross DH8 . . . . . .77 C2
Handy Dr NE11 . . . . .54 E2
Hangmans La SR3,SR7 . . .91 F7
Hanlon Ct Hebburn NE32 . .57 F7
Jarrow NE32 . . . . .58 A8
Hann Terr NE37 . . . . .83 F8
Hannington Pl 3 NE6 . . . .56 A6
Hannington St 2 NE6 . . . .56 A6
Hanover Cl 2 NE5 . . . . . . .36 C2
Hanover Ct
Annitsford NE23 . . . . .22 B1
5 Gateshead NE9 . . . . . . .71 A2

Hanover Dr NE21 . . . . . . .53 A1
Hanover Gdns 3 NE28 . . .41 A1
Hanover Ho NE32 . . . . . . .58 B4
Hanover Pl
Cramlington NF23 . . . . . . .16 A2
Sunderland SR4 . . . . .102 B4
Hanover Sq NE1 . . . . .101 A4
Hanover St NE1 . . . . .101 A4
Hanover Wlk
Blaydon NE21 . . . . .68 A8
1 Newcastle-u-T NE5 . . . .36 C2
Harbord Terr NE26 . . . . . .23 F5
Harbottle Ave
Newcastle-u-T NE3 . . . . . .38 A6
Shiremoor NE27 . . . . .31 A2
Harbottle Cres NE32 . . . . .58 B2
Harbottle Ct NE6 . . . . .56 C4
Harbottle St 4 NE6 . . . . . .56 C4
Harbour Dr NE33 . . . . .42 E4
Harbour The DH4 . . . . .90 B6
Harbour View
Cambois NE24 . . . . .12 B3
South Shields NE33 . . . . . .42 D5
Sunderland SR6 . . . . .75 F2
Harcourt Pk 1 NE9 . . . . . .71 A5
Harcourt Rd SR2 . . . . .86 D1
Harcourt St 2 NE9 . . . . . .71 A5
Hardgate Rd SR2 . . . . .86 D1
Hardie Ave NE16 . . . . .69 A8
Hardie Dr NE36 . . . . .74 B7
Hardman Gdns NE40 . . . . .52 D5
Hardwick Ct NE8 . . . . .56 A1
Hardwick Pl NE3 . . . . .38 A3
Hardwick Rise SR6 . . . . . .103 B4
Hardy Ave NE34 . . . . .59 B3
Hardy Ct 5 NE30 . . . . .42 B6
Hardy Gr NE28 . . . . .40 A5
Hardy Sq SR5 . . . . .75 A2
Hardyards Ct NE34 . . . . . .59 C5
Harebell Rd NE9 . . . . .71 C4
Harehills Ave NE5 . . . . . . .37 D3
Harehills Twr NE3 . . . . . . .37 D3
Harelaw Dr Ashington NE63 .6 B1
Sunderland SR6 . . . . .75 E1
Harelaw Gr NE5 . . . . .36 D1
Hareshaw Rd NE25 . . . . . .31 B5
Hareside NE23 . . . . .22 A5
Hareside Cl NE15 . . . . .52 F8
Hareside Ct NE15 . . . . .52 F8
Hareside Wlk NE15 . . . . . .52 F8
Harewood Cl
Whickham NE16 . . . . .69 A4
Whitley Bay NE25 . . . . . . .31 B4
Harewood Cres NE25 . . . .31 B4
Harewood Ct NE25 . . . . . .31 B4
Harewood Dr NE22 . . . . . .11 C2
Harewood Gdns
Pegswood NE61 . . . . .4 E4
Sunderland SR3 . . . . .86 A3
Harewood Gn NE9 . . . . . . .71 B2
Harewood Rd NE3 . . . . . . .38 C6
Hareydene NE5 . . . . .36 F5
Hargill Dr NE38 . . . . .83 A1
Hargrave Ct NE24 . . . . . . .17 C6
Harland Way NE38 . . . . . . .83 D5
Harle Cl NE5 . . . . .36 E1
Harle Rd NE27 . . . . .30 D3
Harle St NE28 . . . . .40 B2
Harlebury NE27 . . . . .30 C1
Harlequin Lodge 9
NE10 . . . . .71 D8
Harleston Way NE10 . . . . .71 E6
Harley Terr NE3 . . . . .38 D5
Harlow Ave
Backworth NE27 . . . . .30 D3
Newcastle-u-T NE3 . . . . . .37 F7
Harlow Cl NE23 . . . . .16 A1
Harlow Green Com Inf Sch
NE9 . . . . .71 A2
Harlow Green Jun Sch
NE9 . . . . .71 A2
Harlow Green La NE9 . . . . .71 A2
Harlow Pl NE7 . . . . .39 B3
Harlow St SR4 . . . . .102 B2
Harnham Ave NE29 . . . . . .41 D5
Harnham Gdns NE5 . . . . . .37 C1
Harnham Gr NE23 . . . . . . .22 A5
Harold Sq SR2 . . . . .103 B1
Harold St NE32 . . . . .58 C7
Harper St NE24 . . . . .17 D7
Harperley Dr SR3 . . . . .86 B2
Harperley La DH9 . . . . . . .79 B1
Harraby Gdns NE9 . . . . . . .71 B3
Harras Bank DH3 . . . . .82 C3
Harraton Terr
15 Birtley DH3 . . . . .82 C4
Bournmoor DH3 . . . . .89 C7
Harriet Pl 22 NE6 . . . . . . .56 C6
Harriet St Blaydon NE21 . .53 C2
Newcastle-u-T NE6 . . . . . .56 D6
Harrington Gdns NE62 . . . .11 C8
Harrington St 6 NE28 . . . .40 B2
Harriot Dr NE12 . . . . .29 B2
Harrison Ct
Annitsford NE23 . . . . .29 B8
Birtley DH3 . . . . .82 C3
Harrison Gdns NE8 . . . . . . .70 D7
Harrison Pl NE2 . . . . .99 B3
Harrison Rd NE28 . . . . .41 A3
Harrogate St SR2 . . . . . . .103 B1
Harrow Cres DH4 . . . . .90 A6
Harrow Gdns NE13 . . . . . . .28 C5
Harrow Sq SR4 . . . . .85 D5
Harrow St NE27 . . . . .30 E4
Hart Ct SR1 . . . . .103 A3
Hart Sq SR4 . . . . .85 E5
Hart Terr SR6 . . . . .75 F6
Hartburn NE10 . . . . .72 A6

Hartburn Dr NE5 . . . . .36 D3
Hartburn Pl NE4 . . . . .54 F7
Hartburn Rd NE30 . . . . . . .32 A1
Hartburn Terr NE25 . . . . . .23 D3
Hartburn Wlk NE3 . . . . . . .37 D5
Hartford NE12 . . . . .29 D5
Hartford Bank NE15 . . . . . .15 C4
Hartford Bridge Farm
NE22 . . . . .15 C5
Hartford Cres
Ashington NE63 . . . . .6 D2
Bedlington NE22 . . . . .15 E8
Hartford Ct NE22 . . . . .15 E8
Hartford Cvn Pk NE22 . . . .15 B5
Hartford Dr NE22 . . . . .15 C5
Hartford Ho NE4 . . . . .98 B2
Hartford Rd
Bedlington NE22 . . . . .15 D6
Newcastle-u-T NE3 . . . . . .38 D7
South Shields NE34 . . . . . .59 A5
Sunderland SR4 . . . . .85 D5
Hartford Rd E NE22 . . . . . .15 F8
Hartford Rd W NE22 . . . . .15 F8
Hartford St 1 NE6 . . . . . . .56 C8
Harthope NE61 . . . . .1 E5
Harthope Ave SR5 . . . . . . .74 C3
Harthope Cl NE38 . . . . . . .88 F8
Harthope Dr NE29 . . . . . . .41 E3
Hartington Rd NE30 . . . . . .32 B2
Hartington St
Gateshead NE8 . . . . .101 C1
Newcastle-u-T NE4 . . . . . .98 A1
Sunderland SR6 . . . . .75 E1
Hartington Terr NE33 . . . . .59 D8
Hartland Dr DH3 . . . . .82 D3
Hartlands NE22 . . . . .15 E8
Hartleigh Pl NE24 . . . . . . .17 B7
Hartley Ave NE26 . . . . .31 E5
Hartley Ct
Brunswick Village NE13 . . .27 F5
New Hartley NE25 . . . . . . .23 D6
Hartley Gdns NE25 . . . . . . .23 C3
Hartley Ho NE26 . . . . .31 F5
Hartley La Holywell NE25 . .31 B7
Whitley Bay SR5,NE26 . . . .24 C2
Hartley Sq NE26 . . . . .24 D4
Hartley St
Seaton Delaval NE25 . . . . .23 C3
Sunderland SR1 . . . . .103 C3
Hartley St N NE25 . . . . . . .23 C3
Hartley Terr NE24 . . . . . . .17 E7
Hartleyburn Ave NE31 . . . .57 D3
Hartoft Cl DH4 . . . . .90 D3
Harton Gr NE34 . . . . .59 E7
Harton House Rd NE34 . . . .59 F7
Harton House Rd E NE34 . .60 A7
Harton Inf Sch NE34 . . . . . .60 B6
Harton Jun Sch NE34 . . . . .60 A6
Harton La NE34 . . . . .59 D6
Harton Lea NE34 . . . . .59 F6
Harton Quay NE33 . . . . . . .42 B2
Harton Rise NE34 . . . . .60 A6
Harton Sch NE34 . . . . .60 A6
Harton View NE36 . . . . . . .74 A7
Hartside Birtley DH3 . . . . . .82 D1
Newcastle-u-T NE15 . . . . .53 C7
Hartside Cres
Backworth NE27 . . . . .30 D4
Blaydon NE21 . . . . .68 A8
Cramlington NE23 . . . . . . .16 A2
Hartside Gdns
Easington Lane DH5 . . . . . .95 C1
Newcastle-u-T NE2 . . . . . .38 F1
Hartside Pl NE3 . . . . .28 C1
Hartside Rd SR4 . . . . .85 D4
Hartside Sq SR4 . . . . .85 D4
Harvard Rd NE3 . . . . .37 E6
Harvest Cl SR3 . . . . .91 F5
Harvey Cl Ashington NE63 . .7 A3
Washington NE38 . . . . . . .82 F5
Harvey Combe NE12 . . . . .29 B2
Harvey Cres NE10 . . . . . . .72 B8
Harwood Cl
Cramlington NE23 . . . . . . .22 A5
Washington NE38 . . . . . . .83 A1
Harwood Dr NE12 . . . . . . .30 A3
Hascombe Cl NE25 . . . . . .31 D6
Haslemere Dr SR3 . . . . . . .86 A3
Hassop Way NE22 . . . . . . .10 F2
Hasting Hill Prim Sch
SR3 . . . . .85 C1
Hastings Ave
Longbenton NE12 . . . . . . .39 D7
Newcastle-u-T NE3 . . . . . .37 D7
Seaton Sluice NE26 . . . . . .24 B7
Whitley Bay NE26 . . . . . . .24 F1
Hastings Ct
Bedlington NE22 . . . . .11 C2
New Hartley NE25 . . . . . . .23 D6
Hastings Dr NE30 . . . . . . .42 C8
Hastings Gdns NE25 . . . . .23 D6
Hastings Par NE31 . . . . . . .58 A3
Hastings St
Cramlington NE23 . . . . . . .22 C5
Sunderland SR2 . . . . .86 E3
Hastings Terr
Cramlington NE23 . . . . . . .16 D1
New Hartley NE25 . . . . . . .23 D7
Sunderland SR2 . . . . .86 F3
Haswell Cl NE10 . . . . .72 D7
Haswell Gdns NE30 . . . . . .42 A6
Hatfield Ave NE31 . . . . . . .57 F6
Hatfield Dr NE23 . . . . .23 A2

Hatfield Gdns
Sunderland SR3 86 A3
Whitley Bay NE25 31 B5
Hatfield Ho [10] NE29 42 A4
Hatfield Sq [11] NE33 42 D3
Hathaway Gdns SR3 86 A3
Hathersage Gdns NE34 59 D5
Hatherton Ave NE30 32 B3
Hathery La NE24 16 D5
Haugh La Hexham NE46 45 B5
Ryton NE15,NE40 52 E6
Ryton,Ryton Haugh NE21 53 A5
Haugh Lane Ind Est NE46 45 A6
Haughs The NE42 50 D3
Haughton Cres
Hedworth NE32 58 B2
Newcastle-u-T NE5 36 E1
Haughton Ct NE4 100 A3
Haughton Terr NE24 17 E7
Hautmont Rd NE31 57 F4
Hauxley NE12 29 D5
Hauxley Dr
Cramlington NE23 16 A1
Newcastle-u-T NE3 37 F7
Hauxley Gdns NE5 37 D2
Havanna NE12 29 D5
Havannah Cres NE13 27 B6
Havannah Rd NE37 83 B7
Havant Gdns NE13 28 B7
Havelock Cl NE8 101 B2
Havelock Cres NE22 11 F3
Havelock Ct SR4 85 D6
Havelock Ho SR4 85 D6
Havelock Mews NE22 11 F3
Havelock Pl NE4 98 B1
Havelock Prim Sch SR4 85 D6
Havelock Rd NE27 30 D3
Havelock St Blyth NE24 17 E8
South Shields NE33 42 B1
South Shields NE33 42 C1
Sunderland SR1 103 C3
Havelock Terr
Chopwell NE17 66 B1
Gateshead NE8 101 B2
Jarrow NE32 58 B5
Sunderland SR2 102 B1
Tantobie DH9 79 B2
Havelock Villas NE22 11 F3
Haven Ct Blyth NE24 17 C6
Sunderland SR6 75 F1
Haven The
North Shields NE29 42 A3
Penshaw DH4 90 B6
Prudhoe NE42 50 D2
Haven View NE64 7 E4
Havercroft NE10 72 B7
Haverley Dr [1] SR7 92 E1
Haversham CL NE7 39 A5
Haversham Pk SR5 75 C5
Hawarden Cres SR4 102 A1
Hawes Ave DH2 88 C1
Hawes Ct SR6 75 C5
Hawesdale Cres NE21 68 B8
Haweswater Cl NE34 59 D6
Haweswater Cres NE64 7 C4
Hawick Cres NE6 56 B4
Hawk Terr DH3 82 E2
Hawkesley Rd SR4 85 D5
Hawkey's La NE29 41 F6
Hawkhills Terr [6] DH3 82 C5
Hawkhurst NE38 83 E2
Hawkins Ct SR3 91 F6
Hawks St NE8 56 A4
Hawksbury NE16 69 A7
Hawksfeld NE10 71 E4
Hawkshead Ct NE3 37 D7
Hawkshead Pl NE9 71 B4
Hawksley NE5 36 F2
Hawksmoor Cl NE63 6 C1
Hawkwell Rise NE15 35 D1
Hawsker Cl SR3 92 C7
Hawthorn Ave
Brunswick Village NE13 28 A6
New Silksworth SR3 92 B8
Hawthorn CE Fst Sch
NE63 6 D1
Hawthorn Cl NE16 69 B5
Hawthorn Cres NE38 83 C1
Hawthorn Ct Morpeth NE61 8 E8
Newcastle-u-T NE3 38 C4
Hawthorn Dr
Dunston NE11 69 F8
Hedworth NE32 58 D2
Hawthorn Gdns
[5] Gateshead NE10 56 D1
Newcastle-u-T NE3 37 F4
Ryton NE40 52 E4
Tynemouth NE29 41 F7
Whitley Bay NE26 31 F5
Hawthorn Gr NE28 40 B2
Hawthorn Mews NE3 38 C4
Hawthorn Pl
Killingworth NE12 29 C4
Newcastle-u-T NE4 100 B4
Hawthorn Prim Sch
NE4 100 A4
Hawthorn Rd
Ashington NE63 6 E3
Blaydon NE21 53 C1
Newcastle-u-T NE3 38 C4
Hawthorn Rd W NE3 38 C4
Hawthorn St
Burnside DH4 90 C2
Jarrow NE32 58 A7
Sunderland SR4 102 A2
Hawthorn St *continued*
Walbottle NE15 35 F2
Hawthorn Terr
Chester le S DH3 88 D2
Crawcrook NE40 51 E3
[8] Dunston NE11 69 F8
Gateshead NE9 71 D1
Newcastle-u-T NE4 100 A4
[12] Springwell NE9 71 F1
Sunderland SR6 75 E6
Hawthorn Villas NE23 22 D6
Hawthorn Way NE20 25 D3
Hawthorn Wlk NE4 100 B4
Hawthorne Ave
Hebburn NE31 57 F6
South Shields NE34 59 F4
Hawthorne Gdns NE9 70 F6
Hawthorne Rd NE24 17 F7
Hawthorne Terr DH9 79 D3
Hawthorns The
East Boldon NE36 74 D7
Gateshead NE9 71 D1
Newcastle-u-T NE4 100 A3
Hay St SR5 102 C4
Haydock Dr NE10 72 C7
Haydon NE38 83 E1
Haydon Cl NE3 37 F8
Haydon Dr NE25 31 F3
Haydon Gdns NE27 30 D4
Haydon Rd NE63 6 D2
Haydon Sq SR4 85 D5
Hayes Wlk NE13 28 B6
Hayfield La NE16 69 B6
Hayhole Rd NE29 41 E2
Haylands Sq NE34 59 D5
Hayleazes Rd NE15 53 F7
Haymarket NE1 99 A2
Haymarket Sta NE1 99 A2
Haynyng The NE10 71 E7
Hayricks The DH9 79 D4
Hayton Ave NE34 60 A5
Hayton Cl NE23 22 C7
Hayton Rd NE30 32 A2
Hayward Ave NE25 23 D3
Hazard La DH5 94 E3
Hazel Ave
[3] Houghton-le-S DH4 94 C8
New Silksworth SR3 92 B8
Tynemouth NE29 41 F7
Hazel Ct NE12 39 D7
Hazel Gr Burnopfield NE16 79 C6
Chester le S DH2 88 A5
Ellington NE61 1 E5
Gateshead NE10 72 B7
Killingworth NE12 29 B2
South Shields NE34 59 F4
Hazel Rd Blaydon NE21 53 D2
Gateshead NE8 70 C8
Hazel St NE32 58 A7
Hazel Terr DH4 90 C2
Hazeldene Hedworth NE32 73 C8
Whitley Bay NE25 31 E5
Hazeldene Ave NE3 37 C5
Hazeldene Ct NE30 42 C7
Hazeley Gr [4] NE3 37 D5
Hazeley Way NE3 37 D5
Hazelmere Ave
Bedlington NE22 10 E1
Newcastle-u-T NE3 28 D1
Hazelmere Cres NE23 22 C8
Hazelmere Dene NE23 22 E1
Hazelmoor NE31 57 D7
Hazelwood Jarrow NE32 58 D6
Killingworth NE12 29 F3
Hazelwood Ave
Newbiggin-by-t-S NE64 7 D5
Newcastle-u-T NE2 38 E2
Sunderland SR5 74 F2
Hazelwood Cl NE9 71 D2
Hazelwood Com Prim Sch
NE13 28 B5
Hazelwood Gdns NE38 83 C1
Hazelwood Terr NE28 41 A3
Hazledene Terr [2] SR4 85 F6
Hazlitt Ave NE34 59 B3
Hazlitt Pl NE23 23 A1
Headlam Gn [2] NE6 56 C5
Headlam Ho [12] NE6 56 C6
Headlam St [4] NE6 56 C6
Headlam View NE28 41 A2
Healey Dr SR3 86 B2
Heartsbourne Dr NE34 59 F3
Heath Cl NE11 70 B7
Heath Cres NE15 54 A4
Heath Grange DH5 90 E1
Heath Sq SR4 85 E5
Heathcote Gn NE5 37 B3
Heathdale Gdns NE7 39 B3
Heather Cl SR6 60 A2
Heather Dr DH5 95 A5
Heather Hill [4] NE9 71 F1
Heather Lea DH9 78 E2
Heather Lea La NE42 50 D3
Heather Pl
Crawcrook NE40 52 A4
Newcastle-u-T NE4 54 E8
Heather Terr NE16 79 B6
Heatherdale Terr NE9 71 B3
Heatherlaw
Gateshead NE9 71 C5
Washington NE37 82 F6
Heatherlea Gdns [1] SR3 86 B3
Heatherlea Pl NE37 72 D1
Heatherlee Gdns NE62 11 A8
Heatherslaw Rd NE5 54 C8
Heatherwell Gn NE10 71 C7
Heathery La NE3 38 E7
Heatheryhill NE46 44 A4
Heathfield Morpeth NE61 9 B6
Sunderland SR2 86 C2
Heathfield Cres NE5 37 D3
Heathfield Farm NE40 52 A1
Heathfield Gdns NE40 52 A1
Heathfield Ho NE9 70 F6
Heathfield Pl
Gateshead NE9 70 F6
Newcastle-u-T NE3 28 D1
Heathfield Rd NE9 70 F6
Heathway NE32 58 C2
Heathwell Gdns NE16 69 B8
Heathwell Rd NE15 53 F7
Heathwood Ave [1] NE16 69 A7
Heaton Cl NE6 56 B7
Heaton Gdns NE34 59 C2
Heaton Gr NE6 56 B7
Heaton Hall Rd NE6 56 B7
Heaton Manor Sch NE7 39 A2
Heaton Park Ct [9] NE6 56 B7
Heaton Park Rd NE6 56 B7
Heaton Park View NE6 56 B7
Heaton Pl NE6 56 B6
Heaton Rd NE6 56 B7
Heaton Terr
Newcastle-u-T NE6 56 A6
North Shields NE29 41 E6
Heaton Wlk [4] NE6 56 B6
Hebburn Comp Sch NE31 57 E4
Hebburn Hospl NE31 57 D4
Hebburn Sta NE31 57 D6
Heber St NE1 98 C1
Hebron Ave NE61 4 E4
Hebron Pl NE63 6 F3
Hebron Way NE23 22 A5
Hector St NE27 30 F4
Heddon Ave NE13 28 A4
Heddon Banks NE15 34 E1
Heddon Cl
Newcastle-u-T NE3 38 A6
Ryton NE40 52 D5
Heddon View
Blaydon NE21 53 B2
Ryton NE40 52 D5
Heddon Way NE34 59 B6
Hedge Cl NE11 70 B7
Hedgefield Ave NE21 52 F5
Hedgefield Cotts NE21 52 F5
Hedgefield Ct NE21 52 F5
Hedgefield Gr NE24 17 C3
Hedgefield View NE23 22 A1
Hedgehope [6] NE37 83 A6
Hedgehope Rd NE5 37 A4
Hedgelea NE40 52 B5
Hedgelea Rd DH5 94 C3
Hedgeley Rd
Hebburn NE31 57 E6
Newcastle-u-T NE5 53 E8
Tynemouth NE29 41 D7
Hedgeley Terr NE6 56 F6
Hedgerow Mews NE63 6 B2
Hedley Ave NE24 17 F6
Hedley Cl [7] NE33 42 C4
Hedley Ct NE24 17 F6
Hedley La NE11,NE16 80 C6
Hedley Pl NE28 40 B1
Hedley Rd
North Shields NE29 41 F3
Seaton Delaval NE25 23 E2
Wylam NE41 51 B6
Hedley St Gateshead NE8 70 D8
Newcastle-u-T NE3 38 C5
[5] South Shields NE33 42 C4
Hedley Terr
Newcastle-u-T NE3 38 C5
Ryhope SR2 93 A6
South Hetton DH6 97 F7
Hedworth Ave NE34 59 A4
Hedworth Ct SR1 103 B2
Hedworth La
Boldon Colliery NE35 58 E1
Hedworth NE32 58 D2
Hedworth Lane Prim Sch
NE35 58 D1
Hedworth Pl NE9 71 C3
Hedworth St DH3 88 C3
Hedworth Terr DH4 90 B6
Hedworth View NE32 58 D3
Hedworthfield Prim Sch
NE32 58 D1
Heighley St NE15 53 F5
Helen St Blaydon NE21 53 A2
East Cramlington NE23 22 F5
Sunderland SR6 75 E4
Helena Ave NE26 32 B5
Helena Ho SR2 102 B1
Hellpool La NE46 44 F5
Helmdon NE37 83 E8
Helmsdale Ave [13] NE10 56 D1
Helmsdale Rd SR4 85 D5
Helmsley Cl DH4 90 A6
Helmsley Ct SR5 74 E3
Helmsley Dr NE28 40 F2
Helmsley Gn NE9 71 B2
Helmsley Rd NE2 99 C3
Helston Ct NE15 53 B7
Helvellyn Ave NE38 83 A3
Helvellyn Cl NE21 68 C8
Helvellyn Rd SR2 86 D2
Hemel St [8] DH3 88 C2
Hemlington Cl [12] SR2 92 F6
Hemming St [9] SR2 86 F2
Hemsley Rd NE34 43 A1
Hencotes NE46 45 A4
Hencotes Ct [7] NE46 45 A4
Hencotes Mews [4] NE46 45 A4
Henderson Ave NE16 69 A8
Henderson Cl NE46 44 F3
Henderson Ct NE29 41 F3
Henderson Gdns NE10 72 B8
Henderson Rd
South Shields NE34 58 F4
Sunderland SR4 85 F6
Wallsend NE28 40 B3
Wallsend NE28 40 B4
Henderson's Bldgs NE64 7 E5
Hendersyde Cl NE5 37 B3
Hendon Burn Ave SR2 103 B1
Hendon Burn Ave W [2]
SR2 86 E4
Hendon Cl
North Shields NE29 42 A3
Sunderland SR1 103 B2
Hendon Gdns NE32 58 D2
Hendon Ho NE63 6 A4
Hendon Rd
Gateshead NE8,NE9 71 B8
Sunderland SR1 103 B3
Sunderland,Hendon SR1,
SR2 103 C2
Hendon Rd E SR1 103 C2
Hendon St SR1 103 C2
Hendon Valley Ct [7] SR2 86 E4
Hendon Valley Rd SR2 103 B1
Henley Cl NE23 22 D7
Henley Gdns NE28 41 B4
Henley Ho NE35 73 E8
Henley Rd Sunderland SR4 85 D5
Tynemouth NE30 32 C1
Henley Sq NE61 2 A3
Henley Way NE35 73 E8
Henlow Rd NE15 53 C7
Henry Nelson St NE33 42 D4
Henry Robson Way NE33 42 C2
Henry Sq NE2 99 C2
Henry St Hetton le H DH5 95 A5
Houghton-le-S DH5 90 E1
Newcastle-u-T NE3 38 C5
North Shields NE29 42 A4
Shiney Row DH4 90 B6
South Shields NE33 42 D4
Henry St E SR2 103 C2
Henry Terr DH4 89 F2
Hensby Ct NE5 37 B4
Henshaw Ct NE63 6 B2
Henshaw Gr NE25 23 F2
Henshaw Pl NE5 54 B7
Henshelwood Terr [2]
NE2 38 E1
Henson Cl NE38 83 D4
Hepburn Gdns NE10 56 C1
Hepburn Gr SR5 73 F1
Hepple Ct NE24 17 C6
Hepple Rd NE64 7 C3
Hepple Way NE3 38 A6
Hepscott Dr NE25 31 D6
Hepscott Manor Cotts
NE61 9 D3
Hepscott Terr NE33 59 D8
Hepscott Wlk NE61 4 E3
Herbert St NE8 56 A1
Herbert Terr SR5 75 B5
Herd Cl NE21 53 A1
Herd House La NE21 52 F2
Herdinghill NE37 82 F6
Herdlaw NE23 22 A6
Hereford Ct
Newcastle-u-T NE3 37 D8
Sunderland SR2 86 D1
Hereford Rd SR2 86 D1
Hereford Sq SR2 86 D1
Hereford Way NE32 58 B2
Heritage Cl NE8 100 C1
Hermiston NE25 31 E5
Hermitage Gdns DH2 88 B1
Hermitage Pk DH3 88 C1
Hermitage Sch The DH2 88 A2
Heron Cl Ashington NE63 6 E1
Blyth NE24 17 E4
Washington NE38 83 A2
Heron Dr NE33 42 C4
Heron Pl NE12 39 A7
Heron Villas NE34 59 B4
Herrick St NE5 37 A3
Herring Gull Cl NE24 17 E3
Herrington Mews DH4 90 E6
Herrington Rd SR3,DH4 91 B6
Hersham Cl NE3 37 D7
Hertburn Gdns NE37 83 D7
Hertburn Ind Est NE37 83 E7
Hertford NE9 70 F2
Hertford Ave NE34 60 C7
Hertford Cl NE25 31 D6
Hertford Cres DH5 94 F4
Hertford Gr NE23 22 C7
Hesket Ct NE3 37 E7
Hesleyside [4] NE63 6 F2
Hesleyside Dr NE5 54 C8
Hesleyside Rd NE25 31 B5
Hessewelle Cres DH6 97 E1
Hester Ave NE25 23 D6
Hester Bglws NE25 23 D6
Hester Gdns NE25 23 E6
Heswall Rd NE23 16 A2
Hetton Lyons Ctry Pk*
DH5 95 C4
Hetton Lyons Ind Est
DH5 95 B3
Hetton Lyons Prim Sch
DH5 95 A2
Hetton Moor Terr DH5 95 B2
Hetton Prim Sch DH5 94 F3
Hetton Rd DH5 94 E7
Hetton Sch DH5 94 F3
Heugh Hill NE9 72 A2
Hewitson Terr NE10 71 C8
Hewitt Ave SR2 92 E8
Hewley Cres NE15 35 D1
Heworth Burn Cres NE10 71 E8
Heworth Cres [1] NE37 83 D8
Heworth Ct [6] NE34 59 A5
Heworth Dene Gdns
NE10 56 E1
Heworth Gr NE37 83 C8
Heworth Grange Comp Sch
NE10 71 F8
Heworth Rd NE37 72 D1
Heworth Sta (BR & Metro)
NE10 71 F8
Heworth Way NE10 71 A8
Hewson Pl NE9 71 B6
Hexham NE38 82 F4
Hexham Abbey* NE46 45 B5
Hexham Ave
Cramlington NE23 22 D7
Hebburn NE31 57 E3
Newcastle-u-T NE6 56 F5
Hexham Bsns Pk NE46 45 A6
Hexham Cl NE29 41 C7
Hexham Ct NE11 69 F6
Hexham East Fst Sch
NE46 45 C4
Hexham General Hospl
NE46 45 C4
Hexham Ho [8] NE6 57 A6
Hexham Mid Sch NE46 45 B4
Hexham Old Rd NE21,
NE40 52 E5
Hexham Priory Sch NE46 45 C4
Hexham Race Course
NE46 44 D1
Hexham Rd
Heddon-on-t-W NE15 34 E2
Sunderland SR4 85 D5
Throckley NE15 35 C2
Whickham NE16 54 A1
Hexham Sta NE46 45 C5
Hextol Cres NE46 45 A4
Hextol Ct NE46 44 F4
Hextol Gdns NE15 53 F7
Hextol Terr NE46 44 F4
Heybrook Ave NE29 41 F8
Heyburn Gdns NE15 54 D5
Hi-Tec Village NE35 73 D7
Hibernia Rd NE6 57 A4
Hibernian Rd NE32 58 B7
Hickling Ct NE5 37 C4
Hickstead Cl NE28 40 E7
Hickstead Gr NE23 22 D7
Hiddleston Ave NE7 39 B5
High Axwell NE21 53 D2
High Back Cl NE32 58 A4
High Barnes Terr SR4 102 A1
High Bridge NE1,NE99 99 A1
High Burswell NE46 44 F5
High Chare DH3 88 D3
High Cl NE42 50 F3
High Croft NE37 72 C1
High Croft Cl NE31 57 D4
High Dene NE7 39 B1
High Dewley Burn NE15 35 D3
High Downs Sq DH5 95 A5
High Flatworth NE29 41 B4
High Friar La NE1 99 A1
High Friarside NE16 78 E6
High Gables [9] NE46 45 B4
High Gate The NE3 37 E4
High Gosforth Park
(Newcastle Race Course)
NE3 28 D2
High Gr NE40 52 D4
High Grindon Ho SR4 85 C3
High Hamsterley Rd
NE39 78 A5
High Hedgefield Terr
NE21 52 E5
High Heworth La NE10 71 E7
High Horse Cl NE39 68 A4
High Horse Close Wood
NE39 68 A4
High House Cl NE61 8 D8
High House Gdns NE10 56 E1
High La DH4 90 F4
High Lane Row NE31 57 F7
High Lanes NE10 71 F7
High Laws NE3 38 F4
High Level Rd NE8 101 B3
High Market NE63 6 A4
High Mdw
South Shields NE34 59 F8
South Shields NE34 59 F8
High Mdws NE3 37 E3
High Mill Rd NE39 78 A5
High Moor Ct NE5 37 E2
High Moor Pl NE34 59 C5
High Pasture NE38 83 E1
High Pk NE61 9 A7
High Primrose Hill DH4 89 D3
High Quay Blyth NE24 17 F8
Newcastle-u-T NE1 56 A5
High Rd The NE34 60 A6
High Reach NE10 57 A2
High Reins NE46 44 E5
High Ridge
Bedlington NE22 10 E1
Hazlerigg NE13 28 B4
High Row
Great Lumley DH4 89 E1
Newcastle-u-T NE15 53 C6
Ryton NE40 52 E4
Washington NE37 72 D1
High Sandgrove SR6 60 A1
High Shaw NE42 50 B1
High Spen Ct NE39 67 A4

High Spen Ind Est NE39 .66 F5
High Spen Prim Sch
NE39 . . . . .66 F3
High St Blyth NE24 . . . .17 D7
Blyth NE24 . . . . .17 E7
Choppington NE62 . . . . .10 E6
Easington Lane DH5 . . . .95 C1
Gateshead NE8 . . . . . .101 C3
Gateshead,Felling NE10 . .71 D8
Gateshead,Wrekenton NE9 .71 C3
Guide Post NE62 . . . . . .10 E7
High Pittington DH6 . . . .96 B6
Jarrow NE32 . . . . .58 C7
Jarrow NE32 . . . . .58 D7
Newbiggin-by-t-S NE64 . . . .7 F5
Newburn NE15 . . . . . . .52 F7
Newcastle-u-T NE3 . . . . .38 C4
Sunderland SR4 . . . . . . .85 A6
High St Bk NE3 . . . . . . .38 C5
High St E Sunderland SR1 103 B3
Wallsend NE28 . . . . . . .40 C1
High St W
Sunderland SR1 . . . . . .103 A3
Wallsend NE28,NE6 . . . . .40 A1
High Stanners NE61 . . . . .3 F1
High Stobhill NE61 . . . . . .9 A6
High Swinburne Pl NE4 .98 B1
High View
Hedley on t H NE43 . . . .64 F3
Ponteland NE20 . . . . . . .25 D2
Wallsend NE28 . . . . . . .40 B3
High View N NE28 . . . . .40 B4
High Weetslade Farm Cotts
NE23 . . . . .29 A6
High Well Gdns NE10 . . .56 E1
High West St NE8 . . . . .101 C4
Higham Pl NE1 . . . . . . .99 B2
Highbridge NE3 . . . . . . .38 C7
Highburn NE23 . . . . . . .22 A5
Highbury Gateshead NE10 .71 E8
Newcastle-u-T NE2 . . . . .38 D2
Whitley Bay NE25 . . . . . .31 E5
Highbury Ave NE9 . . . . .72 A2
Highbury Cl NE9 . . . . . .72 A2
Highbury Pl NE29 . . . . .41 F6
Highclere DH4 . . . . .89 F5
Highclere Dr SR2 . . . . . .92 D6
Highcliffe Gdns NE8 . . . .71 A8
Highcroft Dr SR6 . . . . . .60 E1
Highcroft Pk SR6 . . . . . .60 F1
Highcrofts NE15 . . . . . . .50 C8
Highcross Rd NE30 . . . . .32 A3
Highfield Birtley DH3 . . . .82 C6
Blyth NE24 . . . . .16 F7
Prudhoe NE42 . . . . .50 D2
Sunniside NE16 . . . . . . .69 B3
Highfield Ave NE12 . . . . .39 D8
Highfield Cl NE5 . . . . . .36 F3
Highfield Com Prim Sch
NE39 . . . . .67 C2
Highfield Cres DH3 . . . . .88 C5
Highfield Ct NE10 . . . . . .71 E7
Highfield Day Hospl DH3 88 C5
Highfield Dr
Ashington NE63 . . . . .7 A2
Fence Houses DH4 . . . . .94 B7
South Shields NE34 . . . . .59 F8
Highfield Gdns DH3 . . . .88 C5
Highfield Grange DH4 . . .94 B7
Highfield Inf Sch NE34 . . .43 A1
Highfield La NE42 . . . . . .50 C1
Highfield Pl
Brunswick Village NE13 . .28 A5
⑥ Sunderland SR4 . . . . .85 F6
Highfield Rd
Gateshead NE8 . . . . .56 A1
Newcastle-u-T NE5 . . . . .36 F3
Rowlands Gill NE39 . . . . .67 C1
Shiney Row DH4 . . . . . . .90 A6
South Shields NE33,NE34 .59 F8
Highfield Rise DH3 . . . . .88 C5
Highfield Terr
Newcastle-u-T NE6 . . . . .57 A4
Prudhoe NE42 . . . . .50 B2
Highfields Mid Sch NE42 50 C2
Highford Gdns NE61 . . . . .8 E7
Highford La NE46 . . . . . .44 E4
Highgate Gdns NE32 . . . .58 D2
Highgate Rd SR4 . . . . . .85 D5
Highgreen Chase NE16 . .69 A4
Highgrove NE5 . . . . .36 D2
Highheath ⚊ NE37 . . . . .83 A6
Highland Rd NE5 . . . . . .37 D3
Highlaws Gdns NE9 . . . .71 B2
Highmoor NE61 . . . . .8 D7
Highridge DH3 . . . . .82 C5
Highside Dr SR3 . . . . . . .86 A3
Highstead Ave NE23 . . . .16 A1
Highsteads DH8 . . . . . . .77 B1
Hightree Cl SR3 . . . . . . .91 F5
Highwell La ⚊ NE5 . . . . .36 E1
Highwood Rd NE15 . . . . .53 F7
Highworth Dr
Newcastle-u-T NE7 . . . . .39 D3
⑶ Springwell NE9 . . . . .71 F1
Hilda Pk DH2 . . . . .88 B5
Hilda St Gateshead NE8 . .101 A1
Sunderland SR6 . . . . . . .75 D3
Hilda Terr
Chester le S DH2 . . . . . .88 B4
⑺ Throckley NE15 . . . . .35 D2
Hilden Bldgs NE7 . . . . . .39 C2
Hilden Gdns NE7 . . . . . .39 C2
Hill Ave NE23 . . . . .23 A2
Hill Brow SR3 . . . . .92 B6
Hill Crest Burnopfield NE16 79 B6
Gateshead NE10 . . . . . . .71 E6
Hill Crest Gdns NE2 . . . .38 E4

Hill Croft NE15 . . . . .33 C1
Hill Dyke NE9 . . . . .71 C2
Hill Head Dr NE5 . . . . . .36 D1
Hill House Rd NE15 . . . . .35 C2
Hill La DH4 . . . . .84 C1
Hill Pk NE20 . . . . .25 D2
Hill Park Rd NE32 . . . . . .58 C5
Hill Rise Crawcrook NE40 .51 F3
Washington NE38 . . . . . .83 E6
Hill St Corbridge NE45 . . .46 F5
Jarrow NE32 . . . . .58 A7
New Silksworth SR3 . . . .92 A7
South Shields NE33 . . . . .42 B1
Hill Terr DH4 . . . . .90 E6
Hill The NE42 . . . . .50 B4
Hill Top Birtley DH3 . . . . .82 D4
Blaydon NE21 . . . . .53 B1
Hill Top Ave NE9 . . . . . .71 B5
Hill Top Cl NE62 . . . . . . .10 F8
Hill Top Gdns NE9 . . . . .71 A5
Hill Top Sch NE10 . . . . . .71 E4
Hill View Gdns SR3 . . . . .86 B3
Hill View Inf Sch SR2 . . . .86 D2
Hill View Jun Sch SR2 . . . .86 D2
Hill View Rd SR2 . . . . . . .86 D2
Hill View Sq SR2 . . . . . . .86 D2
Hillary Ave NE12 . . . . . . .39 E8
Hillcrest Ashington NE63 . . .7 A2
Hedworth NE32 . . . . . . .58 D2
Prudhoe NE42 . . . . .50 D2
South Shields NE34 . . . . .60 B5
Sunderland SR3 . . . . . . .91 B8
Whitley Bay NE25 . . . . . .31 E5
Hillcrest Ave NE62 . . . . . .10 F8
Hillcrest Ct NE42 . . . . . .50 D2
Hillcroft ⑧ Birtley DH3 . . .82 C5
Gateshead NE9 . . . . .71 A6
Rowlands Gill NE39 . . . . .67 C2
Hillfield NE25 . . . . .31 D5
Hillfield Gdns SR3 . . . . . .86 B3
Hillfield St NE8 . . . . . . .101 B4
Hillford Terr NE17 . . . . . .66 B1
Hillgate NE8 . . . . .101 B4
Hillhead Gdns NE15 . . . .70 A6
Hillhead La NE16 . . . . . .68 D1
Hillhead Parkway NE5 . . .36 C2
Hillhead Rd NE5 . . . . . . .36 D2
Hillhead Way NE5 . . . . . .36 E3
Hillheads Rd NE25,NE26 . .32 A4
Hillingdon Gr SR4 . . . . . .85 A2
Hillrise Cres SR7 . . . . . . .92 D1
Hills Ct NE21 . . . . .53 E4
Hills St NE8 . . . . .101 B3
Hillsden Rd NE25 . . . . . . .31 D7
Hillside Ashington NE63 . . . .6 C4
Birtley DH3 . . . . .82 D4
Blaydon NE21 . . . . .53 B2
Chester le S DH3 . . . . . . .88 C4
Dunston NE11 . . . . .69 F7
Killingworth NE12 . . . . . .29 E2
Morpeth NE61 . . . . .8 F7
Ponteland NE20 . . . . . . .25 C1
South Shields NE34 . . . . .60 B4
Sunderland SR3 . . . . . . .86 C3
West Boldon NE36 . . . . . .74 A7
Hillside Ave NE15 . . . . . .53 F8
Hillside Cl NE39 . . . . . . .67 E3
Hillside Cres NE15 . . . . .54 A4
Hillside Dr SR6 . . . . .60 E1
Hillside Gdns SR3 . . . . . .86 C3
Hillside Gr DH6 . . . . .96 B5
Hillside Pl NE9 . . . . .71 A6
Hillside Rd NE46 . . . . . . .45 D4
Hillside Way DH4 . . . . . .90 E1
Hillsleigh Rd NE5 . . . . . .37 D2
Hillsview Ave NE3 . . . . . .37 E5
Hillthorne Cl NE38 . . . . .83 E4
Hilltop Gdns SR3 . . . . . .92 C7
Hilltop Ho NE5 . . . . .37 A4
Hilltop View SR6 . . . . . . .60 E2
Hillview SR3 . . . . .91 B7
Hillview Cres DH4 . . . . . .90 D3
Hillview Gr DH4 . . . . . . .90 D3
Hillview Rd DH4 . . . . . . .90 D3
Hilton Ave NE5 . . . . .37 B2
Hilton Cl NE23 . . . . .16 A2
Hilton Prim Sch NE5 . . . .37 B2
Hind St SR1 . . . . .102 C2
Hindley Cl NE40 . . . . . . .51 E3
Hindley Gdns NE4 . . . . . .54 D7
Hindmarch Dr NE35,NE36 .74 B7
Hindson's Cres N DH4 . . .90 A5
Hindson's Cres S DH4 . . .90 A5
Hinkley Ct SR3 . . . . .86 A3
Hippingstones La NE45 . .46 F6
Hipsburn Dr SR3 . . . . . . .86 A3
Hiram Dr NE36 . . . . .74 D7
Hirst Head NE22 . . . . . . .11 A1
Hirst High Sch NE22 . . . . .6 F2
Hirst Terr N NE22 . . . . . .11 A1
Hirst Villas NE22 . . . . . . .11 B1
Histon Ct NE5 . . . . .37 B3
Histon Way NE5 . . . . . . .37 B3
Hither Gn NE32 . . . . .58 D2
Hobart NE26 . . . . .31 F7
Hobart Ave NE34 . . . . . .58 F3
Hobart Gdns NE7 . . . . . .39 A5
Hobson Ind Est NE16 . . . .79 A5
Hodgkin Ho NE3 . . . . . . .99 A3
Hodgkin Park Cres NE15 .54 C5
Hodgkin Park Rd NE15 . .54 C5
Hodgson Terr ⑥ NE37 . . .83 F8
Hodgson's Rd NE24 . . . . .12 D1
Hodkin Gdns NE9 . . . . . .71 B6

Hogarth Cotts NE22 . . . .16 A8
Hogarth Dr NE38 . . . . . . .83 E3
Hogarth Rd NE34 . . . . . .59 C2
Holbein Rd NE34 . . . . . . .59 C3
Holborn Ho NE33 . . . . . .42 B2
Holborn Pl NE5 . . . . .36 E1
Holborn Rd SR4 . . . . . . .85 D5
Holborn Sq SR4 . . . . . . .85 D4
Holburn Cl NE40 . . . . . . .52 D5
Holburn Cres NE40 . . . . .52 E5
Holburn Gdns NE40 . . . .52 E5
Holburn La NE40 . . . . . . .52 D6
Holburn Lane Ct NE40 . . .52 D6
Holburn Terr NE40 . . . . . .52 E5
Holburn Way NE40 . . . . .52 D5
Holburn Wlk NE40 . . . . .52 E5
Holden Pl NE5 . . . . .37 D2
Holder House La NE34 . . .59 E3
Holder House Way NE34 .59 E2
Holderness Rd
Newcastle-u-T NE6 . . . . .39 B1
Wallsend NE28 . . . . . . .41 B3
Hole La Sunniside NE16 . .69 B3
Whickham NE16 . . . . . . .68 F4
Holeyn Hall Rd NE41 . . . .51 A7
Holeyn Rd NE15 . . . . . . .35 C1
Holland Dr NE2 . . . . .98 B3
Holland Park Dr NE32 . . .58 D2
Holland Pk NE28 . . . . . .39 E3
Holley Park Prim Sch
NE38 . . . . .83 A3
Hollinghill Rd NE25 . . . . .23 E2
Hollings Cres NE28 . . . . .40 B4
Hollings Terr NE17 . . . . . .66 A1
Hollingside Way NE34 . . .59 D5
Hollington Ave NE12 . . . .39 B6
Hollington Cl NE12 . . . . .39 B6
Hollinhill NE39 . . . . .68 A5
Hollinhill Rd NE37 . . . . . .83 E7
Hollinhill Terr NE44 . . . . .62 F8
Hollinside Cl NE16 . . . . .69 A5
Hollinside Gdns NE15 . . .54 B6
Hollinside Rd
Sunderland SR4 . . . . . . .85 D4
Whickham NE11 . . . . . . .54 B2
Hollinside Sq SR4 . . . . . .85 C5
Hollinside Terr NE39 . . . .67 D2
Hollon St NE61 . . . . .1 E1
Hollow The Ashington NE63 .7 B2
Hedworth NE32 . . . . . . .58 D2
Hollowdene DH5 . . . . . . .95 A3
Holly Ave Dunston NE11 . .69 F7
Earsdon NE25 . . . . .31 B5
Houghton-le-S DH5 . . . . .94 F8
Longbenton NE12 . . . . . .29 D1
Morpeth NE61 . . . . .8 E7
New Silksworth SR3 . . . .92 B8
Newcastle-u-T,Fawdon NE3 .37 F6
Newcastle-u-T,Jesmond
NE2 . . . . .38 F1
Ryton NE40 . . . . .52 C6
South Shields NE34 . . . . .60 A5
Wallsend NE28 . . . . . . .40 C1
Whitburn SR6 . . . . .75 F8
Whitley Bay NE26 . . . . . .32 A5
Winlaton Mill NE21 . . . . .68 C6
Holly Ave W NE2 . . . . . .38 E1
Holly Bush Gdns NE40 . .52 E4
Holly Ct Hexham NE46 . . .44 E3
Killingworth NE12 . . . . . .29 C4
Holly Cres NE38 . . . . . . .83 C1
Holly Ct Newcastle-u-T NE5 .37 B2
Sunderland SR4 . . . . . .102 A2
Whitley Bay NE26 . . . . . .31 F5
Holly Gdns NE9 . . . . . . .70 D4
Holly Gr NE42 . . . . .50 B3
Holly Haven DH5 . . . . . .94 D4
Holly Hill NE10 . . . . .71 D8
Holly Ho SR1 . . . . .103 C3
Holly Mews NE26 . . . . . .32 A5
Holly Park View NE10 . . .71 D8
Holly Rd NE29 . . . . .41 F7
Holly St Ashington NE63 . . .6 D3
Jarrow NE32 . . . . .58 A7
Holly Terr NE16 . . . . .79 C5
Holly View NE10 . . . . . . .71 C8
Hollybush Rd ⑷ NE10 . .71 C8
Hollycarriside Rd SR2 . . .92 E8
Hollycrest DH2 . . . . .88 B5
Hollydene
Kibblesworth NE11 . . . . .81 D6
Rowlands Gill NE39 . . . . .67 F2
Hollyhock Hebburn NE31 . .57 E3
Washington NE38 . . . . . .83 E2
Hollymount Ave NE22 . . .16 A8
Hollymount Sq NE22 . . . .16 A8
Hollymount Terr NE22 . . .16 A8
Hollyoak Ho NE24 . . . . . .17 B5
Hollys The NE37 . . . . . . .82 B7
Hollywell Gr NE13 . . . . . .36 F8
Hollywell Rd NE29 . . . . . .41 D6
Hollywood Ave
Newcastle-u-T,Gosforth
NE3 . . . . .38 D6
Sunderland SR5 . . . . . . .74 F2
Wallsend NE6 . . . . .40 A1
Hollywood Cres NE3 . . . .38 D6
Hollywood Gdns NE11 . . .70 B5
Holm Gn NE25 . . . . .31 D4
Holman Ct NE33 . . . . . . .42 C2
Holmcroft NE64 . . . . .7 E3
Holmdale Ashington NE63 . .6 C2
Hexham NE46 . . . . .45 C4
Holme Ave
Newcastle-u-T NE6 . . . . .39 F1
Whickham NE16 . . . . . . .69 B7

Holme Gdns
Sunderland SR3 . . . . . . .86 B3
Wallsend NE28 . . . . .41 A2
Holme Rise NE16 . . . . . .69 B7
Holmesdale Rd NE5 . . . .37 D1
Holmeside SR1 . . . . . . .103 A2
Holmewood Dr NE39 . . . .78 D8
Holmfield Ave NE34 . . . .59 E7
Holmland NE15 . . . . .54 C4
Holmlands NE25 . . . . . . .31 E5
Holmlands Cl NE25 . . . . .31 E5
Holmlands Pk DH3 . . . . .88 D2
Holmlands Pk N SR2 . . . .86 C4
Holmlands Pk S SR2 . . . .86 C4
Holmside Ave NE11 . . . . .70 A8
Holmside Terr NE16 . . . . .69 C2
Holmwood Ave
Newbiggin-by-t-S NE64 . . . .7 D5
Whitley Bay NE25 . . . . . .31 D4
Holmwood Gr NE2 . . . . .38 D2
Holyake Ave NE3 . . . . . .38 A2
Holy Island ⚊ NE8 . . . . .45 A5
Holy Jesus Bglws NE2 . . .98 B4
Holyfields NE27 . . . . .30 E2
Holylake Sq SR4 . . . . . . .85 D5
Holyoake Gdns
Birtley DH3 . . . . .82 C4
Gateshead NE9 . . . . .70 F8
South Shields NE42 . . . . .50 D3
Holyoake Terr
Sunderland SR6 . . . . . . .75 E3
⚊ Washington NE37 . . . .83 D8
Holyrood Rd ⚊ SR2 . . . .86 F2
Holystone Ave Blyth NE24 17 C5
Newcastle-u-T NE3 . . . . .38 B6
Whitley Bay NE25 . . . . . .32 B4
Holystone Cl Blyth NE24 . .17 B5
Burnside DH4 . . . . .90 B2
Holystone Cres NE7 . . . . .39 B3
Holystone Ct NE8 . . . . .101 A1
Holystone Dr NE27 . . . . .30 C2
Holystone Gdns NE29 . . .41 D8
Holystone Grange NE27 .30 C1
Holystone Prim Sch
NE27 . . . . .30 C1
Holystone St NE31 . . . . .57 D6
Holystone Way NE12,
NE27 . . . . .40 C8
Holywell Ave
Holywell NE25 . . . . .23 F2
Newcastle-u-T NE6 . . . . .56 E3
Whitley Bay NE26 . . . . . .31 F6
Holywell Cl Blaydon NE21 53 D1
Holywell NE25 . . . . .23 F2
Newcastle-u-T NE4 . . . . .98 B2
Holywell Dene Rd NE25 . .23 F2
Holywell La NE16 . . . . . .69 B3
Holywell Mews NE26 . . . .31 F6
Holywell Rd NE27 . . . . . .30 D1
Holywell Village Fst Sch
NE25 . . . . .23 F2
Home Ave ⚊ NE9 . . . . . .70 F4
Home Farm Cl NE63 . . . . .5 F4
Home Pk NE28 . . . . .39 E3
Homedale NE42 . . . . . . .50 E2
Homedale Pl NE42 . . . . .50 D2
Homedale Terr NE42 . . . .50 D2
Homedowne Ho NE3 . . . .38 C5
Homeprior Ho NE25 . . . .31 E4
Homestall Cl NE34 . . . . .59 D5
Honeycomb Ct ⑺ SR3 . .91 F5
Honeycrook Dr NE34 . . . .59 B5
Honeysuckle Ave NE34 . .59 B5
Honeysuckle Cl SR3 . . . .92 A5
Honister Ave NE2 . . . . . .38 E3
Honister Cl NE15 . . . . . . .53 D7
Honister Dr SR5 . . . . . . .75 C3
Honister Pl NE15 . . . . . . .53 D7
Honister Rd NE30 . . . . . .32 B2
Honister Way NE24 . . . . .17 A8
Honiton Cl DH4 . . . . .90 C4
Honiton Ct NE3 . . . . .37 B6
Honiton Way NE29 . . . . .41 B8
Hood Cl SR5 . . . . .75 C1
Hood Sq NE21 . . . . .53 A1
Hood St Morpeth NE61 . . . .1 F1
Newcastle-u-T NE1 . . . . .99 A1
⑷ Whickham NE16 . . . . .54 A1
Hookergate La NE39 . . . .67 A2
Hookergate Sch NE39 . . .67 B3
Hope Shield NE38 . . . . . .82 F1
Hope St Jarrow NE32 . . . .58 B7
Sunderland SR1 . . . . . .102 C2
Hope View SR2 . . . . .92 F7
Hopedene NE10 . . . . . . .72 A5
Hopgarth Ct DH3 . . . . . . .88 D4
Hopgarth Gdns DH3 . . . .88 D4
Hopkins Ct SR4 . . . . .85 D4
Hopkins Wlk NE34 . . . . . .59 A4
Hopper Pl NE8 . . . . .101 C3
Hopper Rd NE10 . . . . . . .71 C7
Hopper St
Gateshead NE8 . . . . . . .101 C3
⑤ North Shields NE29 . . .41 F5
⑧ Wallsend NE28 . . . . . .40 B2
Horatio St
Newcastle-u-T NE1 . . . . .56 A5
Sunderland SR6 . . . . . . .75 E1
Hornbeam DH4 . . . . .89 F5
Hornbeam Pl NE4 . . . . . .100 B4
Horncliffe Gdns NE16 . . .69 C8
Horncliffe Pl NE15 . . . . .35 B2
Horncliffe Wlk NE15 . . . .53 A7
Horning Ct NE5 . . . . .37 B4

Hornsea Cl NE13 . . . . . . .28 B5
Hornsey Cres DH5 . . . . . .95 B1
Hornsey Terr DH5 . . . . . .95 B1
Horse Crofts NE21 . . . . . .53 C3
Horsegate Bank NE17,
NE40 . . . . .66 D5
Horsham Gdns SR3 . . . . .86 A3
Horsham Gr NE29 . . . . . .41 E4
Horsley Ave
Crawcrook NE40 . . . . . . .51 E3
Shiremoor NE27 . . . . . . .30 F2
Horsley Cl NE62 . . . . . . .10 F8
Horsley Ct NE3 . . . . .37 E6
Horsley Gdns
Dunston NE11 . . . . .70 A8
Holywell NE25 . . . . .23 F2
Horsley Gr SR3 . . . . .86 A3
Horsley Hill Rd NE33 . . . .42 E1
Horsley Hill Sq NE34 . . . .60 B7
Horsley Rd
Newcastle-u-T NE7 . . . . .39 B2
Ovingham NE42 . . . . . . .50 A5
Washington NE38 . . . . . .84 A5
Horsley Terr
Newcastle-u-T NE6 . . . . .56 F5
⑿ Tynemouth NE30 . . . .42 D7
Horsley Vale NE34 . . . . .60 A8
Horsley View NE42 . . . . .50 F3
Horsley Wood Cotts
NE15 . . . . .50 D7
Horsleys Bldgs ⑶ NE61 . . .9 A8
Horton Ave
Bedlington NE22 . . . . . . .15 F8
Shiremoor NE27 . . . . . . .30 F2
Whiteleas NE34 . . . . .59 D3
Horton Cres NE13 . . . . . .27 D4
Horton Dr NE23 . . . . .16 B2
Horton Grange Fst Sch
NE24 . . . . .16 F8
Horton Manor NE24 . . . . .16 D7
Horton Pl NE24 . . . . .17 B4
Horton Rd NE24,NE22 . . .16 C5
Horton St ⑶ NE24 . . . . .17 F7
Hortondale Gr NE24 . . . . .17 B7
Horwood Ave NE5 . . . . . .36 E2
Hospital Dr NE31 . . . . . . .57 D4
Hospital La NE15 . . . . . . .53 B8
Hospital Of King James The
NE8 . . . . .56 B1
Hospl of St Mary the Virgin
The ⚊ NE4 . . . . .100 B4
Hotch Pudding Pl NE5 . . .36 F1
Hotspur Ave
Bedlington NE22 . . . . . . .15 F8
South Shields NE34 . . . . .59 F7
Whitley Bay NE25 . . . . . .32 A4
Hotspur Prim Sch NE2 . . .56 A6
Hotspur Rd NE28 . . . . . .40 A5
Hotspur St
Newcastle-u-T NE6 . . . . .56 A7
Tynemouth NE30 . . . . . . .42 D8
Houghton Ave
Newcastle-u-T NE5 . . . . .37 E3
Tynemouth NE30 . . . . . . .32 B3
Houghton Cut DH5 . . . . .90 E1
Houghton Ent Ctr DH5 . . .94 E8
Houghton Gate DH3 . . . . .89 B3
Houghton Kepier Sch
DH4 . . . . .94 D8
Houghton Rd
Hetton le H DH5 . . . . . . .95 A4
Newbottle DH4 . . . . .90 D3
Houghton Rd W DH5 . . . .95 A4
Houghton St SR4 . . . . . .102 A2
Houghtonside DH4 . . . . .90 E1
Houlet Garth ⚊ NE6 . . . .56 C5
Houlsyke Cl SR3 . . . . . . .92 C7
Houndslow Dr NE63 . . . . .6 B2
Hounslow Gdns NE32 . . .58 D2
House Terr NE37 . . . . . . .83 D8
Housesteads Gdns NE12 .38 F6
Housing La DH8 . . . . .77 D1
Housesteads ⚊ NE28 . . . .40 F4
Houston Ct NE4 . . . . . . .100 B4
Houston St NE4 . . . . . . .100 B4
Houxty Rd NE25 . . . . . . .31 B5
Hovingham Gdns SR3 . . .86 A3
Howard Cl NE27 . . . . . . .30 C1
Howard Ct NE30 . . . . . . .42 B5
Howard Gr NE61 . . . . .4 E3
Howard Ho NE3 . . . . .38 C4
Howard Pl NE3 . . . . .38 C5
Howard Rd NE61 . . . . .4 A1
Howard St
Gateshead,Mount Pleasant
NE8 . . . . .56 B1
Gateshead,Windy Nook
NE10 . . . . .71 C6
Jarrow NE32 . . . . .58 C6
Newcastle-u-T NE1 . . . . .99 C1
North Shields NE30 . . . . .42 B5
⑶ Sunderland SR5 . . . . .75 D1
Howard Terr
High Spen NE39 . . . . . . .66 F4
⑹ Morpeth NE61 . . . . . . .3 F1
Howardian Cl NE38 . . . . .83 B3
Howarth St SR4 . . . . . . .102 A2
Howarth Terr DH6 . . . . . .97 F3
Howat Ave NE5 . . . . .37 E1
Howburn Cres NE61 . . . . .4 E3
Howdene Rd NE15 . . . . . .53 F6
Howdon Green Ind Est
NE28 . . . . .41 B2
Howdon La NE28 . . . . . .41 A2

Howdon Rd
North Shields,Howdon Pans
NE28 . . . . .41 C2
North Shields,Redburn Dene
NE28,NE29 . . . . .41 E3
Howe Sq SR4 . . . . .85 C5
Howe St Gateshead NE8 . . .56 A1
Hebburn NE31 . . . . .58 A6
Howick Ave NE3 . . . . .38 A7
Howick Pk SR6 . . . . .103 A4
Howlett Hall Rd NE15 . . . .53 F6
Howley Ave SR5 . . . . .74 C2
Hownam Cl NE3 . . . . .38 A4
Hoy Cres SR7 . . . . .92 F1
Hoylake Ave NE7 . . . . .39 C5
Hoyle Ave NE4 . . . . .54 E6
Hoyle Fold SR3 . . . . .92 A4
Hubert St NE35 . . . . .73 F8
Hucklow Gdns NE34 . . . . .59 D5
Huddart Terr 2 DH3 . . . . .82 C5
Huddleston Rd NE6 . . . . . .56 D7
Huddlestone Rise SR6 . .103 B4
Hudleston NE26 . . . . .32 C4
Hudshaw Gdns NE46 . . . . .45 D4
Hudson Ave
Bedlington NE22 . . . . .11 B1
Dudley NE23 . . . . .29 B8
Hudson Rd SR1 . . . . .103 B2
Hudson Road Prim Sch
SR1 . . . . .103 B2
Hudson St
Gateshead NE8 . . . . .101 B3
North Shields NE30 . . . . . .42 C6
South Shields NE33 . . . . . .59 B6
Hugar Rd NE39 . . . . .67 A3
Hugh Ave NE27 . . . . .30 F4
Hugh Gdns NE4 . . . . .54 E4
Hugh St Sunderland SR6 . .75 E4
Wallsend NE28 . . . . .40 B1
7 Washington NE38 . . . . .83 F4
Hull St NE4 . . . . .54 F5
Hulne Ave NE30 . . . . .42 D7
Hulne Terr NE15 . . . . .53 C6
Humber CI 11 SR3 . . . . . . .91 F6
Humber Gdns NE8 . . . . . . .56 B1
Humber St NE17 . . . . .66 C1
Humbert St NE32 . . . . . . .58 B6
Humbledon Pk SR3 . . . . . .86 A3
Humbledon View 5 SR2 . .86 C4
Hume St
Newcastle-u-T NE6 . . . . . .56 A5
Sunderland SR4 . . . . .102 A2
Humford Gn NE24 . . . . . . .16 F7
Humford Ho NE24 . . . . . . .17 B6
Humford Way NE24 . . . . . .16 A7
Humsford Gr NE23 . . . . . .22 C8
Humshaugh CI NE12 . . . . .40 A8
Humshaugh Rd NE29 . . . . .41 C6
Hunn's Bldgs NE62 . . . . . .10 E5
Hunstanton Ct NE9 . . . . . .70 E3
Hunt Lea NE16 . . . . .68 E5
Huntcliffe Ave NE6 . . . . . .75 E6
Huntcliffe Gdns NE6 . . . . .39 D1
Huntcliffe Ho NE34 . . . . . .59 C3
Hunter Ave NE24 . . . . .17 F6
Hunter CI NE36 . . . . .74 D6
Hunter Ho NE6 . . . . .57 A4
Hunter St Shiney Row DH4 .90 A5
South Shields NE33 . . . . . .42 D1
Hunter Terr SR2 . . . . .86 E3
Hunter's Moor CI NE2 . . . .98 B4
Hunter's Moor Hospl
NE2 . . . . .98 B4
Hunter's PI NE2 . . . . .98 B4
Hunter's Rd
Newcastle-u-T,South Gosforth
NE3 . . . . .38 F5
Newcastle-u-T,Spital Tongues
NE2 . . . . .98 B3
Hunters CI DH8 . . . . .77 C1
Hunters Ct
Newcastle-u-T NE3 . . . . . .38 E5
Wallsend NE28 . . . . .40 C2
Hunters Hall Rd SR4 . . . .102 B1
Hunters Lodge NE28 . . . . .40 C2
Huntingdon CI NE3 . . . . . .37 D8
Huntingdon Gdns SR3 . . . .86 A3
Huntingdon PI NE30 . . . . .42 D7
Huntington Dr NE23 . . . . . .22 D7
Huntley Cres NE21 . . . . . .68 A8
Huntley Sq SR4 . . . . .85 D5
Huntley Terr 4 SR2 . . . . . .92 F6
Huntly Rd NE25 . . . . .31 D7
Huntsmoor Ho NE2 . . . . . .98 B3
Hurst Terr NE6 . . . . .56 E6
Hurstwood Rd SR4 . . . . . .86 A4
Hurworth Ave NE34 . . . . . .60 B7
Hurworth PI NE32 . . . . . . .58 B6
Hutton CI Chester le S DH3 .88 E1
Houghton-le-S DH4 . . . . . .94 C8
Washington NE38 . . . . . . .82 F5
Hutton Ho NE29 . . . . .41 E8
Hutton Row NE33 . . . . . . .42 E2
Hutton St
Boldon Colliery NE35 . . . . .58 F1
Newcastle-u-T NE3 . . . . . .38 A5
Sunderland SR4 . . . . .102 B1
Hutton Terr
Gateshead NE9 . . . . .70 F4
Newcastle-u-T NE2 . . . . . .99 C3
Huxley CI NE34 . . . . .59 B2
Huxley Cres NE8 . . . . .70 D7
Hyacinth Ct SR4 . . . . . . .102 B3
Hybrid CI DH4 . . . . .89 F5

Hyde Park St NE8 . . . . . . .70 D8
Hyde Pk NE28 . . . . .39 F3
Hyde St
South Shields NE33 . . . . . .42 D2
Sunderland SR2 . . . . .86 F4
Hyde Terr NE3 . . . . .38 D5
Hylton Ave NE34 . . . . .60 B7
Hylton Bank SR4 . . . . . . .85 B6
Hylton Castle★ SR5 . . . . .74 B2
Hylton Castle Prim Sch
SR5 . . . . .74 A2
Hylton Castle Rd SR5 . . . .74 B2
Hylton CI NE22 . . . . .10 D1
Hylton Ct NE38 . . . . .83 B5
Hylton Grange SR5 . . . . . .84 F8
Hylton La NE36,SR5 . . . . . .74 A5
Hylton Park Rd SR5 . . . . . .74 E1
Hylton Pk SR5 . . . . .74 E1
Hylton Rd Jarrow NE32 . . .58 C3
Sunderland SR4 . . . . .85 D5
Hylton Red House Prim Sch
SR5 . . . . .74 E4
Hylton Red House Sch
SR5 . . . . .74 E4
Hylton St Gateshead NE8 . .56 B1
Newbottle DH4 . . . . .90 D2
17 North Shields NE29 . . .42 A5
Sunderland SR4 . . . . .102 A2
Hylton Terr
Newcastle-u-T NE10 . . . . . .57 C2
6 North Shields NE29 . . . .42 A5
Ryhope SR2 . . . . .92 E6
Hylton Wlk SR4 . . . . .85 A5
Hymers Ave NE34 . . . . . . .58 F4
Hyperion Ave NE34 . . . . . .59 A5

I

Ilderton PI NE5 . . . . .53 E8
Ilford Ave NE23 . . . . .16 A1
Ilford PI NE8,NE9 . . . . .71 A8
Ilford Rd
Newcastle-u-T NE2 . . . . . .38 D3
Wallsend NE28 . . . . .40 F3
Ilford Road Sta NE2 . . . . . .38 D3
Ilfracombe Ave NE4 . . . . . .54 E5
Ilfracombe Gdns
Gateshead NE9 . . . . .70 F3
Whitley Bay NE26 . . . . . . .31 F6
Illingworth Ho NE29 . . . . . .41 E3
Ilminster Ct NE3 . . . . .37 C6
Imeary Gr 9 NE33 . . . . . .42 D1
Imeary St NE33 . . . . .42 D1
Imperial Bldgs 9 DH4 . . . .94 E8
Inchberry CI NE4 . . . . .54 E4
Inchcliffe Cres NE5 . . . . . .37 C2
Industrial Rd NE37 . . . . . .83 E7
Industry Rd NE6 . . . . .39 D2
Ingham Gr NE23 . . . . .16 A1
Ingham Grange NE33 . . . . .42 E1
Ingham PI NE2 . . . . .99 C2
Ingham Terr NE41 . . . . . . .51 B6
Ingleborough CI 3 NE37 .83 A6
Ingleby Terr
Lynemouth NE61 . . . . .2 A3
Sunderland SR4 . . . . .102 A1
Ingleby Way NE24 . . . . . . .17 D3
Inglemere PI NE15 . . . . . . .54 A6
Ingleside
South Shields NE34 . . . . . .60 B6
Whickham NE16 . . . . .68 F6
Ingleton Ct SR4 . . . . .102 B1
Ingleton Dr NE15 . . . . .35 B2
Ingleton Gdns NE24 . . . . . .17 C3
Inglewood CI NE24 . . . . . . .16 F7
Inglewood PI NE3 . . . . .28 C1
Ingoe Ave NE3 . . . . .37 F7
Ingoe CI NE24 . . . . .17 C7
Ingoe St
Newcastle-u-T NE15 . . . . . .53 C6
North Shields NE28 . . . . . .41 C2
Ingoldsby Ct SR4 . . . . .85 E4
Ingram Ave NE3 . . . . .37 F8
Ingram CI
Chester le S DH2 . . . . .88 A1
Wallsend NE28 . . . . .40 F5
Ingram Dr Blyth NE24 . . . .17 B7
Newcastle-u-T NE5 . . . . . .36 D4
Ingram Terr NE6 . . . . .57 A6
Inkerman Rd NE37 . . . . . . .72 D1
Inkerman St SR5 . . . . .75 A1
Inleborough Dr NE40 . . . . .52 D4
Innesmoor NE31 . . . . .57 D7
Inskip Ho NE34 . . . . .59 C5
Inskip Terr NE8 . . . . .70 F8
Inst for Higher Rabbinical
Studies Rd NE63 . . . . . .101 B1
Institute Rd NE63 . . . . .6 B4
Intake Way NE46 . . . . .44 F2
International Ctr for Life
The★ NE1 . . . . .100 C4
Inverness Rd NE32 . . . . . .58 E2
Inverness St SR6 . . . . .75 D2
Invertay NE3 . . . . .28 A5
Invincible Dr NE4 . . . . . . .100 A3
Iolanthe Cres NE6 . . . . . . .56 E7
Iolanthe Terr NE33 . . . . . .42 E1
Iona Ct 10 NE28 . . . . .40 F4
Iona PI NE6 . . . . .57 A6
Iona Rd
Brockley Whins NE32 . . . . .58 E3
Gateshead N10,NE9 . . . . . .71 B7
Irene Ave SR2 . . . . .86 F1
Iris CI NE21 . . . . .53 A2
Iris Cres DH2 . . . . .81 F2
Iris PI NE4 . . . . .54 D7
Iris Steedman Ho NE4 . . . .98 A2

Iris Terr Bournmoor DH4 . . .89 E3
Crawcrook NE40 . . . . .51 F3
Ironside St DH5 . . . . .90 E1
Irthing NE61 . . . . .1 E5
Irthing Ave NE6 . . . . .56 D4
Irton St NE3 . . . . .38 C5
Irvine Ho 7 NE12 . . . . .39 D8
Irwin Ave NE28 . . . . .40 C3
Isabella CI NE4 . . . . .54 E3
Isabella Rd NE4 . . . . .17 C6
Isabella Wlk NE15 . . . . . . .35 D1
Islay Ho 9 SR3 . . . . .92 A6
Ivanhoe NE25 . . . . .31 E5
Ivanhoe Cres SR2 . . . . . . .86 B4
Ivanhoe Terr
11 Chester le S DH3 . . . .88 C2
Dipton DH9 . . . . .78 E1
Ivanhoe View NE9 . . . . . . .71 B2
Iveagh CI NE4 . . . . .54 D4
Iveson Rd NE46 . . . . .44 E3
Ivor St SR2 . . . . .87 A2
Ivy Ave
Newbiggin-by-t-S NE64 . . . . .7 C5
Ryton NE40 . . . . .52 C6
Ivy CI Newcastle-u-T NE4 .100 B3
Ryton NE40 . . . . .52 C6
Ivy La NE9 . . . . .71 A3
Ivy PI DH9 . . . . .79 C3
Ivy Rd Longbenton NE12 . . .39 E8
Newcastle-u-T,Gosforth
NE3 . . . . .38 C4
Newcastle-u-T,Walkergate
NE6 . . . . .56 F8
Ivy Road Prim Sch NE12 .39 E8
Ivy St NE13 . . . . .28 C8
Ivy Terr Crawcrook NE40 . . .51 E3
Penshaw DH4 . . . . .90 B6
Ivymount Rd NE6 . . . . .39 B1

J

Jack Common Ho 3 NE6 .56 B7
Jack's Terr NE34 . . . . .59 C5
Jackson Ave NE20 . . . . . . .25 F7
Jackson Rd NE41 . . . . .51 B6
Jackson St
Gateshead NE8 . . . . .101 C3
Newcastle-u-T NE6 . . . . . .56 F6
North Shields NE30 . . . . . .42 B6
Sunderland SR4 . . . . .102 A1
Jackson St W NE30 . . . . . .42 B6
Jackson Terr 13 NE61 . . . . .9 A8
Jacksons PI DH3 . . . . .82 C5
Jacobins Chare 9 NE1 . . .98 C1
Jacques St SR4 . . . . .85 F8
Jacques Terr DH2 . . . . . . .88 B4
Jade CI NE15 . . . . .53 C8
James Armitage St SR5 . .75 B2
James Ave NE27 . . . . .30 F4
James Mather St NE33 . . .42 E3
James PI St NE6 . . . . .56 A6
James St Kip Hill DH9 . . . .79 F1
Newcastle-u-T,Elswick NE4 .54 F4
Sunderland SR5 . . . . .75 A2
10 Whickham NE16 . . . . .69 A7
James Steel Pk The★
NE38 . . . . .84 A2
James Terr
Easington Lane DH5 . . . . . .97 B8
Fence Houses DH4 . . . . . . .94 A8
Wallsend NE28 . . . . .40 B7
James Williams St SR1 .103 B3
Jameson Dr NE45 . . . . . . .47 B7
Jane Eyre Terr NE8 . . . . . .56 B1
Jane St Hetton le H DH5 . . .95 A6
28 Newcastle-u-T NE6 . . .56 C6
Jane Terr NE6 . . . . .57 A4
Janet Sq NE6 . . . . .56 C5
Janet St
17 Newcastle-u-T,St Lawrence
NE6 . . . . .56 C5
Newcastle-u-T,St Peters
NE6 . . . . .56 C4
Janus CI NE5 . . . . .36 C4
Jarrow Cross CE Prim Sch
NE32 . . . . .58 B6
Jarrow Rd NE32,NE34 . . . .58 F6
Jarrow Sch (Cornhill)
NE32 . . . . .58 B5
Jarrow Sch (Field Terrace)
NE32 . . . . .58 B5
Jarrow Sta NE32 . . . . .58 B7
Jasmin Ave NE5 . . . . .36 C4
Jasmine CI NE6 . . . . .56 B7
Jasmine Ct Ashington NE63 .6 C1
Sunderland SR4 . . . . .102 B3
Jasmine Terr DH3 . . . . . . .82 D4
Jasmine Villas 7 NE16 . . .69 A7
Jasper Ave NE40 . . . . .52 B1
Jaycroft Ct NE30 . . . . .42 B5
Jedburgh CI
Gateshead NE8 . . . . .101 C1
Newcastle-u-T NE5 . . . . . .36 C4
Tynemouth NE29 . . . . .41 E8
Jedburgh Ct NE11 . . . . . . .70 E2
Jedburgh Gdns NE15 . . . . .54 B7
Jedburgh Rd DH4 . . . . . . .90 B6
Jedmoor NE31 . . . . .57 D7
Jefferson CI SR5 . . . . .75 C4
Jefferson PI NE4 . . . . .98 B2
Jellicoe Rd NE6 . . . . .56 E3
Jenifer Gr NE7 . . . . .39 A4
Jenison Ave NE15 . . . . . . .54 C5
Jennifer Ave 9 SR5 . . . . . .74 B1
Jersey Sq NE61 . . . . .2 A3
Jervis St NE31 . . . . .57 F6

Jesmond Dene Rd
Newcastle-u-T,Jesmond
NE2 . . . . .38 F2
Newcastle-u-T,West Jesmond
NE2 . . . . .38 D3
Jesmond Gdns
Newcastle-u-T NE2 . . . . . .38 F1
Whiteleas NE34 . . . . .59 C3
Jesmond Park Ct 1 NE7 .39 B1
Jesmond Pk E NE7 . . . . . . .39 B1
Jesmond Pk W NE7 . . . . . .39 A2
Jesmond PI 1 NE2 . . . . . .38 E1
Jesmond Rd NE2 . . . . .99 C4
Jesmond Rd W NE2 . . . . . .99 B3
Jesmond Sta NE2 . . . . .99 B3
Jesmond Terr NE26 . . . . . .32 B4
Jesmond Vale NE2 . . . . . . .56 A7
Jesmond Vale La NE6 . . . .56 B8
Jesmond Vale Terr NE6 . . .56 B8
Jessel St NE9 . . . . .70 F4
Jetty The NE10 . . . . .57 A2
Joan Ave SR2 . . . . .86 F1
Joan St NE4 . . . . .54 D4
Joannah St SR5 . . . . .75 C3
Jobling Ave NE21 . . . . .53 B2
Jobling Cres NE61 . . . . .9 B6
Jobling Ho SR4 . . . . .85 F7
Joel Terr NE10 . . . . .57 B2
John & Margaret Common
Homes for Aged Miners 5
NE24 . . . . .16 F8
John Ave NE40 . . . . .52 B1
John Brown Ct NE2 . . . . . .10 F1
John Candlish Rd SR4 . . .102 A3
John Clay St
3 South Shields NE33 . . .42 D1
5 South Shields,Dean
NE33 . . . . .59 D8
John Dobson St NE1,
NE99 . . . . .99 B2
John F Kennedy Est
NE38 . . . . .83 E5
John F Kennedy Prim Sch
NE38 . . . . .83 E5
John Reid Rd NE34 . . . . . .59 C4
John Spence Community
High Sch NE29 . . . . .42 A8
John St Ashington NE63 . . . .6 C4
Blyth NE24 . . . . .17 B8
Boldon Colliery NE35 . . . . .73 F8
Earsdon NE25 . . . . .31 A5
Fence Houses DH4 . . . . . . .94 A8
Gateshead,Old Fold NE8 . . .56 B1
1 Gateshead,Pelaw NE10 .56 F1
Hetton le H DH5 . . . . .95 A3
Houghton-le-S DH4 . . . . . .94 F8
Newcastle-u-T NE3 . . . . . .38 C5
Pegswood NE61 . . . . .4 F3
Prudhoe NE42 . . . . .50 E3
Ryhope SR2 . . . . .93 A6
Sunderland SR5 . . . . .75 A2
Sunderland,South Hylton
SR4 . . . . .85 A7
Tynemouth NE30 . . . . .32 C3
Wallsend NE28 . . . . .40 B2
John Taylor Ct SR5 . . . . . .75 A3
John Wesley Ct NE42 . . . . .50 D2
John Williamson St
NE33 . . . . .59 C7
Johnson St
6 Dunston NE11 . . . . . . .54 F1
Gateshead NE8 . . . . .100 B1
Newcastle-u-T NE15 . . . . . .53 C6
South Shields NE33 . . . . . .59 C7
Sunderland SR1 . . . . .102 C3
Johnson Terr
High Spen NE39 . . . . .66 F4
5 Washington NE37 . . . .83 F8
Johnston Ave NE31 . . . . . .57 E6
Joicey Aged Miners Homes
7 NE4 . . . . .90 B6
Joicey Rd NE9 . . . . .70 F6
Joicey Road Sch NE9 . . . .70 F6
Joicey St NE10 . . . . .57 A1
Jolliffe St DH3 . . . . .88 D1
Jonadab Rd NE10 . . . . .57 A2
Jonadab St NE10 . . . . .57 A1
Jones St 4 DH3 . . . . .82 C4
Jonquil CI NE5 . . . . .36 C4
Joseph CI NE4 . . . . .54 E4
Joseph Hopper Aged
Miners' Homes DH3 . . .82 C7
Joseph Hopper Meml Homes
NE9 . . . . .71 C6
Joseph Swan Sch NE9 . . . .70 E3
Joseph Terr NE17 . . . . .66 B1
Jowett Sq SR5 . . . . .75 A2
Joyce CI NE10 . . . . .72 D8
Joyce Terr 5 SR5 . . . . .74 B1
Jubilee Ave NE9 . . . . .71 C1
Jubilee Bldgs 3 NE46 . . . .45 B4
Jubilee Cotts
Greenside NE40 . . . . .66 D7
Houghton-le-S DH4 . . . . . .94 D8
Lynemouth NE61 . . . . .2 A3
Jubilee Cres
Newcastle-u-T NE3 . . . . . .38 A5
Sherburn Hill DH6 . . . . . . .96 D1
Jubilee Ct Annitsford NE23 .22 B1
Blyth NE24 . . . . .17 D6
Gateshead NE9 . . . . .70 C8
Hebburn NE31 . . . . .58 A6
Jubilee Est NE63 . . . . .6 D1
Jubilee Ho DH5 . . . . .95 C1
Jubilee Ind Est NE63 . . . . . .6 D1
Jubilee Lodge NE23 . . . . . .22 B4
Jubilee Mews NE3 . . . . . . .38 B5

Jubilee Rd Blyth NE24 . . . .17 E6
Newcastle-u-T NE1 . . . . . .99 C1
Newcastle-u-T,Coxlodge
NE3 . . . . .38 B5
Ovington NE42 . . . . .49 C4
Jubilee Sq
Easington Lane DH5 . . . . . .95 C1
South Hetton DH6 . . . . . . .97 F7
Jubilee St 3 NE28 . . . . . . .40 B2
Jubilee Terr
Bedlington NE22 . . . . .11 D2
Crawcrook NE40 . . . . .51 E3
Newbiggin-by-t-S NE64 . . . .7 E4
Seaton Burn NE13 . . . . . . .28 B8
Tantobie DH9 . . . . .79 A2
Washington NE38 . . . . . . .84 A2
7 Whickham NE16 . . . . . .54 A1
Jubilee Terrs NE6 . . . . .56 D6
Julian Ave
Newcastle-u-T NE6 . . . . . .56 E7
South Shields NE33 . . . . . .42 D4
Julian Rd NE10 . . . . .72 D8
Julian St NE33 . . . . .42 D4
Juliet Ave NE29 . . . . .41 D6
Juliet St NE63 . . . . .6 E4
Julius Caesar St 5 SR5 . . .75 A2
Julius Ct NE33 . . . . .42 C4
June Ave NE21 . . . . .68 C6
Juniper CI Blyth NE24 . . . . .17 C4
Newcastle-u-T NE3 . . . . . .28 D1
5 Sunderland SR2 . . . . . .86 E4
Juniper Ct NE21 . . . . .53 C3
Juniper Wlk NE5 . . . . .36 D4
Jutland Ave NE31 . . . . .57 E6

K

Kane Gdns NE10 . . . . .71 C6
Kateregina DH3 . . . . .82 D4
Katherine St NE63 . . . . .6 E4
Katrine CI DH2 . . . . .88 B1
Katrine Ct SR3 . . . . .92 A5
Kay's Cotts 5 NE10 . . . . . .71 C7
Kayll Rd SR4 . . . . .85 F6
Kearsley CI NE25 . . . . .23 D3
Kearton Ave NE5 . . . . .36 C3
Keats Ave Blyth NE24 . . . . .17 C5
Sunderland SR5 . . . . .75 A2
West Boldon NE35 . . . . . . .74 B8
Keats Gr NE63 . . . . .6 F3
Keats Rd NE15 . . . . .53 A6
Keats Wlk
Biddick Hall NE34 . . . . . . .59 A3
Gateshead NE8 . . . . .56 A2
Keeble CI NE63 . . . . .7 B3
Keebledale Ave NE6 . . . . . .56 F7
Keebledale Ho NE6 . . . . . . .56 F7
Keel Row 11 Blyth NE24 . . .17 E8
Whickham NE11 . . . . .54 B3
Keele Dr NE23 . . . . .21 D6
Keelman's La SR4 . . . . .85 C7
Keelman's Rd SR4 . . . . . . .85 B7
Keelmans Ho 6 NE24 . . . .17 E8
Keelmans Terr NE24 . . . . . .17 E8
Keelmen's Flats NE1 . . . . .99 C1
Keighley Ave SR5 . . . . .74 B1
Keighley Sq SR5 . . . . .74 A4
Keir Hardie Ave NE10 . . . . .72 A8
Keir Hardie Ct NE64 . . . . . . .7 C5
Keir Hardie St
Fence Houses DH4 . . . . . . .94 B8
Rowlands Gill NE39 . . . . . .67 B2
Keir Hardie Way SR5 . . . . .75 C1
Keith CI NE4 . . . . .54 E4
Keith Sq SR5 . . . . .74 B4
Kelburn Ho NE1 . . . . .99 B1
Keldane Gdns NE4 . . . . . . .54 E6
Kelfield Gr NE23 . . . . .16 B2
Kelham Sq SR5 . . . . .74 A4
Kell Cres DH6 . . . . .96 D1
Kell's Way NE39 . . . . .67 E1
Kellfield Ave NE9 . . . . .71 A6
Kellfield Rd NE9 . . . . .71 A5
Kells Gdns NE9 . . . . .71 A5
Kells La NE9 . . . . .70 F5
Kells Lane Prim Sch NE9 .70 F5
Kellsway NE10 . . . . .71 F5
Kellsway Ct NE10 . . . . .71 F5
Kelly Rd NE31 . . . . .57 E3
Kelpie Gdns 3 SR6 . . . . . .75 E1
Kelsey Way NE23 . . . . .16 B2
Kelso CI NE5 . . . . .36 C4
Kelso Dr NE29 . . . . .41 E8
Kelso Gdns
Bedlington NE22 . . . . .11 C1
Newcastle-u-T NE15 . . . . . .54 B6
Wallsend NE28 . . . . .41 A4
Kelso Gr DH4 . . . . .90 A6
Kelso PI NE8 . . . . .100 B1
Kelso Way NE5 . . . . .36 C4
Kelson Way NE5 . . . . .37 C2
Kelvin Gdns 3 NE11 . . . . . .54 F1
Kelvin Gr Cleadon SR6 . . . .59 E1
Gateshead NE8 . . . . .70 D8
Newcastle-u-T NE2 . . . . . .99 C3
South Shields NE33 . . . . . .42 F1
Sunderland SR6 . . . . .75 E2
Tynemouth NE29 . . . . .42 A8
Kelvin Grove Com Prim Sch
NE8 . . . . .70 E8
Kelvin PI NE12 . . . . .30 A1
Kemble CI NE23 . . . . .16 B2
Kemble Sq SR5 . . . . .74 B4
Kempton Gdns NE8 . . . . . .70 C7
Kendal DH3 . . . . .82 E2
Kendal Ave Blyth NE24 . . . .17 C6
Tynemouth NE30 . . . . .32 B2

Kendal Cres NE9 . . . . .71 B5
Kendal Dr
Cramlington NE23 . . . . . . .22 C8
East Boldon NE36 . . . . . .74 C8
Kendal Gdns NF28 . . . . . . .41 A4
Kendal Gn 24 NE6 . . . . . .56 B6
Kendal Ho 27 NE6 . . . . . .56 B6
Kendal Pl 28 NE6 . . . . . .56 B6
Kendal Rise NE22 . . . . . .10 D2
Kendal St 1 NE6 . . . . . . .56 B5
Kendale Wlk NE5 . . . . . .36 E3
Kendor Gr NE61 . . . . .8 F6
Kenilworth NE12 . . . . . . .29 D4
Kenilworth Ct
Newcastle-u-T NE4 . . . . .100 A4
 4 Washington NE37 . . . .83 F8
Kenilworth Rd
Ashington NE63 . . . . .6 C3
Newcastle-u-T NE4 . . . . .100 A4
Whitley Bay NE25 . . . . . .31 F4
Kenilworth Sq SR5 . . . . .74 C4
Kenilworth View 7 NE9 . .71 A2
Kenley Rd
Newcastle-u-T NE5 . . . . . .54 A8
Sunderland SR5 . . . . .74 C4
Kenmoor Way NE5 . . . . .36 C3
Kenmore Cl NE10 . . . . . .72 B8
Kenmore Cres NE40 . . . . .52 B2
Kennersdene NE30 . . . . . .42 C8
Kennet Ave NE32 . . . . . . .58 C3
Kennet Sq SR5 . . . . .74 B4
Kennford NE9 . . . . .71 A2
Kennington Gr NE6 . . . . .56 F6
Kensington Ave NE3 . . . . .38 C7
Kensington Cl NE31 . . . . .31 F5
Kensington Cotts NE61 . . . .9 B8
Kensington Ct
 5 Gateshead NE10 . . . . .71 C8
Hebburn NE31 . . . . .57 D5
South Shields NE33 . . . . .59 E8
Kensington Gdns
 1 North Shields NE30 . . . .42 B6
Wallsend NE28 . . . . .39 E3
Whitley Bay NE25 . . . . . .31 F5
Kensington Gr NE30 . . . . .42 B7
Kensington Terr
 2 Dunston NE11 . . . . . .69 F8
Newcastle-u-T NE2 . . . . . .99 A3
Kensington Villas NE5 . . . .36 E3
Kent Ave 3 Dunston NE11 .70 A8
Hebburn NE31 . . . . .57 D5
Wallsend NE28 . . . . .40 F2
Kent Cl NE63 . . . . .6 A4
Kent Gdns DH5 . . . . .94 E4
Kent Pl NE34 . . . . .60 A6
Kent St NE32 . . . . .58 A6
Kent Terr DH6 . . . . .97 E1
Kentchester Rd SR5 . . . . .74 C4
Kentmere DH3 . . . . .82 E1
Kentmere Ave
Newcastle-u-T NE6 . . . . . .56 F7
Sunderland SR6 . . . . .75 C5
Kentmere Cl NE23 . . . . . .23 A2
Kenton Ave NE3 . . . . . . .38 A3
Kenton Bank NE5 . . . . . .37 C5
Kenton Bar Prim Sch
NE3 . . . . .37 D4
Kenton Cres NE3 . . . . . . .37 F4
Kenton Ct NE33 . . . . .42 D1
Kenton Gr SR6 . . . . .75 D1
Kenton La NE3 . . . . .37 E4
Kenton Park Sh Ctr NE3 . .38 A4
Kenton Rd
Newcastle-u-T NE3 . . . . . .38 A3
Tynemouth NE29 . . . . . . .41 C7
Kenton Sch NE3 . . . . . . .37 F4
Kentucky Rd SR5 . . . . . . .74 A4
Kenwood Gdns NE9 . . . . .71 A2
Kenya Rd SR5 . . . . .74 A4
Kepier Chare Com Prim Sch
NE40 . . . . .51 F3
Kepier Gdns 6 SR4 . . . . .85 A6
Keppel St Dunston NE11 . . .54 F1
 3 South Shields NE33 . . .42 C3
Kepwell Bank Top NE42 . .50 C3
Kepwell Ct NE42 . . . . . . .50 D3
Kepwell Rd NE42 . . . . . . .50 C2
Kerry Cl NE12 . . . . .17 E8
Kerry Sq SR5 . . . . .74 B4
Kesteven Sq SR5 . . . . . . .74 B4
Keston Dr NE23 . . . . .16 B2
Kestrel Cl NE38 . . . . .83 A2
Kestrel Ct 16 DH3 . . . . . .82 C4
Kestrel Dr NE63 . . . . .6 B1
Kestrel Lodge Flats 6
NE33 . . . . .42 D3
Kestrel Mews NE16 . . . . . .69 A4
Kestrel Pl NE12 . . . . .39 A7
Kestrel Sq SR5 . . . . .74 B4
Kestrel Way
North Shields NE29 . . . . . .42 A3
South Shields NE33 . . . . .59 B4
Keswick Ave SR6 . . . . . . .75 D4
Keswick Dr NE30 . . . . . . .32 B2
Keswick Gdns NE28 . . . . .41 A3
Keswick Gr NE5 . . . . .54 A8
Keswick St NE8 . . . . . . .101 B1
Keswick Terr DH6 . . . . . .97 E8
Kettering Pl NE23 . . . . . . .22 C8
Kettering Sq SR5 . . . . . . .74 B4
Kettlewell Terr 7 NE30 . . .42 B7
Ketton Cl NE12 . . . . .39 B6
Kew Gdns NE26 . . . . .31 F6
Keyes Gdns NE2 . . . . . . .38 E3
Kibblesworth Bank NE11 . .81 B6
Kibblesworth Prim Sch
NE11 . . . . .81 D6

Kidd Sq SR5 . . . . .74 B4
Kidderminster Dr NE5 . . . .36 C3
Kidderminster Rd SR5 . . . .74 B3
Kidderminster Sq SR5 . . . .74 B3
Kidland Cl NF63 . . . . .6 F4
Kidlandlee Gn NE5 . . . . . .37 A4
Kidlandlee Pl NE5 . . . . . .37 A4
Kidsgrove Sq SR5 . . . . . .74 B3
Kielder NE38 . . . . .82 F4
Kielder Ave NE23 . . . . . . .21 D6
Kielder Cl Blyth NE24 . . . .17 D5
Killingworth NF12 . . . . . . .29 C4
Newcastle-u-T NE5 . . . . . .37 A4
Kielder Dr NE23 . . . . .21 E6
Kielder Gdns Jarrow NE32 58 B3
Stakeford NE62 . . . . .6 A1
Kielder Ho 11 SR3 . . . . . .92 A6
Kielder Pl NE25 . . . . .31 B5
Kielder Rd Earsdon NE25 . .31 B5
Newcastle-u-T NE15 . . . . .53 C7
Kielder Terr NE30 . . . . . . .42 B6
Kielder Way NE3 . . . . . . .38 B7
Kilburn Cl SR2 . . . . .93 A6
Kilburn Gdns NE29 . . . . . .41 D3
Kilburn Gn NE9 . . . . .71 B1
Kilburne Cl NE7 . . . . .39 E3
Kildale DH4 . . . . .89 E8
Kildare Sq SR5 . . . . .74 B4
Killarney Ave SR5 . . . . . .74 B4
Killarney Sq SR5 . . . . . . .74 B4
Killiebrigs NE15 . . . . .34 E2
Killin Cl NE5 . . . . .36 C4
Killingworth Ctr The
NE12 . . . . .29 D3
Killingworth Dr
Killingworth NE12 . . . . . . .29 B2
Sunderland SR3,SR4 . . . . .85 E4
Killingworth Hall NE12 . . . .29 E2
Killingworth La NE27 . . . . .30 A5
Killingworth Pl NE1 . . . . . .99 A2
Killingworth Rd
Killingworth NE12 . . . . . . .29 E2
Newcastle-u-T NE3 . . . . . .38 F5
Killingworth Way NE12,
NE27 . . . . .29 D4
Killowen St NE9 . . . . .70 E4
Kiln Rise NE16 . . . . .69 A4
Kilnshaw Pl NE3 . . . . .28 D1
Kilsyth Ave NE29 . . . . . . .31 E2
Kilsyth Sq SR5 . . . . .74 B3
Kimberley NE38 . . . . .84 A5
Kimberley Ave NE29 . . . . .41 E6
Kimberley Gdns
Newcastle-u-T NE2 . . . . . .56 A8
Stocksfield NE43 . . . . .6 C1
Kimberley St Blyth NE24 . . .17 D8
Sunderland SR4 . . . . .85 F6
Kimberley Terr 4 NE24 . . .17 E8
Kinfauns Terr 5 NE9 . . . . .71 A5
King Charles Ct SR5 . . . . .74 A4
King Charles Twr NE2 . . . .99 C2
King Edward Prim Sch
NE30 . . . . .42 B7
King Edward Rd
Newcastle-u-T NE6 . . . . . .39 B1
Ryton NE40 . . . . .52 E4
Sunderland SR4 . . . . .85 B4
Tynemouth NE30 . . . . . . .42 C7
King Edward St
Gateshead NE8 . . . . .56 B1
Tanfield Lea DH9 . . . . . . .79 C1
King Edward VI Sch The
NE61 . . . . .3 F1
King George Ave NE11 . . . .69 F8
King George Rd
Newcastle-u-T NE3 . . . . . .37 E6
South Shields NE34 . . . . .59 E5
King George V Sch NE34 . .59 E3
King George's Rd NE64 . . . .7 D5
King Henry Ct SR5 . . . . . .74 A4
King James Ct SR5 . . . . . .74 A4
King James St NE8 . . . . .101 C1
King John St NE6 . . . . . . .56 B8
King John Terr NE6 . . . . . .56 B8
King John's Ct NE20 . . . . .25 A4
King St Birtley DH3 . . . . . .82 B4
Blyth NE24 . . . . .17 E8
Gateshead,Bensham NE8 . . .70 C8
Gateshead,Pelaw NE10 . . . .57 A1
Newbiggin-by-t-S NE64 . . . .7 E5
Newcastle-u-T NE1 . . . . .101 B4
North Shields NE30 . . . . . .42 B6
South Shields NE33 . . . . .42 C3
Sunderland SR1 . . . . . . .103 A3
Sunderland,Fulwell SR6 . . .75 D4
King's Ave NE3 . . . . .3 F1
King's Dr Greenside NE40 . .52 B1
Whitley Bay NE26 . . . . . .32 A4
King's Gdns NE24 . . . . . . .17 C8
King's Pl SR4 . . . . .102 A3
King's Rd Bedlington NE22 11 D2
Newcastle-u-T NE1,NE2 . . .99 A2
Whitley Bay NE26 . . . . . .31 F6
King's Rd The SR5 . . . . . .75 A2
King's School Tynemouth
NE30 . . . . .42 D7
King's Terr SR4 . . . . .102 A3
King's Wlk NE1 . . . . .99 A2
Kingarth Ave SR6 . . . . . . .75 E5
Kingdom Pl NE29 . . . . . . .42 A3
Kingfisher Bvd NE15 . . . . .53 D5
Kingfisher Ct NE11 . . . . . .100 A2
Kingfisher Lodge NE32 . . .58 A6
Kingfisher Rd NE12 . . . . . .39 A7

Kingfisher Way
Blyth NE24 . . . . .17 F4
Shiremoor NE28 . . . . .41 A6
Kingham Ct NF3 . . . . .38 A6
Kinghorn Sq SR5 . . . . . . .74 B4
Kings Ave Hebburn NF31 . .57 F5
Sunderland SR6 . . . . .75 E5
Kings Cl NE8 . . . . .56 B1
Kings Ct NE2 . . . . .99 C2
Kings Lodge NE30 . . . . . .42 B6
Kings Mdw NE32 . . . . . . .58 C1
Kings Mw NE4 . . . . .100 A3
Kings Pk NE62 . . . . .10 F5
Kings Rd NE12 . . . . .29 C1
Kings Road N NE28 . . . . .40 B4
Kings Road S NE28 . . . . .40 B3
Kings Terr 23 NE9 . . . . . .71 F1
Kings Vale NE28 . . . . .40 C4
Kings Wlk NE5 . . . . .36 C4
Kingsbridge NE12 . . . . . . .38 F7
Kingsbridge Cl NE29 . . . . .41 E4
Kingsclere Ave SR5 . . . . . .74 B3
Kingsclere Sq SR5 . . . . . .74 B3
Kingsdale Ave Blyth NE24 .17 A7
Washington NE37 . . . . . . .83 C8
Kingsdale Rd NE12 . . . . . .38 F7
Kingsgate 5 NE46 . . . . . .45 A5
Kingsgate Terr NE46 . . . . .45 A5
Kingsland NE2 . . . . .99 B4
Kingsland Sq SR5 . . . . . . .74 B3
Kingsley Ave
Biddick Hall NE34 . . . . . . .59 A3
Newcastle-u-T NE3 . . . . . .28 D1
Whitley Bay NE25 . . . . . .32 A4
Kingsley Cl 4 SR5 . . . . . .75 A1
Kingsley Pl
 8 Dunston NE11 . . . . . .54 F1
 8 Newcastle-u-T NE6 . . .56 B7
Wallsend NE28 . . . . .40 F3
Whickham NE16 . . . . .69 B8
Kingsley Rd NE61 . . . . .2 C1
Kingsley Terr
Crawcrook NE40 . . . . .51 E4
Newcastle-u-T NE4 . . . . . .98 A1
Kingsmeadow Com Comp
Sch NE11 . . . . .69 B8
Kingsmere DH3 . . . . .88 C7
Kingsmere Gdns NE6 . . . .57 A4
Kingston Ave NE6 . . . . . . .56 D4
Kingston Cl NE26 . . . . . . .31 F5
Kingston Cres DH6 . . . . . .97 E3
Kingston Ct 6 NE26 . . . . .31 F8
Kingston Dr NE26 . . . . . . .31 F8
Kingston Gn NE6 . . . . . . .56 D5
Kingston Mews DH4 . . . . .90 C5
Kingston Park Ave NE3 . . .37 C6
Kingston Park Ctr NE3 . . . .37 C6
Kingston Park Prim Sch
NE3 . . . . .37 C6
Kingston Park Rd NE3 . . . .37 B8
Kingston Park Sta NE3 . . .37 C6
Kingston Rd NE8 . . . . .71 B8
Kingston Terr NE30 . . . . . .75 D2
Kingston Way 3 NE26 . . . .31 F8
Kingsway Blyth NE24 . . . . .17 E6
Houghton-le-S DH5 . . . . . .94 F8
Newcastle-u-T NE4 . . . . . .54 E8
Ponteland NE20 . . . . .25 E6
South Shields NE33 . . . . .42 F2
Sunnisde NE16 . . . . .69 A2
Tynemouth NE30 . . . . . . .42 C8
Kingsway Ave NE3 . . . . . .38 C7
Kingsway Ho NE4 . . . . . . .70 D4
Kingsway Intc NE11 . . . . . .70 C5
Kingsway N NE11 . . . . . . .70 C5
Kingsway Rd SR5 . . . . . . .74 B3
Kingsway S NE11 . . . . . . .70 D3
Kingsway Sq SR5 . . . . . . .74 B3
Kingswell NE61 . . . . .9 B7
Kingswood Ave NE2 . . . . .38 D3
Kingswood Cl NE35 . . . . . .58 E1
Kingswood Cl 18 NE3 . . . .42 D7
Kingswood Dr NE20 . . . . .25 C4
Kingswood Gr SR4 . . . . . .85 A2
Kingswood Rd NE23 . . . . .22 C8
Kingswood Sq SR5 . . . . . .74 B3
Kinlett NE38 . . . . .84 A5
Kinloch Ct DH2 . . . . .88 B1
Kinloss Sq NE23 . . . . .22 C8
Kinnaird Ave NE15 . . . . . .54 A5
Kinnock Cl DH6 . . . . .96 A1
Kinross Cl DH3 . . . . .82 D2
Kinross Dr NE10 . . . . .57 B2
Kinross Dr NE3 . . . . .37 E8
Kinsale Sq SR5 . . . . .74 B4
Kinver Dr NE5 . . . . .36 F2
Kipling Ave Hebburn NE31 .57 F6
West Boldon NE35 . . . . . .74 B8
Whickham NE16 . . . . .69 B8
Kipling Cl NE16 . . . . .69 B8
Kipling St SR5 . . . . .75 A1
Kipling Wlk NE8 . . . . .56 A2
Kirby Cl NE34 . . . . .58 F4
Kirk St NE6 . . . . .56 C5
Kirk View NE40 . . . . .90 D3
Kirkbride Pl NE23 . . . . . . .22 C8
Kirkdale Ct 2 NE34 . . . . . .59 A4
Kirkdale Gn NE4 . . . . . . .100 B4
Kirkdale Sq SR5 . . . . .74 B3
Kirkdale St DH5 . . . . .94 F2
Kirkham NE38 . . . . .83 D4
Kirkham Ave NE3 . . . . . . .37 C7
Kirkharle Dr NE61 . . . . .4 C1
Kirkheaton Pl NE5 . . . . . .54 C8
Kirkland Wlk NE27 . . . . . .30 E1
Kirklands NE23 . . . . .29 C5
Kirklea Rd DH5 . . . . .94 F8
Kirkleatham Gdns NE6 . . .39 D2

Kirkley Ave NE34 . . . . . . .60 A6
Kirkley Cl NE3 . . . . .38 B6
Kirkley Dr Ashington NE63 . .6 C2
Ponteland NE20 . . . . .25 E7
Kirkley Lodge NE3 . . . . . .38 R6
Kirkley Rd NF27 . . . . .30 F7
Kirklinton Rd NE30 . . . . . .32 A2
Kirknewton Cl 7 DH5 . . . .94 F8
Kirkside DH4 . . . . .90 E6
Kirkston Ave NE15 . . . . . .53 D7
Kirkstone DH3 . . . . .82 D2
Kirkstone Ave
Hedworth NE32 . . . . .58 D3
Sunderland SR5 . . . . .75 C5
Tynemouth NE30 . . . . . . .32 A2
Kirkstone Cl Blaydon NE21 68 C8
 8 Houghton-le-S DH5 . . .94 F8
Kirkstone Gdns NE7 . . . . .39 A3
Kirkstone Rd NE10 . . . . . .71 F8
Kirkwall Cl SR5 . . . . .74 A1
Kirkwood NE23 . . . . .29 C5
Kirkwood Ave SR4 . . . . . .85 A2
Kirkwood Dr NE3 . . . . . . .37 F5
Kirkwood Gdns NE10 . . . . .72 B8
Kirkwood Pl NE3 . . . . .28 B1
Kirton Ave NE4 . . . . .54 E6
Kirton Park Terr NE29,
NE30 . . . . .42 A7
Kirton Way NE23 . . . . . . .22 C8
Kismet St SR5 . . . . .75 A2
Kitchener Rd SR6 . . . . . . .60 F4
Kitchener St
Gateshead NE9 . . . . .71 A8
Sunderland SR4 . . . . .85 A4
Kitchener Terr
Jarrow NE32 . . . . .58 B5
New Herrington DH4 . . . . .90 D6
North Shields NE30 . . . . . .42 C7
Sunderland SR2 . . . . .86 F2
Kittiwake Cl Blyth NE24 . . .17 F4
Shiremoor NE28 . . . . .41 A7
Kittiwake Dr NE38 . . . . . .82 F3
Kittiwake Ho NE26 . . . . . .32 B5
Kitty Brewster Ind Est
NE24 . . . . .12 B1
Kitty Brewster Rd NE24 . . .16 F8
Knaresborough Cl NE10 . . .72 D2
Knaresborough Sq SR5 . . .74 C4
Knaresdale DH3 . . . . .82 D1
Knarsdale Ave NE29 . . . . .41 D6
Knarsdale Pl 3 NE5 . . . . .36 E1
Knightsbridge
Newcastle-u-T NE3 . . . . . .38 C6
Sunderland SR3 . . . . .38 C6
Knightsbridge Ct NE3 . . . .38 C6
Knightside Gdns NE11 . . . .70 A7
Knightside Wlk NE5 . . . . . .36 C3
Knivestone Ct NE12 . . . . . .29 E4
Knobbyends La NE21 . . . . .67 F8
Knoll Rise NE11 . . . . .69 F7
Knoll The Ellington NE61 . . .1 C5
Sunderland SR2 . . . . . . .102 B1
Knollside Cl SR3 . . . . .91 F5
Knop Law Fst Sch NE5 . . .36 C3
Knott Meml Flats 13
NE30 . . . . .42 D7
Knott Pl NE15 . . . . .54 B5
Knoulberry Rd NE37 . . . . .83 A6
Knowe Pl NE12 . . . . .39 B5
Knowle Pl NE12 . . . . .39 B5
Knowledge Hill NE21 . . . . .53 B1
Knowsley Ct NE3 . . . . . . .37 B5
Knox Cl NE22 . . . . .11 D2
Knox Rd NE22 . . . . .16 B8
Knox Sq SR5 . . . . .75 A2
Knutsford Wlk NE23 . . . . .22 C8
Kristin Ave NE32 . . . . . . .58 C4
Kyffin View NE34 . . . . . . .60 B5
Kyle Cl NE4 . . . . .100 B4
Kyle Rd NE8 . . . . .70 C8
Kylins The NE61 . . . . .9 A6
Kyloe Ave NE25 . . . . .23 D2
Kyloe Cl NE3 . . . . .37 E7
Kyloe Pl Bedlington NE22 . .10 F1
Newcastle-u-T NE5 . . . . . .37 A3
Kyloe Villas NE5 . . . . . . .37 A3
Kyo Bog La NE41,NE42 . . .51 B1
Kyo La NE40 . . . . .66 D7

L

L'Arbre Cres NE16 . . . . . .68 F7
La Sagesse Sch NE2 . . . . .38 E3
Laburnum Ave Blyth NE24 17 D8
Gateshead NE10 . . . . .72 A7
Newcastle-u-T NE6 . . . . . .56 F8
Wallsend NE28 . . . . .40 B2
Washington NE38 . . . . . . .83 B1
Whitley Bay NE26 . . . . . .32 A5
Laburnum Cl SR4 . . . . . . .85 A6
Laburnum Cres NE11 . . . . .81 C6
Laburnum Gdns
 6 Gateshead,Felling NE10 .72 A7
Gateshead,Low Fell NE9 . . .70 F6
Jarrow NE32 . . . . .58 A4
Laburnum Gr Cleadon SR6 60 A1
Hebburn NE31 . . . . .57 E3
South Shields NE34 . . . . .59 F5
Sunderland SR5 . . . . .85 A8
Sunnisde NE16 . . . . .69 B2
Whickham NE16 . . . . .69 A7
Laburnum Ho NE28 . . . . . .40 C1
Laburnum Rd
Blaydon NE21 . . . . .53 C2
Sunderland SR6 . . . . .75 D4

Laburnum Terr
Ashington NE63 . . . . .6 D3
Wylam NE41 . . . . .51 A6
Laburnum Ct NE62 . . . . . .10 E7
Lacebark Shiney Row DH4 .89 F6
Silksworth SR3 . . . . .91 E4
Ladock Cl SR3 . . . . .93 A8
Lady Beatrice Terr DH4 . . .90 E7
Lady St DH5 . . . . .95 A5
Lady's Piece La DH6 . . . . .96 A5
Lady's Wlk Morpeth NE61 . . .3 E1
South Shields NE33 . . . . .42 C4
Ladybank NE5 . . . . .36 A5
Ladycutters La NE45 . . . . .46 F3
Ladyhaugh Dr NE16 . . . . .69 A4
Ladykirk Rd NE4 . . . . .54 E5
Ladykirk Way NE23 . . . . . .21 E6
Ladyrigg NE20 . . . . .25 C4
Ladysmith St NE33 . . . . . .42 D2
Ladywell NE43 . . . . .64 D6
Ladywell Rd NE21 . . . . . . .53 C2
Ladywell Way NE20 . . . . . .25 D7
Ladywood Pk DH4 . . . . . . .89 F8
Laet St NE29 . . . . .42 B5
Laindon Ave SR6 . . . . . . .75 D4
Laing Art Gallery & Mus*
NE1 . . . . .99 B2
Laing Gr NE28 . . . . .41 B3
Laith Rd NE3 . . . . .37 E5
Lake App NE21 . . . . .53 F1
Lake Ave NE34 . . . . .60 C6
Lake Ct SR3 . . . . .92 A6
Lake Rd DH5 . . . . .94 E8
Lake View NE31 . . . . .57 E4
Lakeside Blaydon NE21 . . .53 F1
South Shields NE34 . . . . .60 D6
Laleham Ct NE3 . . . . .37 D7
Lamara Dr SR5 . . . . .75 C3
Lamb St
East Cramlington NE23 . . . .22 F5
Newcastle-u-T NE6 . . . . . .57 A5
Lamb Terr 6 NE27 . . . . . .30 E1
Lambden Cl NE29 . . . . . . .41 E3
Lambert Rd NE37 . . . . . . .82 F7
Lambert Sq NE3 . . . . .38 A5
Lambeth Pl NE8 . . . . .71 A8
Lambley Ave NE30 . . . . . .32 B2
Lambley Cl NE16 . . . . .69 A2
Lambley Cres NE31 . . . . . .57 D3
Lambourn Ave
Longbenton NE12 . . . . . . .39 C7
North Shields NE29 . . . . . .41 E4
Lambourne Cl NE38 . . . . . .89 E3
Lambourne Rd SR2 . . . . . .86 C3
Lambrook Ho NE24 . . . . . .17 A7
Lambton Ave NE16 . . . . . .69 C8
Lambton Cl NE40 . . . . . . .51 F4
Lambton Ct
Sunderland SR3 . . . . .91 C7
Washington NE38 . . . . . . .88 E8
Lambton Dr DH5 . . . . .95 A1
Lambton Gdns NE16 . . . . .78 E5
Lambton Lea DH4 . . . . . . .90 A4
Lambton Prim Sch NE38 . .83 B3
Lambton Rd Hebburn NE31 57 F2
Newcastle-u-T NE2 . . . . . .99 B4
Lambton St
Chester le S DH3 . . . . . . .88 D2
Gateshead NE8 . . . . .101 B3
Sunderland SR1 . . . . . . .103 A3
Lambton Terr
Jarrow NE32 . . . . .58 B4
Penshaw DH4 . . . . .89 F8
Lambton Twr SR1 . . . . . .103 B3
Lamonby Way NE23 . . . . .22 A4
Lampeter Cl NE5 . . . . . . .37 B4
Lamport St NE31 . . . . .57 C7
Lampton Ct NE22 . . . . . . .11 C2
Lanark Cl NE29 . . . . .41 C8
Lanark Dr NE32 . . . . .58 E2
Lancaster Ct NE3 . . . . . . .37 D7
Lancaster Dr NE28 . . . . . .40 D7
Lancaster Ho NE3 . . . . . . .22 D5
Lancaster Rd NE11 . . . . . .54 E1
Lancaster St NE4 . . . . . . .98 B1
Lancaster Terr
Chester le S DH3 . . . . . . .88 D2
Morpeth NE61 . . . . .4 A1
Lancaster Way NE32 . . . . .58 A1
Lancastrian Rd NE23 . . . . .22 A5
Lancefield Ave NE6 . . . . . .56 F4
Lancet Ct NE8 . . . . .101 C2
Lanchester Ave NE9 . . . . .71 E3
Lanchester Cl NE10 . . . . . .72 C6
Lanchester Gn NE22 . . . . .10 F2
Lanchester Pk NE38 . . . . .83 C2
Lancing Ct NE3 . . . . .37 C7
Landscape Terr NE40 . . . . .52 B1
Landsdowne Gdns NE62 . . .11 A8
Landseer Gdns
Gateshead NE9 . . . . .71 B7
Whiteleas NE34 . . . . .59 D2
Landswood Terr NE21 . . . .68 D7
Lane Cnr NE34 . . . . .59 C5
Lane Head NE34 . . . . .52 C5
Lanercost NE38 . . . . .83 D5
Lanercost Ave NE21 . . . . . .53 B2
Lanercost Dr NE5 . . . . . . .54 C8
Lanercost Gdns
Gateshead NE10 . . . . .71 C6
Throckley NE15 . . . . .35 D2
Lanercost Pk NE23 . . . . . .29 C5
Lanercost Rd NE29 . . . . . .41 E5
Lanesborough Ct NE3 . . . .38 A5
Langdale Birtley DH3 . . . . .82 E1

Langdale continued
Washington NE37 ....83 C7
Whitley Bay NE25 ....31 E5
Langdale Cl NE12 ....39 A6
Langdale Cres NE21 ...68 B8
Langdale Dr NE23 .....21 E6
Langdale Gdns
Newcastle-u-T NE6 ......57 A6
Wallsend NE28 ....41 A5
Langdale Rd
Gateshead NE9 ....71 A5
Penshaw NE5 ....90 A8
Langdale St DH5 ......95 A2
Langdale Terr NE17 ...77 A5
Langdale Way NE36 ...74 C7
Langdon Cl NE29 .....31 F1
Langdon Rd NE5 ......36 E2
Langeeford Pl 4 SR6 ..75 E1
Langford NE35 ....58 F2
Langham Rd NE15 .....54 A5
Langholm Ave NE29 ...41 C8
Langholm Rd
East Boldon NE36 ....74 D8
Newcastle-u-T NE3 ......38 C7
Langhorn Cl NE6 ......56 B7
Langhurst SR2 ....92 E8
Langleeford Rd NE5 ...37 A4
Langley Ave Blyth NE24 ..17 B8
Gateshead NE10 ....72 B6
Hexham NE46 ....45 D4
Shiremoor NE27 ....31 A3
Whitley Bay NE25 ....31 D3
Langley Cl NE38 ......83 B4
Langley Fst Sch NE25 ..31 D3
Langley Mere 8 NE12 ..39 D8
Langley Rd Ashington NE63 ...6 C3
Newcastle-u-T,Walker NE6 ..56 F6
Newcastle-u-T,West Denton
NE5 ....53 F8
North Shields NE29 ......41 D6
Sunderland SR3 ....86 B2
Langley St DH4 ....90 D6
Langley Tarn 1 NE29 ..42 A4
Langley Terr NE32 ....58 B3
Langport Rd SR2 ......86 D3
Langton Cl SR4 ....102 B2
Langton Ct NE20 ......25 B4
Langton Dr NE23 ......16 C2
Langton St NE8 ......101 C1
Langton Terr
Bournmoor DH4 ....89 C2
Newcastle-u-T NE7 ......39 B2
Langwell Cres NE63 ....6 C4
Langwell Terr NE61 ....4 F4
Lanivet Cl 4 SR2 .....92 F8
Lannerwood 5 NE29 ...42 A4
Lansbury Cl DH3 ......82 B6
Lansbury Dr DH3 ......82 B5
Lansbury Gdns NE10 ...72 A8
Lansbury Rd NE16 .....69 C6
Lansbury Way SR5 .....74 B1
Lansdowne SR2 ....92 E7
Lansdowne Cres NE3 ...38 C5
Lansdowne Ct NE46 ....44 F3
Lansdowne Gdns NE2 ..56 A8
Lansdowne Pl NE3 .....38 C5
Lansdowne Rd NE12 ...39 D8
Lansdowne St SR4 ....102 A3
Lansdowne Terr
Newcastle-u-T NE3 ......38 C5
North Shields NE29 ......41 F6
Lansdowne Terr E NE3 ..38 C5
Lansdowne Terrace W
NE29 ....41 F6
Lanthwaite Rd NE9 ....71 A4
Lanton St DH4 ....90 D6
Lapford Dr NE23 ......16 C1
Lapwing Cl Blyth NE24 ..17 E4
Washington NE38 ....82 F3
Lapwing Ct
Burnopfield NE16 ....79 C5
Haswell DH6 ....97 F3
South Shields NE34 ......59 E5
Larch Ave
Houghton-le-S DH4 ......90 D1
South Shields NE34 .....60 A5
Whitburn SR6 ....61 A2
Larch Cl NE9 ....71 D2
Larch Gr NE24 ....17 C4
Larch Rd NE21 ....53 D3
Larch St 2 NE16 ......69 B2
Larch Terr DH9 ....79 A1
Larches The
Burnopfield NE16 ....79 B7
Newcastle-u-T NE4 .....100 A3
Larchlea NE20 ....25 C2
Larchlea S NE20 ......25 C2
Larchwood NE38 ......83 B1
Larchwood Ave
Newcastle-u-T,Fawdon NE3 ..37 F7
Newcastle-u-T,Walkergate
NE6 ....56 E8
Wideopen NE13 ....28 C5
Larchwood Dr NE63 ....6 C1
Larchwood Gdns NE11 ..70 B5
Larchwood Gr SR2 .....86 C2
Larkfield Cres DH4 ....90 A5
Larkfield Rd SR2 ......86 C3
Larkhill SR2 ....92 F7
Larkrise Cl NE7 ....39 D3
Larkspur NE9 ....71 C4
Larkspur Com Prim Sch
NE9 ....71 C4
Larkspur Rd NE16 .....69 B6
Larkspur Terr NE2 .....38 E1

Larkswood NE34 ......60 B7
Larne Cres NE9 ....71 A5
Larriston NE42 ....50 B1
Larriston Pl NE23 .....21 F6
Lartington Gdns NE3 ..38 F5
Larwood Cl DH3 ....88 E1
Lascelles Ave NE34 ...59 E5
Laski Gdns NE10 ......72 B8
Lassells Rigg NE42 ...50 D4
Latimer St NE30 ......42 D8
Latrigg Ct 25 SR3 ....91 F6
Latton Cl NE23 ....22 A4
Lauderdale Ave NE28 ..40 C4
Launceston Cl NE3 ....37 D8
Launceston Dr SR3 ....91 C7
Laura St SR1 ....103 B2
Laurel Ave
Longbenton NE12 ....30 A1
Newcastle-u-T NE3 ......38 A7
Laurel Cres Burnside DH4 ..90 C3
Newcastle-u-T NE6 ......39 F1
Laurel Ct Chester le S DH2 ..88 B5
North Shields NE30 ......42 B5
Laurel Dr NE63 ....6 C1
Laurel End NE12 ......30 A1
Laurel Gr SR2 ....86 D2
Laurel Rd NE21 ....53 D2
Laurel St Throckley NE15 ..35 D3
Wallsend NE28 ....40 C1
Laurel Terr
Burnopfield NE16 ....78 F6
Seaton Delaval NE25 ....23 E2
Laurel Way NE40 ......52 A3
Laurel Wlk NE3 ....38 C5
Laurelwood Gdns NE11 ..70 B5
Laurens Ct NE37 ......83 D8
Laurel Terr
Gateshead NE9 ....70 F6
Newcastle-u-T NE2 ......38 D1
Lavender Gr
Hedworth NE32 ....73 C8
Sunderland SR5 ....74 A1
Lavender La NE34 .....59 B5
Lavender Rd NE16 .....69 A6
Lavender Row 2 NE9 ..71 B5
Lavender St 4 SR4 ....85 A6
Lavender Wlk NE31 ....57 E3
Lavendon Cl NE23 .....22 A4
Laverick NE10 ....71 F6
Laverock Ct 12 NE6 ...56 C5
Laverock Hall Rd NE24 ..17 B3
3 Newcastle-u-T NE3 ..37 D5
Lavers Rd DH3 ....82 C5
Lavington Rd NE34 ....59 E8
Lawe Rd NE33 ....42 D4
Lawn Cotts SR3 ....91 F6
Lawn Ct NE63 ....6 B3
Lawn Dr NE36 ....73 F6
Lawn The NE40 ....52 C6
Lawnhead Sq NE3 .....92 B6
Lawns The
Easington Lane DH5 .....95 C1
Newcastle-u-T NE2 ......38 F2
Silksworth SR3 ....91 F6
Whitburn SR6 ....75 F8
Lawnsway NE32 ....58 C1
Lawnswood DH5 ......94 F7
Lawrence Ave
Blaydon NE21 ....53 C3
Whiteleas NE34 ....59 D3
Lawrence Ct NE21 .....53 C3
Lawrence Hill Ct NE10 ..72 C8
Lawrence St SR1 .....103 C2
Laws St SR6 ....75 D4
Lawson Ave NE32 .....58 D3
Lawson Cres SR6 .....75 D4
Lawson Ct
Boldon Colliery NE35 ....73 F7
3 Chester le S DH2 ...88 C2
Lawson St
North Shields NE29 .....42 A4
Wallsend NE28 ....40 C1
Lawson St W 8 NE29 ..42 A4
Lawson Terr
Hetton le H DH5 ....95 B1
Newcastle-u-T NE4 .....54 E4
Laxford DH3 ....82 D2
Laxford SR3 ....92 A5
Laybourn Gdns 5 NE34 ..59 A4
Layburn Gdns NE15 ...53 E8
Laycock Gdns NE23 ...22 F1
Layfield Rd NE3 ....28 C1
Laygate NE33 ....42 C1
Laygate Pl NE33 ......42 C1
Laygate Sch NE33 .....42 C1
Laygate St NE33 ......42 B1
Lea Ave NE32 ....58 C2
Lea Gn DH3 ....82 E1
Lea Riggs DH4 ....94 A2
Leabank NE15 ....53 D8
Leaburn Terr NE42 ....50 B2
Lead La Horsley NE15 ..33 C1
Newlands DH8 ....76 C6
Lead Rd Greenside NE40 ..52 B1
High Spen NE17,NE40 ...66 D6
Stocksfield NE43 ....64 B2
Leadgate Cotts NE17 ..66 A4
Leafield Cl DH3 ....82 D6
Leafield Cres NF34 ...60 A8
Leagreen Ct NE3 ......38 A5
Leaholme Cres NE24 ...17 C6
Lealholm Rd NE7 ......39 A5
Leam Gdns NE10 ......72 C8
Leam La Gateshead NE10 ..72 B6
Jarrow NE32 ....58 C3

Leam La/Newcastle Rd
NE32,NE34 ....58 F5
Leamington St SR4 ...102 B1
Leamside Gateshead NE10 ..71 F6
Jarrow NE32 ....58 C4
Leander Ave
Chester le S DH3 ....88 D7
Stakeford NE62 ....11 B8
Leander Ct NE62 ......11 B8
Leander Dr NE35 ......73 E8
Leaplish NE38 ....83 F2
Leas The Newbottle DH4 ..90 D3
Whitley Bay NE25 ....31 D4
Leasyde Wlk NE16 .....68 F5
Leatham SR2 ....92 E8
Leaway NE42 ....50 B2
Leazes Arc NE1 ....99 A2
Leazes Cres Hexham NE46 ..44 F5
Newcastle-u-T NE1 .....98 C2
Leazes Ct NE4 ....98 B2
Leazes La Corbridge NE45 ..47 A8
Hexham NE46 ....44 F5
Newcastle-u-T NE1 .....99 A2
Leazes Par NE2 ....98 B2
Leazes Park Rd NE1 ...99 A2
Leazes Parkway NE15 ..35 D1
Leazes Pk NE46 ....44 E5
Leazes Terr
Corbridge NE45 ....46 F6
Hexham NE46 ....44 F5
Newcastle-u-T NE1 .....98 C2
Leazes The
Burnopfield NE16 ....78 F6
South Shields NE34 .....59 F6
Sunderland SR1 ....102 B2
Throckley NE15 ....35 C1
Leazes View
Ovington NE42 ....49 D4
Rowlands Gill NE39 .....67 D2
Leazes Villas NE16 ....79 A6
Lecondale NE10 ......71 F5
Lecondale Ct NE10 ....71 F5
Ledbury Rd SR2 ......86 D3
Lee Cl NE38 ....84 B6
Lee St
Sunderland,Fulwell SR6 ..75 D4
6 Sunderland,Southwick
SR5 ....75 B1
Lee Terr DH5 ....95 B2
Leechmere Cres SR7 ..92 F1
Leechmere Ind Est SR2 ..86 E1
Leechmere Rd SR2 ....86 D1
Leechmere View 5 SR2 ..92 F8
Leechmere Way SR2 ...92 F8
Leeds St SR6 ....75 E2
Leeholme DH5 ....94 F7
Leeming Gdns NE9 ....71 B6
Legg Ave NE22 ....11 E3
Legges Dr NE13 ......20 D6
Legion Gr NE15 ....53 F7
Legion Rd NE15 ......53 F7
Leicester Cl NE28 .....40 A5
Leicester St NE6 ......56 E5
Leicester Way NE32 ...58 A1
Leighton Rd SR2 ......86 D2
Leighton St
7 Newcastle-u-T NE6 ..56 A6
South Shields NE33 .....42 E2
Leighton Terr DH3 ....82 B5
Leith Ct NE34 ....59 C5
Leith Gdns DH9 ....79 D1
Leland Pl NE61 ....8 D7
Lemington Gdns NE5 ..54 F2
Lemington Rd NE15 ...53 B6
Lemington Riverside Prim
Sch NE15 ....53 D6
Lemon St NE33 ....59 B6
Lena Ave NE25 ....31 E4
Lenin Terr NE17 ......77 C8
Lenore Terr NE40 .....52 A5
Lenthorn Mews 2 SR6 ..75 E1
Leominster Rd SR2 ...86 D2
Leopold Ho SR2 ......102 C1
Leopold St NE32 ......58 B6
Lesbury Ave
Ashington NE63 ....6 D2
Shiremoor NE27 ....30 E3
Stakeford NE62 ....6 A1
Wallsend NE28 ....40 F3
Lesbury Chase NE3 ...38 B7
Lesbury Gdns NE13 ...28 C6
Lesbury Rd NE6 ......56 B8
Lesbury St
Newcastle-u-T NE15 ....53 C6
North Shields NE28 .....41 C1
Lesbury Terr NE17 ....77 B8
Lesley Ct NE3 ....38 C5
Leslie Ave NE31 ......57 E5
Leslie Cl NE40 ....52 E4
Leslie Cres NE3 ......38 C3
Leslies View NE61 .....3 E2
Letch Way NE15 ......53 C7
Letchwell Villas NE12 ..39 F1
Leuchars Ct DH3 ......82 C3
Leven Ave DH2 ....88 B1
Leven Ho 10 SR3 .....92 A6
Levens Wlk NE23 ......21 E7
Levisham Cl SR3 ......92 C7
Lewis Cres SR2 ......103 C1
Lewis Dr NE4 ....54 F6
Lewis Gdns NF34 .....59 C3
Leybourne Ave NE12 ..29 D2
Leybourne Dene NE12 ..29 D2
Leybourne Hold DH3 ...82 C6
Leyburn Cl
Houghton-le-S DH4 ......90 D1
Urpeth DH2 ....81 D1
Leyburn Ct NE23 ......22 A4

Leyburn Dr NE7 ....39 A3
Leyburn Gr DH4 ....90 D1
Leyburn Pl DH3 ....82 B6
Leyfield Cl SR3 ....92 B5
Leyton Pl NE8 ....71 B8
Liberty Ho NE2 ....38 E1
Liberty Terr DH9 ......79 B2
Lichbarn Cl DH9 ......36 C8
Lichfield Ave NE6 .....56 E4
Lichfield Cl Ashington NE63 ..6 F2
Newcastle-u-T NE3 ......37 E7
Lichfield Rd SR5 ......75 A3
Lichfield Way NE32 ...58 A1
Lidcombe Cl SR3 ......92 C7
Liddell Ct SR3 ....75 F2
Liddell St
North Shields NE29,NE30 ..42 B5
Sunderland SR6 ....103 A4
Liddell Terr
Gateshead NE8 ....70 D8
Kibblesworth NE11 .....81 C6
Liddle Ct NE4 ....98 A1
Liddle Rd NE4 ....98 A1
Liddles St 1 NE22 .....11 D3
Lieven St NE13 ....28 A4
Liffey Rd NE31 ....57 F3
Lightbourne Rd NE6 ...57 A6
Lightfoot Sports Ctr The
NE6 ....56 F4
Lightwood Ave NE15 ..54 A4
Lilac Ave NE34 ....17 D8
Longbenton NE12 ......39 F8
New Silksworth SR3 ....92 B8
South Shields NE34 ....60 A5
Whitburn SR6 ....60 F3
Lilac Cl NE5 ....36 B4
Lilac Cres NE16 ......79 A6
Lilac Ct Ashington NE63 ..6 C1
Ellington NE61 ....1 E6
Lilac Gdns Cleadon SR6 ..60 A2
Gateshead NE9 ....70 F6
Washington NE38 ......83 C1
Whickham NE16 ....69 A6
Lilac Gr Chester le S DH2 ..88 A5
Sunderland SR5 ....75 D3
Lilac Rd NE6 ....40 A1
Lilac Sq DH4 ....89 E3
Lilac St SR4 ....85 A6
Lilac Wlk NE31 ....57 E3
Lilburn Cl 5 NE6 .....56 C4
Lilburn Gdns NE3 .....38 F4
Lilburn Pl SR5 ....75 A1
Lilburn Rd NE27 ......30 E2
Lilburn St NE29 ......41 F5
Lilburne Cl SR1 ......103 B3
Lilian Ave Sunderland SR2 ..92 E8
Wallsend NE28 ....40 A1
Lilley Gr SR5 ....74 B1
Lilley Terr NE39 ......67 F4
Lilleycroft NE39 ......67 F2
Lillico Ho NE2 ....99 C3
Lily Ave Bedlington NE22 ..16 B8
Newcastle-u-T NE2 .....38 E1
Lily Bank NE28 ....40 C2
Lily Cl NE21 ....53 A2
Lily Cres
Newcastle-u-T NE2 .....38 E1
Whitburn SR6 ....60 F3
Lily Est NE35 ....35 D3
Lily Gdns DH9 ....78 E1
Lily St SR4 ....102 B3
Lily Terr Newbottle DH4 ..90 D4
Newcastle-u-T NE5 .....37 A3
Lilywhite Terr DH5 ....95 B1
Lime Ave NE34 ....90 C1
Lime Gr Prudhoe NE42 ..50 B3
Ryton NE40 ....52 C5
Lime St Blaydon NE21 ..53 D1
Newcastle-u-T,Heaton NE1,NE6 ..56 A5
Sunderland SR4 ....102 B3
Throckley NE15 ....35 D3
Limecroft NE32 ......58 C1
Limekiln Ct NE28 .....40 D2
Limekiln Rd NE28 .....40 D2
Limes Ave NE24 ......12 C1
Limes The Penshaw DH4 ..90 B8
Stannington NE61 ......14 C3
Sunderland SR2 ....86 D4
Limestone La NE20 ...25 B7
Limetree NE38 ....83 E2
Limetrees Gdns NE9 ..70 F7
Limewood Ct NE2 .....98 B4
Limewood Gr NE13 ...28 B5
Linacre Cl NE3 ....37 B6
Linbridge Dr NE5 .....36 E1
Linburn NE38 ....89 B8
Lincoln Ave
New Silksworth SR3 ....92 A8
Wallsend NE28 ....40 A5
Lincoln Cres DH5 .....94 F4
Lincoln Ct NE31 ......57 D5
Lincoln Gn NE3 ......28 C1
Lincoln Rd
Cramlington NE23 ......16 C1
South Shields NE34 ....60 B7
Lincoln St
Gateshead NE8 ....101 B1
Sunderland SR4 ....85 F7
Lincoln Way NE32 ....58 B1
Lincrest Ct NE5 ....36 F2
Lindale Ave NE16 .....69 A5
Lindale Rd NE4 ....54 E8
Lindean Pl NE23 ......21 F6
Linden NE9 ....71 D4
Linden Ave
Newcastle-u-T,Fenham NE4 ..54 D7

Linden Ave, continued
Newcastle-u-T,Gosforth
NE3 ....38 C4
Linden Cl NE62 ....11 A8
Linden Gdns SR2 ......86 C3
Linden Gr
1 Dunston NE11 ......70 A8
Houghton-le-S DH4 .....94 D8
Linden Rd Blaydon NE21 ..53 D2
Longbenton NE12 ......39 D6
Newcastle-u-T NE3 .....38 C4
Seaton Delaval NE25 ...23 B3
Sunderland SR2 ....86 C3
Linden Sch NE12 ....39 D8
Linden Terr
Longbenton NE12 ......39 D6
25 Springwell NE9 .....71 F1
Whitley Bay NE26 ......32 B5
Linden Way Ellington NE61 ..1 D2
Gateshead NE9 ....71 D2
Ponteland NE20 ....25 C3
Lindfield Ave NE5 .....37 C1
Lindisfarne Ryhope SR2 ..92 E4
Washington NE38 ......83 C4
Lindisfarne Ave DH3 ..88 D3
Lindisfarne Cl
Burnside DH4 ....90 C2
Chester le S DH2 ....88 A1
Morpeth NE61 ....9 A6
Newcastle-u-T NE5 .....36 F1
Newcastle-u-T,Jesmond
NE2 ....38 F2
Pegswood NE61 ....5 A4
Lindisfarne Com Prim Sch
NE8 ....56 A2
Lindisfarne Ct NE32 ...58 F6
Lindisfarne Dr NE8 ...101 C2
Lindisfarne La NE61 ....9 A6
Lindisfarne Pl NE28 ...40 D3
Lindisfarne Rd
Hebburn NE31 ....57 E3
Jarrow NE32 ....58 D4
Newcastle-u-T NE2 .....38 F2
Lindisfarne Recess NE32 ..58 D4
Lindisfarne Terr NE30 ..42 A7
Lindisfarne Wlk NE62 ..10 E7
Lindom Ave DH3 ......88 D3
Lindrick Ct NE10 ......72 C7
Lindsay Ave NE24 .....17 C8
Lindsay Cl SR2 ....103 B1
Lindsay Ct SR6 ....60 F2
Lindsay Rd SR2 ......103 B1
Lindsay St DH5 ....95 B5
Lindsey Cl NE23 ......21 E6
Lindum Rd NE9 ....70 F8
Linfield SR2 ....92 E7
Lingcrest NE9 ....71 C5
Lingdale Ave SR6 .....75 E6
Lingey Gdns NE10 ....72 C8
Lingey House Prim Sch
NE10 ....72 B7
Lingey La NE10 ....72 B7
Lingfield DH5 ....94 F7
Lingholme DH2 ....88 A4
Lingmell NE37 ....83 B6
Lingshaw NE10 ....72 B7
Lingside NE32 ....58 C1
Linhope Ave NE3 ......37 F7
Linhope PRU NE5 .....36 F2
Linhope Rd NE5 ......36 F2
Link Ave NE22 ....10 D1
Link Rd Hazlerigg NE13 ..28 A4
Newcastle-u-T NE5 .....37 E2
Link The NE46 ....44 F5
Links Ave Tynemouth NE30 ..32 C2
Whitley Bay NE26 ......31 F7
Links Ct NE26 ....32 A7
Links Gn NE3 ....38 D6
Links Green Wlk NE3 ..38 D6
Links Rd Blyth NE24 ...17 F4
Seaton Sluice NE24 .....18 A2
Tynemouth NE30 ....32 C2
Links The NE26 ......32 A7
Links View
Ashington NE63 ....12 A8
Blyth NE24 ....17 C4
Links Wlk NE5 ....36 F2
Linkway NE32 ....58 D1
Linley Hill NE16 ......68 E4
Linnel Dr NE15 ....53 E7
Linnet Cl NE38 ....83 A3
Linnet Ct NE63 ....6 B2
Linnet Gr SR5 ....74 C1
Linnetsfield NE6 ......56 F8
Linney Gdns NE34 ....59 A4
Linnheads NE42 ......50 B1
Linshiels Gdns 1 NE63 ..6 F2
Linskell SR2 ....92 E8
Linskill Ctr PRU NE30 ..42 B7
Linskill Pl
Newcastle-u-T NE3 .....37 F3
North Shields NE30 ....42 B7
Linskill St NE30 ......42 B5
Linskill Terr
North Shields NE30 ....42 B7
Tynemouth NE30 ....42 B7
Linslade Wlk NE23 ....21 F6
Lintfort NE38 ....88 E7
Linthorpe Ct 1 NE34 ..59 A5
Linthorpe Rd
Newcastle-u-T NE3 .....38 C7
Tynemouth NE30 ....32 B3
Linton NE12 ....29 D5
Linton Fst Sch NE61 ....1 A3
Linton Rd Gateshead NE9 ..70 F2
Whitley Bay NE26 ......24 E1
Lintonville Ent Pk NE63 ..6 D5
Lintonville Parkway NE63 ..6 C5

Lintonville Rd NE63 ......6 C4
Lintz Green La NE16,NE39 78 C6
Lintz La NE16 ....78 E4
Lintz Terr NE16 ....78 F6
Lintzford Gdns
  Newcastle-u-T NE15 .....53 E7
  Rowlands Gill NE39 .....78 D8
Lintzford La NE39 ....67 B1
Lintzford Rd NE39 ......78 C7
Linum Ct NE4 ....54 E8
Linwood Pl NE3 ....28 C1
Lion Wlk NE29 ....42 A3
Lisa Ave SR4 ....85 A5
Lisburn Terr SR4 ......102 A3
Lish Ave NE26 ....32 C4
Lishman Terr NE40 ......52 A4
Lisle Ct ⑪ NE28 ....40 B2
Lisle Gr NE28 ....41 A3
Lisle Rd NE34 ....60 A6
Lisle St Newcastle-u-T NE1 99 A2
  Wallsend NE28 ....40 B2
Lismor Terr ⑩ NE9 ......71 F1
Lismore Ave NE33 ....59 D7
Lismore Pl NE15 ....54 D6
Lister Ave Dunston NE11 .54 F1
  Greenside NE40 ....66 F8
Lister Cl DH5 ....94 D6
Lister St NE15 ....53 F5
Listers La NE9 ....71 A4
Litchfield Cres ② NE21 .53 B1
Litchfield La NE21 .....53 B1
Litchfield St ⓵ NE21 ...53 B1
Litchfield Terr ③ NE21 .53 B1
Little Bedford St NE30,
  NE30 ....42 B5
Little Bldgs NE42 ......49 D4
Little Dene NE2 ....38 D3
Little Villiers St SR1 ..103 B3
Little Way NE15 ....54 B4
Littleburn Cl DH4 ......90 C2
Littledene NE9 ....70 F7
Littletown La DH6 ......96 D3
Litton Ct ⑭ SR3 ....91 F6
Littondale NE28 ....39 F4
Livingstone Pl ⑧ NE33 .42 C4
Livingstone Rd SR1 ....102 C3
Livingstone St ② NE33 .42 D4
Livingstone View NE30 .42 C7
Lizard La NE34,SR6 .....60 E4
Lizard View SR6 ....60 E2
Lloyd Ave DH5 ....94 C4
Lloyd Ct NE11 ....54 E2
Lloyd St ⑥ NE40 ....51 F3
Lobban Ave NE31 ....57 D3
Lobelia Ave NE10 ......56 B2
Lobelia Cl NE5 ....36 B3
Lobley Gdns NE11 ......70 A6
Lobley Hill Prim Sch
  NE11 ....70 A6
Lobley Hill Rd NE11,NE8 .70 C7
Lobleyhill Rd
  Byermoor NE16 ....79 D8
  Sunniside NE16 ....79 D8
Local Ave DH6 ....96 C1
Locarno Pl NE64 ....7 A4
Lochcraig Pl NE23 ......21 F6
Lochfield Gdns NE11 ...81 C6
Lochmaben Terr SR5 ....75 D2
Lockerbie Gdns NE15 ...53 E7
Lockerbie Rd NE23 .....21 F6
Lockhaugh Rd NE39 .....68 A4
Locksley Ct NE29 ......31 B1
Locomotion Way
  Killingworth NE12 .....29 B5
  North Shields NE29 ....42 A4
Locomotive Ct NE42 ....50 C2
Lodge Cl NE39 ....78 A5
Lodges Rd The NE9 .....70 F3
Lodgeside Mdw SR3 .....92 B5
Lodore Ct ⑤ NE16 ......91 F6
Lodore Gr NE32 ....58 D3
Lodore Rd NE2 ....38 D3
Lodsworth Dr NE23 .....22 A4
Lofthill ⑥ SR3 ....91 E5
Logan Rd NE6 ....39 F1
Logan St DH5 ....95 A3
Logan Terr DH6 ....97 E8
Lola St NE13 ....27 F4
Lombard Dr DH3 ....88 D7
Lombard St
  Newcastle-u-T NE1 ....101 B4
  Sunderland SR1 ....103 B3
Lomond Cl NE38 ....83 B3
Lomond Ct ⑪ SR3 ......92 A6
Lomond Pl DH2 ....88 B1
London Ave NE37 ....72 B1
Londonderry Mews ⑤
  SR3 ....92 B7
Londonderry St SR3 ....92 A7
Londonderry Terr SR3 ..92 B7
Londonderry Twr ..103 B3
Londonderry Way DH4 ..90 A7
Long Bank Birtley DH3 ..82 C7
  Gateshead NE9 ....71 C1
Long Close Rd NE39 ....77 F5
Long Crag NE37 ....83 A5
Long Dr NE61 ....8 F5
Long Gair NE21 ....68 A8
Long Headlam ⑪ NE6 ...56 C6
Long Meadow Cl NE40 ..52 A3
Long Pk NE64 ....7 D4
Long Ridge Rd NE21,
  NE40 ....52 D2
Long Rigg NE16 ....54 A2
Long Row NE33 ....42 B4
Long Row Cl NE40 ......66 F8
Longacre
  Houghton-le-S DH4 .....94 C8

Longacre continued
  Washington NE38 ....83 E1
Longbenton Com Coll
  NE12 ....39 C7
Longbenton Sta NE12 ...39 A5
Longborough Ct NE7 ....39 A4
Longclose Bank DH8,
  NE39 ....77 E3
Longdean Cl NE31 ......57 C5
Longdean Pk DH3 ......88 D6
Longfellow St DH5 .....94 E7
Longfield Cl NE34 .....59 D4
Longfield Rd SR6 ......75 D3
Longfield Terr NE6 ....57 A4
Longhirst Gateshead NE10 72 A7
  Killingworth NE12 .....29 D5
  Newcastle-u-T NE7 .....36 F2
Longhirst Ct NE61 ......4 F4
Longhirst Dr
  Cramlington NE23 ......22 A4
  Wideopen NE13 ....28 B5
Longhirst Rd NE61 ......4 F4
Longhirst Village NE61 ..4 F7
Longlands ⑪ NE46 .....45 A4
Longlands Dr DH5 ......94 E7
Longleat Gdns
  Pegswood NE61 ....4 E4
  ⑩ South Shields NE33 ..42 D3
Longley St NE4 ....98 A2
Longmeadows
  Ponteland NE20 ....25 B3
  Sunderland SR3 ....91 C6
Longniddry NE37 ....72 C3
Longniddry Ct NE9 .....70 E3
Longridge NE21 ....53 A2
Longridge Ave
  Newcastle-u-T NE7 .....39 D2
  Washington NE38 ......83 B3
Longridge Ct NE22 .....11 A4
Longridge Dr NE26 .....31 E7
Longridge Sq SR2 .....86 D2
Longridge Way
  Bedlington NE22 ....11 A4
  Cramlington NE23 ......21 F6
Longrigg NE10 ....72 A7
Longriggs The NE44 ....62 E7
Longshank La DH3 .....82 A6
Longstaff Gdns NE34 ...58 F4
Longston Ave NE30 .....32 B3
Longstone Ct NE12 .....29 E4
Longstone Sq NE5 .....36 D1
Longwood Cl NE16 .....69 B3
Lonnen Ave NE4 ....54 D7
Lonnen Dr NE16 ....69 B3
Lonnen The Ryton NE40 .52 E5
  South Shields NE34 ....60 B4
Lonsdale DH3 ....82 E1
Lonsdale Ave Blyth NE24 .16 E8
  Sunderland SR6 ....75 E7
Lonsdale Ct
  Medomsley NE17 ....77 B4
  South Shields NE34 ....59 A4
Lonsdale Gdns NE28 ...41 A4
Lonsdale Rd SR6 ......75 E2
Lonsdale Terr NE2 .....38 E2
Loraine Terr NE15 .....53 C6
Lord Blyton Prim Sch
  NE34 ....59 B6
Lord Byrons Wlk SR7 ..93 B1
Lord Gort Cl ⓵ SR5 ...75 A1
Lord Lawson of Beamish Com
  Sch DH3 ....82 D3
Lord Nelson St NE33 ...59 B6
Lord St New Silksworth SR3 92 B7
  Newcastle-u-T NE1 ....100 C4
  South Shields NE33 ....42 E1
Lordenshaw NE5 ....36 F2
Lorne St DH5 ....97 B8
Lorne Terr SR2 ....103 A4
Lorrain Rd NE34 ......59 D2
Lort Ho NE2 ....99 C2
Lorton Ave NE30 ......32 A2
Lorton Rd NE9 ....71 A4
Losh Terr NE6 ....56 F5
Lossiemouth Rd NE29 ..41 C5
Lothian Cl Birtley DH3 ..82 D1
  Sunderland SR4 ....85 D3
Lothian Ct NE5 ....37 C3
Lotus Cl NE5 ....36 B3
Lotus Pl NE4 ....54 D7
Loudon St NE34 ....59 C5
Lough Ct NE9 ....71 B5
Loughborough Ave
  Sunderland SR2 ....86 C3
  Tynemouth NE30 ....32 C1
Loughraw Pk NE46 .....45 B2
Loughrigg Ave NE23 ...21 F6
Louie Terr NE9 ....71 A5
Louis Ave SR6 ....75 D3
Louise Ho SR2 ....102 C1
Louise Terr DH3 ......88 C3
Louisville NE20 ....25 C7
Loup St NE21 ....53 C3
Louvain Terr
  Guide Post NE62 ....10 F7
  Hetton le H DH5 ....95 A5
Louvain Terr W DH5 ...95 A5
Lovaine Ave
  ⑧ North Shields NE29 .42 A5
  Whitley Bay NE25 .....32 A4
Lovaine Flats NE1 .....99 B2
Lovaine Pl NE29 ......42 A5
Lovaine Place W ⑨ NE3 41 F5
Lovaine Row NE30 .....42 E8
Lovaine Terr NE29 ....42 A6
Love Ave NE23 ....29 B7
Love Avenue Cotts NE23 29 B8

Love La NE1 ....99 C1
Loveless Gdns NE10 ...72 B8
Lovett Wlk NE8 ......100 C2
Low Burswell NE46 ....44 F5
Low Chare DH3 ....88 D3
Low Cl NE42 ....50 E3
Low Downs Rd DH5 ....95 A6
Low Downs Sq DH5 ....95 B6
Low Farm NE61 ....1 D4
Low Flatts Rd DH3 ....88 C6
Low Fold NE6 ....56 B5
Low Friar La ② NE1 ...99 A1
Low Friar St NE1 .....99 A1
Low Gate Fst Sch NE46 .44 A4
Low Gosforth Ct NE3 ..28 D1
Low Haugh NE20 ....25 F7
Low Heworth La NE10 ..56 F1
Low La NE34 ....59 C5
Low Main Pl NE23 .....22 B6
Low Mdw SR6 ....60 A1
Low Prudhoe Ind Est
  NE42 ....50 D4
Low Quay NE24 ....17 F8
Low Reach NE10 ....57 A2
Low Row Ryton NE40 ...52 E3
  Sunderland SR1 ....102 C2
Low St SR1 ....103 B3
Low Stobhill NE61 ......9 A7
Low Well Gdns NE10 ...56 E1
Low West Ave NE39 ....67 D1
Lowbiggin NE5 ....36 E5
Lowdham Ave NE29 ....41 E4
Lowdon Ct NE2 ....98 C3
Lower Crone St NE27 ..30 F4
Lower Dundas St SR6 .103 A4
Lower Rudyerd St NE29 .42 B5
Lowerson Ave DH4 ....90 A5
Lowery Rd NE42 ......99 C2
Loweswater Ave
  Chester le S DH2 .....88 B1
  Easington Lane DH5 ...97 C8
Loweswater Cl NE24 ...11 F1
Loweswater Rd
  Gateshead NE9 ....71 A4
  Newcastle-u-T NE5 ....54 B8
Loweswood Cl NE7 ....39 A1
Lowfield Terr NE6 ....56 F4
Lowfield Wlk NE6 .....69 A6
Lowgate NE15 ....35 D1
Lowick Cl DH3 ....82 D1
Lowick Ct NE3 ....38 E4
Lowland Cl SR3 ....92 A5
Lowlean Ct NE5 ....36 F1
Lownds Terr NE6 .....56 E6
Lowrey's La NE9 ....70 F5
Lowry Gdns NE34 .....59 D2
Lowry Rd SR6 ....75 E5
Lowther Ave DH2 ......88 B2
Lowther Cl NE63 ....6 F1
Lowther Sq NE23 ......21 E6
Lowthian Cres NE6 ....56 E5
Lowthian Terr NE38 ...83 F4
Loxton Sq NE23 ....22 A3
Lucknow St SR1 ......103 C3
Lucock St NE34 ....59 B5
Lucombe Cl DH4 ......89 F5
Lucy St Blaydon NE21 ..53 D3
  ④ Chester le S DH3 ...88 C4
Ludlow Ave NE29 ......41 E8
Ludlow Ct NE3 ....37 E7
Ludlow Dr NE25 ....31 B5
Ludlow Rd SR2 ....86 D3
Luffness Dr NE34 .....59 F3
Luke's La NE10,NE31 ..57 F1
Lukes Lane Com Sch
  NE31 ....58 A3
Lulsgate SR5 ....74 A1
Lulworth Ave NE32 ....58 D5
Lulworth Ct SR3 ......91 C7
Lulworth Gdns SR2 ...86 C3
Lumley Ave
  South Shields NE34 ....60 B6
  Whickham NE16 ....54 B1
Lumley Cl
  Chester le S DH2 .....88 B2
  Washington NE38 ......83 B3
Lumley Cres DH4 .....90 C4
Lumley Ct Bedlington NE22 11 C2
  Hebburn NE31 ....57 F8
  Sunderland SR3 ....91 C7
Lumley Gdns
  Burnopfield NE16 .....78 E5
  Gateshead NE8 ....56 B1
Lumley New Rd DH3,DH4 89 F1
Lumley St Newbottle DH4 .90 C7
  Sunderland SR4 ....102 B2
Lumley Terr
  Chester le S DH3 .....88 D2
  Jarrow NE32 ....58 C4
  ⓵ Ryhope SR2 ....92 F6
Lumley Thicks DH3 ....89 C1
Lumley Twr SR1 ......103 B3
Lumley Wlk NE11 .....100 A1
Lumley's La NE43 .....65 B6
Lumsden's La NE61 .....3 F1
Lune Gn NE32 ....58 C2
Lunedale Ave SR6 .....75 C5
Lunedale St DH5 ......95 A2
Lupin Cl NE5 ....36 C4
Luss Ave NE32 ....58 E3
Lutterworth Cl NE12 ..39 B6
Lutterworth Pl NE12 ..39 B6
Lutterworth Rd
  Longbenton NE12 ......39 B5
  Sunderland SR2 ....86 C3
Luxembourg Rd SR4 ...85 D7
Lychgate Ct NE8 .....101 C3
Lydbury Cl NE23 ......16 C1

Lydcott NE38 ....84 B5
Lyden Gate NE9 ......71 A3
Lydford Ct Newbottle DH4 .90 C3
  Newcastle-u-T NE5 ....37 C6
Lydford Way DH3 .....82 D3
Lydney Cl NE15 ....35 C1
Lyncroft NE63 ....6 C2
Lyncroft Rd NE29 .....41 E6
Lyndale NE23 ....16 C1
Lynden Gdns NE5 .....37 A3
Lynden Rd SR2 ....92 F8
Lyndhurst Ave
  Chester le S DH3 .....88 C6
  Gateshead NE9 ....71 A4
  Newcastle-u-T NE2 ....38 E2
Lyndhurst Cl NE21 ....68 A8
Lyndhurst Cres NE9 ..71 A4
Lyndhurst Dr NE9 ....71 A3
Lyndhurst Gdns NE2 ..38 D2
Lyndhurst Gn NE9 ....70 F4
Lyndhurst Gr NE9 ....71 A4
Lyndhurst Lodge NE25 .31 E5
Lyndhurst Rd
  Ashington NE63 ....6 F1
  Longbenton NE12 .....39 D7
  Whitley Bay NE25 .....31 E5
Lyndhurst St ③ NE33 ..42 D2
Lyndhurst Terr
  Sunderland SR4 ....85 E8
  ⓵ Whickham NE16 ....54 A1
Lyndon Cl NE36 ......74 B7
Lyndon Dr NE36 ......74 B7
Lyndon Gr NE36 ......74 B7
Lyndon Wlk NE24 .....16 F8
Lyne Terr NE61 ....1 F3
Lyneburn Grange NE61 ..1 D5
Lynemouth Fst Sch NE61 .2 B3
Lynemouth Rd NE61 ....1 D4
Lynfield NE26 ....31 F7
Lynfield Ct NE5 ......37 B3
Lynfield Pl NE5 ......37 B3
Lynford Gdns SR2 ....86 C3
Lyngrove SR2 ....92 F8
Lynholm Gr NE12 .....39 D8
Lynholme Cl ⑨ NE8 ...71 A8
Lynmouth Pl NE7 .....39 B3
Lynmouth Rd
  Gateshead NE9 ....70 F3
  North Shields NE29 ...41 C5
  Wallsend NE28 ....40 A1
Lynn St Blyth NE24 ....17 B7
  ⑬ Chester le S DH3 ...88 C2
Lynndale Ave NE24 ...17 A7
Lynnholm Cl NE7 .....39 B2
Lynnholme Gdns
  ④ Gateshead NE9 .....70 F8
  Gateshead,Deckham NE9 .71 A8
Lynnwood Ave NE4 ...54 F5
Lynnwood Terr NE4 ..54 F5
Lynthorpe SR2 ....92 F8
Lynthorpe Gr SR6 ....75 E3
Lynton Ave NE32 .....58 E5
Lynton Ct Newbottle DH4 .90 C3
  Newcastle-u-T NE5 ....37 B3
Lynton Pl NE5 ....37 B3
Lynton Way NE5 .....37 B3
Lynwood Ave
  Blaydon NE21 ....53 C3
  Newbiggin-by-t-S NE64 .7 D5
  Sunderland SR4 ....85 A2
Lynwood Bsns Dev Ctr
  NE4 ....54 F5
Lynwood Cl NE20 .....25 C2
Lyon St NE31 ....57 D7
Lyons Ave DH5 ....95 B2
Lyons Cotts DH5 .....95 B2
Lyons La DH5 ....95 B1
Lyons The DH5 ....95 B2
Lyric Cl NE29 ....41 C8
Lysdon Ave NE25 .....23 D6
Lyster Cl SR7 ....92 F1
Lytchfeld NE10 ......72 B7
Lytham Cl
  Cramlington NE23 .....21 E6
  Wallsend NE28 ....40 E7
  Washington NE37 .....72 C2
Lytham Dr NE25 ......31 D5
Lytham Grange DH4 ..90 A4
Lytham Pl NE6 ....56 E5
Lythe Way NE12 ......39 C6

M

Mabel St NE21 ....53 C3
Macadam St NE8 ......70 D7
Macdonald Rd NE4 ...54 D7
Maclynn Cl SR3 ......91 E6
Macmerry Cl SR5 .....84 F8
Macmillan Gdns NE10 .72 A8
Maddison Ct SR1 ....103 C3
Maddison Gdns NE23 ..22 E1
Maddison St NE24 ....17 E8
Maddox Rd NE12 .....39 D6
Madeira Ave NE26 ....31 F7
Madeira Cl NE5 ......36 C4
Madeira Terr ⑧ NE33 .42 D1
Madras St NE34 ......58 E3
Madrona Cl DH4 .....89 F5
Mafeking Pl NE29 ....31 B1
Mafeking St
  ⑤ Gateshead NE9 ....71 A8
  Newcastle-u-T NE6 ...56 B6
  Sunderland SR4 ......85 F7
  Whitley Bay NE26 ....32 B5
Magdalene Ct NE2 ....98 B4

Magdalene Pl SR4 ....85 F7
Magenta Cres NE5 ....36 C4
Magnet Ct ⓵ NE1 ....99 A1
Magnolia Cl NE4 .....54 D7
Magnolia Dr NE63 .....6 C1
Magnolia Gr NE16 ....79 B6
Magpie Ct NE63 ....6 B2
Mahogany Row DH9 ..80 D1
Maiden La NE40 ......52 A2
Maiden Law DH4 .....94 A7
Maiden St NE4 ......100 B3
Maiden's Wlk NE46 ...45 C4
Maidenhair DH4 .....89 F5
Maidens Croft NE46 ..44 F4
Maidstone Cl SR3 ....91 D6
Maidstone Terr DH4 ..90 D4
Main Cres NE28 ......39 F4
Main Rd Dinnington NE13 27 C6
  Newcastle-u-T NE3 ...37 B6
  Ryton NE40 ....52 B5
  Wylam NE41 ....51 B6
Main St Corbridge NE45 47 A5
  Crawcrook NE40 ......51 F4
  Ponteland NE20 ......25 E6
Main St N NE23 ....22 F1
Main St S NE23 ......22 F1
Mains Park Rd DH3 ..88 D3
Mains Pl NE61 ....3 F1
Mainsforth Terr SR2 .103 C1
Mainsforth Terr W SR2 .86 E4
Mainstone Cl NE23 ...22 A6
Maitland Terr NE64 ...7 D4
Makendon St NE8 ...101 C4
Makepeace Terr ⑧ NE9 71 F1
Malaburn Way ② SR5 75 A1
Malaga Cl NE5 ....36 C4
Malaya Dr NE6 ....57 B5
Malcolm Ct NE25 ....31 D4
Malcolm St NE6 ......56 A6
Malden Cl NE23 ......21 F6
Maling Ct NE6 ....56 B4
Maling Pk SR4 ....85 B7
Maling St NE6 ....56 A5
Malings Cl SR1 .....103 C2
Mallard Cl Ashington NE63 11 D8
  Washington NE38 .....82 F4
Mallard Ct NE12 .....29 C3
Mallard Lodge ⑪ NE10 .71 D8
Mallard Way NE24 ...17 F3
  Fence Houses DH4 ....94 B7
Mallory Pl NE8 .....101 C2
Malmo Cl NE29 ......41 B5
Malone Gdns DH3 ....82 D6
Malory Pl NE8 ......101 C2
Maltby Cl
  ② Silksworth SR3 ....91 E5
  Washington NE38 ....83 D4
Maltings The SR3 ....92 C7
Maltkiln NE46 ....45 A4
Malton Cl Blyth NE24 ..17 B7
  Newcastle-u-T NE15 ..53 E6
Malton Cres NE29 ....41 F4
Malton Ct NE32 ......58 A7
Malton Gdns NE28 ...40 B4
Malton Gn NE9 ......71 B1
Malvern Ave DH2 ....88 B2
Malvern Ct Cleadon SR6 .59 F1
  Dunston NE11 ....70 A6
  Newcastle-u-T NE15 ..53 B7
Malvern Gdns
  Dunston NE11 ....70 A7
  Sunderland SR6 ......75 E3
Malvern Rd
  Seaton Sluice NE26 ..24 D5
  Tynemouth NE29 .....41 E8
  Wallsend NE28 ......41 A3
  Washington NE38 ....83 B3
Malvern St
  Newcastle-u-T NE4 ..100 A4
  South Shields NE33 ..59 C7
Malvin's Close Fst Sch
  NE24 ....17 C7
Malvins Close Rd NE24 .17 C7
Malvins Rd NE24 ....17 B8
Manchester St NE61 ...3 F1
Mandale Cres NE30 ..32 A3
Mandarin Cl NE5 .....36 C3
Mandarin Lodge ⑧ NE10 71 D8
Mandarin Way NE38 ..84 C6
Mandela Cl SR1 .....103 C3
Mandela Way NE11 ..54 D3
Mandeville NE37 .....83 F8
Manet Gdns NE34 ....59 D4
Mangrove Cl NE5 ....36 C4
Manila St SR2 ....86 E4
Manisty Ho NE4 .....54 E4
Manley View NE63 ....7 A3
Manners Gdns NE25 ..23 C4
Manningford Cl NE23 .22 A5
Manningford Dr SR3 .91 E5
Manor Chare NE1 ....99 B1
Manor Cl
  Newcastle-u-T NE3 ...38 D5
  Riding Mill NE44 .....62 F7
Manor Cotts NE45 ...46 F6
Manor Ct NE33 ......42 E1
Manor Dr Newcastle-u-T NE7 39 C5
  Newburn NE15 ....52 F8
Manor Gdns
  Gateshead NE10 .....72 C8

Manor Gdns continued
Longbenton NE7 ......**39** C5
Newburn NE15 ......**52** F7
Manor Gr Longbenton NE7 .**39** C5
New Herrington DH4 ......**90** F7
Manor House Cl 1 NE6 .**56** C5
Manor House Farm Cotts
NE5 ......**37** D4
Manor House Rd NE2 ...**38** F1
Manor Pk Corbridge NE45 .**46** F6
Washington NE37 ......**83** D8
Manor Pl NE7 ......**39** C5
Medomsley DH8 ......**77** C1
Tynemouth NE30 ......**42** D7
Washington NE37 ......**83** D8
Manor Rd Longbenton NE7 .**39** C5
Manor The NE37 ......**72** E2
Manor Terr Blaydon NE21 .**53** A1
Winlaton Mill NE21 ......**68** C7
Manor The NE37 ......**72** E2
Manor View
High Pittington DH6 ......**96** B4
Newbiggin-by-t-S NE64 ....**7** B5
Washington NE37 ......**83** E8
Manor View E 2 NE37 ..**83** E8
Manor Walks Sh Ctr
NE23 ......**22** A6
Manor Wlk NE7 ......**39** C5
Manorfields NE12 ......**39** D6
Manors Sta NE1 ......**99** B1
Manors Sta (Metro) NE1 .**99** B1
Manors The NE42 ......**50** E3
Manorway Hedworth NE32 .**58** C1
Tynemouth NE30 ......**42** D8
Mansel Terr NE24 ......**16** E7
Mansell Pl NE3 ......**37** E3
Mansfield Cres SR6 ....**75** E2
Mansfield Ct NE36 ......**74** A7
Mansfield Pl NE4 ......**98** B1
Mansfield St NE4 ......**98** B1
Mansion Ho NE4 ......**74** A7
Mansion Hts NE11 ......**69** E7
Manston Ct SR3 ......**91** D6
Manx Sq SR5 ......**75** B3
Maple Ave Dunston NE11 .**70** A7
New Silksworth SR3 ......**92** B8
Whitley Bay NE25 ......**31** F4
Maple Cl Bedlington NE22 .**10** F1
Newcastle-u-T NE15 ......**53** E6
Maple Cres NE4 ......**16** F8
Maple Ct Killingworth NE12 **29** C4
New Hartley NE25 ......**23** D6
Maple Gr
Gateshead,Felling NE10 ...**71** E8
Gateshead,Saltwell NE8 ..**70** E7
Prudhoe NE42 ......**50** E3
South Shields NE34 ......**59** F5
Whitburn SR6 ......**60** F1
Maple Rd NE21 ......**53** C2
Maple Row NE11 ......**54** B2
Maple St Ashington NE63 ...**6** D3
Jarrow NE32 ......**58** A7
Newcastle-u-T NE4 ......**100** B4
Maple Terr
Burnopfield NE16 ......**78** F6
Newcastle-u-T NE4 ......**100** B4
Shiney Row DH4 ......**90** A5
Maplebeck Cl SR3 ......**91** D5
Mapledene NE38 ......**83** E2
Mapledene Rd NE3 ......**37** F6
Maplewood
Chester le S DH2 ......**88** B4
Newcastle-u-T NE6 ......**56** B8
Maplewood Ave SR5 ....**74** F3
Maplewood Cres NE38 ...**83** B1
Maplewood Dr DH6 ......**97** F3
Maplewood Sch SR5 ....**74** F3
Maplewood St DH4 ......**89** E1
Mapperley Dr NE15 ......**53** E7
Marblet Ct NE11 ......**70** B7
Marbury Cl SR3 ......**91** D6
March Rd NE23 ......**29** B7
March Terr NE13 ......**27** A7
Marchburn La NE44 ......**62** E7
Marcia Ave SR6 ......**75** D3
Marconi Way NE11 ......**54** B2
Marcross Cl NE15 ......**36** B2
Marcross Dr SR3 ......**91** E5
Mardale NE37 ......**83** B7
Mardale Gdns NE9 ......**71** A3
Mardale Rd NE5 ......**37** B1
Mardale St DH5 ......**95** A2
Marden Ave NE30 ......**32** C3
Marden Bridge Mid Sch
NE25 ......**32** A4
Marden Cl NE61 ......**8** D7
Marden Cres NE26 ......**32** C4
Marden Ct NE26 ......**24** B7
Marden Farm Dr NE30 ...**32** B3
Marden High Sch NE30 ..**32** B3
Marden Rd NE26 ......**32** A4
Marden Rd S NE25 ......**32** B4
Marden Terr NE30 ......**32** C3
Mare Cl NE23 ......**23** A3
Mareburn Cres NE10 ....**71** E8
Maree Cl SR3 ......**91** E5
Margaret Alice St SR4 ..**85** E7
Margaret Collins Ho NE6 .**56** D6
Margaret Cotts NE25 ....**31** F2
Margaret Dr NE12 ......**40** A8
Margaret Gr NE34 ......**59** A5
Margaret Rd NE26 ......**32** C4
Margaret St SR2 ......**87** A2
Margaret Sutton Sch
NE34 ......**59** D6

Margaret Terr
Penshaw DH4 ......**90** C6
Rowlands Gill NE39 ......**67** C1
Tanfield Lea NE39 ......**79** C1
Margate St SR3 ......**92** A8
Marguerite Ct SR4 ......**102** B3
Maria St
New Silksworth SR3 ......**92** A7
Newcastle-u-T NE4 ......**54** E4
Marian Ct NE8 ......**101** A1
Marian Dr NE10 ......**57** C3
Marian Way
Ponteland NE20 ......**25** B3
South Shields NE34 ......**59** F3
Marie Curie Dr NE4 ....**54** F4
Marigold Ave NE10 ......**56** B2
Marigold Cres DH4 ......**89** E3
Marigold Ct SR4 ......**102** B3
Marigold Wlk NE34 ......**59** B5
Marina Ave SR6 ......**75** D3
Marina Ct SR6 ......**75** D3
Marina Dr
South Shields NE33 ......**42** E3
Whitley Bay NE25 ......**31** C4
Marina Gr SR6 ......**75** D3
Marina Terr
8 Ryhope SR2 ......**92** F6
Whitburn SR6 ......**60** F1
Marina View
Hebburn NE31 ......**57** D6
Wallsend NE28 ......**40** F2
Marine App NE33 ......**42** E2
Marine Ave NE26 ......**31** F5
Marine Ct E NE26 ......**32** A6
Marine Ct W NE26 ......**32** A6
Marine Dr Jarrow NE31 ...**58** A3
Ryhope SR2 ......**93** A8
Marine Gdns NE26 ......**32** A6
Marine Park Fst Sch
NE26 ......**32** A6
Marine Park Prim Sch
NE33 ......**42** D3
Marine St NE64 ......**7** E5
Marine Terr NE24 ......**17** E7
Marine View NE26 ......**24** C7
Marine Wlk SR6 ......**75** F2
Mariner Sq SR1 ......**103** C4
Mariners Point 8 NE30 .**42** D7
Mariners Wharf NE1 ....**56** A5
Mariners' Cotts NE33 ...**42** E3
Mariners' La NE30 ......**42** C7
Marion St SR2 ......**86** E4
Maritime Pl 4 NE61 ....**3** F1
Maritime St SR1 ......**103** A2
Maritime Terr SR1 ......**102** C2
Marius Ave NE15 ......**34** F2
Mariville E SR2 ......**93** A5
Mariville W SR2 ......**93** A5
Marjorie St NE23 ......**22** F5
Mark Rise DH5 ......**95** A5
Mark's La DH4 ......**94** A3
Markby Cl 3 SR3 ......**91** E5
Market La
Dunston NE11,NE16 ......**69** D8
Newcastle-u-T NE1 ......**99** B1
Market Pl Bedlington NE22 **15** F8
Blyth NE24 ......**17** E8
Corbridge NE45 ......**46** F5
2 Hexham NE46 ......**45** B5
Houghton-le-S DH5 ......**94** F8
Morpeth NE61 ......**8** F8
South Shields NE33 ......**42** C3
Market Place Ind Est
DH5 ......**90** F1
Market Sq Jarrow NE32 ..**58** B7
Lynemouth NE61 ......**2** B2
Sunderland SR1 ......**103** A2
Market St Blyth NE24 ....**17** E8
Dudley NE23 ......**29** A8
Hetton le H DH5 ......**95** B4
Hexham NE46 ......**45** B5
Newcastle-u-T NE1 ......**99** B1
Market Way NE11 ......**70** D6
Markham Ave SR6 ......**61** A1
Markham St SR2 ......**86** F2
Markington Dr SR2 ......**92** F5
Markle Gr DH5 ......**94** D5
Marlboro Ave NE16 ......**69** B8
Marlborough App NE3 ...**38** C7
Marlborough Ave NE3 ...**38** C7
Marlborough Cres
Gateshead NE9 ......**71** C3
Newcastle-u-T NE1 ......**100** C4
Marlborough Ct
Houghton-le-S DH5 ......**94** E6
Jarrow NE32 ......**58** B5
Newcastle-u-T NE3 ......**37** D7
Marlborough Ho NE26 ...**31** F6
Marlborough Rd
Sunderland SR4 ......**85** A3
Washington NE37 ......**83** F8
Marlborough St N NE33 .**59** D8
Marlborough St S NE33 .**59** D8
Marlborough Terr NE62 .**10** F4
Marleen Ave NE6 ......**56** C8
Marleen Ct 2 NE6 ......**56** C8
Marlesford Cl SR3 ......**91** D6
Marley Cres SR5 ......**74** F3
Marley Hill Com Prim Sch
NE16 ......**80** A8
Marlfield Ct NE5 ......**37** B3
Marlow Dr SR3 ......**91** D5
Marlow Pl NE12 ......**39** C6
Marlow St NE24 ......**17** D7
Marlow Way NE16 ......**68** F5
Marlowe Gdns NE8 ....**101** C1
Marlowe Pl DH5 ......**94** F7

Marlowe Wlk NE34 ......**59** A3
Marmion Rd NE6 ......**57** A8
Marmion Terr NE25 ......**31** F4
Marne St DH4 ......**90** C6
Marondale Ave NE6 ......**56** F7
Marquis Ave NE5 ......**36** C4
Marquis Cl NE12 ......**39** D5
Marquis Ct
Gateshead NE11 ......**70** D3
4 New Silksworth SR3 ...**92** B7
Prudhoe NE42 ......**50** E4
Marquisway NE11 ......**70** D2
Marr Ho SR4 ......**85** F7
Marr Rd NE31 ......**57** F5
Marris Ho NE2 ......**98** C3
Marsden Ave SR6 ......**60** F3
Marsden Cl NE34 ......**94** C8
Marsden Cliffs Nature
Reserve* NE34 ......**60** E6
Marsden Ct
Gateshead NE9 ......**71** D3
Whitburn SR6 ......**60** F1
Marsden La
Newcastle-u-T NE5 ......**37** A3
South Shields NE34 ......**60** C7
Marsden Prim Sch SR6 ..**60** F3
Marsden Rd Cleadon SR6 .**74** F8
South Shields NE34 ......**60** A7
Marsden St 6 NE33 ....**59** D8
Marsden View SR6 ......**60** F3
Marsh Ct NE11 ......**70** B7
Marshall St SR6 ......**75** D4
Marshall Wallis Rd NE33 .**59** C8
Marsham Cl Cleadon SR6 .**60** A2
Newcastle-u-T NE15 ......**53** E7
Marsham Rd 3 NE5 ....**36** E3
Marshes' Houses NE62 ..**11** D7
Marshmont Ave NE30 ...**32** C1
Marske Terr NE6 ......**56** E6
Marston NE12 ......**29** D4
Marston Wlk NE16 ......**68** F5
Martello Gdns NE7 ......**39** D2
Martha St DH9 ......**79** B2
Martin Ct NE38 ......**82** F2
Martin Hall NE32 ......**58** C6
Martin Rd NE28 ......**41** A4
Martin Terr 7 SR4 ......**85** F7
Martin Way NE13 ......**28** A6
Martindale Ave SR6 ....**75** C5
Martindale Pk DH5 ......**94** E8
Martindale Pl NE25 ......**23** E3
Martindale Wlk NE12 ....**29** C2
Marwell Dr NE37 ......**72** E2
Marwood Ct NE25 ......**31** D6
Marx Terr NE17 ......**77** C8
Mary Agnes St NE3 ....**38** A5
Mary Ave DH3 ......**82** B6
Mary Magdalene Bglws
NE2 ......**98** B4
Mary St Blaydon NE21 ...**53** C3
Blaydon,Winlaton NE21 ...**53** A2
New Silksworth SR3 ......**92** A8
Sunderland SR1 ......**102** C2
Mary Terr NE5 ......**37** A3
Mary's Pl NE6 ......**57** B6
Maryhill Cl NE4 ......**54** E4
Maryside Pl NE40 ......**51** F7
Mascot Ho 3 NE1 ......**98** C1
Masefield Ave NE16 ....**54** B1
Masefield Dr NE34 ......**59** A2
Masefield Pl NE8 ......**101** C2
Mason Ave NE26 ......**32** B5
Mason Rd NE28 ......**40** A4
Mason St
Brunswick Village NE13 ...**28** A6
4 Newcastle-u-T NE6 ...**56** C5
Mason View NE13 ......**28** B8
Massingham Way NE34 ..**59** B5
Mast La NE30 ......**32** B3
Master Mariners' Homes
NE30 ......**42** C7
Master's Cres NE42 ....**50** B2
Matamba Terr SR4 ......**102** B2
Matanzas St SR2 ......**86** E3
Matfen Ave
Hazlerigg NE13 ......**28** A4
Shiremoor NE27 ......**31** A2
Matfen Cl Blyth NE24 ....**17** C7
Newcastle-u-T NE15 ......**53** E6
Matfen Ct DH2 ......**88** A3
Matfen Dr SR3 ......**91** D6
Matfen Gdns NE28 ......**40** F5
Matfen Pl
Newcastle-u-T,Fawdon NE3 .**38** A6
Newcastle-u-T,Fenham NE4 .**54** F7
Matfen Terr NE64 ......**7** D3
Mather Rd NE4 ......**100** B4
Mathesons Gdns NE61 ...**8** F8
Matlock Gdns NE5 ......**36** F3
Matlock Rd NE32 ......**58** C5
Matlock Sq NE61 ......**2** A2
Matlock St SR1 ......**103** A3
Matthew Bank NE2 ......**38** E3
Matthew Cl NE6 ......**56** B6
Matthew Rd NE24 ......**17** F5
Matthew St 13 NE6 ....**56** B6
Maud St
Newcastle-u-T NE15 ......**53** C6
Sunderland SR6 ......**75** E4
Maud Terr
5 Shiremoor NE27 ......**30** E1
Tanfield DH9 ......**79** D3
Maud's Terr NE64 ......**7** E5
Maude Gdns 7 NE28 ...**40** B1
Maudlin Pl 2 NE5 ......**37** D1
Maudlin St DH5 ......**95** B6
Mauds La SR1 ......**103** B3
Maughan St NE24 ......**17** F7

Maurice Rd NE28 ......**57** B8
Maurice Road Ind Est
NE28 ......**57** B8
Mautland St DH4 ......**90** E1
Maxton Cl SR3 ......**91** D5
Maxwell NE33 ......**42** C2
Maxwell St Gateshead NE8 **70** D7
South Shields NE33 ......**42** C2
2 Sunderland SR4 ......**85** F7
Maxwell St Ind Est 6
NE33 ......**42** C2
May Ave Ryton NE40 ....**52** C6
Winlaton Mill NE21 ......**68** C7
May Gr SR6 ......**60** F3
May St Birtley DH3 ......**82** C4
Blaydon NE21 ......**53** B1
South Shields NE33 ......**42** D1
Sunderland SR4 ......**102** B3
Maybury Villas NE12 ....**39** A5
Maydown Cl SR5 ......**84** F8
Mayfair Ct NE31 ......**57** D5
Mayfair Gdns
Gateshead NE8 ......**71** A8
Ponteland NE20 ......**25** F6
South Shields NE34 ......**59** E7
Mayfair Rd NE2 ......**38** C2
Mayfield Morpeth NE61 ...**8** E7
Whickham NE16 ......**69** B5
Mayfield Ave
Cramlington NE23 ......**22** C6
Throckley NE15 ......**35** C1
Mayfield Ct SR6 ......**75** D3
Mayfield Dr SR6 ......**75** B8
Mayfield Gdns
Jarrow NE32 ......**58** A6
Throckley NE15 ......**35** C1
Wallsend NE28 ......**40** A3
Mayfield Gr SR4 ......**85** A2
Mayfield Pl NE13 ......**28** A5
Mayfield Rd
Newcastle-u-T NE3 ......**38** C4
Sunderland SR4 ......**85** A6
Mayfield Terr NE5 ......**37** E1
Mayo Dr 1 SR3 ......**91** E5
Mayoral Way NE11 ......**70** D3
Maypole Ct 8 SR5 ......**75** B2
Mayswood Rd SR6 ......**75** D3
Maytree Ho NE4 ......**100** A4
Maywood Cl NE3 ......**37** E4
Mazine Terr DH6 ......**97** E2
McAnany Ave NE34 ......**59** D5
McAteer Ct DH6 ......**97** E1
McClaren Way DH4 ......**90** F7
McCracken Cl NE3 ......**38** C8
McCracken Dr NE13 ......**28** C7
McCutcheon Ct NE6 ....**56** E3
McCutcheon St 7 SR7 ..**92** E1
McErlane Sq NE10 ......**57** A1
McEwan Gdns NE4 ......**54** F5
McGowen Ct 6 NE6 ....**56** C5
McIlvenna Gdns NE28 ...**40** B4
Mcintyre Hall NE31 ....**57** F7
Mcintyre Rd NE31 ......**57** F7
McKendrick Villas NE5 ..**37** D1
McLennan Ct NE38 ......**83** D6
McNamara Rd NE28 ......**40** F3
Mcnulty Ct NE23 ......**28** F8
Meacham Way NE16 ....**69** A5
Mead Ave NE12 ......**39** E8
Mead Cres NE12 ......**39** E8
Mead Way NE12 ......**39** F8
Mead Wlk NE6 ......**56** F6
Meadow Bank Dr NE62 ..**10** E8
Meadow Brook Dr NE17 .**66** C2
Meadow Cl Blaydon NE21 .**52** F1
Dunston NE11 ......**54** C1
Houghton-le-S DH5 ......**94** F7
Longbenton NE12 ......**39** B7
Ryton NE40 ......**52** D5
Seghill NE23 ......**22** F2
Meadow Ct
Bedlington NE22 ......**10** E1
Ponteland NE20 ......**25** E5
Meadow Dr
Seaton Burn NE13 ......**28** C8
Sunderland,East Herrington
SR3 ......**91** B6
Sunderland,South Hylton
SR4 ......**85** A5
Meadow Gdns SR3 ......**86** B3
Meadow Gr SR4 ......**85** B5
Meadow Grange DH4 ...**89** E2
Meadow Ho SR3 ......**92** A5
Meadow La
Crawcrook NE40 ......**52** A4
Dunston NE11 ......**54** F1
Sunderland SR3 ......**91** B6
Meadow Laws NE34 ....**60** A5
Meadow Pk NE44 ......**62** F7
Meadow Rd
Newcastle-u-T NE15 ......**53** D8
Seaton Sluice NE26 ......**24** B6
Wallsend NE28 ......**40** F1
Whitley Bay NE25 ......**31** D4
Meadow Rise
Gateshead NE9 ......**71** C5
Newcastle-u-T NE5 ......**37** B4
Meadow St DH5 ......**94** C3
Meadow Terr DH4 ......**90** C6
Meadow Vale SR2 ......**86** B4
Meadow View Dipton DH9 **78** E1
Hedworth NE32 ......**73** D8
New Hartley NE25 ......**23** D6
North Shields NE29 ......**41** A4
Sunderland SR3 ......**91** B6
Meadow Well Sta NE29 ..**41** E4
Meadow Well Way NE29 .**41** E4
Meadow Wlk NE40 ......**52** D5

Meadowbank NE23 ......**29** A8
Meadowbrook Dr NE10 ..**72** C7
Meadowcroft Mews
NE8 ......**101** A1
Meadowdale Cres
Bedlington NE22 ......**10** D1
Newcastle-u-T NE5 ......**37** D3
Meadowdale Mid Sch
NE22 ......**10** E1
Meadowfield
Ashington NE63 ......**7** A2
Ponteland NE20 ......**25** E7
Whitley Bay NE25 ......**31** D5
Meadowfield Ave NE3 ...**38** A6
Meadowfield Cres NE40 .**52** A4
Meadowfield Ct NE20 ...**25** E7
Meadowfield Dr SR6 ....**60** B1
Meadowfield Est NE9 ...**71** F1
Meadowfield Gdns NE6 ..**40** A1
Meadowfield Ind Est
NE20 ......**25** E6
Meadowfield Pk NE20 ...**25** E6
Meadowfield Pk S NE43 .**64** C5
Meadowfield Rd
Newcastle-u-T NE3 ......**38** B4
Stocksfield NE43 ......**64** C5
Meadowfield Terr
Longbenton NE12 ......**29** F1
Stocksfield NE43 ......**64** D7
Meadows Crest NE43 ....**65** A3
Meadows La DH4,DH5 ...**94** B3
Meadows The
Bournmoor DH4 ......**89** D3
Burnopfield NE16 ......**79** A4
Newcastle-u-T NE3 ......**37** F6
Ryton NE40 ......**52** D5
West Rainton DH4 ......**94** A3
Meadowside SR2 ......**86** B4
Meadowsweet Cl 3
NE24 ......**17** C4
Meadowvale
Backworth NE27 ......**30** D3
Ponteland NE20 ......**25** A2
Meadway Dr NE12 ......**39** F8
Meal Mkt 7 NE46 ......**45** B5
Means Ct NE23 ......**29** B6
Means Dr NE23 ......**29** B5
Medburn Ave NE30 ......**32** C2
Medburn Rd
Newcastle-u-T NE15 ......**53** C7
Seaton Delaval NE25 ......**23** E2
Medina Cl SR3 ......**91** E5
Medlar NE9 ......**71** D4
Medlar Cl DH4 ......**89** F6
Medomsley Gdns NE9 ...**71** E4
Medomsly St SR4 ......**102** A3
Medway NE32 ......**58** C2
Medway Ave NE31 ......**57** E3
Medway Cres NE8 ......**71** B8
Medway Gdns
Sunderland SR4 ......**85** D4
Tynemouth NE30 ......**42** A7
Medway Pl NE23 ......**16** D1
Medwood Ct NE3 ......**37** E5
Medwyn Cl Blyth NE24 ..**17** D5
Bournmoor DH4 ......**89** E3
Megstone Ave NE23 ....**22** A5
Megstone Ct NE12 ......**29** E4
Melbeck Dr DH2 ......**81** E2
Melbourne Cres NE25 ...**31** E3
Melbourne Ct
Gateshead NE8 ......**101** B3
Newcastle-u-T NE1 ......**99** C1
Melbourne Gdns NE34 ..**58** F3
Melbourne Pl SR4 ......**85** E4
Melbourne St NE1 ......**99** B1
Melbury NE25 ......**31** D6
Melbury Ct SR6 ......**75** D3
Melbury Rd NE7 ......**39** A1
Meldon Ave
Newcastle-u-T NE3 ......**37** F7
Sherburn DH6 ......**96** A1
South Shields NE34 ......**59** E6
Meldon Cl NE28 ......**40** E3
Meldon Ct NE40 ......**51** E3
Meldon Gdns
Dunston NE11 ......**70** A5
Stakeford NE62 ......**10** F8
Meldon Ho NE24 ......**17** B8
Meldon Rd SR4 ......**85** F7
Meldon St NE28 ......**41** C1
Meldon Terr
Greenside NE40 ......**51** F1
Newbiggin-by-t-S NE64 ....**7** D3
Newcastle-u-T NE6 ......**56** B8
Newcastle-u-T NE21 ......**67** F8
Melgarve Dr SR3 ......**91** E5
Melkington Ct NE5 ......**37** B3
Melkridge Gdns NE7 ....**39** D3
Melkridge Pl NE23 ......**22** A5
Mellendean Cl NE5 ......**37** B3
Melling Rd NE23 ......**22** A6
Melmerby Cl NE3 ......**38** D7
Melness Rd NE13 ......**28** A5
Melock Ct NE13 ......**28** A5
Melrose NE38 ......**83** D3
Melrose Ave
Backworth NE27 ......**30** C5
Bebside NE22 ......**11** D1
Gateshead NE9 ......**71** A5
Hebburn NE31 ......**57** E3
Seaton Delaval NE25 ......**23** D2
Tynemouth NE30 ......**32** A2
Whitley Bay NE25 ......**31** F4
Melrose Cl
Newcastle-u-T NE3 ......**28** B2
Newcastle-u-T,Bell's Close
NE15 ......**53** E6

Melrose Ct NE22 ....11 D2

Melrose Gdns
Newbottle DH4 ....90 C3
Sunderland SR6 ....75 D4
Wallsend NE28 ....41 A4

Melrose Gr NE32 ....58 E4

Melrose Terr
Bedlington NE22 ....11 D2
Newbiggin-by-t-S NE64 ....7 D3

Melrose Villas NE22 .....11 D2

Melsonby Cl SR3 ....91 D6

Meltham Ct NE15 ....36 B2

Meltham Dr SR3 ....91 E5

Melton Ave NE6 ....56 F5

Melton Cres NE26 ....24 D5

Melton Dr NE25 ....23 D6

Melvaig Cl SR3 ....91 E5

Melville Ave NE24 ....17 D5

Melville Gdns NE25 ......31 C4

Melville Gr NE7 ....39 A4

Melville St DH3 ....88 C2

Melvin Pl **5** NE5 ......37 B2

Melvyn Gdns SR6 ....75 E3

Membury Cl **4** SR3 ....91 E5

Memorial Sq NE64 ....7 D5

Menai Ct **9** SR3 ......91 F6

Menceforth Cotts DH2 ...88 B4

Mendham Cl NE10 ....71 E6

Mendip Ave DH2 ....88 C2

Mendip Cl Ashington NE63 .6 E1
Tynemouth NE29 ....31 F1

Mendip Dr NE38 ....83 B3

Mendip Gdns NE11 ....70 B6

Mendip Way NE12 ....38 F6

Mentieth Cl NE38 ....83 B3

Menvill Pl SR1 ....103 B2

Mercantile Rd DH4 ......94 C7

Merchants Wharf **10** NE6 56 C4

Mercia Way NE15 ....53 E5

Mere Knolls Rd SR6 .....75 E4

Meredith Gdns NE10 ....101 C1

Meresyde NE10 ....72 A7

Meresyde Ct NE10 ....72 A7

Merevale Cl NE37 ....72 E2

Merganser Lodge **10**
NE10 ....71 D8

Meridan Way NE7 ....39 D3

Meridian Ho **3** NE33 ...59 E8

Merlay Dr NE13 ....27 B6

Merlay Hall NE6 ....57 A4

Merle Gdns Morpeth NE61 .3 C2
16 Newcastle-u-T NE6 ...56 C5

Merle Terr SR4 ....85 E7

Merley Gate NE61 ....9 A6

Merlin Cres NE28 ....40 F3

Merlin Ct **17** NE10 .....56 D1

Merlin Dr DH3 ....88 D7

Merlin Pl NE12 ....39 A7

Merlin Way Earsdon NE27 .31 A1
Shiremoor NE27 ....41 A8

Merrick Ho **21** SR3 ....91 F6

Merrington Cl
New Hartley NE25 ....23 D7
Silksworth SR3 ....91 D6

Merrion Cl SR3 ....91 D6

Merryfield Gdns NE16 ...75 E3

Merryshields Terr NE43 ..64 C8

Mersey Ct **17** SR3 .....91 F6

Mersey Pl NE8 ....71 B8

Mersey Rd Gateshead NE8 71 B8
Hebburn NE31 ....57 F3

Mersey St NE17 ....66 C1

Merton Ct NE4 ....54 D4

Merton Rd NE20 ....25 E6

Merton Sq **3** NE24 .....17 E8

Merton Way NE20 ....25 E6

Methuen St NE9 ....71 A8

Methven Way NE23 ......16 C2

Metro Ctr Sta NE11 ......54 D2

Metro Ret Pk NE11 ....54 B2

MetroCentre The NE11 ...54 C2

MetroCentre Indoor Theme
Pk★ NE11 ....54 C2

Mews Ct DH5 ....94 E8

Mews Gdns NE1 ....99 B1

Mews The Blaydon NE21 ..53 E2
Fence Houses DH4 ....94 A7
Gateshead NE10 ....72 B8
Newcastle-u-T NE1 ......99 A2
North Shields NE30 .....42 A6
Sunderland SR3 ....91 B7
Tynemouth NE30 ....42 E8

Michaelgate **24** NE6 ...56 C6

Mickle Cl NE37 ....83 A6

Mickleton Gdns SR3 .....86 B2

Micklewood Cl NE61 ......4 E6

Mickley Fst Sch NE43 ....49 E1

Middle Chare DH3 ....88 D3

Middle Cl NE38 ....83 B1

Middle Dr Ponteland NE20 25 C3
Woolsington NE13 ....26 C4

Middle Engine La
Shiremoor NE27,NE28,NE29 41 A7
Wallsend NE27,NE28,NE29 .40 F5

Middle Farm Ct NE22 ....22 B7

Middle Garth **1** NE5 ...37 D2

Middle Gate Morpeth NE61 .8 F6
Newcastle-u-T NE5 ......36 D1

Middle Gn NE25 ....31 C4

Middle Row
Great Lumley DH4 ....89 E1
Ryton NE40 ....52 E3

Middle St Blyth NE24 ....17 B4
Corbridge NE45 ....46 F5
Newcastle-u-T NE6 ......56 F6
Sunderland SR1 ....102 C3
Sunderland SR1 ....103 A3
Tynemouth NE30 ....42 E7

Middle St E NE6 ....57 A6

Middlebrook NE20 ....25 B3

Middlefields Ind Est
NE33 ....59 B6

Middleham Cl DH2 ....81 E1

Middleham Ct SR5 ....74 E3

Middleton Ave
Newcastle-u-T NE4 ......54 E6
Rowlands Gill NE39 .....67 F1

Middleton Cl SR7 ....92 E1

Middleton Ct NE2 ....99 C3

Middleton St NE24 ......17 E7

Middlewood Pk NE4 .....54 E7

Midfield Dr **11** SR6 ....75 E2

Midgley Dr SR3 ....91 E5

Midhurst Ave NE34 ......60 A8

Midhurst Cl SR3 ....91 D6

Midhurst Rd NE12 ....39 D7

Midlothian Cl SR4 ......85 D3

Midmoor Rd SR4 ....85 E7

Midsomer Cl SR3 ....91 D5

Midway NE6 ....57 A6

Milbanke Cl DH2 ....81 F1

Milbanke St DH2 ....81 F1

Milburn Cl
Chester le S DH3 ....88 C2
Hexham NE46 ....44 F2

Milburn Dr NE15 ....54 B6

Milburn Rd NE63 ....6 D2

Milburn Terr
Shiney Row DH4 ....90 B6
Stakeford NE62 ....11 C6

Milcombe Cl SR3 ....91 D6

Milecastle Ct NE5 ......36 D2

Milecastle Fst Sch NE5 .36 C2

Milfield Ave
Shiremoor NE27 ....31 A3
Wallsend NE28 ....40 C4

Milford Gdns NE3 ......28 B1

Milford Rd NE15 ....54 C5

Military Rd
Heddon-on-t-W NE15 ....34 C3
North Shields NE30 ....42 B6

Military Vehicle Mus★
NE2 ....99 A4

Milk Mkt NE1 ....99 C1

Milkhope Ctr NE13 ......20 D5

Milkwell NE45 ....47 A6

Milkwell La NE45 ....47 A7

Mill Bank SR5 ....75 C4

Mill Cl North Shields NE29 41 A8
Riding Mill NE44 ....62 F7

Mill Cres Hebburn NE31 .57 C2
Penshaw DH4 ....90 B6

Mill Ct Bournmoor DH4 ..89 E2
Ellington NE61 ....1 C4
Hamsterley NE17 ....77 B6

Mill Dam NE33 ....42 B2

Mill Dene View NE32 ....58 C5

Mill Dyke Cl NE25 ......31 C6

Mill Farm Cl NE4 ......98 B1

Mill Farm Rd NE39 .....78 A5

Mill Gr South Shields NE34 60 B4
Tynemouth NE30 ....42 C8

Mill Grange NE44 ......63 A8

Mill Hill DH5 ....94 D6

Mill Hill Prim Sch SR3 .92 A5

Mill Hill Rd
Newcastle-u-T NE5 .....53 F8
Silksworth SR3 ....92 A6

Mill Ho NE2 ....98 B4

Mill La Ebchester DH8 ...76 E4
Hebburn NE10,NE31 .....57 E2
Heddon-on-t-W NE15 ....34 F3
Newcastle-u-T NE4 ....100 A4
North Shields NE29 ....42 B4
Seghill NE23 ....22 D1
Sherburn DH6 ....96 A1
Slaley NE44 ....62 A1
Urpeth DH2 ....81 D1
Whitburn SR6 ....60 F2
Winlaton Mill NE21 ....68 B7

Mill Pit DH4 ....90 B6

Mill Race Cl NE17 ......77 B6

Mill Rd Chopwell NE17 ...77 B8
Gateshead NE8 ....101 C4

Mill Rise NE3 ....38 C4

Mill St SR4 ....102 B3

Mill Terr
Houghton-le-S DH5 .....94 D6
Shiney Row DH4 ....90 B6

Mill View Gateshead NE10 72 B7
West Boldon NE36 ......74 A7

Mill View Ave SR6 ......75 D3

Mill View Rise NE42 ....50 D4

Mill Way NE15,NE42 ....50 D7

Millais Gdns NE34 ......59 C2

Millbank Cres NE22 .....11 A1

Millbank Ind Est **3** NE33 42 C2

Millbank Pl NE22 ....16 B8

Millbank Rd
Bedlington NE22 ....11 B1
Newcastle-u-T NE6 .....57 A4

Millbank Terr NE22 .....11 B1

Millbeck Gdns NE9 .....71 B2

Millbeck Gr DH5 ....94 E7

Millbrook Gateshead NE10 71 E7
North Shields NE29 .....41 B5

Millbrook Rd NE23 ......16 D1

Millburn St SR4 ....102 B3

Milldale Ave NE24 ......17 D6

Milldene Ave NE30 ......42 C8

Millennium Way SR5 ...102 C4

Miller St NE8 ....70 D8

Miller Terr SR3 ....92 A8

Miller's La NE16 ....54 B1

Millers Hill NE4 ....90 C6

Millers Rd NE6 ....56 C7

Millfield Bedlington NE22 16 A7
Seaton Sluice NE26 .....24 D5

Millfield Ave NE3 ......37 E3

Millfield Cl
Chester le S DH2 ....88 A1
Newburn NE15 ....52 F7

Millfield Ct
Bedlington NE22 ....16 A8
Hexham NE46 ....44 F5
Seaton Sluice NE26 ....24 D5
Whickham NE16 ....69 C7

Millfield E NE22 ....16 A7

Millfield Gdns Blyth NE24 12 D1
Gateshead NE10 ....71 C8
Hexham NE46 ....44 F5
Tynemouth NE30 ....42 C8

Millfield Gr NE30 ......42 C8

Millfield La NE15 ....52 F8

Millfield N NE22 ....16 A8

Millfield Rd
Riding Mill NE44 ......62 F7
Whickham NE16 ....69 B6

Millfield S NE22 ....16 A7

Millfield Sta SR4 .....102 B3

Millfield Terr
Hexham NE46 ....44 F5
Whitburn SR6 ....60 F2

Millfield W NE22 ....16 A8

Millford Cl NE10 ....72 B6

Millford Ct NE10 ....72 B6

Millgrove View NE3 .....37 F3

Milling Ct NE8 ....100 C2

Millne Ct NE22 ....10 F1

Millom Pl NE9 ....71 B4

Mills Gdns NE28 ....40 B3

Millside NE6 ....8 F8

Millthorp Cl SR2 ....87 A1

Millview Dr NE30 ......42 C8

Millway Gateshead NE9 ..71 A7
Seaton Sluice NE26 ....24 D5

Millway Gr NE26 ....24 D5

Milne Way NE3 ....37 F6

Milner Cres NE21 ......53 A1

Milner St NE33 ....42 E2

Milrig Cl SR3 ....91 E5

Milsted Ct SR3 ....91 D5

Milton Ave Hebburn NE31 .57 E6
Houghton-le-S DH5 .....94 F7

Milton Cl NE2 ....99 C3

Milton Gn NE2 ....99 C3

Milton Gr Ashington NE63 .6 F3
North Shields NE29 .....41 F6
Prudhoe NE42 ....50 B2

Milton Pl
Newcastle-u-T NE2 .....99 C3
North Shields NE29 .....41 F6
22 Springwell NE9 ....71 F1

Milton Rd NE16 ....69 B8

Milton Sq NE8 ....56 A2

Milton St Greenside NE40 .51 E1
Jarrow NE32 ....58 B8
1 South Shields NE33 ..59 D8
Sunderland SR4 ....102 A3

Milton Terr NE29 ....41 F6

Milvain Ave NE4 ....54 E6

Milvain Cl NE8 ....101 C1

Milvain St NE8 ....101 C1

Milverton Ct NE3 ....37 C6

Mimosa Dr NE31 ....57 E3

Mimosa Pl NE4 ....54 D8

Minden St NE1 ....99 B1

Mindrum Terr
Newcastle-u-T NE6 .....56 F5
North Shields NE29 .....41 D4

Mindrum Way NE25 ......23 D3

Minehead Gdns **9** SR3 .92 A8

Miner's Cotts NE16 .....69 C6

Miners Cotts NE15 ......54 A7

Minerva Cl NE5 ....36 C4

Mingarry DH3 ....82 E2

Mingary Cl DH5 ....94 C4

Minorca Cl SR1 ....103 C2

Minorca Pl NE3 ....37 F3

Minskip Cl SR3 ....91 E5

Minster Ct NE8 ....101 C3

Minster Gr NE15 ....36 B3

Minster Par NE32 ......58 C7

Minting Pl NE23 ....22 A5

Minton Ct NE29 ....41 F4

Minton La NE29 ....41 F4

Minton Sq **4** SR4 .....85 E7

Mirk La NE8 ....101 B4

Mirlaw Rd NE23 ....21 F5

Mistletoe Rd NE2 ......38 E1

Mitchell Ave
Newcastle-u-T NE2 .....38 E2
Whitley Bay NE25 ......31 D4

Mitchell Dr NE63 ....7 D3

Mitchell Gdns NE34 ....59 F7

Mitchell St Birtley DH3 ..82 C4
Crawcrook NE40 ....51 A4
Newcastle-u-T NE6 .....57 B5

Mitchell Terr DH9 .....79 B2

Mitchell's Bldgs NE9 ...72 A1

Mitford Ave Blyth NE24 ..17 C6
Pegswood NE61 ....4 E4
Seaton Delaval NE25 ...23 C3

Mitford Cl
Chester le S DH3 ....88 D8
Washington NE38 ......83 B4

Mitford Dr Ashington NE63 .6 D2
Newcastle-u-T NE5 .....37 B2

Mitford Dr continued
Sherburn DH6 ....96 A2

Mitford Gdns
Dunston NE11 ....70 A5
Stakeford NE62 ....10 F8
Wallsend NE28 ....40 F5
Wideopen NE13 ....28 C6

Mitford Pl NE3 ....38 A6

Mitford Rd Morpeth NE61 .3 E1
South Shields NE34 ....59 E6

Mitford St
North Shields NE28 ....41 C2
Sunderland SR6 ....75 D4

Mitford Terr NE32 .....58 B2

Mitford Way NE13 ......27 B7

Mithras Gdns NE15 ....34 C2

Mitre Ind Est NE33 ....59 B7

Mitre Pl NE33 ....59 B7

Moat Gdns NE10 ....72 C8

Mobray First Sch NE62 .10 C7

Modder St NE6 ....56 F3

Model Dwellings **1**
NE38 ....83 E4

Model Terr NE4 ....90 A8

Modigars La NE43 ......64 F6

Moffat Ave NE32 ....58 E4

Moffat Cl NE29 ....41 C8

Moine Gdns SR6 ....75 E3

Moir Terr SR2 ....93 A6

Molesdon Cl NE30 ......32 A1

Molineux Cl **6** NE6 ...56 B6

Molineux Ct **8** NE6 ...56 B6

Molineux St NE6 ....56 B6

Mollyfair Cl NE40 ......52 A4

Monarch Rd NE4 ......100 A2

Monarch Terr NE21 ....53 C2

Monarch Way SR3 ......91 C5

Monastery Ct **11** NE32 .58 B7

Monday Cres NE4 ......98 B2

Monday Pl NE4 ....98 B2

Monk Ct NE8 ....101 C2

Monk St
Newcastle-u-T NE1 .....98 C1
Sunderland SR6 ....75 D1

Monk's Terr NE46 ......45 D4

Monkchester Gn NE6 ...56 E4

Monkchester Rd NE6 ...56 E4

Monkdale Ave NE24 .....17 A6

Monkhouse Ave NE30 ...32 A1

Monkhouse Prim Sch
NE30 ....32 B1

Monkridge
Newcastle-u-T NE15 ...36 B2
Whitley Bay NE26 ......31 E7

Monkridge Ct NE3 .....38 E4

Monkridge Gdns NE11 ..70 A7

Monks Ave NE25 ....31 D3

Monks Mdws NE46 ......45 D4

Monks Park Way NE12 ..39 A6

Monks Rd NE25 ....31 C3

Monks Ridge NE61 ....8 D7

Monks Way NE30 ....32 C1

Monks Wood NE29 .....41 F8

Monkseaton Com High Sch
NE25 ....31 E2

Monkseaton Dr NE25,
NE26 ....31 E6

Monkseaton Mid Sch
NE25 ....31 E4

Monkseaton Rd NE25 ...31 B5

Monkseaton Sta NE25 ..31 D5

Monkseaton Terr NE63 ..6 E1

Monksfeld NE10 ....71 E7

Monksfield Cl **6** SR3 ..91 F5

Monkside
Cramlington NE23 ......21 F5
Newcastle-u-T NE6 .....56 D8

Monkside Cl NE38 .....83 B2

Monkstone Ave NE30 ...42 C8

Monkstone Cl NE30 ....42 C8

Monkstone Cres NE30 ..32 C1

Monkstone Grange NE30 32 B1

Monksway NE32 ....58 E6

Monkswood Sq SR3 ....92 B6

Monkton NE10 ....71 E6

Monkton Ave NE34 .....59 A4

Monkton Bsns Pk NE31 .57 F2

Monkton Bsns Pk S NE10 57 F1

Monkton Hall NE31 .....57 F4

Monkton Hall Hospl
NE31 ....57 F4

Monkton Inf Sch NE34 ..59 A4

Monkton Jun Sch NE34 .58 F4

Monkton La Hebburn NE32 57 F4
Jarrow NE31,NE32 ......57 F2

Monkton Rd NE32 ......58 B7

Monkton Terr NE32 ....58 C6

Monkwearmouth Hospl
SR5 ....75 C2

Monkwearmouth Sch
SR5 ....75 C5

Monkwearmouth Station
Mus★ SR5 ....103 A4

Monmouth Gdns NE28 ..41 A4

Monroe Pl NE5 ....37 D2

Mons Ave NE31 ....57 E6

Mons Cres DH4 ....90 C6

Montagu Ave NE3 ......38 A2

Montagu Prim Sch NE3 .37 E2

Montague Ct NE9 ......70 F8

Montague St
Newcastle-u-T NE15 ...53 D6
Sunderland SR6 ....75 D3

Monterey Silksworth SR3 .91 E5
Washington NE37 ......72 C1

Montford Cl SR3 ....91 D5

Montgomery Pl NE3 ....37 F3

Montpellier Pl NE3 ....37 F3

Montpellier Terr SR2 ..86 E3

Montrose Cl NE25 ......23 D6

Montrose Cres NE9 ....71 B7

Montrose Dr NE10 .....72 C7

Montrose Gdns
Morpeth NE61 ....8 F7
Sunderland SR3 ....86 A3

Monument Mall Sh Ctr
NE1 ....99 A1

Monument Sta NE1 .....99 A1

Monument Terr
11 Birtley DH3 ......82 C4
Penshaw DH4 ....90 A8

Monument View DH4 ....90 B8

Moonfield NE46 ....45 B4

Moor Cl Sunderland SR1 103 C3
Tynemouth NE29 ....41 C8

Moor Cres NE3 ....38 C3

Moor Crest Terr **2** NE29 41 F8

Moor Croft NE64 ....7 E5

Moor Ct Bournmoor DH4 .89 E3

Moor Edge
Newcastle-u-T NE5 .....38 B2
Whitburn SR6 ....75 E8

Moor Edge Prim Sch
NE12 ....29 C3

Moor Edge Rd NE27 ...30 E4

Moor Gdns NE29 ....41 C8

Moor Grange NE42 .....50 D1

Moor Ho NE4 ....98 B2

Moor La Cleadon SR6 ...75 A7
Newcastle-u-T NE5 .....37 D4
Ponteland NE20 ....25 C4
South Shields NE34 ....59 E6
Stannington NE61 ......14 C6
Whitburn SR6 ....75 D8

Moor La E NE34 ....59 F7

Moor Park Ct NE29 ....41 C7

Moor Park Rd NE29 ....41 C7

Moor Pl NE3 ....38 C3

Moor Rd NE42 ....65 E7

Moor Rd N NE3 ....38 D4

Moor Rd S NE2,NE3 ....38 D3

Moor St SR1 ....103 B3

Moor Terr SR1 ....103 C3

Moor View
Crawcrook NE40 ....52 A4
High Pittington DH6 ...96 D4
Killingworth NE12 .....29 C4
Newbiggin-by-t-S NE64 ..7 E5
Whitburn SR6 ....75 E8

Moor View Cl NE61 ......4 E3

Moor View Wlk NE12 ...29 C4

Moorcroft Cl NE15 .....53 D7

Moorcroft Rd NE15 ....53 E6

Moordale Ave NE24 ....17 A6

Moore Ave Dunston NE11 70 A8
South Shields NE34 ....59 F6

Moore Cres DH3 ....82 C6

Moore Cres N DH5 .....94 E7

Moore Cres S DH5 .....94 E7

Moore Ct NE15 ....52 B7

Moore St NE8 ....56 A1

Moorfield NE2 ....38 D3

Moorfield Gdns SR6 ....75 A8

Moorfields NE61 ....9 A6

Moorfoot Ave DH2 .....88 C2

Moorfoot Gdns NE11 ...70 A7

Moorhead NE5 ....37 E1

Moorhead Mews NE5 ...37 E1

Moorhouse Cl NE34 ....59 D5

Moorhouse Est NE63 ....6 F3

Moorhouse Gdns DH5 ..95 B2

Moorhouse La NE63 ....6 F3

Moorhouses Rd NE29 ..41 C7

Moorings The **8** NE6 ..56 C4

Moorland Ave NE22 ...11 E3

Moorland Cotts **6** NE22 11 D3

Moorland Cres
Bedlington NE22 ....11 E3
Newcastle-u-T NE6 .....56 E7

Moorland Ct NE22 .....11 E3

Moorland Dr NE22 .....11 E3

Moorland Ho NE5 ......37 C2

Moorland Villas NE22 ..11 E3

Moorland Way NE23 ...15 E1

Moorlands Dipton DH9 ..78 E1
Hedworth NE32 ....58 D1
Prudhoe NE42 ....50 E1

Moormill NE11 ....81 D6

Moormill La NE11 .....81 E6

Moors Cl DH4 ....94 B8

Moorsburn Dr DH4 ....90 C1

Moorsfield DH4 ....94 B8

Moorside Hedworth NE32 58 C1
Longbenton NE12 ......29 B2
Washington NE37 ......83 B7

Moorside Com Prim Sch
NE4 ....98 A2

Moorside Cl NE5 ....37 E1

Moorside N NE4 ....54 F8

Moorside Pl NE4 ......54 F8

Moorside Rd SR3 ......91 D5

Moorside S NE4 ....54 F7

Moorsley Rd DH5 ......94 F2

Moorvale La NE5 ......37 E2

Moorview Cres NE5 ...37 E2

Moorway NE37 ....83 B6

Moorway Dr NE15 .....53 E7

Moraine Cres NE17 ....77 B6

Moralee Cl NE7 ....39 D3

Moran St SR6 ....75 D4

Moray Cl DH3 ....82 D1

Moray St SR6 ....75 D3

Morcott Gdns NE29 ....41 F4

Morden St NE1 ....99 A2
Mordey Cl SR2 ....103 B1
Morecambe Par NE31 ..58 A2
Moreland Rd NE34 ......59 D3
Moreland St SR6 ....75 D2
Moresby Rd NE23 ....16 C2
Morgan Bsns Ctr NE12 ..29 B5
Morgan St SR5 ....75 B2
Morgans Way NE21 ....53 A2
Morinda Cl DH4 ....89 F5
Morland Ave NE38 .....83 E4
Morland Gdns NE9 .....71 B7
Morley Ave NE10 ......57 B2
Morley Ct **16** NE6 ....56 C7
Morley Hill Rd NE5 ....53 F8
Morley Pl NE27 ....30 F4
Morley Terr
Fence Houses DH4 .....90 A1
6 Gateshead NE10 ...71 D8
Morningside NE38 .....88 B8
Morningside Ct **5** DH3 ..88 C4
Mornington Ave NE3 ...37 F3
Morpeth All Saints CE Fst
Sch NE61 ....3 D2
Morpeth Ave Jarrow NE32 58 B3
Pegswood NE61 ....4 E4
South Shields NE34 ...59 E7
Wideopen NE13 ....28 C7
Morpeth Chantry Bagpipe
Mus★ NE61 ....9 A8
Morpeth Chantry Mid Sch
NE61 ....3 E1
Morpeth Cl
Guide Post NE62 ......10 C1
Washington NE38 .....83 A4
Morpeth Clock Twr★
NE61 ....8 F8
Morpeth Collingwood Sch
NE61 ....9 B7
Morpeth Cottage Hospl
NE61 ....8 F6
Morpeth Ct NE61 ......9 A8
Morpeth Dr SR3 ....91 D6
Morpeth Fst Sch NE61 ..9 A8
Morpeth Newminster Mid
Sch NE61 ....3 E1
Morpeth Rd Ashington NE63 5 F4
Guide Post NE62 ......10 E7
Morpeth Road Fst Sch
NE24 ....17 D8
Morpeth St NE2 ......98 B4
Morpeth Sta NE61 .....9 B4
Morpeth Stobhillgate Fst Sch
NE61 ....9 B7
Morpeth Terr NE34 ....59 B3
Morris Ave NE34 ....59 B3
Morris Cres NE35 .....74 A8
Morris Ct NE23 ....29 B8
Morris Gdns NE10 ....72 B8
Morris Rd NE16 ......69 B8
Morris St Birtley DH3 ...82 C4
Gateshead NE8 ......70 C8
Washington NE37 .....83 C8
Morrison Rd NE61 .....4 A1
Morrison St NE8 ......100 C2
Morriss Terr DH5 ......94 F7
Morrit Ct NE7 ....39 C5
Morston Dr NE15 .....53 E6
Mortimer Ave
Newcastle-u-T NE5 ...36 F3
North Shields NE29 ...41 D6
Mortimer Chase NE23 ..16 C3
Mortimer Comp Sch
NE33 ....59 D7
Mortimer Prim Sch NE34 59 D7
Mortimer Rd NE33,NE34 .59 D7
Mortimer St SR4 ......85 F7
Mortimer Terr
Pegswood NE61 ....4 F4
Seaton Delaval NE25 ..23 E2
Morton Cl NE38 .....83 D4
Morton Cres
Great Lumley DH4 .....89 F1
Woolsington NE5 .....36 B6
Morton Grange Terr DH4 89 F1
Morton St
Newcastle-u-T NE6 ....56 D6
1 South Shields NE33 ..42 C4
Morton Wlk **6** NE33 ..42 C4
Morval Cl SR3 ....91 D5
Morven Dr NE10 ......57 B1
Morven Lea NE21 .....53 B2
Morven Pl NE63 ......6 B4
Morven Terr NE63 .....6 B4
Morwick Cl NE23 .....22 A5
Morwick Pl **3** NE5 ....37 D1
Morwick Rd NE29 .....41 D8
Mosley St NE1 ....99 B1
Moss Bank NE9 ......71 B3
Moss Cl NE15 ....53 C8
Moss Cres NE40 .....52 A4
Moss Side NE9 ......71 C3
Mosspool NE21 ......53 A2
Mostyn Gn NE3 ......37 F5
Motcombe Way NE23 ..16 C2
Moulton Cl NE5 ......37 C2
Moulton Pl NE5 ......37 C2
Mount Cl
Killingworth NE12 ....29 D4
Sunderland SR4 ......85 B6
Whitley Bay NE25 .....31 D5
Mount Ct DH3 ....82 D5
Mount Gr Dunston NE11 ..69 F7

Mount Gr continued
Sunderland SR4 ......86 A4
Mount La NE9 ....82 E8
Mount Lonnen NE9 ....82 E8
Mount Pleasant
Birtley DH3 ....82 C5
5 Blaydon NE21 ....53 B1
Dipton DH9 ....78 E1
Houghton-le-S DH5 ...94 F8
10 Newcastle-u-T NE6 ..56 C6
3 Sunderland SR5 ...75 A1
Mount Pleasant Bglws **4**
DH3 ....82 C5
Mount Pleasant Ct NE15 .35 D2
Mount Pleasant Gdns
NE8 ....56 A1
Mount Rd Birtley DH3 ..82 D5
Gateshead NE9 ......82 E8
Sunderland SR4 ......85 F4
Mount Terr NE33 .....42 C2
Mount The Ryton NE40 ..52 C5
Throckley NE15 ......35 C2
Mount View
17 Crawcrook NE40 ..51 F3
Wickham NE16 ......69 B8
Mount View Terr NE43 ..64 A7
Mountbatten Ave NE31 ..57 E4
Mountfield Gdns NE3 ..37 F5
Mountfield Prim Sch
NE3 ....37 E5
Mountford Rd NE25 ...23 D7
Mountside Gdns NE11 ..69 F7
Mourne Gdns NE11 ...70 A6
Mowbray Cl SR2 ......103 A1
Mowbray Mews NE33 ..42 E2
Mowbray Rd
Longbenton NE12 ....39 E8
North Shields NE29 ...41 D6
South Shields NE33 ...42 C1
Sunderland SR2 ......103 B1
Mowbray St NE6 .....56 A7
Mowbray Terr NE62 ...10 F7
Mowden Hall (Prep Sch)
NE43 ....48 E7
Moyle Terr NE16 .....79 A4
Mozart St NE33 .....42 D2
Muirfield
South Shields NE33 ...42 F1
Whitley Bay NE25 ....31 D5
Muirfield Dr
Gateshead NE10 .....71 E6
Washington NE37 ....72 C2
Muirfield Rd NE7 .....39 C5
Mulben Cl NE4 ......54 E4
Mulberry Cl NE24 ....17 D4
Mulberry Gdns NE10 ..56 C2
Mulberry Gr NE16 ....79 A4
Mulberry Pk NE9 .....70 F5
Mulberry Pl NE4 .....100 B3
Mulberry St NE10 ....56 C1
Mulcaster Gdns NE28 ..40 A3
Mulgrave Dr SR6 .....75 F4
Mulgrave Terr NE8 ....101 B3
Mulgrave Villas NE8 ...101 B2
Mull Gr NE32 ....58 E3
Mullen Dr NE40 .....52 D4
Mullen Gdns NE28 ...40 A4
Mullen Rd NE28 .....40 B4
Mundella Terr NE6 ...56 B7
Mundle Ave NE21 ....68 C6
Mundles La NE36 ....74 D6
Municipal Terr NE38 ..83 D6
Munslow Rd SR3 .....91 D8
Murphy Gr SR2 ......92 E7
Murray Ave DH4 .....90 A1
Murray Ct DH2 ......88 B3
Murray Gdns **1** NE11 ..70 A7
Murray Pl DH2 ......88 C3
Murray Rd
Chester le S DH2,DH3 ..88 C3
Wallsend NE28 ......40 F3
Murray St NE21 .....53 C3
Murrayfield NE23 ....22 F2
Murrayfield Rd NE5 ...37 D3
Murston Ave NE23 ...16 C2
Murton La
Easington Lane DH5 ..95 A3
Tynemouth NE27,NE29 .31 B2
Murton St SR1 ......103 B2
Muscott Gr NE15 ....54 A6
Musgrave Prim Sch NE9 .70 F6
Musgrave Rd NE9 ....70 F6
Musgrave Terr
Gateshead NE10 .....57 A1
Newcastle-u-T NE6 ...56 E6
Washington NE38 ....83 D6
Muswell Hill NE15 ...54 A5
Mutual St NE28 .....40 B1
Mylord Cres NE12 ...29 B5
Myrella Cres SR2 ....86 C2
Myreside Pl NE12 ....39 B7
Myrtle Ave Dunston NE11 ..69 F7
Whitburn SR6 ....60 F1
Myrtle Cres NE12 ....29 D1
Myrtle Gr Burnopfield NE16 78 F6
Gateshead NE11 .....70 F5
Newcastle-u-T NE2 ...38 C2
South Shields NE34 ..59 F4
Wallsend NE28 ......40 D1
Myrtle Rd NE21 .....53 C1
Myrtle St NE63 ......6 D4
Myrtles DH2 ....88 B5

N

Nafferton Pl NE5 .....54 C8

Nailsworth Cl NE35 ..58 E2
Nairn Cl Birtley DH3 ...82 D2
Sunderland SR4 ......85 D4
Washington NE37 ....72 C2
Nairn Rd NE23 ......22 B7
Nairn St NE32 ......58 E3
Nansen Cl NE5 ......36 F2
Napier Cl DH3 ......88 D8
Napier Ct NE16 .....69 B4
Napier Rd NE16 .....54 A1
Napier St Jarrow NE32 ..58 B7
Newcastle-u-T NE2 ...99 C2
South Shields NE33 ...59 B6
Napier Way NE21 ....53 A2
Napoleon Cl SR2 ....92 F7
Narvik Way NE29 ....41 B4
Nash Ave NE34 ......59 D3
Naters St NE26 .....32 C4
National Glass Ctr (Mus)★
SR6 ....103 B4
Natley Ave NE36 ....74 E7
Navan Cl NE62 ......11 D8
Navenby Cl
Newcastle-u-T NE3 ...38 D8
Seaham SR7 ....93 A1
Naworth Ave NE30 ...32 A1
Naworth Dr NE5 .....36 E3
Naworth Terr NE32 ...58 D4
Nawton Ave SR5 ....75 C2
Nayland Rd NE23 ....22 A7
Naylor Ave NE21 ....68 C6
Naylor Bldgs NE21 ...68 C6
Naylor Ct NE21 .....53 E4
Naylor Pl NE26 .....24 B7
Neale St Prudhoe NE42 ..50 D3
Sunderland SR6 .....75 E3
Tantobie DH9 ....79 B2
Neale Terr **1** DH3 ....82 C4
Nearlane Cl NE13 ...28 C8
Neasdon Cres NE30 ..32 B1
Neasham Rd SR7 ....93 A1
Nedderton Cl NE5 ...36 B4
Needham Pl NE23 ...22 B7
Neil St DH5 ....95 C1
Neill Dr NE16 ....69 B2
Neilson Rd NE10 ....56 B3
Nell Terr NE39 ......67 C1
Nellie Gormley Ho NE8 .29 B2
Nelson Ave
Cramlington NE23 ....21 F8
Newcastle-u-T NE3 ...38 A5
South Shields NE33 ...42 E2
Nelson Cl Ashington NE63 ..6 E2
Sunderland SR2 ......103 B1
Nelson Cres NE29 ...41 D2
Nelson Dr NE23 .....15 F1
Nelson Ho **14** NE30 ..42 D7
Nelson Ind Est NE23 ..15 E2
Nelson Park Ind Est
NE23 ....15 E1
Nelson Park Networkctr
NE23 ....15 E1
Nelson Park W NE23 ..15 D1
Nelson Rd
Cramlington NE23 ....15 D1
Earsdon NE25 ....31 B5
Newcastle-u-T NE6 ...57 B4
Stakeford NE62 .....11 A7
Nelson St Chester le S DH3 88 C2
Dunston NE11 ......54 F2
Gateshead NE8 .....101 C3
Greenside NE40 .....51 F1
Hetton le H DH5 .....95 A3
Newcastle-u-T NE1 ...99 A1
11 South Shields NE33 ..42 C3
Sunderland SR2 ......92 F7
Washington NE38 ....83 E4
Nelson Terr
Chopwell NE17 ......66 B1
North Shields NE29 ...41 D3
Sherburn DH6 ....96 A1
Nelson Way NE23 ...15 E2
Nene Ct **11** NE37 ....83 E8
Neptune Rd
Newcastle-u-T,Denton Burn
NE15 ....53 E7
Newcastle-u-T,Lemington
NE15 ....53 D6
Wallsend NE28 ......57 B8
Nesburn Rd SR4 ....102 A1
Nesham Pl DH5 .....94 F8
Nesham Terr SR1 ....103 C3
Ness Ct NE21 ....53 A2
Nest Rd NE10 ......56 D2
Nether Farm Rd NE10 ..56 F1
Nether Riggs NE22 ..15 F1
Netherburn Rd SR5 ..75 C2
Netherby Dr NE5 ....54 C8
Netherdale NE22 ....10 D1
Netherton Cl NE12 ...29 C4
Netherton Ave NE29 ..41 D7
Netherton Gdns NE13 ..28 B6
Netherton Gr NE29 ...41 D7
Netherton La NE22 ..10 C1
Netherwitton Way NE3 ..28 B1
Nettleham Rd SR5 ...75 C2
Nettles La SR3 ......92 B6
Nevill Rd NE43 .....64 D7
Neville Cres DH3 ....82 C6
Neville Ct **3** NE37 ...83 F8
Neville Rd
Newcastle-u-T NE15 ..53 E7
Sunderland SR4 ......85 F7
Neville Sq NE61 .....2 A2
Neville St NE1 ......101 A4
Neville's Cross Rd NE31 .57 F5
Nevinson Ave NE34 ..59 E3

Nevis Cl NE26 ......31 E8
Nevis Ct NE26 ......31 E8
Nevis Gr NE36 ......74 B7
Nevis Way NE26 ....31 E7
New Bridge St NE1 ..99 C1
New Bridge St W NE1,
NE99 ....99 B2
New Cotts NE61 .....3 A1
New Delaval Fst Sch
NE24 ....17 B4
New Durham Rd SR2 ..102 C2
New Front St DH9 ...79 D1
New George St NE8 ..42 C1
New Green St NE33 ..42 C1
New Hartley Fst Sch
NE25 ....23 D6
New Herrington Ind Est
DH4 ....90 D6
New Horton Grange Cotts
NE13 ....19 F4
New King St NE64 ...7 F5
New Mills NE4 ......98 B2
New Mills Ho NE4 ...98 B2
New Moor Cl NE63 ...5 F4
New Penshaw Prim Sch
DH4 ....90 B8
New Phoenix Yd **1** NE61 .9 A8
New Quay NE29 .....42 B4
New Queen St NE64 ..7 E5
New Rainton St DH4 ..90 B8
New Rd Burnopfield NE16 ..79 B7
Dunston NE11 ......70 B6
Gateshead NE10 .....72 C5
Washington NE38 ....89 C8
West Boldon NE35 ...74 B8
New Ridley Rd NE43 ..64 D5
New Sandridge NE64 ..7 F5
New Seaham Prim Sch
SR7 ....92 F1
New Silksworth Inf Sch
SR3 ....92 B7
New Silksworth Jun Sch
SR3 ....92 B7
New South Terr DH3 ..82 D4
New St Sherburn DH6 ..96 A1
5 Sunderland SR4 ...85 A4
New York Ind Pk NE27 ..41 A8
New York Prim Sch
NE29 ....41 C8
New York Rd
Shiremoor NE27 .....30 E2
Tynemouth NE29 ....31 B1
New York Way NE27 ..41 A8
Newark Cl NE22 ....10 D2
Newark Cres SR7 ....93 A1
Newark Dr SR6 .....75 F8
Newark Sq NE29 ....41 F4
Newarth Cl NE15 ....53 E7
Newbank Wlk NE21 ..53 A1
Newbiggin La NE5 ...37 A5
Newbiggin Mid Sch NE64 .7 C4
Newbiggin Rd NE63 ..6 E1
Newbiggin-by-the-Sea
Mooride Fst Sch NE64 .7 D5
Newbold Ave SR5 ...75 C2
Newbold St NE6 ....56 D5
Newbolt Ct NE8 ....56 A2
Newbottle Prim Sch DH4 90 D3
Newbottle St DH4 ...90 E1
Newbridge Ave SR5 ..75 C2
Newbridge Bank DH3 ..88 F5
Newbrough Cres NE2 ..38 C2
Newburgh Ave NE25 ..23 D2
Newburn Ave SR5 ...75 C2
Newburn Bridge Rd
NE15,NE21 ....52 E6
Newburn Cres DH4 ..90 D1
Newburn Ct NE33 ...42 D1
Newburn Hall Motor Mus★
NE15 ....53 C6
Newburn Haugh Ind Est
NE15 ....53 C6
Newburn Ind Est NE21 ..53 A6
Newburn Lane End NE15 35 D2
Newburn Manor Fst Sch
NE15 ....52 F8
Newburn Rd
Newburn NE15 ......52 F8
Throckley NE15 .....35 E1
Newbury NE12 ......29 D4
Newbury Ave NE8 ...70 D8
Newbury Cl NE15 ...53 D7
Newbury St
South Shields NE33 ..59 D7
Sunderland SR5 .....75 D3
Newby Cl NE22 .....11 C3
Newby La DH6 ......96 C5
Newby Pl NE9 ......71 B4
Newcastle Arena NE4 ..100 C3
Newcastle Bank NE9 ..82 D4
Newcastle Bsns Pk NE4 100 A3
Newcastle Coll Trevelyan
Bldg NE4 ....100 B4
Newcastle Discovery Mus★
NE1 ....100 C4
Newcastle General Hospl
NE4 ....54 F6
Newcastle International
Airport NE13 ....26 D3
Newcastle Nuffield Hospl The
NE2 ....99 B4
Newcastle Rd Birtley DH3 ..82 C6
Blyth NE24 ....17 C4
Chester le S DH3 ....88 C5
Corbridge NE45 .....47 B5
Sunderland SR5 .....75 C3
West Boldon NE10,NE36 ..73 C7

Newcastle Rd/Leam La
NE34 ....58 F5
Newcastle St NE29 ..42 A5
Newcastle Terr **5** NE30 ..42 D7
Newcastle Trade Ctr
NE4 ....100 B3
Newcastle Upon Tyne Central
Sta NE1 ....101 A4
Newdene Wlk NE15 ..53 D7
Newfield Wlk NE16 ..69 A6
Newgate Sh Ctr NE1 ..99 B1
Newgate St Morpeth NE61 .3 F1
Newcastle-u-T NE1 ...99 A1
Newham Ave NE13 ...28 A4
Newhaven Ave SR5 ..75 C2
Newington Ct
Sunderland SR5 .....75 C1
Washington NE37 ....83 C8
Newington Dr NE29 ..31 F1
Newington Rd NE6 ...56 C6
Newker Prim Sch DH2 ..88 B2
Newland Ct NE34 ...59 C5
Newlands NE30 .....32 A2
Newlands Ave Blyth NE24 ..17 D5
Newcastle-u-T NE3 ...28 D1
Sunderland SR3 .....86 B3
Whitley Bay NE25 ...31 D3
Newlands Pl NE24 ...17 D5
Newlands Rd Blyth NE24 ..17 D5
Newcastle-u-T NE2 ...38 D3
New Rd W SR7 ....93 A1
Newlands Sch NE3 ..38 D4
Newlynn Cres NE29 ..41 E5
Newlyn Dr
Cramlington NE23 ....22 B8
Jarrow NE32 ....58 D6
Newlyn Rd NE3 .....37 E5
Newman Pl **10** NE8 ...71 A8
Newman Terr NE8 ...71 A8
Newman's Way **2** NE46 .45 B4
Newmarch St NE32 ..58 A7
Newmarket Wlk **1** NE33 ..42 D1
Newmin Way NE16 ..68 F5
Newminster Cl DH4 ..90 B2
Newminster Rd NE4 ..54 D7
Newport Gr **6** SR3 ...92 A8
Newquay Gdns **4** NE9 ..71 A2
Newriggs NE38 .....83 E2
Newsham Cl NE5 ....36 B4
Newsham Fst Sch NE24 ..17 C6
Newsham Rd NE24 ..17 C6
Newstead Ct NE38 ...83 C5
Newstead Rd DH4 ...90 C2
Newstead Sq SR3 ...92 A6
Newsteads Cl NE25 ..31 D5
Newsteads Dr NE25 ..31 D5
Newton Ave
Tynemouth NE30 ....32 B3
Wallsend NE28 ......40 F3
Newton Cl NE15 .....53 E7
Newton Gr NE34 ....59 A5
Newton Ho NE4 .....98 B3
Newton Pl NE7 .....39 B2
Newton Rd NE7 .....39 B2
Newton St Dunston NE11 ..54 F2
Gateshead NE8 .....70 D8
Newton Terr NE43 ...49 E1
Nichol Ct NE4 ......54 D5
Nichol St NE4 ......54 D5
Nicholas Ave SR6 ...75 F8
Nicholas St DH5 ....95 B5
Nicholson Cl SR1 ...103 B2
Nicholson Terr NE12 ..29 E1
Nidderdale Ave DH5 ..94 F2
Nidderdale Cl NE24 ..17 A8
Nidsdale Ave NE6 ...57 A7
Nightingale Cl SR4 ..85 B4
Nile Cl NE15 ....53 C8
Nile Ct NE8 ....56 A1
Nile St North Shields NE29 ..42 A5
South Shields NE33 ...42 B2
Sunderland SR1 .....103 B3
Nilverton Ave SR2 ...86 D3
Nimbus Ct **13** SR3 ...92 A6
Nine Lands DH4 .....94 C8
Ninth Ave Blyth NE24 ..17 D6
Chester le S DH2 ....88 B3
Gateshead NE11 .....70 D3
Morpeth NE61 ....9 B7
Newcastle-u-T NE6 ...56 C8
Ninth Ave E NE11 ...70 D3
Ninth Row NE63 ....6 B4
Nissan Way SR5 ....84 B7
Nithdale Cl NE6 ....57 B8
Nixon St NE8 ......56 A4
Nixon Terr NE24 ....17 F6
Noble Gdns NE34 ...58 F4
Noble St
2 Gateshead NE10 ...56 D1
Newcastle-u-T NE4 ..54 F3
Sunderland SR2 .....103 C1
Noble Terr
16 Morpeth NE61 ....9 A8
Sunderland SR2 .....103 C1
Noble's Bank Rd SR2 ..103 C1
Noel Ave NE21 .....68 C6
Noel Terr NE21 .....68 D7
Noirmont Way SR3 ..91 E6
Nolan Hall NE32 ....58 B6
Nook The
North Shields NE29 ..41 F5
Whitley Bay NE25 ...31 F5
Nookside SR4 ......85 C4
Nookside Ct SR4 ...85 C4
Nora St South Shields NE34 59 F5
Sunderland SR4 .....85 F4
Norbury Gr NE6 ....56 D5
Nordale Ho NE24 ...17 A8

Nordale Way NE24 . . . . . .17 A8
Norfolk Ave Birtley DH3 . .82 D1
New Silksworth SR3 . . . . .91 F8
Norfolk Cl Ashington NE63 . .6 A4
Seaham SR7 . . . . .93 A1
Norfolk Ct **10** NE30 . . . . .42 B6
Norfolk Dr NE37 . . . . .72 D2
Norfolk Gdns NE28 . . . . .40 E4
Norfolk Mews **11** NE30 . .42 A6
Norfolk Pl NE37 . . . . .72 D1
Norfolk Rd Gateshead NE8 56 A4
South Shields NE34 . . . . . .60 C7
Norfolk Sq **19** NE30 . . . . .56 B6
Norfolk St Hetton le H DH5 94 F4
North Shields NE30 . . . . . .42 B5
Sunderland SR1 . . . . .103 A3
Norfolk Way NE15 . . . . . .53 E7
Norham Ave N NE34 . . . . .60 A8
Norham Ave S NE34 . . . . .60 A8
Norham Cl Blyth NE24 . . . .17 C7
Brunswick Village NE13 . . .28 A5
Norham Com Tech Coll
NE29 . . . . .41 D5
Norham Ct
Bournmoor DH4 . . . . .89 D1
Washington NE38 . . . . . . .83 B4
Norham Dr Morpeth NE61 . .9 B5
Newcastle-u-T NE5 . . . . . .36 E3
Norham Gdns NE62 . . . . . .6 A1
Norham Pl NE2 . . . . .38 C1
Norham Rd Ashington NE63 6 D2
Newcastle-u-T NE3 . . . . . .38 B6
North Shields NE30 . . . . . .41 C5
Whitley Bay NE25,NE26 . . .31 F5
Norham Road N NE29 . . . .41 B7
Norham Terr NE32 . . . . . .58 B3
Norhurst NE16 . . . . .68 E5
Norland Rd NE15 . . . . . . .53 F6
Norley Ave SR5 . . . . .75 C2
Norma Cres NE26 . . . . . . .32 C4
Norman Ave SR3 . . . . . . .92 B7
Norman Rd NE39 . . . . . . .67 F1
Norman Terr
High Pittington DH6 . . . . . .96 C5
Morpeth NE61 . . . . .9 A8
Wallsend NE28 . . . . .41 B8
Normanby Cl SR7 . . . . . . .93 A1
Normanby Ct SR6 . . . . . . .75 F1
Normandy Cres DH5 . . . . .94 F8
Normanton Terr NE4 . . . . .98 A1
Normount Ave **2** NE4 . . .54 E5
Normount Gdns NE4 . . . . .54 E6
Normount Rd NE4 . . . . . . .54 E5
North App DH2 . . . . .102 B2
North Ave Guide Post NE62 10 E7
Longbenton NE12 . . . . . . .39 D6
Newcastle-u-T NE5 . . . . . .36 F2
Newcastle-u-T,Gosforth
NE3 . . . . .38 C4
South Shields NE34 . . . . . .59 F6
Washington NE37 . . . . . . .72 C1
North Balkwell Farm Ind Est
NE29 . . . . .41 B7
North Bank Ct **5** SR5 . . .75 B2
North Bridge St SR5 . . . .103 A4
North Burns DH3 . . . . .88 C4
North Church St **2** NE30 42 B6
North Cl
4 Newcastle-u-T NE6 . . .56 C7
Ryton NE40 . . . . .52 C5
South Shields NE34 . . . . . .59 F6
North Cres NE38 . . . . .83 B1
North Croft NE12 . . . . .39 E7
North Cross St NE3 . . . . . .38 C5
North Ct **5** NE32 . . . . . .58 B7
North Dene DH3 . . . . .82 C7
North Dr Chester le S NE38 88 E7
Cleadon SR6 . . . . .59 F1
Hebburn NE31 . . . . .57 C4
North Durham St SR1 . . . .103 B3
North East Aircraft Mus★
SR5 . . . . .73 E3
North East Bus Mus★
NE10 . . . . .72 B6
North Eastern Ct NE16 . . .69 E8
North Farm Ave NE22 . . . .15 A8
North Farm Ave SR3 . . . . .85 B2
North Farm Rd NE31 . . . . .57 D5
North Fawdon Prim Sch
NE3 . . . . .37 F7
North Gr Ryton NE40 . . . . .52 D5
Sunderland SR6 . . . . .75 E3
North Grange NE20 . . . . . .25 E8
North Guards SR6 . . . . . . .75 F8
North Hall Rd SR4 . . . . . . .85 D4
North Hylton Rd NE5 . . . . .42 B6
North Hylton Road Ind Est
SR5 . . . . .74 D2
North Jesmond Ave NE2 . .38 C2
North King St NE30 . . . . . .42 B6
North La East Boldon NE36 74 E4
Hetton le H DH5 . . . . .95 E5
North Leech NE61 . . . . .3 D2
North Leigh DH9 . . . . .79 D1
North Lodge DH3 . . . . .88 D7
North Lodge Apartments **11**
NE21 . . . . .53 B1
North Magdalene DH8 . . . .77 B1
North Mason Lodge
NE13 . . . . .27 B8
North Mdws NE42 . . . . . . .50 B5
North Milburn St SR4 . . . .102 B3
North Moor Ct SR3 . . . . . .91 E8
North Moor La SR3 . . . . . .91 E8
North Moor Rd SR3 . . . . . .85 E1
North Par
Choppington NE62 . . . . . . .10 E6
Whitley Bay NE26 . . . . . . .32 B5

North Pl NE61 . . . . .3 E1
North Ravensworth St
SR4 . . . . .102 B3
North Rd
Doldon Colliery NE35 . . . . .58 E1
Boldon Colliery,New Town
NE35,NE36 . . . . .73 F7
Chester le S DH3 . . . . .88 C7
Dipton DH9 . . . . .78 E1
East Boldon NE36 . . . . . . .74 C7
Hetton le H DH5 . . . . .94 E4
Houghton-le-S DH5 . . . . . .94 E4
Ponteland NE20 . . . . .25 E8
Seaham SR7 . . . . .93 D1
Slaley NE47 . . . . .62 A4
Tynemouth NE29 . . . . .42 A8
Wallsend NE28 . . . . .40 B2
North Ridge
Bedlington NE22 . . . . .10 D1
Bedlington NE22 . . . . .10 E1
Whitley Bay NE25 . . . . . . .31 C6
North Row NE42 . . . . .50 A2
North Sands Bsns Ctr
SR6 . . . . .103 B4
North Seaton Ind Est NE63 6 F1
North Seaton Rd
Ashington NE63 . . . . .6 D2
Newbiggin-by-t-S NE64 . . . .7 D3
North Shields Sta NE29 . . .42 A5
North Side NE13 . . . . . . .100 B2
North St Birtley DH3 . . . . .82 E3
Blaydon NE21 . . . . .53 A2
Cleadon SR6 . . . . .60 A1
East Rainton DH5 . . . . .94 D4
New Silksworth SR3 . . . . . .92 A8
Newbottle DH4 . . . . .90 D4
Newcastle-u-T NE1 . . . . . .99 A2
South Shields NE33 . . . . . .42 C3
5 Sunderland SR5 . . . . .75 C1
West Rainton DH4 . . . . . . .94 A1
North St E NE1 . . . . .99 B2
North Terr Chopwell NE17 .66 B2
Hexham NE46 . . . . .45 B4
11 New Silksworth SR3 . .92 A8
Newcastle-u-T NE2 . . . . . .98 C3
1 Shiremoor NE27 . . . . .30 E1
Wallsend NE28 . . . . .40 E2
North Tyne Ind Est NE12 .40 A8
North Tyneside Coll
NE28 . . . . .40 E5
North Tyneside General
Hospl NE29 . . . . .31 E1
North Tyneside Steam Rly★
NE28,NE29 . . . . .41 C5
North View Ashington NE63 .6 C4
7 Bedlington NE22 . . . . .11 D3
Bournmoor DH4 . . . . .89 E2
Cambois NE24 . . . . .12 C6
Crawcrook NE40 . . . . .51 E7
Dinnington NE13 . . . . .27 B7
Easington Lane DH5 . . . . . .95 C1
Gateshead NE9 . . . . .71 B3
Haswell DH6 . . . . .97 E1
Hazlerigg NE13 . . . . .28 A4
High Spen NE39 . . . . .66 F3
Jarrow NE32 . . . . .58 A6
4 Longbenton NE12 . . . .39 D8
Medomsley DH8 . . . . .77 B1
Mickley Square NE43 . . . . .49 E1
Newbiggin-by-t-S NE64 . . . .7 D3
Newcastle-u-T NE6 . . . . . .56 B7
Newcastle-u-T NE6 . . . . . .56 C7
Ouston DH2 . . . . .81 F1
Rowlands Gill NE39 . . . . . .67 C2
Ryton NE40 . . . . .52 A5
Sherburn Hill DH6 . . . . . . .96 D1
South Shields NE34 . . . . . .59 F8
Stakeford NE62 . . . . .11 C8
Sunderland,Castletown SR5 74 C1
Sunderland,Monkwearmouth
SR6 . . . . .75 D3
Sunderland,South Hylton
SR4 . . . . .85 B5
Tynemouth NE28 . . . . .41 F8
Wallsend NE28 . . . . .40 C2
Washington NE37 . . . . . . .83 D8
Whickham NE11 . . . . .69 A7
Whitley Bay NE30 . . . . . . .32 C4
North View Terr
Fence Houses DH4 . . . . . . .94 B8
Gateshead NE8 . . . . .56 C1
Prudhoe NE42 . . . . .50 B2
Stocksfield NE43 . . . . .64 C7
North View W NE39 . . . . . .67 C2
North Villas NE23 . . . . . . .22 A1
North Walbottle Rd
Newcastle-u-T NE5 . . . . . .36 B4
Walbottle NE15 . . . . .36 A2
North West Side NE8 . . .100 B2
North Wylam View NE42 . .50 B2
Northbourne Ave NE61 . . . .3 F2
Northbourne Ho NE9 . . . . .70 F5
Northbourne Rd NE31,
NE32 . . . . .58 A6
Northbourne St
Gateshead NE8 . . . . .70 F8
Newcastle-u-T NE4 . . . . . .54 F7
Northburn Fst Sch NE23 . .16 A1
Northcote NE16 . . . . .69 A5
Northcote Ave
Newcastle-u-T NE5 . . . . . .36 C1
Sunderland SR1 . . . . .103 B2
Whitley Bay NE25 . . . . . . .31 D4
Northcote St
Newcastle-u-T NE4 . . . . . .98 A1
8 South Shields NE33 . . .59 D8
Northcott Gdns NE23 . . . .22 E1

Northern Counties Sch
NE2 . . . . .38 D1
Northern Terr NE23 . . . . . .22 A1
Northern Way SR5 . . . . . . .75 A2
Northfield NE22 . . . . .12 B4
Northfield Cl NE16 . . . . . . .68 F5
Northfield Dr
Killingworth NE12 . . . . . . .29 B2
Sunderland SR4 . . . . .85 B2
Northfield Gdns NE34 . . . .59 F8
Northfield Rd
Newcastle-u-T NE3 . . . . . .38 B4
South Shields NE33 . . . . . .42 F1
Northfields Cl **23** NE6 . . .56 C7
Northfields Ho **22** NE6 . .56 C7
Northgate NE12 . . . . .29 D4
Northgate & Prudhoe NHS
Trust Northgate Hospl
NE61 . . . . .3 D4
Northland Cl SR4 . . . . .85 B2
Northlands Blaydon NE21 . .53 B1
Chester le S DH3 . . . . .88 C5
Tynemouth NE30 . . . . .32 B1
Northlands Rd NE61 . . . . . .3 F2
Northlea NE15 . . . . .53 E8
Northmoor Rd NE6 . . . . . .56 E8
Northolt Ave NE23 . . . . . . .22 B7
Northside DH3 . . . . .82 D6
Northside Pl NE25 . . . . . . .23 E2
Northumberland Aged
Mineworkers Homes
NE23 . . . . .22 D5
Northumberland Ave
Bedlington NE22 . . . . .10 E1
Longbenton NE12 . . . . . . .39 D7
Newbiggin-by-t-S NE64 . . . .7 D4
Newcastle-u-T NE3 . . . . . .38 A3
Wallsend NE28 . . . . .40 F2
Northumberland Cl NE63 . .6 A4
Northumberland Coll
NE63 . . . . .6 E2
Northumberland Ct
Hebburn NE31 . . . . .57 D5
Prudhoe NE42 . . . . .50 E4
Northumberland Dock Rd
NE28 . . . . .41 C1
Northumberland Gdns
Newcastle-u-T NE5 . . . . . .36 B3
Newcastle-u-T,Jesmond Vale
NE2 . . . . .56 A8
Northumberland Pl
Birtley DH3 . . . . .82 D1
1 Newcastle-u-T NE1 . . .99 A2
9 North Shields NE30 . . .42 A6
Northumberland Rd
Newcastle-u-T NE1,NE99 . .99 B2
Newcastle-u-T,Lemington
NE15 . . . . .53 C6
Ryton NE40 . . . . .52 C6
Northumberland Sq
4 North Shields NE30 . . .42 B6
Whitley Bay NE26 . . . . . . .32 A5
Northumberland St
Gateshead NE8 . . . . .100 C1
Newcastle-u-T NE1 . . . . . .99 A2
North Shields NE30 . . . . . .42 A6
Wallsend NE28 . . . . .40 C2
Northumberland Terr
29 Newcastle-u-T NE6 . .56 B6
Tynemouth NE30 . . . . .42 D7
Wallsend NE28 . . . . .40 D7
Northumberland Villas
NE28 . . . . .40 E2
Northumberland Way
Washington,Columbia NE37,
NE38 . . . . .83 F4
Washington,Usworth NE10,
NE37 . . . . .72 D3
Northumbria Ctr For Ent
NE63 . . . . .6 D5
Northumbria Lodge NE5 . .37 E1
Northumbria Police
Headquarters NE20 . . . . .25 D8
Northumbria Univ, Coach
Lane Campus NE7 . . . . . .39 C4
Northumbria Wlk
Newcastle-u-T NE5 . . . . . .36 F1
Newcastle-u-T,East Denton
NE5 . . . . .37 A2
Northumbrian Rd NE23 . . .22 B6
Northumbrian Way
Killingworth NE12 . . . . . . .29 C2
North Shields NE29 . . . . . .42 A3
Northway Gateshead NE9 . .71 B7
Guide Post NE62 . . . . .10 F7
Throckley NE15 . . . . .35 D3
Northwood Ct SR5 . . . . . . .75 C2
Norton Ave SR7 . . . . .93 A1
Norton Cl **1** DH2 . . . . . .88 A1
Norton Rd SR5 . . . . .75 A3
Norton Way NE15 . . . . . . .53 E6
Norway Ave SR4 . . . . .85 E4
Norwich Ave NE13 . . . . . . .28 B5
Norwich Cl NE63 . . . . .7 A2
Norwich Way
Cramlington NE23 . . . . . . .22 A7
Hedworth NE32 . . . . .58 B1
Norwood Ave
Newcastle-u-T,Brunton Park
NE3 . . . . .28 C1
Newcastle-u-T,Heaton NE6 .39 B1
Norwood Cres NE39 . . . . . .67 F2
Norwood Ct
Gateshead NE9 . . . . .71 C2
Longbenton NE12 . . . . . . .39 D6
Norwood Gdns **4** NE9 . .71 A8
Norwood Rd
Gateshead NE11 . . . . .70 B7

Norwood Rd continued
Newcastle-u-T NE15 . . . . .53 D8
Nottingham Ct NE22 . . . . .10 D2
November Ctyd NE8 . . . .100 B2
Numbers Garth SR1 . . . .103 B3
Nun St NE1 . . . . .99 A1
Nuneaton Way NE5 . . . . . .36 B4
Nunn Gdns **12** NE16 . . . .69 A7
Nunn St DH4 . . . . .90 A5
Nunnykirk Cl NE42 . . . . . .50 A4
Nuns La Gateshead NE8 . .101 C3
Newcastle-u-T NE1 . . . . . .99 A1
Nuns Moor Cres NE4 . . . . .54 E7
Nuns Moor Rd NE4 . . . . . .54 E7
Nunthorpe Ave SR2 . . . . . .86 F1
Nunwick Gdns NE29 . . . . .41 C6
Nunwick Way NE7 . . . . . . .39 D4
Nursery Cl SR3 . . . . .86 A2
Nursery Ct NE17 . . . . .77 B6
Nursery Gdns NE5 . . . . . . .54 B8
Nursery Grange NE46 . . . .44 F1
Nursery La Cleadon SR6 . .60 A1
Gateshead NE10 . . . . .71 C7
Nursery Pk NE63 . . . . .6 E1
Nursery Rd SR3 . . . . .86 A2
Nutley Pl NE15 . . . . .54 A5
Nye Bevan Ho NE24 . . . . .17 F6
Nye Dene SR5 . . . . .74 B1

O

O'Hanlon Cres NE28 . . . . .40 A4
Oak Ave Dinnington NE13 . .27 C7
Dunston NE11 . . . . .69 F7
5 Houghton-le-S DH4 . . .94 D8
South Shields NE34 . . . . . .60 A5
Oak Cl NE6 . . . . .44 E3
Oak Cres SR6 . . . . .61 A3
Oak Gr Longbenton NE12 . .39 D8
Wallsend NE28 . . . . .40 D1
Oak Rd NE29 . . . . .41 B7
Oak Sq NE8 . . . . .100 C1
Oak St Great Lumley DH4 . .89 E1
Jarrow NE32 . . . . .58 A7
Mickley Square NE43 . . . . .64 E8
Seaton Burn NE13 . . . . . . .28 C8
Sunderland SR1 . . . . .103 C2
1 Throckley NE15 . . . . .35 D2
Washington NE38 . . . . . . .83 F4
Oak Terr Blaydon NE21 . . .53 C1
Burnopfield NE16 . . . . .79 C6
Tantobie DH9 . . . . .79 B2
Oakapple Cl NE22 . . . . . . .10 F1
Oakdale NE22 . . . . .15 B8
Oakdale Cl NE15 . . . . .53 D6
Oakdale Terr DH3 . . . . . . .88 C2
Oakenshaw NE15 . . . . . . .53 E6
Oakey's Rd DH9 . . . . .79 F1
Oakfield Ave NE16 . . . . . . .69 B6
Oakfield Cl
Sunderland SR3 . . . . .91 C6
Whickham NE16 . . . . .69 B6
Oakfield Ct SR3 . . . . .91 C6
Oakfield Dr
Killingworth NE12 . . . . . . .29 F3
Whickham NE16 . . . . .69 B6
Oakfield Gdns
Newcastle-u-T NE15 . . . . .54 D5
Wallsend NE28 . . . . .39 F3
Oakfield Grange NE13 . . . .27 B7
Oakfield Inf & Jun Schs
NE9 . . . . .70 F3
Oakfield N NE40 . . . . .52 B5
Oakfield Pk NE42 . . . . . . .50 D2
Oakfield Rd Dunston NE11 70 A6
Newcastle-u-T NE3 . . . . . .38 B3
Whickham NE16 . . . . .69 A5
Oakfield Terr
Gateshead NE10 . . . . .57 A1
Killingworth NE12 . . . . . . .29 E1
Newcastle-u-T NE3 . . . . . .38 B4
Oakfield Way NE23 . . . . . .22 E7
Oakfields NE16 . . . . .79 B7
Oakham Ave NE16 . . . . . . .68 F6
Oakham Gdns NE29 . . . . .41 E5
Oakhurst Dr NE3 . . . . .38 A3
Oakhurst Terr NE12 . . . . . .39 D7
Oakland Rd
Newcastle-u-T NE2 . . . . . .38 D2
Whitley Bay NE25 . . . . . . .31 F3
Oakland Terr
Ashington NE63 . . . . .6 C3
Lynemouth NE61 . . . . .2 A2
Oaklands
Newcastle-u-T NE3 . . . . . .38 C3
Ponteland NE20 . . . . .25 D4
Riding Mill NE44 . . . . .62 F7
Whickham NE16 . . . . .69 C8
Oaklands Ave NE3 . . . . . . .38 C3
Oaklands Cres SR5 . . . . . .75 A2
Oaklands Ct NE20 . . . . . . .25 D4
Oaklands Pl NE42 . . . . . . .50 E2
Oaklands Rise NE44 . . . . .62 F7
Oaklands Terr SR4 . . . . . .102 A1
Oaklea Chester le S DH2 . .88 A5
Shiney Row DH4 . . . . .89 F4
Oakleigh Gdns SR6 . . . . . .60 A2
Oakley Cl NE23 . . . . .29 B8
Oakley Dr NE23 . . . . .29 B8
Oakley Gardens Sch SR6 .60 B2
Oakmere Cl **2** DH4 . . . . .90 B6
Oakridge NE16 . . . . .68 F6
Oaks The Greenside NE40 .52 B1
Hexham NE46 . . . . .44 F3
Penshaw DH4 . . . . .90 B8
Sunderland SR2 . . . . .103 B1
Oaks W The SR2 . . . . .103 B1

Oaktree Ave NE6 . . . . .40 A1
Oaktree Gdns NE25 . . . . . .31 E3
Oaktree Terr NE42 . . . . . . .50 D2
Oakville NE63 . . . . .7 A2
Oakwell Ct NE17 . . . . .77 C5
Oakwell Terr NE42 . . . . . . .50 D2
Oakwellgate NE8 . . . . . . .101 C4
Oakwood Gateshead NE10 .71 E5
Hebburn NE31 . . . . .57 C7
Oakwood Ave
Gateshead NE9 . . . . .71 A3
Newbiggin-by-t-S NE64 . . . .7 D5
Wideopen NE13 . . . . .28 C5
Oakwood Bank NE46 . . . . .45 C7
Oakwood Cl NE9 . . . . .71 F1
Oakwood Gdns NE11 . . . . .70 B5
Oakwood Pl **2** NE5 . . . . .37 C1
Oakwood St SR2 . . . . .102 B3
Oatens Bank NE15 . . . . . .33 A2
Oates St SR4 . . . . .102 A2
Oatfield Cl NE63 . . . . .6 B2
Oatlands Rd SR4 . . . . .85 E4
Oban Ave NE28 . . . . .40 F4
Oban Ct NE6 . . . . .56 C5
Oban Gdns **9** NE6 . . . . . .56 C5
Oban St
Brockley Whins NE32 . . . . .58 E3
Gateshead NE10 . . . . .56 C1
Ocean Rd
South Shields NE33 . . . . . .42 D3
Sunderland SR2 . . . . .86 F2
Ocean Rd N **6** SR2 . . . . .86 F2
Ocean Rd S **7** SR2 . . . . .86 F2
Ocean View
Newbiggin-by-t-S NE64 . . . .7 E4
Sunderland SR2 . . . . .92 F8
Whitley Bay NE26 . . . . . . .32 B5
Ochiltree Ct NE26 . . . . . . .24 D6
Octavia Cl NE22 . . . . .10 E2
Octavia Ct NE28 . . . . .40 F4
Octavian Way NE11 . . . . . .70 C3
October Ctyd NE8 . . . . . .100 B2
Odinel Ct NE42 . . . . .50 D3
Off Quay Bldg The NE6 . .56 B5
Offerton Ct **1** SR4 . . . . .85 A6
Offerton La
Sunderland,Offerton SR4 . .84 F4
Sunderland,South Hylton
SR4 . . . . .85 A5
Offerton St SR4 . . . . .102 B2
Office Pl DH5 . . . . .95 A3
Office Row
New Herrington DH4 . . . . .90 E7
Washington NE38 . . . . . . .83 A1
Ogden St SR4 . . . . .102 B2
Ogle Ave Hazlerigg NE13 . .28 A4
Morpeth NE61 . . . . .8 E8
Ogle Dr NE24 . . . . .17 C7
Ogle Gr NE32 . . . . .58 A3
Oil Mill Rd NE6 . . . . .57 B7
Okehampton Ct **2** NE9 . .71 A2
Okehampton Dr DH4 . . . . .90 C4
Okehampton Sq SR5 . . . . .75 A3
Old Bakehouse Yd **11**
NE61 . . . . .3 E1
Old Brewery Sq NE42 . . . .49 C4
Old Brewery The **10** DH4 .94 E8
Old Coastguard Cotts
NE30 . . . . .42 E7
Old Coronation St NE33 . . .42 C2
Old Course Rd SR6 . . . . . .75 A8
Old Custom Ho NE29 . . . . .42 B4
Old Durham Rd NE8,NE9 . .71 B6
Old Farm Ct NE16 . . . . . . .69 B2
Old Fold Rd NE10,NE8 . . . .56 B7
Old Forge The NE43 . . . . .48 C5
Old George Yd **7** NE1 . . .99 A1
Old Main St NE40 . . . . . . .51 E4
Old Mill Rd
Sunderland SR5 . . . . .75 A3
Sunderland,Hendon SR2 . .103 C1
Old Orchard The NE44 . . . .63 A7
Old Rectory Cl DH9 . . . . . .79 D4
Old Sawmill NE61 . . . . .8 A8
Old Station Ct NE20 . . . . . .25 C3
Old Vicarage Wlk NE6 . . . .56 C6
Old Well Ave **4** NE21 . . .53 B1
Old Well La NE21 . . . . .53 B1
Oldfield Rd NE6 . . . . .56 F3
Oldgate NE61 . . . . .8 F8
Oldgate Ct NE61 . . . . .8 F8
Oldstead Gdns SR4 . . . . . .85 E4
Olga Terr NE39 . . . . .67 C1
Olive Gdns NE9 . . . . .71 A6
Olive Pl NE4 . . . . .54 E6
Olive St South Shields NE33 59 B6
Sunderland SR1 . . . . .102 C2
Oliver Ave NE4 . . . . .54 E6
Oliver Cres DH3 . . . . .82 C6
Oliver St **2** NE38 . . . . . . .83 E4
Olivers Mill NE61 . . . . .8 F8
Ollerton Dr NE15 . . . . .35 B2
Ollerton Gdns NE10 . . . . .71 C6
Olney Cl NE23 . . . . .22 D7
Olympia Ave NE62 . . . . . . .10 F7
Olympia Gdns NE61 . . . . . .4 A1
Olympia Hill NE61 . . . . .3 F2
Ongar Way NE12 . . . . .39 B7
Onslow Gdns NE5 . . . . . . .70 F5
Onslow St SR4 . . . . .85 E4
Open The NE1 . . . . .99 A2
Oram Ct NE11 . . . . .9 B8
Orange Gr Annitsford NE23 22 B1
Whickham NE16 . . . . .69 C8
Orchard Ave NE39 . . . . . . .67 D1

Orchard Cl
Killingworth NE12 ....29 F2
Morpeth NE61 ....9 B8
Prudhoe NE42 ....50 D1
Rowlands Gill NE39 ....78 D8
Sunniside NE16 ....69 B3
Orchard Cres NE45 .....47 A5
Orchard Ct
Greenside NE40 ....51 F1
Ryton NE40 ....52 C5
Tynemouth NE29 ....42 A8
Orchard Dene NE39 ....67 D1
Orchard Gdns
Chester le S DH3 ....88 C1
Gateshead NE9 ....71 A4
Wallsend NE28 ....40 A4
Whitburn SR6 ....75 E8
Orchard Gn NE5 ....37 D4
Orchard Hill NE42 ......50 D3
Orchard Mews NE61 .....3 F1
Orchard Pk [8] DH3 .....82 C4
Orchard Pl NE2 ....38 F1
Orchard Rd
Rowlands Gill NE39 ....67 D1
Whickham NE16 ....69 C7
Orchard Rise NE15 ......53 B7
Orchard St Birtley DH3 ..82 C4
Newcastle-u-T NE1 ....101 A4
Sunderland SR4 ....85 F7
Orchard Terr
Chester le S DH3 ....88 C1
[4] Hexham NE46 ....45 B5
Newcastle-u-T NE15 ......53 C6
Rowlands Gill NE39 ....78 D8
[8] Throckley NE15 ....35 D2
Orchard The
Chester le S DH3 ....88 D4
East Boldon NE36 ....74 C7
Hepscott NE61 ....9 E5
Newcastle-u-T NE15 ......53 D6
[4] North Shields NE29 ...42 A6
Whickham NE16 ....69 C7
Wylam NE41 ....51 A6
Orchard View NE45 ......46 F6
Orchard-Leigh NE15 .....53 E6
Orchards The NE24 ......17 B8
Orchid Cl Ashington NE63 .6 C2
South Shields NE34 ......59 B5
Ord Cl NE4 ....54 D7
Ord St NE4 ....100 C3
Ord Terr NE62 ....11 B8
Orde Ave NE28 ....40 E3
Ordley Cl NE15 ....53 E6
Oriole Ho NE12 ....39 D7
Orkney Dr SR2 ....92 D8
Orlando Rd NE29 ....41 E6
Ormesby Rd SR6 ....75 D3
Ormiscraig NE15 ....53 E6
Ormiston NE15 ....53 E6
Ormonde Ave NE15 ......54 A6
Ormonde St Jarrow NE32 .58 B7
Sunderland SR4 ....102 A1
Ormsby Gn NE5 ....54 A8
Ormskirk Cl NE15 ....53 D6
Ormskirk Gr NE23 ....22 C7
Ormston St NE23 ....16 B3
Orpen Ave NE34 ....59 C3
Orpine Ct NE63 ....6 C2
Orpington Ave NE6 ......56 E6
Orpington Rd NE23 ......22 C7
Orr Ave SR3 ....92 B6
Orton Cl NE4 ....54 E4
Orwell Cl NE34 ....59 B2
Orwell Gn NE3 ....37 E3
Osbaldeston Gdns NE3 ..38 B3
Osborne Ave
Hexham NE46 ....44 F5
Newcastle-u-T NE2 ....99 C4
South Shields NE33 ......42 E1
Osborne Cl NE22 ....11 C2
Osborne Ct NE2 ....99 C4
Osborne Gdns
Tynemouth NE29 ....42 A7
Whitley Bay NE26 ....31 F5
Osborne Ho NE28 ....40 E2
Osborne Pl NE12 ....29 F1
Osborne Rd
Chester le S DH3 ....88 C3
Newcastle-u-T NE2 ....38 E2
Sunderland SR5 ....85 A7
Osborne St
South Shields NE33 ......42 E2
Sunderland SR4 ....75 D2
Osborne Terr
Cramlington NE23 ....22 A7
Gateshead NE8 ....101 A1
Newcastle-u-T NE2 ....99 B3
Osborne Villas NE2 ......99 B4
Osier Ct NE62 ....11 C7
Oslo Cl NE29 ....41 B4
Osman Cl SR2 ....103 B1
Osmund Terr [10] DH4 ...90 B6
Osprey Dr Blyth NE24 ...17 F5
Shiremoor NE28 ....41 A6
Osprey Ho [4] NE2 ......38 E1
Osprey Way NE34 ....59 B4
Oswald Rd
Hetton le H DH5 ....95 A5
Morpeth NE61 ....4 A2
Newbiggin-by-t-S NE64 ....7 D5
Oswald St
Sunderland SR4 ....102 A3
Whiteleas NE34 ....59 C3
Oswald Terr
Gateshead NE8 ....101 A1

Oswald Terr continued
Sunderland SR5 ....74 C1
[11] Sunderland,Grangetown
SR2 ....86 F2
Oswald Terr S SR5 ......74 C1
Oswald Wlk NE3 ....38 E5
Oswestry Pl NE23 ....22 C7
Oswin Ave NE12 ....39 D8
Oswin Ct NE12 ....29 E1
Oswin Rd NE12 ....29 E1
Oswin Terr NE29 ....41 D5
Otley Cl NE23 ....22 D7
Otter Burn Way NE42 ...50 B1
Otterburn Ave
Earsdon NE25 ....31 B4
Newcastle-u-T NE3 ....38 A4
Otterburn Cl NE12 ......39 F8
Otterburn Cres DH4 .....90 C1
Otterburn Ct
Gateshead NE8 ....101 A1
Whitley Bay NE25 ....31 B4
Otterburn Dr NE63 ....6 B1
Otterburn Gdns
Dunston NE11 ....70 A7
Gateshead NE9 ....70 D5
South Shields NE34 ......59 E6
Whickham NE16 ....69 B7
Otterburn Gr NE24 ......17 B5
Otterburn Rd NE29 ......41 F7
Otterburn Terr NE2 .....38 E1
Otterburn Villas S NE2 ..99 B4
Ottercap Cl NE15 ....53 D6
Ottercops NE42 ....50 B1
Otterington NE38 ....84 B4
Ottershaw NE15 ....53 E6
Otto Terr SR2 ....102 B1
Ottovale Cres NE21 .....53 A1
Ottringham Cl NE15 .....53 D6
Oulton Cl
Cramlington NE23 ....22 C7
Newcastle-u-T NE5 ....37 D4
Our Lady & St Anne's RC
Prim Sch NE4 ....100 C4
Our Lady Queen of Peace RC
Prim Sch DH4 ....90 A7
Ousby Ct NE3 ....37 D7
Ouse St NE1 ....56 A5
Ouseburn Cl SR2 ....92 F8
Ouseburn Rd
Newcastle-u-T,Jesmond Vale
NE2,NE6 ....56 A3
Newcastle-u-T,St Ann's NE1 56 A6
Ouselaw NE11 ....81 D6
Ouslaw La NE11 ....81 B6
Ouston Cl NE10 ....72 C7
Ouston Inf Sch DH2 .....82 A1
Ouston Jun Sch DH2 ....81 F1
Outram St DH5 ....90 E1
Oval Park View NE10 ....71 D7
Oval The Bedlington NE22 .11 C1
Blyth NE24 ....17 B3
Houghton-le-S DH4 ......94 D8
Longbenton NE12 ....39 E6
Newcastle-u-T NE6 ....56 D4
Ouston DH2 ....81 F2
[4] Sunderland SR5 ......75 B2
Washington NE37 ....83 D8
Woolsington NE13 ....36 F8
Overdale Ct NE62 ....10 E6
Overdene NE15 ....53 F7
Overfield Rd NE3 ....37 F5
Overhill NE15 ....34 E2
Overhill Terr NE8 ......101 A1
Overstone Ave NE40 .....51 F2
Overstone Gdns NE46 ...45 A3
Overton Cl NE15 ....53 D6
Overton Rd NE29 ....41 E8
Ovett Gdns NE8 ....56 B2
Ovingham CE Fst Sch
NE42 ....50 A3
Ovingham Cl NE38 ....83 F5
Ovingham Gdns NE13 ...28 B6
Ovingham Mid Sch NE42 50 A3
Ovingham Rd NE41 ......51 A6
Ovington Gr NE5 ....54 D8
Ovington View NE42 .....50 B1
Owen Brannigan Dr
NE23 ....29 B7
Owen Ct NE2 ....98 C3
Owen Dr NE35,NE36 .....74 B8
Owen Terr Chopwell NE17 .77 C8
Tantobie DH9 ....79 B2
Owlet Cl NE21 ....53 A1
Owlet Grange NE39 .....77 E5
Oxberry Gdns NE10 .....71 C7
Oxbridge St SR2 ....86 F2
Oxclose Com Sch NE38 ..83 A4
Oxclose Rd NE38 ....83 E4
Oxclose Village Prim Sch
NE38 ....83 A5
Oxford Ave
Cramlington NE23 ....22 C7
[10] South Shields NE33 ..59 D8
Wallsend NE28 ....40 A3
Washington NE37 ....83 B8
Oxford Cl SR3 ....91 F8
Oxford Cres Hebburn NE31 57 F6
Hetton le H DH5 ....94 F4
Oxford Pl DH3 ....82 C1
Oxford Rd NE62 ....11 A7
Oxford Sq SR4 ....85 E7
Oxford St Blyth NE24 ...17 F7
Newcastle-u-T NE1 ....99 B2
South Shields NE33 ......59 D8
Sunderland SR4 ....85 E7
Tynemouth NE30 ....42 D7
Whitley Bay NE26 ....32 B5

Oxford Terr
Gateshead NE8 ....101 B1
Shiney Row DH4 ....90 A6
Oxford Way NE32 ....58 B1
Oxley Mews [7] NE35 ...58 E1
Oxnam Cres NE2 ....98 B3
Oxted Cl NE23 ....22 D7
Oxted Pl NE6 ....56 C3
Oystershell La NE4 ......98 C1
Oyston St NE33 ....42 C2
Ozanan Cl NE23 ....29 B7

P

Packham Rd SR4 ....85 C5
Paddock Cl Cleadon SR6 .59 E1
Prudhoe NE42 ....50 E2
Shiney Row DH4 ....89 F5
Paddock Hill NE20 ......25 F7
Paddock La SR3 ....92 C7
Paddock Rise NE63 ....6 B2
Paddock The
Ashington NE63 ....7 B2
Blyth NE24 ....17 C7
East Cramlington NE23 ...22 D5
Gateshead NE10 ....71 F6
New Herrington DH4 .....90 F7
Seaton Delaval NE25 .....23 E3
Stocksfield NE43 ....64 C5
Walbottle NE15 ....35 F1
Woolsington NE13 ....36 F8
Paddock Wood NE42 ....50 E2
Paddocks The NE24 .....12 C7
Pader Cl NE13 ....28 B5
Padgate Rd SR4 ....85 C6
Padonhill [5] SR3 ....91 E5
Padstow Cl [2] SR2 ......92 F8
Padstow Gdns NE9 ......70 F2
Padstow Rd NE29 ....41 E4
Page Ave NE34 ....59 E7
Page St NE31 ....57 F7
Page's Bldgs NE35 ......73 E8
Paignton Ave
Newcastle-u-T NE4 ....54 F5
Whitley Bay NE25 ....31 E4
Paignton Sq SR3 ....85 E2
Painshawfield Rd NE43 .64 C6
Paisley Sq SR3 ....85 E2
Palace Rd NE22 ....11 D2
Palace St NE4 ....100 B4
Palatine View DH6 ....96 C1
Palermo St SR4 ....85 F8
Paley St SR1 ....102 C3
Palgrove Rd SR4 ....85 C5
Palgrove Sq SR4 ....85 C5
Pallinsburn Ct NE5 ......37 B3
Pallion Ind Est SR4 .....85 D7
Pallion New Rd SR4 .....85 F8
Pallion Pk SR4 ....85 F7
Pallion Prim Sch SR4 ...85 E8
Pallion Rd SR4 ....85 F6
Pallion Ret Pk SR4 ......85 E8
Pallion Sta SR4 ....85 E8
Pallion Subway SR4 .....85 F8
Pallion Way SR4 ....85 E8
Pallion West Ind Est SR4 85 D7
Palm Ave
Newcastle-u-T NE4 ....54 D7
South Shields NE34 ......60 A5
Palm Ct NE12 ....29 F1
Palm Terr DH9 ....79 C3
Palmer Community Hospl
NE32 ....58 B7
Palmer Cres NE31 ....57 F6
Palmer Gdns NE10 ......72 C8
Palmer Rd DH9 ....78 E1
Palmer St NE32 ....58 A7
Palmer's Hill Rd SR6 ...103 A4
Palmers Gn NE12 ....29 F1
Palmerston Ave NE6 ....56 E7
Palmerston Rd SR4 ......85 B3
Palmerston Sq SR4 ......85 C4
Palmerston St NE33 .....59 C8
Palmerston Wlk NE8 ...101 A2
Palmersville NE12 ....29 F1
Palmersville Sta NE12 ...30 A1
Palmstead Rd SR4 ....85 C5
Palmstead Sq SR4 ....85 C5
Pancras Rd SR3 ....85 E2
Pandon NE1 ....99 B1
Pandon Bank NE1 ....99 B1
Pandon Ct NE2 ....99 C2
Pandon Quays NE1 ......99 C1
Panfield Terr DH4 ....89 C2
Pangbourne Cl NE15 ....53 C8
Pann La SR1 ....103 A3
Panns Bank SR1 ....103 A3
Pantiles The NE37 ......72 D2
Parade Cl NE6 ....57 A5
Parade The
Chester le S DH3 ....88 D1
Newcastle-u-T NE6 ....57 A5
Sunderland SR2 ....103 C1
Wallsend NE28 ....40 D5
Washington NE38 ....83 E4
Paradise Row NE23 .....22 B6
Park Ave Bedlington NE22 .11 E3
Blaydon NE21 ....53 B2
Blaydon,Bleach Green NE21 53 B2
Dunston NE11 ....69 E7
Hexham NE46 ....44 F5
New Silksworth SR3 ......92 B7
Newcastle-u-T,Fawdon NE3 .37 F7
Newcastle-u-T,Gosforth
NE3 ....38 B6
North Shields NE30 ......42 C7

Park Ave continued
Prudhoe NE42 ....50 E1
Shiremoor NE27 ....31 A3
South Shields NE34 ......59 F4
Sunderland SR6 ....75 E4
Wallsend NE28 ....40 B2
Washington NE37 ....83 D8
Whitley Bay NE26 ....32 A5
Park Chare NE38 ....83 D5
Park Cl NE4 ....100 A4
Park Cotts NE17 ....77 B6
Park Cres
North Shields NE30 ......42 B7
Shiremoor NE27 ....30 F3
Park Cres E NE30 ....42 C7
Park Ct Gateshead NE8 ..101 C3
Gateshead,Chowdene NE11 70 D3
Wallsend NE6 ....40 A1
Park Dr Blyth NE24 ......17 B4
Longbenton NE12 ....39 E8
Morpeth NE61 ....8 F7
Newcastle-u-T NE3 ....28 C1
Stannington NE61 ....9 E1
Whickham NE16 ....69 C8
Park Farm Villas NE24 ..17 C2
Park Field NE40 ....52 C5
Park Field Terr NE26 ....24 C6
Park Gate SR6 ....75 E3
Park Gdns NE26 ....32 A5
Park Gr Shiremoor NE27 ..30 F3
Washington NE37 ....72 D1
Park Hall SR2 ....103 D1
Park Head Rd NE7 ....39 A1
Park House Gdns NE6 ...96 A2
Park La Blaydon NE21 ...68 B8
Gateshead NE8 ....56 A3
Prudhoe NE42 ....50 D1
Shiremoor NE27 ....30 F2
Sunderland SR1 ....103 A2
Park Lane Intc SR1 .....103 A2
Park Lane Sta SR1 .....103 A2
Park Lea SR3 ....91 B6
Park Lea Rd SR6 ....75 E3
Park Par Sunderland SR6 .75 E2
Whitley Bay NE26 ....32 A5
Park Pl DH3 ....88 D5
Park Pl E SR2 ....103 A1
Park Pl W SR2 ....103 A1
Park Rd Ashington NE63 ..6 B3
Bedlington NE22 ....16 A8
Blyth NE24 ....17 F7
Gateshead NE10,NE8 ....56 B2
Hebburn NE31 ....57 E5
Jarrow NE32 ....58 A6
Lynemouth NE61,NE63 ....2 A2
Newburn NE15 ....52 F8
Newcastle-u-T NE4 ......100 A3
Rowlands Gill NE39 ......67 D2
Seaton Delaval NE25 .....23 C3
Shiremoor NE27 ....30 F3
Sunderland SR2 ....103 A1
Wallsend NE28 ....40 C1
Whitley Bay NE26 ....32 A6
Park Rd N DH3 ....88 D4
Park Rd S DH3 ....88 D1
Park Rise NE15 ....54 A6
Park Road Central DH3 ..88 D3
Park Road E NE63 ....6 C4
Park Row
[3] Gateshead NE10 .....71 D8
Sunderland SR5 ....75 A1
Park Side NE61 ....9 F5
Park St S SR5 ....74 C1
Park Terr Bedlington NE22 .11 D3
Blaydon NE21 ....53 D2
Burnopfield NE16 ....79 A6
Dunston NE11 ....69 F8
Killingworth NE12 ....29 B2
Newcastle-u-T NE1,NE2 ..99 A3
North Shields NE30 ......42 C7
Sunderland SR5 ....75 A2
Wallsend NE28 ....40 B2
Washington NE37 ....72 D1
Whickham NE16 ....54 A1
Whitley Bay NE26 ....32 A6
Park View Ashington NE63 .6 B4
Blaydon NE21 ....68 C8
Blyth NE24 ....17 F7
Bournmoor DH3 ....89 D4
Burnopfield NE16 ....79 A6
Chester le S DH3 ....88 B5
Hetton le H DH5 ....95 A3
Jarrow NE32 ....58 B4
Longbenton NE12 ....29 B2
Longbenton,Forest Hall
NE12 ....39 D8
Lynemouth NE61 ....2 A2
Newcastle-u-T NE6 ....57 A5
Seaton Delaval NE25 .....23 D3
Shiney Row DH4 ....90 B6
Wallsend NE28 ....40 B2
Widopen NE13 ....28 C6
Park View Cl NE40 ......52 D5
Park View Com Sch DH3 .88 D3
Park View Com Sch (Lower)
DH3 ....88 D7
Park View Ct NE26 ......32 A5
Park View Gdns NE40 ...52 D5
Park View Sh Ctr NE26 ..32 A5
Park Villas Ashington NE63 .6 B4
Wallsend NE28 ....40 B2
Park Wall Cnr SR3 ....91 B6
Parkdale Rise NE16 .....69 A7
Parker Ave NE3 ....38 B3
Parker Ct NE11 ....54 E2
Parkfield NE32 ....58 C1
Parkgate DH5 ....95 C3

Parkgate La NE21 ......68 B8
Parkham Cl NE23 ....16 B1
Parkhead Com Prim Sch
NE21 ....68 C8
Parkhead Gdns NE21 ....68 B8
Parkhead Sq NE21 ......53 C1
Parkhouse Ave SR5 .....85 B8
Parkhurst Rd SR4 ......85 B4
Parkin Gdns NE10 ......71 F7
Parkinson's Cotts NE40 .52 E4
Parkland Longbenton NE12 39 D6
Ryton NE40 ....53 A4
Parkland Ave NE21 .....68 B8
Parklands Gateshead NE10 72 C8
Hamsterley Mill NE39 ....77 F5
Ponteland NE20 ....25 B2
Parklands Ct NE10 ......57 C1
Parklands Way NE10 ....72 C8
Parklea NE26 ....24 C6
Parkmore Rd SR4 ....85 A3
Parks The DH3 ....88 E1
Parkshiel NE34 ....60 A4
Parkside Bedlington NE22 .11 E3
Dunston NE11 ....69 F8
Hebburn NE31 ....57 D4
Sunderland SR3 ....91 B6
Tanfield Lea DH9 ....79 C1
Throckley NE15 ....35 E1
Tynemouth NE30 ....32 C1
Wallsend NE28 ....40 D3
Parkside Ave
Blaydon NE21 ....53 C1
Newcastle-u-T NE7 ......39 B5
Parkside Cotts DH9 .....79 C1
Parkside Cres NE30 .....42 D8
Parkside Ct Ashington NE63 .6 C2
Whitley Bay NE26 ....31 F5
Widopen NE13 ....28 C6
Parkside S SR3 ....91 B6
Parkside Sch NE28 ......40 A5
Parkside Terr NE28 .....40 A4
Parkstone Cl SR4 ....85 A2
Parkville NE6 ....56 A7
Parkway Guide Post NE62 .10 F8
Washington,Biddick NE38 .83 C4
Washington,Washington Village
NE38 ....83 D5
Whickham NE16 ....68 E6
Parkwood Ave NE42 .....50 F3
Parliament St NE31 .....57 C7
Parmontley St NE15 ....53 F5
Parnell St DH4 ....94 B8
Parrish View NE1 ....99 A1
Parry Dr SR6 ....60 E1
Parson Rd NE41 ....51 B6
Parson's Ave NE6 ......56 F5
Parsons Ind Est NE37 ..83 B8
Parsons Rd NE37 ....83 B8
Parsons St [10] NE24 ...17 E8
Parsons' Gdns [5] NE11 .54 F1
Partick Rd SR4 ....85 B4
Partick Sq SR4 ....85 C4
Partnership Ct SR7 .....92 E2
Partridge Cl NE38 ....82 F4
Pasteur Rd DH6 ....97 F7
Paston Rd NE25 ....23 D2
Pastures The Blyth NE24 .17 D4
Morpeth NE61 ....8 D7
Stocksfield NE43 ....64 B4
Path The [8] NE9 ....70 F4
Pathside NE32 ....58 C2
Patience Ave NE13 ......28 C8
Patina Cl NE15 ....53 C8
Paton Rd SR3 ....85 F2
Paton Sq SR3 ....85 F2
Patrick Cain Ho NE33 ...59 B8
Patrick Cres DH6 ....97 E8
Patrick Terr NE23 ....29 B7
Patterdale Cl NE36 ......74 C7
Patterdale Gdns NE7 ....39 B4
Patterdale Gr SR5 ......75 C4
Patterdale Ho NE24 .....17 A8
Patterdale Rd NE24 .....17 A8
Patterdale St DH5 ......95 A2
Patterdale Terr NE8 ....70 F8
Patterson Cl NE46 ......44 E3
Patterson St NE21 ......53 E4
Pattinson Gdns
Gateshead,Carr Hill NE9 ..71 B7
Gateshead,Old Fold NE10 .56 C2
Pattinson Ind Est
Washington NE38 ....84 B6
Washington,Swan NE38 ...83 F3
Pattinson Rd NE38 ......84 B4
Patton Way NE61 ....4 E3
Pauline Ave SR6 ....75 D3
Pauline Gdns NE15 .....54 A4
Pauls Gn DH5 ....95 A6
Pauls Rd SR1 ....103 B2
Paulsway NE32 ....58 E6
Pavilion Mews NE2 .....99 C4
Pavilion Terr DH5 ....95 A3
Pavilion The NE16 ......53 F1
Pavillion Ct SR1 ....103 B2
Pawston Rd NE21,NE39 ..67 B5
Paxford Cl NE7 ....39 A5
Paxton Terr SR4 ....102 A3
Peacehaven Ct NE37 ....72 C2
Peacock Ct NE11 ....70 B7
Peacock St W SR4 ......85 F6
Pear Tree Terr
Chopwell NE17 ....77 B8
Great Lumley DH3 ....89 B1
Pearth Edge [2] NE9 ....71 F1
Peareth Ct NE8 ....101 C3
Peareth Gr SR6 ....75 F3
Peareth Hall Rd NE37,
NE9 ....72 A2

Peareth Rd SR6 ....75 F4
Peareth Terr DH3 ....82 C3
Pearey Ho NE29 ....42 A7
Pearl Rd SR3 ....85 F2
Pearson Pl Jarrow NE32 ...58 C0
  North Shields NE30 .....42 B6
Pearson St NE33 ....42 D4
Pearson's Terr 1 NE46 ...45 A5
Peartree Bglws NE17 ....77 C6
Peartree Ct NE17 ....77 C6
Peartree Gdns NE6 ......40 A1
Peartree Mews 8 SR2 ...86 C4
Peary Cl NE5 ....36 F2
Pease Ave NE15 ....54 C6
Peasemoor Rd SR4 ......85 B5
Pebble Beach SR6 ....75 F7
Pecket Cl NE24 ....17 A5
Peddars Way NE34 ......59 B5
Peebles Cl NE29 ....41 C8
Peebles Rd SR3 ....85 E2
Peel Ct NE13 ....28 B8
Peel Ctr The NE37 ......83 F7
Peel Gdns NE34 ....58 E4
Peel La NE1 ....100 C4
Peel St
  Newcastle-u-T NE1 ....100 C4
  Sunderland SR2 ....103 B1
Peepy Cotts NE43 ......48 D2
Pegswood Fst Sch NE61 ..4 F4
Pegswood Ho NE4 ....98 B2
Pegswood Ind Est NE61 ...4 F4
Pegswood Prec NE61 .....4 F3
Pegswood Sta NE61 ......4 F3
Pegswood Village NE61 ...4 F4
Pegwood Rd SR4 ....85 C5
Pelaw Ave
  Chester le S DH2 ....88 C5
  Newbiggin-by-t-S NE64 ..7 D5
Pelaw Bank DH3 ....88 C4
Pelaw Cres DH2 ....88 B5
Pelaw Grange Ct DH3 ....88 B5
Pelaw Ind Est NE10 .....72 A8
Pelaw Pl DH2 ....88 C5
Pelaw Rd DH2 ....88 C5
Pelaw Sq Chester le S DH2 88 B5
  Sunderland SR4 ....85 C7
Pelaw Sta NE10 ....57 A1
Pelaw Way NE10 ....57 A1
Peldon Cl NE7 ....38 F5
Pelham Ct NE3 ....37 D7
Pelton Fell Rd DH2 .....88 C2
Pelton La DH2 ....88 B5
Pelton Rd SR4 ....85 C7
Peltondale Ave NE24 ....17 A6
Pemberton Bank DH5 ....95 C1
Pemberton Cl 7 SR5 ....75 B1
Pemberton Gdns 3 SR3 ..86 B3
Pemberton St DH5 ......95 A4
Pembridge NE38 ....83 A5
Pembroke Ave
  Birtley DH3 ....82 D1
  Newcastle-u-T NE6 .....56 E7
  Silksworth SR3 ....92 A6
Pembroke Ct
  1 Blyth NE24 ....17 F7
  Newbiggin-by-t-S NE64 ..7 E5
  Newcastle-u-T NE3 .....37 F7
Pembroke Dr NE20 ......25 B4
Pembroke Gdns
  Ashington NE63 ....7 A1
  Wallsend NE28 ....41 A4
Pembroke Terr NE33 ....59 C7
Pembrooke Ave NE6 .....56 E7
Pendamor Ct NE61 ......5 D8
Pendeford NE38 ....84 A4
Pendle Cl NE38 ....83 B3
Pendle Gn SR4 ....102 A1
Pendleton Dr NE23 .....16 B1
Pendower Way NE15 ....54 C5
Penfold Cl NE7 ....39 C4
Penhale Dr SR2 ....92 F7
Penhill Cl DH2 ....81 F1
Penistone Rd NE34 .....85 A4
Penman Pl NE29 ....42 A4
Penman Sq SR4 ....85 C4
Penman St NE29 ....42 A4
Penn Sq SR4 ....85 C6
Penn St NE4 ....100 B3
Pennant Sq SR4 ....85 C6
Pennine Ave 23 DH2 ....91 F6
Pennine Ct NE63 ....6 E1
Pennine Dr NE63 ....6 E1
Pennine Gdns NE11 .....70 A6
Pennine Gr NE36 ....74 B7
Pennine View NE17 .....77 B8
Pennine Way NE12 .....39 A6
Pennycross Rd SR4 .....85 A4
Pennycross Sq SR4 .....85 A5
Pennyfine Cl NE29 .....42 A8
Pennyfine Rd NE16 .....69 C2
Pennygate Sq SR4 .....85 A5
Pennygreen Sq SR4 ....85 A5
Pennymore Sq SR4 .....85 A4
Pennywell Bsns Ctr SR4 .85 C5
Pennywell Ind Est SR4 ..85 A3
Pennywell Rd SR4 .....85 C4
Pennywell Sch SR4 ....85 B4
Pennywell Sh Prec SR4 .85 C4
Penrith Ave NE30 ......32 A2
Penrith Ct NE22 ....10 D2
Penrith Gdns NE9 ......71 B4
Penrith Gr NE9 ....71 B4
Penrith Rd Hebburn NE31 .57 F4
  Sunderland SR5 ....75 C4
Penrose Gn NE3 ....37 F5
Penrose Rd SR4 ....85 B4
Pensford Ct NE3 ....37 C6

Penshaw Gn NE5 ....37 D3
Penshaw La DH4 ....90 B8
Penshaw Monument*
  SR4 ....84 C1
Penshaw View
  Birtley DH3 ....82 E3
  Gateshead NE10 ....72 C8
  Hebburn NE31 ....57 E4
  Jarrow NE32 ....58 B4
Penshaw Way DH3 ......82 E4
Pensher St
  Gateshead NE10 ....56 C1
  Sunderland SR4 ....102 C1
Pensher St E NE10 .....56 C1
Pensher View NE37 ....72 C1
Pent Ct NE40 ....52 A1
Pentland Cl Ashington NE63 6 E1
  Cramlington NE23 .....16 B1
  Tynemouth NE29 ....31 F1
  Washington NE38 .....83 B3
Pentland Ct 5 DH2 ....88 C2
Pentland Gdns NE11 ...70 A7
Pentland Gr NE12 .....29 B1
Pentridge Cl NE23 ....22 C7
Penwood Rd SR4 ......85 C5
Penyghent Way NE37 ...83 A6
Penzance Par NE31 ....58 A2
Penzance Rd SR4 ......85 B4
Peplow Sq SR4 ....85 C7
Peppercorn Ct NE1 ....101 B4
Percival St SR4 ....85 F7
Percy Ave
  Tynemouth NE30 ......32 C3
  Whitley Bay NE26 .....32 A5
Percy Cl NE46 ....44 F3
Percy Cotts NE25 .....23 E2
Percy Cres NE29 ......41 D3
Percy Ct NE29 ....41 D3
Percy Gardens Cotts
  NE30 ....42 D8
Percy Gdns Dunston NE11 70 A7
  Longbenton NE12 .....39 D8
  Stakeford NE62 ....11 A8
  Tynemouth NE30 ......42 E8
  Whitley Bay NE25 .....32 A4
Percy Hedley Sch NE12 .39 D7
Percy Hedley Senior Sch The
  NE12 ....29 C7
Percy Lonnen NE42 ....50 D3
Percy Main Prim Sch
  NE29 ....41 D2
Percy Main Sta NE29 ..41 D3
Percy Main Village Sta
  NE29 ....41 C3
Percy Park Rd NE30 ...42 D8
Percy Pk NE30 ....42 D8
Percy Rd NE26 ....32 B5
Percy Scott St NE34 ..58 C1
Percy St Ashington NE63 ..6 E4
  Blyth NE24 ....17 F8
  Cramlington NE23 ....22 C5
  Hetton le H DH5 ......95 B4
  Jarrow NE32 ....58 C7
  Longbenton NE12 .....29 F1
  Newcastle-u-T NE1 ...99 C3
  Newcastle-u-T,Lemington
  NE15 ....53 C6
  5 South Shields NE33 .42 D2
  Tynemouth NE30 ......42 E7
  Wallsend NE28 ....40 C2
Percy St S NE24 ......17 F7
Percy Terr Newburn NE15 52 F7
  Newcastle-u-T NE3 ....38 E5
  Penshaw DH4 ....90 A8
  Sunderland SR2 ....86 E4
  4 Whitburn SR6 ......60 F1
  Whitley Bay NE25 ....31 E5
Percy Terr S SR2 .....86 F3
Percy Way NE15 ....36 A1
Peregrine Ct NE28 ....41 F6
Peregrine Pl NE12 ....39 A7
Perivale Rd SR4 ......85 B4
Perry St NE8,NE9 .....70 F8
Perry Stone Mews NE22 16 A8
Perrycrofts SR3 ......92 A4
Perth Ave NE32,NE34 ..58 E1
Perth Cl Tynemouth NE29 41 C8
  Wallsend NE28 ....40 F4
Perth Ct Gateshead NE11 70 E3
  Sunderland SR3 ....85 E1
Perth Gdns NE28 ......40 F4
Perth Rd SR3 ....85 F2
Perth Sq SR3 ....85 F2
Pescott Ct 7 NE46 ...45 B4
Pesspool Ave DH6 ....97 F3
Pesspool Bglws DH6 ..97 F3
Pesspool La DH6 .....97 F3
Pesspool Terr DH6 ...97 F3
Peter Stracey Ho SR6 .75 D4
Peterborough Cl NE8 .101 B2
Peterborough Way NE32 58 B1
Petersfield Rd SR4 ...85 B4
Petersham Rd SR4 ....85 C6
Peth Gn DH5 ....95 B4
Peth Head NE46 ......45 C5
Peth La NE40 ....52 D6
Petherton Ct NE3 ....37 C6
Pethgate Ct 10 NE61 ..9 A8
Petrel Cl 12 NE33 ...42 C4
Petrel Way NE24 .....17 F4
Petteril NE38 ....83 A1
Petworth Cl NE33 ....42 B1
Petworth Gdns NE61 ..4 E4
Pevensey Cl NE29 ....31 F1
Pexton Way NE5 .....54 A8
Pheasantmoor 3 NE37 83 A7
Philadelphia Aged Miners
  Homes 6 DH4 ....90 B6

Philadelphia Complex
  DH4 ....90 D6
Philadelphia La DH4 ...90 C4
Philip Pl NE4 ....98 A2
Philip Sq SR4 ....85 E2
Philip St NE4 ....98 A2
Philip's Ct 3 NE9 ....71 B5
Philiphaugh NE28 .....57 B8
Philipson St NE6 .....56 F6
Phillips Ave NE16 ....69 A8
Phillips Cl DH6 ......97 E3
Phobe Grange Cotts
  NE42 ....50 D2
Phoenix Chase NE9 ...41 C8
Phoenix Ct Morpeth NE61 .8 F8
  Tynemouth NE29 ......41 C8
Phoenix Rd
  Sunderland SR4 ....85 C6
  Washington NE38 .....82 E6
Phoenix St NE24 .....17 B4
Phoenix Way DH4 .....94 C7
Piccadilly SR3 ......91 E8
Picherwell NE10 .....71 D7
Pickard St SR4 ......102 A3
Pickering Ct NE32 ...58 A7
Pickering Gn NE9 ....71 B2
Pickering Rd SR4 ....85 B3
Pickering Sq SR4 ....85 B4
Pickersgill Ho SR5 ..74 C3
Pickhurst Rd SR4 ....85 B3
Pickhurst Sq SR4 ....85 B3
Picktree Cotts 2 DH3 .88 D4
Picktree Cotts E 3 DH3 88 D4
Picktree Farm Cotts
  NE38 ....88 E7
Picktree La
  Chester le S DH3 .....88 D4
  Chester le S,Picktree DH3,
  NE38 ....88 E7
Picktree Lodge
  Birtley NE38 ....82 E8
  Chester le S DH3 .....88 D8
Picktree Mews 6 DH3 .88 D4
Picktree Terr 1 DH3 .88 D4
Pier Par NE33 ....42 E4
Pier Rd NE30 ....42 E7
Pier View SR6 ....75 F2
Pikestone Cl NE38 ...83 A3
Pilgrim Cl SR5 ......75 C1
Pilgrim St
  Newcastle-u-T NE1 ...101 B4
  Newcastle-u-T NE1 ...99 B1
Pilgrims Ct NE2 .....99 B4
Pilgrims Way NE61 ...8 D7
Pilgrimsway
  Gateshead NE9 ......71 B7
  Jarrow NE32 ....58 E6
Pilton Rd NE5 ....36 F3
Pilton Wlk 4 NE5 ...36 F3
Pimlico Ct NE9 .....70 F4
Pimlico Rd
  Hetton le H DH5 .....95 B1
  Sunderland SR4 .....85 B4
Pinders Way DH6 ....96 D1
Pine Ave Burnopfield NE16 78 F6
  Dinnington NE13 .....27 C7
  Guide Post NE62 .....10 D7
  3 Houghton-le-S DH4 ..94 D8
  Newcastle-u-T NE34 ..37 F7
  South Shields NE34 ..60 A5
Pine Rd NE21 ....53 C2
Pine St Birtley DH3 ..82 C5
  4 Chester le S DH3 ..88 C3
  Greenside NE40 .....52 B1
  Jarrow NE32 ....58 A6
  Seaton Burn NE13 ...28 C8
  Sunderland SR4 .....85 F7
  Throckley NE15 .....35 D3
Pinedale Dr NE46 ....97 F7
Pinegarth NE20 .....25 C2
Pines The Greenside NE40 52 B1
  Newcastle-u-T NE4 ..100 A3
Pinesway 4 SR3 ....86 B3
Pinetree Gdns NE25 ..31 E3
Pinetree Way NE11 ..54 B2
Pinewood NE31 .....57 C7
Pinewood Ave
  Cramlington NE23 ...16 B1
  Washington NE38 ...83 C1
  Wideopen NE13 .....28 C5
Pinewood Cl
  Newcastle-u-T,Kingston Park
  NE3 ....37 B7
  Newcastle-u-T,Walkerville
  NE6 ....39 F1
  Washington NE38 ...83 F3
Pinewood Dr NE61 ...3 D2
Pinewood Gdns NE11 .70 A5
Pinewood Rd SR5 ...74 F2
Pinewood Sq 8 SR5 .74 F2
Pinewood St DH4 ...89 E1
Pinewood Villas NE34 60 A6
Pink La NE1 ....100 C4
Pinner Pl NE6 ......56 E4
Pinner Rd SR4 .....85 C5
Pintail Ct 10 NE34 .59 A4
Pioneer Terr NE22 ..11 C2
Pipe Track La NE4 ..54 D4
Piper Rd NE42 .....50 B5
Pipershaw NE37 ....82 F6
Pipewellgate NE8 ..101 B3
Pit Row SR3 ......91 F8
Pitcairn Rd SR4 ...85 C5
Pitt St NE4 ....98 B2
Pittington La DH6 .96 A6
Pittington Prim Sch DH6 96 B5
Pittington Rd DH5,DH6 .96 A5

Plains Farm Prim Sch
  SR3 ....85 F2
Plains Rd SR3 ......85 F2
Plaistow Sq SR4 ....85 C6
Plaistow Way NE23 ..16 B1
Plane Tree Ct SR3 ..91 E6
Planesway NE10 ...71 E5
Planet Ho SR1 .....103 A3
Planet Pl NE12 ....29 C2
Planetree Ave NE4 .54 D8
Plantagenet Ave DH3 88 D2
Plantation Ave
  High Pittington DH6 .96 E3
  Whickham NE16 .....69 A8
Plantation Ct NE40 .66 E8
Plantation Gr NE10 .57 C2
Plantation Rd SR4 ..85 E7
Plantation Sq 2 SR4 85 E7
Plantation St NE28 .57 B8
Plantation The NE9 .71 A4
Plantation Wlk NE9 .97 F7
Plawsworth Gdns NE9 71 A4
Pleasant Pl 5 DH4 ..82 C5
Plenmeller Pl NE16 .69 A3
Plessey Ave NE24 ...17 F6
Plessey Cres NE25 ..32 B4
Plessey Ct NE24 ....17 B4
Plessey Gdns NE29 ..41 D5
Plessey Rd NE24 ...17 D5
Plessey Road Fst Sch
  NE24 ....17 F7
Plessey Road Workshops
  NE24 ....17 B4
Plessey St NE23 ...16 B3
Plessey Terr NE7 ..39 B2
Plessey Woods Ctry Pk*
  NE22 ....15 B4
Plough Rd SR3 .....91 F5
Plover Cl Blyth NE24 17 E4
  5 Washington NE38 .82 F3
Plover Dr NE16 ....79 C5
Plover Lodge DH3 ..82 C6
Ploverfield Cl NE63 ..6 C2
Plummer St NE4 ...100 C3
Plunkett Rd DH9 ...78 E1
Plymouth Sq SR3 ..85 C6
Point Pleasant Ind Est
  NE28 ....40 F1
Point Pleasant Terr NE28 40 F1
Polden Cres NE29 ..31 F1
Polebrook Rd SR4 ..85 C6
Pollard St NE33 ...42 D3
Polmaise St NE21 ..53 C2
Polmuir Rd SR3 ...85 F2
Polperro Cl DH3 ...82 D3
Polperro Cl 6 SR2 .92 F8
Polton Sq SR4 ....85 C6
Polwarth Cres NE3 .38 C8
Polwarth Dr NE3 ..28 C1
Polwarth Pl NE3 ...38 C8
Polwarth Rd NE3 ..28 C1
Polworth Sq SR3 ..85 F2
Pont Haugh NE20 ..25 F7
Pont St NE63 .....6 D3
Pont View NE20 ...25 F7
Pontdyke NE10 ...71 F4
Pontefract Rd 2 SR4 85 B3
Ponteland Cl
  Tynemouth NE29 ...41 C7
  Washington NE38 ..82 F4
Ponteland Com High Sch
  NE20 ....25 F5
Ponteland Fst Sch NE20 25 F7
Ponteland Mid Sch NE20 25 F5
Ponteland Rd
  Newcastle-u-T,Blakelaw
  NE5 ....37 D3
  Newcastle-u-T,Kenton Bankfoot
  NE3 ....37 B6
  Newcastle-u-T,Spital Tongues
  NE2 ....98 A3
  Ponteland NE20 ....26 A5
  Throckley NE15 ....35 D5
  Woolsington NE13 ..37 A7
Ponthaugh NE39 ...67 F3
Pontop Sq SR4 ....85 C7
Pontop St DH5 ....94 C4
Pontop View NE39 .67 D2
Poole Cl NE23 ....22 C7
Poole Rd SR4 .....85 C6
Pooley Cl NE5 ....37 B1
Pooley Rd NE5 ....37 B1
Poplar Ave Blyth NE24 12 D1
  Burnopfield NE16 ..78 F6
  Dinnington NE13 ...27 C7
  1 Houghton-le-S DH4 94 D8
  Newcastle-u-T NE6 .39 F1
Poplar Cl NE31 ...57 E3
Poplar Cres Birtley DH3 82 B5
  Dunston NE11 .....69 F7
  Gateshead NE8 ....101 B2
Poplar Dr SR6 ....75 D4
Poplar Gr Bedlington NE22 11 C1
  South Shields NE34 .59 F5
  7 Sunderland SR2 ..92 E8
Poplar Pl NE3 ....38 C5
Poplar Rd NE21 ...53 C1
Poplar St Ashington NE63 .6 D4
  3 Chester le S DH3 .88 C3
  Throckley NE15 ...35 D3
Poplar Terr DH3 ..88 D3
Poplars The
  Easington Lane DH5 .95 C1
  Newcastle-u-T,Elswick
  NE4 ....100 A3

Poplars The continued
  Newcastle-u-T,Gosforth
  NE3 ....38 C3
  Penshaw NE38 .....90 B8
  1 Sunderland SR5 ..74 F2
  1 Sunderland,South Hylton
  SR4 ....85 A6
  Washington NE38 ..83 D4
Popplewell Gdns NE9 71 A4
Popplewell Terr NE29 42 A8
Popular Ct 1 DH3 ..88 C3
Porchester Dr NE23 .22 C7
Porlock Ct NE23 ...16 A1
Porlock Ho NE32 ..58 D5
Porlock Rd NE32 ..58 D5
Portadown Rd 1 SR4 85 B3
Portberry St NE33 ..42 B1
Portberry Street Ind Est
  NE33 ....59 B8
Portberry Way NE33 42 B1
Portchester Gr NE35 73 E8
Portchester Rd SR4 .85 C5
Portchester Sq SR4 .85 C4
Porthcawl Dr NE37 .72 C2
Portia St NE63 ....6 E4
Portland Cl DH2 ..88 A1
Portland Gdns
  Cramlington NE23 .22 C7
  1 Gateshead NE9 ..70 F2
  Tynemouth NE30 ..42 A7
Portland Ind Pk NE63 5 F5
Portland Mews NE2 .99 C3
Portland Rd
  Newcastle-u-T NE2 .99 C2
  Sunderland SR3 ...85 F2
  Throckley NE15 ...35 E2
Portland Sch
  Silksworth SR3 ...91 E5
  Sunderland SR3 ..85 F3
Portland Sq SR3 ..85 F3
Portland St 1 Blyth NE24 17 D8
  Gateshead NE10 ..57 A1
  Newcastle-u-T NE4 .54 C4
Portland Terr
  Ashington NE63 ...5 F5
  Hexham NE46 .....44 F5
  Newcastle-u-T NE2 .99 C3
Portman Mews NE2 .99 C2
Portman Pl NE6 ...56 E3
Portman Sq SR4 ..85 C5
Portmarnock NE37 .72 B2
Portmeads Rd DH3 .82 D4
Portmeads Rise DH3 82 D4
Portobello Ind Est DH3 82 E4
Portobello La SR5,SR6 75 D1
Portobello Prim Sch
  DH3 ....82 D2
Portobello Terr DH3 82 D2
Portobello Way DH3 82 D2
Portree Cl DH3 ...82 D1
Portree Sq SR3 ..85 E2
Portrush Cl NE37 .72 C2
Portrush Rd SR4 .85 C6
Portrush Way NE7 .39 C5
Portslade Rd SR4 .85 B4
Portsmouth Rd
  North Shields NE29 41 C5
  Sunderland SR4 ..85 B5
Portsmouth Sq SR4 85 B5
Portugal Pl NE28 .40 B1
Post Office La NE2 .42 A8
Post Office St 4 NE24 17 F8
Postern Cres NE61 .8 F7
Potland View NE61 .1 A3
Potter Sq SR3 ....85 F2
Potter St Jarrow NE32 58 A7
  Wallsend NE28 ....41 A1
Potteries The NE33 42 E1
Pottersway NE9 ..71 B7
Pottery Bank Morpeth NE61 3 E2
  Newcastle-u-T NE6 .56 F3
Pottery Bank Ct NE61 3 E2
Pottery La
  Newcastle-u-T NE1 .100 C3
  Sunderland SR4 ..85 A7
Pottery Rd SR5 ..75 A1
Pottery Yd 3 DH4 .94 E8
Potts St NE6 ....56 C6
Poulton Cl NE38 .89 B8
Powburn Cl DH2 ..88 A1
Powburn Gdns NE4 54 E8
Powis Rd SR3 ....85 F2
Powis Sq SR3 ...85 F2
Powys Pl NE4 ...98 B2
Poynings Cl NE5 .37 C5
Praetorian Dr NE28 40 B1
Precinct The
  Blaydon NE21 ....53 D3
  Sunderland SR4 ..102 B2
  Sunderland,Hillview SR2 86 C2
Prefect Pl NE9 ..71 A7
Premier Rd SR3 ..85 F2
Prendwick Ave NE31 57 D3
Prendwick Cl NE31 57 D3
Prengarth Ave SR6 75 D3
Prensgarth Way NE34 58 F3
Prescot Rd SR4 ..85 C6
Press La SR1 ....103 A3
Prestbury Ave NE23 16 A1
Prestbury Rd SR4 .85 A3
Prestdale Ave NE24 17 A7
Presthope Rd SR4 .85 B4
Prestmede NE10 ..71 E7
Preston Ave NE30 .42 B7
Preston Ct NE29 ..42 A8

Preston Gate NE29 31 F1
Preston Grange Prim Sch NE29 31 E1
Preston North Rd NE29 31 F1
Preston Pk NE29 42 A7
Preston Rd
Sunderland SR2 86 F4
Tynemouth NE29,NE30 42 A7
Preston Terr
12 Shiremoor NE27 30 E1
1 Tynemouth NE29 41 F8
Preston Twrs NE29 42 A7
Preston Wood NE30 32 A1
Prestonhill 7 SR3 91 E5
Prestwick NE10 71 E5
Prestwick Ave NE29 41 C6
Prestwick Carr Rd NE13 27 A8
Prestwick Cl NE37 72 C2
Prestwick Dr NE10 72 C7
Prestwick Gdns NE3 37 F4
Prestwick Ho NE4 98 B2
Prestwick Rd SR4 85 C6
Prestwick Terr NE20 26 C3
Pretoria Ave NE61 8 F8
Pretoria Sq SR3 85 E2
Pretoria St NE15 54 A5
Price St Hebburn NE31 57 C7
Morpeth NE61 3 E1
Priestclose Cotts NE42 50 F2
Priestclose Rd NE42 50 D2
Priestfield Cl SR3 91 F5
Priestfield Gdns NE16 78 F6
Priestlands Ave 12 NE46 45 A4
Priestlands Cl NE46 45 A3
Priestlands Cres NE46 45 A4
Priestlands Dr NE46 45 A4
Priestlands Gr NE46 45 A3
Priestlands La NE46 45 A4
Priestlands Rd NE46 45 A4
Priestley Ct NE34 59 A3
Priestley Gdns NE10 72 B7
Priestly Cres SR4 102 B4
Priestman Ct SR4 85 D6
Priestpopple NE46 45 B4
Primary Gdns SR2 103 C1
Primate Rd SR3 85 E2
Primrose Ave NE34 59 B5
Primrose Cl NE23 29 A8
Primrose Cres
Bournmoor DH4 89 E3
Sunderland SR6 75 D3
Primrose Ct NE63 6 B1
Primrose Gdns
Ouston DH2 81 F2
Wallsend NE28 40 A4
Primrose Hill NE9 71 A5
Primrose Hill Hospl NE32 58 C4
Primrose Hill Terr NE32 58 C3
Primrose Prec SR6 75 D3
Primrose St 3 SR4 85 A6
Primrose Terr Birtley DH3 82 D4
Jarrow NE32 58 C4
Prince Albert Terr NE2 99 C2
Prince Consort Ind Est NE31 57 C7
Prince Consort La NE31 57 D6
Prince Consort Rd
Gateshead NE8 101 C1
Hebburn NE31 57 C6
Jarrow NE32 58 C6
Prince Consort Way NE29 42 A3
Prince Edward Ct NE34 60 A5
Prince Edward Gr NE34 60 C6
Prince Edward Rd NE34 60 A5
Prince Edward Rd E NE34 60 C6
Prince George Ave SR6 75 D3
Prince George Sq 15 NE33 42 D3
Prince Of Wales Cl NE34 59 E5
Prince Philip Cl NE15 54 C5
Prince Rd NE28 40 B3
Prince St Chopwell NE17 66 B1
Sunderland SR1 103 A3
Prince's Gdns NE24 17 C8
Prince's Mdw NE3 38 A5
Princes Ave
Newcastle-u-T NE3 38 B7
Sunderland SR6 75 E5
Princes Cl NE3 38 B8
Princes Gdns
Sunderland SR6 75 E5
Whitley Bay NE25 31 E5
Princes Pk Dunston NE11 70 B6
Gateshead NE8 70 C5
Princes Rd NE3 28 B1
Princes St Corbridge NE45 47 A5
Shiney Row DH4 90 A5
Tynemouth NE30 42 B7
Princess Ct NE42 50 D4
Princess Dr NE8 100 A1
Princess Gdns DH5 95 A5
Princess Louise Fst Sch NE24 17 D7
Princess Louise Rd NE24 17 E7
Princess Mary Ct NE2 99 A4
Princess Sq NE1 99 B2
Princess St
Gateshead NE10 57 A1
Sunderland SR2 102 C1
Sunniside NE16 69 B2
Princess Way NE42 50 C4
Princesway NE11 70 C5
Princesway Central NE11 70 C4
Princesway S NE11 70 C3
Princetown Terr SR3 85 E2
Princeway NE30 42 D8
Prinn Pl NE16 69 B2
Prior Terr Corbridge NE45 46 F6
Hexham NE46 45 A6
Prior's Ho NE30 42 E7
Prior's Terr NE30 42 D7
Priors Grange DH6 96 B5
Priors Way NE28 40 E2
Priors Wlk NE61 8 E7
Priory Ave NE25 31 F4
Priory Ct Gateshead NE8 101 C3
Gateshead,Wardley NE10 72 B8
South Shields NE33 42 D5
Tynemouth NE30 42 E8
Priory Gdns NE45 46 F7
Priory Gn 20 NE6 56 B6
Priory Gr SR4 85 F5
Priory Grange NE24 17 C8
Priory Mews 7 NE30 42 D7
Priory Pl
Brunswick Village NE13 28 A5
Newcastle-u-T NE6 56 C5
Stakeford NE62 11 A8
Priory Prim Sch NE30 42 D8
Priory Rd NE32 58 C8
Priory Way NE5 36 F4
Proctor Ct NE6 57 A5
Proctor Sq SR3 85 F2
Proctor St NE6 57 A5
Promenade
Newbiggin-by-t-S NE64 7 E4
Seaham SR7 93 D1
South Shields NE33 42 F3
Sunderland SR2 87 A3
Whitley Bay NE26 32 B5
Promontory Terr NE26 32 C4
Promotion Cl 9 SR6 75 E2
Prospect Ave
Seaton Delaval NE25 23 C3
Wallsend NE28 40 B3
Prospect Avenue N NE28 40 B4
Prospect Cotts NE22 11 C5
Prospect Cres DH5 97 C8
Prospect Ct NE4 98 A1
Prospect Gdns NE36 74 A7
Prospect Pl
Newbiggin-by-t-S NE64 7 F5
Newcastle-u-T NE4 98 A1
Prospect Row SR1 103 C3
Prospect St 2 DH3 88 C4
Prospect Terr
Burnopfield NE16 79 A4
1 Chester le S DH3 88 C4
East Boldon NE36 74 C7
Ebchester DH8 76 F4
Gateshead NE9 71 D1
Kibblesworth NE11 81 C6
North Shields NE30 42 C6
Prudhoe NE42 50 B2
Prospect Terr Ind Est NE30 42 C6
Providence Pl 18 NE10 56 D1
Provident Terr NE28 40 A2
Provost Gdns NE4 54 D4
Prudhoe Castle* NE42 50 C3
Prudhoe Castle Fst Sch NE42 50 B2
Prudhoe Chare NE1 99 A2
Prudhoe Com High Sch NE42 50 D1
Prudhoe Ct NE3 37 E7
Prudhoe Gr NE32 58 B3
Prudhoe Hospl NE42 50 F1
Prudhoe Pl NE1 99 A2
Prudhoe St
Newcastle-u-T NE1 99 A2
North Shields NE29 42 A5
8 Sunderland SR4 85 F7
Prudhoe Sta NE42 50 B4
Prudhoe Street Back 19 NE29 42 A5
Prudhoe Terr
18 North Shields NE29 42 A5
Tynemouth NE30 42 D8
Prudhoe West Fst Sch NE42 50 C2
Pudding Chare NE1 99 A1
Pudding Mews 3 NE46 45 B5
Puffin Cl NE24 17 F3
Pullman Ct NE9 70 E5
Purbeck Cl NE29 31 F2
Purbeck Gdns NE23 22 C7
Purbeck Rd NE12 39 B6
Purdy's Ho NE61 3 E1
Purley NE38 84 A4
Purley Cl NE28 40 F4
Purley Gdns NE3 37 F4
Purley Rd SR3 85 E2
Purley Sq SR3 85 E2
Putney Sq SR4 85 B4
Pykerley Mews NE25 31 E4
Pykerley Rd NE25 31 E5

Q

Quadrant The
North Shields NE29 41 E5
Sunderland SR1 103 C3
Quality Row NE6 56 A5
Quality Row Rd NE16 54 A1
Quantock Ave DH2 88 A2
Quantock Cl NE29 31 F2
Quarry Bank Ct NE4 98 B1
Quarry Cotts NE63 7 B6
Quarry Edge NE46 45 C3
Quarry Hos NE23 29 C6
Quarry House Gdns DH5 94 C4
Quarry House La DH5 94 D4
Quarry La
South Shields NE34 60 B5
South Shields NE34 60 D6
Quarry Rd Hebburn NE31 57 E5
New Silksworth SR3 92 B7
Newcastle-u-T NE15 53 C6
Quarry Row 19 NE10 56 D1
Quarry Sq DH9 79 B2
Quarry St SR3 92 A7
Quarry View Prim Sch SR4 85 C6
Quarryfield Rd NE8 101 C4
Quatre Bras NE46 44 F5
Quay Corner Ave NE32 58 D8
Quay Rd NE24 18 A7
Quay The DH5 95 A3
Quay View NE28 41 A2
Quayside Blyth NE24 17 F8
Newcastle-u-T NE1 101 B4
Newcastle-u-T,St Lawrence NE1,NE6 56 A5
Quayside Ct 7 Blyth NE24 17 F8
North Shields NE30 42 B5
Quayside Ho SR1 103 B3
Queen Alexandra Mews SR2 86 D3
Queen Alexandra Rd
Sunderland SR2 86 D3
Tynemouth NE29 42 A7
Queen Alexandra Road W NE29 41 E7
Queen Ann Ct 21 NE6 56 C7
Queen Elizabeth Ave NE9 71 B6
Queen Elizabeth Ct NE34 58 F3
Queen Elizabeth Dr DH5 97 D8
Queen Elizabeth High Sch NE46 44 E4
Queen Elizabeth Hospl NE9 71 B6
Queen Elizabeth II Ctry Pk* NE63 6 F6
Queen St Ashington NE63 6 E4
Birtley DH3 82 B4
Gateshead NE8 70 C8
Hetton le H DH5 95 A5
Lynemouth NE61 2 A2
Morpeth NE61 9 A8
Newbiggin-by-t-S NE64 7 E5
Newcastle-u-T NE1 101 B4
North Shields NE30 42 B6
South Shields NE33 42 C3
Sunderland SR1 103 A3
Sunderland,Grangetown SR2 92 F8
Queen St E SR1 103 B3
Queen Victoria Rd NE1, NE2 99 A3
Queen Victoria St NE10 57 A1
Queen's Cres
Hebburn NE31 57 D4
Sunderland SR4 102 A1
Wallsend NE28 40 B3
Queen's Dr NE26 32 A5
Queen's Gdns Blyth NE24 17 C8
Morpeth NE61 8 E7
Queen's Par SR6 75 F5
Queen's Pk DH3 88 D2
Queen's Rd
Bedlington NE22 11 D2
Newcastle-u-T NE2 38 F1
Sunderland SR5 75 B1
Whitley Bay NE26 31 F6
Queen's Terr NE2 38 F1
Queens Ave SR6 75 E5
Queens Ct
Gateshead NE8 100 C1
Newcastle-u-T NE4 98 B2
Newcastle-u-T,Brunton Park NE3 28 C2
Walbottle NE15 36 A1
Queens Dr Sunniside NE16 69 B2
Whickham NE16 69 C5
Queens Gdns
Annitsford NE23 22 B1
Longbenton NE12 39 D6
Queens La NE1 101 A4
Queens Pl NE64 7 E5
Queens Rd
Annitsford NE23 22 B1
Newcastle-u-T NE5 37 A3
Seaton Sluice NE26 24 D6
Walbottle NE15 36 A1
Queens Terr NE28 40 C3
Queens Way NE46 44 E5
Queensberry St SR4 102 B3
Queensbridge NE12 38 F7
Queensbury Dr NE15 36 B2
Queensbury Gate NE12 39 A6
Queensland Ave NE34 58 F4
Queensmere DH3 88 C7
Queensway
Houghton-le-S DH5 94 F8
Morpeth NE61 8 D7
Newcastle-u-T,Brunton Park NE3 28 B1
Newcastle-u-T,Fenham NE4 54 D8
Ponteland NE20 25 D2
Tynemouth NE30 42 D8
3 Washington NE38 83 E4
Queensway Ct NE11 70 C6
Queensway N NE11 70 C5
Queensway S NE11 70 D4
Quentin Ave NE3 37 D5
Quick Silver Way NE27 30 E1
Quigley Terr DH3 82 B6

R

Rabbit Banks Rd NE8 101 A3
Raby Cl Bedlington NE22 10 D1
Fence Houses DH4 90 A1
Raby Cres 8 NE6 56 C6
Raby Cross 10 NE6 56 C5
Raby Dr SR3 91 C7
Raby Gdns
Burnopfield NE16 78 E6
Jarrow NE32 58 B4
Raby Rd NE38 83 A5
Raby St Gateshead NE8 70 F8
16 Newcastle-u-T,Byker NE6 56 B6
Newcastle-u-T,St Lawrence NE6 56 C5
Sunderland SR4 102 B2
Raby Way NE6 56 C5
Rabygate 7 NE6 56 C6
Rachel Cl SR2 92 C7
Rackly Way SR6 75 F8
Radcliffe Cotts 5 NE15 35 D2
Radcliffe Pl 3 NE5 37 D2
Radcliffe Rd
Hexham NE46 45 C4
Sunderland SR5 74 E2
Radcliffe St DH3 82 C3
Radlett Rd SR5 74 D2
Radnor Gdns NE28 41 A3
Radnor St NE1 99 B2
Radstock Pl NE12 39 C7
Rae Ave NE28 40 B4
Raeburn Ave NE38 83 E4
Raeburn Gdns NE9 71 B7
Raeburn Rd
Sunderland SR5 74 C3
Whiteleas NE34 59 D2
Raglan NE38 83 A5
Raglan Ave SR2 86 E3
Raglan Pl NE16 79 B6
Raglan Row DH4 90 C5
Raglan St NE32 58 C7
Railton Gdns NE9 71 B6
Railway Arches NE1 99 B1
Railway Cotts Birtley DH3 82 B4
Blyth,Bebside NE24 16 E8
Blyth,South Newsham NE24 17 C2
Cleadon NE36 59 D1
Penshaw DH4 90 A8
Riding Mill NE44 63 A8
Wylam NE41 50 F5
Railway Mus* NE41 51 B6
Railway Row SR1 102 B3
Railway St Dunston NE11 100 A1
Dunston NE11 54 F2
Hebburn NE31 57 F7
Hetton le H DH5 95 A4
Jarrow NE32 58 A7
Newbottle DH4 90 D2
Newcastle-u-T NE4 100 B3
10 North Shields NE29 42 A5
Sunderland SR1 103 C2
Railway Terr Blyth NE24 17 D7
New Herrington DH4 90 D6
Newcastle-u-T NE4 100 B3
North Shields NE29 42 A5
Penshaw DH4 90 A8
2 Sunderland SR4 85 A6
Wallsend NE28 40 D1
4 Washington NE38 83 F4
Railway Terr N DH4 90 D7
Raine Gr SR1 103 B2
Rainford Ave SR2 86 E3
Rainhill Cl NE37 72 F1
Rainhill Rd NE37 72 F1
Rainton Bridge Ind Est DH4 94 C7
Rainton Cl NE10 72 C6
Rainton Gr DH5 94 E6
Rainton Meadows (Nature Reserve)* DH4 94 B6
Rainton St Penshaw DH4 90 B8
Sunderland SR4 102 A2
Rainton View DH4 94 A2
Rake La NE29 31 E1
Raleigh Cl NE33 59 B8
Raleigh Rd SR5 74 E2
Raleigh Sq SR5 74 D2
Ralph Ave SR2 92 E8
Ralph St NE31 57 F7
Ramilies SR2 92 D6
Ramillies Rd SR5 74 C3
Ramillies Sq SR5 74 C3
Ramparts The NE15 53 F8
Ramsay Rd NE17 66 B2
Ramsay Sq SR5 74 E3
Ramsay St Blaydon NE21 53 B1
High Spen NE39 67 A5
Ramsey St DH3 88 C2
Ramsgate Rd SR5 74 E3
Ramshaw Cl NE7 39 E3
Randolph St NE32 58 C7
Rangoon Rd SR5 74 C3
Ranmere Rd NE15 54 A5
Ranmore Cl NE23 22 B7
Rannoch Ave DH2 88 B1
Rannoch Cl NE10 72 C8
Rannoch Ho NE2 38 F2
Rannoch Rd SR5 74 C3
Ranson Cres NE34 58 F5
Ranson St SR4,SR2 86 B4
Raphael Ave NE34 59 C2
Rapperton Ct 7 NE5 36 F3
Rathmore Gdns NE30 42 A7
Ratho Ct NE10 71 E6
Ravel Ct NE32 58 C6
Raven Terr 7 DH3 82 C5
Ravenburn Gdns NE15 53 F6
Ravenna Rd SR5 74 B3
Ravens Hill Dr NE63 6 A2
Ravensbourne Ave NE36 74 D8
Ravensburn Wlk 6 NE15 35 D2
Ravenscar Cl NE16 68 F5
Ravenscourt Pl NE8 101 A1
Ravenscourt Rd SR5 74 C3
Ravensdale Cres 3 NE9 71 A6
Ravensdale Gr NE24 17 A7
Ravenshill Rd NE5 36 E1
Ravenside Rd NE4 54 E8
Ravenside Terr NE17 66 A1
Ravenstone NE37 83 B7
Ravenswood 5 NE9 71 A6
Ravenswood Cl NE12 39 E8
Ravenswood Gdns NE9 70 F3
Ravenswood Prim Sch NE6 39 C1
Ravenswood Rd
Newcastle-u-T NE6 39 C1
Sunderland SR5 74 B3
Ravenswood Sq SR5 74 B3
Ravensworth SR2 92 D6
Ravensworth Apartments 6 NE11 70 A8
Ravensworth Ave
Fence Houses DH4 90 A1
Gateshead NE9 71 C2
Ravensworth Cl NE28 40 F2
Ravensworth Cres NE16 79 D8
Ravensworth Ct
Bedlington NE22 11 D3
Dunston NE11 100 A1
Newcastle-u-T NE3 37 D7
South Hetton DH6 97 F7
Ravensworth Gdns NE61 1 D4
Ravensworth Rd
Birtley DH3 82 B5
Dunston NE11 100 A1
Fence Houses DH4 89 F1
Ravensworth St
2 Bedlington NE22 11 D3
Sunderland SR4 102 B3
Wallsend NE28 40 F2
Ravensworth Terr
3 Bedlington NE22 11 D3
Dunston NE11 70 A8
Jarrow NE32 58 B3
Newcastle-u-T NE4 98 B1
South Shields NE33 59 C8
Sunniside NE16 69 B2
Ravensworth Terrace Prim Sch DH3 82 C4
Ravine Ct SR6 75 F3
Ravine Terr SR6 75 F3
Rawdon Rd SR5 74 E3
Rawling Rd NE8 70 D8
Rawlston Way NE5 37 C3
Rawmarsh Rd SR5 74 C3
Raydale SR5 74 E3
Raydale Ave NE37 83 B8
Raylees Gdns NE11 70 A7
Rayleigh Dr NE13 28 B7
Rayleigh Gr NE8 70 D8
Raynes Cl NE61 8 D7
Raynham Cl NE23 21 F3
Raynham Ct 8 NE33 42 C2
Readhead Ave NE33 42 E1
Readhead Bldgs 2 NE33 42 C2
Readhead Dr NE6 56 F4
Readhead Rd NE34 59 F8
Reading Rd
South Shields NE33 59 D7
Sunderland SR5 74 D3
Reading Sq SR5 74 D3
Reasby Gdns NE40 52 B5
Reasby Villas NE40 52 B5
Reavley Ave NE22 11 E3
Reay Cres NE35 74 B8
Reay Ct 4 DH2 88 C2
Reay Gdns NE5 37 A3
Reay Pl Newcastle-u-T NE3 38 A5
South Shields NE34 59 B5
Reay St NE10 57 B2
Rectory Ave NE3 38 E4
Rectory Bank NE36 74 A7
Rectory Ct 6 NE16 69 B7
Rectory Dene NE61 8 F7
Rectory Dr NE3 38 E4
Rectory Gn NE36 73 F7
Rectory Gr NE3 38 D5
Rectory La Blaydon NE21 68 B8
Ebchester DH8 76 E3
Whickham NE16 69 B7
Rectory Pk NE61 8 F7
Rectory Pl NE8 101 A1
Rectory Rd
Gateshead,Carr Hill NE10 71 C7
Gateshead,Shipcote NE8, NE9 70 E8
Hetton le H DH5 95 A3
Newcastle-u-T NE3 38 D4
Rectory Rd E NE10 71 D7
Rectory Terr NE3 38 E4
Red Admiral Ct NE11 70 B7
Red Barns NE1 99 C1
Red Bglws NE9 71 E1
Red Hall Dr NE7 39 D3
Red House Dr NE25 31 C6
Red House Farm NE22 15 D8
Red House Rd NE31 58 A6
Red Lion Bldgs NE10 71 D1
Red Lion La NE37 72 C2

Red – Ros 137

Red Rose Prim Sch DH3 88 D1
Red Rose Terr DH3 88 D2
Red Row Ct NE22 11 C4
Red Row Dr NE22 11 C3
Red Wlk NE7 39 A1
Redberry Way NE34 59 B4
Redburn Cl DH4 94 C8
Redburn Rd NE5 36 F4
Redby Cl SR6 75 D2
Redby Prim Sch SR6 75 E2
Redcar Rd
Newcastle-u-T NE6 39 D1
Sunderland SR5 74 E2
Wallsend NE28 41 A3
Redcar Sq SR5 74 E2
Redcliffe Way NE5 37 B3
Redcroft Gn NE5 37 B3
Redditch Sq SR5 74 D3
Rede Ave Hebburn NE31 57 E6
Hexham NE46 45 C4
Rede Ct NE61 1 E5
Rede St Gateshead NE11 70 C5
Jarrow NE32 58 A5
Rede Terr NE46 45 C4
Redemarsh NE10 71 F6
Redesdale Ave
Blaydon NE21 67 F8
Newcastle-u-T NE3 38 A6
Redesdale Cl
Longbenton NE12 39 C8
Newcastle-u-T NE15 53 E7
Redesdale Gdns NE11 69 F7
Redesdale Gr NE29 41 D6
Redesdale Pl NE24 17 B7
Redesdale Prim Sch
NE28 39 F4
Redesdale Rd
Chester le S DH2 88 A1
North Shields NE29 41 D6
Sunderland SR5 74 C3
Redewater Gdns NE16 69 A6
Redewater Rd NE4 54 E8
Redewood Cl NE5 37 A1
Redford Pl NE23 29 C5
Redheugh Bridge Rd
NE1,NE4 100 C3
Redheugh Ct NE8 70 B8
Redheugh Rd NE25 31 B5
Redhill SR6 75 E8
Redhill Dr NE16 68 E4
Redhill Rd SR5 74 D3
Redhill Wlk NE23 22 B7
Redhills Way DH5 95 A2
Redland Ave NE3 37 E6
Redlands DH4 90 A7
Redmayne Ct 1 NE10 71 D8
Redmires Cl DH2 81 E1
Redmond Rd SR5 74 E3
Redmond Sq SR5 74 E3
Rednam Pl NE5 37 B2
Redruth Gdns NE9 70 F2
Redruth Sq SR5 74 D3
Redshank Cl NE38 82 F2
Redshank Dr NE24 17 E4
Redstart Ct NE39 67 D2
Redwell Ct Prudhoe NE42 50 D2
South Shields NE34 60 C7
Redwell La NE34 60 D7
Redwell Rd NE42 50 E2
Redwing Cl NE38 82 F3
Redwing Ct NE6 56 E7
Redwood Cl
Hetton le H DH5 94 F4
Killingworth NE12 29 C4
Redwood Ct NE63 6 E2
Redwood Gdns NE11 70 B5
Redwood Gr SR3 92 B7
Reed Ave NE12 29 C4
Reed St North Shields NE30 42 B6
South Shields NE33 59 C8
Reedham Ct NE5 37 B4
Reedling Ct SR5 74 C4
Reedside NE40 52 D5
Reedsmouth Pl NE5 54 B8
Reedswood Cres NE23 22 E5
Reestones Pl NE3 37 D5
Reeth Rd SR5 74 D2
Reeth Sq SR5 74 D2
Reeth Way NE15 35 C1
Regal Rd SR4 102 A3
Regency Ct NE2 99 C4
Regency Dr
New Silksworth SR3 92 B8
Whickham NE16 68 F6
Regency Gdns NE29 41 E7
Regency Way NE20 25 A5
Regent Ave NE3 38 B5
Regent Centre Sta NE3 38 C6
Regent Ct Blyth NE24 17 D7
Gateshead NE8 101 C2
Hebburn NE31 57 D5
Longbenton NE12 29 B2
South Shields NE33 42 C1
Regent Ctr The NE3 38 C6
Regent Dr NE16 68 F4
Regent Farm Ct NE3 38 C5
Regent Farm Fst Sch
NE3 38 A6
Regent Farm Rd NE3 38 B6
Regent Rd Jarrow NE32 58 C6
Newcastle-u-T NE3 38 C5
Ryhope SR2 93 A5
Wallsend NE28 40 A3
Regent Rd N NE3 38 C5
Regent St Blyth NE24 17 E8
Hetton le H DH5 95 A5
Regent Terr
Gateshead NE8 101 B2
Regent Terr *continued*
North Shields NE29 41 E6
Sunderland SR2 86 F2
Regents Cl SR6 75 F8
Regents Ct NE28 39 F4
Regents Dr Prudhoe NE42 50 F4
Tynemouth NE30 32 C1
Regents Pk NE28 39 E3
Regina Sq SR5 74 D3
Reginald St
Boldon Colliery NE35 73 F8
Gateshead NE8 56 B1
4 Sunderland SR4 85 F7
Regrave Cl NE8 56 B2
Reid Ave NE28 40 B3
Reid Park Cl NE2 38 F2
Reid Park Ct NE2 38 F2
Reid Park Rd NE2 38 F2
Reid St NE61 9 A8
Reid's La NE23 22 E1
Reigate Sq NE23 22 B7
Reins Ct NE46 44 E5
Reiverdale Rd NE63 6 D4
Rekendyke Ind Est NE33 42 B1
Rekendyke La NE33 42 B1
Relton Ave NE6 56 D4
Relton Cl DH4 94 A7
Relton Ct NE25 31 E5
Relton PL NE25 31 E5
Relton Terr
Chester le S DH3 88 C2
Whitley Bay NE25 31 E5
Rembrandt Ave NE34 59 C2
Remscheid Way NE63 6 C1
Remus Ave NE15 34 D2
Remus Cl NE13 28 B5
Renaissance Point NE30 42 C6
Rendel St NE11 54 F1
Rendle Rd NE6 57 B4
Renforth Cl NE8 56 B2
Renforth St NE11 69 F8
Renfrew Cl NE29 41 C8
Renfrew Gn NE5 37 B3
Renfrew Pl DH3 82 D2
Renfrew Rd SR5 74 D3
Rennie Rd SR5 74 B3
Rennie Sq SR5 74 B3
Rennington NE10 72 A5
Rennington Ave NE30 32 C1
Rennington Cl
Morpeth NE61 9 B5
Tynemouth NE30 32 C1
Rennington Pl 5 NE5 37 D2
Renoir Gdns NE34 59 D2
Renwick Ave NE3 37 E6
Renwick Ct NE8 70 C8
Renwick Ho NE61 8 E7
Renwick Rd NE24 17 D7
Renwick St NE6 56 D6
Renwick Wlk NE61 8 E8
Rescue Station Cotts
DH5 94 F6
Resida Cl NE15 53 C8
Retford Rd SR5 74 D3
Retford Sq SR5 74 D3
Retreat The
Newburn NE15 52 F7
Sunderland SR2 102 B2
Revell Terr NE5 37 E1
Revelstoke Rd SR5 74 C3
Revesby St NE33 59 C6
Reynolds Ave
Killingworth NE12 29 B2
Washington NE38 83 E4
Whiteleas NE34 59 D3
Reyrolle Ct NE31 57 D5
Rheims Ct SR4 85 D7
Rheydt Ave NE28 39 F2
Rhoda Terr SR2 86 F1
Rhodes St NE6 57 A5
Rhodesia Rd SR5 74 D3
Rhondda Rd SR5 74 B3
Rhuddlan Ct NE5 37 B4
Rhyl Par NE31 58 A2
Rhyl Sq SR5 74 E3
Ribble Rd SR5 74 C2
Ribble Wlk NE32 58 C2
Ribbledale Gdns NE7 39 B3
Ribblesdale Penshaw DH4 90 B7
Wallsend NE28 39 F4
Ribblesdale Ave NE24 17 A8
Richard Ave SR4 86 A4
Richard Avenue Prim Sch
SR4 86 B4
Richard Browell Rd NE15 35 E1
Richard Coates CE Mid Sch
NE20 25 E7
Richard St Blyth NE24 17 E7
Hetton le H DH5 95 A3
Richard Stannard Ho 11
NE24 17 F8
Richardson Ave 2 NE34 58 F4
Richardson Dees Prim Sch
NE28 40 D2
Richardson Rd NE1,NE2 98 C3
Richardson St
Ashington NE63 6 E1
3 Newcastle-u-T NE6 56 C8
Wallsend NE28 40 C2
Richardson Terr
Chopwell NE17 66 B1
Ryhope SR2 93 A6
5 Washington NE37 83 D8
Richardson's Bldgs NE62 10 E5
Richmond SR2 92 D7
Richmond Ave
Gateshead NE10 57 C2
Washington NE38 83 D6
Richmond Ave *continued*
Whickham NE16 54 B1
Richmond Cl NE22 10 E2
Richmond Ct
Gateshead NE8 101 C1
1 Gateshead,Low Fell NE9 70 F4
Jarrow NE32 58 A7
Richmond Dr DH4 89 D1
Richmond Fields NE20 25 A5
Richmond Gdns NE28 40 E3
Richmond Gr NE29 41 E5
Richmond Lodge NE3 38 D4
Richmond Mews NE3 38 B3
Richmond Pk NE28 39 E3
Richmond Rd NE34 59 C6
Richmond St SR5 102 C4
Richmond Terr
Gateshead NE8 101 B1
13 Gateshead,Felling NE10 71 D8
Haswell DH6 97 F3
Walbottle NE15 35 F1
Whitley Bay NE26 31 F7
Richmond Way
Cramlington NE23 22 A3
Ponteland NE20 25 A5
Rickaby St SR1 103 C4
Rickgarth NE10 71 F5
Rickleton Ave DH3 88 D5
Rickleton Prim Sch NE38 88 F8
Rickleton Village Ctr
NE38 88 F8
Rickleton Way NE38 83 A1
Riddell Ave NE15 54 C5
Riddell Ct 7 DH2 88 C2
Riddings Rd SR5 74 D3
Riddings Sq SR5 74 D3
Ridge Ct NE13 28 B4
Ridge Terr NE22 10 E1
Ridge The NE40 52 C4
Ridge Villas NE22 10 E1
Ridge Way The NE3 37 F4
Ridgely Cl NE20 26 A6
Ridgely Dr NE20 26 A6
Ridgeway Ashington NE63 7 A2
Birtley DH3 82 C6
Gateshead NE10 72 B6
Newcastle-u-T NE4 54 E8
Ryhope SR2 92 C6
Seaton Delaval NE25 23 E1
Stakeford NE62 11 A8
Ridgeway Cres SR3 86 B3
Ridgeway Prim Sch NE34 59 F4
Ridgeway The NE34 59 F3
Ridgewood Cres NE3 38 F5
Ridgewood Gdns NE3 38 E5
Ridgewood Villas NE3 38 E5
Riding Barns Way NE16 69 A2
Riding Cl NE40 51 E3
Riding Cotts NE46 45 A8
Riding Dene NE43 49 F1
Riding Grange NE44 62 E8
Riding La DH2,NE11 81 B4
Riding Lea NE21 53 A1
Riding Mill Sta NE44 62 F8
Riding Terr NE43 49 F1
Riding The NE3 37 E3
Ridings Ct NE40 51 E3
Ridings The NE25 31 C6
Ridley Ave Blyth NE24 17 F7
Chester le S DH2 88 B2
Sunderland SR2 92 F7
Wallsend NE28 41 B4
Ridley Cl Hexham NE46 44 F3
Morpeth NE61 8 E8
Newcastle-u-T NE3 37 F8
Ridley Gdns NE16 54 A1
Ridley Gr NE34 60 A7
Ridley Mill Cotts NE43 64 B6
Ridley Mill Rd NE43 64 B5
Ridley Pl NE1,NE99 99 A2
Ridley St Blyth NE24 17 F8
Cramlington NE23 22 C5
Gateshead NE8 70 E8
Sunderland SR5 75 B2
Ridley Terr Cambois NE24 12 D4
Gateshead NE10 71 E8
Hexham NE46 45 A6
Sunderland SR2 103 C1
Ridsdale NE42 50 B1
Ridsdale Ave NE5 36 E1
Ridsdale Cl
Seaton Delaval NE25 23 C3
Wallsend NE28 40 C4
Ridsdale Ct NE8 101 A1
Ridsdale Sq NE63 6 C3
Rievaulx NE38 83 C4
Riga Sq SR5 74 C3
Riggs The Corbridge NE45 46 F7
Houghton-le-S DH5 94 F8
Rignall NE38 84 A5
Riley St NE32 58 A7
Riley Street Ind Est NE32 58 A7
Ringlet Cl NE11 70 B7
Ringmore Ct SR2 86 C2
Rington Ct 19 NE30 42 D7
Ringway Stakeford NE62 6 A1
Sunderland SR5 85 A8
Ringwood Dr NE23 22 B7
Ringwood Gn NE12 39 C7
Ringwood Rd SR5 74 D3
Ringwood Sq SR5 74 D3
Rink St NE24 17 F8
Ripley Ave NE29 41 E4
Ripley Cl NE22 10 D2
Ripley Ct NE9 71 B1
Ripley Dr NE23 22 A3
Ripley Terr NE6 56 E6
Ripon Cl NE23 21 F3
Ripon Gdns
Newcastle-u-T NE2 56 A8
Wallsend NE28 40 E3
Ripon Sq NE32 73 B8
Ripon St Chester le S DH3 88 C1
Gateshead NE8 101 B1
Sunderland SR6 75 E1
Rise The
Newcastle-u-T NE3 37 E4
Ponteland NE20 25 B2
Ryton NE21 53 A4
Seaton Sluice NE26 24 E4
Rishton Sq SR5 74 C3
Rising Sun Cotts NE28 40 B5
Rising Sun Ctry Pk*
NE28 40 B6
Ritson Cl NE29 41 E7
Ritson St SR6 75 E4
River Bank NE62 11 C8
River Bank E NE62 11 C8
River Dr NE33 42 C4
River La NE40 52 C6
River Terr 5 DH3 88 D4
River View Bebside NE22 11 D1
Blackhall Mill NE17 77 B6
Blaydon NE21 53 B2
Lynemouth NE61 2 A3
North Shields NE30 42 C6
Ovingham NE42 50 A4
Prudhoe NE42 50 C2
Ryton NE40 52 E5
River View Cl NE22 11 D1
Riverbank Rd SR5 74 D2
Riverdale SR5 85 B8
Rivermead NE38 83 E1
Rivermede NE20 25 F7
Riversdale NE17 77 B6
Riversdale Ave NE62 11 A8
Riversdale Ct
Newcastle-u-T NE15 53 C6
Stakeford NE62 11 A7
Riversdale Ho NE62 11 A7
Riversdale Terr SR2 102 B1
Riversdale Way NE15 53 C6
Riverside Morpeth NE61 8 F8
Ponteland NE20 25 E6
Riverside Ave NE62 10 D7
Riverside Bsns Pk NE28 41 A1
Riverside Ct
Dunston NE11 100 A1
South Shields NE33 42 B2
Riverside Lodge NE15 52 E7
Riverside Pk SR4 85 B7
Riverside Prim Sch NE29 41 F4
Riverside Rd SR5 74 F2
Riverside The NE31 57 C7
Riverside Way
Rowlands Gill NE39 78 D8
Whickham NE11,NE16 54 C3
Riverslea NE34 60 A6
Riverview Lodge NE4 54 D4
Roachburn Rd NE5 36 E2
Robert Allan Ct NE13 28 A6
Robert Owen Gdns NE10 71 C7
Robert St Blyth NE24 17 E7
New Silksworth SR3 92 B7
South Shields NE33 42 D1
Sunderland SR4 102 A3
Robert Terr NE39 66 F4
Robert Terr Cotts NE39 66 F4
Robert Westall Way
NE29 42 A3
Robert Wheatman Ct
SR2 86 E2
Roberts St NE15 54 A5
Roberts Terr NE32 58 B5
Robertson Ct 14 DH3 88 C2
Robertson Rd SR5 74 B2
Robertson Sq SR5 74 B3
Robin Ct DH5 94 C3
Robin Gr SR5 74 C1
Robin La
East Rainton DH4,DH5 94 C2
West Rainton DH4,DH5 94 C2
Robinson Gdns
Wallsend NE28 41 A3
2 Whitburn SR6 60 F1
Robinson Sq NE64 7 E5
Robinson St
5 Newcastle-u-T NE6 56 C6
8 South Shields NE33 42 D2
Robinson Terr
Burnopfield NE16 79 A4
Sunderland SR2 103 C1
2 Washington NE38 83 F4
Robinswood 8 NE9 70 F5
Robsheugh Pl NE5 54 C8
Robson Dr NE46 44 F3
Robson Pl SR2 93 A6
Robson St
7 Gateshead NE9 70 F5
Newcastle-u-T NE6 56 B6
Robson Terr
High Spen NE39 67 B3
Tantobie DH9 78 F1
Rochdale Rd SR5 74 D3
Rochdale St
Hetton le H DH5 95 A2
Wallsend NE28 40 B1
Rochdale Way SR5 74 D3
Roche Ct NE38 83 C4
Rochester Cl NE63 7 A2
Rochester Gdns NE11 70 A8
Rochester Sq NE32 58 B1
Rochester St NE6 57 A4
Rochester Terr 1 NE10 71 E8
Rochford Gr NE23 22 A3
Rochford Rd SR5 74 C3
Rock Gr 4 NE9 70 F5
Rock Lodge Gdns SR6 75 F3
Rock Lodge Rd SR6 75 F3
Rock Terr
Newcastle-u-T NE2 99 C2
9 Washington NE37 83 E8
Rockcliffe
South Shields NE33 42 F1
Whitley Bay NE26 32 C5
Rockcliffe Ave NE26 32 C4
Rockcliffe Fst Sch NE26 32 C4
Rockcliffe Gdns
Newcastle-u-T NE15 53 F7
Whitley Bay NE26 32 C4
Rockcliffe St NE26 32 C4
Rockcliffe Way NE9 71 D1
Rocket Way NE12 39 F8
Rockhope NE38 88 F8
Rockingham Cl SR7 93 C1
Rockingham Rd SR5 74 C3
Rockingham Sq SR5 74 C3
Rockmore Rd NE21 53 C1
Rockville SR6 75 E4
Rockwood Gdns NE40 51 E1
Rockwood Hill Est NE40 66 E8
Rockwood Hill Rd NE40 51 F1
Rockwood Terr NE40 51 F1
Rodin Ave NE34 59 D2
Rodney Cl Ryhope SR2 92 C6
Tynemouth NE30 42 D7
Rodney Ct NE26 31 D7
Rodney St NE6 56 B5
Rodney Way NE26 31 D7
Rodsley Ave NE8,NE9 70 F8
Roeburn Way NE3 37 F3
Roedean Rd SR5 74 E3
Roehedge NE10 72 B6
Rogan Ave 8 NE37 83 A6
Roger St NE6 56 B6
Rogerson Terr NE5 36 E3
Rogues La NE39 67 A5
Rokeby Ave NE15 53 D6
Rokeby Dr NE3 37 F4
Rokeby St
Newcastle-u-T NE15 53 D6
Sunderland SR4 102 B2
Rokeby Terr NE6 39 C1
Rokeby View NE9 71 A1
Roker Ave Sunderland SR6 75 E1
Whitley Bay NE25 31 F3
Roker Baths Rd SR6 75 E2
Roker Park Cl 10 SR6 75 E2
Roker Park Rd SR6 75 E3
Roker Park Terr SR6 75 F2
Roker Terr SR6 75 F3
Rokerby Ave NE16 69 C6
Roland Rd NE28 40 E2
Roland St NE38 83 E4
Rollesby Ct NE5 37 B4
Rolley Way NE42 50 E3
Rolling Mill Rd NE32 58 A8
Romaldskirk Cl SR4 85 B5
Roman Ave
Chester le S DH3 88 D3
Newcastle-u-T NE6 56 E6
Roman Ct NE28 40 E4
Roman Rd Hedworth NE10 72 E8
South Shields NE33 42 D4
Roman Rd N NE33 42 C4
Roman Road Prim Sch
NE10 72 A5
Roman Way NE45 46 F6
Roman Way The NE5 53 D8
Romford Cl NE23 22 A3
Romford Pl NE9 71 A8
Romford St 4 SR4 85 F6
Romiley Gr NE10 72 D7
Romilly St NE33 42 D2
Romney Ave
Sunderland SR2 86 E3
Washington NE38 83 E4
Whiteleas NE34 59 D3
Romney Cl
Shiney Row DH4 90 C5
Whitley Bay NE26 32 C4
Romney Gdns NE9 71 B7
Romney Villas 5 NE38 83 E4
Romsey Cl NE23 22 B7
Romsey Dr NE35 73 E8
Romsey Gr NE15 53 C8
Ronald Dr NE15 54 A6
Ronald Gdns NE31 57 D4
Ronald Sq SR6 75 D3
Ronaldsay Cl 4 SR2 92 E8
Ronan Mews DH4 94 A2
Ronsdorf Ct NE32 58 B6
Rookery Cl NE24 17 B7
Rookery La NE16 68 E4
Rookery The NE16 78 F6
Rooksleigh 6 NE21 53 B1
Rookswood NE61 9 A6
Rookswood Gdns NE39 67 E3
Rookwood Dr NE13 28 C8
Rookwood Rd NE5 54 A8
Ropery La Bournmoor DH3 88 F3
Chester le S DH3 88 D2
Hebburn NE31 57 D6
Wallsend NE28 40 F2
Ropery Rd Gateshead NE8 70 B8
Sunderland SR4 102 B4
Ropery The NE6 56 D4
Rosa St NE33 42 D2
Rosalie Terr SR2 86 F4
Rosalind Ave NE22 11 B1
Rosalind St Ashington NE63 6 E4

138 Ros – St C

Rosalind St *continued*
Ashington,Hirst NE63 6 E3
Rosamond Pl NE24 17 F7
Rose Ave
Cramlington NE23 21 F8
Fence Houses DH4 89 F1
Whickham NE16 69 B7
Rose Bery Cres NE2 56 A8
Rose Cotts NE41 51 A6
Rose Cres Bournmoor DH4 89 D3
Whitburn SR6 60 F2
Rose Ct NE31 57 D5
Rose Gdns
Kibblesworth NE11 81 C6
Wallsend NE28 40 B4
Rose St Gateshead NE8 100 C2
Hebburn NE31 57 D5
7 Houghton-le-S DH4 94 D8
Sunderland SR4 102 B3
Rose St E DH4 90 B8
Rose St W DH4 90 B8
Rose Terr Greenside NE40 52 C2
Newcastle-u-T NE5 37 E1
Rose Villa La NE16 69 B7
Rosebank Cl SR2 92 E8
Rosebank Hall NE28 40 F2
Roseberry Ct 12 NE37 83 E8
Roseberry Grange NE12 30 A1
Roseberry Pl NE2 99 C4
Roseberry Terr 1 NE35 58 E1
Rosebery Ave Blyth NE24 17 D7
Gateshead NE8 71 A8
South Shields NE33 42 E1
Tynemouth NE29 42 A8
Rosebery Pl NE2 56 A8
Rosebery St 4 SR5 75 D1
Rosebud Cl 8 NE16 54 A1
Rosedale Bedlington NE22 10 E1
Wallsend NE28 39 F4
Rosedale Ave SR6 75 E6
Rosedale Cres DH4 90 C2
Rosedale Ct NE5 36 D2
Rosedale Rd NE40 51 F3
Rosedale St
Hetton le H DH5 94 E1
Sunderland SR1 102 B2
Rosedale Terr
Newcastle-u-T NE2 99 C3
North Shields NE30 42 B7
Sunderland SR6 75 E4
Roseden Ct NE12 39 C7
Rosedene Villas NE23 22 D6
Rosefinch Lodge NE9 70 F5
Rosegill NE37 83 B6
Rosehill NE28 40 E2
Rosehill Rd NE28 40 F2
Rosehill Way NE5 37 C1
Roselea NE32 58 C1
Roselea Ave SR2 92 F7
Rosella Pl NE29 42 A6
Rosemary Gdns NE9 71 D2
Rosemary Rd SR5 74 D3
Rosemary Terr NE24 17 F6
Rosemount Haswell DH6 97 F4
Morpeth NE61 9 A7
Newcastle-u-T NE5 36 F2
Sunderland SR4 85 A5
Rosemount Ave NE10 72 B7
Rosemount Cl NE37 72 C2
Rosemount Ct NE36 74 B7
Rosemount Way
Newcastle-u-T NE7 39 C5
Whitley Bay NE25 31 C5
Roseneath Ct NE63 6 D3
Roseville St SR4 102 B1
Rosewell Pl NE16 69 A4
Rosewood NE12 29 F3
Rosewood Ave NE3 38 E6
Rosewood Cres
Newcastle-u-T NE6 39 F1
Seaton Sluice NE26 24 D4
Rosewood Gdns
Chester le S DH2 88 B5
Gateshead NE9 71 B5
Newcastle-u-T NE3 37 F4
Rosewood Sq SR4 85 A2
Rosewood Terr
Birtley DH3 82 B5
Wallsend NE28 41 A2
Roseworth Ave NE3 38 D3
Roseworth Cl NE3 38 D4
Roseworth Cres NE3 38 D3
Roseworth Terr
Newcastle-u-T NE3 38 C4
Whickham NE16 69 B7
Roslin Pk NE22 11 C1
Roslin Way NE23 22 A3
Ross Ouston DH2 82 A1
Ouston DH2 81 F2
Ross Ave NE11 54 F1
Ross Gr NE23 21 F7
Ross Lea DH4 90 A5
Ross St SR5 75 C1
Ross Way
Newcastle-u-T NE3 37 F8
Whitley Bay NE26 31 E7
Rossdale 1 NE40 51 F3
Rosse Cl NE37 83 B8
Rossendale Pl NE12 38 F6
Rosslyn Ave
Gateshead NE9 71 A6
Newcastle-u-T NE3 37 E5
Sunderland SR2 92 F7
Rosslyn Mews SR4 102 A2
Rosslyn Pl DH3 82 D2
Rosslyn St SR4 102 A2
Rosslyn Terr SR4 102 A2
Rosyth Rd SR5 74 E3
Rosyth Sq SR5 74 E3
Rotary Parkway NE63 6 B4
Rotary Way Blyth NE24 17 F5
Hexham NE46 45 C6
North Shields NE29 41 E3
Ponteland NE20 26 A4
Rothay Pl NE5 37 C2
Rothbury SR2 92 D6
Rothbury Ave Blyth NE24 17 B6
Gateshead NE10 57 A1
Hebburn NE32 58 A4
Newcastle-u-T NE3 38 B6
Rothbury Cl
Chester le S DH2 88 A1
Killingworth NE12 29 C4
Rothbury Gdns
Dunston NE11 70 A5
Wallsend NE28 40 F3
Wideopen NE13 28 C6
Rothbury Rd SR5 74 D3
Rothbury Terr
Newcastle-u-T NE6 56 C8
North Shields NE29 41 D4
Rotherfield Cl NE23 22 B7
Rotherfield Gdns 8 NE9 71 A2
Rotherfield Rd SR5 74 C3
Rotherfield Sq SR5 74 C3
Rotherham Cl DH5 94 D6
Rotherham Rd SR5 74 C3
Rothesay DH2 81 F1
Rothesay Terr NE22 11 C2
Rothlea Gdns NE62 11 A8
Rothley NE38 83 F2
Rothley Ave Ashington NE63 6 D2
Newcastle-u-T NE5 54 C7
Rothley Cl
Newcastle-u-T NE3 38 D5
Ponteland NE20 25 D7
Rothley Ct
Killingworth NE12 29 D3
Sunderland SR5 74 F4
Rothley Gdns NE30 32 B1
Rothley Gr NE25 23 C3
Rothley Terr DH8 77 B1
Rothley Way NE26 31 E7
Rothsay Terr NE64 7 D3
Rothwell Rd
Newcastle-u-T NE3 38 C5
Sunderland SR5 74 C2
Roundhill NE32 58 D1
Roundhill Ave NE5 37 C2
Roundstone Cl NE7 39 D4
Roundway The NE12 39 B7
Row's Terr NE3 38 E5
Rowan Ave NE38 83 C1
Rowan Cl Bedlington NE22 10 F2
Sunderland SR4 85 B5
Rowan Ct Blyth NE24 17 D6
Burnopfield NE16 79 B6
Longbenton NE12 39 F8
4 South Shields NE34 59 A4
Rowan Dr Hetton le H DH5 94 F4
Newcastle-u-T NE3 37 F6
Ponteland NE20 25 E7
Rowan Gr
Cramlington NE23 22 D5
Prudhoe NE42 50 B2
Rowanberry Rd NE12 39 B6
Rowans The NE9 71 D2
Rowantree Rd NE6 40 A1
Rowanwood Gdns NE11 70 B5
Rowedge Wlk NE5 37 A2
Rowell Cl SR2 92 C6
Rowes Mews NE6 56 C4
Rowland Burn Way NE39 67 E2
Rowlands Gill Inf Sch
NE39 67 F3
Rowlands Gill Jun Sch
NE39 67 F3
Rowlandson Cres NE10 71 D8
Rowlandson Terr
12 Gateshead NE10 71 D8
9 Sunderland SR2 86 E4
Rowley St NE24 17 E7
Rowlington Terr NE63 6 D2
Rowntree Way NE29 42 A3
Rowsley Rd NE32 58 C5
Roxburgh Cl NE21 68 A8
Roxburgh Ho NE26 32 A5
Roxburgh Pl 2 NE6 56 B7
Roxburgh St SR6 75 D2
Roxburgh Terr NE26 32 A5
Roxby Gdns NE29 41 E5
Royal Arc NE1 99 B1
Royal Cres NE4 54 E8
Royal Gram Sch NE2 99 B3
Royal Ind Est NE32 57 F8
Royal Quays Outlet Shopping
NE28 41 E2
Royal Victoria Infmy NE2 98 C3
Royalty The SR2 102 B2
Roydon Ave SR2 86 E3
Royle St SR2 86 F2
Royston Terr NE6 57 A4
Ruabon Cl NE23 22 A3
Rubens Ave NE34 59 D3
Ruby St DH4 90 D2
Rudby Cl NE3 38 D8
Rudchester Pl NE5 54 C8
Ruddock Sq 1 NE6 56 C4
Rudyard Ave SR2 86 E3
Rudyerd Ct NE29 42 B5
Rudyerd St
13 North Shields NE29 42 A5
North Shields NE29 42 B5
Rugby Gdns
Gateshead NE9 71 C3
Wallsend NE28 40 E3
Ruislip Pl NE23 21 F3
Ruislip Rd SR4 85 A5
Runcorn SR2 92 C7
Runcorn Rd SR5 74 C3
Runhead Est NE40 52 D4
Runhead Gdns NE40 52 D5
Runhead Terr NE40 52 E5
Runnymede SR2 92 D7
Runnymede Gdns NE17 77 B7
Runnymede Rd
Ponteland NE20 25 C5
Sunderland SR5 74 D3
Whickham NE16 69 A6
Runnymede Way
Newcastle-u-T NE3 37 E4
Sunderland SR5 74 D3
Runswick Ave NE12 38 F6
Runswick Cl SR3 92 C7
Runswick Dr SR7 93 D1
Rupert Sq SR5 74 E3
Rupert St SR6 60 F1
Rupert Terr NE15 52 F8
Rushall Pl NE12 39 B6
Rushbury Ct NE27 30 C5
Rushcliffe SR6 75 D3
Rushford SR2 92 D6
Rushie Ave NE15 54 C5
Rushley Cres NE21 53 C3
Rushsyde Cl NE16 68 E5
Rushton Ave SR2 86 E3
Rushyrig NE37 83 A6
Ruskin Ave Ashington NE63 6 F2
7 Dunston NE11 54 F1
Easington Lane DH5 97 D8
Longbenton NE12 29 D1
Ruskin Cres NE34 59 B3
Ruskin Ct NE42 50 B1
Ruskin Dr
Newcastle-u-T NE7 39 E3
West Boldon NE35 74 A8
Ruskin Rd Birtley DH3 82 C4
Gateshead N10,NE9 71 B7
Whickham NE16 69 A8
Russel Ct NE2 38 F2
Russell Ave NE34 60 A6
Russell Ct NE8 100 C1
Russell Ho SR1 103 B3
Russell Sq NE13 28 B8
Russell St Jarrow NE32 58 C7
8 North Shields NE29 42 A5
7 South Shields NE33 42 C3
Sunderland SR1 103 B3
Washington NE37 83 C8
Russell Terr
Bedlington NE22 15 F8
Birtley DH3 82 B6
Newcastle-u-T NE1,NE2 99 C2
Rustic Terr NE64 7 E5
Ruswarp Dr SR3 92 B6
Ruth Ave NE21 53 C2
Rutherford Ave 4 SR7 92 F1
Rutherford Cl NE62 10 E7
Rutherford Pl NE61 8 F7
Rutherford Rd
Sunderland SR5 74 B3
Washington NE37 72 E2
Rutherford Sq SR5 74 B3
Rutherford St Blyth NE24 17 D7
Newcastle-u-T NE1 98 C1
Wallsend NE28 41 B3
Rutherglen Rd SR5 74 E3
Rutherglen Sq SR5 74 E3
Ruthven Ct NE2 38 F2
Rutland Ave
New Silksworth SR3 91 F7
Newcastle-u-T NE6 57 A7
Rutland Pl
North Shields NE29 41 F6
Washington NE37 72 D2
Rutland Rd Hebburn NE31 57 F3
Wallsend NE28 40 A1
Rutland Sq DH3 82 B5
Rutland St Ashington NE63 6 C3
Hetton le H DH5 94 F4
Sunderland SR4 85 F7
Rutland Terr DH6 97 E1
Ryal Cl Blyth NE24 17 C7
Seaton Delaval NE25 23 E3
Ryal Terr NE6 56 F5
Ryal Wlk NE3 37 D4
Ryall Ave NE13 28 A4
Rydal NE10 72 A8
Rydal Ave
Easington Lane DH5 97 C8
Tynemouth NE30 32 A2
Rydal Cl East Boldon NE36 74 C8
Killingworth NE12 29 F3
Rydal Cres NE21 68 B8
Rydal Gdns NE34 59 E6
Rydal Mount
Newbiggin-by-t-S NE64 7 C4
Sunderland SR5 75 C3
Sunderland,Castletown SR5 85 A8
Rydal Rd Chester le S DH2 88 C1
Newcastle-u-T,Gosforth
NE3 38 D5
Newcastle-u-T,Lemington
NE15 53 D8
Rydal St NE8 101 B1
Rydal Terr NE13 28 B4
Ryde Pl NE23 22 B7
Ryde Terr NE11 100 A1
Rye Cl NE15 35 E1
Rye Hill
Newcastle-u-T NE4 100 B4
Rye Hill *continued*
Newcastle-u-T NE4 100 C4
Rye Terr NE46 44 F5
Rye View SR2 92 F7
Ryedale Sunderland SR6 75 F7
Wallsend NE28 39 F5
Ryedale Cl NE63 6 B2
Ryedale Ct 7 NE34 59 A4
Ryedale Ho NE24 16 F8
Ryehaugh NE20 25 F6
Ryehill View DH5 94 C5
Ryemount Rd SR2 92 D7
Ryhope Engine Mus*
SR2 92 E5
Ryhope Gdns NE9 71 D4
Ryhope General Hospl
SR2 92 F5
Ryhope Grange Ct SR2 86 F1
Ryhope Inf Sch SR2 92 F7
Ryhope Jun Sch SR2 92 F7
Ryhope Rd Ryhope SR2 93 A8
Sunderland SR2 86 E3
Ryhope St
Houghton-le-S DH5 94 F8
Ryhope SR2 92 E7
5 Sunderland SR2 86 F2
Ryhope St S SR2 92 F7
Ryhope Village CE Prim Sch
SR2 92 F6
Ryton Com Inf Sch NE40 52 A5
Ryton Comp Sch NE40 52 B5
Ryton Ct NE33 42 D1
Ryton Hall Dr NE40 52 C6
Ryton Ind Est NE21 52 F5
Ryton Jun Sch NE40 52 A5
Ryton Sq SR2 86 E3
Ryton Terr
Newcastle-u-T NE6 56 F4
Shiremoor NE27 30 D1

S

Sackville Rd
Newcastle-u-T NE6 39 C1
Sunderland SR3 85 E3
Sacred Heart Lower Sch
NE4 54 F6
Sacred Heart RC High Sch
NE4 54 D7
Sacred Heart RC Mid Sch
NE4 54 E7
Sacred Heart RC Prim Sch
Byermoor NE16 79 D7
Newcastle-u-T NE4 54 D7
Sacriston Ave SR3 85 F3
Sacriston Gdns NE9 71 C2
Saddleback NE37 83 B7
Saffron Pl NE6 57 A5
Saga Ct NE6 39 F1
Sage Cl NE15 53 C8
Sage Gateshead The
NE8 101 C4
Saint Aidan's Ho NE29 41 D8
Saint Ct SR3 92 A5
Saint Wilfrid's RC Comp Sch
NE34 59 D6
Saints Peter & Paul RC Prim
Sch NE33 59 B6
St Acca's Ct NE46 44 F5
St Agnes RC Prim Sch
NE40 51 E4
St Agnes' Gdns NE40 51 E4
St Agnes' Gdns N NE40 51 E4
St Agnes' Gdns W NE40 51 E4
St Agnes' Terr NE40 51 E4
St Aidan's Ave
Sunderland SR2 86 F2
Wallsend NE28 30 C1
St Aidan's Cl NE29 41 D8
St Aidan's Cres NE61 9 A6
St Aidan's Ct NE30 42 C7
St Aidan's Prim Sch
NE8 100 C1
St Aidan's RC Comp Sch
SR2 86 C4
St Aidan's RC Fst Sch
NE63 6 D1
St Aidan's Rd
South Shields NE33 42 D4
Wallsend NE28 40 A1
St Aidan's Sq NE12 30 C1
St Aidan's St NE8 101 A1
St Aidan's Terr DH4 90 E6
St Aidans Ct DH4 90 E6
St Alban's Cl NE25 31 A5
St Alban's Cres NE10 71 C7
St Alban's Cres NE6 39 D2
St Alban's Pl
Gateshead NE10 71 C7
Tynemouth NE30 42 D7
St Alban's RC Prim Sch
NE10 57 A1
St Alban's RC Sch NE6 56 F7
St Alban's St SR2 86 F3
St Alban's Terr NE8 101 C1
St Albans Cl NE63 7 A2
St Albans View NE27 30 F2
St Aldate's Ct SR4 85 A2
St Aloysius RC Inf Sch
NE31 57 F7
St Aloysius RC Jun Sch
NE31 57 E7
St Aloysius View NE31 57 D6
St Andrew's CE Fst Sch
NE15 34 E2
St Andrew's Ct NE7 39 C5
St Andrew's Dr NE9 70 E3
St Andrew's La NE42 49 D4
St Andrew's RC Fst Sch
NE24 17 C7
St Andrew's Rd
Hexham NE46 45 A4
Kip Hill DH9 79 F1
St Andrew's St
Hebburn NE31 57 C7
Newcastle-u-T NE1 98 C1
St Andrew's Terr
Ashington NE63 6 E3
3 Sunderland SR6 75 E2
St Andrews DH4 94 B8
St Andrews Ave NE37 83 B8
St Andrews Cl NE25 31 D5
St Andrews Ct 4 NE29 41 F8
St Ann's Cl NE1 56 A5
St Ann's Quay NE1 99 C1
St Ann's St NE1 99 C1
St Anne's Ct NE25 31 E3
St Anne's RC Prim Sch
NE9 71 B2
St Anne's RC Prim Sch
SR4 85 B5
St Anselm Cres NE29 41 C7
St Anselm Rd NE29 41 C7
St Anthony's CE Prim Sch
NE6 56 F3
St Anthony's Ct NE6 56 F6
St Anthony's Ho NE6 56 F3
St Anthony's RC Girls Sch
SR2 102 C1
St Anthony's Rd NE6 56 E4
St Anthony's Wlk NE6 56 F3
St Asaph Cl NE12 39 D4
St Augustine's RC Prim Sch
NE10 72 A6
St Austell Cl NE5 37 C4
St Austell Gdns NE9 70 F2
St Barnabas DH4 89 D3
St Barnabas Way SR2 103 C1
St Bartholomew's CE Prim
Sch NE12 39 D5
St Bartholomews Cl NE61 2 A7
St Bede's NE36 74 D7
St Bede's Cl DH5 95 A4
St Bede's Dr NE8 101 C2
St Bede's Ho NE9 71 A7
St Bede's Pk SR2 103 A1
St Bede's RC Fst Sch
NE22 15 E8
St Bede's RC Prim Sch
Jarrow NE32 58 C7
Newcastle-u-T NE15 54 A6
South Shields NE33 42 D2
Washington NE37 72 D1
St Bede's Terr SR2 103 A1
St Bedes Pl NE24 17 B4
St Bedes Rd NE24 17 B4
St Bedes Wlk NE27 30 C1
St Benedict's RC Mid Sch
NE63 6 F3
St Benet Biscop RC High Sch
NE22 15 E8
St Benet's RC Prim Sch
DH2 81 F1
St Benet's RC Prim Sch
SR6 75 D2
St Bernadette's RC Prim Sch
NE28 40 B5
St Buryan Cres NE5 37 C4
St Catherine's Ct SR5 74 D1
St Catherine's RC Prim Sch
NE2 56 A8
St Catherines Gr NE2 56 A7
St Cecilia's Cl SR2 86 F4
St Chad's Cres SR3 91 B7
St Chad's Rd SR3 91 B7
St Chad's Villas 6 NE36 74 D7
St Charles' RC Prim Sch
NE3 38 B6
St Christopher Way NE29 41 C2
St Christopher's Ho NE61 8 E8
St Christopher's Rd SR3 86 A2
St Christophers Cl NE63 6 F5
St Clements Ct
Ashington NE63 7 A2
3 Longbenton NE12 39 A6
Newcastle-u-T NE3 37 F8
Sunderland SR4 85 D6
St Columba's Ct SR5 75 C2
St Columba's RC Prim Sch
NE28 40 A2
St Cuthbert Ave DH3 88 D3
St Cuthbert's Ave NE34 60 A8
St Cuthbert's Cl DH5 95 A4
St Cuthbert's Ct
Gateshead NE8 101 A2
Newcastle-u-T NE3 38 A5
St Cuthbert's Dr NE10 71 F7
St Cuthbert's Gn NE5 54 C7
St Cuthbert's High Sch
NE15 54 B6
St Cuthbert's La NE46 45 A4
St Cuthbert's Pl NE8 101 A1
St Cuthbert's RC Prim Sch
Newcastle-u-T NE5 37 D4
North Shields NE29 42 A5
Sunderland SR4 85 D3
Walbottle NE15 35 F2
St Cuthbert's Rd
Gateshead NE8 101 A2
Gateshead,Windmill Hills
NE8 101 B3
New Herrington DH4 90 F7
Newbottle DH4 90 D3
Newcastle-u-T,Benwell NE5 54 B7
Newcastle-u-T,Fenham NE5 54 C8

St Cuthbert's Rd *continued*
Sunniside NE16 .....80 B7
Wallsend NE28 .....40 E3
Wallsend,Holystone NE27 ..30 C1
St Cuthbert's Terr NE22 ..11 B1
St Cuthbert's Terr
Hexham NE46 .....45 A4
Sunderland SR4 .....102 B3
St Cuthbert's Wlk DH3 ..88 C3
St Cuthberts Cl
Hexham NE46 .....45 A4
Prudhoe NE42 .....50 C2
Wallsend NE27 .....30 C1
St Cuthberts Ct NE24 ....17 F7
St Cuthberts Lower Sch
NE15 .....54 C6
St Cuthberts Pk NE16 ...80 A8
St Cuthberts RC Prim Sch
DH3 .....88 D2
St Cuthberts Way
Blaydon NE21 .....53 D3
Wallsend NE27 .....30 C1
St David's Cl NE26 .....31 F8
St David's Way
Hedworth NE32 .....58 C1
Whitley Bay NE26 .....31 F8
St Ebba's Way DH8 .....76 E3
St Edmund Campion RC Sch
NE9 .....71 D4
St Edmund's Ct NE8 .....56 A1
St Edmund's Dr NE10 ...71 F7
St Edmund's Rd NE8 ...101 C1
St Etienne Ct 12 NE10 ...56 D1
St Gabriel's Ave
Newcastle-u-T NE6 .....39 B1
Sunderland SR4 .....85 F5
St George's Ave NE33,
NE34 .....59 E8
St George's Cl NE2 .....38 E2
St George's Cres NE29 ...41 F5
St George's Est NE38 ...83 C1
St George's Hospl NE61 ..4 A2
St George's Pl NE15 .....53 E5
St George's RC Prim Sch
NE15 .....53 D5
St George's Rd
Hexham NE46 .....45 A4
Newcastle-u-T NE15 .....53 E5
Tynemouth NE30 .....32 C3
St George's Terr
East Boldon NE36 .....74 D7
Newcastle-u-T,Lemington
NE15 .....53 E5
Newcastle-u-T,West Jesmond
NE2 .....38 E2
Sunderland SR6 .....75 F2
St George's Way SR2 ..103 A1
St Georges Cres NE25 ...31 F4
St Georges Ct NE10 .....72 B7
St Godric's Dr DH4 .....94 A2
St Gregory's Ct NE34 ....59 F5
St Gregory's RC Prim Sch
NE34 .....60 A7
St Helen's Cres NE9 .....70 E5
St Helen's La NE45 .....47 A6
St Helen's St NE45 .....46 F6
St Helens Terr NE9 .....70 F5
St Hilda Ind Est 4 NE33 .42 C2
St Hilda St NE33 .....42 C2
St Hilda's Ave NE28 .....40 E3
St Hilda's Rd NE46 .....45 A3
St Ignatius Cl SR2 .....103 B1
St Ives Way NE5 .....37 C4
St James Bvld NE1,NE4 .100 C4
St James Cl NE44 .....62 F7
St James Ct NE8 .....56 B1
St James Gate NE1 ....100 C4
St James Lodge 4 NE4 .54 D5
St James RC Prim Sch
NE31 .....57 F4
St James Rd NE8 .....56 A2
St James Sq NE8 .....56 A2
St James St NE3 .....38 E5
St James Sta NE1 .....98 C1
St James Terr
7 Morpeth NE61 .....3 F1
Newcastle-u-T NE1 .....98 C2
Riding Mill NE44 .....63 A7
St James' Cres NE15 ....54 D4
St James' Gdns 6 NE15 .54 D5
St James' Mall NE31 ....57 D5
St James' Pk (Newcastle Utd
FC) NE1 .....98 C2
St James' Rd NE15 .....54 D5
St James' St NE1 .....98 C2
St James' Terr NE29 .....41 D3
St John & St Patrick's Church
Prim Sch SR1 .....103 C3
St John Bosco RC Prim Sch
SR5 .....74 A4
St John Boste RC Prim Sch
NE38 .....83 A5
St John St NE1 .....99 A1
St John the Baptist's RC
Prim Sch NE10 .....71 D8
St John Vianney RC Prim Sch
NE5 .....36 D1
St John's Ave NE31 .....57 D5
St John's Cl NE26 .....31 F8
St John's Cres NE22 .....11 D3
St John's Ct
Backworth NE27 .....30 C5
Newcastle-u-T NE4 .....54 E4
North Shields NE29 .....41 D3
St John's Ct NE33 .....42 D2
St John's Gn NE29 .....41 D3
St John's Mall NE31 ....57 D5
St John's Pl
Bedlington NE22 .....11 D3
Birtley DH3 .....82 C4
Whitley Bay NE26 .....31 F8
St John's Rd NE22 .....11 D2
St John's Rd DH6 .....96 B5
St John's Rd NE4 .....54 E4
St John's St NE29 .....41 D3
St John's Terr
East Boldon NE36 .....74 E7
Jarrow NE32 .....58 B7
North Shields NE29 .....41 D3
3 Seaham SR7 .....92 E1
St John's W NE22 .....11 D3
St John's Wlk
Hebburn NE31 .....57 E5
Newcastle-u-T NE4 .....54 E4
North Shields NE29 .....41 D3
St Johns SR1 .....103 C4
St Johns Ct NE12 .....29 D1
St Johns Pl NE10 .....71 D8
St Johns Rd NE46 .....45 A3
St Johns Vale SR4 .....85 A4
St Joseph's Ct
8 Birtley DH3 .....82 C5
Hebburn NE31 .....57 D3
St Joseph's RC Comp Sch
NE31 .....57 D2
St Joseph's RC Inf Sch
DH3 .....82 C5
St Joseph's RC Jun Sch
DH3 .....82 C4
St Joseph's RC Mid Sch
NE46 .....44 F4
St Joseph's RC Prim Sch
Blaydon NE21 .....53 B3
Gateshead NE8 .....101 C2
Hedworth NE32 .....58 B1
Newcastle-u-T NE15 .....54 D4
North Shields NE29 .....41 E5
St Joseph's RC Prim Sch
NE39 .....67 B2
St Joseph's RC Prim Sch
SR4 .....102 A3
St Joseph's Washington RC
Sch NE38 .....83 D6
St Joseph's Way NE32 ...58 C1
St Jude's Terr NE33 .....59 C8
St Julien Gdns
Newcastle-u-T NE7 .....39 D2
Wallsend NE28 .....41 B3
St Just Pl NE5 .....37 C4
St Keverne Sq NE5 .....37 C4
St Kitt's Cl NE26 .....31 F8
St Lawerence's RC Prim Sch
NE6 .....56 C6
St Lawrence Cl DH6 .....96 C5
St Lawrence Rd
High Pittington DH6 .....96 B5
Newcastle-u-T NE6 .....56 C4
St Lawrence Sq NE6 .....56 B5
St Leonard St SR2 .....86 F4
St Leonard's La NE61 .....3 B2
St Leonard's RC Prim Sch
SR3 .....92 B7
St Leonard's Wlk NE61 ...3 C2
St Lucia Cl
Sunderland SR2 .....103 B1
Whitley Bay NE26 .....31 E8
St Luke's Rd
North Shields NE29 .....41 D3
Sunderland SR4 .....85 D7
St Luke's Terr SR4 .....85 F7
St Lukes Ct NE31 .....57 D4
St Lukes Rd NE46 .....45 A4
St Margaret's Ave SR5 ..74 A1
St Margaret's Ct SR5 ....74 A1
St Margaret's Dr DH9 ...79 D4
St Margaret's Rd NE15 ..54 A4
St Margarets Ave NE12 ..39 D6
St Margarets Ct NE26 ....32 C4
St Mark's Cl 11 NE6 .....56 C7
St Mark's Cres SR4 ....102 B2
St Mark's Ct NE29 .....41 D2
St Mark's RC Prim Sch
NE5 .....36 F4
St Mark's Rd SR4 .....102 B2
St Mark's Rd N SR4 ....102 A2
St Mark's St Morpeth NE61 .3 E1
13 Newcastle-u-T NE6 .....56 C7
Sunderland SR4 .....102 B2
St Mark's Terr SR4 .....102 B2
St Mark's Way NE33 .....42 C1
St Marks Ct
Backworth NE27 .....30 E3
Newcastle-u-T NE5 .....36 F4
St Marks Rd NE46 .....45 A3
St Martin's Cl NE26 .....31 E7
St Martin's Ct NE26 .....31 E7
St Martin's Way NE26 ...31 E7
St Mary's & St Thomas
Aquinas RC Prim Sch
NE21 .....53 A4
St Mary's Ave
South Shields NE34 .....59 F6
Whitley Bay NE26 .....31 F7
St Mary's Chare 9 NE46 .45 B5
St Mary's Church (Mus)*
NE63 .....7 C6
St Mary's Coll NE4 .....54 E7
St Mary's College Flats
NE4 .....54 E7
St Mary's Ct
Gateshead NE8 .....101 C2
South Shields NE33 .....59 B7
St Mary's Dr Blyth NE24 ..17 B6
West Rainton DH4 .....94 A2
St Mary's Field NE61 .....8 F7
St Mary's Gn 4 NE16 ....69 B7
St Mary's Lodge NE26 ...31 F5
St Mary's or Bait Island*
NE26 .....24 G2
St Mary's Pl
Newcastle-u-T NE1 .....99 A2
Throckley NE15 .....35 E2
St Mary's Pl E NE1 .....99 A2
St Mary's RC Cath NE1 .100 C4
St Mary's RC Comp Sch
NE7 .....39 A5
St Mary's RC Fst Sch
NE46 .....45 A4
St Mary's RC Prim Sch
Brockley Whins NE32 .....58 D3
Longbenton NE12 .....29 D1
Sunderland SR2 .....86 B4
Tynemouth NE30 .....32 A2
Whickham NE16 .....69 C7
St Mary's St NE1 .....99 C1
St Mary's Terr
East Boldon NE36 .....74 E7
Ryton NE40 .....52 B5
South Shields NE33 .....59 B7
St Mary's Training &
Enterprise Ctr NE4 .....98 B1
St Mary's Way SR1 .....103 A3
St Mary's Wynd
8 Hexham NE46 .....45 B5
Seaton Sluice NE26 .....24 E4
St Marys CE Prim Sch
NE33 .....59 B7
St Marys Cl DH2 .....88 B1
St Mathews La NE42 .....50 D2
St Matthew's RC Fst Sch
NE42 .....50 C2
St Matthew's RC Prim Sch
NE32 .....58 B2
St Matthew's Terr DH4 ..90 D4
St Matthews Rd NE46 ....44 F3
St Matthews View SR3 ...92 A7
St Michael's Ave
New Hartley NE25 .....23 D6
South Shields NE33 .....42 E1
St Michael's Ave N NE33 42 D1
St Michael's Mount 3
NE6 .....56 C5
St Michael's RC Prim Sch
DH5 .....94 D7
St Michael's Rd NE6 .....56 B5
St Michael's Way NE11 ..54 C1
St Michaels DH4 .....94 B8
St Michaels RC Prim Sch
NE4 .....100 A3
St Michaels Way SR1 ...102 C2
St Michaels Workshops 10
NE6 .....56 B5
St Nichola's Cath* NE1 .99 B1
St Nicholas Ave
Newcastle-u-T,Gosforth
NE3 .....38 C4
Newcastle-u-T,South Gosforth
NE3 .....38 D4
Sunderland SR3 .....86 B3
St Nicholas Cl NE63 .....6 F5
St Nicholas Hospl NE3 ..38 A5
St Nicholas Rd
Hexham NE46 .....45 A4
West Boldon NE36 .....74 A7
St Nicholas View NE36 ..74 A7
St Nicholas' Church Yd
NE1 .....99 A1
St Nicholas' Sq 8 NE1 ..99 A1
St Nicholas' St NE1 ....101 A4
St Omers Rd NE11 .....54 F2
St Oswald's Ave NE6 .....56 E6
St Oswald's Gn NE6 .....56 E7
St Oswald's RC Prim Sch
NE9 .....71 C3
St Oswald's RC Prim Sch
Newcastle-u-T NE3 .....38 D7
Whiteleas NE34 .....59 D3
St Oswald's Rd
Hebburn NE31 .....57 F7
14 Hexham NE46 .....45 A4
Wallsend NE28 .....40 E4
St Oswald's Terr 8 DH4 .90 B6
St Oswalds C of E Prim Sch
NE31 .....57 F7
St Oswalds Ct NE42 .....50 E3
St Oswin's Ave NE30 ....32 C3
St Oswin's Pl NE30 .....42 D7
St Oswin's St NE33 .....59 D7
St Patrick's Cl NE10 ....71 D8
St Patrick's RC Prim Sch
SR2 .....92 F6
St Patrick's Terr SR2 ....92 F6
St Patrick's Wlk NE10 ...71 D8
St Paul's CE Prim Sch
Newcastle-u-T NE4 .....100 B4
Ryhope SR2 .....92 F6
St Paul's Gdns NE25 .....32 A4
St Paul's Pl NE4 .....98 A1
St Paul's RC Fst Sch
NE23 .....22 B5
St Paul's Rd NE32 .....58 C7
St Paul's Terr 5 SR2 ....92 F6
St Pauls Cl NE63 .....6 F5
St Pauls Ct NE8 .....100 C1
St Pauls Dr DH4 .....89 E8
St Pauls Monastery*
NE32 .....58 D7
St Pauls Rd NE46 .....44 F4
St Peter's Ave NE34 .....59 E7
St Peter's Ct NE6 .....56 C5
St Peter's Quayside E
NE6 .....56 D4
St Peter's Quayside W 9
NE6 .....56 C4
St Peter's RC Mid Sch
NE23 .....22 B4
St Peter's RC Prim Sch
NE9 .....71 A6
St Peter's Rd
Newcastle-u-T NE6 .....56 C5
Wallsend NE28 .....40 D3
St Peter's Sta SR5 .....103 A4
St Peter's View SR6 ....103 A4
St Peter's Wharf NE6 ...56 C4
St Peters' Way SR6 ....103 B4
St Philip Neri RC Prim Sch
NE11 .....70 A8
St Philips Cl NE4 .....98 B1
St Philips Way NE4 .....98 B1
St Robert of Newminster RC
Sch NE38 .....83 D2
St Robert's RC Fst Sch
NE61 .....8 F8
St Rollox St NE31 .....57 D5
St Ronan's Dr NE26 .....24 B7
St Ronan's Rd NE25 .....31 F4
St Ronans View NE9 .....71 A2
St Simon St NE34 .....59 A4
St Stephen's Cl NE25 ....23 B3
St Stephen's RC Prim Sch
NE12 .....39 B7
St Stephen's Way NE29 ..41 D3
St Stevens Cl DH4 .....89 E8
St Teresa's RC Prim Sch
NE6 .....56 B8
St Thomas Cl NE42 .....50 D2
St Thomas Mews NE42 ...50 D2
St Thomas More RC High Sch
NE29 .....41 D7
St Thomas More RC Sch
NE21 .....53 B3
St Thomas St 6 NE9 ....71 A5
St Thomas' Cres NE1 ....99 A2
St Thomas' Sq NE1 .....99 A2
St Thomas' St
Newcastle-u-T NE1 .....99 A2
Sunderland SR1 .....103 A3
St Thomas' Street Bsns Ctr
NE1 .....99 A2
St Thomas' Terr NE1 .....99 A2
St Vincent Ct NE8 .....56 A1
St Vincent St
Gateshead NE8 .....56 A1
South Shields NE33 .....42 E1
Sunderland SR2 .....103 B1
St Vincent's Pl NE26 .....31 F8
St Vincent's RC Sch NE6 .56 E4
St Vincent's Way 1 NE26 31 F8
St Vincents Cl NE15 .....53 E8
St Vincents Ho NE30 .....42 D7
St Wilfred's RC Mid Sch
NE24 .....17 D7
St Wilfred's Rd NE45 ....47 A6
St Wilfrid's Ct 9 NE46 ..45 A4
St Wilfrid's RC Prim Sch
NE10 .....56 B2
St Wilfrid's Rd NE46 ....45 A4
Saker Pl 1 NE28 .....40 B1
Salcombe Ave NE32 .....58 D6
Salcombe Gdns NE9 .....70 F2
Salem Hill SR2 .....103 B1
Salem Rd SR2 .....103 B1
Salem St Jarrow NE32 ....58 C7
South Shields NE33 .....42 C3
Sunderland SR2 .....103 B1
Salem St S SR2 .....103 B1
Salem Terr SR2 .....103 B1
Salisbury Ave
10 Chester le S DH3 .....88 C2
Tynemouth NE29 .....42 A7
Salisbury Cl
7 Ashington NE63 .....6 F2
Cramlington NE23 .....21 E6
Salisbury Gdns NE2 .....56 A8
Salisbury Ho NE6 .....56 A6
Salisbury Pl NE33 .....42 C3
Salisbury St Blyth NE24 ..17 D8
Gateshead NE10 .....57 A1
Morpeth NE61 .....9 B8
South Shields NE33 .....42 D2
Sunderland SR1 .....103 B2
Sunderland,South Hylton
SR4 .....85 A7
Salisbury Way NE32 .....58 B1
Salkeld Gdns NE9 .....71 A8
Salkeld Rd NE9 .....71 A6
Sallyport Cres NE1 .....99 B1
Sallyport Ho NE1 .....99 B1
Salmon St NE33 .....42 D4
Saltburn Cl DH4 .....90 C1
Saltburn Gdns NE28 .....41 B3
Saltburn Rd SR3 .....85 E3
Saltburn Sq SR3 .....85 E3
Salter's La Haswell DH6 ..97 E6
Houghton-le-S SR3 .....91 E1
Seaham SR7 .....95 F6
Salterfen La SR2 .....93 A8
Salterfen Rd SR2 .....93 A8
Salters Cl NE3 .....38 E6
Salters Ct NE3 .....38 E6
Salters' La NE3,NE12 ....38 F7
Salters' Rd NE3 .....38 B4
Saltford NE9 .....71 A2
Saltmeadows Rd NE10,
NE8 .....56 B4
Saltwell Park Mansion Mus*
NE9 .....70 E6
Saltwell Pl NE8 .....70 D8
Saltwell Rd NE8 .....70 D7
Saltwell Rd S NE9 .....70 E4
Saltwell St NE8 .....70 D8
Saltwell View NE8 .....70 E7
Sam's Ct NE23 .....28 F8
Samson Cl NE12 .....29 C2
Sancroft Dr DH5 .....94 E7
Sand Point Rd SR6 .....75 F1
Sandalwood NE34 .....59 E3
Sandalwood Sq SR4 .....85 B2
Sanderling Cl NE40 .....52 D4
Sanderlings 3 NE28 .....40 B1
Sanders Gdns DH3 .....82 C5
Sanders' Meml Homes
DH2 .....88 C3
Sanderson Hospl NE3 ...38 B4
Sanderson Rd
Newcastle-u-T NE2 .....38 E2
Whitley Bay NE26 .....31 F5
Sanderson St NE4 .....54 F3
Sandfield Rd
Cambois NE22 .....12 B4
Tynemouth NE30 .....32 B3
Sandford Ave NE23 .....16 B1
Sandford Ct SR2 .....86 C3
Sandford Mews NE13 ....28 A5
Sandgate NE1 .....99 C1
Sandgrove SR6 .....60 A1
Sandhill NE1 .....101 B4
Sandhill View Sch SR3 ...85 D2
Sandholm Cl NE28 .....40 F5
Sandhurst Ave NE30 .....32 C2
Sandiacres NE32 .....58 C1
Sandison Ct NE13 .....27 F6
Sandmartin Cl NE63 .....11 E8
Sandmere Pl NE15 .....54 A5
Sandmere Rd SR2 .....86 D1
Sandoe Gdns NE15 .....54 B5
Sandon Cl NE27 .....30 C5
Sandown NE25 .....31 D5
Sandown Cl NE25 .....23 D2
Sandown Ct NE28 .....41 A4
Sandown Gdns
Gateshead NE8 .....70 D8
New Silksworth SR3 .....91 F8
Wallsend NE28 .....40 F4
Sandpiper Cl Blyth NE24 ..17 F4
Ryton NE40 .....52 D4
Washington NE38 .....82 F2
Sandpiper Ct NE30 .....42 D8
Sandpiper Pl NE12 .....39 A7
Sandpiper Way NE63 .....6 D1
Sandray Cl DH3 .....82 D1
Sandridge NE64 .....7 F5
Sandringham Ave NE12 ..39 D6
Sandringham Cl NE25 ...31 B4
Sandringham Cres SR3 ..91 C6
Sandringham Ct
2 Longbenton NE12 .....39 A6
6 Gateshead NE10 .....71 C8
Sandringham Dr
Blyth NE24 .....17 D3
Whickham NE16 .....69 A7
Whitley Bay NE25 .....31 C4
Sandringham Gdns NE29 42 A7
Sandringham Mews 8
NE28 .....40 F4
Sandringham Rd
Newcastle-u-T,South Gosforth
NE3 .....38 E4
Newcastle-u-T,West Denton
NE5 .....53 E8
Sunderland SR6 .....75 D2
Sandringham Terr SR6 ...75 E2
Sandringham Way NE20 .25 C4
Sands Ind Est The NE16 .54 A1
Sands Rd NE16 .....54 A1
Sandsay Cl SR2 .....92 D8
Sandstone Cl NE34 .....58 F3
Sandwell Dr DH4 .....89 F8
Sandwich Rd NE29 .....31 F1
Sandwich St NE6 .....56 F3
Sandy Bank NE44 .....62 F7
Sandy Bay Cvn Pk NE63 .12 C8
Sandy Chare SR6 .....75 E8
Sandy Cres NE6 .....56 E4
Sandy La Ashington NE63 ...7 B2
Brunswick Village NE13 ....27 E6
Gateshead NE9 .....71 D1
Riding Mill NE44 .....62 E8
Wideopen NE3,NE12 .....28 E4
Sandy Lane Ind Area NE3 28 E4
Sandyford Ave NE42 .....50 F3
Sandyford Pk NE2 .....99 C4
Sandyford Rd NE2 .....99 B3
Sandygate Mews NE16 ...69 B1
Sandypath la NE16 .....79 A7
Sandysykes NE42 .....50 B2
Sans St SR1 .....103 B3
Sans St S SR1 .....103 B2
Sarabel Ave NE62 .....10 E7
Sargent Ave NE34 .....59 D2
Satley Gdns
Gateshead NE9 .....71 C2
Sunderland SR3 .....86 B2
Saunton Ct DH4 .....90 C3
Saville Lodge 5 NE33 ...42 D3
Saville Pl
Newcastle-u-T NE1 .....99 B2
Sunderland SR1 .....103 B2
Saville Row NE1 .....99 A2
Saville St
North Shields NE30 .....42 B5
4 South Shields NE33 ...42 D3
Saville St W NE29 .....42 A5
Savory Rd NE28 .....40 F3
Sawmill Cotts DH9 .....78 E1

Saxilby Dr NE3 38 D8
Saxon Cl SR6 59 E1
Saxon Cres SR3 85 F3
Saxon Dr NE30 32 C1
Saxon Way NE32 58 C7
Saxondale Rd NE3 37 E5
Saxton Gr NE7 39 A4
Scafell DH3 82 D1
Scafell Ct 22 SR3 91 F6
Scafell Dr NE5 37 D3
Scafell Gdns NE11 70 A6
Scalby Cl NE3 38 D8
Scales Cres NE42 50 F2
Scarborough Ct
Cramlington NE23 22 B5
Newcastle-u-T NE6 56 D6
Scarborough Par NE31 58 A2
Scarborough Rd
New Silksworth SR3 91 F8
Newcastle-u-T NE6 56 D6
Sceptre Ct NE4 100 A4
Sceptre Pl NE4 98 A1
Sceptre St NE4 98 A1
Schalksmuhle Rd NE22 10 F1
Schimel St SR5 75 B2
School App NE34 60 A6
School Ave Dunston NE11 69 F8
Guide Post NE62 10 F7
School Cl NE9 71 D6
School La High Spen NE39 67 A3
Whickham NE16 69 C7
School Rd
Bedlington NE22 11 D3
East Rainton DH5 94 C4
School Row
Hedley on t H NE43 64 F3
Prudhoe NE42 50 E3
School St Birtley DH3 82 C4
Hebburn NE31 57 F7
Whickham NE16 69 A7
School Terr DH4 89 E1
School View DH5 97 D8
Schoolhouse La NE16 79 E7
Scorer St NE29 41 F5
Scorer's La DH3 89 B1
Scot Terr NE17 66 B1
Scot's Ho NE36 73 B6
Scotby Gdns NE9 71 B3
Scotland Ct NE21 53 A1
Scotland Head NE21 68 A8
Scotland St SR2 93 A6
Scotswood Rd NE15,NE4 54 B4
Scotswood View NE11 54 C2
Scott Ave NE23 21 F8
Scott Cl NE46 44 F2
Scott Ct NE34 59 A3
Scott St
East Hartford NE23 16 B3
Houghton-le-S DH4 94 D8
Scott's Ave 13 NE40 51 F3
Scott's Ct NE10 72 B6
Scott's Terr DH5 95 A4
Scottish Life Ho NE2 99 B3
Scoular Dr NE63 7 A3
Scrogg Rd NE6 56 F6
Scruton Ave SR3 85 F3
Sea Banks NE30 42 E8
Sea Crest Rd NE64 7 E6
Sea La SR6 75 E4
Sea Rd South Shields NE33 42 E4
Sunderland SR6 75 E4
Sea View Ashington NE63 12 A8
Lynemouth NE61 2 B3
Ryhope SR2 93 A6
Sea View Gdns SR6 75 E3
Sea View La NE64 7 E5
Sea View Pk
Cramlington NE23 22 D6
Whitburn SR6 75 D8
Sea View Rd SR2 86 E3
Sea View Rd W SR2 86 D2
Sea View St SR2 86 F2
Sea View Villas NE23 22 D6
Sea Way NE33 42 E3
Sea Winnings Way
South Shields NE33 42 E2
South Shields NE33 42 F2
Seaburn Ave NE25 23 D6
Seaburn Cl 1 SR6 75 E4
Seaburn Dene Prim Sch
SR6 75 D5
Seaburn Dr 1 DH4 94 C8
Seaburn Gdns
Gateshead NE9 71 D3
Sunderland SR6 75 E4
Seaburn Gr NE26 24 C6
Seaburn Hill SR6 75 E4
Seaburn Sta SR5 75 C4
Seaburn Terr SR6 75 F4
Seaburn View NE25 23 D6
Seacombe Ave NE30 32 C3
Seacrest Apartments
NE30 32 C1
Seacrest Ave NE30 32 C2
Seafield Rd NE24 17 E5
Seafield Terr NE33 42 E3
Seafield View NE30 42 D8
Seafields SR6 75 E5
Seaforth Rd SR3 86 A3
Seaforth St NE24 17 E8
Seaham Cl NE34 60 B6
Seaham Gdns NE9 71 C2
Seaham Grange Ind Est
SR7 92 E2
Seaham Rd
Houghton-le-S DH5 95 A8
Ryhope SR2 93 A6
Seaham Sch of Technology
SR7 93 A1
Seaham St SR3 92 A7
Seal Terr 3 NE46 45 A4
Seascale Pl NE9 71 B4
Seatoller Ct 3 SR3 91 F6
Seaton Ave
Annitsford NE23 22 B1
Bedlington NE22 11 B1
Blyth NE24 17 C4
Houghton-le-S DH5 95 A7
Newbiggin-by-t-S NE64 7 D4
Seaton Burn Coll NE13 28 C8
Seaton Cl NE10 72 B6
Seaton Cres Holywell NE25 23 F2
Seaham SR7 92 E1
Whitley Bay NE25 31 E5
Seaton Croft NE23 29 C8
Seaton Delaval Fst Sch
NE25 23 B4
Seaton Delaval Hall★
NE26 24 A6
Seaton Gdns NE9 71 C3
Seaton Hirst CE Mid Sch
NE63 7 A2
Seaton La SR7 92 E1
Seaton Pl
Brunswick Village NE13 28 A6
Newcastle-u-T NE6 56 E3
Seaton Rd Shiremoor NE27 31 A4
Sunderland SR3 85 D3
Seaton Sluice Fst Sch
NE26 24 D5
Seaton Sluice Mid Sch
NE26 24 B7
Seatonville Cres NE25 31 E3
Seatonville Gr NE25 31 E3
Seatonville Rd NE25 31 E3
Seaview Terr NE33 42 E3
Second Ave Ashington NE63 6 D4
Blyth NE24 17 D6
Chester le S,Canada DH2 88 B2
Chester le S,South Pelaw
DH2 88 B8
Dunston NE11 70 B6
Morpeth NE61 9 B7
Newcastle-u-T NE6 56 C7
North Shields NE29 41 B4
Second Row Ellington NE61 1 E4
Linton NE61 1 A3
Second St NE8 101 A1
Secretan Way NE33 42 C2
Sedbergh Rd NE30 32 B2
Sedgefield Ct NE12 29 D3
Sedgeletch Ind Est DH4 90 A2
Sedgeletch Rd DH4 90 A2
Sedgemoor NE12 29 D4
Sedgemoor Ave NE15 54 A4
Sedgewick Pl NE8 101 B1
Sedley Rd NE28 40 B1
Sedling Rd NE38 83 B2
Sefton Ave NE6 39 C1
Sefton Ct NE23 16 C1
Sefton Sq SR3 85 E3
Segedunum Cres NE28 40 E4
Segedunum Way NE28 40 B1
Segendum Roman Fort Ctr★
NE28 40 C1
Seghill Fst Sch NE23 22 F1
Seine Ct NE32 58 C6
Selborne Ave NE9 70 E4
Selborne Gdns NE2 56 A8
Selbourne Cl NE23 21 E6
Selbourne St
2 South Shields NE33 42 D2
Sunderland SR6 75 E1
Selbourne Terr NE24 12 D3
Selby Cl NE23 16 B1
Selby Ct 2 Jarrow NE32 58 B7
Newcastle-u-T NE6 56 F4
Selby Gdns
Newcastle-u-T NE6 56 F8
Wallsend NE28 40 B3
Selby Sq SR3 85 E3
Selby's Grave NE21 67 F8
Sele Ct 5 NE46 45 A4
Sele Fst Sch The NE46 45 A5
Selina Pl SR6 75 E1
Selkirk Cres DH3 82 C6
Selkirk Gr NE23 16 C1
Selkirk Sq SR3 85 D3
Selkirk St NE32 58 E3
Selkirk Way NE29 41 C8
Selsdon Ave SR4 85 A2
Selsey Ct NE10 71 E6
Selwood Ct NE34 59 F5
Selwyn Ave NE25 31 D3
Selwyn Cl NE5 37 D4
Senet Enterprise Workshops
NE63 6 D2
Serin Ho NE5 37 A3
Serlby Cl NE37 72 C1
Seton Ave NE34 58 F4
Seton Wlk NE34 58 F4
Setting Stones NE38 89 A8
Settlingstone Cl NE7 39 E3
Sevenoaks Dr SR4 85 A2
Seventh Ave
Ashington NE63 6 E2
Blyth NE24 17 D6
Chester le S DH2 88 B4
Gateshead NE11 70 D4
Morpeth NE61 9 B7
Newcastle-u-T NE6 56 C7
Seventh Row NE63 6 B4
Severn Ave NE31 57 E3
Severn Ct 8 SR3 91 F6
Severn Dr NE32 58 C2
Severn Gdns NE8 71 B8
Severn Hos NH37 84 A8
Severn St NE17 66 C1
Severs Terr NE5 36 B6
Severus Rd NE4 54 E7
Sextant Ho 6 NE24 17 F8
Seymour Ct Ashington NE63 7 B3
Dunston NE11 100 A1
Seymour Sq SR3 85 E3
Seymour St
Dunston NE11 100 A1
North Shields NE29 42 A4
Seymour Terr
Hetton le H DH5 95 B1
Ryton NE40 52 A5
Sezze Bldg 6 NE46 45 B4
Shadfen Cres NE61 4 E3
Shadfen Park Rd NE30 32 A3
Shadon Way DH3 82 E3
Shaftesbury Ave
Jarrow NE32 58 E5
Ryhope SR2 92 E7
Whitley Bay NE26 31 F6
Shaftesbury Cres
Sunderland SR3 85 F3
Tynemouth NE30 32 A3
Shaftesbury Gr NE6 56 B7
Shaftesbury Ho NE33 59 B6
Shaftesbury Wlk NE8 100 C2
Shafto Ct NE15 54 B5
Shafto St
Newcastle-u-T NE15 54 A5
Wallsend NE28 40 E3
Shaftoe Cl NE40 51 F3
Shaftoe Cres NE46 45 A5
Shaftoe Ct
Killingworth NE12 29 D3
Newcastle-u-T NE3 38 A7
Shaftoe Leazes NE46 44 F4
Shaftoe Rd SR3 85 D2
Shaftoe Sq SR3 85 D2
Shaftoe Way NE13 27 B7
Shakespeare Ave NE31 57 E6
Shakespeare St
Houghton-le-S DH5 94 E7
Jarrow NE32 58 B8
Newcastle-u-T NE1 99 A1
13 South Shields NE33 42 D1
Sunderland SR5 75 B2
Wallsend NE28 40 F3
Shakespeare Terr SR2 102 C1
Shalcombe Cl SR3 92 A6
Shallcross SR2 86 B4
Shallon Ct NE63 6 C2
Shalstone NE37 72 F1
Shamrock Cl NE15 53 C8
Shandon Way NE3 37 E5
Shanklin Pl NE23 21 E6
Shannon Cl SR5 74 A1
Shannon Ct NE3 37 C7
Shap Cl NE38 83 D3
Shap Ct 2 SR3 91 F6
Shap La NE5 37 A1
Shap Rd NE30 32 A2
Sharnford Cl NE27 30 D5
Sharon Cl NE12 29 B2
Sharpendon St NE31 57 E7
Sharperton Dr NE3 28 A1
Sharpley Dr 5 SR7 92 E1
Shaw Ave NE34 59 B4
Shaw Gdns NE10 72 B8
Shaw La DH8,NE17 76 F4
Shawbrow Cl NE7 39 E3
Shawdon Cl NE5 37 B4
Shaws La Hexham NE46 44 D4
Hexham NE46 44 D5
Shaws Pk NE46 44 E6
Shearlegs Rd NE8 56 A3
Shearwater SR6 60 F3
Shearwater Ave NE12 39 A7
Shearwater Cl NE5 37 B4
Shearwater Way NE24 17 F4
Sheelin Ave DH2 88 C1
Sheen Cl DH4 94 A2
Sheen Ct NE3 37 B5
Sheep Hill NE16 79 B6
Sheepfolds N SR5 103 A4
Sheepfolds Rd SR5 103 A4
Sheepwash Ave NE62 10 E7
Sheepwash Bank NE62 10 E7
Sheepwash Rd NE61,NE62 5 E3
Shefton Mus of Greek Art & Archaeology★ NE1 99 A2
Sheldon Ct NE12 29 C1
Sheldon Gr
Cramlington NE23 16 B1
Newcastle-u-T NE3 38 A3
Sheldon Rd NE34 42 F1
Sheldon St NE32 58 B7
Shelford Gdns NE15 53 E7
Shellbark DH4 89 F6
Shelley Ave
Easington Lane DH5 97 D8
South Shields NE34 60 B5
Springwell NE9 71 F1
West Boldon NE35 74 A8
Shelley Cres NE24 17 C5
Shelley Dr NE8 56 A2
Shelley Rd NE15 53 A7
Shepherd St SR4 102 A3
Shepherd Way NE38 83 F2
Shepherd's Quay NE29 42 B4
Shepherds Way NE36 74 A7
Sheppard Terr 1 SR5 74 B1
Sheppey Ct SR3 92 A6
Shepton Cotts NE16 69 C3
Sheraton NE10 72 A5
Sheraton St NE2 98 B4
Sherborne Ave NE29 41 D8
Sherburn Gn NE39 67 F3
Sherburn Gr DH4 90 C1
Sherburn Grange N NE32 58 A5
Sherburn Grange S NE32 58 A5
Sherburn Hill Prim Sch
DH6 96 D1
Sherburn Park Dr NE39 67 F3
Sherburn Terr
Gateshead NE9 71 C2
Hamsterley NE17 76 F5
Sherburn Village Prim Sch
DH6 96 A2
Sherburn Way NE10 72 C7
Sherfield Dr NE7 39 D2
Sheridan Gn NE38 83 A1
Sheridan Rd NE34 59 A3
Sheridan St 5 SR4 85 F7
Sheriff's Highway NE9 71 A6
Sheriff's Moor Ave DH5 97 C8
Sheriffs Cl NE10 71 B8
Sheriffs Hall Villas 7
NE9 71 A5
Sheringham Ave NE29 41 D7
Sheringham Cl SR3 92 A4
Sheringham Dr NE23 21 E6
Sheringham Gdns NE15 35 B2
Sheringham Ho 8 NE38 83 F4
Sherringham Ave NE3 37 E4
Sherwood NE27 31 B2
Sherwood Cl
Tynemouth NE27 31 B2
Washington NE38 83 D5
Sherwood Ct 5 SR3 92 A6
Sherwood Pl NE3 28 C2
Sherwood View NE28 40 A4
Shetland Ct 1 SR3 92 A6
Shibdon Bank NE21 53 D2
Shibdon Bsns Pk NE21 53 E3
Shibdon Cres NE21 53 D2
Shibdon Ct NE21 53 C3
Shibdon Park View NE21 53 D2
Shibdon Pond Nature Reserve★ NE21 53 E2
Shibdon Rd Blaydon NE21 53 D3
Blaydon NE21 53 E2
Shibdon Way NE21 53 F2
Shiel Gdns NE23 21 E6
Shield Ave NE16 54 B1
Shield Ct Hexham NE46 45 A5
Newcastle-u-T NE2 99 C3
Shield Gr NE3 38 D6
Shield La 1 NE6 56 C6
Shield St NE2 99 C2
Shieldclose 2 NE37 83 A6
Shieldfield Gn NE2 99 C2
Shieldfield Ho NE2 99 C2
Shieldfield La NE2 99 C2
Shields Pl DH5 90 E1
Shields Rd
Chester le S DH3 88 D5
Cleadon NE34 60 A3
Cleadon SR6 60 A2
Gateshead NE10 71 F8
Morpeth NE61 9 B7
Nedderton NE22 15 C5
Newcastle-u-T NE6 56 C7
Sunderland SR5,SR6 75 B5
Whitley Bay NE25 31 F3
Shields Rd W 5 NE6 56 A6
Shillaw Pl NE23 29 B5
Shilmore Rd NE3 37 F5
Shilton Cl NE34 60 B5
Shincliffe Ave SR5 74 C2
Shincliffe Gdns NE9 71 D3
Shiney Row Prim Sch
DH4 90 B5
Shipcote La NE8 70 F8
Shipcote Terr NE8 70 F8
Shipley Art Gallery★
NE8 70 F8
Shipley Ave
Newcastle-u-T NE4 54 E6
Sunderland SR6 75 E4
Shipley Ct NE8 101 C1
Shipley Pl 18 NE6 56 B6
Shipley Rd NE30 42 C7
Shipley Rise 9 NE6 56 C6
Shipley St NE15 53 C6
Shipley Wlk 23 NE6 56 B6
Shipton Cl NE35 58 E1
Shire Farm Gr NE63 6 A2
Shiremoor Prim Sch
NE27 30 E3
Shiremoor Sta NE27 30 F4
Shirlaw Cl NE5 36 F4
Shirley Gdns SR3 86 B3
Shirwood Ave NE16 69 A5
Shop Row DH4 90 C5
Shop Spouts NE21 53 C3
Shopping Ctr The NE5 36 C2
Shore St SR6 75 D1
Shoreham Ct NE3 37 C7
Shoreham Sq SR3 85 E3
Shorestone Ave NE30 32 B3
Shoreswood Dr 3 SR3 92 B7
Short Row NE5 36 B6
Shortridge St 1 NE33 42 D3
Shortridge Terr NE2 38 F1
Shot Factory La NE4 100 C3
Shotley Ave SR5 75 B3
Shotley Ct NE63 6 B2
Shotley Gdns NE9 71 A7
Shotley Gr NE36 74 B7
Shotton Ave NE24 17 E6
Shotton La
Cramlington NE23 15 C2
Shotton NE61,NE13 20 F8
Shotton St NE23 16 B3
Shotton Way NE10 72 E6
Shrewsbury Cl NE12 39 D4
Shrewsbury Cres SR3 85 F3
Shrewsbury Dr NE27 30 C5
Shrewsbury St NE11 69 F8
Shrewsbury Terr NE33 59 C7
Shrigley Cl NE38 89 B8
Shrigley Gdns NE3 37 F5
Shummard Cl DH4 89 F5
Shunner Cl NE37 83 A6
Sibthorpe St NE29 42 B5
Side NE1 101 B4
Side Cliff Rd SR6 75 E3
Sidlaw Ave
Chester le S DH2 88 A2
Tynemouth NE29 31 F1
Sidlaw Ct NE63 6 E1
Sidmouth Cl DH4 90 C4
Sidmouth Rd
Gateshead NE9 70 F3
North Shields NE29 41 C5
Sidney Gr Gateshead NE8 101 A1
Newcastle-u-T NE4 98 A2
Sidney St Blyth NE24 17 D7
Boldon Colliery NE35 73 F8
North Shields NE29 42 A5
Silkey's La NE29 41 F5
Silkstun Ct 8 SR3 92 A7
Silksworth Cl SR3 91 F8
Silksworth Gdns NE9 71 C2
Silksworth Hall Dr SR3 91 F6
Silksworth La
New Silksworth SR3 91 F7
Sunderland SR3 86 A2
Silksworth Rd
New Silksworth SR3 92 A7
Sunderland SR3 91 C6
Silksworth Row SR1 102 C3
Silksworth Terr SR3 92 A7
Silkwood Cl NE23 16 B1
Silkworth La 1 SR3 92 A8
Silksworth Way SR3 91 E6
Silloth Ave NE5 54 A8
Silloth Dr NE37 72 C2
Silloth Pl NE30 32 B2
Silloth Rd SR3 85 D2
Silvas Ct NE61 4 A1
Silver Ct 3 NE9 71 A8
Silver Fox Way
Earsdon NE27 31 A1
Wallsend NE27 40 F8
Silver Lonnen NE5 54 B8
Silver St Sunderland SR1 103 C3
Tynemouth NE30 42 D7
Silverbirch Ind Est NE12 29 B4
Silverbriar SR5 74 F1
Silverdale SR3 92 A4
Silverdale Ave NE10 72 D8
Silverdale Dr NE21 68 A8
Silverdale Rd NE23 16 B1
Silverdale Sch NE28 41 A5
Silverdale Terr NE8 70 F8
Silverdale Way
Brockley Whins NE34 58 F3
Whickham NE16 68 F4
Silverhill Dr NE5 54 B7
Silverhill Sch The NE5 54 C7
Silverlink N The
Shiremoor NE27 30 E1
Wallsend NE27 40 F8
Silverlink Ret Pk NE28 41 A6
Silverlink The NE28 41 A6
Silvermere Dr NE40 52 D4
Silverstone NE12 29 E3
Silverstone Rd NE37 83 E8
Silvertop Gdns NE40 52 A1
Silvertop Terr NE40 66 F8
Silverwood Gdns NE11 70 B5
Simon Pl NE13 28 A5
Simonburn NE38 82 F4
Simonburn Ave
Newcastle-u-T NE4 54 E8
North Shields NE29 41 C6
Simonburn La 2 NE63 6 F2
Simonside Prudhoe NE42 50 B1
Seaton Sluice NE26 24 D4
Simonside Ave
Stakeford NE62 11 B8
Wallsend NE28 40 F4
Simonside Cl
Morpeth NE61 8 D7
Seaton Sluice NE26 24 D4
Simonside Hall NE34 58 F5
Simonside Ind Est NE32 58 E5
Simonside Pl 2 NE9 71 D3
Simonside Prim Sch
Brockley Whins NE32 58 D4
Newcastle-u-T NE5 36 F5
Simonside Rd
Blaydon NE21 53 C1
Sunderland SR3 85 D3
Simonside Terr
Newbiggin-by-t-S NE64 7 E4
Newcastle-u-T NE6 56 C8
Simonside View
Jarrow NE32 58 C4
Ponteland NE20 25 D7
13 Whickham NE16 69 A7
Simonside Way NE12 29 F4
Simonside Wlk NE11 70 A5
Simpson Cl NE35 73 E8
Simpson Ct NE63 7 A3
Simpson St Blyth NE24 17 E8
North Shields NE29 41 E5

Simpson St *continued*
Ryton NE40 . . . . .52 E4
Sunderland SR4 . . . . .102 B4
Tynemouth NE30 . . . . .32 C4
Simpson Terr
Newcastle-u-T NE15 . . . . . . .36 B1
Newcastle-u-T,Shieldfield
NE2 . . . . .99 B2
Simpsons Meml Homes
NE40 . . . . .52 A4
Sinclair Dr DH3 . . . . .88 D8
Sinclair Gdns NE25 . . . . . . .23 D3
Sinderby Cl NE3 . . . . .38 D8
Sir Charles Parsons Sch
NE6 . . . . .56 F7
Sir GB Hunter Meml Hospl
NE28 . . . . .40 C2
Sir Godfrey Thomson Ct
NE10 . . . . .71 C8
Siskin Ho NE12 . . . . .39 E8
Sixth Ave Ashington NE63 . . . .6 E2
Blyth NE24 . . . . .17 D6
Chester le S DH2 . . . . .88 B3
Gateshead NE11 . . . . .70 C4
Morpeth NE61 . . . . .9 B7
Newcastle-u-T NE6 . . . . . . .56 C7
Skaylock Dr NE38 . . . . .83 A3
Skegness Par NE31 . . . . . . .58 A2
Skelder Ave NE12 . . . . .39 B6
Skelton Ct NE3 . . . . .37 E8
Ski View SR3 . . . . .91 F8
Skiddaw Dr SR6 . . . . .75 C5
Skiddaw Pl NE9 . . . . .71 B4
Skinnerburn Rd NE1,
NE4 . . . . .100 C3
Skipper Cl NE11 . . . . .70 B7
Skipsea View SR2 . . . . .92 D7
Skipton Cl
Bedlington NE22 . . . . .10 D2
Cramlington NE23 . . . . .16 C1
Skipton Gn NE9 . . . . .71 B2
Skirlaw Cl NE38 . . . . .83 D4
Skye Cl 2 SR3 . . . . .92 A6
Skye Gr NE32 . . . . .58 E2
Slake Rd NE32 . . . . .58 D8
Slaley NE38 . . . . .83 E1
Slaley Cl NE10 . . . . .72 C7
Slaley Ct Bedlington NE22 . . .11 A1
4 Silksworth SR3 . . . . .92 A6
Slatyford La NE5 . . . . .54 A8
Sled La NE40,NE41 . . . . .51 D3
Sleekburn Ave NE31 . . . . . .11 E3
Sleekburn Bsns Ctr NE22,
NE24 . . . . .12 A6
Sleekburn Ho NE22 . . . . . . .11 D2
Slingley Cl 4 SR7 . . . . .92 E1
Slingsby Gdns NE7 . . . . . . .39 D3
Slipway The NE10 . . . . .57 A2
Sloane Ct NE2 . . . . .99 B3
Smailes La NE39 . . . . .67 C2
Smallholdings NE64 . . . . . . .7 C6
Smeaton Ct 5 NE28 . . . . . .41 A1
Smeaton St 2 NE28 . . . . . .41 A1
Smith Gr SR2 . . . . .92 E6
Smith St Ryhope SR2 . . . . . .92 F6
South Shields NE33 . . . . . . .59 B8
Smith St S SR2 . . . . .92 F6
Smith's Terr SR5 . . . . .95 B1
Smithburn Rd NE10 . . . . . . .71 E7
Smithy La NE11,NE9 . . . . . . .70 F1
Smithy Sq NE23 . . . . .22 B6
Smithy St 2 NE33 . . . . .42 C3
Smithyford NE15 . . . . .71 A1
Smyrna Pl SR1 . . . . .103 B2
Snipes Dene NE39 . . . . .67 E3
Snowdon Gdns NE11 . . . . . .70 A6
Snowdon Gr NE36 . . . . .74 B7
Snowdon Terr NE39 . . . . . . .66 F5
Snowdrop Cl NE21 . . . . .53 A2
Soane Gdns NE34 . . . . .59 D3
Softley Pl NE15 . . . . .53 F7
Solar Ho SR1 . . . . .102 C2
Solingen Est NE24 . . . . .17 F5
Solway Ave NE30 . . . . .32 B2
Solway Rd NE31 . . . . .57 F4
Solway Sq SR3 . . . . .85 E3
Solway St NE6 . . . . .56 C4
Somerford NE9 . . . . .71 F2
Somersby Dr NE3 . . . . .37 E5
Somerset Cl NE63 . . . . .6 A4
Somerset Cotts 4 SR3 . . . .92 A8
Somerset Gdns NE28 . . . . . .40 A2
Somerset Gr NE29 . . . . .41 D8
Somerset Pl NE4 . . . . .98 A1
Somerset Rd
Hebburn NE31 . . . . .57 F3
Sunderland SR3 . . . . .85 D3
Somerset Sq SR3 . . . . .85 D3
Somerset St SR3 . . . . .92 A8
Somerton Ct NE3 . . . . .37 C6
Somervyl Ave NE12 . . . . . . .38 F6
Sophy St SR5 . . . . .75 B2
Sorley St SR4 . . . . .102 A2
Sorrel Cl NE63 . . . . .6 C2
Sorrel Gdns NE34 . . . . .59 E3
Sorrell Cl NE4 . . . . .54 D7
Soulby Cl NE3 . . . . .37 D8
Sourmilk Hill La NE9 . . . . . .71 A6
Souter Lighthouse ★ SR6 . .60 F5
Souter Rd NE3 . . . . .38 A5
Souter View SR6 . . . . .60 F2
South App DH2 . . . . .88 C2
South Ave Ryton NE40 . . . . .52 E4
South Shields NE34 . . . . . . .59 F5
Washington NE37 . . . . .83 C8
Whickham NE16 . . . . .69 B5
South Beach Fst Sch
NE24 . . . . .17 E4

South Bend NE3 . . . . .28 B1
South Bents Ave SR6 . . . .75 F6
South Benwell Prim Sch
NE4 . . . . .54 E4
South Benwell Rd NE15 . . .54 C4
South Burn Terr DH4 . . . . . .90 C6
South Burns DH3 . . . . .88 C4
South Cl
Easington Lane DH5 . . . . . . .97 D8
Ryton NE40 . . . . .52 C4
South Shields NE34 . . . . . . .59 F5
South Cliff SR6 . . . . .75 F2
South Cres
Boldon Colliery NE35 . . . . . .73 F8
Great Lumley DH4 . . . . .89 F1
Washington NE38 . . . . .89 B8
South Croft NE12 . . . . .39 E7
South Cross St NE3 . . . . . . .38 C5
South Dene NE34 . . . . .59 B6
South Dr Cleadon SR6 . . . . .59 F1
Shotton NE13 . . . . .20 E6
Woolsington NE13 . . . . .37 A8
South Durham Ct SR1 . . . .103 B2
South East Farm NE15 . . . .50 D8
South Eldon St NE33 . . . . . .59 B8
South End Cleadon SR6 . . . .74 E8
High Pittington DH6 . . . . . . .96 C5
South Farm
Nedderton NE22 . . . . .15 B8
Ryhope SR2 . . . . .93 A6
South Frederick St NE33 . . .59 B7
South Front NE2 . . . . .99 B4
South Gosforth Fst Sch
NE3 . . . . .38 E4
South Gosforth Sta NE3 . . .38 E4
South Gr NE40 . . . . .52 D4
South Grange Pk SR7 . . . . .92 F2
South Hetton Ind Est
DH6 . . . . .97 F7
South Hetton Prim Sch
DH6 . . . . .97 F7
South Hetton Rd DH5,
DH6 . . . . .97 D8
South Hill Cres SR2 . . . . . .102 B1
South Hill Rd NE8 . . . . . . .101 A1
South Hylton Prim Sch
SR4 . . . . .85 A6
South Hylton Sta SR4 . . . . .85 B6
South La NE36 . . . . .74 C7
South Lea Blaydon NE21 . . . .53 C1
Horsley NE15 . . . . .50 C8
South Leigh DH9 . . . . .79 D1
South Lodge Wood NE61 . . .9 B4
South Magdalene DH8 . . . . .77 B1
South Market St DH5 . . . . . .95 B4
South Nelson Ind Est
NE23 . . . . .21 E8
South Nelson Rd NE23 . . . .21 E8
South Newsham Rd
NE24 . . . . .17 D3
South Par
Choppington NE62 . . . . .10 E6
Gateshead NE10 . . . . .57 B2
Stocksfield NE43 . . . . .64 A7
Whitley Bay NE26 . . . . .32 C5
South Pelaw Inf Sch DH2 . .88 B5
South Pk NE6 . . . . .45 B3
South Preston Gr 1
NE29 . . . . .42 A5
South Preston Terr 2
NE29 . . . . .42 A5
South Rd Chopwell NE17 . . .66 C1
Prudhoe NE42 . . . . .50 D2
South Ridge
Ashington NE63 . . . . .7 B2
Newcastle-u-T NE3 . . . . . . .38 B8
South Riggs NE22 . . . . .15 F8
South Row NE8 . . . . .56 A4
South Sherburn NE39 . . . . .67 E1
South Shields Sta NE33 . . .42 C3
South Shore Rd
Gateshead,East Gateshead
NE8 . . . . .56 B3
Gateshead,Saltmeadows
NE8 . . . . .56 A4
South Side Cresswell NE61 . . .2 B1
South St Chester le S DH2 . .88 C4
East Rainton DH5 . . . . .94 C4
9 Fence Houses DH4 . . . . .94 A8
Gateshead NE8 . . . . .101 C1
Hebburn NE31 . . . . .57 F7
High Spen NE39 . . . . .66 F4
Newbottle DH4 . . . . .90 D3
Newcastle-u-T NE1 . . . . . . .101 A4
Newcastle-u-T,Coxlodge
NE3 . . . . .38 A5
Sherburn DH6 . . . . .96 A1
Shiremoor NE27 . . . . .30 F4
Sunderland SR1 . . . . .103 A3
West Rainton DH4 . . . . .94 A2
South Street Prim Sch
NE8 . . . . .101 C1
South Terr Chopwell NE17 . .77 B8
Morpeth NE61 . . . . .3 F1
Sunderland SR5 . . . . .75 B1
Wallsend NE28 . . . . .40 E2
South Tyneside Coll
Hebburn NE31 . . . . .57 C2
South Shields NE33 . . . . . . .59 E8
South Tyneside Coll
Seamanship Ctr NE33 . .42 C4
South Tyneside General
Hospl NE34 . . . . .59 D5
South View
Annitsford NE23 . . . . .22 B1
Ashington NE63 . . . . .6 C4

South View *continued*
Birtley DH3 . . . . .82 D4
Blyth NE24 . . . . .17 C4
Cambois NE24 . . . . .12 C6
Chopwell NE17 . . . . .77 A8
Crawcrook NE40 . . . . .51 F4
Crawcrook,Clara Vale NE40 .51 F7
East Sleekburn NE22 . . . . . .11 F3
Easington Lane DH5 . . . . . . .97 D8
15 Gateshead NE10 . . . . . .56 E3
Guide Post NE62 . . . . .10 E7
Hazlerigg NE13 . . . . .28 A4
High Spen NE39 . . . . .66 F3
Jarrow NE32 . . . . .58 A6
Longbenton NE7 . . . . .39 D1
Mickley Square NE43 . . . . . .49 E1
Newcastle-u-T NE5 . . . . . . .53 E8
Pegswood NE61 . . . . .4 F1
Prudhoe NE42 . . . . .50 B2
Sherburn Hill DH6 . . . . .96 B1
Shiney Row DH4 . . . . .90 B6
Sunderland SR6 . . . . .75 D3
Sunderland,South Hylton
SR4 . . . . .85 B5
Tantobie DH9 . . . . .79 B2
Washington NE38 . . . . .83 E1
Whitburn SR6 . . . . .60 F3
South View E NE39 . . . . . . .67 C2
South View Gdns NE46 . . . .45 A4
South View Pl NE23 . . . . . . .22 B6
South View Rd SR4 . . . . . . .85 B5
South View Terr
Fence Houses DH4 . . . . .94 B8
Whickham NE16 . . . . .69 B6
Whickham,Swalwell NE16 . . .69 B8
South View W
Newcastle-u-T NE6 . . . . . . .56 A6
Rowlands Gill NE39 . . . . . . .67 C2
South Wellfield Fst Sch
NE25 . . . . .31 B4
South Woodbine St 1
NE33 . . . . .42 D2
Southburn Cl DH4 . . . . .94 C8
Southcliff NE26 . . . . .32 C4
Southcote NE16 . . . . .69 A5
Southcroft NE38 . . . . .83 D1
Southdowns DH2 . . . . .88 C2
Southend Ave NE24 . . . . . . .17 C6
Southend Par NE31 . . . . . . .58 A2
Southend Rd
Gateshead NE9 . . . . .71 B5
Sunderland SR3 . . . . .85 E2
Southend Terr NE9 . . . . . . .71 B6
Southern Cl NE63 . . . . .7 B3
Southern Rd NE6 . . . . .56 F4
Southern Way NE40 . . . . . . .52 C4
Southey St NE33 . . . . .59 D8
Southfield Gn NE16 . . . . . . .69 C6
Southfield La NE39 . . . . . . .77 F3
Southfield Rd
Longbenton NE12 . . . . .39 D6
2 South Shields NE34 . . . .60 A8
Whickham NE16 . . . . .69 C6
Southfield Terr
Newcastle-u-T NE6 . . . . . . .57 A4
Whickham NE16 . . . . .69 C6
Southfields NE23 . . . . .29 A8
Southfields Ho 1 NE6 . . . . .56 B6
Southfork NE15 . . . . .53 C8
Southgarth E 2 NE33 . . . . .59 E8
Southgate NE12 . . . . .29 D3
Southgate Ct NE12 . . . . . . .38 F6
Southgate Wood NE61 . . . . .9 A5
Southhill Rd NE34 . . . . .60 A6
Southlands
Gateshead NE9 . . . . .71 C2
Hedworth NE32 . . . . .58 D1
Hexham NE46 . . . . .44 D4
Newcastle-u-T NE7 . . . . . . .39 A2
Tynemouth NE30 . . . . .32 B1
Southlands Mid Sch
NE23 . . . . .22 B3
Southlands Sch NE30 . . . . .32 A1
Southleigh NE26 . . . . .32 B5
Southmayne Rd SR4 . . . . . .85 D4
Southmead Ave NE5 . . . . . .37 C1
Southmoor Com Sch SR2 . .86 E3
Southmoor Rd NE6 . . . . . . .56 F7
Southport Par NE31 . . . . . . .58 A3
Southridge Fst Sch NE25 . .31 D6
Southward NE26 . . . . .24 D5
Southward Cl NE26 . . . . . . .24 D5
Southward Way NE25 . . . . . .23 E1
Southway Gateshead NE9 . . .71 B6
Newcastle-u-T NE15 . . . . . .53 E7
Southwick Ind Est SR5 . . . .74 F2
Southwick Prim Sch SR5 . .75 A2
Southwick Rd SR5 . . . . .75 C1
Southwold Pl NE23 . . . . . . .21 E6
Southwood Cres NE39 . . . . .67 F2
Southwood Gdns NE3 . . . . .37 F4
Sovereign Ct
Newcastle-u-T NE4 . . . . . . .100 A4
Newcastle-u-T,Jesmond
NE2 . . . . .99 C4
Sovereign Ho 16 NE30 . . . .42 D7
Sovereign Pl NE4 . . . . .100 A4
Spa Well Cl NE21 . . . . .68 B8
Spa Well Dr SR5 . . . . .74 C2
Spa Well Turn NE21 . . . . . .68 E7
Spalding NE7 . . . . .39 C4
Sparkwell Cl DH4 . . . . .90 F7
Spartylea NE38 . . . . .83 F1
Speculation Pl NE37 . . . . . .83 D8
Speedwell NE9 . . . . .71 C5

Speedwell Ct NE63 . . . . .6 B1
Spelter Works Rd SR2 . . . . .86 F3
Spelvit La NE61 . . . . .8 F7
Spen Burn NE39 . . . . .67 A4
Spen La
Greenside NE39,NE40 . . . . . .66 F7
High Spen NE39 . . . . .67 B3
Spen Rd NE39 . . . . .66 F5
Spence Terr 1 NE29 . . . . . .41 F5
Spencer Cl NE24 . . . . .12 B1
Spencer Dr NE61 . . . . .4 E3
Spencer Gr NE16 . . . . .69 A8
Spencer Rd NE24 . . . . .12 B1
Spencer St Hebburn NE31 . . .57 F7
Newcastle-u-T NE6 . . . . . . .56 C8
20 North Shields NE29 . . . . .42 A5
Spencer Terr NE15 . . . . . . .36 B1
Spencers Bank 3 NE16 . . . .54 A1
Spenfield Rd NE5 . . . . .37 D3
Spenser St NE32 . . . . .58 B8
Spenser Wlk NE34 . . . . .59 A3
Spetchells NE42 . . . . .50 D3
Spinney Terr NE6 . . . . .56 F6
Spinney The
Annitsford NE23 . . . . .22 C1
Killingworth NE12 . . . . .29 E2
Morpeth NE61 . . . . .9 A6
Newcastle-u-T NE7 . . . . . . .39 B2
Washington NE38 . . . . .83 D2
Spinneyside Gdns NE11 . . . .69 F7
Spire Rd NE37 . . . . .83 F7
Spires La NE6 . . . . .56 C6
Spital Cres NE64 . . . . .7 D3
Spital La NE46 . . . . .44 F7
Spital Rd NE64 . . . . .7 C3
Spital Terr NE3 . . . . .38 D5
Spital Villas NE15 . . . . .33 A3
Spittal Terr NE46 . . . . .45 A4
Split Crow Rd NE10,NE8 . . . .71 B8
Spohr Terr NE33 . . . . .42 D2
Spoor St NE11 . . . . .100 A1
Spoors Cotts NE16 . . . . .69 A6
Spout La Washington NE37 . . .83 D7
Washington,Concord NE37 . . .83 D8
Washington,Washington Village
NE38 . . . . .83 D6
Spoutwell La NE45 . . . . .47 A5
Spring Cl DH8 . . . . .76 E2
Spring Garden Cl SR1 . . . . .103 B3
Spring Garden La NE4 . . . . .98 B2
Spring Gardens Ct 12
NE29 . . . . .42 A6
Spring Gardens Prim Sch
NE29 . . . . .41 F6
Spring Gdns NE29 . . . . .41 F5
Spring St NE4 . . . . .98 B2
Spring Terr NE29 . . . . .42 A6
Spring Ville NE22 . . . . .11 F4
Springbank Ho NE2 . . . . . . .56 A7
Springbank Rd
Newcastle-u-T NE2 . . . . . . .56 A7
Sunderland SR3 . . . . .85 D3
Springbank Sq SR3 . . . . . . .85 D3
Springfeld NE10 . . . . .71 F4
Springfell DH3 . . . . .82 D3
Springfield
5 North Shields NE29 . . . . .42 A6
Ovington NE42 . . . . .49 D4
Springfield Ave NE9 . . . . . . .71 C1
Springfield Cl NE42 . . . . . . .49 D4
Springfield Gdns
Chester le S DH3 . . . . .88 C5
Wallsend NE28 . . . . .39 F3
Springfield Gr NE25 . . . . . . .31 E3
Springfield Pl NE9 . . . . .71 A6
Springfield Rd
Blaydon NE21 . . . . .53 C1
Hexham NE46 . . . . .45 C4
Newbottle DH4 . . . . .90 D3
Newcastle-u-T NE5 . . . . . . .37 D2
Springfield Terr 1 NE10 . . .71 C7
Springhill Gdns NE15 . . . . . .54 D6
Springhill Wlk NE61 . . . . .8 E7
Springhouse La DH8 . . . . . .76 E2
Springs The DH3 . . . . .82 E3
Springsyde Cl NE16 . . . . . . .68 E5
Springwell Ave
Gateshead NE9 . . . . .71 C3
Jarrow NE32 . . . . .58 C6
Newcastle-u-T NE6 . . . . . . .56 E4
Springwell Cl NE21 . . . . . . .53 C1
Springwell Dene Sch
SR3 . . . . .85 D3
Springwell Dr NE61 . . . . .1 E4
Springwell Rd
Gateshead NE9 . . . . .71 D3
Jarrow NE32 . . . . .58 B5
Springwell NE9 . . . . .71 F1
Springwell Sta ★ NE9 . . . . .71 F3
Springwell Terr
Gateshead NE9 . . . . .71 E3
Hetton le H DH5 . . . . .95 A2
17 Springwell NE9 . . . . . . .71 F1
Springwell Village Prim Sch
NE9 . . . . .71 F1
Springwood NE31 . . . . .57 C7
Square Hos 4 NE10 . . . . . .71 C2
Square The
Guide Post NE62 . . . . .10 F7
Ponteland NE20 . . . . .26 C5
Riding Mill NE44 . . . . .63 A8
3 Hexham NE46 . . . . .69 B7
Squires Gdns NE10 . . . . . . .71 D7
Stable Block NE45 . . . . .47 C5
Stable Cl NE61 . . . . .4 E7
Stable La NE3 . . . . .37 F8
Stables The DH4 . . . . .90 F7

Stadium Ind Pk NE10 . . . .56 B3
Stadium of Light (Sunderland
FC) SR5 . . . . .102 C4
Stadium of Light Sta
SR5,SR6 . . . . .75 D1
Stadium Rd NE10 . . . . .56 B3
Stadium Villas NE28 . . . . . .40 C2
Stadium Way SR5 . . . . . . .102 C4
Stafford Gr Ryhope SR2 . . . .92 E6
Sunderland SR5 . . . . .75 B2
Stafford St
Hetton le H DH5 . . . . .94 F4
Sunderland SR1 . . . . .103 C4
Stafford Villas 19 NE9 . . . .71 F1
Staffords La 3 SR6 . . . . . . .75 F8
Stagshaw NE12 . . . . .29 C5
Stagshaw Rd NE45 . . . . . . .46 F6
Staindrop NE10 . . . . .72 A5
Staines Rd NE6 . . . . .56 D4
Stainthorpe Ct 1 NE46 . . . .45 B4
Stainton Dr NE10 . . . . .71 D8
Stainton Gdns NE9 . . . . .71 C2
Stainton Gr SR6 . . . . .75 C5
Staith La NE21 . . . . .53 A4
Staithes Ave NE12 . . . . .39 C6
Staithes La NE61 . . . . .4 A1
Staithes Rd
Dunston NE11 . . . . .100 A2
Penshaw NE38 . . . . .84 A3
Staithes St NE6 . . . . .57 B6
Stakeford Cres 11 B8
Stakeford Fst Sch NE62 . . .11 C8
Stakeford La NE62 . . . . .11 A7
Stakeford Rd NE22 . . . . . . .11 C3
Stakeford Terr NE62 . . . . . .11 A7
Stalks Rd NE13 . . . . .28 B6
Stamford NE12 . . . . .29 D4
Stamford Ave
Seaton Delaval NE25 . . . . . .23 E1
Sunderland SR3 . . . . .85 F3
Stamfordham Ave NE29 . . . .41 D5
Stamfordham Cl NE28 . . . . .40 A2
Stamfordham Mews 7
NE5 . . . . .37 D1
Stamfordham Rd
Newcastle-u-T NE5 . . . . . . .36 C4
Ponteland NE5,NE15 . . . . . .35 D7
Stamp Exchange NE1 . . . . .101 A4
Stampley Cl NE21 . . . . .68 A8
Stamps La SR1 . . . . .103 C3
Stanley Rd NE42 . . . . .50 E2
Standfield Gdns NE10 . . . . . .72 C8
Stanelaw Way DH9 . . . . .79 F1
Staneway NE10 . . . . .71 E5
Stanfield Bsns Ctr SR2 . . . .103 C1
Stanfield Ct NE7 . . . . .39 E3
Stang Wlk NE12 . . . . .39 C7
Stanhope NE38 . . . . .83 A5
Stanhope Cl DH4 . . . . .94 D7
Stanhope Par 7 NE33 . . . . .59 D8
Stanhope Prim Sch NE33 . . .59 D7
Stanhope Rd Jarrow NE32 . . .58 D5
South Shields NE33 . . . . . . .59 C7
Sunderland SR6 . . . . .75 E4
Stanhope St
Greenside NE40 . . . . .51 F1
Newcastle-u-T NE4 . . . . . . .98 B2
South Shields NE33 . . . . . . .42 C3
Stanhope Way NE4 . . . . . . .98 B2
Stanley Cres
Prudhoe NE42 . . . . .50 E3
9 Whitley Bay NE26 . . . . . .32 B4
Stanley Gdns
Gateshead NE9 . . . . .71 C2
Seghill NE23 . . . . .22 F1
Stanley Gr
Bedlington NE22 . . . . .11 B1
Newcastle-u-T NE7 . . . . . . .39 B4
Stanley St Blyth NE24 . . . . . .17 F7
Houghton-le-S DH5 . . . . . . .90 E1
Jarrow NE32 . . . . .58 C7
Newcastle-u-T NE4 . . . . . . .54 F4
North Shields NE29 . . . . . . .42 A5
South Shields NE34 . . . . . . .59 B5
2 Sunderland SR5 . . . . . . .74 F2
Wallsend NE28 . . . . .40 F3
Stanley St W NE29 . . . . . . .42 A5
Stanley Terr
Chester le S DH3 . . . . .88 D2
4 Penshaw DH4 . . . . .90 B6
Stanmore Rd NE6 . . . . .39 C1
Stannerford Rd NE40 . . . . . .51 F6
Stannington Ave NE6 . . . . . .56 B7
Stannington Fst Sch
NE61 . . . . .14 B4
Stannington Gdns SR2 . . . .86 C2
Stannington Gr
5 Newcastle-u-T NE6 . . . . .56 B7
Sunderland SR2 . . . . .86 C2
Stannington Pl
1 Newcastle-u-T NE6 . . . . .56 B7
Ponteland NE20 . . . . .25 E8
Stannington Rd NE29 . . . . . .41 D5
Stannington St NE24 . . . . . .17 F7
Stannington Station Rd
NE61 . . . . .14 D8
Stannington Vale NE61 . . . .14 D1
Stansfield St SR6 . . . . .75 E1
Stanstead Cl SR5 . . . . .85 A8
Stanton Ave Blyth NE24 . . . .17 B5
South Shields NE34 . . . . . . .59 E2
Stanton Cl NE10 . . . . .72 D7
Stanton Dr NE61 . . . . .4 E3
Stanton Gr NE30 . . . . .32 A1

Stanton Rd
Shiremoor NE27 30 E3
Tynemouth NE30 32 A1
Stanton St NE4 98 A2
Stanway Dr NE7 39 A3
Stanwick St NE30 42 D8
Stanwix 1 NE28 40 F4
Stapeley Ct 5 NE3 37 D5
Stapeley View NE3 37 D5
Staple Rd NE32 58 C7
Stapleford Cl NE5 37 B1
Stapylton Dr SR2 86 B4
Star of the Sea RC Prim Sch NE25 31 E2
Starbeck Ave NE2 99 C3
Starbeck Mews NE2 99 C3
Stardale Ave NE24 17 A6
Stargate Gdns NE9 71 C2
Stargate Ind Est NE40 52 E3
Stargate La NE40 52 E4
Starlight Cres NE25 23 C3
Starling Wlk NE16 69 C2
Station App Cleadon NE36 74 E8
Gateshead NE11,NE9 70 D3
Longbenton NE12 39 D6
1 South Shields NE33 42 C3
Station Ave DH5 95 A3
Station Ave N DH4 90 A1
Station Ave S DH4 90 A1
Station Bank
Mickley Square NE43 49 E2
Ryton NE40 52 C6
Station Cl NE44 62 F8
Station Cotts
Burnopfield NE39 78 C6
Longhirst NE61 5 B7
Morpeth NE61 9 A7
Ponteland NE20 25 E6
Seghill NE23 23 A1
Station Field Rd DH9 79 F1
Station First Sch The NE22 11 D3
Station Ind Est NE42 50 B3
Station La DH2,DH3 82 B4
Station Mews 10 NE30 42 D7
Station Rd Ashington NE63 6 B4
Backworth NE27 30 D3
Bedlington NE22 11 C2
Boldon Colliery NE35 58 E2
Chester le S DH3 88 C3
Corbridge NE45 46 F4
Cramlington NE23 22 A7
Crawcrook NE41 51 C5
Dudley NE23 28 F8
East Boldon NE36 74 D7
Gateshead,Bill Quay NE10 57 B2
Gateshead,Low Fell NE9 70 E5
Hebburn NE31 57 D6
Heddon-on-t-W NE15 35 A1
Hetton le H DH5 95 A3
Hexham NE46 45 C5
High Pittington DH6 96 A6
Houghton-le-S DH4 90 D1
Killingworth NE12 29 B3
Longbenton NE12 39 D7
Newburn NE15 52 F7
Newcastle-u-T,Kenton Bankfoot NE13 37 B6
Newcastle-u-T,South Gosforth NE3 38 E5
Newcastle-u-T,Wincomblee NE6 57 A5
North Shields NE29 41 D4
Penshaw DH4 89 E8
Prudhoe NE42 50 C3
Rowlands Gill NE39 67 F1
Ryhope SR2 93 A6
Seghill NE23 23 A1
Shiney Row DH4 90 A6
South Shields NE33 42 C2
Sunderland SR5,SR6 75 D4
Tynemouth NE30 32 C3
Wallsend NE28 40 B2
Wallsend NE28 40 C1
Wallsend,Willington Quay NE28 41 A1
Washington NE38 84 A4
Washington,Columbia NE38 83 E4
Washington,Fatfield DH4, NE38 83 E1
Whitley Bay NE26 32 B4
Wylam NE41 51 B5
Station Rd N
Hetton le H DH5 95 A3
Longbenton NE12 39 D8
Station Sq 1 NE26 32 B4
Station St
4 Bedlington NE22 11 D3
Blyth NE24 17 E8
Haswell DH6 97 F3
Jarrow NE32 58 B7
Sunderland SR1 103 A3
Station Terr
Choppington NE62 10 F3
East Boldon NE36 74 E7
Fence Houses DH4 89 F1
Tynemouth NE30 42 D7
10 Washington NE37 83 E8
Station View DH5 95 A3
Staveley Rd SR6 75 C5
Stavordale Terr NE9 71 A7
Staward Ave NE25 23 D2
Staward Terr NE6 56 F4
Staynebrigg NE10 72 A6
Stead La NE22 11 C1
Stead Lane Fst Sch NE22 11 C1
Stead St NE28 41 A3
Steadings The
Ashington NE63 6 A2
Seaton Sluice NE26 24 E4
Steadlands Sq NE22 11 C1
Steads The NE61 9 A6
Stedham Cl NE37 72 E2
Steenbergs 8 NE1 56 A6
Steep Hill SR3 91 C7
Stella Bank NE21 52 F5
Stella Hall Dr NE21 53 A4
Stella La NE21 53 A4
Stella Rd Blaydon NE21 53 B4
Ryton NE21 53 B4
Stephen Ct NE32 58 C6
Stephen St Blyth NE24 17 E8
East Hartford NE23 16 B3
Newcastle-u-T NE6 56 A6
Stephenson Bldg NE2 99 C2
Stephenson Cl DH5 95 B4
Stephenson Ct
North Shields NE30 42 B5
Wylam NE41 51 C6
Bedlington NE22 11 A3
Stephenson Ho 15 NE46 45 A5
Stephenson Ind Est
Killingworth NE12 29 C2
Washington NE37 72 E2
Stephenson Meml Prim Sch NE28 41 A2
Stephenson Railway Mus* NE29 41 A7
Stephenson Rd
Newcastle-u-T NE7 39 B1
Washington NE37 72 E2
Stephenson St
Gateshead NE8 70 D8
North Shields NE30 42 B5
1 Tynemouth NE30 42 D7
Wallsend NE28 41 B1
Stephenson Terr
Gateshead NE10 71 D8
Newcastle-u-T NE15 36 B1
Throckley NE15 35 D2
Wylam NE41 51 B6
Stephenson Way
Bedlington NE22 11 A4
Blaydon NE21 68 B8
Stephenson's La NE1 101 A4
Stepney Bank NE1 56 A6
Stepney La NE1 99 C1
Stepney Rd 1 NE1,NE2 56 A6
Sterling Cotts NE10 71 C7
Sterling St SR4 102 A2
Stevenson St DH4 94 D8
Steward Cres NE34 60 B6
Stewart Ave SR2 92 E6
Stewart Dr NE36 74 B7
Stewart St
New Silksworth SR3 92 A7
Sunderland SR4 102 B1
Stewartsfield NE39 67 D1
Stileford NE10 72 A7
Stillington Cl 4 SR2 92 F5
Stirling Ave
Brockley Whins NE32 58 E4
Rowlands Gill NE39 67 E1
Stirling Cl NE38 84 A4
Stirling Ct NE11 70 E2
Stirling Dr
Bedlington NE22 11 C2
Tynemouth NE29 41 C8
Stirling La NE39 67 F1
Stobart St SR5 102 C4
Stobhill Villas NE61 9 A7
Stockfold NE38 83 E2
Stockholm Cl NE29 41 B5
Stockley Ave SR5 74 C2
Stockley Rd NE38 83 F6
Stocksfield Ave NE5 54 C7
Stocksfield Avenue Prim Sch NE5 54 B7
Stocksfield Gdns NE9 71 B2
Stocksfield Hall NE43 64 A8
Stocksfield Sta NE43 64 A7
Stockton Rd
North Shields NE29 41 F3
Ryhope SR2,SR7 92 F2
Sunderland SR2 103 A1
Stockton Terr 8 SR2 86 F2
Stockwell Gn NE6 56 F8
Stoddart Ho NE2 99 C2
Stoddart St
Newcastle-u-T NE1,NE2 99 C2
South Shields NE34 59 C6
Stoker Ave NE34 58 F4
Stoker Terr NE39 67 A3
Stokesley Gr NE7 39 A3
Stokoe Dr NE63 7 A3
Stone Cellar Rd NE37 72 C2
Stone St NE10 71 C6
Stonechat Cl 3 NE38 82 F3
Stonechat Mount NE21 53 A4
Stonechat Pl NE12 39 A7
Stonecroft Gdns NE7 39 D3
Stonecrop NE9 71 C5
Stonecross NE63 6 C2
Stonefold Cl NE5 37 B3
Stonegate NE15 33 D1
Stonehaugh Way NE20 25 B2
Stonelaw Mid Sch NE23 22 A4
Stoneleigh NE61 9 E4
Stoneleigh Ave NE12 39 A7
Stoneleigh Cl DH4 90 C2
Stoneleigh Pl 1 NE12 39 A6
Stonesdale DH4 89 E8
Stonethwaite NE29 41 E3
Stoney La Springwell NE9 71 F1
Sunderland SR5 75 A1
Stoneycroft E NE12 29 E2
Stoneycroft W NE12 29 E2
Stoneycroft Way SR7 93 C1
Stoneygate Cl NE10 56 E1
Stoneygate Gdns NE10 56 E1
Stoneygate La NE10 56 E1
Stoneyhurst Ave NE15 54 B5
Stoneyhurst Rd NE3 38 E4
Stoneyhurst Rd W NE3 38 D4
Stoneylea Cl NE40 51 E3
Stoneylea Rd NE5 53 F8
Stoneywaites NE40 66 E8
Stonybank Way NE43 64 E8
Stonycroft NE37 83 C7
Stonyflat Bank NE42 50 E2
Store Bldgs NE35 73 E8
Store Farm Rd NE64 7 C5
Store St Blaydon NE21 53 B1
Newcastle-u-T NE15 53 C6
Store Terr DH5 95 B1
Storey Cres NE64 7 C5
Storey La NE21 53 A4
Storey St NE23 22 C5
Stormont Gn NE3 37 F3
Stormont St NE29 42 A5
Stothard St NE32 58 C7
Stott's Pasture DH4 90 A4
Stotts Rd NE6 57 A8
Stowe Gdns NE61 4 E4
Stowell Sq NE1 98 C1
Stowell St NE1 98 C1
Stowell Terr NE10 71 E8
Straker Dr NE46 44 E3
Straker St NE32 58 D6
Straker Terr NE34 59 C5
Strand The SR3 91 E8
Strangford Ave 2 DH2 88 B1
Stranton Terr SR6 75 D2
Stratfield St SR4 85 E7
Stratford Ave SR2 86 E3
Stratford Cl
Cramlington NE23 21 E7
Killingworth NE12 29 E3
Stratford Gdns NE9 70 F6
Stratford Gr NE6 56 A7
Stratford Gr W NE6 56 A7
Stratford Grove Terr NE6 56 A7
Stratford Rd NE6 56 A7
Stratford Villas NE6 56 A7
Strathearn Way NE3 37 F7
Strathmore Ave NE39 67 E1
Strathmore Cres
Byermoor NE16 79 D8
Newcastle-u-T NE4 54 E6
Strathmore Rd
Gateshead N10,NE9 71 B7
Newcastle-u-T NE3 38 C7
Rowlands Gill NE39 67 E1
Sunderland SR3 85 E2
Strathmore Sq SR3 85 E2
Stratton Cl SR2 93 A8
Stratus Ct 12 SR3 92 A6
Strawberry Ave NE23 29 C5
Strawberry Cotts NE62 11 B8
Strawberry Gdns NE28 40 A4
Strawberry La NE1 98 C1
Strawberry Pl NE1 98 C2
Strawberry Terr NE13 27 F4
Street Gate Pk NE16 69 D3
Street The NE30 42 B5
Stretford Ct NE9 71 A1
Stretton Cl DH4 94 A7
Stretton Way NE27 30 C5
Stridingedge NE37 83 B6
Stronsay Cl 2 SR2 92 E8
Strothers Rd NE39 66 F5
Strothers Terr NE39 66 E4
Struan Terr NE36 74 E7
Struddars Farm Ct NE21 53 F2
Stuart Ct NE3 37 C6
Stuart Gdns NE15 35 D2
Stuart Terr NE10 56 D1
Stubbs Ave NE16 69 A8
Studdon Wlk NE3 37 D5
Studland Cl NE29 31 F1
Studley Gdns
2 Gateshead NE9 70 F5
Whitley Bay NE25 32 A4
Studley Terr NE4 98 A3
Studley Villas NE12 39 E7
Sturdee Gdns NE2 38 E3
Styan Ave NE26 32 B5
Styford Gdns NE15 53 E7
Success Rd DH4 90 B4
Sudbury Way NE23 21 E6
Suddick St 2 SR5 75 B1
Suez St NE30 42 B6
Suffolk Cl NE63 6 A4
Suffolk Gdns
South Shields NE34 60 C7
Wallsend NE28 40 E4
Suffolk Pl Birtley DH3 82 D1
Gateshead NE8 56 A4
Suffolk Rd NE31 57 F3
Suffolk St Hetton le H DH5 94 F4
Jarrow NE32 58 B6
Sunderland SR2 103 B1
Sugley Dr NE15 53 D6
Sugley St NE15 53 D6
Sugley Villas NE15 53 D6
Sulgrave Ind Est NE37 72 E1
Sulgrave Rd NE37 72 F1
Sullivan Wlk NE31 57 E5
Summer St NE10 56 D1
Summerfield NE17 77 A5
Summerfield Rd NE9 70 F7
Summerhill Blaydon NE21 53 B3
Hedworth NE32 58 D1
Newcastle-u-T NE4 100 A4
Sunderland SR2 102 B2
Sunderland,Middle Herrington SR3 91 B7
Summerhill Ave NE3 28 D1
Summerhill Gr NE4 98 B1
Summerhill Rd NE34 60 A7
Summerhill St NE4 98 B1
Summerhill Terr NE1 100 C4
Summerhouse Farm DH5 94 D5
Summerhouse La
Ashington,North Seaton NE63 7 B3
Ashington,Woodbridge NE63 7 B4
Summers St 7 NE24 17 E8
Summerson St DH5 95 B4
Summerson Way NE22 11 D2
Sun St 8 NE16 69 B2
Sun View Terr SR6 59 E1
Sunbury Ave NE2 38 E2
Sunderland Ent Pk SR5 85 B8
Sunderland Eye Infmy SR2 86 D3
Sunderland High Sch SR2 103 A1
Sunderland High Sch Jun Sch SR2 86 D4
Sunderland Highway NE37,NE38 83 C6
Sunderland Mus & Winter Gdns* SR1 103 A2
Sunderland Rd
Cleadon SR6 75 B7
East Boldon NE36,SR5 74 E6
Gateshead,Felling NE10 71 E8
Gateshead,Heworth NE10 71 F8
Gateshead,Wardley NE10 72 C7
Newbottle DH4 90 E4
South Shields NE33 59 E8
South Shields,Harton NE34 59 F6
Sunderland SR5 75 A2
Sunderland Ret Pk SR6 75 D1
Sunderland Royal Hospl SR4 102 A2
Sunderland Ski Ctr* SR3 85 F1
Sunderland St
Houghton-le-S DH5 90 E1
2 Houghton-le-S,New Town DH4 94 E8
Newcastle-u-T NE1 100 C4
Sunderland SR1 103 B3
Sunderland Sta SR1 103 A2
Sunderland Tech Pk SR2 102 C2
Sundew Rd NE9 71 C4
Sundridge Dr NE10 72 C7
Sunhill NE16 69 B2
Sunholme Dr NE28 40 A5
Sunlea Ave NE30 32 C2
Sunnidale NE16 68 E5
Sunnilaws NE34 60 A3
Sunningdale
South Shields NE33 42 E1
Whitley Bay NE25 31 D5
Sunningdale Ave
Newcastle-u-T NE6 57 A6
Wallsend NE28 40 C2
Sunningdale Cl NE10 71 D7
Sunningdale Dr NE37 72 C2
Sunningdale Rd SR3 85 E3
Sunningdale Sch SR3 85 E2
Sunnirise NE34 60 A4
Sunniside
North Shields NE29 41 E5
Sunderland SR4 85 A6
Sunniside Ct NE16 69 B3
Sunniside Dr NE34 60 A4
Sunniside Gdns
Gateshead NE9 71 C2
Newcastle-u-T NE15 54 B6
Sunniside La NE34,SR6 60 B2
Sunniside Rd NE16 69 B3
Sunniside Sta* NE16 69 B1
Sunniside Terr SR6 60 A2
Sunny Brae NE40 66 F8
Sunnybank Ave NE15 54 D5
Sunnybrow SR3 91 F8
Sunnycrest Ave NE6 56 F6
Sunnygill Terr NE40 51 F2
Sunnyside NE23 22 A6
Sunnyway NE5 37 C2
Sunrise Ent Pk SR5 85 A8
Sunrise La 1 DH4 90 D1
Surrey Ave SR3 92 A6
Surrey Cl NE63 6 A4
Surrey Pl
Newcastle-u-T NE4 98 A1
Penshaw DH4 90 C6
Surrey Rd Hebburn NE31 57 F3
North Shields NE29 41 D6
Surrey St Hetton le H DH5 94 F4
Jarrow NE32 58 A6
Penshaw DH4 90 C6
Surrey Terr DH3 82 C1
Sussex Gdns NE28 40 E3
Sussex Pl NE37 72 D1
Sussex St 2 Blyth NE24 17 F8
Jarrow NE32 58 A6
3 New Silksworth SR3 92 A8
Sutherland Ave
Newbiggin-by-t-S NE64 7 D4
Newcastle-u-T NE4 54 E7
Sutherland Ct NE34 59 D2
Sutherland Dr SR4 85 D4
Sutherland Grange DH4 90 D6
Sutherland St
Gateshead NE8 101 C1
Seaham SR7 93 B1
Sunderland SR6 75 D2
Sutton Cl DH4 90 A6
Sutton Ct NE28 39 F5
Sutton St NE6 56 E7
Sutton Way NE34 60 B5
Swainby Cl NE3 38 D8
Swaledale Sunderland SR6 75 F7
Wallsend NE28 39 F5
Swaledale Ave NE24 17 A7
Swaledale Cl DH5 94 F1
Swaledale Cres DH4 90 A8
Swaledale Ct NE24 17 A7
Swaledale Gdns
Newcastle-u-T NE7 39 B3
Sunderland SR4 85 F5
Swallow Cl NE63 11 E8
Swallow Ct NE12 29 C4
Swallow Tail Ct NE34 59 B5
Swallow Tail Dr NE11 70 B7
Swallows The NE28 40 E7
Swalwell Bank NE16 69 A8
Swalwell Cl NE42 50 C2
Swalwell Cty Prim Sch NE16 69 B8
Swan Ave NE28 40 D3
Swan Ct NE11 100 A1
Swan Dr NE11 100 A1
Swan Ind Est NE38 83 F4
Swan Ind Est (South) NE38 83 F3
Swan Rd
Newcastle-u-T NE6 57 B4
Washington NE38 83 F4
Swan St Gateshead NE8 101 C3
Sunderland SR5 75 C1
Swansfield NE61 8 E7
Swanton Cl NE5 37 B4
Swanway NE9 71 B7
Swards Rd NE10 71 E7
Swarland Ave NE7 39 B5
Swarland Rd NE25 23 D2
Swarth Cl NE37 83 A6
Sweetbriar Cl NE61 3 E2
Sweetbriar Way NE24 17 C4
Sweethope Ave
Ashington NE63 6 F2
Blyth NE24 17 D8
Sweethope Dene NE61 9 A6
Swiftdale Cl NE22 10 F1
Swiftden Dr SR4 85 A4
Swinbourne Gdns NE26 31 F6
Swinbourne Terr NE32 58 B3
Swinburn Rd NE25 23 D2
Swinburne Pl Birtley DH3 82 C3
Gateshead NE8 101 C3
Newcastle-u-T NE4 98 C1
Swinburne St
Gateshead NE8 101 B3
Jarrow NE32 58 E6
Swindale Cl NE21 68 C8
Swindale Cotts NE41 51 B6
Swindale Dr NE12 29 C3
Swindon Rd SR3 85 D3
Swindon Sq SR3 85 E3
Swindon St NE31 57 D6
Swindon Terr NE6 39 B1
Swinhoe Gdns NE13 28 B6
Swinhope NE38 89 A8
Swinley Gdns NE15 53 F6
Swinton Cl NE61 9 B6
Swirle The NE1 99 C1
Swirral Edge NE37 83 C7
Swyntoft NE10 72 B7
Sycamore DH2 88 A5
Sycamore Ave Blyth NE24 12 D1
Dinnington NE13 27 C7
Guide Post NE62 10 E7
Ponteland NE20 25 D4
South Shields NE34 59 F4
Washington NE38 83 B1
Whitley Bay NE25 31 F4
Sycamore Cl
Newcastle-u-T NE2 38 F2
South Hetton DH6 97 F7
Sycamore Dr SR5 75 B3
Sycamore Gr
Gateshead NE10 71 E8
Prudhoe NE42 50 A2
Springwell NE9 71 F1
Sycamore Pl NE12 29 C4
Sycamore Rd
Blaydon NE21 53 C2
Whitburn SR6 60 F1
Sycamore St
Ashington NE63 6 D3
Throckley NE15 35 D3
Wallsend NE28 40 C1
Sycamore Terr DH6 97 F3
Sycamores The
Burnopfield NE16 79 C5
Guide Post NE62 10 E7
Newcastle-u-T NE4 100 A3
Sunderland SR2 86 E3
Sydenham Terr
14 South Shields NE33 42 D3
Sunderland SR4 102 A1
Sydney Ct NE8 101 B3
Sydney Gdns NE34 58 F3
Sydney Gr NE28 40 A5
Sydney St DH4 89 E2
Syke Rd NE16 78 F5
Sylvan Cl NE61 8 D7
Sylverton Gdns NE33 42 F1
Symington Gdns SR3 91 F8

Symon Terr NE17 ....77 B8
Synclen Ave NE45 ....47 A6
Synclen Rd NE45 ....47 A6
Synclen Terr NE45 ....47 A6
Syon St NE30 ....42 D8
Syron NE16 ....68 F7
Syston Cl DH4 ....94 A7

T

Taberna Cl NE15 ....34 E2
Tadcaster Rd SR3 ....85 C1
Tadema Rd NE33 ....42 F2
Talbot Cl NE38 ....83 D4
Talbot Cotts DH3 ....82 C4
Talbot Gn NE5 ....53 F8
Talbot House Sch NE15 ..35 F2
Talbot Rd
  South Shields NE34 ....59 C6
  Sunderland SR6 ....75 E3
Talbot Terr 12 DH3 ....82 C4
Talgarth NE38 ....84 B5
Talisman View 6 NE9 ..71 A2
Talley Ct NE38 ....83 C5
Tamar Cl NE29 ....41 D8
Tamar Ct 6 SR3 ....91 F6
Tamar St DH5 ....97 C8
Tamarisk Way NE16 ....71 C5
Tamerton Dr DH3 ....82 D2
Tamerton St NE4 ....85 F6
Tamworth Sq SR3 ....85 C1
Tanbark DH4 ....89 F6
Tanfield Gdns NE34 ....60 B6
Tanfield Lea Ind Est DH9 79 D2
Tanfield Lea Jun & Inf Sch DH9 ....79 C1
Tanfield Lea South Ind Est DH9 ....79 F1
Tanfield Pl NE9 ....71 C2
Tanfield Rd
  Gateshead NE9 ....71 C2
  Newcastle-u-T NE15 ....54 A6
  Sunderland SR3 ....85 D1
Tanfield Rly* NE16 ....80 B6
Tanfield St SR4 ....85 E7
Tangmere Cl NE23 ....22 C7
Tankerville Pl 3 NE2 ..38 E1
Tankerville Terr NE2 ....38 E1
Tanners Row 10 NE46 ..45 A5
Tanners' Bank NE30 ....42 C6
Tantallon DH3 ....82 D2
Tantallon Ct DH4 ....89 D1
Tantobie Rd NE15 ....54 A6
Tarlton Cres NE10 ....71 C8
Tarn Dr SR2 ....86 F1
Tarragon Way NE34 ....59 E3
Tarrington Cl NE28 ....40 F5
Tarset Dr NE42 ....50 D2
Tarset Pl NE3 ....38 A6
Tarset Rd NE25 ....31 B5
Tarset St NE1 ....56 A5
Tasman Rd SR3 ....91 C8
Tasmania Rd NE34 ....58 F3
Tate St 8 NE24 ....17 F8
Tatham St SR1 ....103 B2
Tatham Street Back SR1 ....103 B2
Tattershall SR2 ....86 B4
Taunton Ave Jarrow NE32 .58 E3
  Tynemouth NE29 ....31 D1
Taunton Cl NE28 ....40 F5
Taunton Pl NE23 ....22 B8
Taunton Rd SR3 ....85 D2
Taunton Sq SR3 ....85 D2
Tavistock Ct DH4 ....90 C3
Tavistock Ho SR1 ....103 A2
Tavistock Pl Jarrow NE32 .58 D5
  Sunderland SR1 ....103 A2
Tavistock Rd NE2 ....38 E2
Tavistock Sq SR3 ....92 A8
Tavistock Wlk NE23 ....22 B8
Tay Rd SR3,SR4 ....85 C2
Tay St Chopwell NE17 ....66 C1
  Easington Lane DH5 ....97 D8
Taylor Ave Ashington NE63 ..7 B3
  Rowlands Gill NE39 ....67 F1
  Wideopen NE13 ....28 C4
Taylor Gdns
  Gateshead NE10 ....57 A1
  Seaton Sluice NE26 ....24 D6
  10 Sunderland SR2 ....86 E4
Taylor St Blyth NE24 ....17 A8
  South Shields NE33 ....59 B8
Taylor Terr 8 NE27 ....30 B1
Taylor's Bldgs NE22 ....11 D2
Taylors Ct 5 NE1 ....99 A1
Taynton Gr NE23 ....22 F2
Teal Ave NE24 ....17 F4
Teal Cl Longbenton NE7 ..3 D9
  8 Washington NE38 ....82 F3
Team St NE8 ....100 B1
Team Valley Bsns Ctr NE11 ....70 D6
Team Valley Trad Est NE11 ....70 D4
Teasdale Ho NE5 ....37 A5
Teasdale St SR2 ....103 C1
Tebay Dr NE5 ....53 F8
Tedco Bsns Ctr NE32 ..57 F8
Tedco Bsns Wks 1 NE33 42 C2
Teddington Cl NE3 ....37 B7
Teddington Rd SR3 ....85 C2
Teddington Sq SR3 ....85 C2
Tedham Rd NE15 ....53 C7
Tees Ct 18 Silksworth SR3 .91 F6
  South Shields NE34 ....59 C6

Tees Rd NE31 ....57 E3
Tees St Chopwell NE17 ..66 C1
  Easington Lane DH5 ....97 D8
Tees Terr 9 NE37 ....83 D8
Teesdale Ave DH4 ....90 A8
Teesdale Gdns NE7 ....39 B3
Teesdale Gr NE12 ....39 D8
Teesdale Pl 3 NE24 ..16 F8
Teindland Cl NE4 ....54 E4
Tel-el-Kebir Rd SR2 ....86 E4
Telford Cl NE27 ....30 C5
Telford Ct
  Morpeth,Loansdean NE61 ..8 F5
  North Shields NE28 ....41 C2
Telford Rd SR3 ....85 D2
Telford St
  Newcastle-u-T NE1 ....100 C4
  North Shields NE28 ....41 C2
Temperley Pl NE46 ....45 A4
Tempest St
  10 New Silksworth SR3 ..92 A7
  Ryton NE21 ....53 A4
Temple Ave NE17 ....17 C8
Temple Bldgs 4 NE1 ..98 C1
Temple Gn Gateshead NE8 70 C8
  South Shields NE34 ....59 E5
Temple Park Inf Sch NE34 ....59 D3
Temple Park Jun Sch NE34 ....59 D4
Temple Park Rd NE34 ..59 D6
Temple St
  Gateshead NE10 ....56 D1
  Newcastle-u-T NE1 ....100 C4
  South Shields NE33 ....59 B7
Temple St W NE33 ....59 B7
Temple Town NE33 ....59 B8
Ten Fields DH5 ....95 A3
Tenbury Cres
  Longbenton NE12 ....39 C7
  Tynemouth NE29 ....31 E1
Tenby Rd SR3 ....91 C8
Tenby Sq NE23 ....22 C8
Tennant St Hebburn NE31 .57 D5
  3 South Shields NE34 ..59 A4
Tennyson Ave
  Hebburn NE31 ....57 F6
  West Boldon NE35 ....74 B8
Tennyson Cres NE16 ....69 A8
Tennyson Ct
  Gateshead NE8 ....56 A2
  Prudhoe NE42 ....50 B1
Tennyson Gn NE3 ....37 F3
Tennyson St
  11 South Shields NE33 ..42 D2
  6 Sunderland SR5 ....75 A2
Tennyson Terr NE29 ....42 B4
Tenter Garth NE15 ....35 C2
Tenter Terr NE61 ....9 A8
Tenth Ave Blyth NE24 ..17 E6
  Chester le S DH2 ....88 B3
  Gateshead NE11 ....70 D2
  Morpeth NE61 ....9 B6
  Newcastle-u-T NE6 ....56 C8
Tenth Ave W NE11 ....70 D2
Tern Cl NE24 ....17 F4
Terrace Pl NE1 ....98 C2
Terrace The
  6 Boldon Colliery NE35 ..58 E7
  5 East Boldon NE36 ....74 D7
  Longbenton NE12 ....39 C6
  Ovingham NE42 ....50 A4
Terraces The NE38 ....83 E4
Terrier Cl NE22 ....11 C1
Tesla St DH4 ....90 D4
Tetford Pl NE12 ....39 C7
Teviot NE38 ....83 A1
Teviot St
  Easington Lane DH5 ....97 C8
  Gateshead NE8 ....71 A8
Teviot Way NE32 ....58 A5
Teviotdale Gdns NE7 ..39 B3
Tewkesbury NE12 ....29 D4
Tewkesbury Rd NE15 ..53 C7
Thackeray Rd SR3 ....85 D2
Thackeray St DH4 ....94 D8
Thames Ave NE32 ....58 C2
Thames Cres DH4 ....94 A8
Thames Gdns NE28 ....40 B1
Thames Rd Hebburn NE31 .57 F3
  Sunderland SR3 ....91 C8
Thames St Chopwell NE17 .66 C1
  Easington Lane DH5 ....97 C8
  Gateshead NE8 ....56 A1
Thanet Rd SR3 ....85 D1
Tharsis Rd NE31 ....57 D5
Thatcher Cl NE16 ....69 A5
Theatre Pl 21 NE29 ....42 A5
Thelma St SR4 ....102 B1
Theme Rd SR3 ....91 C8
Theresa Russell Ho NE6 .56 C6
Theresa St NE21 ....53 C3
Thetford NE38 ....83 D4
Thieves Bank NE61 ....5 E1
Third Ave Ashington NE63 ..6 E3
  Blyth NE24 ....17 D6
  Chester le S,Canada DH2 ..88 B3
  Chester le S,South Pelaw DH2 ....88 B7
  Gateshead NE11 ....70 C6
  Morpeth NE61 ....9 B7
  Newcastle-u-T NE6 ....56 C7
  North Shields NE29 ....41 B5
Third Row Ellington NE61 ..1 E4
  Linton NE61 ....1 A3
Third St NE8 ....40 D1
Thirkeld Pl DH4 ....90 A7
Thirlington Cl NE5 ....37 B3
Thirlmere Birtley DH3 ..82 E2

Thirlmere *continued*
  Cleadon SR6 ....60 A1
  Gateshead NE10 ....72 A8
Thirlmere Ave
  Chester le S DH2 ....88 B1
  Easington Lane DH5 ....97 C8
  Tynemouth NE30 ....32 A2
Thirlmere Cl NE12 ....29 F3
Thirlmere Cres
  Blaydon NE21 ....68 B8
  Penshaw DH4 ....90 B6
Thirlmere Ct NE31 ....57 F4
Thirlmere Terr NE64 ....7 E4
Thirlmere Way Blyth NE24 12 A1
  Newcastle-u-T NE5 ....37 B1
Thirlmoor NE37 ....83 A6
Thirlmoor Pl NE62 ....11 A8
Thirlwall Ct NE12 ....38 F6
Thirlwell Gr NE32 ....58 B3
Thirlwell Rd NE8 ....56 A3
Thirsk Rd SR3 ....85 D2
Thirston Dr NE23 ....22 C6
Thirston Pl NE29 ....41 D7
Thirston Way NE3 ....37 D5
Thistle Ave NE40 ....52 A4
Thistle Cl NE31 ....57 D5
Thistle Ho SR3 ....92 A5
Thistle Rd SR3 ....85 C1
Thistlecroft DH5 ....94 E7
Thistledon Ave NE16 ..68 F6
Thistley Cl NE6 ....56 E8
Thistley Gn NE10 ....57 B1
Thomas Bell Ho 8 NE34 .59 A4
Thomas Bewick Sch NE5 36 C2
Thomas Dr NE31 ....57 D6
Thomas Ferguson Ct NE30 ....42 C6
Thomas Hawksley Pk SR3 ....86 A3
Thomas Hepburn Com Comp Sch NE10 ....71 E7
Thomas Holliday Homes 10 NE22 ....11 D3
Thomas Horsley Ho NE15 54 B5
Thomas St
  9 Chester le S DH3 ....88 C2
  Gateshead NE9 ....71 D1
  Hetton le H DH5 ....95 B5
  Newcastle-u-T NE5 ....36 F2
  Ryhope SR2 ....92 F6
  South Shields NE33 ....42 C3
  8 Washington NE37 ....83 E8
  Whickham NE16 ....69 A7
Thomas St N SR6 ....103 A4
Thomas St S Ryhope SR2 .92 F6
  Sunderland SR5 ....75 A1
Thomas Taylor Cotts NE27 ....30 C5
Thomas Walling Prim Sch NE5 ....37 C2
Thompson Ave NE12 ..29 C4
Thompson Cres 7 SR5 .74 B1
Thompson Gdns NE28 ..40 B2
Thompson Pl NE10 ....71 D8
Thompson Rd SR5 ....75 B2
Thompson St
  9 Bedlington NE22 ....11 D3
  Blyth NE24 ....12 D1
  Blyth NE24 ....12 E1
Thompson Terr SR2 ....93 A6
Thompson's Bldgs DH4 .90 C5
Thorburn St SR6 ....75 D4
Thorn Cl NE13 ....28 A5
Thorn Ho SR3 ....92 A5
Thorn Tree Dr NE24 ..10 F2
Thornbank Cl SR3 ....92 A4
Thornbeck Coll SR2 ..102 C1
Thornborough Ho 18 NE6 ....56 C6
Thornbridge NE38 ....84 A5
Thornbury 8 NE21 ....53 B1
Thornbury Ave NE23 ..23 A2
Thornbury Cl
  Boldon Colliery NE35 ..58 E1
  Newcastle-u-T NE3 ....37 B5
Thornbury Dr NE25 ....31 C6
Thornbury St SR4 ....102 A3
Thorncliffe Pl NE29 ..41 E5
Thorndale Pl NE24 ..17 A8
Thorndale Rd
  Newcastle-u-T NE15 ..53 F5
  Sunderland SR3 ....85 D1
Thorne Ave NE10 ....72 B8
Thorne Brake NE10 ....72 A7
Thorne Rd SR3 ....85 C1
Thorne Sq SR3 ....85 C1
Thorne Terr NE6 ....56 E7
Thornehill Gdns NE62 ..11 A8
Thorney Close Prim Sch SR3 ....85 D1
Thorney Close Rd SR3 .85 D1
Thorneyburn Ave NE25 .31 B5
Thorneyburn Cl DH4 ..90 C2
Thorneyburn Way NE24 .17 C7
Thorneyfield Dr NE12 ..29 B2
Thorneyford Pl NE20 ..25 E7
Thornfield Gr SR2 ....86 E2
Thornfield Pl NE39 ....67 E3
Thornfield Rd NE3 ....38 B4
Thorngill NE37 ....83 C6
Thornhaugh Ave NE16 .68 F6
Thornhill Cl
  Gateshead NE11 ....70 A8
  Seaton Delaval NE25 ..23 D2
Thornhill Cres SR2 ....102 C2
Thornhill Gdns
  Burnopfield NE16 ....78 F5
  Sunderland SR2 ....102 C1

Thornhill Park Sch SR2 102 C1
Thornhill Pk
  Ponteland NE20 ....25 E7
  Sunderland SR2 ....102 C1
Thornhill Rd
  Longbenton NE12 ....39 D6
  Ponteland NE20 ....25 E7
Thornhill Sch SR2 ....102 C1
Thornhill St DH4 ....94 D8
Thornhill Terr SR2 ....102 C1
Thornholme Ave NE34 ..60 B6
Thornholme Rd SR2 ....102 C1
Thornhope Cl NE38 ....83 F6
Thornlea NE61 ....9 E4
Thornlea Gdns NE9 ....70 F6
Thornleigh Gdns SR6 ..60 A3
Thornleigh Rd NE2 ....38 E1
Thornley Ave
  Cramlington NE23 ....22 C6
  Gateshead NE10 ....72 B6
Thornley Cl NE16 ....69 A4
Thornley La NE21,NE39 ..68 A6
Thornley Rd NE5 ....53 F8
Thornley Terr NE12 ....11 C6
Thornley View NE39 ....67 F2
Thornley Wood* NE21 ..68 B6
Thornton Cl Morpeth NE61 .9 B6
  Penshaw DH4 ....90 B7
Thornton Cotts NE40 ..52 C6
Thornton Cres NE21 ..53 C3
Thornton Ct NE38 ....83 C5
Thornton Ho 10 NE1 ..98 C1
Thornton St NE1 ....98 C1
Thornton Terr NE12 ..30 A1
Thorntree Ave NE13 ..21 B1
Thorntree Cl NE25 ....31 B4
Thorntree Cotts NE13 ..21 B1
Thorntree Ct NE12 ....39 F8
Thorntree Dr
  Newcastle-u-T NE15 ..54 A7
  Whitley Bay NE25 ....31 C4
Thorntree Gdns NE63 ..7 A2
Thorntree Mews SR3 ..85 C2
Thorntree Way NE24 ..16 F7
Thornwood Gdns NE11 .70 B6
Thornyford Ho NE4 ....98 A2
Thornygarth NE10 ....71 E7
Thoroton St NE24 ....17 E8
Thorp Ave NE61 ....4 A2
Thorp Cl NE24 ....17 B5
Thorp Cotts NE40 ....52 A5
Thorpe Cl NE4 ....98 A2
Thorpe Dr NE4 ....52 E5
Thorpe St NE4 ....98 A2
Thorpeness Rd SR3 ....85 C1
Threap Gdns NE28 ....40 E4
Three Mile Ct NE3 ....38 C8
Three Rivers Ct NE36 ..74 A7
Threlkeld Gr SR6 ....75 C5
Thrift St NE29 ....42 A4
Thristley Gdns SR2 ....86 C3
Throckley Fst Sch NE15 .35 C2
Throckley Way NE34 ..59 B5
Thropton Ave Blyth NE24 .17 C5
  Newcastle-u-T NE7 ....39 B5
Thropton Cl
  Chester le S DH2 ....88 A1
  Gateshead NE10 ....72 C6
Thropton Cres NE24 ..17 C7
Thropton Pl NE29 ....41 D7
Thropton Terr NE7 ....39 B7
Thrunton Cl DH5 ....94 F8
Thrush Gr 2 SR5 ....74 C1
Thurleston DH4 ....90 A8
Thurlow Way DH5 ....94 D6
Thursby DH3 ....82 E2
Thursby Ave NE30 ....32 B2
Thursby Gdns NE9 ....71 B3
Thurso Cl SR3 ....85 B1
Tiberius Cl 6 NE28 ..40 B1
Tidings The NE10 ....57 B2
Tilbeck Sq SR3 ....92 A5
Tilbury Cl DH4 ....90 C5
Tilbury Gdns SR3 ....91 C8
Tilbury Gr NE30 ....32 A2
Tilbury Rd SR3 ....91 C8
Tileshed La NE36 ....59 D1
Till Ave NE21 ....53 B2
Till Gr NE61 ....1 E5
Till St 7 NE6 ....56 C4
Tilley Cres NE42 ....50 D3
Tilley Rd NE38 ....82 F5
Tillmouth Ave NE25 ..23 E2
Tillmouth Gdns NE4 ..54 C6
Tillmouth Park Rd NE15 .35 D1
Tilson Way NE3 ....37 F6
Timber Beach Rd SR5 ..74 D1
Times Sq NE1 ....100 C4
Timlin Gdns NE28 ....41 B3
Timothy Duff Ct NE30 ..42 E7
Tindal Cl NE4 ....98 B1
Tindal St NE4 ....98 B1
Tindale Ave NE23 ....22 C6
Tindale Dr NE16 ....69 A6
Tinkler's Bank NE45 ..46 F3
Tintagel Cl
  Cramlington NE23 ....22 B8
  Sunderland SR3 ....85 B1
Tintern NE38 ....83 C3
Tintern Cl DH4 ....90 C2
Tintern Cres
  Newcastle-u-T NE6 ....56 B7
  Tynemouth NE29 ....41 D8
Tintern St SR4 ....102 B2

Tiree Ct SR3 ....92 A6
Tirril Pl NE5 ....37 A1
Titan Ho 7 NE6 ....57 A6
Titan Rd NE6 ....57 A5
Titchfield Rd NE38 ....83 C4
Titchfield Terr
  Ashington NE63 ....6 D2
  Pegswood NE61 ....4 F4
Tithe Cotts NE20 ....25 E7
Titian Ave NE34 ....59 C2
Titlington Gr NE31 ....57 D3
Tiverton Ave
  1 Newcastle-u-T NE4 ..54 E5
  Tynemouth NE29 ....41 D5
Tiverton Cl Newbottle DH4 90 C4
  Wallsend NE28 ....41 A5
Tiverton Gdns NE9 ....70 F3
Tiverton Pl NE23 ....22 B8
Tiverton Sq SR3 ....85 C1
Tivoli Bldgs DH4 ....90 C6
Toberty Gdns NE10 ..72 B8
Todd's Nook NE4 ....98 B1
Togstone Pl 4 NE5 ..37 C1
Toll Bar Ho SR3 ....93 A8
Toll Bar Rd SR2 ....92 E8
Toll Bridge Rd NE21 ..53 F3
Tollerton Dr SR5 ....74 A1
Tollgate Rd NE39 ....77 F5
Tolls Cl NE25 ....31 C6
Tom Urwin Ho 11 SR3 .92 A7
Tomlea Ave NE22 ....11 D1
Tonbridge Ave NE29 ..41 E4
Toner Ave NE31 ....57 D4
Toner Avenue Prim Sch NE31 ....57 D3
Topcliff SR6 ....103 B4
Topcliffe Gn NE9 ....71 B2
Toppings St NE35 ....58 E1
Tor Mere Cl NE37 ....83 A6
Torcross Way NE23 ..22 B8
Toronto Ct SR3 ....85 D2
Toronto Sq SR3 ....85 D2
Torquay Gdns NE9 ....70 F3
Torquay Par NE31 ....58 A3
Torquay Rd SR3 ....85 D2
Torrens Rd SR3 ....85 D2
Torrington Cl DH4 ....90 C4
Torver Cl NE13 ....28 B5
Torver Cres SR6 ....75 D5
Torver Pl NE9 ....71 B4
Torver Way NE30 ....31 F2
Tosson Cl NE22 ....11 B1
Tosson Pl Ashington NE63 ..6 E3
  North Shields NE29 ..41 D5
Tosson Terr NE6 ....39 C1
Totnes Cl SR3 ....85 B1
Totnes Dr NE23 ....22 B8
Toward Rd
  Sunderland SR1,SR2 ..103 A2
  Sunderland SR2 ....103 B1
Tower Ct Dunston NE11 ..100 A1
  Easington Lane DH5 ..95 C1
Tower Gdns NE40 ....52 C5
Tower Ho NE1 ....99 C1
Tower Pl 1 SR2 ....86 E4
Tower Rd NE37 ....83 E7
Tower St
  Newcastle-u-T NE1 ....99 B1
  Sunderland SR1 ....103 C1
Tower St W SR2 ....103 B1
Tower View NE15 ....54 C6
Towers Ave NE2 ....38 E3
Towers Cl NE22 ....16 A8
Towers Pl NE34 ....58 E5
Towers The SR4 ....85 B5
Town End Prim Sch SR5 .73 F4
Town Farm Field NE45 ..46 F6
Towne Gate The NE15 ..34 E2
Towneley Cotts NE42 ..50 A4
Towneley Terr NE39 ..66 E4
Townend Ct NE34 ....59 C5
Townfield Gdns NE15 ..52 F8
Townley Fields NE39 ..67 F2
Townley Rd NE39 ....67 D2
Townsend Cres NE61 ..8 D6
Townsend Rd SR3 ....85 D1
Townsend Sq SR3 ....91 C8
Townsville Ave NE25 ..31 D3
Towton NE12 ....29 D4
Toynbee NE38 ....84 A5
Tracey Ave NE36 ....74 B8
Trafalgar Ho 17 NE30 ..42 D7
Trafalgar Rd NE37 ....72 F1
Trafalgar Sq SR1 ....103 C3
Trafalgar St NE1 ....99 B1
Trafford NE9 ....71 A1
Trafford Rd SR5 ....75 A1
Trafford Wlk NE5 ....36 E1
Trajan Ave NE33 ....42 D4
Trajan St NE33 ....42 D4
Trajan Wlk NE15 ....34 D2
Transbritannia Ct NE21 .53 E4
Tranwell Cl
  Newcastle-u-T NE3 ....37 F8
  Pegswood NE61 ....4 E3
Tranwell Cotts NE61 ..8 D4
Tranwell Ct NE61 ....8 D4
Tranwell Dr NE25 ....23 E2
Travers St DH4 ....90 C6
Treby St SR4 ....102 A3
Tredegar Cl NE5 ....37 A1
Tree Ct 28 SR3 ....91 F6
Tree Top Mews 7 NE28 .40 E5
Treecone Cl SR3 ....92 A5

Treetops The NE32 ......58 A4
Treherne Rd NE2 ......38 D3
Trent Ave NE31 ......57 E3
Trent Dr NE32 ......58 C2
Trent Gdns NE8 ......71 B8
Trent Rd SR3 ......85 C1
Trent St Chopwell NE17 ..66 C1
  Easington Lane DH5 ......97 C8
Trentham Ave NE7 ......39 B5
Trentham Gdns NE61 ......4 F4
Trenton Ave NE38 ......83 D6
Trevarren Dr SR2 ......92 F7
Trevelyan Ave
  Bedlington NE22 ......11 B1
  Blyth NE24 ......17 C6
Trevelyan Ct SR3 ......85 B1
Trevelyan Dr NE5 ......37 A4
Trevethick St NE8 ......70 D8
Trevone Pl NE23 ......23 A2
Trevor Gr SR6 ......75 A8
Trevor Terr NE30 ......42 B7
Trewit Rd NE26 ......32 B5
Trewhitt Rd NE6 ......56 C8
Triangle Ho 5 NE1 ......98 C1
Tribune Pl NE9 ......71 B6
Trident Rd SR3 ......92 A7
Trimdon Gr NE9 ......71 D3
Trimdon St SR4 ......102 B3
Trimdon St W SR4 ......102 B4
Trinity Bldgs NE30 ......42 C5
Trinity Cl 2 NE29 ......42 A4
Trinity Ct Corbridge NE45 ..46 F6
  Gateshead NE8 ......101 C3
  9 North Shields NE29 ......42 A4
Trinity Ctyd NE6 ......56 D4
Trinity Gr NE23 ......23 A4
Trinity Maritime Mus★
  NE1 ......101 B4
Trinity Pk DH4 ......90 B5
Trinity Pl NE29 ......42 A4
Trinity Sch (Deneview Site)
  NE3 ......38 F4
Trinity Sch (Kenton Lodge
  Site) NE3 ......38 B2
Trinity Sch (Oakfield Coll)
  NE4 ......54 D6
Trinity Sq Gateshead NE8 101 C3
  Sunderland SR1 ......103 B3
Trinity St
  North Shields NE29 ......42 A4
  Sunderland SR5 ......74 F2
Trinity Terr
  Corbridge NE45 ......46 F6
  3 North Shields NE29 ......42 A4
Trinity Wlk NE33 ......42 B1
Trojan Ave NE6 ......56 E7
Tromso Cl NE29 ......41 C5
Trool Ct SR3 ......92 A5
Troon Cl NE37 ......72 C2
Trotter Gr NE22 ......11 C1
Trotter Terr SR2 ......92 F6
Troutbeck Ave NE6 ......56 F5
Troutbeck Gdns NE9 ......71 A3
Troutbeck Rd SR6 ......75 C5
Troutbeck Way NE34 ......58 F3
Troutdale Pl NE12 ......38 F6
Troves Cl NE4 ......54 E4
Trowbridge Way NE3 ......37 F5
Truro Gr NE29 ......41 D8
Truro Rd SR3 ......85 D1
Truro Way NE32 ......58 C1
Tuart St DH3 ......88 C3
Tudor Ave NE29 ......41 E6
Tudor Ct NE20 ......25 C4
Tudor Dr DH9 ......79 D3
Tudor Gr SR3 ......85 F3
Tudor Rd Chester le S DH3 88 D5
  South Shields NE33 ......42 C2
Tudor Way NE3 ......37 B6
Tudor Wlk NE3 ......37 C6
Tudor Wynd NE6 ......39 D2
Tulip Cl NE21 ......53 B2
Tulip Ct DH4 ......90 B8
Tulip St Gateshead NE8 ..56 C1
  Prudhoe NE42 ......50 B2
Tummel St SR3 ......92 A6
Tunbridge Rd SR3 ......85 D2
Tundry Way NE21 ......53 F4
Tunis Rd SR3 ......85 E2
Tunstall Ave
  Newcastle-u-T NE6 ......56 D6
  South Shields NE34 ......60 B6
Tunstall Bank SR2,SR3 ..92 D7
Tunstall Hill Cl SR2 ......86 C2
Tunstall Hope Rd SR3 ..92 C8
Tunstall Rd SR3 ......86 B2
Tunstall Terr
  New Silksworth SR2 ......92 B7
  Ryhope SR2 ......92 D7
  Sunderland SR2 ......102 C2
Tunstall Terr W SR2 ......102 C2
Tunstall Vale SR2 ......86 C4
Tunstall View SR3 ......92 B8
Tunstall Village Gn SR3 ..92 C7
Tunstall Village Rd SR3 ..92 B7
Tunstall Villas SR3 ......92 B7
Turbinia Gdns NE7 ......39 B8
Turfside Gateshead NE10 ..72 B7
  Hedworth NE32 ......58 D1
Turn The NE61 ......9 B7
Turnberry Ouston DH2 ....81 F2
  South Shields NE33 ......42 E1
  Whitley Bay NE25 ......31 C5

Turnberry Cl NE37 ......72 C2
Turnberry Ct NE10 ......72 B7
Turnberry Way
  Cramlington NE23 ......22 C6
  Newcastle-u-T NE3 ......38 E6
Turnbull Ho 5 SR5 ......75 B1
Turnbull St SR1 ......103 C4
Turnbull The NE1 ......101 A4
Turner Ave NE34 ......59 D2
Turner Cl NE40 ......52 D4
Turner Cres NE3 ......38 A5
Turner St NE27 ......30 E1
Turners Way NE61 ......8 D7
Turnham Rd SR3 ......85 C1
Turnstile Mews 7 SR6 ..75 E2
Turret Rd NE15 ......53 F7
Tuscan Rd SR3 ......91 C8
Tweed Ave NE61 ......1 E5
Tweed Cl SR2 ......92 F8
Tweed Dr NE61 ......9 E1
Tweed Gr NE15 ......53 C7
Tweed St Ashington NE63 ....6 E4
  Chopwell NE17 ......66 C1
  Easington Lane DH5 ......97 C8
  Hebburn NE31 ......57 E5
  Jarrow NE32 ......58 A5
  Newcastle-u-T NE4 ......54 F5
  Washington NE38 ......83 F4
Tweedy St NE24 ......17 A8
Tweedy Terr NE6 ......56 F5
Tweedy's Bldgs NE40 ....52 B5
Twelfth Ave Blyth NE24 ..17 D6
  Chester le S DH2 ......88 B4
Twentieth Ave NE24 ....17 C5
Twentyfifth Ave NE24 ....17 C5
Twentysecond Ave NE24 ..17 C5
Twentysixth Ave NE24 ....17 C5
Twentythird Ave NE24 ....17 C5
Twickenham Ct NE23 ....22 F2
Twickenham Rd SR3 ....85 C2
Twizell Ave NE21 ......53 B2
Twizell Pl NE20 ......25 E7
Twizell St NE24 ......17 F6
Two Ball Lonnen NE4 ....54 D8
Twyford Ct NE23 ......22 B8
Tyldesley Sq SR3 ......85 C1
Tyndal Gdns 4 NE11 ....54 F1
Tyne App NE32 ......58 A8
Tyne Ct NE46 ......45 A6
Tyne Dock Sta NE33 ....59 B6
Tyne Gdns Ovingham NE42 50 B4
  Ryton NE40 ......52 E4
  Washington NE37 ......72 D1
Tyne Gn NE46 ......45 A6
Tyne Green Ctry Pk★
  NE46 ......45 B6
Tyne Green Rd
  Hexham NE46 ......45 A6
  Hexham NE46 ......45 B6
Tyne Ho 20 SR3 ......91 F6
Tyne Main Rd NE10 ....56 C3
Tyne Mills Ind Est NE46 ..45 C6
Tyne Point Ind Est NE32 58 E5
Tyne Rd E NE8 ......100 C2
Tyne Riverside Ctry Pk
  ★ Prudhoe NE42 ......50 B3
  ★ Throckley NE15 ......52 B8
Tyne St Ashington NE63 ....6 E4
  Blaydon NE21 ......53 B1
  Chopwell NE17 ......66 B1
  Easington Lane DH5 ......97 C8
  Gateshead,Bill Quay NE10 ..57 A2
  Gateshead,Felling Shore
  NE10 ......56 E2
  Gateshead,Pelaw NE10 ..56 F2
  Jarrow NE32 ......58 B8
  North Shields NE30 ......42 B5
Tyne Terr NE34 ......59 C5
Tyne Tunnel (Tynemouth)
  Trad Est NE29 ......41 B5
Tyne Valley Gdns NE40 ..52 A5
Tyne View Blaydon NE21 ..53 C1
  Crawcrook NE40 ......51 F7
  Hebburn NE31 ......57 C7
  Newcastle-u-T NE15 ......53 D6
  Wylam NE41 ......51 B6
Tyne View Ave NE16 ....69 C8
Tyne View Com Prim Sch
  NE8 ......100 C2
Tyne View Gdns NE10 ..56 F1
Tyne View Pl NE8 ......100 C1
Tyne View Terr
  North Shields NE28 ......41 C1
  Prudhoe NE42 ......50 D3
  Stocksfield NE43 ......64 D7
Tyne Wlk NE15 ......35 D1
Tynebank NE21 ......53 B2
Tynedale Ave
  Wallsend NE28 ......40 B4
  Whitley Bay NE26 ......31 F6
Tynedale Cl NE41 ......51 B6
Tynedale Cres DH4 ......90 B7
Tynedale Ct NE28 ......41 A4
Tynedale Dr NE24 ......17 A7
Tynedale Gdns NE43 ....64 D5
Tynedale Ho NE15 ......54 B5
Tynedale Mews NE45 ....46 F5
Tynedale Mid Sch NE41 17 A7
Tynedale Rd
  South Shields NE34 ......59 F8
  Sunderland SR3 ......85 C1
Tynedale Ret Pk NE46 ..45 B5
Tynedale St DH5 ......94 E1
Tynedale Terr
  Hexham NE46 ......44 F4

Tynedale Terr continued
  Longbenton NE12 ......39 D6
Tynegate Office Prec
  NE8 ......101 C2
Tynell Wlk NE3 ......37 B5
Tynemouth Castle★
  NE30 ......42 E7
Tynemouth Cl 3 NE6 ..56 B6
Tynemouth Coll NE29 ....41 F6
Tynemouth Ct 7 NE6 ..56 C7
Tynemouth Gr 9 NE6 ..56 C7
Tynemouth Pl 6 NE30 ..42 D7
Tynemouth Priory★
  NE30 ......42 E7
Tynemouth Rd
  Jarrow NE32 ......58 B2
  Newcastle-u-T NE6 ......56 C7
  North Shields NE30 ......42 C6
  Wallsend NE28 ......41 A3
Tynemouth Sq SR3 ......85 D1
Tynemouth Sta NE30 ....42 D7
Tynemouth Terr NE30 ..42 D7
Tynemouth Watch House
  (Mus)★ NE30 ......42 E7
Tynemouth Way 8 NE6 ..56 C7
Tyneside Rd NE4 ......100 B3
Tynevale Ave NE21 ......53 C1
Tynevale Terr
  Gateshead NE8 ......100 C1
  Newcastle-u-T NE15 ......53 C6
Tyneview Prim Sch NE6 57 A5
Tyneview Terr NE46 ......45 C3
Tynewold Cl NE8 ......100 C1
Tyzack Cres SR6 ......75 D2

U

Uldale Ct NE3 ......37 E7
Ullswater Ave
  Easington Lane DH5 ......97 C8
  Hedworth NE32 ......58 D3
Ullswater Cl NE24 ......16 E8
Ullswater Cres NE21 ....68 B8
Ullswater Dr NE12 ......29 F3
Ullswater Gdns NE34 ....59 D6
Ullswater Gr SR5 ......75 C4
Ullswater Rd
  Chester le S DH2 ......88 B1
  Newbiggin-by-t-S NE64 ....7 C3
Ullswater Terr DH6 ......97 E8
Ullswater Way NE5 ......54 B8
Ulverston Gdns NE9 ....71 B4
Ulverstone Terr NE6 ....56 E7
Umfraville Dene NE42 ..50 D3
Underhill Dr NE62 ......10 E6
Underhill Rd SR6 ......59 F1
Underhill Terr NE9 ......72 A1
Underwood NE10 ......72 A6
Underwood Gr NE23 ....16 A1
Union Alley NE33 ......42 C3
Union Ct 16 DH3 ......88 C2
Union Hall Rd NE15 ....53 D7
Union La SR1 ......103 B3
Union Quay NE30 ......42 C5
Union Rd
  Newcastle-u-T NE6 ......56 C6
  North Shields NE30 ......42 C6
Union St Blyth NE24 ....17 F7
  Hetton le H DH5 ......95 A4
  Jarrow NE32 ......58 B8
  Newcastle-u-T NE2 ......99 C2
  North Shields NE30 ......42 B5
  South Shields NE33 ......59 B6
  Sunderland SR1 ......103 A3
  Sunderland,South Hylton
  SR4 ......85 A6
  Wallsend NE28 ......57 B8
Union Strs NE30 ......42 B5
Unity Hall NE33 ......42 B2
Unity Terr Cambois NE24 ..12 D4
  Tantobie DH9 ......79 B2
Univ of
  Newcastle-upon-Tyne
  NE1 ......99 A3
Univ of Northumbria at
  Newcastle NE1 ......99 B2
Univ of Sunderland SR1 102 C2
Univ of Sunderland Ashburne
  Ho (School of Arts,Design &
  Media) SR2 ......86 A4
Univ of Sunderland Bede Twr
  SR2 ......103 A1
Univ of Sunderland Benedict
  Bldg SR2 ......103 A1
Univ of Sunderland Langham
  Twr SR2 ......103 A1
Univ of Sunderland Liby
  Sunderland SR1 ......102 C2
  Sunderland SR2 ......103 A1
Univ of Sunderland Sir Tom
  Cowie Campus SR6 ..103 B4
University Sta SR1 ......102 C2
Uplands NE25 ......31 D5
Uplands The Birtley DH3 ..82 D5
  Newcastle-u-T NE3 ......37 F4
Uplands Way NE9 ......71 F2
Upper Camden St NE10
  NE30 ......42 A6
Upper Crone St NE27 ..30 F4
Upper Elsdon St 6 NE29 42 A4
Upper Fenwick Gr NE61 ..4 A2
Upper Norfolk St NE30 ..42 B6
Upper Pearson St NE30 42 B6
Upper Precinct The
  NE21 ......53 D3
Upper Queen St NE30 ..42 B6
Upton St NE8 ......100 C1

Urban Gdns NE37 ......83 D7
Urfa Terr 4 NE33 ......42 D4
Urswick St NE33 ......37 B5
Urwin St DH5 ......95 B3
Ushaw Rd NE31 ......57 F6
Usher St 3 SR5 ......75 B1
Usk Ave NE32 ......58 C3
Usworth Colliery Prim Sch
  NE37 ......72 E1
Usworth Cotts SR5 ......73 D3
Usworth Grange Prim Sch
  NE37 ......72 F1
Usworth Hall NE37 ......72 E2
Usworth Sch NE37 ......72 D2
Usworth Station Rd
  4 Washington,Concord
  NE37 ......83 E8
  Washington,Sulgrave NE37 83 F8
Uxbridge Terr 3 NE10 ..56 D1

V

Vale Ho NE2 ......56 A8
Vale St Easington Lane DH5 97 B8
Vale St E SR4 ......102 B1
Vale Wlk NE2 ......56 A8
Valebrook NE46 ......44 F4
Valebrooke SR2 ......102 C1
Valebrooke Ave SR2 ....102 C1
Valebrooke Gdns SR2 ..102 C1
Valehead NE25 ......31 D5
Valentia Ave NE6 ......56 E7
Valeria Cl NE28 ......40 E6
Valerian Ave NE15 ......34 F2
Valerian Ct NE63 ......6 B1
Valeshead Ho 12 NE28 ..40 B2
Valeside NE15 ......35 C2
Valley Cres NE21 ......53 A2
Valley Ct SR2 ......103 B1
Valley Dene NE17 ......77 B7
Valley Dr Dunston NE11 ..69 F7
  Gateshead NE9 ......70 F7
  Whickham NE16 ......69 A8
Valley Forge NE38 ......83 D6
Valley Gardens Mid Sch
  NE25 ......31 D6
Valley Gdns
  Gateshead NE9 ......71 A7
  Wallsend NE28 ......40 D3
  Whitley Bay NE25 ......31 D5
Valley Gn NE40 ......51 F2
Valley La NE34 ......60 C6
Valley Rd NE25 ......23 F2
Valley Road Com Prim Sch
  SR2 ......86 F4
Valley Shopping Village
  NE11 ......70 D4
Valley View Birtley DH3 ..82 B6
  Burnopfield NE16 ......78 F7
  Hetton le H DH5 ......94 D1
  Hexham NE46 ......45 C4
  Jarrow NE32 ......58 B4
  Newcastle-u-T,Jesmond
  NE2 ......38 F1
  Newcastle-u-T,Lemington
  NE15 ......53 C7
  Prudhoe NE42 ......50 E1
  Rowlands Gill NE39 ......67 D2
  Washington NE38 ......83 E1
Valley View Prim Sch
  NE32 ......58 B4
Vallum Ct NE4 ......98 B1
Vallum Pl NE9 ......71 B6
Vallum Rd
  Newcastle-u-T NE6 ......56 E6
  Throckley NE15 ......35 E2
Vallum Way NE4 ......98 B1
Vanborough Ct NE25 ....23 D2
Vanburgh Gdns NE61 ......8 D7
Vance Bsns Pk NE11 ....70 B7
Vance Ct NE21 ......53 E4
Vancouver Dr NE7 ......39 D2
Vane St 12 SR3 ......92 A7
Vane Terr SR2 ......103 C1
Vanguard Ct SR3 ......91 F6
Vardy Terr DH4 ......90 E6
Vauxhall Rd NE6 ......57 A8
Vedra St 1 SR5 ......75 B1
Velville Ct NE3 ......37 B4
Venerable Bede CE Sec Sch
  SR2 ......92 C7
Ventnor Ave NE4 ......54 F5
Ventnor Cres NE9 ......70 E5
Ventnor Gdns
  Gateshead NE9 ......70 E6
  Whitley Bay NE26 ......32 A6
Vera St NE40 ......66 F8
Vermont NE37 ......83 D8
Vermont Ho NE37 ......83 E8
Verne Rd NE29 ......41 D6
Vernon Cl NE33 ......59 B8
Vernon Dr NE25 ......31 E4
Vernon Pl NE64 ......7 E5
Vernon St NE37 ......83 D8
Veryan Gdns SR3 ......86 B3
Vespasian Ave NE33 ....42 D4
Vespasian St NE33 ......42 D4
Viador DH3 ......88 C4
Viaduct St NE28 ......40 E2
Vicarage Cl SR3 ......91 F7
Vicarage La SR4 ......85 A6
Vicarage Rd SR3 ......92 A7
Vicarage St NE29 ......42 A4
Vicarage Terr NE22 ....16 A4
Vicaridge Cl DH5 ......95 A4

Vicars' La NE7 ......39 A5
Vicarsholme Cl SR3 ......91 E5
Victor St
  5 Chester le S DH3 ......88 C3
  6 Sunderland SR6 ......75 E1
Victoria Ave
  Gateshead NE10 ......71 C7
  Longbenton NE12 ......39 D7
  Sunderland,Grangetown
  SR2 ......86 E2
  Sunderland,South Hylton
  SR4 ......85 B6
  Wallsend NE28 ......40 B2
  Whitley Bay NE26 ......32 B5
Victoria Ave W SR2 ......86 E2
Victoria Bglws NE11 ......100 A1
Victoria Bldgs SR1 ......102 C2
Victoria Cl NE25 ......23 D3
Victoria Cres
  8 North Shields NE29 ....41 F5
  Tynemouth NE30 ......32 C3
Victoria Ct
  Gateshead NE8 ......100 C1
  Hebburn NE31 ......57 D5
  Longbenton NE12 ......29 C1
  Sunderland SR2 ......102 C2
  Tynemouth NE30 ......32 C3
Victoria Gr NE42 ......50 E4
Victoria Ho NE8 ......100 C1
Victoria Ind Est NE31 ..57 C3
Victoria Mews Blyth NE24 17 D7
  Newcastle-u-T NE2 ......56 A8
  Whickham NE16 ......69 A7
  Whitley Bay NE26 ......32 B5
Victoria Pl
  15 Chester le S DH3 ......88 C3
  Sunderland SR1 ......103 B2
  7 Washington NE37 ......83 D8
  Whitley Bay NE25 ......31 F4
Victoria Rd
  Gateshead NE8 ......70 C8
  South Shields NE33 ......42 C1
  Washington NE37 ......83 D8
Victoria Rd E NE31 ......57 F6
Victoria Rd W NE31 ......57 D4
Victoria Sq
  4 Gateshead NE10 ......71 D8
  Newcastle-u-T NE2 ......99 B3
Victoria St
  Crawcrook NE40 ......51 F4
  Dunston NE11 ......100 A1
  Hebburn NE31 ......57 C6
  Hetton le H DH5 ......95 A4
  Newcastle-u-T NE4 ......100 B4
  North Shields NE29 ......42 A4
Victoria Terr
  Bedlington NE22 ......11 C1
  East Boldon NE36 ......74 C4
  5 Gateshead,Felling NE10 ..71 D8
  Gateshead,Wrekenton NE9 71 C3
  Hamsterley NE17 ......77 B6
  Jarrow NE32 ......58 A6
  Newbiggin-by-t-S NE64 ....7 E4
  Penshaw DH4 ......90 C8
  Prudhoe NE42 ......50 D2
  Rowlands Gill NE39 ......67 C1
  14 Springwell NE9 ......71 F4
  3 Throckley NE15 ......35 D2
  Whitley Bay NE26 ......32 B5
Victoria Villas NE22 ....11 B1
Victory Cotts NE23 ......22 A1
Victory Ho 15 NE30 ......42 D7
Victory St SR4 ......85 E7
Victory St E DH5 ......95 B4
Victory St W DH5 ......95 B4
Victory Way SR3 ......91 C5
Viewforth Dr SR5 ......75 C3
Viewforth Gn 1 NE5 ....37 C1
Viewforth Rd SR2 ......92 F5
Viewforth Terr SR5 ......75 C3
Viewlands NE63 ......6 C4
Vigo La Birtley DH3 ......88 D8
  Washington NE38 ......83 A1
  Washington NE38 ......83 B1
Vigodale DH3 ......82 E1
Viking Ind Est NE32 ....58 A8
Viking Prec 8 NE32 ....58 B7
Villa Cl SR4 ......85 F4
Villa Pl NE8 ......101 B1
Villa View NE9 ......71 A4
Village Cl NE26 ......31 F5
Village Ctr
  Washington,Biddick NE38 ..83 D4
  Washington,Donwell NE37 ..72 B1
  Washington,Glebe NE38 ..83 D5
  Washington,Lambton NE38 83 B3
Village E NE40 ......52 C6
Village Farm NE15 ......36 A1
Village Hts NE8 ......101 B2
Village La NE38 ......83 D6
Village Rd NE23 ......22 C6
Village The SR2 ......93 A6
Villas The Ryhope SR2 ..92 F5
  Stannington NE61 ......13 C7
  7 Sunderland SR5 ......74 C1
  Wideopen NE13 ......28 C5
Villette Brook St 6 SR2 86 E4
Villette Path SR2 ......86 E4
Villette Rd SR2 ......86 E4
Villiers Pl 3 DH3 ......88 C4
Villiers St SR1 ......103 B3
Villiers St S SR1 ......103 B2
Vimy Ave NE31 ......57 E6
Vindolanda 2 NE28 ....40 F4
Vindomora Rd DH8,NE17 76 D3
Vindomora Roman Fort★
  DH8 ......76 E4

Vindomora Villas DH8 . . .76 E4
Vine Cl NE8 . . . . .100 C1
Vine Ct NE46 . . . . .45 B4
Vine La NE1 . . . . .99 A2
Vine Pl
6 Houghton-le-S DH4 . . . .94 E8
Sunderland SR1 . . . . .102 C2
Vine St South Shields NE33 59 C6
Wallsend NE28 . . . . .40 C1
Vine Terr NE46 . . . . .45 B4
Viola Cres DH2 . . . . .81 F2
Viola St NE37 . . . . .83 D8
Viola Terr NE16 . . . . .69 B7
Violet Cl NE4 . . . . .54 D4
Violet St
6 Houghton-le-S DH4 . . . .94 D8
Sunderland SR4 . . . . .102 B3
Sunderland,South Hylton SR4 . . . . .85 A6
Violet Terr DH4 . . . . .89 D3
Viscount Rd 4 SR3 . . . . .92 A7
Vivian Cres 1 DH2 . . . . . .88 C2
Vivian Sq SR6 . . . . .75 D3
Voltage Terr DH4 . . . . . . .90 D4
Vulcan Pl Bedlington NE22 16 A8
Sunderland SR6 . . . . .75 D1
Vulcan Terr NE12 . . . . .29 E1

W

Wade Ave NE15 . . . . .33 A7
Wadham Ct SR2 . . . . .92 E7
Wadham Terr NE34 . . . . . .59 B5
Wadsley Sq SR2 . . . . .86 E3
Waggonway The NE42 . . .50 D3
Wagon Way NE28 . . . . . . .40 D1
Wagonway Rd NE31 . . . . .57 E7
Wagtail Cl NE21 . . . . .68 C8
Wakefield Ave NE34 . . . . .60 B5
Walbottle Campus Tech Coll NE15 . . . . .35 F2
Walbottle Hall Gdns NE15 . . . . .36 A1
Walbottle Rd
Newburn NE15 . . . . .52 F8
Walbottle NE15 . . . . .35 F1
Walbottle Village Fst Sch NE15 . . . . .35 F1
Walden Cl DH2 . . . . .81 D2
Waldo St NE29 . . . . .42 B5
Waldridge Cl NE37 . . . . . .83 A6
Waldridge Gdns NE9 . . . .71 D4
Waldridge La DH2 . . . . . .88 A2
Waldridge Rd DH2 . . . . . .88 B2
Waldron Sq SR2 . . . . .86 E3
Walker Ct 11 NE16 . . . . . .69 A7
Walker Gate Hospl NE6 . .39 E1
Walker Gate Ind Est NE6 .57 B6
Walker Gr NE6 . . . . .56 F8
Walker Park Cl NE6 . . . . .57 A4
Walker Park Gdns NE6 . .57 A4
Walker Pl NE30 . . . . .42 C6
Walker Rd NE6 . . . . .56 E3
Walker Riverside Ind Pk NE6 . . . . .57 B4
Walker Riverside Pk* NE6 . . . . .56 F3
Walker Tech Coll NE6 . . . .56 F6
Walker Terr NE8 . . . . . . .101 B2
Walker View NE10 . . . . . .71 D8
Walkerburn NE23 . . . . . . .22 B3
Walkerdene Ho NE6 . . . . .57 B8
Walkergate Hospl NE6 . . .56 E8
Walkergate Prim Sch NE6 . . . . .56 E8
Walkergate Sta NE6 . . . . . .56 E8
Walkers Bldgs 22 NE29 . .42 A5
Wall Cl NE3 . . . . .38 A5
Wall St NE3 . . . . .38 A5
Wall Terr NE6 . . . . .56 E7
Wallace Ave NE16 . . . . . . .69 C8
Wallace Gdns NE9 . . . . . .71 E3
Wallace St Dunston NE11 100 A1
Houghton-le-S DH4 . . . . . . .94 D8
Newcastle-u-T NE2 . . . . . . .98 B4
Sunderland SR5 . . . . .75 C1
Wallace Terr NE40 . . . . . .52 C6
Waller Terr DH5 . . . . .94 E7
Wallinfen NE10 . . . . .71 F5
Wallingford Ave SR2 . . . .86 E2
Wallington Ave
Brunswick Village NE13 . . .28 A6
Tynemouth NE30 . . . . .32 A1
Wallington Cl NE22 . . . . . .11 C2
Wallington Ct
Killingworth NE12 . . . . .29 C3
Newcastle-u-T NE3 . . . . . . .37 D7
Seaton Delaval NE25 . . . . .23 D3
Tynemouth NE30 . . . . .32 B1
Wallington Dr NE15 . . . . .53 E8
Wallington Gr 9 NE33 . . .42 D3
Wallington Rd NE63 . . . . . .6 F2
Wallis St Penshaw DH4 . . .90 B8
12 South Shields NE33 . . . .42 C3
Wallridge Dr NE25 . . . . . .23 E1
Wallsend Jubilee Prim Sch NE28 . . . . .40 A4
Wallsend Rd
North Shields NE29 . . . . . . .41 C3
North Shields NE29 . . . . . . .41 D4
Wallsend St Peter's CE Prim Sch NE28 . . . . .40 E2
Wallsend Sta NE28 . . . . . .40 C1
Walmer Terr NE9 . . . . . . .71 D1
Walnut Gdns NE8 . . . . . . .70 C8
Walnut Pl NE3 . . . . .37 F3
Walpole Ct 1 SR4 . . . . . .85 F6
Walpole St
Newcastle-u-T NE6 . . . . . . .56 E8
South Shields NE33 . . . . . .42 C1
Walsh Ave NE31 . . . . .57 E7
Walsham Cl NE24 . . . . . . .17 B5
Walsingham NE38 . . . . . . .83 C4
Walter St
Brunswick Village NE13 . . .28 A6
Jarrow NE32 . . . . .58 B7
Walter Terr
Hetton le H DH5 . . . . .95 B1
Newcastle-u-T NE4 . . . . . . .98 A2
Walter Thomas St 3 SR5 74 F2
Waltham NE38 . . . . .83 D4
Waltham Cl NE28 . . . . . . .39 F3
Waltham Pl 4 NE5 . . . . . .37 B2
Walton Ave Blyth NE24 . . .17 C8
Tynemouth NE29 . . . . .41 F7
Walton Dr NE62 . . . . .10 F8
Walton La SR1 . . . . .103 B3
Walton Pk NE29 . . . . .41 F8
Walton Rd
Newcastle-u-T NE5 . . . . . . .37 A1
Washington NE38 . . . . .84 B5
Walton Terr DH8 . . . . .76 E4
Walwick Ave NE29 . . . . . .41 D6
Walwick Rd NE25 . . . . . . .31 B5
Walworth Ave NE34 . . . . .60 C6
Walworth Gr NE32 . . . . . .58 B3
Wandsworth Rd NE6 . . . .56 B7
Wanless La NE46 . . . . . . .45 B4
Wanley St NE24 . . . . .17 E8
Wanlock Cl NE23 . . . . .22 C3
Wanny Rd NE22 . . . . .11 B1
Wansbeck NE38 . . . . .83 A1
Wansbeck Ave Blyth NE24 17 E5
Stakeford NE62 . . . . .11 A8
Tynemouth NE30 . . . . .32 C2
Wansbeck Bsns Pk NE63 . .6 B5
Wansbeck Cl Ellington NE61 1 E5
Sunniside NE16 . . . . .69 A3
Wansbeck Cres NE61 . . . . .4 E3
Wansbeck Ct
Bedlington NE22 . . . . .16 A8
19 Silksworth SR3 . . . . .91 F6
Wansbeck General Hospl NE63 . . . . .6 F4
Wansbeck Gr NE25 . . . . . .23 D6
Wansbeck Ho NE15 . . . . .53 C6
Wansbeck Mews
Ashington NE63 . . . . .6 B4
South Shields NE34 . . . . . . .59 C5
Wansbeck Pl NE61 . . . . . . .3 E1
Wansbeck Rd
Ashington NE63 . . . . .6 B2
Dudley NE23 . . . . .28 F8
Jarrow NE32 . . . . .58 B5
Newcastle-u-T NE3 . . . . . . .38 A6
Wansbeck Rd S NE3 . . . . .38 A6
Wansbeck Riverside Pk* NE62,NE63 . . . . .5 F1
Wansbeck Road Sta NE3 38 A6
Wansbeck Sq NE63 . . . . . . .6 C4
Wansbeck St
Ashington NE63 . . . . .12 A8
Chopwell NE17 . . . . .66 C1
Morpeth NE61 . . . . .9 A8
Wansbeck Terr NE62 . . . .11 D7
Wansbeck View NE62 . . . .11 B8
Wansdyke NE61 . . . . .3 D1
Wansfell Ave NE5 . . . . . . .37 D3
Wansford Ave NE5 . . . . . .37 B1
Wansford Way
Whickham NE16 . . . . .68 F5
Whickham NE16 . . . . .69 A4
Wantage Ave NE29 . . . . . .41 D4
Wantage St NE33 . . . . . . .59 D7
Wapping 1 NE24 . . . . .17 F8
Wapping St NE33 . . . . . . .42 B4
Warbeck Cl NE3 . . . . .37 B6
Warburton Cres NE9 . . . .71 A8
Warcop Ct NE3 . . . . .37 E7
Ward Ct SR2 . . . . .103 B1
Warden Gr DH5 . . . . .94 F7
Warden Law La SR3 . . . . .91 F6
Wardenlaw NE10 . . . . .71 F5
Wardill Gdns NE9 . . . . . . .71 B7
Wardle Ave NE33 . . . . .42 E1
Wardle Dr NE23 . . . . .29 B8
Wardle Gdns NE10 . . . . . .71 E7
Wardle St NE3 . . . . .38 E5
Wardle Terr NE40 . . . . . . .51 F4
Wardley Ct NE10 . . . . . . .72 D8
Wardley Dr NE10 . . . . .72 D7
Wardley La NE10,NE31 . . .57 C1
Wardley Prim Sch NE10 .72 B8
Wardroper Ho NE6 . . . . . .57 A4
Warenford Cl NE23 . . . . . .22 C4
Warenford Pl NE5 . . . . . . .54 C7
Warenmill Cl NE15 . . . . . .53 B7
Warennes St 3 SR4 . . . . .85 E7
Warenton Pl NE29 . . . . . . .31 B1
Waring Ave NE26 . . . . . . .24 B7
Wark Ave
North Shields NE29 . . . . . . .41 C6
Shiremoor NE27 . . . . .30 F4
Wark Cres NE32 . . . . .58 B2
Wark Ct NE3 . . . . .38 E4
Wark St DH3 . . . . .88 C1
Warkdale Ave NE24 . . . . .17 A6
Warkworth Ave
Blyth NE24 . . . . .17 E5
South Shields NE34 . . . . . . .60 B7
Wallsend NE28 . . . . .40 C4
Whitley Bay NE26 . . . . .32 A5
Warkworth Cl NE38 . . . . .83 B4
Warkworth Cres
Ashington NE63 . . . . .6 C3
Warkworth Cres *continued*
Newburn NE15 . . . . .52 F7
Newcastle-u-T NE3 . . . . . . .38 B6
Warkworth Dr
Chester le S DH2 . . . . .88 A1
Ellington NE61 . . . . .1 E5
Pegswood NE61 . . . . .4 F3
Wideopen NE13 . . . . .28 C6
Warkworth Gdns NE10 . .71 C8
Warkworth La NE61 . . . . . .1 C6
Warkworth St
3 Newcastle-u-T,Byker NE6 . . . . .56 C6
Newcastle-u-T,Lemington NE15 . . . . .53 C6
Warkworth Terr
Jarrow NE32 . . . . .58 B3
Tynemouth NE30 . . . . .42 D8
Warkworth Woods NE3 . .28 B2
Warnham Ave SR2 . . . . . .86 E2
Warnhead Rd NE22 . . . . . .11 B1
Warren Ave NE6 . . . . .57 A8
Warren Cl DH4 . . . . .90 C4
Warren Ct NE63 . . . . .6 C2
Warren Sq SR1 . . . . .103 C4
Warrenmor NE10 . . . . . . .72 A7
Warrens Wlk NE21 . . . . . .53 A1
Warrington Rd
Newcastle-u-T,Elswick NE4 . . . . .100 A4
Newcastle-u-T,Fawdon NE3 .37 E6
Warton Terr NE6 . . . . .56 C8
Warwick Ave NE16 . . . . . .69 B5
Warwick Cl Seghill NE23 . .22 E1
Whickham NE16 . . . . .69 A5
Warwick Ct
Gateshead NE8 . . . . .101 C2
Newcastle-u-T NE3 . . . . . . .37 D7
Warwick Dr
Houghton-le-S DH5 . . . . . . .94 E7
Sunderland SR3 . . . . .91 C7
Washington NE37 . . . . .72 D2
Whickham NE16 . . . . .69 B5
Warwick Gr NE22 . . . . . . .10 D1
Warwick Hall Wlk NE7 . .39 D3
Warwick Rd Hebburn NE31 57 F3
Newcastle-u-T NE5 . . . . . . .53 E8
South Shields NE34 . . . . . . .59 D7
Wallsend NE28 . . . . .40 B1
Warwick St Blyth NE24 . . .17 C4
Gateshead NE8 . . . . .101 C2
Newcastle-u-T NE6 . . . . . . .56 A7
Sunderland SR5 . . . . .75 D1
Warwick Terr SR3 . . . . . . .92 A8
Warwick Terr W SR3 . . . .92 A8
Wasdale Cl NE23 . . . . .22 C3
Wasdale Ct SR6 . . . . .75 C5
Wasdale Rd NE5 . . . . .54 B8
Washington 'F' Pit Mus* NE37 . . . . .83 C7
Washington Arts Ctr NE38 . . . . .83 D2
Washington Gdns NE9 . . .71 C3
Washington Highway
Penshaw DH4,NE38 . . . . . . .89 E8
Washington NE37,NE38 . . . .83 B4
Washington Hospl The NE38 . . . . .88 E8
Washington Old Hall* NE38 . . . . .83 E6
Washington Rd SR5 . . . . .74 B2
Washington Sch NE37 . . .83 D7
Washington Service Area DH3,NE38 . . . . .82 E3
Washington St SR4 . . . . . .85 F6
Washington Terr NE30 . . .42 C7
Washington Waterfowl & Wetlands Ctr* NE38 . . .84 C5
Washingwell Com Prim Sch NE16 . . . . .69 C6
Washingwell La NE16 . . . .69 D6
Washingwell Pk NE16 . . .69 C6
Waskdale Cres NE21 . . . .68 B8
Waskerley Cl NE16 . . . . . .69 B3
Waskerley Gdns 3 NE9 . .71 D3
Waskerley Rd NE38 . . . . .83 F5
Watch House Cl NE29 . . .42 A3
Watcombe Cl NE37 . . . . . .72 F2
Water Row NE15 . . . . .52 E7
Water St NE4 . . . . .100 B3
Waterbeach Pl NE5 . . . . .37 B2
Waterbeck Cl NE23 . . . . . .22 C3
Waterbury Cl SR5 . . . . . . .74 F3
Waterbury Rd NE3 . . . . . .28 B1
Waterfield Rd NE22 . . . . . .12 B4
Waterford Cl
East Rainton DH5 . . . . .94 D4
Seaton Sluice NE26 . . . . . . .24 D6
Waterford Cres 6 NE26 . .32 B4
Waterford Gn NE63 . . . . . .11 D8
Waterford Pk NE13 . . . . . .27 F6
Watergate NE1 . . . . .101 B4
Waterloo Ct 5 NE37 . . . . .83 E8
Waterloo Pl
North Shields NE29 . . . . . . .42 A6
Sunderland SR1 . . . . .103 A2
Waterloo Rd Blyth NE24 . . .17 E7
Earsdon NE25 . . . . .31 A5
Washington NE37 . . . . .72 F3
Washington,Sulgrave NE37 .72 E1
Waterloo Sq 10 NE33 . . . .42 C3
Waterloo St Blaydon NE21 53 A1
Newcastle-u-T NE1 . . . . . .100 C4
Waterloo Vale 8 NE33 . . .42 C3
Waterloo Wlk NE37 . . . . .83 E8
Waterlow Cl SR5 . . . . .74 F4
Watermark The NE11 . . . .54 C3
Watermill NE40 . . . . .52 C5
Watermill La NE10 . . . . . .71 E8
Watermill Pk NE10 . . . . . .71 D7
Waterside NE61 . . . . .8 F8
Waterside Dr NE11 . . . . . .54 E2
Waterside Pk NE31 . . . . . .57 C6
Waterville Pl 16 NE29 . . . .42 A5
Waterville Prim Sch NE29 . . . . .41 F4
Waterville Rd NE29 . . . . . .41 E4
Waterville Terr 9 NE29 . .42 A5
Waterworks Rd SR1 . . . .102 C2
Waterworks The SR2 . . . .92 E5
Watford Cl SR5 . . . . .74 F4
Watling Pl NE9 . . . . .71 B6
Watling St NE45 . . . . .46 F5
Watson Ave Dudley NE23 .29 A8
South Shields NE34 . . . . . . .60 B5
Watson Gdns NE28 . . . . . .41 A3
Watson Pl NE34 . . . . .60 B5
Watson St
Burnopfield NE16 . . . . .79 B6
Gateshead NE8 . . . . .100 C1
High Spen NE39 . . . . .67 A5
Jarrow NE32 . . . . .58 C8
Watson Terr
Boldon Colliery NE35 . . . . . .73 F7
17 Morpeth NE61 . . . . .9 A8
Watt St NE8 . . . . .70 D7
Watt's La NE64 . . . . .7 E5
Watt's Rd NE26 . . . . .32 A6
Watts Moses Ho SR1 . . .103 C3
Wavendon Cres SR4 . . . .85 E4
Waverdale Ave NE6 . . . . .57 A7
Waverdale Way NE33 . . . .59 B7
Waverley Ave
Bedlington NE22 . . . . .11 B1
Bedlington NE22 . . . . .11 C2
Whitley Bay NE25 . . . . .31 F4
Waverley Cl NE21 . . . . . . .67 F8
Waverley Cres NE15 . . . . .53 D7
Waverley Ct NE22 . . . . . . .11 C2
Waverley Dr NE22 . . . . . . .11 C2
Waverley Lodge NE2 . . . .99 C3
Waverley Pl NE64 . . . . .7 E5
Waverley Prim Sch NE15 53 E6
Waverley Rd
Gateshead NE9 . . . . .71 B1
Newcastle-u-T NE4 . . . . . .100 B4
Waverley Terr Dipton DH9 .78 E1
Sunderland SR4 . . . . .85 E7
Waverly Dr NE22 . . . . .11 D2
Waverton Cl NE23 . . . . . . .22 B3
Wawn St NE33 . . . . .59 D8
Wayfarer Rd SR5 . . . . .75 A1
Wayland Sq SR2 . . . . .86 E1
Wayman St SR5 . . . . .75 C1
Wayside
Newcastle-u-T NE15 . . . . . .54 B5
South Shields NE34 . . . . . . .60 B6
Sunderland SR2 . . . . .86 B4
Wealcroft NE10 . . . . .71 F5
Wealcroft Ct NE10 . . . . . . .71 F5
Wealleans Cl NE63 . . . . . . .7 B3
Wear Ct NE34 . . . . .59 C5
Wear Lodge DH3 . . . . .88 C7
Wear Rd NE31 . . . . .57 E3
Wear St Chester le S DH3 .88 D2
Chopwell NE17 . . . . .66 B1
Fence Houses DH4 . . . . . . .94 A7
Hetton le H DH5 . . . . .95 A3
Jarrow NE32 . . . . .58 B7
Sunderland,Hendon SR1 . .103 C2
Sunderland,Low Southwick SR5 . . . . .75 A1
Sunderland,South Hylton SR4 . . . . .85 A7
Wear Terr NE38 . . . . .83 E4
Wear View SR4 . . . . .85 B7
Weardale Ave Blyth NE24 .17 A8
Longbenton NE12 . . . . .39 D8
Newcastle-u-T NE6 . . . . . . .57 A6
Sunderland SR6 . . . . .75 E7
Wallsend NE28 . . . . .40 B4
Washington NE37 . . . . .83 C8
Weardale Cres DH4 . . . . .90 B7
Weardale St DH5 . . . . .94 E1
Weardale Terr DH3 . . . . .88 D2
Wearfield SR5 . . . . .74 F1
Wearhead Dr SR2,SR4 . .102 B1
Wearmouth Ave SR5 . . . .75 D2
Wearmouth Dr SR5 . . . . .75 D2
Wearmouth St SR6 . . . . . .75 D1
Weathercock La NE9 . . . .70 F5
Weatherside NE21 . . . . . .53 B1
Webb Gdns NE10 . . . . . . .72 A8
Wedder Law NE23 . . . . . . .22 B3
Wedderburn Sq NE63 . . . . .6 C3
Wedgewood Cotts NE15 .53 D6
Wedmore Rd NE5 . . . . . . .36 D3
Weetman St NE33 . . . . . . .42 B1
Weetslade Cres NE23 . . . .29 A7
Weetslade Rd NE23 . . . . .29 A7
Weetslade Terr NE23 . . . .29 C5
Weetwood Rd NE23 . . . . .22 C4
Weidner Rd NE15,NE4 . . .54 D6
Welbeck Com Fst Sch NE63 . . . . .7 A2
Welbeck Gn NE6 . . . . .56 E5
Welbeck Prim Sch NE6 . .56 D5
Welbeck Rd
Guide Post NE62 . . . . .10 E7
Newcastle-u-T NE6 . . . . . . .56 E5
Welbeck Terr
Ashington NE63 . . . . .6 D2
Pegswood NE61 . . . . .4 F4
Welburn Cl NE42 . . . . .50 C5
Welbury Way NE23 . . . . . .22 B3
Weldon Ave SR2 . . . . .86 E2
Weldon Cres NE7 . . . . . . .39 B2
Weldon Pl NE29 . . . . .41 D8
Weldon Rd
East Cramlington NE23 . . . .22 E5
Longbenton NE12 . . . . .39 B6
Weldon Terr DH3 . . . . . . .88 D2
Weldon Way NE3 . . . . .38 B6
Welfare Cres
Ashington NE63 . . . . .6 F3
Newbiggin-by-t-S NE64 . . . . .7 C4
Welfare Rd DH5 . . . . .95 A4
Welford Ave NE3 . . . . .38 A5
Well Bank NE45 . . . . .46 F5
Well Bank Rd NE37 . . . . . .72 B1
Well Close Wlk NE16 . . . .69 A6
Well Dean NE42 . . . . .50 D3
Well La Tynemouth NE27 . .31 B2
Tynemouth NE27 . . . . .31 C2
Well Rd NE43 . . . . .64 B5
Well Ridge Cl NE25 . . . . .31 C6
Well Ridge Pk NE25 . . . . .31 C7
Well St SR4 . . . . .85 F7
Well Way NE61 . . . . .3 F1
Wellands Cl SR6 . . . . .60 E1
Wellands Ct SR6 . . . . .60 E1
Wellands Dr SR6 . . . . .60 E1
Wellands La SR6 . . . . .60 E1
Wellburn Rd NE37 . . . . . . .72 B1
Wellesley St NE32 . . . . . . .58 B5
Wellesley Terr NE4 . . . . . .98 A1
Wellfield Cl NE15 . . . . . . .35 C1
Wellfield Ct NE40 . . . . . . .51 E3
Wellfield La NE5 . . . . .37 B2
Wellfield Mews SR2 . . . . .92 E5
Wellfield Mid Sch NE25 . .31 B4
Wellfield Rd
Newcastle-u-T NE4 . . . . . . .54 D5
Newcastle-u-T NE4 . . . . . . .54 E5
Rowlands Gill NE39 . . . . . . .67 C2
Wellfield Terr
3 Gateshead NE10 . . . . . . .71 C7
Newcastle-u-T NE10 . . . . . .57 B1
Ryhope SR2 . . . . .92 E5
Wellgarth Rd NE37 . . . . . .72 B1
Wellhead Dean Rd NE62 . .5 F2
Wellhead Terr NE63 . . . . . .6 A4
Wellhope NE38 . . . . .88 F8
Wellington Ave NE25 . . . .31 A5
Wellington Ct
2 Gateshead NE10 . . . . . . .71 C8
6 Washington NE37 . . . . . .83 E8
Wellington Dr NE33 . . . . .42 C4
Wellington La SR4 . . . . .102 B4
Wellington Rd
Dunston NE11 . . . . .54 E1
Dunston NE11 . . . . .54 F1
Stakeford NE62 . . . . .11 A7
Wellington Row DH4 . . . .90 C5
Wellington St Blyth NE24 .17 F7
Gateshead NE8 . . . . .101 B3
Gateshead,Felling NE10 . . .71 C8
Hebburn NE31 . . . . .57 D5
High Pittington DH6 . . . . . .96 B5
Newcastle-u-T NE4 . . . . . . .98 C1
Newcastle-u-T,Lemington NE15 . . . . .53 D6
11 North Shields NE29 . . . .42 A5
Wellington St E 10 NE24 .17 F8
Wellington St W 12 NE29 42 A5
Wellington Wlk 2 NE37 . .83 F8
Wellmere Rd SR2 . . . . . . .86 F1
Wells Cl NE12 . . . . .39 D4
Wells Gdns NE9 . . . . .70 F2
Wells Gr NE34 . . . . .60 A7
Wells St NE35 . . . . .58 E1
Wellshede NE10 . . . . .72 B7
Wellway NE32 . . . . .58 B2
Wellway Ct 8 NE61 . . . . . .3 F1
Wellwood Gdns NE61 . . . . .4 A1
Welton Cl NE43 . . . . .64 D6
Welworth Way SR1 . . . . .102 C3
Welwyn Ave NE22 . . . . . . .11 D3
Welwyn Cl Sunderland SR5 85 A8
Wallsend NE28 . . . . .39 F4
Wembley Ave NE25 . . . . . .31 E4
Wembley Cl SR5 . . . . .74 F3
Wembley Gdns NE24 . . . .12 B6
Wembley Rd SR5 . . . . .74 F3
Wembley Terr NE24 . . . . .12 C6
Wendover Cl SR5 . . . . . . .74 E4
Wendover Way SR5 . . . . .74 E4
Wenham Sq SR2 . . . . .86 B4
Wenlock NE38 . . . . .83 C4
Wenlock Dr NE29 . . . . . . .41 F8
Wenlock Pl 6 NE34 . . . . .59 A4
Wenlock Rd NE34 . . . . . . .59 A5
Wensley Cl
Newcastle-u-T NE5 . . . . . . .37 C4
Urpeth DH2 . . . . .81 E1
Wensley Ho 2 SR3 . . . . . .91 F5
Wensleydale NE28 . . . . . .39 F5
Wensleydale Ave
Penshaw DH4 . . . . .90 A7
Washington NE37 . . . . .83 C8
Wensleydale Dr NE12 . . .39 D8
Wensleydale Mid Sch NE24 . . . . .17 F6
Wensleydale Terr NE24 . .17 F6
Wentworth NE33 . . . . .42 E1
Wentworth Cl NE10 . . . . .71 D7
Wentworth Ct NE20 . . . . .25 C4
Wentworth Dr NE37 . . . . .72 C2
Wentworth Gdns NE25 . . .31 C4
Wentworth Grange NE3 .38 D4

Wentworth Pl
Hexham NE46 . . . .**45** B5
Newcastle-u-T NE4 . . . . . .**100** B4
Wentworth Terr SR4 . . . . .**102** B3
Werhale Gn NE10 . . . .**71** D8
Wesley Ct Blaydon NE21 . . .**53** D3
1 Gateshead,Felling NE10 .**71** C8
Wesley Dr NE12 . . . .**30** B1
Wesley Gr NE40 . . . .**51** E3
Wesley Mount NE40 . . . . . .**51** E3
Wesley St
Gateshead,Low Fell NE9 . . .**70** F5
Newcastle-u-T NE2 . . . .**99** C2
Prudhoe NE42 . . . .**50** D2
15 South Shields NE33 . . . . .**42** C3
Wesley Terr
Chester le S DH3 . . . .**88** C3
Dipton DH9 . . . .**78** D1
Prudhoe NE42 . . . .**50** D2
Sherburn Hill DH6 . . . .**96** C1
Wesley Way
Longbenton NE12 . . . .**30** B1
Throckley NE15 . . . .**35** D2
Wessex Cl SR5 . . . .**74** F4
Wessington Terr NE37 . . .**83** D7
Wessington Way
Sunderland SR5 . . . .**74** E1
Sunderland,Castletown SR5 .**85** B8
West Acres Blaydon NE21 .**53** D2
Dinnington NE13 . . . .**27** B8
West Ave Guide Post NE62 .**10** D7
Longbenton NE12 . . . .**39** D6
Longbenton,Forest Hall
NE12 . . . .**29** F1
Newcastle-u-T NE5 . . . .**36** F2
Newcastle-u-T,Gosforth
NE3 . . . .**38** C4
North Shields NE29 . . . .**41** D5
Rowlands Gill NE39 . . . .**67** D1
South Shields NE34 . . . .**59** E6
Washington NE38 . . . .**83** B1
Whitburn SR6 . . . .**60** E1
Whitley Bay NE25 . . . .**31** E5
West Bailey NE12 . . . .**29** B3
West Boldon Prim Sch
NE36 . . . .**74** A7
West Bridge St
Cambois NE24 . . . .**12** D3
Penshaw DH4 . . . .**89** E8
West Brunton Farm Cotts
NE13 . . . .**27** D2
**West Chirton (Middle) Ind
Est** NE29 . . . .**41** B7
West Chirton (South) Ind Est
NE29 . . . .**41** C5
West Chirton North Ind Est
NE29 . . . .**41** B7
West Clifton NE12 . . . .**29** C4
West Copperas NE15 . . . . .**53** F7
West Cres Chopwell NE17 .**77** B7
Gateshead NE10 . . . .**72** C8
West Ct NE24 . . . .**17** C6
West Dene Dr NE30 . . . . . .**42** A7
West Denton Cl NE15 . . . . .**53** D8
West Denton Prim Sch
NE5 . . . .**36** D1
West Denton Rd NE15 . . . .**53** D8
West Denton Ret Pk NE5 .**37** A2
West Denton Way NE5 . . .**36** E1
West Dr Blyth NE24 . . . .**17** C4
Cleadon SR6 . . . .**74** E8
West End NE26 . . . .**24** C6
West End Terr 1 NE46 . . . .**45** A4
West Farm Burdon SR3 . . . .**92** B3
Medomsley DH8 . . . .**77** C2
West Farm Ave NE12 . . . .**39** A6
West Farm Ct
Cramlington NE23 . . . .**22** B7
Killingworth NE12 . . . .**29** E2
West Farm La DH8 . . . .**77** C2
West Farm Rd
Cleadon SR6 . . . .**75** B8
Newcastle-u-T NE6 . . . .**56** E7
Wallsend NE28 . . . .**40** F3
West Farm Wynd NE12 . . .**38** F6
West Ford Rd NE62 . . . .**11** B8
West Gate Com Coll NE4 .**54** D6
West George Potts St 17
NE33 . . . .**42** D1
West Gns 11 NE61 . . . .**9** A8
West Gr SR4 . . . .**85** B5
West Grange SR5 . . . .**75** C3
West Hextol NE46 . . . .**44** F4
West Hextol Cl NE46 . . . . .**44** F4
West High Horse Cl
NE39 . . . .**68** A4
West Hill Morpeth NE61 . . . .**8** E7
Sunderland SR4 . . . .**85** E4
West Holborn NE33 . . . . . .**42** B1
West Jesmond Ave NE2 . .**38** E2
West Jesmond Prim Sch
NE2 . . . .**38** E1
West Jesmond Sta NE2 . . .**38** E2
West La Blaydon NE21 . . . . .**68** A8
Byermoor NE16 . . . .**68** C1
Chester le S DH3 . . . .**88** C2
Killingworth NE12 . . . .**29** D2
Medomsley NE17 . . . .**77** B4
West Law Rd DH8 . . . .**76** D1
West Lawn SR2 . . . .**86** C4
West Lawrence St SR1 .**103** B2
West Lea Blaydon NE21 . . . .**68** C8
New Herrington DH4 . . . . . .**90** D6
West Market St NE61 . . . . .**2** B3
West Mdws NE5 . . . .**36** D4

West Meadows Dr SR6 . . .**75** A8
West Meadows Rd SR6 . . .**75** B8
West Moffett St 6 NE33 .**42** D1
West Monkseaton Sta
NE25 . . . .**31** D4
West Moor Ct NE12 . . . .**29** B1
West Moor Dr SR6 . . . .**75** A7
West Moor Terr 1 SR4 . .**85** E7
West Mount
Killingworth NE12 . . . .**29** C3
Sunderland SR4 . . . .**85** E5
West Par Hebburn NE31 . . .**57** D5
Newcastle-u-T NE4 . . . .**100** B4
West Park Gdns NE21 . . . .**53** C1
West Park Rd
Cleadon SR6 . . . .**60** A1
Gateshead NE8,NE9 . . . .**70** E7
South Shields NE33 . . . .**59** C7
West Park View NE23 . . . .**28** F8
West Pastures
Ashington NE63 . . . .**6** B2
West Boldon NE36 . . . .**73** C5
West Percy Rd NE29 . . . . . .**41** F5
West Percy St NE29 . . . . . .**42** A5
West Pk Dunston NE11 . . . .**54** F1
Morpeth NE61 . . . .**8** E7
Sunderland SR3 . . . .**91** B6
West Quarter NE46 . . . . . .**44** F5
West Quay Rd SR5 . . . .**74** F1
West Rd Bedlington NE22 . . .**11** D2
Newcastle-u-T NE15,NE5 . . .**54** C6
Ponteland NE20 . . . .**25** E6
Prudhoe NE42 . . . .**50** B2
Tantobie DH9 . . . .**79** A1
West Rig The NE3 . . . .**37** E4
West Riggs NE22 . . . .**15** F8
West Row DH3 . . . .**82** E3
West Salisbury St 4
NE24 . . . .**17** D8
West Sleekburn Ind Est
NE22 . . . .**11** D6
West Sleekburn Mid Sch
NE62 . . . .**11** F6
West Spencer Terr NE15 .**36** F4
West St 5 Birtley DH3 . . . .**82** C4
Gateshead NE8 . . . .**101** B3
Hebburn NE31 . . . .**57** F7
High Spen NE39 . . . .**66** F4
New Silksworth SR3 . . . .**92** A8
Shiremoor NE27 . . . .**30** D1
Sunderland SR1 . . . .**102** C3
Wallsend NE28 . . . .**40** A2
Whickham NE16 . . . .**69** A7
West Stainton St 5
NE33 . . . .**42** D1
West Stevenson St 7
NE33 . . . .**42** D1
West Sunniside SR1 . . . .**103** A3
West Terr Corbridge NE45 .**46** F6
Seaton Sluice NE26 . . . .**24** D6
Stakeford NE62 . . . .**11** C7
West Thorn Wlk NE16 . . . .**69** A6
West Thorp NE5 . . . .**36** F5
West Vallum NE15 . . . .**53** F7
West View Ashington NE63 . .**6** D3
Bedlington NE22 . . . .**11** C3
Blaydon NE21 . . . .**53** C3
Bournmoor DH4 . . . .**89** E3
Burnopfield NE16 . . . .**79** A6
Cambois NE24 . . . .**12** C6
Chester le S DH3 . . . .**88** C4
Crawcrook NE40 . . . .**51** E6
Dudley NE23 . . . .**29** A8
Earsdon NE25 . . . .**31** A5
Gateshead NE9 . . . .**71** C4
Kibblesworth NE11 . . . .**81** D6
5 Longbenton NE12 . . . . . .**39** D8
Morpeth NE61 . . . .**3** C5
Newbiggin-by-t-S NE64 . . . .**7** E5
Newbottle DH4 . . . .**90** D2
Newcastle-u-T,Elswick NE4 .**54** F4
NE15 . . . .**53** C6
Pegswood NE61 . . . .**4** E3
Penshaw DH4 . . . .**90** B8
Ryhope SR2 . . . .**92** E6
Seghill NE23 . . . .**22** F1
Sherburn Hill DH6 . . . .**96** C1
Shiney Row DH4 . . . .**90** B4
3 Sunderland,Castletown
SR5 . . . .**74** B1
Sunderland,Monkwearmouth
SR6 . . . .**75** D3
Wideopen NE13 . . . .**28** B7
Wylam NE41 . . . .**51** B6
West View Bldgs NE46 . . .**32** C3
West View Terr NE46 . . . . .**45** C3
West Walker Prim Sch
NE6 . . . .**57** A2
West Walls NE1 . . . .**98** C1
West Walpole St NE33 . . . .**42** B1
West Way Dunston NE11 . . .**70** A7
South Shields NE33 . . . .**59** C7
West Wear St SR1 . . . . . .**103** A3
West Wylam Dr NE42 . . . . .**50** E3
West Wynd NE12 . . . .**29** D3
Westacres Gdns NE5 . . . . .**54** C7
Westacres Ave NE16 . . . . .**69** B5
Westacres Cres NE15 . . . .**54** C6
Westbourne Ave
Gateshead NE8 . . . .**70** E8
3 Newcastle-u-T NE6 . . . . .**57** A6
Newcastle-u-T,Gosforth
NE3 . . . .**38** C7
Newcastle-u-T,Walker NE6 .**56** F7
Stakeford NE62 . . . .**6** A1
Westbourne Cotts 11
DH4 . . . .**90** B6

Westbourne Dr DH4 . . . . . .**90** B5
Westbourne Gdns 2
NE6 . . . .**57** A6
Westbourne Gr NE46 . . . . .**44** F5
Westbourne Rd SR1 . . . . .**102** B2
Westbourne Terr
Seaton Delaval NE25 . . . . . .**23** E3
2 Shiney Row DH4 . . . .**90** A6
Westbrooke 2 SR2 . . . .**86** D4
Westburn Gdns NE28 . . . . .**39** F4
Westburn Mews NE40 . . . .**51** E3
Westburn Terr SR6 . . . .**75** E2
Westbury Ave NE6 . . . .**57** A8
Westbury Ct NE12 . . . .**39** A5
Westbury Rd NE29 . . . .**41** F8
Westbury St SR4 . . . .**102** B3
Westcliffe Rd SR6 . . . .**75** F4
Westcliffe Way NE34 . . . . .**58** F3
Westcott Ave NE33 . . . .**42** E1
Westcott Rd NE34 . . . .**59** C6
Westcott Terr DH4 . . . .**90** C8
Westcroft SR6 . . . .**60** E1
Westcroft Rd NE12 . . . .**39** E8
Wester Ct 1 SR3 . . . .**91** F5
Westerdale Penshaw DH4 . .**89** E8
Wallsend NE28 . . . .**39** F4
Westerdale Pl NE6 . . . .**57** B6
Westerham Cl SR5 . . . .**74** F3
Westerhope Gdns 11
NE5 . . . .**37** D1
Westerhope Prim Sch
NE5 . . . .**36** E3
Westerhope Rd NE38 . . . . .**83** B5
Westerkirk NE23 . . . .**22** C3
Western App
South Shields,High Shields
NE33 . . . .**42** C1
South Shields,Tyne Dock
NE34 . . . .**59** A6
Western App Ind Est 7
NE33 . . . .**42** C2
Western Ave
Gateshead NE11 . . . .**70** C4
Newcastle-u-T NE5 . . . .**36** D1
Newcastle-u-T,Elswick NE4 .**54** F5
Prudhoe NE42 . . . .**50** B2
Seaton Delaval NE25 . . . . . .**23** C3
Western Com Prim Sch
NE28 . . . .**40** A2
Western Ct 5 NE26 . . . .**31** F8
Western Dr NE4 . . . .**54** F5
Western Highway NE38 . . .**83** B2
Western Hill Ryhope SR2 . .**92** E7
Sunderland SR2 . . . .**102** B2
Western Rd Jarrow NE32 . . .**58** A7
Wallsend NE28 . . . .**40** F2
Western Terr Dudley NE23 .**28** F8
Washington NE37 . . . .**83** D7
West Boldon NE36 . . . .**74** B7
Western View NE9 . . . .**71** C1
Western Way
Blaydon NE21 . . . .**53** E2
Ponteland NE20 . . . .**25** A2
Ryton NE40 . . . .**52** C4
Whitley Bay NE26 . . . .**31** F8
Westernmoor NE37 . . . . . .**82** F6
Westfield Dudley NE23 . . . .**28** F8
Gateshead NE10 . . . .**71** E6
Hedworth NE32 . . . .**58** C1
Morpeth NE61 . . . .**8** F5
Newcastle-u-T NE3 . . . .**38** B2
Westfield Ave
Brunswick Village NE13 . . .**28** A6
Crawcrook NE40 . . . .**51** F3
Newcastle-u-T NE3 . . . .**38** C3
Whitley Bay NE25 . . . .**31** D4
Westfield Cl NE46 . . . .**44** F5
Westfield Cres
Crawcrook NE40 . . . .**51** F3
Newbiggin-by-t-S NE64 . . . .**7** D4
20 Springwell NE9 . . . .**71** F1
Westfield Ct Jarrow NE32 .**58** B6
Sunderland SR4 . . . .**85** E4
Wallsend NE28 . . . .**57** B8
Westfield Dr NE3 . . . .**38** C3
Westfield Gr
Newcastle-u-T NE3 . . . .**38** B3
Sunderland SR4 . . . .**85** E4
Westfield La NE40 . . . .**52** B6
Westfield Lodge NE9 . . . . .**70** E4
Westfield Pk
Newcastle-u-T NE3 . . . .**38** C3
Wallsend NE28 . . . .**40** A2
Westfield Rd
Gateshead NE8 . . . .**70** E8
Newcastle-u-T NE15 . . . .**54** C5
Westfield Sch NE3 . . . .**38** B3
Westfield Terr
Gateshead NE8 . . . .**70** E8
Hexham NE46 . . . .**44** F5
1 Springwell NE9 . . . .**71** E1
Westgarth NE5 . . . .**36** F4
Westgarth Terr 7 NE37 . .**83** E8
Westgate NE61 . . . .**8** D7
Westgate Ave SR3 . . . .**92** A8
Westgate Cl NE25 . . . .**31** C6
Westgate Ct NE4 . . . .**98** B1
Westgate Gr SR3 . . . .**92** A8
Westgate Hill Prim Sch
NE4 . . . .**98** A1
Westgate Hill Terr NE4 . .**98** C1
Westgate Rd NE1,NE4 . . . . .**98** B1
Westgreen NE62 . . . .**10** F5
Westheath Ave SR2 . . . . . .**86** E1
Westhills DH9 . . . .**79** A2
Westholme Gdns NE15 . . .**54** D6
Westholme Terr 1 SR2 . . .**86** F2
Westhope Cl NE34 . . . .**60** A7

Westhope Rd NE34 . . . .**60** A7
Westlands Hedworth NE32 .**58** D1
Newcastle-u-T NE5 . . . .**36** C1
Newcastle-u-T,High Heaton
NE7 . . . .**39** A2
Seaton Sluice NE26 . . . .**24** C6
Tynemouth NE30 . . . .**32** B1
Westlea NE22 . . . .**15** D8
Westleigh Rd DH4 . . . .**90** C3
Westley Ave NE26 . . . .**24** F1
Westley Cl NE26 . . . .**24** F1
Westline Ind Est DH2 . . . . .**82** B2
Westloch Rd NE23 . . . .**22** B3
Westmacott St NE15 . . . . . .**52** E8
Westminster Ave NE29 . . .**41** B8
Westminster Cl NE26 . . . . .**32** C4
Westminster Cres NE31 . . .**57** E2
Westminster Dr NE11 . . . . .**69** F6
Westminster St NE8 . . . . . .**70** D8
Westminster Terr 4 SR2 .**86** F2
Westminster Way NE12 . . .**39** D4
Westmoor Dr NE12 . . . .**29** B1
Westmoor Prim Sch
NE12 . . . .**29** C2
Westmoor Rd SR4 . . . .**85** D7
Westmoreland St NE4 . . . .**40** C2
Westmorland Ave
Bedlington NE22 . . . .**10** E1
Newbiggin-by-t-S NE64 . . . .**7** D4
2 Wallsend NE28 . . . .**41** B1
Washington NE37 . . . .**72** D1
Westmorland Ct NE31 . . . .**57** D5
Westmorland Gdns NE9 . .**70** F5
Westmorland Ho NE9 . . . . .**70** E5
Westmorland La NE1 . . . .**100** C4
Westmorland Rd
Newcastle-u-T NE4 . . . . . .**100** C4
Newcastle-u-T,Elswick
NE1,NE4 . . . .**100** A4
Shiremoor NE29 . . . .**41** B7
South Shields NE34 . . . .**60** C7
Westmorland Way NE23 .**22** A6
Westmorland Wlk NE4 . . . .**54** F3
Westoe Ave NE33 . . . .**42** E1
Westoe Crown Prim Sch
NE33 . . . .**42** E2
Westoe Cty Inf Sch NE33 .**42** D1
Westoe Dr NE33 . . . .**42** E1
Westoe Hall 1 NE33 . . . . . .**59** E8
Westoe Rd NE33 . . . .**42** D1
Westoe Village NE33 . . . . . .**59** E8
Weston Ave NE16 . . . .**68** F5
Westover Gdns NE9 . . . . . .**70** F7
Westport Cl SR5 . . . .**74** F4
Westray DH2 . . . .**88** B1
Westray Cl 3 SR2 . . . .**92** E8
Westsyde NE20 . . . .**25** B3
Westvale NE15 . . . .**35** B2
Westward Ct NE5 . . . .**36** E3
Westward Gn NE25 . . . .**31** C4
Westward Pl NE38 . . . .**83** B1
Westway Blaydon NE21 . . . .**53** B2
Throckley NE15 . . . .**35** E2
Westway Ind Est NE15 . . .**35** D3
Westwell Ct NE3 . . . .**38** F4
Westwood Ave NE6 . . . .**39** B1
Westwood Cl NE16 . . . .**79** B7
Westwood Gdns
Ashington NE63 . . . .**5** F1
6 Gateshead NE9 . . . .**71** D3
Newcastle-u-T NE3 . . . .**37** E4
Westwood La NE17 . . . .**77** B5
Westwood Rd NE3 . . . .**28** C1
Westwood St SR4 . . . .**85** F6
Westwood View
Chester le S DH3 . . . .**88** C1
Crawcrook NE40 . . . .**51** F3
Wetheral Gdns NE9 . . . . . .**71** A3
Wetheral Terr NE6 . . . .**56** F4
Wetherby Cl NE63 . . . .**6** C2
Wetherby Gr NE8 . . . .**70** D7
Wetherby Rd SR2 . . . .**87** A1
Wettondale Ave NE24 . . . .**17** A7
Weybourne Sq SR2 . . . .**86** E2
Weyhill Ave NE29 . . . .**41** D4
Weymouth Dr DH4 . . . .**89** F5
Weymouth Gdns NE9 . . . . .**71** A2
Whaggs La NE16 . . . .**69** B6
Whalebone La NE61 . . . .**8** F8
Whalton Ave NE3 . . . .**38** A6
Whalton Cl
Gateshead NE10 . . . .**72** C7
Morpeth NE61 . . . .**9** B5
Sherburn DH6 . . . .**96** A1
Whalton Ct
Newcastle-u-T NE3 . . . .**38** A6
South Shields NE34 . . . .**59** E6
Wharfdale Pl NE6 . . . .**57** B7
Wharfedale Penshaw DH4 .**90** A8
Wallsend NE28 . . . .**39** F5
Wharfedale Ave NE37 . . . .**83** C8
Wharfedale Dr NE33 . . . . . .**59** C7
Wharfedale Gdns NE24 . . .**17** A8
Wharfedale Gn NE9 . . . . . .**71** B1
Wharmlands Gr NE15 . . . . .**53** F7
Wharmlands Rd NE15 . . . .**53** F7
Wharncliffe St SR1 . . . . . .**102** B2
Wharrier St NE6 . . . .**56** F4
Wharrier Street Prim Sch
NE6 . . . .**56** F4
Wharton Cl DH5 . . . .**94** D4
Wharton St Blyth NE24 . . . .**17** C5
South Shields NE33 . . . .**42** D2
Wheatall Dr SR6 . . . .**60** F2
Wheatear Cl 1 NE38 . . . . . .**82** F4
Wheatfield Cl NE42 . . . .**50** B5
Wheatfield Ct NE5 . . . .**36** F3

Wheatfield Gr NE12 . . . . . .**39** C7
Wheatfield Rd NE5 . . . .**36** F3
Wheatfields NE25 . . . .**23** B4
Wheatley Gdns NE36 . . . . .**74** A7
Wheatridge NE25 . . . .**23** B4
Wheatsheaf Ct SR6 . . . .**75** F1
Wheler St 3 DH4 . . . .**90** D1
Whernside Cl 4 NE37 . . . .**83** A6
Whernside Ct 24 SR3 . . . . .**91** F6
Whernside Pl NE23 . . . .**22** B3
Whernside Wlk NE40 . . . . .**52** D4
Whetstone Bridge Rd
NE46 . . . .**44** F4
Whetstone Gn NE46 . . . . . .**44** F4
Whickham Ave 6 NE11 . . .**69** F8
Whickham Bank 6 NE16 .**69** A7
Whickham Cl DH4 . . . .**94** C8
Whickham Gdns 14 NE6 . .**56** C5
Whickham Highway
NE11,NE16 . . . .**69** E7
Whickham Ind Est NE16 . .**68** F8
Whickham Lodge NE16 . . . .**69** C7
Whickham Lodge Rise
NE16 . . . .**69** C7
**Whickham Parochial CE Prim
Sch** NE16 . . . .**68** F5
Whickham Pk NE16 . . . .**69** C7
Whickham Rd NE31 . . . .**57** E6
Whickham Sch NE16 . . . . . .**69** A6
Whickham St SR6 . . . .**75** E1
Whickham St E SR6 . . . . . .**75** E1
Whickham View
Gateshead NE9 . . . .**71** A4
Newcastle-u-T NE15 . . . .**54** A6
Whickhope NE38 . . . .**83** E2
Whinbank NE20 . . . .**25** D2
Whinbrooke NE10 . . . .**72** A6
Whinbush Pl NE15 . . . .**54** A5
Whinchat Ho NE28 . . . .**40** D5
Whinfell NE37 . . . .**83** B7
Whinfell Cl NE23 . . . .**22** C3
Whinfell Ct 4 SR3 . . . .**91** F6
Whinfell Rd NE20 . . . .**25** D3
Whinfield Ind Est NE39 . . .**67** C1
Whinfield Terr NE39 . . . . . .**67** D2
Whinfield Way NE39 . . . . . .**67** C1
Whinham Way NE61 . . . .**9** B5
Whinlatter Gdns NE9 . . . . .**71** A4
Whinlaw NE9 . . . .**71** C4
Whinmoor Pl NE5 . . . .**37** E1
Whinney Cl NE21 . . . .**68** A8
Whinneyfield Rd NE6 . . . . .**56** F7
Whinny La Ebchester DH8 .**76** E1
Morpeth NE61 . . . .**3** A8
Whinshaw NE10 . . . .**71** F7
Whinstone Mews NE12 . . .**39** D6
Whinway NE37 . . . .**83** B7
Whistler Gdns NE34 . . . . . .**59** D3
Whitbeck Ct NE5 . . . .**37** A1
Whitbeck Rd NE5 . . . .**54** A8
Whitbourne Cl NE37 . . . . . .**72** C2
Whitburn Bents Rd SR6 . .**75** F7
Whitburn CE Sch SR6 . . . . .**75** F8
Whitburn Coastal Pk★
SR6 . . . .**61** A4
Whitburn Gdns NE9 . . . . . .**71** D3
Whitburn Hall SR6 . . . .**75** F8
Whitburn Pl NE23 . . . .**22** B3
Whitburn Rd Cleadon SR6 .**74** F8
Sunderland SR6 . . . .**75** F4
Whitburn Rd E SR6 . . . .**60** B1
Whitburn St SR6 . . . .**103** A4
Whitburn Terr
East Boldon NE36 . . . .**74** D7
Sunderland SR6 . . . .**75** F6
Whitburn Village Prim Sch
SR6 . . . .**75** E8
Whitby Ave Hexham NE46 . .**44** F5
Sunderland SR5 . . . .**75** F6
Whitby Cl NE8 . . . .**101** C1
Whitby Cres NE12 . . . .**39** C6
Whitby Dr NE38 . . . .**83** D3
Whitby Gdns NE28 . . . .**40** E4
Whitby St NE30 . . . .**42** B6
Whitchester Ho NE4 . . . . . .**98** B2
Whitchurch Cl
Boldon Colliery NE35 . . . . . .**58** E1
Sunderland SR5 . . . .**74** F4
Whitchurch Rd SR5 . . . .**74** F4
Whitdale Ave NE24 . . . .**17** A6
White Cross NE46 . . . .**45** C4
White Gates Dr DH5 . . . . . .**95** B2
White Hill Rd DH5 . . . .**97** C8
White Horse View NE34 . .**60** C6
White House Pl SR2 . . . . .**103** C2
White House Rd SR2 . . . . .**103** B2
White House Way NE10 . .**71** F5
White Mere Com Prim Sch
NE10 . . . .**72** C7
White Mere Gdns NE10 . . .**72** C8
White Oaks NE10 . . . .**71** E5
White Rocks Gr SR6 . . . . . .**60** F3
White Rose Way NE10 . . . .**72** E5
White St NE6 . . . .**57** B6
White-le-Head Gdns
DH9 . . . .**79** A1
Whiteacres NE61 . . . .**9** A7
Whitebark SR3 . . . .**91** E4
Whitebeam Pl NE4 . . . .**100** B3
Whitebridge Cl NE3 . . . .**38** D7
Whitebridge Ct NE3 . . . .**38** C7
Whitebridge Parkway
NE3 . . . .**38** D8
Whitebridge Pk NE3 . . . . . .**38** D8
Whitebridge Wlk NE3 . . . . .**38** D8
Whiteburn NE42 . . . .**50** B1
Whitecliff Cl NE29 . . . .**41** F8
Whitecroft Rd NE12 . . . .**29** B2

Whitefield Cres
Pegswood NE61 . . . . .4 E3
Penshaw DH4 . . . . .90 A7
Whitefield Farm Cotts
NE61 . . . . .5 A2
Whitefield Gdns NE40 . . . .66 F8
Whitefield Gr NE10 . . . . .71 D8
Whitefield Terr NE6 . . . . .39 D1
Whiteford Pl NE23 . . . . . .23 A2
Whitefriars Way NE12 . . . .39 A6
Whitegate Cl NE11 . . . . .54 F2
Whitehall Rd
Gateshead NE8 . . . . . . .101 B1
Gateshead,Shipcote NE8 . .70 D8
Walbottle NE15 . . . . .35 F2
Whitehall St NE33 . . . . . .59 C6
Whitehall Terr 7 SR4 . . . .85 F6
Whitehead St
South Shields NE33 . . . . .59 B7
South Shields,West Harton
NE33 . . . . .59 B6
Whitehill NE10 . . . . .71 F5
Whitehill Dr NE10 . . . . . .71 D8
Whitehill Hall Gdns DH2 .88 A4
Whitehill Rd NE23 . . . . . .16 A1
Whitehouse Cres NE9 . . .71 E4
Whitehouse Farm Ctr★
NE61 . . . . .13 E8
Whitehouse La
Gateshead NE9 . . . . .71 E4
Tynemouth NE29 . . . . . . .41 D8
Whitehouse Mews NE28 .40 C2
Whitehouse Prim Sch
NE29 . . . . .41 E8
Whitehouse Rd
Newcastle-u-T,Delaval
NE15 . . . . .54 C4
Newcastle-u-T,Old Benwell
NE15 . . . . .54 B4
Whiteladies Cl NE38 . . . . .83 D6
Whitelaw Pl NE23 . . . . . . .22 C4
Whiteleas Way NE34 . . . .59 C3
Whitelees Ct NE3 . . . . . . .37 E7
Whiteley Cl NE40 . . . . . . .52 A1
Whiteley Rd NE21 . . . . . . .53 E4
Whites Gdns NE31 . . . . . .57 D6
Whiteside NE44 . . . . .62 F7
Whitethorn Cres NE37 . . .37 E2
Whitethroat Cl 6 NE38 . . .82 F3
Whitewell Cl NE40 . . . . . .52 C5
Whitewell La NE40 . . . . . .52 C5
Whitewell Rd NE21 . . . . . .53 C2
Whitfield Dr NE12 . . . . . .39 C6
Whitfield Rd
6 Longbenton NE12 . . . . .39 D8
Newcastle-u-T NE15 . . . . .53 F5
Seaton Delaval NE25 . . . .23 D3
Whitfield Villas NE33 . . . .59 B6
Whitgrave Rd NE5 . . . . . .37 D3
Whithorn Ct NE12 . . . . . . .17 C7
Whitley Bay High Sch
NE26 . . . . .31 E6
Whitley Bay Sta NE25 . . . .32 B4
Whitley Ct 7 NE9 . . . . . .71 D3
Whitley Lodge Fst Sch
NE26 . . . . .31 E8
Whitley Meml CE Fst Sch
NE22 . . . . .16 A8
Whitley Pl NE25 . . . . .23 E2
Whitley Rd Earsdon NE25 .31 A5
Longbenton NE12 . . . . . . .40 A8
Whitley Bay NE26 . . . . . . .32 B4
Whitley Terr
5 Bedlington NE22 . . . . . .11 D3
Seaton Delaval NE25 . . . .23 E2
Whitmore Rd NE21 . . . . . .53 C3
Whitsun Ave NE22 . . . . . .11 A1
Whitsun Gdns NE22 . . . . .11 A1
Whitsun Gr NE22 . . . . . . .11 A1
Whittingham Cl
Ashington NE63 . . . . .6 A2
Tynemouth NE30 . . . . . . .32 C2
Whittingham Ct NE8 . . . .101 A1
Whittingham Rd
Newcastle-u-T NE5 . . . . . .37 A4
Tynemouth NE30 . . . . . . .32 C1
Whittington Gr NE5 . . . . .54 C8
Whittleburn NE10 . . . . . .71 F5
Whitton Ave NE24 . . . . . .17 B5
Whitton Gdns NE29 . . . . .41 D7
Whitton Pl
Newcastle-u-T NE7 . . . . . .39 B4
Seaton Delaval NE25 . . . .23 D3
Whitton Way NE3 . . . . . . .38 B6
Whittonstall NE38 . . . . . .83 F1
Whittonstall Rd NE17 . . . .66 A1
Whittonstall Terr NE17 . . .66 A1
Whitwell Terr NE40 . . . . .52 C6
Whitworth Cl
Gateshead NE8 . . . . .70 D7
Newcastle-u-T NE6 . . . . . .57 A5
Whitworth Pl NE6 . . . . . .57 A5
Whitworth Rd NE37 . . . . .82 F7
Whorlton Grange Cotts
NE5 . . . . .36 E4
Whorlton La NE5 . . . . . . .36 D5
Whorlton Pl 1 NE5 . . . . .36 E3
Whorlton Terr NE5 . . . . . .36 B4
Whorral Bank NE61 . . . . . .4 B2
Whyndyke NE10 . . . . .71 F5
Whytrig Com Mid Sch
NE25 . . . . .23 C4
Whytrigg Cl NE25 . . . . . .23 B3
Wickets The NE3 . . . . . . .38 D4
Wickham Ind Est NE16 . . .54 A1
Wicklow Ct NE62 . . . . . . .11 D8
Widdrington Ave NE34 . . .60 B8

Widdrington Gdns NE13 . .28 C6
Widdrington Rd NE21 . . . .53 C2
Widdrington Terr
4 North Shields NE29 . . . .42 A5
Ryton NE21 . . . . .53 A4
Widnes Pl NE12 . . . . .39 C7
Wigeon Cl NE38 . . . . .83 A2
Wigham Terr NE16 . . . . . .79 A4
Wigmore Ave NE6 . . . . . . .56 E4
Wilber Ct 9 SR4 . . . . . . .85 F7
Wilber St SR4 . . . . .85 F6
Wilberforce St
Jarrow NE32 . . . . .58 C7
Wallsend NE28 . . . . .57 B8
Wilberforce Wlk NE8 . . . .100 C2
Wilbury Pl NE15 . . . . .37 C2
Wildbriar NE38 . . . . .83 E2
Wilden Ct SR3 . . . . .86 B2
Wilden Rd NE38 . . . . .84 A3
Wildshaw Cl NE23 . . . . . .22 C3
Wilfred St
Boldon Colliery NE35 . . . .73 F8
Chester le St DH3 . . . . . .88 C2
Newcastle-u-T NE6 . . . . . .56 A6
Sunderland SR4 . . . . .85 E7
Wilfrid St DH3 . . . . .82 C3
Wilkes Cl NE5 . . . . .36 F2
Wilkinson Ave NE31 . . . . .57 D3
Wilkinson Ct 4 NE32 . . . .58 B7
Wilkinson Terr SR2 . . . . .92 E6
Wilkwood Cl NE23 . . . . . .22 C4
Willerby Dr NE3 . . . . .38 D8
William Allan Homes
NE22 . . . . .15 D8
William Armstrong Dr
NE4 . . . . .54 F3
William Cl NE12 . . . . .40 A8
William Doxford Ctr SR3 . .91 F6
William IV Yd NE8 . . . . . .101 B4
William Morris Ave NE39 67 B2
William Roberts Ct NE12 29 D1
William St Blyth NE24 . . . .17 E6
Chester le St DH3 . . . . . .88 C3
Chopwell NE17 . . . . .66 B1
Gateshead NE10 . . . . . . .56 D1
Hebburn NE31 . . . . .57 D7
Newcastle-u-T NE3 . . . . . .38 E5
North Shields NE29 . . . . .42 A5
Pegswood NE61 . . . . .4 F3
6 South Shields NE33 . . . .42 C3
Sunderland SR1 . . . . . . .103 A3
8 Sunderland,South Hylton
SR4 . . . . .85 A6
9 Whickham NE16 . . . . . .69 A7
William St W
Hebburn NE31 . . . . .57 D6
14 North Shields NE29 . . .42 A5
William Terr NE31 . . . . . . .57 D7
William Whiteley Homes
NE40 . . . . .52 A1
Williams Pk NE12 . . . . . . .39 C6
Williams Terr SR2 . . . . . .92 E6
Williamson Terr SR6 . . . .103 A4
Willington Terr NE28 . . . .40 E3
Willis St DH5 . . . . .95 A5
Willmore St SR4 . . . . . . .102 A2
Willoughby Dr NE26 . . . . .31 E7
Willoughby Rd NE29 . . . . .41 E6
Willoughby Way NE26 . . .31 E7
Willow Ave Blyth NE24 . . .12 D1
Dunston NE11 . . . . .69 F8
Newcastle-u-T NE4 . . . . . .54 D8
Willow Bank Rd SR2 . . . .86 C3
Willow Cl Morpeth NE61 . . .9 B8
Whickham NE16 . . . . .69 B6
Willow Cres Blyth NE24 . .17 C4
Easington Lane DH5 . . . . .95 D1
Willow Ct Ryton NE40 . . . .52 D6
Stakeford NE62 . . . . .11 B7
Willow Dyke NE45 . . . . . .47 A6
Willow Gdns NE12 . . . . . .29 C4
Willow Gn 7 SR2 . . . . . . .86 C4
Willow Gr Gateshead NE10 71 E8
South Shields NE34 . . . . .59 F5
Wallsend NE28 . . . . .40 D1
Willow Grange NE32 . . . . .58 A7
Willow Pl NE20 . . . . .25 E4
Willow Rd Blaydon NE21 . .53 D2
Houghton-le-S DH4 . . . . . .94 C8
Willow View NE16 . . . . . . .79 A6
Willow Way NE20 . . . . . . .25 E3
Willow's Cl 1 NE38 . . . . .83 F4
Willowbank Gdns NE2 . . .38 E4
Willowdene NE12 . . . . . . .29 E1
Willowfield Ave NE3 . . . . .37 F6
Willows Cl NE13 . . . . .28 A5
Willows The
Hebburn NE31 . . . . .57 E4
Hedworth NE32 . . . . .58 C1
Morpeth NE61 . . . . .9 A8
Newcastle-u-T NE4 . . . . .100 A3
Seaton Burn NE13 . . . . . .21 B1
Throckley NE15 . . . . .35 D1
Washington NE38 . . . . . . .84 A4
Willowvale DH2 . . . . .88 A5
Wills Mews NE7 . . . . .39 E2
Wills Oval NE7 . . . . .39 E2
Wilmington Cl NE3 . . . . . .37 B6
Wilson Ave Birtley DH3 . . .82 C5
Cambois NE22 . . . . .12 B3
Wilson Dr NE36 . . . . .74 B8
Wilson Gdns NE3 . . . . . . .38 B3
Wilson St Dunston NE11 . .69 F8
South Shields NE33 . . . . .42 C2
Sunderland SR4 . . . . .85 F6
Wallsend NE28 . . . . .40 B2
Wilson St N SR5 . . . . . . .102 C4

Wilson Terr
1 Longbenton NE12 . . . . .39 D8
New Silksworth SR3 . . . . .92 A8
Wilson's Ct 6 NE1 . . . . . .99 A1
Wilson's La NE9 . . . . .70 F5
Wilsway NE15 . . . . .35 C2
Wilton Ave NE6 . . . . .56 E4
Wilton Cl
Cramlington NE23 . . . . . .22 C3
Whitley Bay NE25 . . . . . .31 C5
Wilton Cotts 6 NE35 . . . .58 E1
Wilton Dr NE25 . . . . .31 B5
Wilton Gdns N NE35 . . . . .58 E1
Wilton Gdns S NE35 . . . . .58 E1
Wilton Manse NE25 . . . . .31 B4
Wilton Sq SR2 . . . . .86 E1
Wiltshire Cl SR5 . . . . .74 E4
Wiltshire Dr NE28 . . . . . . .39 F4
Wiltshire Gdns NE28 . . . . .40 A3
Wiltshire Pl NE37 . . . . . . .72 D2
Wiltshire Rd SR5 . . . . . . .74 E3
Wimbledon Cl SR5 . . . . . .74 F3
Wimborne Cl NE35 . . . . . .73 E8
Wimbourne Ave SR4 . . . . .85 E4
Wimbourne Gn 1 NE5 . . . .36 F3
Wimpole Cl NE37 . . . . . . .72 E2
Wimslow Cl NE28 . . . . . . .39 F3
Winalot Ave SR2 . . . . . . .86 E2
Wincanton Pl NE29 . . . . . .41 E4
Winchcombe Pl NE7 . . . . .39 A3
Winchester Ave NE24 . . . .17 E7
Winchester Cl NE63 . . . . . .6 F1
Winchester Ct NE32 . . . . .58 B1
Winchester St 7 NE33 . . .42 D3
Winchester Terr NE4 . . . . .98 B1
Winchester Way NE22 . . . .10 F2
Winchester Wlk NE13 . . . .28 B6
Wincomblee Rd NE6 . . . . .57 B4
Windburgh Dr NE23 . . . . .22 B3
Windermere Birtley DH3 . .82 D2
Cleadon SR6 . . . . .60 A1
Windermere Ave
Chester le S DH2 . . . . . . .88 C1
Easington Lane DH5 . . . . .97 C8
Gateshead NE10 . . . . . . .71 F8
Windermere Cl NE23 . . . . .22 B3
Windermere Cres
Blaydon NE21 . . . . .68 B8
Hebburn NE31 . . . . .57 F4
Hedworth NE32 . . . . .58 D3
Penshaw DH4 . . . . .90 C6
South Shields NE34 . . . . .59 E6
Windermere Dr NE12 . . . . .29 C3
Windermere Gdns NE16 .69 C7
Windermere Rd
Newbiggin-by-t-S NE64 . . . .7 C3
Newcastle-u-T NE5 . . . . . .54 B8
Windermere St
Gateshead NE8 . . . . .101 B1
Sunderland SR2 . . . . .86 F2
Windermere St W NE8 . . .101 B1
Windermere Terr NE29 . . .41 F6
Windhill Rd NE6 . . . . .56 F3
Winding The NE13 . . . . . . .27 B7
Windlass Ct NE34 . . . . . . .59 C5
Windlass La NE37 . . . . . . .83 C7
Windmill Ct NE2 . . . . .98 C4
Windmill Gr NE24 . . . . . . .17 A8
Windmill Hill Ellington NE61 1 E5
Hexham NE46 . . . . .45 A5
South Shields NE33 . . . . .42 B1
Windmill Hill Cl NE61 . . . . .1 E6
Windmill Hills Prim Sch
NE8 . . . . .101 B2
Windmill Hts NE61 . . . . . . .1 E6
Windmill Ind Est NE23 . . .15 C2
Windmill Sq SR5 . . . . . . .75 C4
Windmill Way
Gateshead NE8 . . . . .101 A2
Hebburn NE31 . . . . .57 E8
Morpeth NE61 . . . . .9 B8
Windshields Wlk NE15 . . .35 C1
Windsor Ave
Gateshead NE8 . . . . .70 E8
Newcastle-u-T NE3 . . . . . .38 E4
Whitley Bay NE26 . . . . . .32 C4
Windsor Cl Wallsend NE28 41 A4
Whickham NE16 . . . . .69 A4
Windsor Cotts NE28 . . . . .41 A4
Windsor Cres
Hebburn NE31 . . . . .57 F6
Houghton-le-S DH5 . . . . .94 F8
Newcastle-u-T NE5 . . . . . .37 A3
Ovingham NE42 . . . . .50 B5
Whitley Bay NE26 . . . . . .32 C4
Windsor Ct
Bedlington NE22 . . . . . . .15 F8
Corbridge NE45 . . . . .47 A6
Cramlington NE23 . . . . . .16 A1
7 Gateshead NE10 . . . . . .71 C8
Newcastle-u-T,Kingston Park
NE3 . . . . .37 E7
Newcastle-u-T,South Gosforth
NE3 . . . . .38 E5
Rowlands Gill NE39 . . . . .67 F2
Windsor Dr Blyth NE24 . . .17 D3
Cleadon SR6 . . . . .59 F1
Houghton-le-S DH5 . . . . .94 E6
New Silksworth SR3 . . . . .92 A7
South Hetton DH6 . . . . . .97 F8
Wallsend NE28 . . . . .41 A4
Windsor Fst Sch NE64 . . . .7 D3
Windsor Gdns
Bedlington NE22 . . . . . . .15 F8
Gateshead NE10 . . . . . . .71 C8
South Shields NE34 . . . . .59 E7
Tynemouth NE29 . . . . . . .42 A7
Whitley Bay NE26 . . . . . .31 F6

Windsor Gdns W NE26 . . .31 F6
Windsor Pk NE28 . . . . . . .39 F3
Windsor Pl
Longbenton NE27 . . . . . . .30 C1
Newcastle-u-T NE2 . . . . . .99 B3
Ponteland NE20 . . . . .25 R4
Windsor Rd Birtley DH3 . . .82 B6
Newbiggin-by-t-S NE64 . . . .7 D4
Springwell NE9 . . . . .71 F1
Whitley Bay NE25 . . . . . .31 E5
Windsor St 2 NE28 . . . . . .40 B2
Windsor Terr
Choppington NE62 . . . . . .10 F4
Corbridge NE45 . . . . .47 A6
Crawcrook NE40 . . . . .52 A4
Haswell DH6 . . . . .97 F2
Hexham NE46 . . . . .44 F5
Newbiggin-by-t-S NE64 . . . .7 D4
Newcastle-u-T NE2 . . . . . .99 B3
Newcastle-u-T,South Gosforth
NE3 . . . . .38 E4
1 Springwell NE9 . . . . . . .71 F1
Sunderland,East Herrington
SR3 . . . . .91 C6
3 Sunderland,Grangetown
SR2 . . . . .86 F2
Whitley Bay NE26 . . . . . .32 C4
Windsor Villas NE62 . . . . .11 A7
Windsor Way NE3 . . . . . . .37 D7
Windsor Wlk
Ashington NE63 . . . . .7 A2
Newcastle-u-T NE7 . . . . . .37 D7
Windt St NE13 . . . . .28 A5
Windy Gyle NE63 . . . . .6 E4
Windy Nook Prim Sch
NE10 . . . . .71 D6
Windy Nook Rd NE10,NE9 . .71 B6
Windy Ridge NE10 . . . . . .71 C7
Windy Ridge Villas NE10 .71 C7
Wingate Cl
Houghton-le-S DH4 . . . . . .94 D8
Newcastle-u-T NE15 . . . . .53 E6
Wingate Gdns NE9 . . . . . .71 D3
Wingrove NE39 . . . . .67 D1
Wingrove Ave
Newcastle-u-T NE4 . . . . . .54 F6
Sunderland SR6 . . . . .75 E3
Wingrove Gdns NE4 . . . . .54 F7
Wingrove Ho NE33 . . . . . .59 C6
Wingrove Prim Sch NE4 . .54 F6
Wingrove Rd N NE4 . . . . .54 F7
Wingrove Terr 11 NE9 . . . .71 F1
Winifred Gdns NE28 . . . . .40 C1
Winifred St SR6 . . . . .75 E3
Winifred Terr SR1 . . . . . .103 B2
*Winlaton West Lane Com
Prim Sch* NE21 . . . . . . .68 A8
Winsford Ave 1 NE29 . . . .31 F1
Winshields NE23 . . . . .22 C4
Winship Cl NE34 . . . . .59 C3
Winship St NE24 . . . . .17 C4
Winship Terr 15 NE6 . . . . .56 C6
Winskell Rd NE34 . . . . . . .59 A4
Winslade Cl SR3 . . . . .92 B8
Winslow Cl
Boldon Colliery NE35 . . . .58 F2
Newcastle-u-T NE6 . . . . . .57 A6
Sunderland SR5 . . . . .74 F4
Winslow Gdns NE9 . . . . . .70 E5
Winslow Pl NE6 . . . . .57 A6
Winster NE38 . . . . .83 A1
Winster Pl NE23 . . . . .22 B3
Winston Cres SR4 . . . . . . .85 E4
Winston Ct NE9 . . . . .71 F1
Winston Gn DH4 . . . . .89 F8
Winston Way NE43 . . . . . .64 C3
Winton Cl NE23 . . . . .23 A2
Winton Way NE3 . . . . .37 F5
Wirralshir NE10 . . . . .72 A6
Wiseton Ct NE7 . . . . .38 F5
Wishart Ho NE4 . . . . .54 E4
Wishart Terr NE39 . . . . . .66 F4
Wishaw Cl NE23 . . . . .22 C4
Wishaw Rise NE15 . . . . . .53 E7
Witham Gn NE32 . . . . .58 C2
Witham Rd NE31 . . . . .57 F3
Witherington Cl NE7 . . . . .39 E3
Withernsea Gr SR2 . . . . . .92 D7
Witherwack Prim Sch
SR5 . . . . .74 F4
Witney Cl SR5 . . . . .74 F4
Witney Way NE36 . . . . . . .73 E7
Witton Ave NE34 . . . . .60 A6
Witton Ct
Newcastle-u-T NE3 . . . . . .37 E6
Sunderland SR3 . . . . .86 B2
Washington NE38 . . . . . . .83 B4
Witton Gdns
1 Gateshead NE9 . . . . . . .71 D2
Jarrow NE32 . . . . .58 B3
Witton Gr DH4 . . . . .94 C7
Witton Rd Hebburn NE31 . .57 F8
Shiremoor NE27 . . . . .30 F3
Wittonstone Ho NE4 . . . . .98 B2
Witty Ave NE31 . . . . .57 F5
Woburn NE38 . . . . .83 D4
Woburn Cl
Cramlington NE23 . . . . . .16 A1
Wallsend NE28 . . . . .39 F3
Woburn Dr
Bedlington NE22 . . . . . . .11 C2
Silksworth SR3 . . . . .92 A6
Woburn Way NE5 . . . . . . .37 A2
Wolmer Rd NE24 . . . . . . .17 F5
Wolseley Cl NE8 . . . . . . .100 C1
Wolseley Gdns NE2 . . . . .56 A8
Wolseley Terr SR4 . . . . . .102 A1
Wolsey Ct NE34 . . . . .59 C6

Wolsingham Ct NE23 . . . .21 F7
Wolsingham Gdns 5
NE9 . . . . .71 D3
Wolsingham Rd NE3 . . . . .38 B4
Wolsingham St NE4 . . . . .100 A3
Wolsley Rd NE24 . . . . . . .17 E7
Wolveleigh Terr NE3 . . . . .38 D5
Wolviston Gdns 4 NE9 . .71 D3
Wood Fields NE20 . . . . . .25 F6
Wood Gr NE15 . . . . .53 E7
Wood Ho 8 SR3 . . . . .91 F5
Wood La NE22 . . . . .11 B1
Wood Lea DH5 . . . . .95 A7
Wood St Burnopfield NE16 .79 A6
Dunston NE11 . . . . .69 F8
Sunderland SR4 . . . . .102 A3
Wood Terr
Gateshead NE10 . . . . . . .57 B2
High Spen NE39 . . . . .67 A2
Jarrow NE32 . . . . .58 A4
South Shields NE33 . . . . .59 D8
4 Washington NE37 . . . . .83 D8
Woodbine Ave
Newcastle-u-T NE3 . . . . . .38 C4
Wallsend NE28 . . . . .40 B2
Woodbine Cl NE4 . . . . . . .54 F4
Woodbine Cotts NE40 . . . .52 B5
Woodbine Pl NE8 . . . . . . .101 B1
Woodbine Rd NE3 . . . . . . .38 C5
Woodbine St
Gateshead NE8 . . . . .101 B1
2 South Shields NE33 . . . .42 D3
Sunderland SR1 . . . . . . .103 C2
Woodbine Terr
Birtley DH3 . . . . .82 D4
Blyth NE24 . . . . .17 F6
Corbridge NE45 . . . . .47 A6
Gateshead,Bensham NE8 .101 B1
Gateshead,Bill Quay NE10 .57 A1
Gateshead,Felling NE10 . .71 B8
Hexham NE46 . . . . .44 F5
Sunderland SR4 . . . . .85 F8
Woodbine Villas NE8 . . . .101 B1
Woodbrook Ave NE5 . . . . .54 A8
Woodburn NE10 . . . . .71 E5
Woodburn Ave NE4 . . . . . .54 E8
Woodburn Cl
Blaydon NE21 . . . . .68 A8
Bournmoor DH4 . . . . .89 E2
Woodburn Dr
Burnside DH4 . . . . .90 C1
Whitley Bay NE26 . . . . . .31 E7
Woodburn Gdns NE11 . . . .70 A6
Woodburn Sq NE26 . . . . .31 D7
Woodburn St NE15 . . . . . .53 C7
Woodburn Terr NE42 . . . .50 B2
Woodburn Way NE26 . . . .31 E7
Woodchurch Cl NE12 . . . .39 D4
Woodcroft Cl NE23 . . . . . .22 B1
Woodcroft Rd NE41 . . . . .51 A6
Woodend NE20 . . . . .25 D2
Woodend Way NE3 . . . . . .37 D8
Woodford NE9 . . . . .70 F1
Woodford Cl SR5 . . . . . . .74 F4
Woodgate Gdns NE10 . . . .57 B2
Woodgate La NE10 . . . . . .57 B2
Woodhall Cl DH2 . . . . . . .81 E2
Woodhall Ct NE25 . . . . . . .23 C3
Woodhall Spa DH4 . . . . . .90 A4
Woodhead Rd
Newcastle-u-T NE6 . . . . . .56 F8
Prudhoe NE42 . . . . .50 F3
Woodhill Dr NE61 . . . . .8 E8
Woodhill Rd NE23 . . . . . . .22 C4
Woodhorn Colliery Mus★
NE63 . . . . .6 F5
Woodhorn Cotts NE63 . . . .6 F5
Woodhorn Cres NE64 . . . .7 D5
Woodhorn Ct NE63 . . . . . .6 F5
Woodhorn Dr NE62 . . . . . .10 F8
Woodhorn Farm NE64 . . . .7 D6
Woodhorn Gdns NE13 . . . .28 B6
Woodhorn La NE64 . . . . . .7 E5
Woodhorn Pk NE63 . . . . . .6 D4
Woodhorn Rd
Ashington NE63 . . . . .6 E4
Newbiggin-by-t-S NE64 . . . .7 D5
Woodhorn Villas NE63 . . . .6 F5
Woodhouse Ct NE34 . . . . .60 C7
Woodhouses La
Whickham,Fellside NE16 . .68 E6
Whickham,Swalwell NE16 .69 A8
Woodhurst Gr SR4 . . . . . .85 A2
Woodkirk Cl NE23 . . . . . . .23 A2
Woodland Cres NE15 . . . . .54 C4
Woodland Dr SR4 . . . . . . .85 E4
Woodland Grange DH4 . . .89 F1
Woodland Mews NE2 . . . . .38 F2
Woodland Rise SR3 . . . . .91 E6
Woodland Terr
Penshaw DH4 . . . . .90 A8
Washington NE37 . . . . . . .83 E8
Woodland View DH4 . . . . .94 A1
Woodlands
Burnopfield NE16 . . . . . . .79 B6
Chester le S DH3 . . . . . . .88 C4
Great Lumley DH4 . . . . . .89 F1
Hexham NE46 . . . . .45 D4
Newcastle-u-T NE3 . . . . . .38 C3
Ponteland NE20 . . . . .25 D3
Seaham SR7 . . . . .93 A1
Throckley NE15 . . . . .35 C2
Tynemouth NE29 . . . . . . .42 A7
Washington NE38 . . . . . . .88 E8

Woodlands Cl
Earsdon NE25 . . . .**31** A5
High Spen NE39 . . . . . .**67** A3
Woodlands Ct
Kibblesworth NE11 . . . . . .**81** D6
Throckley NE15 . . . .**35** C2
Woodlands Dr SR6 . . . . . .**75** A8
Woodlands Grange NE12 **29** E1
Woodlands Ho NE24 . . . . .**17** B8
Woodlands Park Dr
NE21 . . . .**53** D2
Woodlands Park Villas
NE13 . . . .**28** C4
Woodlands Pk NE13 . . . . .**28** C5
Woodlands Rd
Ashington NE63 . . . .**7** A2
Cleadon SR6 . . . .**75** A8
Newcastle-u-T NE15 . . . . .**53** D7
Rowlands Gill NE39 . . . . . .**67** D2
Woodlands Terr
Gateshead NE10 . . . .**71** C8
Longbenton NE12 . . . .**29** E1
5 South Shields NE33 . . . .**42** D4
Woodlands The NE11 . . . .**81** D6
Woodlands View SR6 . . . .**75** A8
Woodlawn Sch NE25 . . . .**31** D3
Woodlea Longbenton NE12 **29** D1
Newbiggin-by-t-S NE64 . . . .**7** E5
Woodlea Cl DH5 . . . .**95** A4
Woodlea Cres NE46 . . . . .**45** C4
Woodlea Ct NE29 . . . . . .**41** E3
Woodlea Gdns NE3 . . . . .**38** E6
Woodlea Prim Sch DH4 . .**89** E1
Woodlea Rd NE39 . . . . . .**67** B2
Woodlea Sq NE29 . . . . . .**41** E3
Woodleigh Rd NE25 . . . .**31** E4
Woodleigh View NE5 . . . .**37** E3
Woodman Cl NE61 . . . . . .**8** E7
Woodman St NE28 . . . . .**41** B3
Woodmans Way NE16 . . .**68** F4
Woodpack Ave NE16 . . . .**68** F6
Woods Gn NE10 . . . .**57** C1
Woods Terr NE8 . . . .**101** C1
Woodside Bedlington NE22 **11** C1
Blyth NE24 . . . .**17** F6
Hexham NE46 . . . .**45** D4
Morpeth NE61 . . . .**8** D7
Ponteland NE20 . . . .**25** C2
Prudhoe NE42 . . . .**50** F2
Sunderland SR2 . . . .**102** C1
Sunderland,East Herrington
SR3 . . . .**91** C6
Woodside Ave
Corbridge NE45 . . . .**47** B6
Newcastle-u-T NE6 . . . . . .**57** B7
Seaton Delaval NE25 . . . .**23** D2
Throckley NE15 . . . .**35** E2

Woodside Cl NE40 . . . . . .**52** C5
Woodside Cres NE12 . . . .**39** E8
Woodside Ct NE12 . . . . .**39** E8
Woodside Gdns NE11 . . . .**69** F7
Woodside Gr
Sunderland SR3 . . . .**91** C6
Tantobie DH9 . . . .**79** C3
Woodside La
Greenside NE40 . . . .**52** B3
Ryton NE40 . . . .**52** B4
Woodside Rd NE40 . . . . .**52** B5
Woodside Terr
Chopwell NE17 . . . .**77** B8
Sunderland SR3 . . . .**91** C6
Woodside Villas NE46 . . .**45** D4
Woodside Way
Ryton NE40 . . . .**52** C5
South Shields NE33 . . . . .**59** B7
Woodside Wlk NE39 . . . . .**67** C1
Woodstock Ave SR2 . . . .**86** E2
Woodstock Rd
Gateshead NE9 . . . .**71** B2
Newcastle-u-T NE15 . . . . .**54** A5
Woodstone Terr DH4 . . . .**89** D1
Woodthorne Rd NE2 . . . .**38** E3
Woodvale NE20 . . . .**25** C2
Woodvale Dr NE31 . . . . .**57** C4
Woodvale Gdns
Gateshead NE9 . . . .**71** C6
Newcastle-u-T NE15 . . . . .**53** E7
Wylam NE41 . . . .**51** B6
Woodvale Rd
Blaydon NE21 . . . .**53** D2
Killingworth NE12 . . . .**29** C4
Woodville Cres SR4 . . . . .**85** E4
Woodville Ct SR4 . . . . . .**85** E4
Woodville Rd NE15 . . . . .**53** D8
Woodwynd NE10 . . . .**71** F6
Wooler Ave NE29 . . . . . .**41** D4
Wooler Cres NE8 . . . . . .**70** C8
Wooler Gn NE15 . . . .**53** B7
Wooler Sq Sunderland SR2 **86** E3
Wideopen NE13 . . . .**28** C7
Wooler Wlk NE32 . . . . . .**58** A4
Woolerton Dr
Gateshead N10,NE9 . . . . .**71** C6
Gateshead NE9 . . . .**71** B6
Newcastle-u-T NE15 . . . . .**53** E7
Wooley St NE28 . . . .**40** B1
Woolmer Ct NE7 . . . .**39** E3
Woolsington Ct NE22 . . . .**10** F1
Woolsington Gdns NE13 . .**36** F8
Woolsington Pk S NE13 . .**36** F8
Woolsington Rd NE29 . . . .**41** C7
Woolwich Cl SR5 . . . .**74** F4
Woolwich Rd SR5 . . . . . .**74** F4
Wooperton Gdns NE5 . . .**54** C7
Worcester Gn NE8 . . . . .**101** B2
Worcester St SR2 . . . . . .**102** C1
Worcester Terr SR2 . . . . .**102** C2

Worcester Way NE13 . . . .**28** C5
Wordsworth Ave
Blyth NE24 . . . .**17** C6
Easington Lane DH5 . . . . .**97** D8
Hebburn NE31 . . . .**57** E6
Whickham NE16 . . . .**69** B8
Wordsworth Ave E DH5 . .**94** E7
Wordsworth Ave W DH5 . .**94** E7
Wordsworth Cres NE9 . . .**71** F1
Wordsworth St NE8 . . . . .**56** A2
Worley Ave NE9 . . . .**70** F4
Worley Cl NE4 . . . .**98** B1
Worley Mews NE9 . . . . . .**70** F4
Worley St NE4 . . . .**98** B1
Worley Terr DH9 . . . .**79** A1
Worm Hill Terr NE38 . . . .**83** E1
Worsdell St NE24 . . . . . .**12** E1
Worsley Cl NE28 . . . .**39** F4
Worswick St NE1 . . . .**99** B1
Worthing Cl NE28 . . . . . .**39** F3
Worthington Ct NE2 . . . .**99** C4
Wouldhave Ct NE33 . . . . .**42** E3
Wouldhave St NE33 . . . . .**42** E3
Wraith Terr SR2 . . . .**92** E6
Wraysbury Ct NE3 . . . . . .**37** D7
Wreay Wlk NE23 . . . .**22** C3
Wreigh St NE31 . . . .**57** D6
Wreken Gdns NE10 . . . . .**72** C8
Wrekenton Row NE9 . . . .**71** C2
Wrekenton Sta* NE9 . . . .**71** D2
Wren Cl NE38 . . . .**83** A3
Wren Gr **1** SR5 . . . .**74** C1
Wretham Pl NE2 . . . .**99** C2
Wright Dr NE23 . . . .**29** A7
Wright St NE24 . . . .**17** D8
Wright Terr DH4 . . . .**90** A5
Wrightson St NE23 . . . . .**16** B3
Wroxham Ct
Newcastle-u-T NE5 . . . . . .**37** B4
Sunderland SR2 . . . .**86** C2
Wroxton NE38 . . . .**83** C3
Wuppertal Ct NE32 . . . . .**58** B6
Wych Elm Cl NE61 . . . . . .**1** D4
Wych Elm Cres NE7 . . . . .**39** C3
Wychcroft Way NE5 . . . . .**37** C2
Wycliffe Ave NE3 . . . .**37** F3
Wycliffe Rd SR4 . . . .**85** F4
Wydon Pk NE46 . . . .**45** A3
Wye Ave NE32 . . . .**58** C3
Wye Rd NE31 . . . .**57** E3
Wylam Ave NE25 . . . .**23** F2
Wylam Cl
South Shields NE34 . . . . .**59** C5
Washington NE37 . . . .**72** E1
Wylam Fst Sch NE41 . . . .**51** B6
Wylam Gdns NE28 . . . . . .**40** F4
Wylam Gr SR1 . . . .**103** B2
Wylam Mill NE41 . . . .**51** B6
Wylam Rd NE29 . . . .**41** F3
Wylam St NE32 . . . .**58** B7

Wylam Sta NE41 . . . .**51** C5
Wylam View NE21 . . . . . .**53** B2
Wylam Wood Rd NE41 . . .**51** B5
Wynbury Rd NE9 . . . .**71** A5
Wyncote Ct NE7 . . . .**39** B2
Wynd The
Longbenton NE12 . . . .**29** F1
Newcastle-u-T NE3 . . . . . .**38** A4
Throckley NE15 . . . .**35** D1
Tynemouth NE30 . . . .**42** A8
Wynde The
Ponteland NE20 . . . .**25** D4
South Shields NE34 . . . . .**59** D5
Wyndfall Way NE3 . . . . . .**38** A3
Wyndham Ave NE3 . . . . .**37** F3
Wyndham Prim Sch NE3 .**38** A3
Wyndham Way NE29 . . . .**41** B8
Wynding The
Annitsford NE23 . . . .**22** B1
Bedlington NE22 . . . .**10** E1
Wyndley Cl NE16 . . . .**68** F5
Wyndley Ho NE3 . . . .**37** F3
Wyndley Pl NE3 . . . .**37** F3
Wyndrow Pl NE3 . . . .**37** F3
Wyndsail Pl NE3 . . . .**38** A3
Wyndtop Pl NE3 . . . .**38** A3
Wyndward Pl NE3 . . . . . .**38** A3
Wyndways Dr DH9 . . . . . .**78** E1
Wynn Gdns NE10 . . . . . .**56** F1
Wynyard DH2 . . . .**88** A3
Wynyard Dr NE22 . . . . . .**11** C3
Wynyard Gdns NE9 . . . . .**71** C2
Wynyard Sq SR2 . . . .**86** E2
Wynyard St Dunston NE11 .**69** F8
Fence Houses DH4 . . . . . .**94** A8
New Silksworth SR3 . . . . .**92** A7
Wythburn Pl NE9 . . . .**71** B4
Wyvern Sq SR2 . . . .**86** E2

Y

Yardley Gr NE23 . . . .**22** A8
Yarmouth Dr NE23 . . . . .**22** A8
Yatesbury Ave NE5 . . . . .**37** B3
Yeadon Ct NE3 . . . .**37** C7
Yeavering Cl NE3 . . . .**38** B4
Yellow Leas Farm NE36 . .**74** C7
Yelverton Cres NE6 . . . . .**56** F3
Yelverton Ct NE23 . . . . . .**22** A8
Yemeni Sch The NE33 . . .**42** B1
Yeoman St NE29 . . . .**42** B5
Yeovil Cl NE23 . . . .**22** A8
Yetholm Ave DH2 . . . . . .**88** B2
Yetholm Pl NE5 . . . .**37** A4
Yetholm Rd NE8 . . . .**100** B1
Yetlington Dr NE3 . . . . . .**38** A4
Yew Tree Dr NE22 . . . . . .**10** F2
Yewburn Way NE12 . . . . .**39** C6
Yewcroft Ave NE15 . . . . .**54** A6

Yewdale Gdns NE9 . . . . .**71** A4
Yewtree Ave SR5 . . . .**74** F2
Yewtree Gdns NE6 . . . . .**40** A1
Yewtrees NE10 . . . .**71** E5
Yewvale Rd NE5 . . . .**37** D1
York Ave NE32 . . . .**58** B3
York Cl NE23 . . . .**22** A8
York Cres DH5 . . . .**94** F4
York Ct Chester le S DH3 . .**88** D2
9 Wallsend NE28 . . . . . .**40** B1
York Dr NE28 . . . .**40** B1
York Gr NE22 . . . .**10** D2
York Ho SR5 . . . .**74** A4
York Rd Birtley DH3 . . . . .**82** C1
Whitley Bay NE26 . . . .**32** B5
York St Blyth NE24 . . . . . .**17** E8
Gateshead NE10 . . . .**57** A1
Hetton le H DH5 . . . .**94** E1
Jarrow NE32 . . . .**58** A6
New Silksworth SR3 . . . . .**92** A8
Newcastle-u-T NE4 . . . . . .**98** B1
Sunderland SR1 . . . .**103** A3
York Terr Chester le S DH3 **88** D2
Gateshead NE10 . . . .**71** D8
7 North Shields NE29 . . . .**42** A5
York Way NE34 . . . .**60** A6
Yorkdale Pl NE6 . . . .**57** A6
Yorkwood NE31 . . . .**57** C2
Young Rd NE12 . . . .**29** F1
Younghall Cl NE40 . . . . . .**52** A1

Z

Zetland Dr NE25 . . . .**31** F2
Zetland Sq **9** SR6 . . . . . .**75** E1
Zetland St SR6 . . . .**75** E1
Zion St SR1 . . . .**103** B3
Zion Terr Blaydon NE21 . .**53** B2
Sunderland SR5 . . . .**75** C3

Addresses

Name and Address	Telephone	Page	Grid reference

Any feature in this atlas can be given a unique reference to help you find the same feature on other Ordnance Survey maps of the area, or to help someone else locate you if they do not have a Street Atlas.

The grid squares in this atlas match the Ordnance Survey National Grid and are at 500 metre intervals. The small figures at the bottom and sides of every other grid line are the National Grid kilometre values (**00** to **99** km) and are repeated across the country every 100 km (see left).

To give a unique National Grid reference you need to locate where in the country you are. The country is divided into 100 km squares with each square given a unique two-letter reference. Use the administrative map to determine in which 100 km square a particular page of this atlas falls.

The bold letters and numbers between each grid line (**A** to **F**, **1** to **8**) are for use within a specific Street Atlas only, and when used with the page number, are a convenient way of referencing these grid squares.

Example   The railway bridge over DARLEY GREEN RD in grid square B1

Step 1: Identify the two-letter reference, in this example the page is in **SP**

Step 2: Identify the 1 km square in which the railway bridge falls. Use the figures in the southwest corner of this square: Eastings **17**, Northings **74**. This gives a unique reference: **SP 17 74**, accurate to 1 km.

Step 3: To give a more precise reference accurate to 100 m you need to estimate how many tenths along and how many tenths up this 1 km square the feature is (to help with this the 1 km square is divided into four 500 m squares). This makes the bridge about **8** tenths along and about **1** tenth up from the southwest corner.

This gives a unique reference: **SP 178 741**, accurate to 100 m.

Eastings (read from left to right along the bottom) come before Northings (read from bottom to top). If you have trouble remembering say to yourself "Along the hall, THEN up the stairs"!

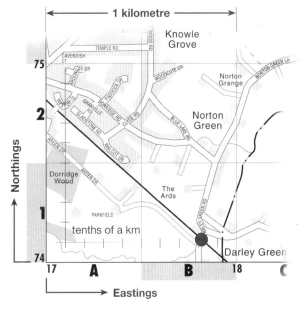

PHILIP'S MAPS

the Gold Standard for serious driving

◆ Philip's street atlases cover every county in England and Wales, plus much of Scotland.

◆ All our atlases use the same style of mapping, with the same colours and symbols, so you can move with confidence from one atlas to the next

◆ Widely used by the emergency services, transport companies and local authorities.

◆ Created from the most up-to-date and detailed information available from Ordnance Survey

◆ Based on the National Grid

BEST BUY • BEST BUY
Auto EXPRESS
BEST BUY • BEST BUY

For national mapping, choose

Philip's Navigator Britain – the most detailed road atlas available of England, Wales and Scotland. Hailed by Auto Express as 'the ultimate road atlas', this is the only one-volume atlas to show every road and lane in Britain.

Street atlases currently available

England

Bedfordshire

Berkshire

Birmingham and West Midlands

Bristol and Bath

Buckinghamshire

Cambridgeshire

Cheshire

Cornwall

Cumbria

Derbyshire

Devon

Dorset

County Durham and Teesside

Essex

North Essex

South Essex

Gloucestershire

North Hampshire

South Hampshire

Herefordshire Monmouthshire

Hertfordshire

Isle of Wight

Kent

East Kent

West Kent

Lancashire

Leicestershire and Rutland

Lincolnshire

London

Greater Manchester

Merseyside

Norfolk

Northamptonshire

Northumberland

Nottinghamshire

Oxfordshire

Shropshire

Somerset

All England and Wales coverage

Staffordshire

Suffolk

Surrey

East Sussex

West Sussex

Tyne and Wear

Warwickshire

Birmingham and West Midlands

Wiltshire and Swindon

Worcestershire

East Yorkshire Northern Lincolnshire

North Yorkshire

South Yorkshire

West Yorkshire

Wales

Anglesey, Conwy and Gwynedd

Cardiff, Swansea and The Valleys

Carmarthenshire, Pembrokeshire and Swansea

Ceredigion and South Gwynedd

Denbighshire, Flintshire, Wrexham

Herefordshire Monmouthshire

Powys

Scotland

Aberdeenshire

Ayrshire

Edinburgh and East Central Scotland

Fife and Tayside

Glasgow and West Central Scotland

Inverness and Moray

How to order

Philip's maps and atlases are available from bookshops, motorway services and petrol stations. You can order direc from the publisher by phoning **01903 828503** or online at **www.philips-maps.co.uk**
For bulk orders only, phone 020 7644 6940